Southern and Northern Quebec
Pages 150–161

Quebec City and the St. Lawrence River
Pages 132–149

Montreal
Pages 110–131

Newfoundland and Labrador
Pages 70–79

New Brunswick, Prince Edward Is., and Nova Scotia
Pages 80–101

Toronto
Pages 170–193

Ottawa and Eastern Ontario
Pages 194–209

P9-DCH-444

Iqaluit

Hudson Bay

Atlantic Ocean

ARIO

QUEBEC

Quebec City

Ottawa

Montreal

Toronto

ATLANTIC CANADA

St. John's

Halifax

0 km   500
0 miles   500

Canada

917.1 CAN

Canada.

EYEWITNESS TRAVEL

Canada

Penguin
Random
House

Produced by Duncan Baird Publishers,
London, England
Managing Editor Rebecca Miles
Managing Art Editor Vanessa Marsh
Editors Georgina Harris,
Michelle de Larrabeiti, Zoë Ross
Designers Dawn Davies-Cook, Ian Midson
Design Assistance Rosie Laing,
Kelvin Mullins
Visualizer Gary Cross
Picture Research Victoria Peel
DTP Designer Sarah Williams

Dorling Kindersley Limited
Project Editor Paul Hines
Art Editor Jane Ewart
US Editor Mary Sutherland
Editor Hugh Thompson

Contributors Bruce Bishop,
Eric and Katharine Fletcher, Paul Franklin,
Sam Ion, Helena Katz, Philip Lee,
Ffion Llywd-Jones, Cam Norton, Lorry Patton,
Sandra Phinney, Geoffrey Roy,
Michael Snook, Donald Telfer, Paul Waters

Photographers Alan Keohane,
Peter Wilson, Francesca Yorke

Illustrators Joanna Cameron,
Gary Cross, Chris Forsey, Paul Guest,
Claire Littlejohn, Robbie Polley,
Kevin Robinson, John Woodcock

Printed and bound in China

First American Edition, 2000
18 19 20 21 10 9 8 7 6 5 4 3 2 1

Published in the United States by
DK Publishing, 345 Hudson Street,
New York, New York 10014

**Reprinted with revisions 2002,
2004, 2006, 2008, 2010, 2012,
2014, 2016, 2018**

Copyright 2000, 2018 ©
Dorling Kindersley Limited, London
A Penguin Random House Company

Published in the UK by
Dorling Kindersley Limited.

A catalog record for this book is available
from the Library of Congress.

ISSN 1542-1554
ISBN 978-1-46546-824-6

MIX
Paper from
responsible sources
FSC
www.fsc.org   FSC™ C018179

Introducing Canada

Atlantic Canada

Quebec

Ontario

Moraine Lake at sunrise, Banff National Park

**The information in this
DK Eyewitness Travel Guide is checked regularly.**
Every effort has been made to ensure that this book is as up-to-date as possible
at the time of going to press. Some details, however, such as telephone numbers,
opening hours, prices, gallery hanging arrangements and travel information are
liable to change. The publishers cannot accept responsibility for any consequences
arising from the use of this book, nor for any material on third party websites, and
cannot guarantee that any website address in this book will be a suitable source of
travel information. We value the views and suggestions of our readers very highly.
Please write to: Publisher, DK Eyewitness Travel Guides, Dorling Kindersley,
80 Strand, London, WC2R 0RL, UK, or email: travelguides@dk.com.

◀ **Title page** The dazzling fall foliage of British Columbia's maple forests.   **Front cover image** Red canoes on Emerald Lake, Yoho
National Park, British Columbia   **Back cover image** Toronto skyline at sunset in Ontario, Canada

Contents

Toronto's skyline from the harbour front

A charming Quebec City street

The Basilica of Sainte-Anne-
de-Beaupré in Quebec

HOW TO USE THIS GUIDE

The detailed information and tips given in this guide will help you to get the most out of your visit to Canada. The guide is divided into 13 areas, including *Toronto* and *Montreal*, and each section describes the main sights using maps, photographs and illustrations. The opening section, *Introducing Canada*, maps the country and sets it in its historical and cultural context. Restaurant and hotel recommendations can be found in the section *Travelers' Needs*, together with information about shopping and entertainment. The *Survival Guide* has tips on everything from transport to making a phone call, as well as other practical matters.

Canada Region by Region

Canada has been divided into six main regions. These have been further divided into 13 color-coded areas. On the inside front cover is a general map of the country showing these 13 areas.

1 Regional Map
This shows a region's major cities, towns and road networks. The introduction provides an overview of its character and geography. There are also useful transport tips on how to get to and around the region.

2 Area Map
This displays the major places of interest in an area. The key sights are numbered, and the introduction gives information about the history, character and natural attractions of the area.

Each area can be easily identified by its color-coded thumb tab.

3 City Map
These maps show the major roads, parks and places of interest in Montreal, Toronto and Vancouver. The most important sights are numbered, and there is information on getting around by car and public transport.

4 Detailed Information
Throughout the guide, the most important towns, city areas and other places to visit are described in detail. They are listed in order and follow the numbering shown on the area or city maps.

The Visitors' Checklist provides practical information about transport, opening times, events, and the closing dates of places of particular interest.

5 Main Towns
Some of the main towns and smaller cities have an individual section where the museums, monuments and other places of interest are listed. All the major sights are located on the town map.

The town map shows the main roads, stations, car parking areas and tourist offices.

6 Street-by-Street Map
This gives a bird's-eye view of the key areas of interest in the main towns and cities with photographs and captions describing the sights.

7 Canada's Top Sights
These are given two full pages. There are cutaways or reconstructions of historic buildings, maps of national parks with information about trails and facilities available, and floorplans of the major museums. There are also photographs of the main sights.

Stars indicate the sights that no visitor should miss.

INTRODUCING CANADA

MAKE THE MOST OF CANADA

The following itineraries have been designed to include as many of the country's highlights as possible, while keeping long-distance travel to a minimum. First come three 2-day tours of Canada's most important cities: Toronto, Montreal, and Vancouver. These itineraries can be followed individually, or, in the case of Montreal and Toronto, included in a week-long provincial tour. Next come four 7-day tours, covering British Columbia (BC) and the Rockies, Ontario, Quebec, and the Maritime Provinces. Select, combine, and follow your favorite tours, or simply dip in and out and be inspired. Booking ahead for major sights is recommended.

Niagara Falls
Located on the border between Canada and the USA, the magnificent Niagara Falls are visited by around 14 million people each year.

British Columbia and the Rockies

Main map

0 kilometers   200

0 miles   200

7 Days in Ontario

- Admire the superb Victorian architecture of **Parliament Hill** in **Ottawa**.

- Canoe the vast, echoing wilderness of **Algonquin Provincial Park**.

- Learn about the early settlement of Ontario at the outstanding National Historic Site of **Sainte-Marie among the Hurons**.

- Boat and hike through the beautiful scenery of **Georgian Bay Islands National Park**.

- Marvel at the magnificent thundering waterfalls of **Niagara Falls**.

- Saunter the streets of **Niagara-on-the-Lake** with its charming assortment of old timber houses.

7 Days in Quebec

- Explore the ancient streets of **Quebec City** and enjoy its fine riverside setting.

- Join the crowds at the mighty **Montmorency Falls** at the **Parc de la Chute Montmorency**.

- Linger at **Sainte-Anne-de-Beaupré**, Quebec's holiest place of pilgrimage.

- Take a whale-watching tour from the agreeable town of **Tadoussac**.

- Experience the rugged landscapes of the **Parc National du Canada Forillon**, at the tip of the **Gaspé Peninsula**.

- Investigate the vineyards of the **Richelieu Valley** near **Montreal**.

◀ *Indian Encampment on Lake Huron*, c1845, by Canadian artist Paul Kane

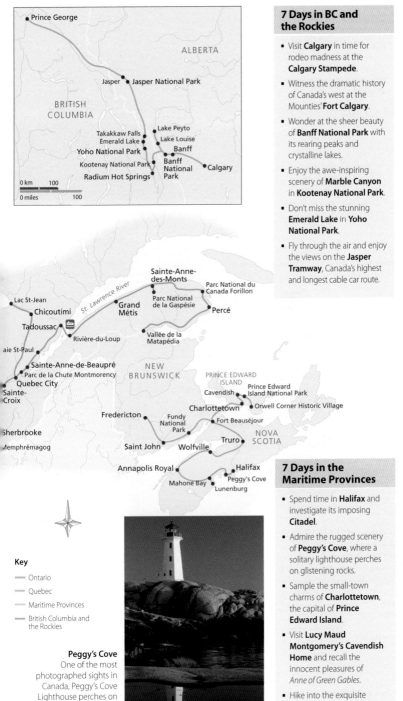

Prince George

ALBERTA

Jasper • Jasper National Park

BRITISH
COLUMBIA

Takakkaw Falls
Emerald Lake
Yoho National Park
Kootenay National Park
Radium Hot Springs

Lake Peyto
Lake Louise
Banff
Banff
National
Park
• Calgary

0 km   100

0 miles   100

7 Days in BC and the Rockies

- Visit **Calgary** in time for rodeo madness at the **Calgary Stampede**.

- Witness the dramatic history of Canada's west at the Mounties' **Fort Calgary**.

- Wonder at the sheer beauty of **Banff National Park** with its rearing peaks and crystalline lakes.

- Enjoy the awe-inspiring scenery of **Marble Canyon** in **Kootenay National Park**.

- Don't miss the stunning **Emerald Lake** in **Yoho National Park**.

- Fly through the air and enjoy the views on the **Jasper Tramway**, Canada's highest and longest cable car route.

Sainte-Anne-
des-Monts

Parc National du
Canada Forillon

St. Lawrence River

Lac St-Jean
Chicoutimi
Tadoussac
aie St-Paul
Sainte-Anne-de-Beaupré
Parc de la Chute Montmorency
Quebec City
Sainte-
Croix

Grand
Métis

Parc National
de la Gaspésie

Percé

Rivière-du-Loup

Vallée de la
Matapédia

NEW
BRUNSWICK

PRINCE EDWARD
ISLAND

Prince Edward
Cavendish   Island National Park

Charlottetown

Orwell Corner Historic Village

Fredericton

Fundy
National
Park

Fort Beauséjour

NOVA
SCOTIA

Sherbrooke
Memphrémagog

Saint John   Wolfville

Truro

Annapolis Royal

Mahone Bay

Halifax
Peggy's Cove
Lunenburg

Key

— Ontario

— Quebec

— Maritime Provinces

— British Columbia and
the Rockies

Peggy's Cove
One of the most photographed sights in Canada, Peggy's Cove Lighthouse perches on granite rocks – a symbol of Nova Scotia's enduring bond with the sea.

7 Days in the Maritime Provinces

- Spend time in **Halifax** and investigate its imposing **Citadel**.

- Admire the rugged scenery of **Peggy's Cove**, where a solitary lighthouse perches on glistening rocks.

- Sample the small-town charms of **Charlottetown**, the capital of **Prince Edward Island**.

- Visit **Lucy Maud Montgomery's Cavendish Home** and recall the innocent pleasures of *Anne of Green Gables*.

- Hike into the exquisite coastal scenery of **Fundy National Park**.

2 Days in Toronto

Canada's economic power-house, Toronto has dozens of great hotels, first-class restaurants, and world-class museums.

- **Arriving** Take the UP Express train (every 15 mins) from Toronto Pearson International Airport to Union Station in the Financial District; the journey takes 25 mins.

- **Moving on** There are regular flights from Toronto to Vancouver, and trains, buses, and flights to Montreal.

The modern Toronto skyline on the northwest side of Lake Ontario

Day 1

Morning Begin a visit to **Toronto** at the **CN Tower** *(p176)*, whose needle-like spire soars high above the city center, offering panoramic views over the lake and across Ontario; be brave and step onto the tower's glass floor. Next, walk to the **TD Gallery of Inuit Art** *(p178)* for a superb collection of Inuit sculptures. Stroll down to the **Harbourfront** *(pp174–5)* to admire the cutting-edge art at the Power Plant. Alternatively, relax at the shoreline and book a cruise.

Afternoon At **Fort York** *(p190)*, see how Toronto began life as a British stockade garrisoned by a handful of Redcoats, before heading to the **Art Gallery of Ontario** *(pp182–3)*, one of Canada's finest galleries, to sample the magnificent collection of art. Nearby is **Kensington Market** *(p184)*, a boho shopping area celebrated for its cosmopolitan vibe and vintage fashion stores.

Day 2

Morning Start the day by exploring the **Royal Ontario Museum** *(p188–9)*, whose huge collection features everything from massive totem poles to intimidating dinosaur skeletons. Then proceed to the **Bata Shoe Museum** *(p186)*, featuring three whole floors of antique shoes and boots of every shape and description.

Afternoon Don't miss the wonderful ceramic collection exhibited at the **Gardiner Museum of Ceramic Art** *(p186)* and then be sure to visit **Casa Loma** *(p190)*, an extravagant Victorian-style folly, built to resemble a medieval castle. Wander down to **Yorkville** *(p187)* for a bite; or in balmy weather, pack a picnic and take a ferry to **Toronto Islands** *(p192)*, where cars are banned and the lake's breeze is welcomed by cyclists. Ferry to **Hanlan's Point** *(p192)* for a clothing-optional beach.

To extend your trip...

Toronto is just two hours by car, train, and bus from the world-famous Niagara Falls, where you can spend a day exploring the famous natural wonder *(see the Ontario itinerary p15, and pp216–19)*.

Gothic Revival façade of Sir Henry Pellatt's Casa Loma, Toronto

2 Days in Montreal

French-speaking Montreal is one of North America's finest cities.

- **Arriving** A shuttle bus covers the 22 km (14 miles) from Montreal airport to down-town; allow 40 minutes.

- **Moving on** There are regular flights from Montreal to Vancouver; trains, buses, and flights go to Toronto.

Day 1

Morning Introduce yourself to **Montreal's** varied charms at the city's finest church, the beautifully decorated **Basilique Notre-Dame-de-Montréal** *(pp116–17)*. From here, stroll down to the **Centre d'histoire de Montréal** *(p118)*, where entertaining displays explore the history of the city, from Canadian origins up to today. Nearby, down on the river, be sure to visit the **Centre des sciences de Montréal** *(p118)*, located on a former pier and crammed with collections on technology and engineering.

Afternoon Begin the afternoon with an easy ramble along the waterfront, where the old port – **Vieux-Port** *(p116)* – has been turned into a leafy park. After-wards, wander back into the heart of **Vieux-Montréal** *(pp114–15)*, where the distinguished **Château**

Ramezay (p116) is a charming, 19th-century copy of a French château. Nearby, **Sir George Etienne-Cartier National Historic Site** (p117) consists of two richly furnished Victorian houses on Rue Notre Dame, which is itself flanked by some of Montreal's most imposing old buildings.

Day 2
Morning Start the day with a promenade along **Rue Sherbrooke** (p126), which is liberally sprinkled with graceful old mansions, sturdy churches, and bijou stores. Montreal's finest art gallery, the **Musée des Beaux-Arts** (pp122–3), which is famous for its collection of European paintings, is also on this street. Nearby, savor the bustling atmosphere of **Square Dorchester** (p123) and **Place du Canada** (p123), a splash of greenery in the heart of the city that is home to statues of famous Canadians of yesteryear. Afterwards, drop by the **Cathédrale Marie-Reine-du-Monde** (p126), whose attractive façade was inspired by St. Peter's Basilica in Rome.

Afternoon Wander the open, airy plaza of the **Place des Arts** (p119) before investigating the **Musée d'art contemporain de Montréal** (pp120–21), whose extensive collection of modern art runs from paintings and photographs to videos and installations. Afterwards, head to **Parc du Mont-Royal** (p127), a hilly slab of parkland, meadow, and wood with look-out points

offering lovely views back over the city. If the weather is good, clamber the steps up to the **Oratoire Saint-Joseph** (p127), Montreal's largest shrine, devoted to the Virgin Mary. Alternatively, head for the **Plateau Mont-Royal** (p119), the city's most atmospheric neighborhood, complete with bistros, bars, bookshops, and bazaars.

2 Days in Vancouver

Laid-back Vancouver is the quintessential West Coast city, with an exquisite setting between the ocean and the mountains, and a scattering of show-stopping attractions.

- **Arriving** Vancouver airport is 13 km (8 miles) south of the city center, a journey covered by the SkyTrain in about 25 minutes.

- **Moving on** There are regular flights from Vancouver to Toronto and Montreal.

Day 1
Morning Explore Vancouver's lively **waterfront** (pp272–3), where boats bob in and out; the modern architecture of **Canada Place** (p272) provides a real aesthetic splash. Look out for the imposing **Waterfront Station** (p272) and the **Harbour Centre Tower** (p272), which offers expansive views. Head inland to **Vancouver Art Gallery** (p275) for its excellent Canadian and international art collection.

Afternoon
Stroll through **Gastown** (pp272–3) with its vibrant street scene and cafés before heading into **Chinatown** (p274), stretching from Carrall to Gore streets. Stalls and storefronts crowd the pavements, offering Chinese delicacies. Recover in the **Dr. Sun Yat-Sen Classical Chinese Garden** (p274). Finish off the day with the inventive exhibits at **Science World** (p274).

Geodesic dome overlooking False Creek at Science World, Vancouver

Day 2
Morning Take a city bus to **Stanley Park** (p279), a slab of greenery that occupies a headland jutting out into English Bay. Hike through the woods, relax on the beach, or cycle the perimeter wall, but above all enjoy the views over city, sea, and mountain.

Afternoon Detour out to the **University of British Columbia Museum of Anthropology** (pp280–81) to examine the country's finest collection of Northwest coast First Nations peoples' art. Exhibits include giant totem poles, ornate headdresses, and exquisite feast dishes. Allow a good couple of hours for the museum and afterwards, on the way back into the city center, stop at **Vanier Park** (p270), a lovely expanse of parkland.

To extend your trip...
Spend two days in Victoria, one of Canada's most beguiling towns, just two hours by ferry from Vancouver (see pp284–9).

Visitors taking in the 18th-century charm of Vieux-Montréal by horse-drawn carriage

Gondolas transporting visitors to and from Sulphur Mountain, Banff

7 Days in BC and the Rockies

- **Airports** Arrive and depart from Calgary airport.
- **Transport** A car is essential for this trip.
- **Booking Ahead** *Jasper National Park:* Jasper Tramway

Day 1: Calgary
Start your tour of the Rockies in **Calgary** *(pp296–9)*, a big and breezy city with a western feel. Calgary is famous for its rodeo, the "Calgary Stampede", but has much more to offer. Be sure to visit the **Glenbow Museum** *(p297)* with its wide-ranging collection of Canadian paintings, and **Fort Calgary Historic Park** *(p298)*, which features a restored Mounties' fort.

Day 2: Banff
With its fine mountain setting, **Banff** *(p307)* is a perfect introduction to the Canadian Rockies. Take the gondola up to the top of **Sulphur Mountain** *(p307)* for breathtaking views; drop by the **Cave and Basin National Historic Site** *(p307)* to learn about the town's colorful history; and relax at the **Upper Hot Springs Pool** *(p307)*.

Day 3: Banff National Park
Head west from Banff for a closer inspection of the white-tipped mountains, deep forests, crystal-clear lakes, and extra-ordinary glaciers that surround the town and punctuate **Banff National Park** *(pp304–7)*. Linger

at the turquoise waters of **Lake Louise** *(p307)*, delve into the depths of **Johnston Canyon** *(p305)*, and stroll off the highway to the well-signed vantage point overlooking **Peyto Lake** *(p306)*.

Day 4: Kootenay National Park and Radium Hot Springs
Drive the dramatic Kootenay Highway as it winds its way through **Kootenay National Park** *(p303)*. Stop at Paint Pots, for the short walk to rust-colored mineral springs, and pause at Marble Canyon, a plunging gorge with dramatic limestone shanks. Take a dip at **Radium Hot Springs** *(p303)*, a pocket-sized town also famous for its mineral springs.

Day 5: Yoho National Park
Begin your exploration of **Yoho National Park** *(pp308–9)* at Emerald Lake, a stunningly beautiful circle of water in the midst of glowering peaks. Sign up for a guided tour of the **Burgess Shale** *(p309)*, where the rock beds hold a remarkable collection of ancient fossils. Finish off the day with a detour to the impressive 254-m (833-ft) high **Takakkaw Falls** *(p309)*.

Day 6: Jasper National Park
No tour of the Canadian Rockies would be complete without a visit to **Jasper National Park** *(pp312–15)*. Sample the magnifi-cent mountains surrounding the pretty little town of Jasper; thrill to the plunging ravine that

comprises **Maligne Canyon** *(p315)*; paddle the cool, green waters of **Pyramid Lake** *(p315)*; and relax in the **Miette Hot Springs** *(p315)*. Alternatively, drive and hike up to the Angel Glacier on **Mount Edith Cavell** *(p315)*; or take the **Jasper Tramway** *(p312)*, Canada's longest and highest cable car, linking Jasper town with a vantage point 9,465 ft (2,885 m) above sea level.

Day 7: Prince George
Round off your tour by visiting **Prince George** *(p316)*, a bustling valley town and transport center at the junction of the Yellowhead Highway and Highway 97. Wander the town center, popping into its several art galleries, and investigate the excellent **Exploration Place Museum and Science Centre** *(p316)*, whose excellent displays journey through the history of the area.

A waterfall coursing through the ravine at Maligne Canyon, Jasper National Park

Stunningly beautiful scenery at Yoho National Park in the Rockies

Trees turning to fall colors on the Thousand Islands, downstream from Kingston, Ontario

7 Days in Ontario

- **Airports** Arrive and depart from either Ottawa or one of Toronto's airports.

- **Transport** Trains run daily between Ottawa, Kingston, and Toronto. The journey from Ottawa to Kingston takes about 2.5 hours, and it's another 2.5 hours to Toronto. You will need a car to see inland Ontario.

- **Booking Ahead** *Algonquin Provincial Park:* Camping and equipment hire

Day 1: Ottawa

Start in the nation's capital, **Ottawa** *(pp196–203)*, a bustling city with a superb range of hotels, restaurants, and sights. Prioritize three key attractions – **Parliament Hill** *(p198)*, with its handsome Victorian buildings; the **Canadian War Museum** *(p199)*, holding an unparalleled range of military artifacts; and the **National Gallery** *(pp202–3)*, which boasts Canada's widest collection of paintings.

Day 2: Kingston and the Thousand Islands

Stroll through the old streets of **Kingston** *(p204)*, a historic town with a fine collection of distinguished Victorian mansions, and admire nautical memorabilia at the **Marine Museum of the Great Lakes** *(p205)*. Allow time for a cruise along the St. Lawrence River: boat trips leave Kingston bound for the scenic **Thousand Islands** *(p204)*.

Day 3: Algonquin Provincial Park

Begin your day at **Algonquin Provincial Park** *(pp208–9)*, a vast forested wilderness latticed with lakes and rivers. Begin by driving along the Parkway Corridor (Hwy 60), the only road to cross the park, visiting the **Algonquin Art Centre** *(p208)* and the **Algonquin Logging Museum** *(p208)* en route. Select one of the park's several lodges for an overnight stop.

Day 4: Algonquin Provincial Park (cont.)

Make an early start, hire the correct outdoors equipment, and explore part of the Algonquin Provincial Park by canoe – either under your own steam or with a guide.

The glass-and-granite building of the National Gallery of Canada, Ottawa

Day 5: Sainte-Marie among the Hurons and Georgian Bay Islands National Park

Enjoy Ontario's prime historical attraction, **Sainte-Marie among the Hurons** *(pp224–5)*, a reconstruction of the Jesuit mission built in the heart of Huronia in the 17th century. Afterwards, head for the hamlet of **Honey Harbour** *(p223)*, where you can take a water taxi through **Georgian Bay Islands National Park** *(p223)* to pine-dusted **Beausoleil Island** *(p223)*, which has a dozen hiking trails to match all abilities.

Day 6: St. Jacobs, Niagara Falls, and Niagara-on-the-Lake

Detour to quaint **St. Jacobs** *(p222)* for craft shops selling traditional Mennonite quilts. Drive out to the **Bell Homestead National Historic Site** *(p222)*, the home of Alexander Graham Bell, the telephone pioneer. Heading southeast, aim for **Niagara Falls** *(pp216–19)*, where Canada's colossal Horseshoe Falls and America's American Falls crash 52 m (170 ft) to the waters below. Clouds of spray drift up, and Hornblower boats take tourists as near to the Falls as they dare. Travel on to **Niagara-on-the-Lake** *(p212)*, a lovely town cocooned within lush gardens and a focal point of the area's wineries.

Day 7: Toronto

Pick from the Toronto itineraries on p12.

The wild landscape of the Parc National du Canada Forillon, Quebec

7 Days in Quebec

- **Airports** Arrive and depart from Montreal airport.

- **Transport** Greyhound Buses serve many destinations around Quebec, and there are regular trips between Montreal and Quebec City, with a journey of about 3 hours. A branch train line inches its way around part of the Gaspé Peninsula, but services are infrequent. A car allows for more flexibility.

Day 1: Quebec City

Start your tour of Quebec in **Quebec City** (pp132–41), which occupies a delightful location on the banks of the Saint Lawrence River. Wander the lovely old town: begin with the citadel and then explore the narrow cobble stone streets. Allow time for the **Musée de la civilisation** (p137), and the extravagant **Fairmont Le Château Frontenac** (p138).

Day 2: Quebec City excursion: Chicoutimi and Lac-Saint-Jean

Spend a day enjoying the environs of Quebec City. Drive to **Chicoutimi** (p144), a sleepy town with a riverside setting. Continue on to **Lac-Saint-Jean** (p145), a well-known beauty spot where tiny villages hug the lakeshores amid spruce forests and rolling hills.

Day 3: Parc de la Chute Montmorency, Sainte-Anne-de-Beaupré, Baie-Saint-Paul, and Tadoussac

Head northeast from Quebec City along the Saint Lawrence River. The first stop has to be the **Parc de la Chute Montmorency** (p143). A mighty waterfall here marks where the Montmorency River crashes down into the Saint Lawrence. Spend time in nearby **Sainte-Anne-de-Beaupré** (pp142–3), Quebec's answer to Lourdes. Visit the church, a richly decorated structure built in the 1920s. Pushing on, take a break at **Baie Saint-Paul** (p143), one of the prettiest coastal towns, and continue to **Tadoussac** (p144), which offers whale-watching tours.

Day 4: The Gaspé Peninsula: the North Shore

Catch the ferry across the Saint

Imposing Fairmont Le Château Frontenac, Quebec City

Lawrence River from Saint-Siméon to **Rivière-du-Loup** (p147) and stroll the town's attractive center. Take the road along the north side of the **Gaspé Peninsula** (pp148–9) with the river on one side and wooded hills on the other. Aim for the lush gardens at **Grand Métis** (p148) and the pretty hamlet of **Sainte-Anne-des-Montes** (p149).

Day 5: The Gaspé Peninsula: the South Shore

Start at the **Parc National du Canada Forillon** (p149), just on the northeast edge of the Peninsula. Then head southwest towards **Percé** (p149), to enjoy small-town life at the village. Proceed to the scenic **Vallée de la Matapédia** (p148), a rural haven noted for its fruit farms and maple syrup.

Day 6: The Eastern Townships

Experience rural Quebec at its most beguiling at the **Sainte-Croix** manor house (p152). Enjoy small-town life in **Sherbrooke** (p152), followed by a detour to the scenic **Lac Memphrémagog** (p152), surrounded by historic villages and rolling hills. Finish the day by driving along the **Richelieu Valley** (p152), whose orchards and vineyards frame the approaches to Montreal.

Day 7: Montreal

Choose from the Montreal itineraries on pp12–13.

For practical information on traveling around Canada, see pp406–19

7 Days in the Maritime Provinces

- **Airports** Arrive and depart from Halifax airport.
- **Transport** A car is essential for this trip.

Day 1: Halifax
In **Halifax** (pp93–5), the capital of Nova Scotia, make a beeline for the **Citadel National Historic Site** (p95), a fortress overlooking the city and the harbor. Then stroll down to the waterfront, Halifax's most atmospheric quarter and home to the elegant **Province House** (p95) and the intriguing **Maritime Museum** (p94).

Day 2: Peggy's Cove and Lunenburg
Don't miss the rugged shoreline running southwest of Halifax. Its surf-battered bays and coves are at their most beguiling at tiny **Peggy's Cove** (p93), with its solitary lighthouse perched on bleak granite rocks. Nearby, enjoy the small-town delights of **Lunenburg** (p92) with its cluster of attractive Victorian houses on a narrow, hilly peninsula.

Day 3: Mahone Bay, Annapolis Royal, Wolfville, and Grand Pré
Stroll the streets of **Mahone Bay** (pp92–3), a pretty place with a trio of old churches. Venture into the heart of Nova Scotia, where **Annapolis Royal** (p91) boasts fanciful Victorian houses

and two old forts. Then savor the charms of gracious **Wolfville** (p91) and head to **Grand Pré National Historic Site** (p91), commemorating the Acadian settlers who were forced out by the British.

Day 4: Truro, Fort Beauséjour, and Charlottetown, PEI
Detour to **Truro** (p90) and watch the tidal bore as it rushes up the Salmon River. Enjoy wide views over the Minas Basin from the immaculately restored **Fort Beauséjour** (p90) and drive over the Confederation Bridge to **Prince Edward Island** (pp86–9). Admire the island's charming capital, **Charlottetown** (p89), and take in **Province House** (p89), the place where the "Fathers of Confederation" began the process of creating Canada from its component parts.

Day 5: PEI: Cavendish, PEI National Park, and Orwell Corner Historic Village
Explore the country roads of **Prince Edward Island** (PEI), where your first port of call should be **Cavendish** (p88), home to all things to do with *Anne of Green Gables*, including **Lucy Maud Montgomery's Cavendish Home** (p89). Proceed to the north shore of the island, where **Prince Edward Island National Park** (p88) boasts wonderful sandy beaches. Finish the day by visiting **Orwell Corner Historic Village** (p89), a careful recreation of country life in the 19th century.

Historic Great George Street, Charlottetown, Prince Edward Island

Day 6: Fundy National Park and Saint John
Marvel at nature's power at **Fundy National Park** (p82), an area of wilderness nudging up to Fundy Bay, which has some of the mightiest tides on earth – reckon on a differential between low and high tide of around 15 m (49 ft). Take a coastal hike before moving on to the vibrant city of **Saint John** (p82).

Day 7: Fredericton
Spend at least a day in pretty **Fredericton** (p83), the capital of New Brunswick. Highlights include the outstanding **Beaverbrook Art Gallery** (p83) and a string of British military buildings dating back to the 19th century.

To extend your trip…
Day 8: Cape Breton Island
Head for the magnificent scenery of **Cape Breton Island** (see pp96–7). A must-see is the **Cape Breton Highlands National Park** (see p98). Take a break in pretty **Chéticamp** (see p96).
Day 9: Cape Breton Island (cont.)
Continue on the highway that circumnavigates Cape Breton Highlands National Park, pausing for a hike on one of the many trails. Press on to **Baddeck** (see p98), which is famous for its connections with Alexander Graham Bell.

The harbor at Peggy's Cove, near Halifax, Nova Scotia

Putting Western and Northern Canada on the Map

Canada lies at the northern end of the American continent and covers 9,970,610 sq km (3,849,652 sq miles). More than 70 percent of this area is uninhabited because of vast tracts of frozen wilderness in the north. In contrast, British Columbia boasts Canada's only temperate rainforest.

Melville Island

Parry Cha

Victoria Island

Holman

Paulatuk

Cambridge Bay

Inuvik

Coronation Gulf

Great Bear Lake

Norman Wells

NORTHWEST TERRITORIES

Dawson City

YUKON

Yellowknife

Great Slave Lake

Whitehorse

Watson Lake

Hay River

Fort Resolution

Fort Smith

Lake Athabasca

Fort Nelson

97

35

BRITISH COLUMBIA

Fort St. John

ALBERTA

Fort McMurray

SASKATCHEW

Athabasca

Saskatchewan

Prince Rupert

Haida Gwaii

Prince George

43

Prince Albert

Pacific Ocean

97

Edmonton

Red Deer

16

Saskatoo

Banff

Calgary

Yorkto

Vancouver Island

Vancouver

Kelowna

Regina

Victoria

1

Seattle

90

0 kilometers   400

0 miles   400

Butte

Portland

15

Key

═══ Expressway

═══ Major road

∙∙∙∙∙ Minor road

─── Principal rail routes

═══ International border

─ ─ Provincial border

UNITED STATES OF AMERICA

94

Salt Lake City

5

80

Denver

Mileage Chart

Banff

128	**Calgary**							
80								
3039	2911	**Dawson City**						
1889	**1809**							
253	146	1976	**Red Deer**					
157	**91**	**1228**						
888	764	2526	610	**Regina**				
552	**475**	**1570**	**379**					
748	630	2297	476	260	**Saskatoon**			
465	**391**	**1427**	**296**	**161**				
928	1057	1917	934	2424	1677	**Vancouver**		
577	**657**	**1191**	**580**	**1506**	**1042**			
2513	2385	440	2188	2871	2614	2697	**Whitehorse**	
1562	**1482**	**274**	**1360**	**1784**	**1624**	**1676**		
1464	1336	2942	1186	888	829	3312	3524	**Winnipeg**
910	**830**	**1828**	**737**	**552**	**515**	**2058**	**2190**	

10 = Distance in kilometers
10 = Distance in miles

Vancouver and Environs

West Vancouver
North Vancouver
Vancouver
Port Moody
Burnaby
Coquitlam
Maple Ridge
Vancouver International
New Westminster
Surrey
Richmond

0 km   5
0 miles   5

Canada

GREENLAND
U.S.A
CANADA
See next page
U.S.A
Pacific Ocean
MEXICO
Atlantic Ocean

Devon Island
Somerset Island
Baffin Island
NUNAVUT
Baker Lake
Rankin Inlet
Arviat
Churchill
MANITOBA
Thompson
Lake Winnipeg
Hudson Bay
Belcher Islands
James Bay
Ungava Bay
QUEBEC
ONTARIO
Seven
Albany
Moosonee
Winnipeg
Thunder Bay
Lake Superior
Sault Ste. Marie
Minneapolis
St. Paul
Lake Huron
Lake Michigan
North Bay
Ottawa
Montreal
Fredericton
Saint John
Sydney
Halifax
Toronto
Lake Ontario
London
Windsor
Lake Erie
Niagara Falls
Boston
Chicago
Pittsburgh
New York

For map symbols *see back flap*

Putting Eastern Canada on the Map

Most of Canada's 30 million people live close to the US border, in a band that stretches from the east coast across to British Columbia in the west. Over 60 percent of all Canadians are concentrated in the southeast corner of the country, in the provinces of Ontario and Quebec. This is the heartland of Canadian industry, including electronics, hydro-electricity, lumber, and paper. The maritime provinces of Nova Scotia, New Brunswick, and Prince Edward Island are Canada's smallest, but the beauty of their landscapes attracts thousands of tourists each year. Newfoundland and Labrador is also known for its rugged charm.

Cape Dor

Ivujivik

Mansel Island

Île Avaqqutaq

Churchill

H u d s o n B a y

MANITOBA

Belcher Islands

Nelson

Fort Sevem

Kuujjuarapik

Thompson

Long Island

Flin Flon

Chisasibi

The Pas

Akiniski Island

Seven

Lake Winnipeg

Eastmain

Albany

Yorkton

Red Lake

ONTARIO

Waskaganish (Fort Rupert)

16

Winnipeg

11

Hearst

Brandon

17

Nipigon

1

Thunder Bay

Timmins

25

Wawa

17

Fargo

Lake Superior

94

Duluth

Sault Ste. Marie

Sudbury

North

55

94

Minneapolis

Lake Michigan

75

Lake Huron

11

Rapid City

Sioux Falls

Lake Erie

Toronto

Windsor

London

Niag. Falls

Toronto

North York

401

Scarborough

Chicago

404

Rexdale

401

2

427

400

Pearson International Airport

York

East York

70

Indianapolis

Pittsburg

5

Toronto

Etobicoke

Lake Ontario

Washington D.

U.S.A.

81

8

Billy Bishop Toronto City Airport

Richmond

0 km   5

0 miles   5

Nashville

Lakeview

81

95

Charlotte

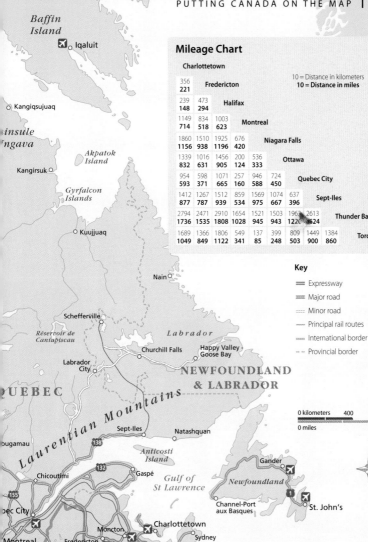

Baffin
Island

🛫 ○ Iqaluit

○ Kangiqsujuaq

insule
ngava

Akpatok
Island

Kangirsuk ○

Gyrfalcon
Islands

○ Kuujjuaq

Mileage Chart

Charlottetown

356 / **221**	**Fredericton**								
239 / **148**	473 / **294**	**Halifax**							
1149 / **714**	834 / **518**	1003 / **623**	**Montreal**						
1860 / **1156**	1510 / **938**	1925 / **1196**	676 / **420**	**Niagara Falls**					
1339 / **832**	1016 / **631**	1456 / **905**	200 / **124**	536 / **333**	**Ottawa**				
954 / **593**	598 / **371**	1071 / **665**	257 / **160**	946 / **588**	724 / **450**	**Quebec City**			
1412 / **877**	1267 / **787**	1512 / **939**	859 / **534**	1569 / **975**	1074 / **667**	637 / **396**	**Sept-Iles**		
2794 / **1736**	2471 / **1535**	2910 / **1808**	1654 / **1028**	1521 / **945**	1503 / **943**	1963 / **1220**	2613 / **1624**	**Thunder Bay**	
1689 / **1049**	1366 / **849**	1806 / **1122**	549 / **341**	137 / **85**	399 / **248**	809 / **503**	1449 / **900**	1384 / **860**	**Toronto**

10 = Distance in kilometers
10 = Distance in miles

Key

— Expressway
— Major road
⋯⋯ Minor road
— Principal rail routes
— International border
- - Provincial border

Nain ○

Scheffervile ○

Réservoir de
Caniapiscau

Labrador

Churchill Falls ○   Happy Valley -
                           Goose Bay ○

Labrador
City ○

**NEWFOUNDLAND
& LABRADOR**

QUEBEC

Laurentian Mountains

0 kilometers   400
0 miles   400

Sept-Iles ○   Natashquan ○

bugamau ○

138

Anticosti
Island

132

Chicoutimi ○   ○ Gaspé

Gulf of
St Lawrence

Gander ○

Newfoundland

155

ec City 🛫

Channel-Port
aux Basques ○

1

○ 🛫 St. John's

Montreal 🛫

Moncton ○   ○ 🛫 Charlottetown

Fredericton ○ 🛫   ○ Sydney

93

🛫 Halifax

89

Yarmouth ○

○ Boston

Atlantic
Ocean

w York ○

elphia ○

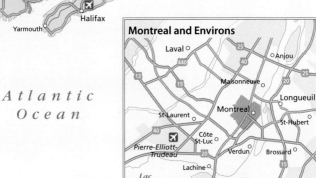

Montreal and Environs

Laval ○   ○ Anjou

440   25   40   25

13   15   Maisonneuve ○   20

St-Laurent ○   Longueuil ○

40   Montreal   ○ St-Hubert

Pierre-Elliott-
Trudeau 🛫   Côte
St-Luc ○

20   Verdun ○   Brossard ○

Lachine ○   15

Lac
St-Louis

0 km   5
0 miles   5

For map symbols *see back flap*

A PORTRAIT OF CANADA

Blessed with ancient forests, rugged mountains, and large cosmopolitan cities, Canada is unimaginably vast, stretching west from the Atlantic to the Pacific, and north to the Arctic Ocean. Around 20,000 years ago the country was inhabited by Aboriginal Peoples, but by the 19th century it had been settled by Europeans. Today Canada, which in 2017 celebrated the 150th anniversary of its confederation as a nation state, is noted as a liberal, multicultural society.

In part, Canada's heritage of tolerance is a result of its conflict-ridden past. Two centuries of compromise were necessary to fully establish the country. Following fighting between the British and French armies in the 1750s, the British won control of the country in 1759. The self-governing colonies of British North America spent three years hammering out the agreement that brought them together as the Dominion of Canada in 1867. Newfoundland did not become part of the nation until 1949. Powerful regional differences, particularly between French- and English-speaking Canada, meant that

the country has had difficulties evolving a national identity. When Pierre Berton, one of Canada's most prolific writers, was prompted to define a Canadian he evaded the question, replying: "Someone who knows how to make love in a canoe."

The second-largest country in the world, Canada has a surface area of 9,970,610 sq km (3,849,674 sq miles). Over 40 percent of the land is north of the treeline at 60° latitude; this extraordinarily hostile and sparsely inhabited wilderness is bitterly cold in winter, averaging -30°C (-22°F), and plagued by millions of insects in summer. Not surprisingly, most Canadians live in

The snow-laden rooftops of Quebec City overlooking the St. Lawrence River at dusk

◀ Royal Canadian Mounted Police riding on Canada Day, Ottawa the more temperate regions farther to the south. Of the country's 30 million inhabitants, more than 80 percent live within 200 km (124 miles) of the US border.

Flora and Fauna

In the far north, the permafrost of the treeless tundra (or taiga) supports the growth of only the toughest flora, such as lichen, mosses, and a range of unusually hardy varieties of flowers and grasses. In spring and fall, however, the tundra flora bursts into an impressive display of color. Animal life is abundant in this region, and includes the polar bear, arctic fox, wolf, seal, musk ox, and caribou.

Farther south, the boreal or coniferous forest covers a wide band from Newfoundland in the east to the Yukon in the west. A variety of trees here, including spruce, balsam fir, and jack pine, provides a home for those animals most typically thought of as Canadian – primarily moose, beaver, lynx, and black bear. The beaver is Canada's national symbol. It was the

European fashion for beaver hats that created and sustained the Canadian fur trade and opened up the interior to European settlers, paving the way for the growth of the modern nation.

In the east, deciduous forests containing the emblematic maple are populated by deer, raccoons, and mink. Across central Canada, the grasslands, known as the Prairies, house elk, gophers, and increasing numbers of buffalo.

British Columbia's temperate rain forests are rich in wildlife such as black-tailed deer, brown bear, and cougar. Rare orchids and ferns grow here, among towering cedars, firs, and spruce trees.

Spring flower from the Bruce Peninsula

The First Nations

Although thought of as a new country, Canada's prehistory dates back about 20,000 years to the end of the first Ice Age. At that time there was a land bridge joining Siberia to Alaska; Siberian hunter-nomads crossed this bridge to become the first human inhabitants of North America, and over the succeeding cen-

The bald eagle, a common sight around the Haida Gwaii archipelago in British Columbia

turies their descendants gradually moved south. Archaeological digs in the Old Crow River Basin in the Yukon have unearthed a collection of tools believed to date to this initial period of migration. These Siberian nomads were the ancestors of the continent's First Peoples.

Inuit children at Bathurst Inlet, Nunavut

By the 16th century, Spanish, French, and Portuguese traders were the first Europeans to have close dealings with the Aboriginal Peoples of the Americas, whom they named "Indians" in the mistaken belief that they had reached India. The "Indian" appellation stuck, and the "Red" was added by British settlers in the 17th century, when they met the Beothuks of Newfoundland, who daubed themselves in red ochre to repel insects. The Aboriginal Peoples of the far north were also given a name they did not want: "Eskimo," literally "eaters of raw meat." Given the history, it is hardly surprising that modern-day leaders of Canada's Aboriginal Peoples have rejected these names in favor of others: Aboriginal and First Nations are both acceptable, though the people of the north prefer Inuit (meaning "the people"). Included among Canada's First Peoples are the Métis, mixed-race descendants of Aboriginal Peoples and French-speaking European traders.

Society

The official languages of Canada are English and French, and the interplay between Canada's two largest linguistic and cultural groups is evident in the capital city of Ottawa, where every federal speech and bill has to be delivered in both languages. All packaging must also be bilingual. Canada's population is about 24 percent French Canadian, predominantly the descendants of French settlers who came to the colony of New France in the 17th and 18th centuries (see p51). Their English-speaking compatriots are largely descended from 18th- and 19th-century British immigrants.

Canada's reputation as a multicultural society began to be established in the 1800s, when successive waves of immigration, along with various settlement plans, brought people from all over the world to Canada. Today, perhaps the best way to experience this modern country's vibrant cultural mix is to visit its three largest cities – Toronto, Montreal, and Vancouver.

Government and Politics

Canada is a parliamentary democracy with a federal political system. Each province or territory has its own democratically elected provincial legislature headed by a Premier, and also sends elected

View from Centre Island's parks and gardens on Lake Ontario toward Toronto's CN Tower

Changing the Guard outside Ottawa's Parliament Building

movement. Twice since 1980 the Quebecois have been asked to vote in referenda seeking their support to leave Canada, and, although the electorate voted "No" both times, both were close results. The issue of Quebec's relationship with the rest of Canada is still unresolved, and further political disputes seem inevitable.

Since the 1980s aboriginal politics has come to the fore with campaigns for constitutional, land, and mineral rights. The Assembly of First Nations has been at the forefront of the establishment of the Inuit homeland, Nunavut. Current issues include battles for self-government and land claims, as well as hunting and fishing rights.

representatives to the federal parliament in Ottawa. The House of Commons is the main federal legislature. The Prime Minister is the head of the political structure, as well as an elected member of the House of Commons, where he must be able to command a majority. Bills passed in the Commons are forwarded to an upper chamber, the Senate, for ratification. At present, the Prime Minister appoints senators, although there is increasing pressure to make the upper chamber elective too. The nominal head of state is the British monarch, currently Queen Elizabeth II, and her Canadian representative is the Governor-General.

In recent decades, the dominant trend in Canadian politics has been regionalism. The provinces have sought to take back power from the center, which makes it difficult for any one political party to win majority support in all parts of the country at once. The most conspicuous aspect of this process has been the conflict over Quebec, where there is a strong separatist

The ceremonial unveiling of the new Nunavut flag in 1999

Canada has played its part in the major events of the 20th century, including both world wars, and today holds a prominent position in international politics. The country is a member of NATO and one of the Group of Eight (G8) countries – along with France, Germany, Italy, Japan, Russia, the UK and the US – which decide on world trade agreements.

Art and Culture

The vast and beautiful landscape of the country is a defining feature of Canadian culture. Outdoor pursuits such as hiking, skiing, and canoeing are high on the list of popular activities. Canadians are also great sports fans, and ice hockey, baseball, basketball, and Canadian football attract huge crowds of spectators, and foster deeply felt allegiances. In addition to their passion for sports, Canadians are also enthusiastic about the arts. This is the country that has produced internationally renowned classical pianist, Glenn Gould, and whose major cities possess well-respected orchestras. Canada has also produced more than its share of popular music stars, from ground breaking singer-songwriters such as Joni Mitchell and Neil Young, to more mainstream artists such as Bryan Adams, Celine Dion, Alanis Morissette, Shania Twain, and Justin Bieber. Canada's cosmopolitan culture also means that visitors are likely to find a wide choice of music in bars, cafés, and at the country's numerous festivals. All kinds of drama from Shakespeare to new writing can be seen at the renowned Stratford Shakespearean Festival, in Ontario. Many Canadian artists have looked to the wilderness as a source of inspiration. The first artist to attempt to express a sense of national identity was Tom Thomson, with his distinctive, brightly colored landscapes of Northern Ontario. He influenced the country's most celebrated group of painters, the Group of Seven (see pp168–9), who evolved a national style of painting capable of representing Canada's wilderness, a theme developed by their contemporaries and successors, notably Emily Carr (see p286).

International pop star Justin Bieber

Author Margaret Atwood, lauded worldwide

Canada's world-class museums and galleries represent the country's pride in its art collections: the outstanding Art Gallery of Ontario in Toronto (see pp182–3) has an extensive display of Group of Seven paintings, as well as Inuit art and cutting-edge contemporary art. Major contemporary Canadian artists on the international circuit include Janet Cardiff and Rodney Graham.

Among Canadian writers, there are distinguished practitioners in both English and French, and an impressive list of contemporary novelists includes such prize-winning authors as Margaret Atwood, Germaine Guèvremont, Yann Martel, Alice Munro, Michael Ondaatje, Jacques Poulin, and Carol Shields.

The Canadian film industry is thriving, with established directors such as David Cronenberg and Atom Egoyan continuing to create daring films. Vancouver, known as Hollywood North, is the third largest centre for the film industry in North America.

Behind Canada's flourishing cultural life lies a pride in its history and cosmopolitan heritage, and an affection for the land's daunting beauty.

Filmmaker and art house favorite Atom Egoyan

Landscape and Geology

Canada is the second-largest country in the world after Russia, covering an area almost as big as Europe. It was created from the world's oldest landmasses. The billion-year-old bowl-shaped Canadian Shield covers much of the country, dipping around Hudson Bay and rising to mountain ranges at its edges. The country is bordered by oceans on three sides, with a coastline 243,800 km (151,500 miles) long and an interior containing some two million lakes. Canada is well known for the diversity of its landscapes: from the frozen, barren north that descends to the mountainous west with its forest and wheat plains, through the wooded, hilly east, and the fertile lowlands of the southeast.

The Great Lakes region covers 3% of Canada's landmass, and comprises a fertile lowland bowl, vital to its agricultural economy.

The Prairies, also known as the Interior Plains, sweep from the Cordillera down to the US border. Once covered by grasslands, this is now one of the largest wheat-producing regions in the world.

The Rockies and the Western Cordillera

This region is part of one of the world's longest mountain chains. In Canada, the Cordillera comprises the Pacific Coastal Mountains and forested basins. Graduated peaks and ridges reveal Ice Age erosion, as does the Columbia Icefield (see p314). The Rockies (see pp262–3) developed from continental plate movement, which began about 120 million years ago.

Geographical Regions

Characterized by its variety, Canadian landscape falls into six main areas. The north of the country offers a landscape of tundra, with the far north ice-covered for much of the year. In the west and south, the warmer, fertile lands of the Cordillera and Prairies support the rural population. To the east, the Great Lakes area is an agricultural center. The vast Canadian Shield cradles the plains and rises to form the northern Innuitian region and the Appalachians in the south.

Innuitian Region and Arctic Lowlands

The Rockies & Western Cordillera

Canadian Shield

Prairies

Appalachians

Great Lakes

The Appalachians' rolling landscape is two-thirds woodland and covers both arable lowland areas and the highest peaks in Quebec. These are found on the Gaspé Peninsula, the outer mountain ring of the Canadian Shield highland. Most of the Appalachian mountain chain lies in the US. These peaks are nature's barrier between the eastern seaboard and the continental interior lowlands.

The Canadian Shield, formed of the 1,100-million-year-old bedrock of the North American continent, is the core of the country. It spreads out from Hudson Bay for 5 million sq km (1.9 million sq miles). The center is scrub and rock, and rises to steep mountains around the rim.

The Innuitian region stretches northward from the Arctic Lowlands' modest height of 100–700 m (330–2,300 ft) above sea level to the peaks of the Innuitian mountain range, at their highest on Elles-mere Island at 2,926 m (9,600 ft). Vigorous glaciation for millenia has developed deep fjords, sharp peaks, and frost patterns on the earth. This region is rich in oil, coal, and gas.

Canada's Wildlife

By the time it emerged from the last Ice Age 10,000 years ago, Canada had developed a geography and climate that remains one of the most diverse on Earth. In the north, the Arctic weather produces a harsh, barren desert, in darkness for several months and frozen most of the year. By contrast, parts of the country's most southerly province, Ontario, share a latitude with northern California and offer fertile forests laced with rivers and lakes. In southern Canada, many varieties of wildlife flourish in the coniferous forest that covers the ancient rocks of the Canadian Shield. In the central plain are wheat-filled open prairies. From here, foothills lead to the Rocky Mountains, which gradually roll westward to coastal mountains and the balmy landscape of temperate rainforest along the Pacific coast.

The muskox is a gregarious herd animal and a remnant of the last Ice Age. Its thick topcoat of guard hair and undercoat of finer, fleecier hair keep it warm even at –45°C (–50°F).

The Boreal Forest
The boreal forest extends from eastern Canada, across most of Quebec and Ontario, and into the northern parts of the prairie provinces. It consists of a mix of spruce, pine, birch, and aspen, and occurs mostly on the giant rock outcrop of the Canadian Shield (*see pp28–9*). Dotted with thousands of lakes, it is a rich habitat for some of Canada's best-known wildlife.

The Prairies
Once referred to as a "sea of grass," the Canadian prairie is now predominantly agricultural in nature, specializing in growing wheat and other grains, and ranching prime beef cattle. While little original prairie wilderness remains, this is still a land of great open spaces that supports a surprising, often rare, wildlife population.

The timber wolf, or gray wolf, was hunted almost to extinction by 1950. It has now returned to the more isolated parts of its range in the boreal forest.

The pronghorn antelope is the last of its species to survive in North America. The fastest American mammal, it can reach speeds of over 75 km (47 miles) per hour.

The loon has a haunting call that rings out over northern lakes and is symbolic of the Canadian wilderness.

The bison now exists in only two remaining wild herds in Alberta and the Northwest Territories.

Canada's Sports Fish

From the northern pike and lake trout in the north to the walleye and smallmouth bass in the south, Canada is blessed with a large number of sports fish species. The arctic char, plentiful in the far north, is also prized for its taste. Some fish that are much sought after as sport in Europe (the common carp, for example) are regarded as "trash," or undesirable, in Canada, and exist in large numbers in lakes and rivers across the Canadian Prairies.

Fishing is one of Canada's most popular sports and is superbly supported by over 40 national parks, each containing plentiful rivers and lakes.

Salmon migrating upriver provide an annual challenge for the keen sports fisherman. Canada has a fifth of the freshwater in the world, but deep sea angling can also prove rewarding.

The Rocky Mountains

The Rocky Mountains begin in the foothills of western Alberta and rise into British Columbia. Along with the Columbia Mountains and the coastal mountains, they form a unique environment that ranges from heavily forested lower slopes, through alpine meadows, to snow-covered rocky peaks. This habitat is home to some of the most majestic wildlife in Canada.

The Canadian Arctic

North of the 60th parallel of latitude, the forest yields to arctic tundra and rock. The tundra is mostly bare, and frozen year-round a few inches below the surface, with the icy ground being known as permafrost. During the brief summer the top layer thaws, and the Arctic bursts into bloom. Even though the Arctic is a freezing desert with little precipitation, wildlife flourishes.

The recurring horns of a mature male bighorn sheep, found in more remote spots of the Rockies, weigh as much as all its bones put together.

The endangered polar bear spends most of its life alone, out on the polar ice pack, hunting for seals.

Canada's grizzly bear stands up to 2.75 m (9 ft) high and weighs up to 350 kg (772 lbs). It feeds on roots, berries, and meat.

The caribou is a North American cousin of the reindeer. Caribou in the arctic migrate with the season in herds of 10,000, heading north on to the tundra in spring, south into the forest during winter.

Multicultural Canada

Canada prides itself on its multiculturalism. The country has evolved a unique way of adjusting to the cultural needs of its increasingly diverse population. In contrast to the US's "melting pot," Canada has opted for what is often called the "Canadian mosaic," a model based on accepting diversity rather than assimilation. The origins of this tolerant and fruitful approach are embedded deep in Canadian history. Fearful of attack by the US in 1793, the British safeguarded the religious and civic institutions of their French-Canadian subjects in the hope that they would not ally with the Americans. This policy set the pattern of compromise that is now a hallmark of Canada. Citizens of British and French ancestry still make up the bulk of the population of 35 million, but over 20 percent are foreign-born, the highest proportion of all the G8 countries.

Inuit mother and daughter on Baffin Island, Nunavut

Aboriginal Canadians

Today there are well over one million Aboriginal Canadians, though national census figures usually break this group down into three sub-sections: Aboriginals (850,000), Métis (Aboriginal and French mixed race 450,000), and Inuit (60,000). Of this, about 60 percent are Status Indians, meaning that they are officially settled on reserve land. However, more than half of Status Indians now live away from reserve land, and only 900 of Canada's 2,370 reserves are still inhabited. These lands are home to 608 First Nations groups, or bands, which exercise varying degrees of self-government through their own elected councils. Since the 1970s, progressive councils have played key roles in the reinvigoration of traditional culture. Most non-Status

Aboriginal Canadians are now integrated into the rest of Canada's population.

Rarely is the membership of a reserve descended from just one tribe. The largest band is the Six Nations of the Grand River, in Ontario, where 19,000 inhabitants come from 13 groups, including the Mohawk, Delaware, and Seneca peoples.

In the far north, where white settlers have always been rare, the Inuit have a small majority. A result of their self-determination was the creation of Nunavut, a semi-autonomous Inuit homeland comprising 349,650 sq km (135,000 sq miles) of the eastern Arctic, created officially in April of 1999. Nunavut means "our land" in the Inuit language, and traditional skills of hunting and igloo-building have been reintroduced to this region.

British and Irish Canadians

Canadians of British and Irish descent constitute a large percentage of the country's population. The first English settlers arrived in the wake of the fleets that fished the waters off Newfoundland in the 16th century. Thereafter, there was a steady trickle of English, Scottish, Welsh, and Irish immigrants and several mass migrations, prompted either by adverse politics at home or fresh opportunities in Canada. The Kingdom of Scotland established Nova Scotia (New Scotland) in 1621, one of the earliest colonies in Canada, and the Irish poured across the Atlantic during and after the potato famine (1845–49). When the Prairie provinces opened up in the 1880s and, later, at the end of both world wars, another large-scale migration took place.

These British and Irish settlers did much to shape Canada, establishing its social and cultural norms and founding its legal and political institutions. Canada's official Head of State is still the British monarch.

British poster of the 1920s promoting emigration to Canada

French Canadians

Canada's French-speakers make up about 20 percent of the total population, and are the country's second-largest ethnic group. They are mainly based in Quebec and New Brunswick, but pockets thrive in other Canadian provinces. The French first reached the Canadian mainland in 1535 when Jacques Cartier sailed up the St. Lawrence River in search of a sea-route to Asia. Fur-traders, priests, and farmers followed in Cartier's footsteps, and by the end of the 17th century, New France, as the colony was known, was well established. After the British captured New France in the Seven Years' War of 1756–63 *(see pp52–3)*, most French colonists stayed on as British subjects. The French-speakers maintained their own religious and civic institutions and a feeling of independence that has grown over time. Since the 1960s, the constitutional link between Quebec and the rest of the country has been the subject of political debate, with a strong minority of Quebecois pressing for full independence *(see p60)*.

German Canadians

Although there have been German-speakers in Canada since the 1660s, the first major migration came between 1850–1900, with other mass arrivals following both world wars. On the whole, the English-speaking majority has absorbed the Germans, but distinctive pockets of German-speakers hold strong today in Lunenburg, Nova Scotia *(see p92)*, and Kitchener-Waterloo in Ontario. The rural communities surrounding Kitchener-Waterloo are strongholds of the Amish *(see p223)*, a religious sect that speaks Pennsylvania Dutch, and whose members shun the trappings of modern life and travel in horse-drawn carts wearing traditional homemade clothes.

German food and drink, especially its beer-making techniques, have added to Canadian cuisine.

Street scene in Chinatown, Toronto

Italian Canadians

The widespread Italian presence in Canada can prove hard to see, as, for the most part, all 600,000 immigrants have merged almost seamlessly with the English speakers. There are, however, exceptions; in Toronto, you can find numerous Italian restaurants and espresso bars in the "Little Italy" neighborhood on College Street, west of Bathurst. The first major influx of Italian Canadians came in the wake of the civil wars that disrupted Italy in the second half of the 19th century; another wave arrived in the 1940s and 1950s after World War II. Immigration continues into the 21st century, with two percent of Canadians today speaking Italian as their first language.

German beer stein

Chinese Canadians

During the 1850s, Chinese laborers arrived in Canada to work in the gold fields of British Columbia. Thereafter, they played a key role in the construction of the railroads, settling new towns and cities, as their work progressed eastward. During this period the Chinese suffered much brutal racism, including laws that enforced statutory discrimination.

Political uncertainties caused a flood of Chinese immigration just before the return of Hong Kong to China by the British in 1997. Most settlers chose Toronto, Montreal, and Vancouver, the latter now having the second-largest Chinatown in North America. With the Chinese focus on keeping large families together, most new arrivals aim for an already established Chinese community. About half of all Canada's immigrants today come from Asia.

Ukrainian Canadians

Although Ukrainians are a small fraction of the Canadian population, numbering less than three percent, they have had a strong cultural influence, especially in the Prairie Provinces, where the cupolas of their churches rise above many midwestern villages. The first major wave of Ukrainian migrants arrived in the 1890s as refugees from Tsarist persecution. The Soviet regime and the aftermath of World War II caused a second influx in the 20th century.

Woman in native Ukrainian dress in Battleford, Saskatchewan

French Canada

Many Canadians are quick to point out that Canada's origins are more French than British; that the first European Canadians were explorers from France, and therefore called *Canadiens*. French Canadians have had a centuries-long history of conquest and battle to preserve their language and culture, which are strongest in Quebec and parts of Atlantic Canada. This has left large parts of the country with a French cultural base that lives on in language, religion, and the arts.

The heart of French Canada is Quebec, a province many times the size of France. Here, 85 percent of people count French as their mother tongue. French is not just the language of food, folklore, and love; it is also the language of business, government, and law. Calls for independence for Quebec throughout the 20th century led to the passing, in 2006, of a qualified government motion recognizing the Quebecois as a "nation within Canada."

Language

French is the joint official language of Canada, but it has mutated in much the same way that North American English has. *Canadiens*, especially those in the bigger cities, have adopted some anglicisms; modern English words relating to industries and trades introduced by English-speakers are favorites. Conversely, some words that have passed out of fashion in France survive here; Canada is one of the few places where a cart remains a *charette*, for example, instead of a *tombereau*, and the *fin-de-semaine* is the time to get away for some relaxation, rather than *le weekend*. Young Quebecois in particular are also far more free in using the informal *tu*, rather than the more formal *vous* that their parents would perhaps consider polite.

Wide varieties exist in the quality and style of French spoken. The Paris-influenced intonation of Montreal's college-educated *haute bourgeoisie*, for example, is quite distinct from the rhythmic gutturals of the Acadian fishermen of the Maritimes. Residents of Quebec's Saguenay-Lac-Saint-Jean region speak a hard, clear French that must sound very like that of their Norman forbears.

Over the years Quebecois have evolved a dialect called *joual*, which is informal, slangy, and peppered with anglicisms. It is also very colorful and viewed with a mix of pride and disdain. The accent may be hard for foreigners to follow.

Food

Canadiens have always considered themselves the epicures of Canada, and with some justice, enjoying the delights of the table more passionately than their English-speaking counterparts. Traditional food is rich and hearty. Meat pies are a specialty: *cipaille* comprises layers of game meat under a flaky crust, and the more common *tourtière* has a filling made of ground beef spiced with cloves. Salmon pie, stews made with pigs' feet, and meatballs in a rich gravy are also typical. Desserts are rich; the Acadian *tarte au sucre* (sugar pie) is popular, as well as *pouding au chômeur* (literally "pudding of the unemployed"), an upside-down cake with a sweet, caramelized base of sugar baked into a rich batter.

Musician Félix Leclerc was a guardian of Quebec's folk music

Music

Chansonniers are the troubadours of French Canada. Rooted in the traditional music of the first settlers, their haunting songs and simple melodies, such as the ballads of Felix Leclerc, might be melancholy or upbeat, but they are almost always romantic. These folk songs, accompanied by guitar, usually reflect optimism and a deep love for the land. Quebec *chansonnier* Gilles Vigneault's *Mon Pays* has become a nationalist anthem for those seeking independence. Of course, French music is not confined to the traditional; there are several successful rock, pop, and independent bands. Acadia's singers are often *chansonnières*, including Edith Butler and Angèle Arseneault vividly evoking the sadness and joy of life by the sea.

Sugar pie, a traditional Acadian family dessert, served at celebrations

Traditional Catholic church in Chéticamp, Cape Breton Island

Faith

The first French settlers were Roman Catholic, many very devout and zealous. The founders of Montreal, Paul Chomédy Sieur de Maisonneuve and Jeanne Mance, had hoped to create a new society based on Christian principles. Much of that devotion has evaporated in the modern age, especially in Quebec, which has one of the lowest church-attendance records in the country. Past fidelity has, however, left permanent monuments. Tiny French villages in Quebec and New Brunswick often have huge stone churches with glittering tin roofs, gilding, and ornate interiors. Some parish churches in Montreal, such as the magnificent Basilique Notre-Dame-de-Montréal (see pp116–17), would pass for cathedrals in larger US cities.

Nationalism

There has been a nationalist strain to most Canadien aspirations since the founding of Modern Canada. Quebecois entered the 1867 Canadian Confederation (see p54) only because French leaders persuaded them that the deal would preserve their faith and language. The 1960s and 1970s took the campaign into a new phase, with the aim being the independence of Quebec, as the politics of mere survival rose to the politics of assertiveness (with French President Charles de Gaulle adding his rallying cry "Vive le Québec – libre!" in 1966).

Acadians in New Brunswick gained real political power to preserve their unique heritage, Franco-Ontarians fought for control over their own schools,

Quebec flag with Bourbon lilies

and Manitobans used the courts to force their provincial government to translate all Manitoba statutes into French.

This resurgence of national pride was felt most strongly in Quebec, where the charismatic and popular politician René Lévesque and his Parti-Québecois won the provincial election in 1976 and made outright separatism respectable. The party now regularly wins local elections and has so far held two referenda on independence. Both times Quebecois said no by the narrowest of margins, but the threat still dominates Canada's political life.

Symbols

The Quebec flag has a white cross on a blue background with a white Bourbon lily in each quarter. Acadians have created their own flag by adding a gold star to the French tricolor, which symbolizes Stella Maris (Star of the Sea), named after the Virgin Mary. The patron saint of French Canada is St. Jean-Baptiste (St. John the Baptist); parades and parties mark his feast day on June 24. The celebrations take on a strongly nationalist style in Quebec, where the big day is called the Fête National. The provincial bird of Quebec is the snowy owl, and the flower remains the white lily, both of which flourish in the province.

Demonstrators during a referendum vote for the independence of Quebec

Aboriginal Canadians

Most archaeologists believe that the first inhabitants of North America crossed from Siberia to Alaska around 25,000 years ago. These hunter-nomads came in search of mammoth and bison, the ice-age animals that constituted their basic diet. The first wave of migrants was reinforced by a steady trickle of Siberian peoples over the next 15,000 years, and slowly the tribes worked their way east and south until they reached the Atlantic and South America. Over the centuries, the descendants of these hunter-nomads evolved a wide range of cultures, which were shaped by their particular environment. In the icy north or across the barren wastes of Newfoundland, life was austere; but the fertile soils of Ontario and the fish-rich shores of British Columbia nourished sophisticated societies based on fishing and farming.

Europeans began to arrive in numbers during the 17th century. In Newfoundland, the first part of Canada settled by whites, interracial relations were initially cordial but soured when new settlers encroached on ancient hunting grounds. In a pattern repeated across the continent, the First Peoples, many dying from European diseases, were driven to inhospitable lands.

The Iroquois

Spread along the St. Lawrence River and the shores of the Great Lakes were the Iroquois-speaking tribes, among whom were the Mohawks, the Huron, and the Seneca. These tribes hunted and fished, but they also cultivated beans, pumpkins, squash, and corn, growing everything in abundance for a year-round food supply. This enabled them to live in large villages, often with several hundred inhabitants. Their traditional dwelling was the longhouse, built of cedar poles bent to form a protective arch and covered with bark. These settlements were all surrounded by high palisades made of sharpened wooden stakes, a

An Iroquois-built longhouse

necessary precaution as warfare between the tribes was endemic.

Cornplanter, a 17th-century chief of the Seneca tribe

The Plains Peoples

War was also commonplace on the plains of southern Manitoba and Saskatchewan (the Prairies), where the majority Blackfoot tribe was totally reliant on the buffalo: they ate the meat, used the hide for clothes and tents, and filed the bones into tools. The first Blackfoot hunted the buffalo by means of cleverly conceived traps, herding the animals and stampeding them off steep cliffs *(see p300)*. The horse was unknown to the original inhabitants of the Americas –

First Nations people on horseback hunting buffalo with arrows

A Blackfoot camp, showing traditional homes

their largest beast of burden was the dog – but the Spanish conquistadores brought the horse with them when they colonized South America in the 1500s. Thereafter, horses were slowly traded north, until they reached the Canadian plains. The arrival of the horse transformed Blackfoot life: it made the buffalo easy to hunt and, with a consistent food supply now assured, the tribe developed a militaristic culture, focusing particularly on the valor of their young men – the "braves."

Peoples of the Pacific Coast

The First Nations peoples of the Pacific Coast were divided into a large number of small tribes such as the Tlingit and the Salish. The ocean was an abundant source of food; with this necessity taken care of, the First Nations developed an elaborate ceremonial life featuring large and lively feasts, the potlachs, in which clans tried to outdo each other with the magnificence of their gifts. The peoples of this region were also superb woodcarvers, their most celebrated works of art being totem poles. Each pole featured a myth from the tribe's religion; magical birds and beasts mix with semi-human figures to tell a story in carved panels rising up the pole.

Totem pole in Stanley Park

Sqylax tribal celebration in British Columbia

Terminology

For Canadians, the words "Eskimo" and "Red Indian" or just "Indian" are unacceptable. They are seen as terms of abuse, as they hark back to times when whites dominated the country and crushed its original population. The word "Eskimo" has been replaced by "Inuit," but modern substitutes for "Indian" are not as clear-cut. Some people choose "Aboriginal", others prefer "Indigenous," and many speak of Canada's "First Peoples" or "First Nations." All are acceptable, but it is preferable to determine a specific tribe or band name, such as "Cree" or "Iroquois."

The Inuit and the Peoples of the Northern Forests

Stretching in a band from Alaska to Greenland, the far north was home to the Inuit, nomadic hunters who lived in skin tents in the summer and igloos in the winter. Arctic conditions and limited food supply meant that they foraged in small family groups and gathered together only in special circumstances – during the annual caribou migration, for instance. To the south of the Inuit, and also widespread across modern-day Canada, were the tribes of the northern forest, including the Naskapi, the Chipewyan, and the Wood Cree. These tribes were also nomadic hunters, dependent on fish and seal, or deer and moose. Successful hunters earned prestige, and the tribal priest (shaman) was expected to keep the spirit world benevolent, but there was little other social organization.

An Inuit hunter by his igloo home

An Inuit using a harpoon to hunt through the ice sheet

Aboriginal Issues

Paul Okalik became Nunavut's first Premier in 1999

Since the 1960s, Canada's Aboriginal peoples have recovered some of their self-confidence. A key development was the creation of the Assembly of First Nations (AFN), an intertribal organization that has become an influential player on the national scene. In the 1980s, the AFN successfully argued for a greater degree of self-government on the reservations and tackled the federal government on land rights, sponsoring a series of court cases that highlighted the ways in which the Aboriginal population had been stripped of its territories. The AFN was also involved in the establishment of Nunavut *(see p61)*, the homeland for the Inuit created in 1999 from part of the Northwest Territories. By comparison with their white compatriots, Canada's Aboriginal population remains, nonetheless, poor and disadvantaged. The rectification of historic wrongs will take decades, even assuming that the political will remains strong enough to improve matters.

Art in Canada

Inuit and other First Nations groups have produced art in Canada since prehistoric times: the Inuit carved wood or antler sculptures, and other groups were responsible for works from rock paintings to richly decorated pottery. Early European immigrants, both French and English, generally eschewed the traditions of the First Peoples and followed European forms. Throughout the 19th and early 20th centuries, artists traveled to Paris, London, and New York to study European art. It was in the 1900s that painters sought to develop a distinctly national style. However, one consistent subject of Canadian painting is the country itself: a preoccupation with its lush forests, stately landscapes, and expanse of freezing northern wilderness. Today, Canadian art reflects a wide range of art movements, with Aboriginal art in particular fetching high prices among collectors.

On the Saint Lawrence (1897) oil painting by Maurice Cullen

Painters in the New World

In the 1600s French settlers in Canada either imported religious paintings or commissioned stock subjects to adorn their new churches. Only Samuel de Champlain, the "Father of New France" *(see p50)*, stands out for his sketches of the Huron tribe. After the English conquest in the 1760s, art moved from religion to matters of politics, the land, and the people. Army officers, such as Thomas Davies (1737–1812), painted fine detailed works, conveying their love of the landscape. Artists such as Robert Field (1769–1819), trained in Neo-Classicism, which was prevalent in Europe at the time, and became very popular, as

did Quebec painters Antoine Plamondon (1804–95) and Théophile Hamel (1817–70). Cornelius Krieghoff (1815–72) settled in Quebec and was famous for his snow scenes of both settlers and First Nations people. His contemporary, Paul Kane (1810–71), recorded the lives of the First Nations on an epic journey across Canada. He then completed over 100 sketches and paintings, of which *Mah-Min*, or *The Feather* (c.1856), is one of the most impressive *(see p48)*. During the 19th century, painters focused on the Canadian landscape. Homer Watson (1855–1936) and Ozias

Leduc (1864–1955) were the first artists to learn their craft in Canada. Watson said, "I did not know enough to have Paris or Rome in mind. … I felt Toronto had all I needed." His canvases portray Ontarian domestic scenes.

After Confederation in 1867, the Royal Canadian Academy of Arts and the National Gallery of Canada were founded in 1883. Artists could now train at home, but many still left to study in Paris. Curtis Williamson (1867–1944) and Edmund Morris (1871–1913) returned from France determined to revitalize their tired national art. In 1907 they formed the Canadian Art Club, where new schools such as Impressionism were shown. James Wilson Morrice (1865–1924), Maurice Cullen (1866–1934), and Marc Aurèle de Foy Suzor-Coté (1869–1937) were key figures in this move toward modernity.

Modern Painters

Before World War I, Toronto artists criticized the influence of Europe and objected to the lack of a national identity in art. By the 1920s, the most influential set of Canadian artists, the Group of Seven *(see pp168–9)*, had defined Canadian painting in their boldly colored landscapes, such as A. Y. Jackson's *Terre Sauvage* (1913). Though he died before the formation of the Group, Tom Thomson is seen as a major influence. Three painters who came to prominence in the 1930s were influenced by the Group but had very different muses. Each artist was distinguished by a passion for their own province: David Milne (1882–1953), was known for his still lifes; LeMoine Fitzgerald (1890–1956) for his domestic and backyard scenes; and Emily Carr (1871–1945) *(see p286)* for her striking depiction

Lawren S. Harris, painter (1885–1970)

Skidegate, Graham Island, BC (1928), a later work by Emily Carr

of the west coast Salish people and their totem poles. Carr was the first woman artist to achieve high regard. A writer as well as painter, her poem *Renfrew* (1929) describes her intense relationship with nature, which is reflected in her paintings: "… in the distance receding plane after plane… cold greens, gnarled stump of gray and brown."

The strong influence of the Group of Seven provoked a reaction among successive generations of painters. John Lyman (1886–1967) rejected the group's rugged nationalism. Inspired by Matisse, he moved away from using land as the dominant subject of painting. Lyman set up the Contemporary Arts Society in Montreal and promoted new art between 1939–48; even Surrealism reached the city.

Since World War II there has been an explosion of new forms based on abstraction. In Montreal, Paul-Emile Borduas (1905–60) and two colleagues formed the Automatists, whose inspirations were Surrealism and Abstract Impressionism. By the 1950s Canadian painters achieved international acclaim. Post-war trends were also taken up in Toronto, where The Painters Eleven produced abstract paintings. Today, artists work across the range of contemporary art movements, incorporating influences from around the world and from Canada's cultural mosaic. Experimental work by painters such as Jack Bush, Greg Carnoe,

and Joyce Wieland continues strongly in the wake of ideas from the 1960s. Canada now boasts a plethora of public and private galleries, and exceptional collections of 20th-century art.

Aboriginal Art

The art of the Inuit *(see pp330–31)* and the Northwest First Nations is highly valued in Canada. Pre-historic Inuit finds reveal beautiful objects, from sculpted figurines to carved harpoon heads, which were largely created for religious use. With the arrival of the Europeans the Inuit quickly adapted their artistic skills to make objects for sale such as sculptures made from ivory, bone, and stone. Today, Inuit artists such as Aqghadluk, Qaqaq Ashoona, and Tommy Ashevak are noted for their contribution to contemporary Canadian art,

Robert Murray's *Sculpture*

especially their sculpture and wallhangings. The sculpture of the Northwest coast First Nations people is known worldwide, particularly the cedar-wood carvings of Haida artist Bill Reid (1920–98), the totem poles of Richard Krentz, and the Kwa Gulth Big House at Fort Rupert by Chief Tony Hunt.

Painters such as Norval Morisseau, Carl Ray, and Daphne Odjig cover a range of styles, from Realism to Abstract. Aboriginal art celebrates the culture of its people, from their legendary survival skills, tales, and myths, to their land and the fight for its preservation.

Sculpture

European sculpture arrived in Canada with the French, who created sacred figures to adorn their churches. Sculptors such as Louis Quévillon (1749–1823) carved decorative altarpieces as well as fine marble statues in Montreal. European traditions continued to dominate through the 19th century, and it was not until the 20th century that civic monuments were required for Canada's new cities. The façade of the Quebec Parliament was designed by Louis-Philippe Hébert (1850–1917).

Native subjects were incorporated into much 20th-century sculpture, as were European styles including Art Nouveau and Art Deco. Since the 1960s, sculptors such as Armand Vaillancourt (b.1929) and Robert Murray (b.1936) have sought to develop a Canadian style. Modern materials and the influence of conceptual art inform the work of current artists including Michael Snow. Their work can be seen not just in museums but also in commercial and civic buildings.

The late Haida sculptor Bill Reid

Literature and Music in Canada

As the Canadian poet the Reverend Edward Hartley Dewart wrote in 1864, "A national literature is an essential element in the formation of a national character." Much Canadian literature and music is concerned with defining a national consciousness and also reflects the cultural diversity of the country. Both English and French speakers have absorbed a variety of influences from the US, Britain, and France, as well as from the other nations whose immigrants make up the population. The Europeans' relationship with First Nations peoples has also affected the style and content of much Canadian fiction and poetry, as have the often harsh realities of living in a land of vast wilderness.

Stars of the popular 1934 film *Anne of Green Gables*

New Beginnings

Much of the earliest writing in Canada (between the mid-1500s and 1700s) was by explorers, fur traders, soldiers, and missionaries. French lawyer Marc Lescarbot's *Histoire de la Nouvelle-France* (1609) is an early example of pioneer commentary and is a lively record of his adventures in Nova Scotia. After the English conquest of 1760, New France was subdued, but by the 19th century, French poets began producing patriotic poems such as *Le Vieux Soldat Canadien* (1855) by Octave Crémazie (1827–79), sparking a renaissance of poetry that continues today.

English writing was concerned with man's struggle with nature and life in the new world. *Roughing it in the Bush* (1852)

by Susanna Moodie is a tale of struggles in isolated northern Ontario. British Columbia was the last region to be settled, and a captivating memoir is *A Pioneer Gentlewoman in British Columbia: the Recollections of Susan Allison* (1876). Allison came from England to teach in the town of Hope and was the first European woman to make the dangerous journey across the Hope Mountains on horseback. Much 19th-century Canadian fiction romanticizes the past, such as *The Golden Dog* (1877) by William Kirby (1817–1906), with its idealized view of 18th-century Quebec. Epic novels of the time focused on the lives and culture of Aboriginal Peoples, notably *Wacousta* (1832) by John Richardson (1796–1852). Archibald Stansfield

Belaney (1888–1938) took on a new identity as an Ojibway writer named Grey Owl *(see p254)*, producing some of Canada's best-loved literature. *Pilgrims of the Wild* (1935) tells of his journey to find sanctuary for the over-hunted beaver. *The Adventures of Sajo and her Beaver People* (1935) and *Tales of an Empty Cabin* (1936) are laments for the wild and lost traditions.

Classics of the early 1900s deal with domesticity. These include *Anne of Green Gables* (1908) by L. M. Montgomery (1874–1942). Humorous writing was led by Stephen Leacock *(see p222)*, and Thomas Chandler Haliburton (1796–1865), a judge who created Sam Slick, narrator of *The Clockmaker* (1836). Painter Emily Carr's *A House of all Sorts* (1944) describes her days as a landlady.

Poetry

Early English language poets Standish O'Grady (1793–1841) and Alexander McLachan (1818–96) wrote verse that reflected a colonial point of view. The genre looked critically at an iniquitous motherland (England), while praising the opportunities available in the New World. Creators of a "new" Canadian poetry in the 1870s and 1980s used detailed descriptions of landscape to highlight man's efforts to conquer landscape. Two notable authors were Charles Mair (1838–1927) and Isabella Valancy Crawford (1850–1887). By the 20th century the idea of the wilderness stayed at

Internationally renowned poet and songwriter Leonard Cohen (1934–2016)

the center of Canadian poetry, but verse was written in a sparer style that mirrored the starkness of the Group of Seven's landscape paintings *(see pp168–9)*. The popular ballads of Robert Service (1874–1958) deal with history, and he is noted for his gold rush poems such as *The Spell of the Yukon* (1907) and the later *Rhymes of a Roughneck* (1950). John McCrae (1872–1918) wrote one of the most famous World War I poems, *In Flanders Fields* (1915).

Modern English and French poetry now have a worldwide audience, with writers such as Anne Wilkinson, Irving Layton, Earle Birney, E. J. Pratt, Leonard Cohen, and Patrick Anderson, whose *Poem on Canada* (1946) looks at the impact of nature on European mentalities. The simple power of French writer Anne Hébert's poems, such as *Le Tombeau des Rois* (The Kings' Tombs) (1953) focuses on the universal themes of childhood, memory, and death. A postwar boom in literature was fostered by the Canada Council for the Arts.

Aboriginal Writing

Despite a powerful oral tradition – where stories are both owned and passed down through families and clans – autobiography, children's books, plays, short stories, poetry, essays, and novels have been produced by Aboriginal writers since the 19th century. One of the most popular autobiographies of this period was written by Ojibway author George Copway (1818–69). Titled *The Life, History, and Travels of Kah-ge-ga-ga-bowh* (1847), it had six editions in a year. The first book to be published by an aboriginal woman is thought to be *Cogewea, The Half-Blood* (1927), by Okanagan author

Mourning Dove (1888–1936). Another Okanagan novelist, Jeannette Armstrong (b.1948), published *Slash* in 1985. The struggles of a Métis woman in modern Canada are described in the best-selling autobiography of Maria Campbell in *Halfbreed* (1973).

Legend and political rights inform much aboriginal fiction, such as Pauline Johnson's *The White Wampum* (1895) and Beatrice (Culleton) Mosionier's *In Search of April Raintree* (1983). The first Inuit work in English was *Harpoon of the Hunter* (1970), a story of coming of age in the northern Arctic by Markoosie (b.1942). One of Canada's top contemporary playwrights is Cree author Thompson Highway (b.1951), who deals with the reality of life on the reservations.

Canadian poet Robert Service in 1942

Modern Fiction

Since the 1940s, many Canadian writers have achieved international fame: Margaret Atwood (b.1939) is well known for her poetry, novels, and criticism, while Carol Shields (1935–2003) won the prestigious Booker Prize for *The Stone Diaries* in 1996. Mordecai Richler (1931–2001) and Robertson Davies (1913–95) are noted for their wry take on contemporary Canadian society. Many authors have reached a wider public through film adaptations of their books. Gabrielle Roy's *Bonheur d'Occasion* (1945) became 1983's *The Tin Flute*; a novel by W. P. Kinsella, *Shoeless Joe* (1982), became *Field of Dreams* in 1989; and the 1996 adaptation of Michael Ondaatje's *The English Patient* (1992) won nine

Michael Ondaatje, the acclaimed author of *The English Patient*

Oscars. There is a strong Canadian tradition of short-story writing, one master being Alice Munro (b.1931). Popular history is highly regarded; noted author Pierre Berton (1920–2004) wrote 40 books on the nation's history.

Music in Canada

Some of the biggest names in the music industry are Canadian. A strong tradition of folk and soft rock has produced such artists as Leonard Cohen, Kate and Anna McGarrigle, Joni Mitchell, and Neil Young. Other singer/songwriters who have continued the tradition of reflective, melodic hits include Alanis Morissette and k. d. lang; and the Cowboy Junkies and Shania Twain have their own takes on country music. Stars such as Justin Bieber, Celine Dion, and Bryan Adams have made a huge impact in Europe and the US. In the classical sphere, orchestras such as the Montréal Orchestre Symphonique are world famous, as is the late-pianist Glenn Gould. Jazz is represented by the pianist Oscar Peterson (1925–2007), and every year Montreal hosts a famous jazz festival.

Legendary composer and folk singer Joni Mitchell

Sports in Canada

Canadians are avid sports fans, and most of the country's cities and towns offer visitors a chance to see year-round sports entertainment. Although the official national game is lacrosse – a First Nations game in which the ball is caught and tossed in a leather cradle on a stick – Canadians' greatest enthusiasm is for ice hockey. Baseball, basketball, and Canadian football (similar to the US game) are also big crowd-pullers. Major cities regularly attract international stars to world-class racing, golf, and tennis tournaments. Even small towns provide the chance to watch minor professionals, amateurs, and student athletes. For visitors who prefer participating in sports, Canada offers a broad choice of activities from skiing to golf, fishing, and hiking.

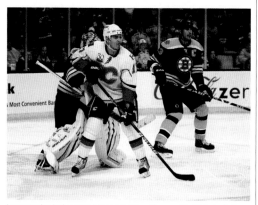

International ice hockey match between the Calgary Flames and the US Boston Bruins

Ice Hockey

The popularity of ice hockey in Canada knows no bounds. Every town has a rink, and every school, college, and university a team. The North American **National Hockey League** (NHL) was founded in 1917, and its principal prize, the Stanley Cup, was instituted in 1892 by Canadian Govenor General, Lord Stanley.

Today, the league has 31 teams, 7 of which belong to Canadian cities; the Montreal Canadiens, Calgary Flames, Edmonton Oilers, Toronto Maple Leafs, Ottawa Senators, Winnipeg Jets, and the Vancouver Canucks. Although most of the players in both the US and Canada are Canadian, there has been an influx of other nationalities such as Russian, American, and Swedish athletes playing for the top teams. Renowned for its toughness, the game usually involves a skirmish or two among the players. The season runs from October to April, when the play-offs for the prestigious Stanley Cup begin.

Hockey stars such as Wayne Gretzky are national icons. He retired in 1999 after 20 years in the game, having captured 61 NHL scoring records.

Tickets to the major games can be hard to come by, and should be booked in advance. It is a good idea to contact the club's ticket lines, or book through **Ticketmaster**. Minor league and college games are easier to get into, and the University of Toronto and York University, both in Toronto, Concordia in Montreal, and the University of Alberta in Edmonton all have good teams. Tickets can be bought from the local arena, or direct from the administration center, and are usually a great bargain.

Baseball

Although baseball is seen as an American sport, the game also has a large following in Canada. There is one Canadian team that plays in the major leagues: the well-known **Toronto Blue Jays**, who won the World Series in 1992 and 1993. Baseball is played in the summer, and the season lasts from April to September (with play-offs through October). It can provide a great family day out, with beer, popcorn, an enthusiastic audience, and plenty of between-innings entertainment, to keep the less baseball-obsessed amused.

The Blue Jays take on their rivals in the Rogers Centre, an architectural marvel with a retractable roof (see p177). Good tickets are easy to come by – just book a day or two in advance. Seats further back are almost always available on the day of the game. Seeing one of the minor league baseball teams can also be fun.

José Bautista winding up for the Toronto Blue Jays

Football

The Canadian version of football (not soccer) is noted for being a more exciting version of American football. Although the best Canadian players tend to move to the US for higher salaries, the game still attracts substantial home audiences. The Canadian Football League has two divisions, whose teams each play over the July to November season.

The games tend to attract a lively family crowd and are fun, especially around the Grey Cup final. Played on the last Sunday of November, the game is preceded by a week of festivities and a big parade in the host city. Football is also played at most universities, where a Saturday afternoon game makes for an entertaining excursion. The annual college championship game is called the Vanier Cup. Tickets are relatively easy to come by and are reasonably priced.

Basketball

What once was an American passion has now spread around the world to become one of the fastest-growing international sports. The game was invented in the United States by a Canadian, Dr. James Naismith, and now enjoys huge popularity in his homeland. The **Toronto Raptors** play in the National Basketball Association, the top professional league in the world, against the likes of the Chicago Bulls, Boston Celtics, Los Angeles Lakers, and New York Knicks. The season lasts from October until late spring, and it is well worth a visit to Toronto's Air Canada Centre to watch one of their fast-paced games. Most of Canada's universities have teams, and although crowds tend to be smaller than those drawn by the professionals, the competition is fierce and the atmosphere truly exhilarating, especially during the annual national championship tournament played each year in March.

Toronto Raptors versus the L. A. Clippers basketball match

Golf

Golf is an immensely popular participation sport in Canada, with an estimated 2,400 courses across the country, from the mountain courses in the west to the many rolling fairways of Prince Edward Island in the east.

The **RBC Canadian Open**, hosted by Golf Canada, is the biggest professional tournament on the golfing calendar each season in Canada. Held annually in July, it rotates between the country's best courses and draws large crowds of spectators to watch many of the world's greatest players. The Glen Abbey golf course in Oakville, Ontario, regularly hosts the RBC Canadian Open. The LPGA's **Canadian Pacific Women's Open** is held annually in August.

Winter Sports

Famous for the plentiful snow and sunshine of its cold winters, Canada is one of the top places both to watch and participate in winter sports. Canadian resorts are less crowded than their European counterparts, and are set among some of the most dramatic scenery in the world.

DIRECTORY

National Hockey League
w nhl.com

Ticketmaster
(for hockey games) **Tel** 1 855 985 5000. w ticketmaster.ca

Baseball
Toronto Blue Jays
Tel Tickets: (416) 341 1234, 1 855 258 3529. w bluejays.com

Football
Canadian Football League
w cfl.ca

Basketball
Toronto Raptors
Tel Tickets: (416) 815 5600.
w raptors.com

Golf
Canadian Pacific Women's Open
Tel 1 866 571 5742.
w cpwomensopen.com

RBC Canadian Open
Tel 1 800 571 6736.
w rbccanadianopen.com

Visitors can enjoy a range of winter sports options in resorts across the country, from Whistler in the Rockies to Mont Ste-Anne in Quebec. As well as downhill skiing, it is also possible to try snowboarding, snow-mobiling, dogsledding, or even heli-skiing on pristine snow (see p395).

Snowboarder descending a slope at speed in powder snow

CANADA THROUGH THE YEAR

Seasonal changes in Canada vary greatly across the country, but in general it is safe to say that the winters are long and cold and run from November to March, while spring and fall tend to be mild. British Columbia is the most temperate zone, with an average temperature of 5°C (40°F) in January. July and August are reliably warm and sunny in most places, even the far

north, and most outdoor festivals are held in the summer months. There are plenty of events in winter, both indoors and out, some of which celebrate Canadians' ability to get the best out of the icy weather, especially activities such as skiing, snowmobiling, and ice-skating. A range of cultural events reflect the country's history, as well as its diverse peoples and culture.

Spring

March to May brings the country some of its most unpredictable weather, moving from snow to sunshine in a day. In the north this is a time for welcoming the end of winter, while farther south spring is the start of an array of fun festivals.

Tapping the trees at the Sugarbush Maple Syrup Festival

March

Sugarbush Maple Syrup Festival *(Mar)* Toronto. Head to Toronto's forested conserved areas to enjoy demonstrations, wagon rides, and pancakes with maple syrup.
Long John Jamboree *(late Mar)* Yellowknife. A celebration of the arrival of spring, featuring ice-carving, snowmobiling, and delicious local foods.

April

Toonik Tyme *(mid-Apr)* Iqaluit. This week-long festival includes igloo building, traditional

games, and community feasts.
Shaw Festival *(Apr–Oct)* Niagara-on-the-Lake. Theater festival with classic plays by George Bernard Shaw and his contemporaries *(see p212)*.

May

Canadian Tulip Festival *(mid-May)* Ottawa. Colorful display of millions of tulips is the center-piece for a variety of events.
Stratford Shakespearean Festival *(May–Nov)* Stratford. World-famous theater festival featuring a range of plays from Elizabethan to contemporary works *(see p215)*.
Vancouver International Children's Festival *(late May–early Jun)* Vancouver. Theater, circus, and music for children aged three and up.

Summer

Warm weather across most of the country means that there is an explosion of festivals, carnivals, and cultural events, from June through August.

June

Pride Week *(Jun)* Toronto. A ten-day celebration of the gay community, featuring a fun, flamboyant parade.
Grand Prix du Canada *(Jun)* Montreal. Annual, weekend-long Formula One event.
Luminato Festival *(Jun)* Toronto. Cutting-edge international arts show, including talks, concerts, and events spanning over ten days.
Red River Exhibition *(mid-Jun)* Winnipeg. A huge fair with varied entertainment.
Banff Summer Arts Festival *(mid-Jun–Aug)* Banff. A summer-long festival of opera, music, drama, and dance at the renowned Banff Centre.
Mosaic – Festival of Cultures *(first weekend)* Regina. A range of cultural events from around the world.
Jazz Fest International *(late Jun–Jul)* Victoria. Jazz and blues musi-cians play in venues all over town.
Festival International de Jazz de Montréal *(late Jun–Jul)* Montreal. Famous jazz festival

Vividly colored tulips at Ottawa's spring event, the Canadian Tulip Festival

Steer wrestling competition in the *Half Million Dollar Rodeo* at Calgary's Stampede

that includes a number of free outdoor concerts.

Royal Nova Scotia International Tattoo *(late Jun–Jul)* Halifax. There are some 2,000 participants in one of the world's largest indoor shows.

July

Folk on the Rocks *(Jul)* Yellowknife. Inuit drummers, dancers, and throat singers perform here along with indie-folk bands, western bands and electro-pop dance groups.

K-Days *(Jul)* Edmonton. Commemorates the city's frontier days.

Calgary Stampede *(Jul)* Calgary. Ten-day celebration of all things western, including a rodeo *(see p298)*.

Honda Indy *(Jul)* Toronto. Indy car race held at Exhibition Place.

Antigonish Highland Games *(early Jul)* Antigonish, Nova Scotia. Oldest traditional highland games in North America, with pipe bands and dancing.

Festival d'été de Québec *(second week)* Quebec City. Ten days of music in historic Old Quebec.

Just for Laughs Festival *(Jul)* Montreal. Two-week comedy festival with more

than 600 comedians from around the world in venues across the city.

Toronto Caribbean Carnival *(Jul–early Aug)*. One of the largest and liveliest Caribbean celebrations in North America. The main event is the parade, which is held on the first weekend in August.

Ana Ivanovic of Serbia competing in the 2014 Rogers Cup

August

Rogers Cup *(Aug)* Montreal, Toronto. Major international tennis tournament.

Royal St. John's Regatta *(first week)* St. John's. Noted as North America's oldest sporting event, features rowing races and a carnival.

Wikwemikong Cultural Festival *(first weekend)* Manitoulin Island.

Ojibway powwow with dancing and drum contests *(see p228)*.

Folklorama *(early Aug)* Winnipeg. Canada's largest and longest-running multicultural festiva.

Festival Acadien de Caraquet *(early Aug)* Caraquet. Celebration of Acadian culture and history.

Halifax International Busker Festival *(early Aug)* Halifax. The best street entertainers from around the world.

Vancouver Gay Pride *(early Aug)*. The parade and festival attracts over 650,000 people.

Victoria Park Arts and Crafts Fair *(mid-Aug)* Moncton. Huge outdoor sale of arts, antiques, and crafts.

Discovery Days Festival *(mid-Aug)* Dawson City. Commemorates Gold Rush days, with costumed parades and canoe races.

Fringe Festival *(mid-Aug)* Edmonton. Theater and live music with international performers in the historic Old Strathcona neighborhood.

Canadian National Exhibition *(Aug–Sep)* Toronto. Annual fair featuring spectacular air show, concerts, and midway rides.

Folkfest *(mid-Aug)* Saskatoon. Saskatchewan's multicultural heritage celebrated in a variety of events.

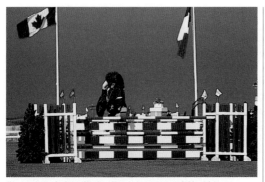
Showjumping in the Spruce Meadows Masters equestrian event held in Calgary

Fall

Cool, but often sunny weather provides the best setting for the dramatic reds and golds of the fall foliage, which is mostly seen in the deciduous forests of the eastern provinces. In Ontario and Quebec, fall signals the end of the humid summer months and heralds crisp days that are perfect for participating in outdoor pursuits.

September

Spruce Meadows Masters *(early Sep)* Calgary. Equestrian event with many top international riders.

Toronto International Film Festival *(Sep)* Toronto. Movie stars and top directors attend this prestigious festival. The Vancouver International Film Festival follows at the end of Sep.

CityFolk *(mid-Sep)* Ottawa. A four-day folk festival at Lansdowne Park by the Rideau Canal.

Ottawa International Animation Festival *(mid-Sep)* Ottawa. Screenings of the world's best animation films are held here.

Niagara Wine Festival *(mid-Sep)* St. Catharines, Ontario. Vineyard tours, wine tastings, and concerts welcome the area's grape harvest.

Autumnfest Outdoor Festival *(weekends in mid-Sep–Oct)* Eastern Townships. Enjoy the fall colors at Owl's Head Ski Resort through hiking, mountain biking, ski-lift rides, and other activities. Similar festivals are held at Orford and Sutton.

Traditional Bavarian costumes and music at the Oktoberfest

Climate

This vast country has a variable climate, despite being famous for having long, cold winters. Most Canadians live in the warmer south of the country, close to the US border. Southern Ontario and British Columbia's south and central coast are the warmest areas, while central and northern Canada have the coldest winters.

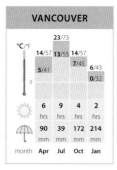

VANCOUVER

°C/°F

	Apr	Jul	Oct	Jan
max	14/57	23/73	14/57	6/43
min	5/41	13/55	7/45	0/32
hrs	6	9	4	2
mm	90	39	172	214

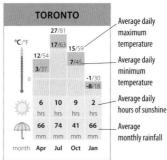

TORONTO

°C/°F

	Apr	Jul	Oct	Jan
max	12/54	27/81	15/59	-1/30
min	3/37	17/63	7/45	-8/18
hrs	6	10	9	2
mm	66	74	41	66

Average daily maximum temperature
Average daily minimum temperature
Average daily hours of sunshine
Average monthly rainfall

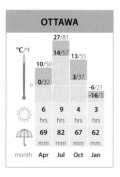

OTTAWA

°C/°F

	Apr	Jul	Oct	Jan
max	10/50	27/81	13/55	-6/21
min	0/32	14/57	3/37	-16/3
hrs	6	9	4	3
mm	69	82	67	62

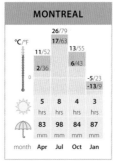

MONTREAL

°C/°F

	Apr	Jul	Oct	Jan
max	11/52	26/79	13/55	-5/23
min	2/36	17/63	6/43	-13/9
hrs	5	8	4	3
mm	83	98	84	87

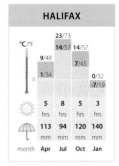

HALIFAX

°C/°F

	Apr	Jul	Oct	Jan
max	9/48	23/73	14/57	0/32
min	1/34	14/57	7/45	-7/19
hrs	5	8	5	3
mm	113	94	120	140

October
Okanagan Wine Festival *(early Oct)* Okanagan Valley. Tours and tastings throughout the valley *(see p321)*.
Oktoberfest *(mid-Oct)* Kitchener-Waterloo. Largest Bavarian festival outside Germany.
Celtic Colours *(mid-Oct)* Cape Breton Island. International Celtic music festival held across the island.

November
Royal Agricultural Winter Fair *(early–mid-Nov)* Toronto. The world's largest indoor agricultural fair features the Royal Horse Show and the Winter Garden Show.
Canadian Finals Rodeo *(mid-Nov)* Saskatoon. Canada's cowboy champions are decided at this event.
Winter Festival of Lights *(mid-Nov–end Jan)* Niagara Falls. Spectacular light displays and concerts.

Winter

Apart from in coastal British Columbia, Canadian winters are typically cold and with lots of snow. Events focus on winter sports, with some of the best skiing in the world available at such resorts as Whistler in British Columbia. The Christmas holidays are a time of fun activities to cheer everyone up in the midst of long, dark days.

Public Holidays
New Year's Day (Jan 1)
Good Friday (variable)
Easter Sunday (variable)
Easter Monday (variable) Vacation for government offices and schools only.
Victoria Day (Mon before May 25)
Canada Day (Jul 1)
Labour Day (first Mon in Sep)
Thanksgiving (second Mon in Oct)
Remembrance Day (Nov 11)
Christmas Day (Dec 25)
Boxing Day (Dec 26)

An illuminated display of Christmas decorations

December
Christmas Carol Ships Parade *(mid-Dec)* Vancouver. Boats are beautifully decorated with Christmas lights, and cruise Vancouver's waters.

January
Rossland Winter Carnival *(last weekend)* Rossland. Snowboarding contests, a torchlit parade, and lots of music and dancing.
Igloofest *(weekends in Jan–Feb)* Montreal. Electronic dance music fest during the city's harshest season, in Vieux-Port.
Quebec Winter Carnival *(Jan–Feb)* Quebec. Witness the famous canoe race across the Saint Lawrence River at these huge winter celebrations.

Jasper in January *(last two weeks)* Jasper. Winter festivities include skiing parties, races, and food fairs.
Fredericton FROSTival *(late Jan–early Feb)* Fredericton. Celebrate winter outdoors with tobogganing, dogsledding, and pond hockey, or head indoors for a slew of cultural activities.
SnowDays *(Jan–early Feb)* Banff and Lake Louise. Variety of fun events, including skating parties, hockey tournaments, and ice-sculpture competitions.

February
Yukon Quest *(Feb)* Whitehorse. Famous 1,600 km (1,000 mile) race from Fairbanks, Alaska, to Whitehorse.
Nova Scotia Icewine Festival *(Feb–Mar)* throughout Nova Scotia. A series of weekends celebrating the region's internationally famed icewines.
Yukon Sourdough Rendezvous *(Feb)* Whitehorse. A "mad trapper" competition and an array of children's events that began as Yukon Carnival Week in 1945.
Available Light Film Festival *(Feb)* Yukon. Exhibits the best of international and Canadian films.
Festival du Voyageur *(mid-Feb)* Winnipeg. Western Canada's largest winter festival, it celebrates Canada's fur-trading past in the French neighborhood of St. Boniface.
Winterlude *(first three weekends)* Ottawa. A wide array of activities including ice-skating on the Rideau Canal.

The international ice canoe race on the Saint Lawrence river, Quebec Winter Carnival

THE HISTORY OF CANADA

Canada is known for its wild and beautiful terrain, yet with the help of the Aboriginal Peoples, European settlers adapted to their new land and built up a prosperous nation. Despite continuing divisions between its English- and French-speaking peoples, Canada has welcomed immigrants from around the globe and is respected as one of the most tolerant countries in the world today.

Long before the first Europeans crossed the Atlantic in AD 986, the landscape we now know as Canada was inhabited by various civilizations. Tribes of hunters came on foot, walking across a land bridge that once joined Asia with North America as part of the ancient land mass of Laurasia.

These first inhabitants, now referred to as the First Nations, endured centuries of hardship and adaptation, eventually developing the skills, technology, and culture required to survive the rigors of life in Canada.

Early Survival

Across most of the country, from the Yukon to the Atlantic, there were two main groups of hunter-gatherers, the Algonquins and the Athapaskans. They lived in small nomadic bands, which developed birch bark canoes and snowshoes to travel across this vast land. Food and clothing were procured through fishing and animal trapping, traditions that gave Canada the lucrative fish and fur trades.

To the north of these two groups were the Innu people, who mastered life in the Arctic, being able to survive in a region of dark, ice-bound winters and brief summers. To the south, the Iroquois settled in forest villages, where they lived in longhouses and grew corn as their staple crop.

On the western plains, other tribes depended on the bison for their livelihood, while communities living along the Pacific Coast relied on fishing and trading. Their towering totem poles indicated a rich culture and spiritual belief system.

The common bond between all the First Nations, despite their disparate lifestyles, was that they saw themselves as part of nature and not as its masters. They believed the animals they hunted had kindred spirits, and misfortune befell those who offended such spirits by gratuitous killing.

The generosity of the First Peoples toward Europeans may have hastened their own downfall. As Canadian historian Desmond Morton points out: "Without the full… assistance of natives showing the Europeans their methods of survival, their territory, and their resources, the early explorers and settlers would have perished in even greater numbers and possibly abandoned their quest, much as the Vikings had done 500 years before."

9,000 BC Aboriginal Peoples are living at least as far south as the Eramosa River near what is now Guelph, Ontario

Viking ship c.AD 980

AD 986 Bjarni Herjolfsson, a Viking sailing from Iceland to Greenland, is the first European to see the coastline of Labrador

1497 The first voyage to North America by Giovanni Caboto (John Cabot)

30,000 BC	20,000 BC	10,000 BC	AD 1	500	1000	1500

30,000–10,000 BC Nomadic hunters arrive in North America across a land bridge from Asia

992 Leif "the Lucky" Ericsson visits Labrador and L'Anse-aux-Meadows, Newfoundland

1003 Thorfinn Karlsefni starts a colony in Labrador (Vinland) to trade with the Aboriginal Peoples, but it is abandoned two years later because of ongoing fighting and hostility

◀ *Mah-Min* or *The Feather*, painting of an Assiniboine chief by Paul Kane, c.1856

The First Europeans

The Norse sagas of Northern Europe tell how Vikings from Iceland first reached the coast of Labrador in AD 986 and made a series of unsuccessful attempts to establish a colony here. Leif "the Lucky" Ericsson sailed from Greenland in 988, naming the country he found in the west Vinland after the wild grapes found growing in abundance there. Around AD 1000 Thorfinn Karlsefni tried to establish a Vinland colony. This group wintered in Vinland but sailed home to Greenland in the spring, convinced that a colony was impossible, as there were too few colonists, and the *skraelings* (aboriginals) were hostile. Remarkably, remains of this early Viking settlement were discovered in Newfoundland in 1963.

Italian navigator and explorer John Cabot

The English Invasion

In 1497, the Italian navigator Giovanni Caboto (John Cabot; 1450–98), on the commission of King Henry VII of England, set sail aboard the *Matthew*, bound for America. On June 24, he found a sheltered place on Newfoundland. Here, he went ashore with a small party to claim the land for England. He then went on to chart the eastern coastline before sailing home, where he was greeted as a hero.

In May 1498, Cabot sailed again with five ships and 300 men, hoping to find the Northwest Passage to China. Harsh weather drove Cabot to relinquish his efforts and head south to Nova Scotia. Cabot then found himself sailing through a sea littered with icebergs. The fleet perished off the coast of Greenland, and English interest in the new land faded.

The French Arrival

Originally from the port of St. Malo, explorer Jacques Cartier (1491–1557) made his first voyage to Canada in 1534. He reached Labrador, Newfoundland, and the Gulf of Saint Lawrence before landing on

Map of the voyage of Jacques Cartier and his followers by Pierre Descaliers c.1534–41

1541 At the mouth of the Cap Rouge River, Cartier founds Charlesbourg-Royal, the first French settlement in America – it is abandoned in 1543

1567 Samuel de Champlain "Father of New France" born

1605 Samuel de Champlain and the Sieur de Roberval found Port Royal, now Annapolis Royal, Nova Scotia

1525   **1550**   **1575**   **1600**

1535 Cartier sails up the Saint Lawrence River to Stadacona (Quebec City) and Hochelaga (Montreal)

Jacques Cartier

1608 Champlain founds Quebec City, creating the first permanent European settlement in Canada

1610 Henry Hudson explores Hudson Bay

Anticosti Island, where he realized he was at the mouth of a great river. A year later, he returned and sailed up the Saint Lawrence River to the site of what is now Quebec City, and then on to an Aboriginal encampment at Hochelega, which he named Montreal. In 1543, Cartier's hopes for a successful colony died when, after a bitter and barren winter, he and his dispirited group returned to France. Seventy more years would pass before French colonists returned to Canada to stay.

Champlain, "Father of New France," fighting the Iroquois

The Father of New France

Samuel de Champlain (1567–1635) was a man of many parts – navigator, soldier, visionary – and first made the journey from France to Canada in 1603. While the ship that carried him across the Atlantic lay at Tadoussac, Champlain ascended the Saint Lawrence River by canoe to the Lachine Rapids.

Champlain's 1605 attempt to found a colony at Port Royal failed, but in 1608 the seeds of a first tiny French colony at Quebec City were planted, with the construction of three two-story houses, a courtyard, and a watchtower, surrounded by a wooden wall.

The economic engine propelling Champlain was the fur trade. In its name he made alliances with the Algonquins and Hurons; fought their dreaded enemies, the Iroquois; traveled to Huron country, now central Ontario; and saw the Great Lakes. Champlain and the other Frenchmen who followed him not only established lasting settlements in the Saint Lawrence Valley but also explored half a continent. They built a

"New France" that, at its zenith, stretched south from Hudson Bay to New Orleans in Louisiana, and from Newfoundland almost as far west as the Rockies. In 1612 Champlain became French Canada's first head of government.

Champlain's efforts also helped to create the religious climate that enabled orders such as the Jesuits to establish missions. But his work also laid the seeds of conflict with the English that would last well into the next century and beyond.

Hudson's last voyage

The Hudson's Bay Company

In 1610, English voyager Henry Hudson landed at the bay that still bears his name. The bay's access to many key waterways and trading routes ensured the fortunes of the fur trade. Founded in 1670, the Hudson's Bay Company won control of the lands that drained into the bay, gaining a fur-trading monopoly over the area. The company was challenged only by Scottish merchants who established the North West Company in Montreal in 1783. By 1821, these two companies amalgamated, and the Hudson's Bay Company (HBC) is today the oldest corporation in Canada.

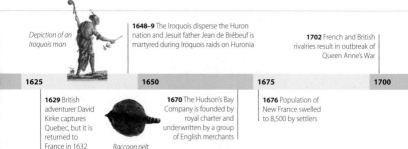

Depiction of an Iroquois man

1648–9 The Iroquois disperse the Huron nation and Jesuit father Jean de Brébeuf is martyred during Iroquois raids on Huronia

1702 French and British rivalries result in outbreak of Queen Anne's War

1625   **1650**   **1675**   **1700**

1629 British adventurer David Kirke captures Quebec, but it is returned to France in 1632

Raccoon pelt

1670 The Hudson's Bay Company is founded by royal charter and underwritten by a group of English merchants

1676 Population of New France swelled to 8,500 by settlers

Anglo-French Hostilities

Throughout the 18th century, hostilities between the French and English in Europe continued to spill over into the New World. By 1713, Britain ruled Nova Scotia, Newfoundland, and the Hudson Bay region and, after the Seven Years' War in 1763, all of French Canada.

Anglo-French tensions were exacerbated by religion: the English were largely Protestant and almost all of the French were Catholic. This resulted in the colony of Quebec being divided in 1791 into the mainly English-speaking Upper Canada (now Ontario), and majority French-speaking Lower Canada (now Quebec).

Taking advantage of the British conflict with Napoleon in Europe, the Americans invaded Canada in 1812. They were defeated by 1814, but the threat of another invasion colored Canadian history during much of the 19th century.

The Acadian Exodus
French-speaking Acadians were ruthlessly expelled from their homes by the British in the 1750s *(see pp68–9)*.

The Plains of Abraham, in Quebec, were the site of victory for the British over the French.

General Isaac Brock
Brock's heroic exploits during the War of 1812, such as the capture of an American post at Detroit, buoyed the spirits of the Canadian people.

United Empire Loyalists
The surrender of British General Cornwallis effectively ended the American Revolution (1775–83). A large number of United Empire Loyalists, refugees from the newly formed United States who remained loyal to the British crown, fled to Canada. They swelled the British population by 50,000.

The Seven Years' War
The famous Battle of the Plains of Abraham in 1759 was the last between British and French forces to take place in Canada. The British launched a surprise assault from the cliffs of the St. Lawrence River at a site now known as Wolfe's Cove. Louis Joseph de Montcalm, the French commander, was defeated by General Wolfe and his army. Both generals were killed, and Quebec fell to the British. The war finally ended in 1763 with the Treaty of Paris, which ceded all French-Canadian territory to the British.

Louisbourg
The French fortress of Louisbourg on Cape Breton Island was built between 1720 and 1740, and was the headquarters for the French fleet until it was destroyed by the British in 1758. Today, the restored fortress is a popular tourist attraction, with historically costumed guides (see pp100–101).

General Wolfe
The distinguished British soldier, shown here fatally wounded at the Plains of Abraham, preceded his 1759 victory in Quebec with the taking of the French fortress, Louisbourg, in 1758.

General Wolfe's forces sailed up the Saint Lawrence River overnight, allowing them to surprise the enemy at Quebec.

French Rights
In 1774 the British government passed the Quebec Act, granting French-Canadians religious and linguistic freedom and giving official recognition to French Civil Law.

Wolfe's infantry scrambled up a steep, wooded cliff. They had to defeat an enemy post before the waiting boats of soldiers could join the battle.

1755 Expulsion of the Acadians from Nova Scotia

1743 The La Vérendrye brothers discover the Rocky Mountains

1758 Louisbourg, the French fortress on Cape Breton Island, falls to the British

Sir Alexander Mackenzie

1793 Scottish explorer and fur trader Alexander Mackenzie crosses the Rockies and reaches the Pacific Ocean by land

1720	1740	1760	1780	1800

1713 British gain control of Nova Scotia, Newfoundland, and Hudson Bay

1759 Wolfe defeats de Montcalm in the Battle of the Plains of Abraham

Medal for the British capture of Quebec, 1759

1760 Montreal falls to the British

1774 The Quebec Act grants French colonists rights to their own language and religion

1812 The US at war with Britain until the Treaty of Ghent in 1814

The Path to Confederation

Twenty-five years after the War of 1812 ended in stalemate, violence of a different sort flared in Canada. The English wanted supremacy in voting power and to limit the influence of the Catholic Church. By 1834 the French occupied one quarter of public positions, although they made up three-quarters of the population. Rebellions in Upper and Lower Canada during 1837–8 were prompted by both French and British reformers, who wanted an accountable government with a broader electorate. The response of the British Government was to join together the two colonies into a united Province of Canada in 1840. The newly created assembly won increased independence, when, in 1849, the majority Reform Party passed an Act compensating the 1837 rebels. Although the Governor-General, Lord Elgin, disapproved, he chose not to use his veto. The Province of Canada now had "responsible government" (the right to pass laws without the sanction of the British colonial representative).

Representatives meet in London to discuss terms of union

The rest of British North America, however, remained a series of self-governing colonies that, despite their economic successes, were anxious about American ambitions. Such fears were reinforced by a series of Fenian Raids on Canadian territory between 1866–70. (The Fenians were New York Irish immigrants hoping to take advantage of French Canada's anti-British feeling to help them to secure independence for Ireland.) The issue of confederation was raised and discussed at conferences held from 1864 onward. Only by uniting in the face of this common menace, said the politicians, could the British colonies hope to fend off these incursions.

The new country was born on July 1, 1867. Under the terms of the British North America Act, the new provinces of Quebec (Canada East) and Ontario (Canada West) were created, and, along with Nova Scotia and New Brunswick, became the Dominion of Canada. The new government was based on the British parliamentary system, with a governor-general (the Crown's representative), a House of Commons, and a Senate. Parliament received power to legislate over matters of national interest, while the provinces ruled over local issues such as education.

Northwest rebel Louis Riel

The Métis Rebellion

Following confederation, the government purchased from the Hudson's Bay Company the area known as Rupert's Land, which extended south and west inland for thousands of kilometers from Hudson's Bay. The Métis people (descendants of mostly French fur-traders and Aboriginal Peoples) who lived here were alarmed by the expected influx of English-speaking settlers. In 1869, local leader Louis Riel took up their cause and led the first of two uprisings. The Red River Rebellion was an attempt to defend what the Métis saw as their ancestral rights to this land. A compromise was reached in 1870 and the new province of Manitoba was created. However, many Métis moved westward to what was to become the province of Saskatchewan in 1905.

Driving home the last spike of the Canadian Pacific Railroad, 1885

Riel was elected to the House of Commons in 1874 but, in 1875, he emigrated to the US. The government's intention to settle the west led the Métis of Saskatchewan to call Riel home in 1884 to lead the North-West Rebellion. It was short-lived. Defeated at Batoche in May, Riel was ultimately charged with treason and hanged in Regina on November 16, 1885.

Birth of a Nation

The defeat of the Métis and the building of a transcontinental railroad were crucial factors in the settlement of the west. British Columbia, a Crown colony since 1858, chose to join the Dominion in 1871 on the promise of a rail link with the rest of the country. The first train to run from Montreal to Vancouver in 1886 paved the way for hundreds of thousands of settlers in the West in the late 1800s. Prince Edward Island, Canada's smallest province, joined the Dominion in 1873.

In 1898, the northern territory of the Yukon was established to ensure Canadian jurisdiction over that area during the Klondike gold rush (see pp56–7). In 1905, the provinces of Saskatchewan and Alberta were created out of Rupert's Land, with the residual area becoming the Northwest Territories. Each province gained its own premier and elected assembly. By 1911 new immigrants had doubled the populations of the new provinces.

For the time being, Newfoundland preferred to remain a British colony, but in 1949 it was made Canada's tenth province.

The Métis People

The Métis people of central Canada were descended from Aboriginal and largely French stock. Proud of their unique culture, this seminomadic group depended almost entirely on buffalo hunting and resisted integration, responding to the unification of the country with two failed rebellions. The Métis won no land rights and were condemned to poverty or enforced integration. Finally, in 2017, the federal government began negotiations with the Métis to advance their rights and settle various claims.

Métis hunt buffalo on the Prairie

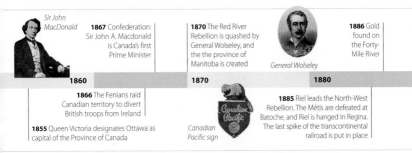

Sir John MacDonald

1867 Confederation: Sir John A. Macdonald is Canada's first Prime Minister

1870 The Red River Rebellion is quashed by General Wolseley, and the the province of Manitoba is created

General Wolseley

1886 Gold found on the Forty-Mile River

1860

1870

1880

1866 The Fenians raid Canadian territory to divert British troops from Ireland

1855 Queen Victoria designates Ottawa as capital of the Province of Canada

Canadian Pacific sign

1885 Riel leads the North-West Rebellion. The Métis are defeated at Batoche, and Riel is hanged in Regina. The last spike of the transcontinental railroad is put in place

The Klondike Gold Rush

There had been rumors of gold in the Yukon since the 1830s, but the harsh land, together with the Chilkoot peoples' guarding of their territory, kept most prospectors away. Then, on August 16, 1896 the most frenzied and fabled gold rush in Canadian history started when George Washington Carmack and two Aboriginal friends, Snookum Jim and Tagish Charlie, found a large gold nugget in the river they later named Bonanza Creek. For the next two years at least 100,000 prospectors set out for the new gold fields.

Only about 40,000 prospectors actually made it. Most took boats as far as Skagway or Dyea, on the Alaskan Panhandle, then struggled across the Coast Mountains by the White or Chilkoot passes to reach the headwaters of the Yukon River. From here boats took them 500 km (310 miles) to the gold fields. In all, the gold rush generated Can $50 million, although few miners managed to hold onto their fortunes.

Klondike Entrepreneur Alex McDonald, a Nova Scotian with a canny business sense, bought up the claims of discouraged miners and hired others to work them for him. Known as "King of the Klondike," he made millions.

The sternwheeler was a steamboat driven by a single paddle at the back.

Skagway, Alaska
The jumping-off point for the Klondike was the tent city of Skagway. There were saloons and swindlers on every corner, and gunfire in the streets was commonplace. The most famous con man was Jefferson Randolph "Soapy" Smith, who died in a shoot-out in 1898.

The Yukon River rises in British Columbia's Coast Mountains, winding for 3,000 km (1,900 miles) to Alaska.

The Mounties Take Control
The safety of the Klondike Gold Rush was secured by Canada's red-coated Mounties. Thanks to them, the rush was remarkably peaceful. A small force of 19 Mounties led by Inspector Charles Constantine was sent to the Yukon in 1895, but by 1898 there were 285, operating out of Fort Herchmer at Dawson.

Klondike Fever
The outside world learnt of the riches in July 1897, when miners docked in Seattle and San Francisco hauling gold. In no time, Klondike fever became an epidemic.

Dawson City
As the gold rush developed in the summer of 1897, the small tent camp at the junction of the Klondike and Yukon rivers grew to a population of 5,000. A year on, it had reached 40,000, making Dawson City one of the largest urban areas in Canada.

Steamboats and other craft brought thousands of prospectors up the long Yukon River to Dawson, where the boats jostled for space at the dock.

Capturing the Mood
Even literature had a place in the Klondike. The gold rush inspired novels such as *The Call of the Wild* (1903) by Jack London (shown here) and the 1907 verses *Songs of a Sourdough* by poet Robert Service.

Crossing the Yukon River
The ferocious Yukon River rapids in Miles Canyon smashed so many boats to splinters that the Mounties decreed that every boat had to be guided by a competent pilot. Experienced sailors could earn up to Can$100 a trip taking boats through the canyon. Past the canyon, only one more stretch of rapids remained before the Yukon's waters grew calmer all the way to Dawson City.

1896 George Carmack and two friends, Tagish Charlie and Snookum Jim, strike it rich on Bonanza Creek. Liberal Wilfred Laurier is elected as the country's first French-Canadian prime minister

Klondike News, 1898

1898 The Yukon is given territorial status, partly to assert British authority in the eyes of the Americans from neighboring Alaska

1896	1897	1898	1899

1897 Steamers from Alaska carry word of the strike to San Francisco and Seattle, setting off a frenzied gold rush

1899 Gold is discovered in Nome, Alaska, and Dawson begins to shrink, as people leave to follow the new dream of riches farther west

New Optimism and Arrivals

The impact of the Klondike gold rush was felt all over Canada. It led to an expansion of cities such as Vancouver and Edmonton, and the establishment of the Yukon territory. A period of optimism was ushered in by the new Liberal government, elected in 1896 under the first French-Canadian premier, Wilfred Laurier, who firmly believed that "the 20th century will belong to Canada."

The new central Canadian provinces provided a home for European immigrants eager to farm large tracts of prairie land. By 1913, this wave of immigration had peaked at 400,000. Finally Canada began to profit from a prosperous world economy and establish itself as an industrial and agricultural power.

1914 poster promoting immigration to Canada

Supporting the Allies

The first overseas test of Canada's military forces came in 1899, when the Boer War broke out in South Africa; the second in 1914, when Europe entered World War I. Initially,

Canadians advance at Paardeberg in the Boer War, 1900

Laurier was cautious in his approach to the South African crisis, but pressure from the English-speaking population led to the dispatch of 1,000 soldiers to Cape Town in 1899. Before the Boer War ended in 1902, some 6,000 men had made the journey to serve with the British on the South African battlefields. They returned with a stronger sense of national identity than many of their compatriots at home had expected. But, while the experience of war infused some with a new sense of national unity, it also laid bare divisions. There were fights between French- and English-speaking university students, as well as disputes among Ontario conservatives and French-speaking Quebec politicians.

Before matters could come to a head, another crisis loomed. Joining the Allies in Flanders, the Canadians found renewed glory during World War I. Canadian pilot Billy Bishop was the Allies' greatest air ace, and another Canadian, Roy Brown, was the pilot credited with downing the Red Baron. Canadian troops were the heroes of two major battles, Ypres (1915) and Vimy Ridge (1917). When peace was declared on November 11, 1918, there were 175,000 Canadian wounded, and 60,000 had died for their country.

Independent Status

Canada had played so significant a role during World War I that it gained recognition as an independent country, winning representation

1899 The first Canadians are sent to fight in the Boer War

1903 Canada loses the Alaska boundary dispute when a British tribunal sides with the US

| 1900 | 1905 | 1910 | 1915 | 1920 |

1911 Robert Borden and the Conservatives win federal election, defeating Liberal party leader Wilfred Laurier on the issue of the Naval Bill

1914 Britain declares war on Germany, automatically drawing Canada into the conflict in Europe. The War Measures Act orders German and Austro-Hungarian Canadians to carry identity cards

1917 Munitions ship explodes in Halifax harbor wiping out 5 sq km (2 sq miles) of the town, killing 2,000, and injuring 9,000

1918 Canadians break through the German trenches at Amiens beginning "Canada's Hundred Days"

1922 Canadians Charles Best, Frederick Banting, and John MacLeod win the Nobel Prize for the discovery of insulin

Dr. Frederick Banting

in the League of Nations. This independence was confirmed in 1931 with the passing of the Statute of Westminster, which gave Canada political independence from Britain and created a commonwealth of sovereign nations under a single crown.

Soup kitchen during the Great Depression

However, national optimism was curtailed by the Great Depression that originated with the Wall Street Crash in 1929. Drought laid waste the farms of Alberta, Saskatchewan, and Manitoba. One in four workers was unemployed, and the sight of men riding boxcars in a fruitless search for work became common.

World War II

The need to supply the Allied armies during World War II boosted Canada out of the Depression. Canada's navy played a crucial role in winning the Battle of the Atlantic (1940–43), and thousands of Allied airmen were trained in Canada. Canadian regiments soon gained a reputation for bravery – for example, many died in the 1942 raid on Dieppe. Thousands battled in Italy, while others stormed ashore at Normandy. In the bitter fighting that followed, the Second and Third Canadian Divisions took more casualties holding the beachheads than any unit under British command. It was also the Canadians who liberated much of Holland.

The Canadian prime minister of the day was the Liberal Mackenzie King (1935–48). He ordered a plebiscite to have conscripts sent overseas to meet an infantry shortage in the last months of the war, monitored the building of the Alaska Highway (see pp266–7), and directed a massive war effort.

An International Voice

When peace finally came in September 1945, Canada had the third-largest navy in the world, the fourth-largest air force, and a standing army of 730,000 men. Although the price Canada had paid during World War II was high – 43,000 people died in action and the national debt quadrupled – the nation found itself in a strong position. A larger population was better able to cope with

German prisoners captured by Canadian Infantry on D-Day, June 6, 1944

1926 The Balfour Report defines British dominions as autonomous and equal in status

Air Canada logo

1937 Trans-Canada Air Lines, now Air Canada, begins regular flights

1942 Around 22,000 Japanese Canadians are stripped of non-portable possessions and interned

1944 Canadian troops push farther inland than any other allied units on D-Day

1925 **1930** **1935** **1940** **1945**

1929 The Great Depression begins

1931 The Statute of Westminster grants Canada full legislative authority

1941 Hong Kong falls to the Japanese, and Canadians are taken as POWs

1945 World War II ends. Canada joins the UN. Canada's first nuclear reactor goes on line in Chalk River, Ontario

Large Canadian grain carrier approaches the Saint Lawrence Seaway in 1959 – its inaugural year

its losses, and much of the debt had been spent on doubling the gross national product, creating durable industries that would power the postwar economy.

Since World War II, Canada's economy has continued to expand. This growth, combined with government social programs such as old-age security, unemployment insurance, and medicare, means that Canadians have one of the world's highest standards of living and a quality of life that draws immigrants from around the world. Since 1945, those immigrants have been made up largely of southern Europeans, Asians, South Americans, and Caribbean islanders, all of whom have enriched the country's multicultural status.

Internationally, the nation's reputation and influence have grown. Canada has participated in the United Nations (UN) since its inception in 1945 and is the only nation to have taken part in almost all of the UN's major peacekeeping operations.

Perhaps it is only fitting that it was a future Canadian prime minister, Lester Pearson, who fostered the peacekeeping process when he won the Nobel Peace Prize in 1957 for helping resolve the Suez Crisis. Canada is also a respected member of the British Commonwealth, la Francophonie, the Group of Eight industrialized nations, the OAS (Organization of American States), and NATO (North Atlantic Treaty Organization).

The French–English Divide

Given all these accomplishments, it seems ironic that the last quarter of a century has also seen Canadians deal with fundamental questions of national identity and unity. The driving force of this debate continues to be the historic English–French rivalry. The best-known players of these late 20th-century events are Prime Minister Pierre Trudeau (served 1968–79 and 1980–84) and Quebec Premier René Lévesque (1976–85).

When Jean Lesage was elected as Quebec Premier in 1960, he instituted the "Quiet Revolution" – a series of reforms that increased provincial power. However, this was not enough to prevent the rise of revolutionary

Quebec Premier René Levesque and Canadian Prime Minister Pierre Trudeau during the 1980 referendum

---

1950 The Canadian Army Special Force joins UN soldiers in the Korean War

1957 Lester Pearson wins the Nobel Peace Prize for helping resolve the Suez Crisis

Lester Pearson

1980 Quebec votes against separation in the 1980 Quebec Referendum

| 1950 | 1955 | 1960 | 1965 | 1970 | 1975 | 1980 |

1949 Newfoundland joins the Confederation. Canada joins NATO

1965 Canada's new flag is inaugurated after a bitter political debate

1976 The Olympic games are held in Montreal under tight security. René Lévesque and the separatist *Parti Québécois* win a provincial election

Marc Garneau

1990 demonstration for Quebec independence in Montreal

nationalists. In October 1970, British Trade Commissioner James Cross and Quebec Labor Minister Pierre Laporte were kidnapped by the French-Canadian terrorist organization, the Front du Libération de Québec (FLQ). Cross was rescued by police, but Laporte was later found murdered. Trudeau invoked the War Measures Act, sent troops into Montreal, and banned the FLQ. His actions eventually led to nearly 500 arrests.

Trudeau devoted his political life to federalism, fighting separatism, and giving Canada its own constitution. In contrast, Lévesque campaigned for a 1980 referendum in Quebec on whether that province should become independent. A majority voted against, but the results were far from decisive, and separatism continued to dominate the country's political agenda. However, in 1982, the Constitution Act fulfilled Trudeau's dream, entrenching federal civil rights and liberties such as female equality.

A Move Toward Conservatism

In 1984 the leader of the Progressive Conservatives, Brian Mulroney, won the general election with the largest majority in Canadian history. Dismissive of Trudeau's policies, Mulroney's emphasis was on closer links with Europe and, in particular, the US. In the years that followed, two major efforts were made to reform the constitutional system. The 1987 Meech Lake Accord aimed to recognize Quebec's claims to special status on the basis of its French culture, but Mulroney failed to implement the amendment since it did not obtain the consent of all provinces. The Charlottetown Accord of 1992, which raised the issue of aboriginal self-government, was triggered by Quebec sovereignty issues. The Accord was rejected in a national referendum held in 1992.

Today, many of these reforms are finally in place and hopefully aiding Canadian unity. Quebec's French heritage has official recognition, and the Inuit rule their own territory of Nunavut.

Independence for Nunavut

On April 1, 1999, Canada gained its newest territory, the Inuit homeland of Nunavut. The campaign for an Inuit state began in the 1960s when the Inuit desire for a political identity of their own was added to aboriginal land claims. Nunavut's first Premier was 34-year-old Paul Okalik, leader of the first-ever Inuit majority government over an 85 percent Inuit population. English is being replaced as the official language by Inuktitut, and traditional Inuit fishing and hunting skills are being reintroduced. By 2012, the federal government had invested over Can $1 billion in public services for Nunavut.

Signing ceremony in Iqaluit, April 1, 1999

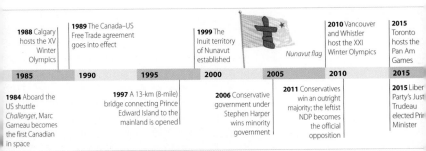

1984 Aboard the US shuttle *Challenger*, Marc Garneau becomes the first Canadian in space

1988 Calgary hosts the XV Winter Olympics

1989 The Canada–US Free Trade agreement goes into effect

1997 A 13-km (8-mile) bridge connecting Prince Edward Island to the mainland is opened

1999 The Inuit territory of Nunavut established

Nunavut flag

2006 Conservative government under Stephen Harper wins minority government

2010 Vancouver and Whistler host the XXI Winter Olympics

2011 Conservatives win an outright majority; the leftist NDP becomes the official opposition

2015 Toronto hosts the Pan Am Games

2015 Liber Party's Just Trudeau elected Prim Minister

1985   1990   1995   2000   2005   2010   2015

ATLANTIC CANADA

Introducing Atlantic Canada

Atlantic Canada is renowned for rocky coastlines, picturesque fishing villages, sun-warmed beaches, cozy country inns, and friendly people. Each province has a distinctive flavor. In northeastern New Brunswick, French-speaking Acadian culture flourishes, while the south coast offers the pristine, tide-carved beauty of the Bay of Fundy. Prince Edward Island is known for its emerald-green farmland, sandy beaches, and rich lobster catches. Nova Scotia, famous for the stunning natural scenery of the Cabot Trail, is also home to historic towns such as seafaring Lunenburg, one of the few towns in Canada designated a National Historic Site. In Newfoundland, the mountains of Gros Morne National Park rise 800 m (2,625 ft) above sparkling blue fjords. Labrador offers an imposing and stunning coastal landscape, often with a backdrop of glittering icebergs.

The fresh maritime scenery of Two Islands beach, known as "The Brothers" for its twin offshore islands, in Parrsboro, Nova Scotia

Contemporary Acadian homesteads flourish after 400 years of a unique culture in northeastern New Brunswick

◀ Nova Scotia lighthouse

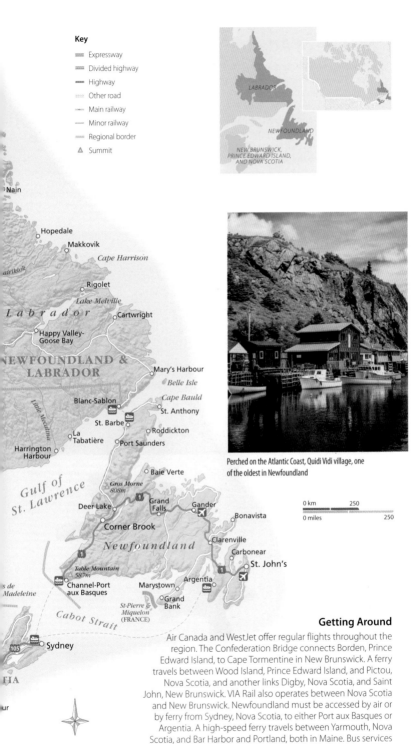

Key

- ▬▬ Expressway
- ▬▬ Divided highway
- ▬▬ Highway
- ┄┄ Other road
- ⤙⤙ Main railway
- ── Minor railway
- ▪▪▪▪ Regional border
- △ Summit

LABRADOR

NEWFOUNDLAND

NEW BRUNSWICK,
PRINCE EDWARD ISLAND,
AND NOVA SCOTIA

Nain

Hopedale

Makkovik

Cape Harrison

airiktok

Rigolet

Lake Melville

Labrador

Cartwright

Happy Valley-
Goose Bay

**NEWFOUNDLAND &
LABRADOR**

Little Mecatina

Mary's Harbour

Belle Isle

Cape Bauld

Blanc-Sablon

St. Anthony

St. Barbe

Roddickton

La
Tabatière

Port Saunders

Harrington
Harbour

Baie Verte

Gros Morne
808m

*Gulf of
St. Lawrence*

Deer Lake

Grand
Falls

Gander

Bonavista

Corner Brook

Newfoundland

Clarenville

Carbonear

St. John's

Table Mountain
587m

Argentia

Channel-Port
aux Basques

Marystown

*s de
Madeleine*

*Grand
Bank*

*St-Pierre &
Miquelon*
(FRANCE)

Cabot Strait

Sydney

IA

ur

Perched on the Atlantic Coast, Quidi Vidi village, one
of the oldest in Newfoundland

0 km   250

0 miles   250

Getting Around

Air Canada and WestJet offer regular flights throughout the region. The Confederation Bridge connects Borden, Prince Edward Island, to Cape Tormentine in New Brunswick. A ferry travels between Wood Island, Prince Edward Island, and Pictou, Nova Scotia, and another links Digby, Nova Scotia, and Saint John, New Brunswick. VIA Rail also operates between Nova Scotia and New Brunswick. Newfoundland must be accessed by air or by ferry from Sydney, Nova Scotia, to either Port aux Basques or Argentia. A high-speed ferry travels between Yarmouth, Nova Scotia, and Bar Harbor and Portland, both in Maine. Bus services cross the provinces, but many areas are remote, so check availability.

For map symbols see back flap

Wildlife of Atlantic Canada

The provinces of Atlantic Canada – Nova Scotia, Prince Edward Island, and New Brunswick – along with Newfoundland and Labrador, the Quebec north shore of the Saint Lawrence River, and the Gaspé Peninsula, constitute a rich and diverse maritime habitat for wildlife. The climate is dominated by the ocean, and influenced by the moderating Gulf Stream that flows north from the Caribbean and by the southward flow of icy waters, often bearing icebergs, from the Canadian Arctic. The terrain of the eastern Canadian coastline varies from rocky headlands to soft, sandy beaches. Both sea and land mammals inhabit this coast, as do hundreds of species of seabirds.

The piping plover is a small, endangered shore bird that lives and breeds along the Atlantic coast of Canada.

Shoreline Habitat

The maritime shoreline encompasses rocky cliffs, sandy beaches, and salt-flat marshes. Moving a little inland, the landscape shifts to bog, forest, and meadow. This is an inviting habitat for many smaller mammals such as raccoons and beavers, and also provides a home for a diversity of bird life. Where the shoreline meets the water, fertile intertidal zones are a habitat for mollusks, algae, and invertebrae.

The river otter lives in "families," frequenting rivers, lakes, and ocean bays, in its search for fish.

The common puffin is a shoreline bird, which lives on cliff edges and is characterized by a brightly colored bill and a curious, friendly nature.

The raccoon, with its ringed tail and black-masked face, preys upon fish, crayfish, birds, and their eggs.

The beaver, the symbol of Canada, lives in marshy woodland near streams and rivers. It gnaws down trees, using them to build dams and its lodge.

Ocean Habitat

The sea around Atlantic Canada is influenced by the cold Labrador Current flowing from the north, the Gulf Stream from the south, and the large outflow of fresh water at the mouth of the St. Lawrence River. The region is home to myriad ocean creatures, and the highest tides in the world at the nutrient-rich Bay of Fundy. Off Newfoundland lie the Grand Banks, once one of the Earth's richest fishing grounds. Over-fishing has endangered fish stocks, and quotas are now limited.

Lobster, a favorite seafood of the area, is caught in traps set near the shore. Rigid conservation rules have been put in force to protect its numbers.

The adult blue whale is the world's largest mammal, reaching up to 30 m (100 ft) long. Today, whale-watching is a growing eco-tourism enterprise, particularly in the Bay of Fundy, where this and other species congregate.

The Atlantic salmon, unlike its Pacific cousins, returns to its home stream to spawn several times during its lifetime. Atlantic salmon are renowned sports fish *(see p31)*.

Bottle-nosed dolphins, characterized by their long beaks and "smiles," live off the east coast, in both New Brunswick and Nova Scotia.

Seabirds of the Atlantic Coast

The maritime coast of eastern Canada is a perfect environment for seabirds. Rocky cliffs and headlands provide ideal rookeries. The rich coastal waters and intertidal zones ensure a generous larder for many species, including the cormorant and storm petrel. Some Atlantic Coast seabirds are at risk due to environmental changes, but puffins and razorbills, in particular, continue to thrive.

The double-crested cormorant, or "sea crow," as it is sometimes known, is a diving fishing bird, capable of capturing food as deep as 10 m (33 ft) under water.

Leach's storm-petrel is part of the Tubenose family of birds, whose acute sense of smell helps them navigate while out at sea.

The Acadians

Few stories surrounding the settlement of the New World evoke as many feelings of tragedy and triumph as the tale of the Acadians. Colonizing Nova Scotia's fertile Annapolis Valley in the 1600s, 500 French settlers adopted the name Acadie, hoping to establish an ideal pastoral land. They prospered and, by 1750, numbered 14,000, becoming the dominant culture in both Nova Scotia and New Brunswick. The threat of this enclave proved too much for a town run by the British, and, in 1755, the Acadians were expelled overseas, many to the US. When England and France made peace in 1763, the Acadians slowly returned. Today their French-speaking culture still thrives in some areas.

Acadian women play a part in summer festivals, displaying local woolcraft and linen textiles.

Ile Sainte-Croix was the earliest Acadian settlement, established by the French in New Brunswick in 1604. The neat, spacious layout of the village is typical.

Acadian Farming

As hardworking farmers, Acadians cleared the land, built villages, and developed an extensive system of dikes to reclaim the rich farmland from tidal waters. Summer crops were carefully harvested for the winter; potatoes and vegetables were put in cellars, and hay stored to feed cattle and goats. By the 19th century, Acadian farmers had expanded their crop range to include tobacco and flax.

An important crop, hay was raked into *"chafauds,"* spiked haystacks that dried in the fields for use as winter animal feed.

The Expulsion of the Acadians took place in August 1755. British troops brutally rounded up the Acadians for enforced deportation. More than 6,000 Acadians were put on boats, some bound for the US, where they became the Cajuns of today. Some returned in later years, and today their descendants live in villages throughout Atlantic Canada.

The Acadian people maintained a traditional farming and fishing lifestyle for centuries, re-created today at the Village Historique Acadien (*see p85*).

The Church of Saint Anne in Sainte-Anne-du-Ruisseau represents Acadian style in its fresh simplicity and elegance. Catholicism was very important to the Acadians, who turned to their priests for succour during the 1755 diaspora.

Acadian musicians have reflected their culture since the 17th century. Playing lively violin and guitar folk music, they are known for their upbeat tunes and ballads of unrequited love and social dispossession.

Acadian life revolved around the farmsteads in each community. Men tilled the fields and fished, while women helped with the annual harvest.

Henry Wadsworth Longfellow

One of the most popular poets of the 19th century, both in the US and Europe, the American Henry Longfellow (1807–82) is best known for his long, bittersweet narrative poems. Based on the trials and injustices of the Acadian civilization, *Evangeline*, published in 1847, traces the paths of a young Acadian couple. The poem, now regarded as a classic, stirringly records Evangeline's tragic loss in this land intended as an idyll, when their love is destroyed through the upheavals and expulsion of the 18th century: "Loud from its rocky caverns, the deep-faced neighbouring ocean [sings], List to the mournful tradition sung by the pines of the Forest, … List to a Tale of Love in Acadie, home of the happy."

NEWFOUNDLAND AND LABRADOR

With towering peaks, vast landscapes, and 17,000 km (10,500 miles) of rugged coastline, both Newfoundland and Labrador display wild, open spaces and grand spectacles of nature. In this captivating landscape, massive icebergs drift lazily along the coast, whales swim in sparkling bays, and moose graze placidly in flat open marshes.

Newfoundland's west coast offers some of the most dramatic scenery east of the Rockies. The granite mountains of Gros Morne National Park shelter deep fjords, while the eastern part of the island has a more rounded terrain, featuring the bays and inlets of Terra Nova National Park. Part of the area's appeal is retracing the history of past cultures that have settled here, including Maritime Archaic Aboriginal Peoples at Port au Choix, Vikings at L'Anse-Aux-Meadows, and Basque whalers at Red Bay in the Labrador Straits.

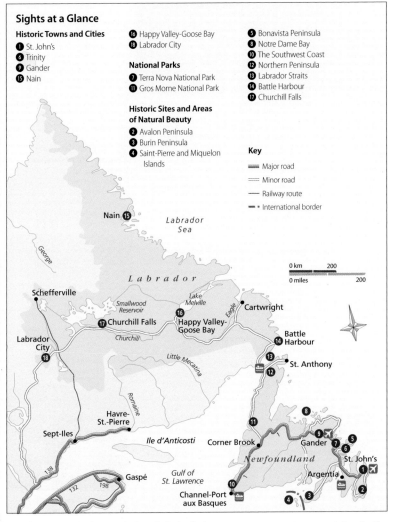

Sights at a Glance

Historic Towns and Cities
1. St. John's
6. Trinity
9. Gander
15. Nain

16. Happy Valley-Goose Bay
18. Labrador City

National Parks
7. Terra Nova National Park
11. Gros Morne National Park

Historic Sites and Areas of Natural Beauty
2. Avalon Peninsula
3. Burin Peninsula
4. Saint-Pierre and Miquelon Islands

5. Bonavista Peninsula
8. Notre Dame Bay
10. The Southwest Coast
12. Northern Peninsula
13. Labrador Straits
14. Battle Harbour
17. Churchill Falls

Key

▦▦ Major road
══ Minor road
── Railway route
▬ ▪ International border

◄ Cape St. Mary's Ecological Reserve, Avalon Peninsula, Newfoundland   **For map symbols** see back flap

❶ St. John's

St. John's is a bustling port, and one of North America's oldest settlements. Rainbow-hued row houses line the hilly streets around the harbour where commercial fishing, oil exploration, and boat servicing are still viable occupations. The province's capital has a longstanding history of sea commerce, beginning with Italian explorer Giovanni Caboto (John Cabot) *(see p50)*, who aroused great interest in Newfoundland in 1497 when he described "a sea so full of fish that a basket thrown overboard is hauled back brimming with cod." The people of St. John's are known for their friendliness, a delightful counterpoint to the rugged beauty that surrounds this historic town.

Downtown St. John's, seen from the approach by sea

Exploring St. John's

The capital of Newfoundland is easily explored on foot. Most of the sights are within a short distance of each other moving east along Water Street. Approaching by sea offers the best view of the harbor, in particular the steep cliff-lined passage on the east side, where pastel-colored old houses cling to the rocks.

🏛 Murray Premises

Cnr Water St. & Beck's Cove.
Open 8am–10:30pm daily. &
Ⓦ murraypremiseshotel.com

At the west end of Water Street stands Murray Premises. Built in 1846, these rambling brick-and-timberframe buildings are the last remaining examples of the large mercantile and fish-processing premises that were common on the St. John's waterfront. Murray Premises once bustled with the work of shipping cod to world markets.

The buildings only just survived a huge fire that engulfed the city in 1892; they mark the western boundary of the fire's devastation. Now a Provincial Historic Site, the restored buildings are home to a boutique hotel and offices.

🏛 The Rooms

9 Bonaventure Ave. **Tel** (709) 757 8000.
Open mid–Jun–mid-Sep: 10am–5pm Mon–Sat (to 9pm Wed; Museum & Art Gallery also open noon–5pm Sun); mid-Sep–mid-Jun: 10am–5pm Wed–Sat.
Closed Jan 1, Dec 25. Ⓦ therooms.ca

A major landmark, The Rooms is a modern facility housing three provincial institutions: the Provincial Archives; the Museum of Newfoundland, which charts the province's history over the past 9,000 years; and the Art Gallery of Newfoundland and Labrador, which showcases the work of local, national, and international artists.

🏛 The Waterfront

Water St.

Tracing the edge of St. John's waterfront, Water Street is the oldest public thoroughfare in North America, dating to the late 1500s when trading first started. Once a brawling wharfside lane of gin mills and brothels, Water Street and Duckworth Street now offer gift shops, art galleries, and some of Newfoundland's top restaurants. Harbour Drive, along the waterfront, is a great place to stroll, while George Street is the hub of the city's nightlife.

🏛 Commissariat House

King's Bridge Rd. ℹ (709) 729 6730.

Commissariat House, now a historical site, was built between 1818 and 1820 and was once the home of 19th-century British officials. The Georgian building now contains a multi-media experience of early-19th-century St. John's. Nearby Government House, built during the 1820s, is the official residence of the province's Lieutenant Governor.

🏛 The Battery

Battery Rd. ℹ (709) 570 2038.

The colorful houses clinging to sheer cliffs at the entrance to the Harbour are known as the Battery. With the look and feel of a 19th-century fishing village, this is one of St. John's most photographed sites. The community is named for the military fortifications built here over centuries to defend the harbor. Local residents used the battery's guns in 1763 to fight off Dutch pirate ships.

🏔 Signal Hill National Historic Site of Canada

Signal Hill Rd. **Tel** (709) 772 5367.
Open Visitor Centre: mid- to end May: 10am–6pm Wed–Sun; Jun–Labour Day weekend: 10am–6pm daily; Labour Day weekend–mid-Oct: 10am–6pm Sat–Wed. 🅿 &

This lofty rise of land presents spectacular views of the open Atlantic, the harbor entrance, and the historic splendor of the city of St. John's.

🏛 Cabot Tower

Signal Hill Rd. **Tel** (709) 772 5367.
Open Visitor Centre: mid- to end May: 10am–6pm Wed–Sun; Labour Day weekend: 10am–6pm daily; Labour Day weekend–mid-Oct: 10am–6pm Sat–Wed. &

View of Signal Hill from St. John's picturesque fishing harbor

The Cabot Tower as it rises above Signal Hill over the harbor

The building of Cabot Tower at the top of Signal Hill began in 1897 to celebrate the 400th anniversary of Cabot's arrival. On summer weekends, soldiers in period dress perform 19th-century marching drills, with firing muskets and cannon. It was here that another Italian, Guglielmo Marconi, received the first transatlantic wireless signal in 1901.

🔲 Quidi Vidi Village

Quidi Vidi Village Rd. **Tel** (709) 570 2038. **Open** daily. Brewery open 10am–5:30pm Mon–Fri, 11:30am–5:30pm Sat. 🛈 for brewery tour. 🔲 quidividibrewery.ca

On the other side of Signal Hill, the weathered buildings of ancient Quidi Vidi Village nestle around a small harbor. Above the village, the Quidi Vidi Battery was a fortified gun emplacement built in 1762 to defend the harbor entrance. The province's most popular microbrewery, Quidi Vidi Brewery, is also located on the harbor and offers tasting tours on Saturdays.

🔲 Pippy Park

Nagles Place. **Tel** (709) 737 3655. **Open** daily. 🛈 🔲 pippypark.com Visitors are sometimes startled to see moose roaming free in St. John's, but it happens often in this 1,400-ha (3,460-acre) nature park, 4 km (2 miles) from the town center. The park is also home to the local Botanical Gardens. The only Fluvarium in North America is based here too, featuring nine underwater windows that look into a rushing freshwater trout stream.

🔲 Cape Spear Lighthouse National Historic Site of Canada

Tel (709) 772 5367. **Open** Visitor Centre: mid- to end May: 10am–6pm Wed–Sun; Jun–Labour Day weekend: 10am–6pm daily; Labour Day weekend–mid-Oct: 10am–6pm Sat–Wed. 🛈 🛈

Ten km (6 miles) southeast of town, Cape Spear marks the most easterly point in North America. Set atop seaside cliffs, the majestic Cape Spear Lighthouse has long been a symbol of Newfoundland's independence. Two lighthouses sit here. The original, built in 1836 and the oldest in Newfoundland, stands beside a graceful, modern, automated lighthouse, added in 1955.

🔲 East End

King's Bridge Rd. 🛈 (709) 570 2038. East End is one of St. John's most architecturally rich neighborhoods, with narrow, cobblestone streets and elegant homes.

St. John's City Center

① Murray Premises
② The Rooms
③ The Waterfront
④ Commissariat House
⑤ The Battery
⑥ Signal Hill
⑦ Cabot Tower

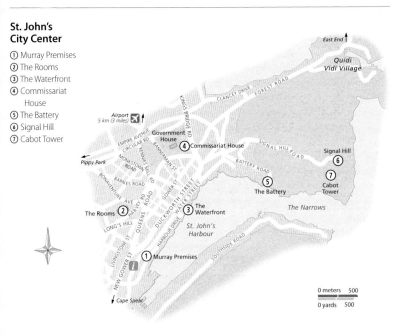

Whale- and bird-watching boats tour the Avalon Peninsula

❷ Avalon Peninsula

🚌 St. John's. ⛴ Argentia. ℹ️ Dept. of Tourism, Confederation Building, St. John's, (709) 576 8106.
🌐 **colonyofavalon.ca**

The picturesque community of Ferryland on the Avalon Peninsula is the site of a large-scale archeological excavation of the Colony of Avalon, a settlement founded by English explorer Lord Baltimore and 11 settlers in 1621. This was Baltimore's first New World venture, intended to be a self-sufficient colony engaged in fishing, agriculture, and trade, with firm principles of religious tolerance.

Boat-tour sign in Witless Bay

By the end of the following year there were 32 settlers. The population continued to grow, and for many years it was the only successful colony in the area. Although excavations to date have unearthed only five percent of the colony, it has proved to be one of the richest sources of artifacts from any early European settlement in North America. A vast array of pieces have been recovered, such as pottery, clay pipes, household implements, and structural parts of many buildings, including defensive works, a smithy, and a waterfront commercial complex. An interpretive center tells the story of the colony and a guided tour includes the chance to watch archeologists working on site and in the laboratory.

At the southern end of the peninsula, **Cape St. Mary's Ecological Reserve** is the only nesting seabird colony in the province that can be approached on foot. A short trail leads along spectacular seacliffs to a site where over 8,000 northern gannets nest on a rock just a few yards over the cliff.

On the southwest side of the peninsula, overlooking the entrance to the historic French town of Placentia, visitors can stroll up to the **Castle Hill National Historic Site**. These are the remains of French fortifications dating back to 1662; from here there are fine coastal views, and in summer the visitor center offers full tours.

🦅 Cape St. Mary's Ecological Reserve
Off Route 100. **Tel** (709) 277 1666.
Open year round. Interpretive Centre: **Open** May–Oct: daily. 🏞️ 🚻

🏰 Castle Hill National Historic Site of Canada
Jerseyside, Placentia Bay. **Tel** (709) 227 2401. Visitor center: **Open** Jun–Labour Day: 10am–6pm. 🚻 📷

❸ Burin Peninsula

🚌 St. John's. ⛴ Argentia. ℹ️ Columbia Drive, Marystown Jun–Nov: (709) 279 1211; Dec–May: (709) 279 1887.

The Burin Peninsula presents some of the most dramatic and impressive scenery in Newfoundland. Short, craggy peaks rise above a patchwork green carpet of heather, dotted by scores of glittering lakes. In the fishing town of Grand Bank, **The Provincial Seamen's Museum** preserves artifacts collected from the daily life of Newfoundland's seamen. The nearby town of Fortune offers a ferry to the French-ruled islands of Saint-Pierre and Miquelon.

🏛️ The Provincial Seamen's Museum
Marine Drive. **Tel** (709) 832 1484.
Open Apr–Oct: 11am–6pm daily.
🚻 limited. 📷

❹ Saint-Pierre and Miquelon Islands

🏔️ 6,400. ✈️ 🚢 ⛴ ℹ️ PO Box 4274, Place du Général de Gaulle.
🌐 **st-pierre-et-miquelon.com**

These two small islands are not Canadian but French, and have been under French rule since the 17th century. Saint-Pierre, the only town on the island of the same name, is a charming French seaside village. The **Saint-Pierre Museum** details the islands' history, including their lively role as a bootlegger's haven during Prohibition in the 1920s, when over three million cases of liquor passed through this port annually. Many of the harbourfront warehouses originally built for this trade are still standing.

Le Cabestan ferry takes visitors to Saint-Pierre and Miquelon

For hotels and restaurants in this region see p350 and p364

Cape Bonavista Lighthouse, built on the spot believed to be near John Cabot's first landing place in the New World

Miquelon Island is made up of two smaller islands, Langlade and Grand Miquelon, joined by a narrow, 12-km- (7-mile-) long strand. The road across this sandy isthmus crosses grassy dunes, where wild horses graze and surf pounds sandy beaches. A ferry leaves Saint-Pierre for the smaller village of Miquelon three times a week, usually on Tuesday, Wednesday, and Sunday. Another ferry goes to Langlade every day except Tuesday.

🏛 **Musée Heritage**
Rue Maître Georges Lefèvre 97500. **Tel** (508) 415 888. **Open** Jun–Oct: Tue–Sun. 🅿 👤 **W** musee-heritage.fr/en/

❺ Bonavista Peninsula

🚌 St. John's. ⛴ Argentia. 🛈 Discovery Trail Tourism Association, (709) 466 3845. **W** the-discovery-trail.com

Bonavista Peninsula juts out into the Atlantic ocean, a rugged coastal landscape of seacliffs, harbor inlets, and enchanting small villages such as Birchy Cove and Trouty.

The town of Bonavista is believed to be where Italian explorer John Cabot (see p50) first stepped ashore in the New World. His monument stands on a high, rocky promontory, near the Cape Bonavista Lighthouse, built in 1843. Along the Bonavista waterfront,

the huge 19th-century buildings of Ryan Premises, once a busy fish merchants' processing facility, are now restored as a National Historic Site. Ryan Premises include three large buildings, where fish were dried, stored, and packed for shipping, and displays on the history of the fisheries in North America. The waterfront salt house offers local music.

❻ Trinity

🏞 300. 🛈 Trinity Visitor Centre, West St., (709) 464 2042.
W townoftrinity.com

The charming village of Trinity, with its colorful 19th-century buildings overlooking the blue waters of Trinity Bay, is easily one of the most beautiful Newfoundland communities. Best explored on foot, Trinity has a range of craft shops and restaurants. The **Trinity Museum** contains over 2,000 artifacts, illustrating the town's past.

Also here is Hiscock House, a turn-of-the-20th-century home, restored to the style of 1910, where merchant Emma Hiscock ran the village store, forge, and post office, while raising her six children.

🏛 **Trinity Museum**
Church Rd. **Tel** (709) 464 3599.
Open mid-Jun–mid-Oct: 10am–5:30pm daily. 🅿 📷

❼ Terra Nova National Park

Trans-Canada Hwy. 🚌 from St. John's. **Open** May–mid-Oct: daily. 🅿 👤 🛈 limited. 🛈 Glovertown, (709) 533 2801. **W** pc.gc.ca

The gently rolling forested hills and deep fjords of northeastern Newfoundland are the setting for Terra Nova National Park. The park's Marine Interpretation Centre offers excellent displays on the local marine flora and fauna, including a fascinating underwater video monitor that broadcasts the busy life of the bay's seafloor. Whale-watching tours are also available.

A lookout over the forested hills of Terra Nova National Park

❽ Notre Dame Bay

🚌 Gander. ⛴ Port-aux-Basques; Argentia (seasonal). ℹ️ Notre Dame Junction, Rte 1.

On the east side, traditional Newfoundland outports maintain a way of life that echoes their history. The Twillingate Museum, located in an Edwardian rectory in Twillingate, has several rooms furnished with period antiques. Twillingate is also touted as the Iceberg Capital since the bulk of the huge icebergs floating down through Iceberg Alley are found here. For a close-up look, and whale-watching, take the boat tours in spring and early summer.

The rugged Fogo Island is a ferry ride away. Located here is the Fogo Island Inn, now a world-famous luxury hotel. Visitors also go to Change Islands, a tiny island home to the critically endangered Newfoundland pony.

The elegant Edwardian rectory that houses the Twillingate Museum

❾ Gander

🏙 10,000. ✈ 🚉 ℹ️ 109 Trans-Canada Hwy, (709) 256 7110. 🌐 **gandercanada.com**

Best known for its illustrious aviation history, Gander is a small town and a useful tourist center for fuel and food. In Grand Falls-Windsor, 100 km (62 miles) west

A display of tools at the Mary March Provincial Museum

of Gander, the Mary March Provincial Museum, named after the last survivor of the now-extinct Beothuk people, traces the span of central Newfoundland's history from the Aboriginal cultures of 9,000 years ago to the industrial age. Behind the museum, visitors can take a guided tour through the historic village.

❿ The Southwest Coast

⛴ Ferry dock terminal. ⛴ Port-aux-Basques. ℹ️ Port-aux-Basques, (709) 695 2262.

In southern Newfoundland the 45-km (28-mile) Granite Coastal Drive along Route 470 from Channel Port-aux-Basques to Rose Blanche leads through a landscape of ancient, jagged, green mountains and along a rocky, surf-carved shoreline. Near Rose Blanche, a 500-m (547-yd) boardwalk trail winds through bright wildflower-strewn heath to the impressive Barachois Falls. There is a charming picnic spot at the foot of the 55 m (180 ft) falls. The area is noted for its many

shipwrecks, and so the Rose Blanche Lighthouse, built in 1873, stands in defiant splendor atop the harbor headland.

⓫ Gros Morne National Park

Tel (709) 458 2417. 🚌 Corner Brook. ⛴ St. Barbe. **Open** daily. ♿ ⛰ 📷 🌐 **pc.gc.ca**

A UNESCO World Heritage Site, Gros Morne is Newfoundland's most scenic landscape master-piece. Here the Long Range Mountains rise 700 m (2,297 ft) above the blue fjord that cuts into the coastal range. Some of the world's oldest mountains, these are pre-Cambrian and several million years older than the Rockies.

The best way to see the North Side of the park is on a boat tour along Western Brook Pond, a narrow fjord cradled between soaring cliffs, where waterfalls vaporize as they tumble from great heights. Wildlife, including moose, caribou, and eagles, is frequently seen and heard.

The Long Range Mountains in Gros Morne National Park, seen from a walkway in the park

For hotels and restaurants in this region see p350 and p364

⑫ Northern Peninsula Tour

A land of legends and mystery, the Northern Peninsula of Newfoundland offers adventurous travelers the chance to experience over 40 centuries of human history, from early aboriginal people through colonization to today's modern fishing life. The road north travels along a harsh and rocky coast. Along the way, important historic sites, such as L'Anse-aux-Meadows, tell the story of the earlier cultures who chose this wild land as their home.

Tips for Drivers

Tour length: 430 km (267 miles) along Hwy 430. **Starting point:** Deer Lake, at junction of Hwy 1. **Stopping off points:** Gros Morne's Wiltondale Visitors' Centre and Tablelands; Port au Choix National Historic Site; Grenfell Museum in St. Anthony.

⑤ **Port au Choix**
This historic site is dedicated to exhibitions of Maritime Archaic people and people of the Paleo-Eskimo culture who lived here between 2000 BC and AD 500.

④ **Hawke's Bay**
A whaling station early in the 20th century, Hawke's Bay boasts excellent salmon-fishing waters.

③ **The Arches**
This lovely spot is named for three limestone arches that are believed to be 400 million years old.

② **Gros Morne National Park**
This is one of the most spectacular parks in Canada, with alpine plateaus, fjords, glacial valleys, and pristine lakes.

⑥ **L'Anse-aux-Meadows National Historic Site**
The reconstructions of three Norse buildings are the focal points of this UNESCO World Heritage Site, which is the earliest known European settlement in the New World.

① **Deer Lake**
A good fuel and refreshment center for those starting on the tour, Deer Lake and its surrounding area are remarkable for their jagged landscape, salmon river (the Humber), forests, lakes, and farms.

Key

▦ Tour route
═ Other roads

0 kilometres 25
0 miles   25

Fishermen's huts in the village of Red Bay on the coast of Labrador

⓭ Labrador Straits

🚢 Blanc Sablon. 🛈 L'Anse au Clair, (709) 931 2013.
🌐 labradorcoastaldrive.com

Hauntingly beautiful coastal landscapes explain why the Labrador Straits is a popular place to visit. A year-round ferry service crosses the strait from St. Barbe, Newfoundland, to Blanc Sablon, Quebec, just a few kilometers from the Labrador border. From there, take Route 510, which leads east along the Labrador Coastal Drive through a wild countryside of high, barren hills, thinly carpeted by heath and wind-twisted spruce. The route takes in small outport fishing villages, where fishing is still the economic mainstay for some. Atlantic Canada's tallest lighthouse was built here in 1854, near L'Anse-Amour. Known as the Point Amour Lighthouse, it stands at 30 m (98 ft) and is now a Provincial Historic Site. Another significant spot to stop is the Maritime Archaic Burial Mound National Historic Site, North America's oldest Burial mound, where a Maritime Archaic child was laid to rest 7,500 years ago.

The highway passes through the town of Red Bay, home to the **Red Bay National Historic Site**, which is now a UNESCO World Heritage site. Visitors can learn about the Basque mariners' presence during the 16th century, view the Right Whale Exhibit Museum, and visit the Interpretation Centre. Visitors can also take a short boat ride to Saddle Island, where a tour leads past the foundations of the shanties, shipworks, and cooper shops, where as many as 1,500 men worked each season, rendering whale oil for lamps in Europe.

🏠 Red Bay National Historic Site
Route 510. **Tel** (709) 920 2142.
Open Jun–early Oct: daily. ♿ ♿

⓮ Battle Harbour

🚢 Mary's Harbour 🛈 Mary's Harbour, Newfoundland, (709) 921 6325. 🌐 battleharbour.com

Once considered the unofficial capital of Labrador (from the 1870s to the 1930s), Battle Harbour, a small settlement on an island just off the southern coast of Labrador, was once a thriving fishing community. In 1965, the dwindling population was relocated to St. Mary's on the mainland, but all of the town's buildings, many of which date back 200 years, were left standing, and in the 1990s the town was restored. Today, it is a National Historic District. Visitors can tour the island and get a taste of the way life once was in remote Labrador.

⓯ Nain

⛰ 1,400. 🚁 🚢 🛈 Town Council, Nain, (709) 922 2842.
🌐 tourismnunatsiavut.com

Nain is Newfoundland and Labrador's most northern community. A large part of the small population is Inuit, and the town is rich with traditional art, much of which can be bought at Torngat Arts & Crafts in the center of town. Nain is also home to world-famous carvers such as John Terriak and Gilbert Hay.

The best way to explore Nain and the Nunatsiavut region is by taking the Northern Ranger ferry from Happy Valley-Goose Bay and visting the small fishing communities along the way. These include Rigolet, the most southern Inuit community in the world; Makkovik, a good place to buy traditional Labrador art; and Postville, which was once a trading post for Inuit families. Nearby Hopedale boasts some of Canada's oldest wooden-framed constructions, including

Inuit children in Nain

Battle Harbour Island, with icebergs on the horizon

A snowy street in Nain during the long winter

the **Hopedale Mission National Historic Site**, where stories and artifacts are displayed.

🏛 Hopedale Mission National Historic Site

Agvituk Historical Society, Hopedale. **Tel** (709) 933 3881. **Open** daily.

The Moravian Church in Happy Valley-Goose Bay

⑯ Happy Valley-Goose Bay

🏙 8,000. ✈ 🚌 ℹ Labrador, (709) 896 8787. 🚗 book ahead.
🌐 tourismlabrador.com

The largest town in the wilderness of Central Labrador, Happy Valley-Goose Bay was a strategically important stopover for transatlantic flights during World War II. German, Italian, and British pilots now train at the NATO base here.

The nearby community of North West River is home to the Labrador Heritage Museum, where exhibitions depict its fascinating history. It pays particular attention to the life of trappers, with displays that include animal furs, trapper's tools, and a traditional tilt (wilderness shelter).

⑰ Churchill Falls

ℹ Churchill Falls Development Corporation, (709) 925 3335. 🚗
🔒 obligatory, book ahead.

The town of Churchill Falls is ideally placed for visitors to stock up on supplies, fill up with gas, and check tyres, as there are no service stations between Happy Valley-Goose Bay and Labrador City. Churchill Falls is famous as the site of one of the largest hydroelectric power stations in the world. Built in the early 1970s, the plant is an extraordinary feat of engineering, diverting the Churchill River (Labrador's largest) and its incredible volume of water to propel the underground turbines that produce 5,225 megawatts of power – enough to supply the needs of a small country. Guided tours are available of this impressive complex.

⑱ Labrador City

🏙 7,700. ✈ 🚌 ℹ Labrador West Tourism Development Corporation, (709) 944 7631.

In the midst of ancient tundra, Labrador City is a mining town that shows the modern, industrial face of Canada. The town is home to the largest open-pit iron mine in the world, and the community has largely grown up around it since the late 1950s.

The vast open wilderness surrounding Labrador City, with its lakes and rivers, is renowned as a sportsman's paradise that attracts hunters and anglers from around the world. The western Labrador wilderness is also home to the 700,000 caribou of the George River herd. The animals move freely through the area for most of the year, grazing the tundra in small bands. Professional outfitters take groups of visitors out to track them through the region. Many tourists make the trip to admire the herd.

The **Gateway Labrador Visitor Center** at Labrador City has an exhibit of artifacts representing the best of Labrador West and its history, culture, and people. It also covers the fur trading and mining history of Labrador.

🏛 Gateway Labrador Visitor Center

1365, Route 500. **Tel** (709) 944 5554. **Open** Jun 15–Sep 25: 9am–6pm daily.

The Northern Ranger Ferry

The Northern Ranger passenger ferry, operated by Nunatsiavut Marine (labradorferry.ca) is the primary mode of transportation for many communities along the coast. It departs from Happy Valley-Goose Bay and Cartwright, and explores the historic region of Nunatsiavut. Stops along the way include Rigolet, Makkovik, Postville, Hopedale and Natuashish, where the ferry docks for 1–3 hours. Nain is the final destination on the journey. Icebergs are a common sight.

NEW BRUNSWICK, PRINCE EDWARD ISLAND AND NOVA SCOTIA

The beauty and lure of the sea is always close at hand here. Stunning coastal scenery, picturesque centuries-old villages, world-class historic sites, and a wealth of family attractions have positioned these three Maritime Provinces among Canada's top vacation destinations. New Brunswick's ruggedly beautiful Bay of Fundy is matched by the gently rolling landscape of Acadian villages tucked into quiet coves and long sandy beaches. Canada's smallest province, Prince Edward Island, is known for its vibrant green farmlands, red bluffs, deep blue waters, and golf courses, and is enjoyed by cyclists, anglers, and hikers. Nova Scotia, with its sparkling bays and weathered fishing towns, embodies the romance of the sea. Elegant country inns and historic sites bring the past to life.

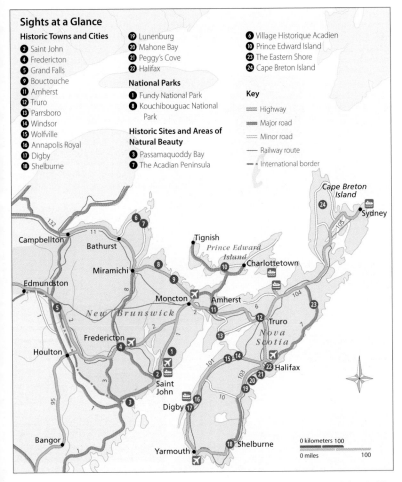

Sights at a Glance

Historic Towns and Cities
2 Saint John
4 Fredericton
5 Grand Falls
9 Bouctouche
11 Amherst
12 Truro
13 Parrsboro
14 Windsor
15 Wolfville
16 Annapolis Royal
17 Digby
18 Shelburne
19 Lunenburg
20 Mahone Bay
21 Peggy's Cove
22 Halifax

National Parks
1 Fundy National Park
8 Kouchibouguac National Park

Historic Sites and Areas of Natural Beauty
3 Passamaquoddy Bay
7 The Acadian Peninsula

6 Village Historique Acadien
10 Prince Edward Island
23 The Eastern Shore
24 Cape Breton Island

Key
▨▨ Highway
▨▨ Major road
═══ Minor road
─── Railway route
▬▪▬ International border

◀ The harbor at Peggy's Cove

For map symbols see back flap

Humpback whales at play in the Bay of Fundy

❶ Fundy National Park

Tel (506) 887 6000. 🚗 Moncton. 🚌 Sussex. 🚢 Saint John. **Open** daily. 🏂 May–Oct. ♿ 📷 🛒 🌐 pc.gc.ca

Along New Brunswick's southern shore, the tremendous tides of the Bay of Fundy are a powerful feature of everyday life. Twice a day, over 100 billion tons of water swirl into and out of the bay, creating a tidal shift of up to 15 m (49 ft) and carving out a stunning wild and rocky shoreline.

Moose in Fundy National Park

One of the best places to experience these world-famous tidal wonders is at Fundy National Park, which is filled with wildlife and hiking trails. Here at low tide, visitors can walk out for over a kilometer. The Bay is a favorite with naturalists, who study the fascinating creatures that live half their lives under water and the other half above.

❷ Saint John

🏙 70,000. ✈ 🚌 🚢 ℹ City Hall, King St., (506) 658 2990. 🌐 discoversaintjohn.com

Saint John still retains the charm of a small town. In 1785, 14,000 loyalists escaping the turmoil of the American Revolution built Saint John in under a year.

More recently, restoration has made Saint John's historic center a delightful place to explore. The Saint John City Market is the oldest continuing farmers' market in Canada, with colorful produce stacked high, fresh seafood vendors, cafés, and an excellent traditional fish restaurant.

In nearby Market Square, an airy atrium links buildings that were once the city's center of commerce. Here visitors will find upscale restaurants and stores. Market Square is also the home of the lively **New Brunswick Museum**. Three floors offer clever and entertaining exhibits on New Brunswick's geological, cultural, and natural history. Children particularly enjoy the Hall of Whales and the three-level Tidal Tower, in which water rises and falls in real-time, re-creating the height of the tides roaring away just outside.

Nearby, the Loyalist House Museum is located in an impressive Georgian house built by Loyalist David Merritt in around 1810. Inside, the house has been renovated to reflect the lifestyle of a wealthy family of that time, with authentic period furnishings.

🏛 **New Brunswick Museum**
Market Square. **Tel** (506) 643 2300. **Open** daily **Closed** Nov–mid-May: Mon. 📷 ♿

❸ Passamaquoddy Bay

🚌 Saint Stephen. 🚢 Black's Harbour & L'Etete. ℹ Saint Andrew's Tourism Bureau, (506) 529 3556.

There is a genteel historic charm to the villages surrounding the island-filled waters of Passamaquoddy Bay, and none is more charming or intriguing than the resort town of Saint Andrews-by-the-Sea. The beautifully renovated Marriott Algonquin Resort, with its elegant grounds and 18-hole golf course, recalls early 20th-century days, when Saint Andrews was renowned as an exclusive getaway of the rich and powerful.

In town, Water Street is lined with intriguing boutiques, craft shops, and fine restaurants housed in century-old buildings. At the town dock, tour companies offer sailing, whale-watching, and kayaking trips. Nearby, the elegant Georgian home built for Loyalist Harris Hatch in 1824 is now the location of the **Ross Memorial Museum**, which contains an extensive collection of antiques and art.

Ferries depart from Blacks Harbour in the Saint George area several times daily for Grand Manan Island, 30 km (18 miles) south of Saint Andrews. For Campobello Island, 20 km (12 miles) south of Saint Andrews, a ferry departs from L'Etete to Deer Island, from where another

View of Saint John from the Saint John River

The charming Victorian vista of Fredericton seen from across the Saint John River

ferry goes to Campobello. The Roosevelt Campobello International Park, on Campobello Island, is a 11-sq-km (4-sq-mile) preserve built around the elegant summer home of US President Franklin D. Roosevelt. The 34-room Roosevelt Cottage has been restored, and includes artifacts belonging to Roosevelt and his family.

Ruggedly beautiful Grand Manan Island has high rocky cliffs, picturesque fishing villages, brightly painted boats, and weathered piers. It is popular with birdwatchers, as it attracts large flocks of seabirds annually.

🏛 The Ross Memorial Museum
188 Montague St. **Tel** (506) 529 5124. **Open** late May–early Oct: Mon–Sat. 🖥 **rossmemorialmuseum.ca**

❹ Fredericton

🏛 48,000. 🚉 🚌 🛈 Carlton Tourism Division, (506) 460 2041. 🖥 **tourismfredericton.ca**

Straddling the Saint John River, Fredericton is New Brunswick's provincial capital. Its Victorian homes and waterfront church make it one of the prettiest small cities in Atlantic Canada. Several historic buildings reflect the town's early role as a British military post. The **Beaverbrook Art Gallery** contains a fine collection of 19th- and 20th-century paintings, including Salvador Dali's masterpiece *Santiago el Grande* (1957). **King's Landing Historical Settlement**, 37 km (23 miles) west of Fredericton,

is a living history museum that re-creates daily life in a rural New Brunswick village of the 19th century. Over a hundred costumed workers bring villagers' homes, church, and school to life.

🏛 Beaverbrook Art Gallery
703 Queen St. **Tel** (506) 458 8545. **Open** daily. 🏛 🦽 📷 🖥 **beaverbrookartgallery.org**

🏛 King's Landing Historical Settlement
Rte 2, W. of Fredericton. **Tel** (506) 363 4999. **Open** Jun–early Oct: 10am–5pm daily. 🏛 🦽 partial. 🖥 **kingslanding.nb.ca**

❺ Grand Falls

🏛 5,900. 🚌 🛈 Malabeam Reception Centre. 🏛

From Fredericton to Edmundston, the Saint John River flows through a pastoral valley of rolling hills, woods, and farmland. The town of Grand Falls consists of one

well-appointed main street, Boulevard Broadway, which is a useful refreshment stop. The town was named Grand Falls for the mighty cataract the Saint John River creates as it tumbles through Grand Falls Gorge. Framed by parkland, the surge of water drops more than 25 m (82 ft). Over time it has carved a gorge 1.5 km (1 mile) long, with steep sides as high as 70 m (230 ft) in places.

Upriver and north through the valley, the town of Edmundston offers the **New Brunswick Botanical Garden**. Paths lead through eight themed gardens and two arboretums that provide dazzling input for the senses. Bright colors, delicate scents, and even soft classical music delight visitors.

🌿 New Brunswick Botanical Garden
Saint-Jacques, Edmundston. **Tel** (506) 737 4444. **Open** May–Oct: 9am–dusk daily. 🏛 🖥 **jardinnb.org/en**

The deep waterfall valley of Grand Falls Gorge

❻ Village Historique Acadien

After the tragic deportation of 1755–63, Acadians slowly returned to the Maritimes, clearing new farmlands and rebuilding their way of life. The Village Historique Acadien portrays a rural Acadian community between 1770 and 1949. The village's 60 restored historic buildings, including several working farms, cover 364 ha (900 acres). Throughout the village, period-costumed bilingual guides re-create the daily activities of the 19th century. Visitors can ride in a horse-drawn wagon, watch the work of the blacksmith, print shop, or gristmill, and also tour working farms and homes where women are busy spinning, weaving, and cooking.

VISITORS' CHECKLIST

Practical Information
Route 11, 10 km (6 miles) W. of Caraquet. **Tel** (506) 726 2600. **Open** 10am–6pm daily. **Closed** Aug 15. 🅿️ ♿ 🅱️ 📷 ✎
W villagehistoriqueacadien.com

Transport
🚌 from Bathurst.

School and Chapel
Through centuries of turmoil, Catholicism was a vital mainstay of the Acadian people. Priests were also schoolteachers; education was highly prized by the community.

Cooper's Shop Tinsmith
Lobster Pound

Men in horse-drawn cart
Traditional methods are used on the farms; tilled by local people arriving each day, the harvest is moved in carts to barns for winter.

The Chapel was built by pioneer Acadians and dates from 1831.

Doucet Farm was first built in 1840 and has been fully restored to its original appearance.

Mazerolle Farm sells fresh bread and rolls, which are baked daily in a large oven in the farmhouse.

Poirier
Tavern

Savoie House
Education Centre

Robin
Shed

Forge
In many ways the center of the community, the blacksmith was a feature of every Acadian village, repairing farm equipment and shoeing horses for the people of the area.

Godin
House

**The Visitors'
Reception Centre** offers an audiovisual presentation, and typical Acadian food in its restaurant.

0 meters 100
0 yards 100

Endless sandy beaches stretch to the horizon at Kouchibouguac National Park

❼ The Acadian Peninsula

🚆 Bathurst. 🚌 Bathurst. 🚢 Dalhousie. ℹ️ Jun-Sep: Water St., Campbellton (506) 789 2367; Oct-May: Campbellton Chamber of Commerce (506) 759 7856.

The quiet coastal villages, beaches, and gentle surf of the Acadian peninsula have made it a favorite vacation destination. Established here since the 1600s, the Acadians have long enjoyed a reputation for fruitful farming, pretty villages, and a strong folk music tradition (see pp68–9).

In Shippagan, a small fishing town, the **Marine Centre and Aquarium** holds tanks with over 3,000 specimens of Atlantic sealife and displays on local fishing industries.

Nearby, the Lamèque and Miscou islands are connected by causeways to the mainland. Visit the Église Ste-Cécile on Lamèque Island, a church with unique painted interiors. It is home to the annual International Baroque Festival. Discover the Acadian Peninsula's flora and fauna at the **Ecological Park**, and learn about the region's five largest ecosystems.

On Miscou Island, a 1-km (0.5-mile) boardwalk leads through a peat bog with signs about this unique ecosystem. The 35-m (85-ft) high Miscou Lighthouse is the oldest operating wooden lighthouse in Canada and also a National Historic Site.

Home to many Acadian artists, Caraquet is the busy cultural center of the peninsula. On the waterfront, adventure centers offer guided kayak trips on the Baie des Chaleurs.

🚢 Marine Centre and Aquarium
100 Aquarium Street, Shippagan. **Tel** (506) 336 3013. **Open** mid-May– mid-Oct: 10am–6pm daily. 🅿️ ♿ 🌐 **aquariumnb.ca**

🌿 Ecological Park
65 Du Ruisseau St., Lamèque. **Tel** (506) 344 3223. **Open** late Jun– Aug: 10am–5pm daily. 🅿️ ♿ 🎫

❽ Kouchibouguac National Park

Tel (506) 876 2443. 🚆 Miramichi. 🚌 Miramichi. 🚢 Miramichi. **Open** daily. 🌐 **parkscanada.gc.ca/ kouchibouguac**

The name of this park comes from the local Mi'kmaq word for "River of Long Tides." The park's 238 sq km (92 sq miles) encompass a salt-spray world of wind-sculpted dunes, salt marshes packed with wild life, and 25 km (16 miles) of fine sand beaches, as well as excellent terrain for cyclists. A popular activity is the Voyageur Canoe Adventure, a three-hour canoe paddle to offshore sandbanks where gray seals bask.

❾ Bouctouche

🏔️ 2,400. 🚌 ℹ️ Jun-Sep: 14 Acadia St. (506) 743 8811; Oct-May: Bouctouche Chamber of Commerce (506) 759 7856. 🌐 **villedebouctouche.ca**

A seaside town with a strong Acadian heritage, Bouctouche is home to **Le Pays de la Sagouine**. This theme village is named for La Sagouine, the wise washer-woman created by Acadian author Antonine Maillet (b. 1929). Theatrical shows here act out her tales. Nearby, the Irving Eco-Centre studies and protects the beautiful 12-km (8-mile) network of dunes, saltmarshes, and beach that extend along the entrance to Bouctouche Harbour.

🎭 Le Pays de la Sagouine
57 Acadia St. **Tel** 1 800 561 9188. **Open** 10am–5:30pm daily. **Closed** Sep 4. 🌐 **sagouine.com**

The raised boardwalk at the Irving Eco-Centre, La Dune de Bouctouche

⑩ Prince Edward Island

Beautiful and pastoral, Prince Edward Island is famous for its lush landscapes. Wherever you look, the island's rich colors, emerald green farmlands, red-clay roads, and sapphire ocean seem to combine and recombine in endless patterns to please the eye. The island is also a popular destination for golfers, who come to tee off on some of Canada's best courses, as well as a haven for sun worshipers, who revel in the sandy beaches around the island. Prince Edward Island seems made for exploring at a leisurely pace. Meandering coastal roads present an ever-changing panorama of sea, sand, and sky. Small historic towns are home to elegant country inns and art galleries. In the evenings, the island's famous lobster suppers await, caught fresh from the surrounding waters.

Green Gables House
Set amid leafy green paths, this 19th-century home was the setting for the popular *Anne of Green Gables* tales.

Malpeque Bay
Cabot Beach Provincial Park covers part of the bay. Ten million of the world-famous Malpeque oysters are caught here each year.

North Cape

Mill River

Portage

Egmont Bay

Malpeque

Cavendish

Kensington

Hunter River

Victoria

Key

▬ Major road

▬ Minor road

▬ Rivers

— National Park boundaries

KEY

① **Cedar Dunes Provincial Park** features a restored 1875 lighthouse, sandy beaches, and a large coastal campground.

② **Confederation Bridge**, opened in 1997 at a cost of Can $840m, runs for 13 km (8 miles) to the mainland.

③ **Brudenell River Provincial Park** is surrounded by rocky coastlines and fine sea views.

④ **Panmure Island** has long stretches of sandy beaches.

Main street, Summerside
This quiet city with its attractive tree-lined streets is known for its Lobster Festival each July.

★ Prince Edward Island National Park

Characterized by 40 km (25 miles) of coastline leading onto red cliffs, pink and white sand beaches, and mild seas, this park offers unbeatable sport and vacationing facilities and has an educational Visitors' Centre for those interested in its marine wildlife.

East Point Lighthouse
The island's easternmost point is home to a 19th-century lighthouse with a restored radio room. Now unmanned and fully automatic, it is open to visitors.

★ Charlottetown

Elegant 19th-century row houses characterize the streets of this sleepy town, the smallest of Canada's provincial capitals. In 1867 the Confederation of Canada was formed here.

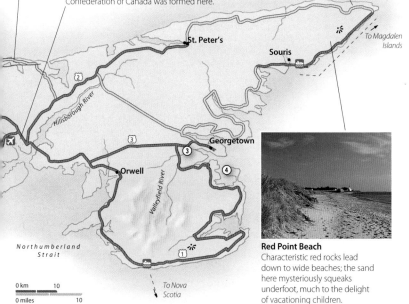

St. Peter's
Souris
To Magdalen Islands
Hillsborough River
Georgetown
Orwell
Valleyfield River
Northumberland Strait
To Nova Scotia

0 km 10
0 miles 10

Red Point Beach
Characteristic red rocks lead down to wide beaches; the sand here mysteriously squeaks underfoot, much to the delight of vacationing children.

For map symbols *see back flap*

Exploring Prince Edward Island

Prince Edward Island is the smallest province in Canada, with a concentration of activity and its every corner easily accessible. Charlottetown, known as the birthplace of Canada, is centrally located, and its tree-lined streets make a gentle start to exploring the outlying country. Red clay roads guide the visitor through farms and fishing villages to tiny provincial parks scattered throughout the island. Traveling the north coast takes in the splendid rolling green scenery of PEI National Park, with its famous beaches, while southward, warm swimming spots abound.

Fishing huts overlooking French River near Cavendish

Cavendish

This is such a busy little town that it can be hard to see the gentle, pastoral home of the *Anne of Green Gables* novels. The best place to get in touch with its charm is at the site of **Lucy Maud Montgomery's Cavendish Home**, where the author lived for many years in a simple homestead. The town is also the location of **Green Gables Heritage Place**, the novels' fictional 19th-century home.

🎦 **Lucy Maud Montgomery's Cavendish Home**
Route 6. **Tel** (902) 963 2231. **Open** mid-May–mid-Oct: 10am–5pm. 🌳 ♿
W peisland.com/lmm

🎦 **Green Gables Heritage Place**
Route 6. **Tel** (902) 963 7874. **Open** May 21–Oct 31. ♿ W **tourismpei. com/green-gables-house**

Cavendish
Routes 6 & 13. 🛈 (902) 963 7830.

Prince Edward Island National Park

Green Gables is part of Prince Edward Island National Park, whose western entrance is in Cavendish. This is the park's busier side. The soft sand and gentle surf of Cavendish Beach make it one of the most popular beaches in the province. The park's coastal road leads to North Rustico Beach, which is a favorite with

sightseers. At the park's western end, the Homestead Trail leads for 8 km (5 miles) through rustic green woodlands and meadows.

The park's quieter eastern side features a long stretch of pristine beach and dunes, and a scenic coastal road. The Reeds and Rushes Trail is a lovely short boardwalk track leading to a freshwater marsh pond, where local species of geese and duck nest and feed.

🦫 **Prince Edward Island National Park**
🚌 Charlottetown. 🚢 Wood Islands. 🛈 (902) 672 6350. **Open** daily. 🌳 ♿ W pc.gc.ca

The South Coast

Enchanting vistas are found along the roads of the south shore, between Confederation Bridge and Charlottetown. Visitors will also find Victoria-by-the-Sea, a small village that is home to some of the island's most interesting craft shops.

En route to Charlottetown, visitors can make a short detour to **Fort Amherst-Port-la-Joye National Historic Site of Canada**. It was here, in 1720, that the French built the island's first permanent settlement. The British captured it in 1758, and built Fort Amherst to protect the entrance to Charlottetown Harbour. While the fort is long gone, the earthworks can still be seen in the park-like surrounds.

🎦 **Fort Amherst-Port-la-Joye National Historic Site of Canada**
Rocky Point. **Tel** (902) 566 7626. **Open** Jul–Sep 2: daily. 🌳 ♿ W pc.gc.ca

The red bluffs of Cavendish Beach, one of the most favored spots in Prince Edward Island National Park

View of the 19th-century church at Orwell Corner Historic Village

Panmure Island

The natural beauty of the island's eastern area is easy to experience on Panmure Island, south of Georgetown. Level roads make it popular with cyclists. In summer, the octagonal wooden **Panmure Island Lighthouse** is open, and the view from the top takes in a long vista of the island's beaches, saltmarshes, and woodlands. The lighthouse still guides ships into port, as it did when it was first built in 1853.

🔲 **Panmure Island Lighthouse**
Panmure Island. **Tel** (902) 838 3568.
Open Jul–Aug: 10am–6pm daily. 🎿

Orwell Corner Historic Village

Just outside of the small hamlet of Orwell, Orwell Corner Historic Village re-creates the day-to-day life of a small 19th-century crossroads community. Orwell Corner was thriving until well into the 20th century, when changes in transportation and commerce lessened the importance of the settlement. This charming village was restored and opened in 1973. Among the buildings are a blacksmith's, church, schoolhouse, and Clarke's store, the social center of the village. At Orwell Corner is the PEI Agricultural Museum, which tells the story of PEI from the mid-1700s to the 1950s.

Just 1 km (0.5 mile) away is the **Sir Andrew Macphail Homestead**. This Victorian house and its surroundings were the much-loved home of Macphail, a local doctor,

journalist, teacher, and soldier who counted among his friends prime ministers and acclaimed writers such as Kipling. The house features many exhibits dealing with Macphail's life. Outside, trails wind through deep woodlands.

🔲 **Orwell Corner Historic Village**
Orwell. **Tel** (902) 651 8513.
Open May–Oct: daily. 🎿 ♿
W peimuseum.com/orwell

🔲 **Sir Andrew Macphail Homestead**
Off Rte 1, Orwell. **Tel** (902) 651 2789.
Open Jul–Sep: 9am–5pm daily.
🎿 ♿ W macphailhomestead.ca

Charlottetown

The birthplace of Canada is a charming coastal city. Voted a Cultural Capital of Canada, the small city has an abundance of performing arts, local shopping, and world-class cuisine. The national **Confederation Centre of the Arts** hosts an array of live entertainment, including the popular musical *Anne of Green*

Gables. **Province House National Historic Site** is where the 1864 Charlottetown Conference was held, which eventually led to the formation of Canada as a nation. Much of the building has been meticulously restored. **Peake's Quay** is perfect for a stroll, waterfront shopping, coastal excursions, live music, dining, or a taste of the ever-popular Cow's ice cream, made to a recipe said to date back to the time of *Anne of Green Gables*.

🏛 **Confederation Centre of the Arts**
145 Richmond St. **Tel** (902) 628 1864.
Open daily. ♿
W confederationcentre.com/en/

🔲 **Province House National Historic Site of Canada**
165 Richmond St. **Tel** (902) 566 7626.
Open daily; call ahead for hours. ♿
W pc.gc.ca

Charlottetown
ℹ Water St., 800 955 1864.
W discovercharlottetown.com

Historic properties on Great George Street, Charlottetown

Lucy Maud Montgomery

The island's most famous author, Lucy Maud Montgomery, was born in Cavendish in 1874. Nearby Green Gables House became the setting of her internationally best-selling novel, *Anne of Green Gables* (1908), set in the late 19th century. The manuscript was accepted only on the sixth attempt. To date, millions of copies of her book have been published, in 16 languages. In 1911, Lucy married and moved to Ontario, where she raised two sons. She continued to write, producing 19 more books, ten of which feature Anne, with all but one set on Prince Edward Island. She died in 1942 and was buried overlooking the farms and fields of her beloved native Cavendish, of which she wrote so often.

Author Lucy Maud Montgomery

⓫ Amherst

🗺 9,500. 🚌 ℹ️ Rte 104, exit 1 (902) 667 8429. 🌐 amherst.ca

The busy commercial and agricultural town of Amherst overlooks the world's largest marsh, the Tantramar. Along its edge, hayfields grow on land reclaimed by Acadian-built dikes in the 1600s. **The Cumberland County Museum** is at the home of Senator R. B. Dickey, one of the Fathers of Confederation. It focuses on the area's development and natural history.

Nearby are **Fort Beauséjour** and its museum, and the archaeological digs at the Acadian village of Beaubassin.

🏛 **Cumberland County Museum**
150 Church St. **Tel** (902) 667 2561. **Open** Tue–Sat. 🅿 ♿
🌐 cumberlandcountymuseum.com

🏛 **Fort Beauséjour**
Trans-Canada Hwy 2, Exit 513A. **Open** Jun–mid-Oct: daily. 🅿 ♿ 📷
🌐 pc.gc.ca

⓬ Truro

🗺 11,700. 🚆 🚌 ℹ️ Victoria Square, (902) 893 2922.

Located at the hub of Nova Scotia's main transportation routes, Truro is the site of a unique geographical phenomenon, the tidal bore. As the great Fundy tides return landward, sweeping into the Minas Basin, they generate a wave, or "bore," that is driven for several kilometers up the rivers that empty into the basin. An information display next to the Salmon River explains the process and posts

Façade of Windsor's Haliburton House, home of the famous humorist

the tidal times. On the nearby Shubenacadie River, visitors can ride the bore in rafts. The waves generated can reach 2 m (7 ft) in height, creating a churn of whitewater that the rafts race through as they follow it for miles upstream.

⓭ Parrsboro

🗺 1,500. ℹ️ Main St., (902) 254 3266. 🌐 town.parrsboro.ns.ca

Located on the north shore of the Minas Basin, Parrsboro is famous as the home of the world's highest tides, which reach over 15 m (49 ft) in height. Rockhounds are drawn to the Minas Basin whose beaches are scattered with semiprecious gems and fossils. The displays at **Fundy Geological Museum** in Parrsboro feature fine examples of local amethysts. There are also dinosaur footprints and bones.

Prosauropod dinosaur skull from Fundy Geological Museum

🏛 **The Fundy Geological Museum**
162 Two Islands Rd. **Tel** (902) 254 3814. **Open** Jun–mid-Oct: daily; late Oct–May: Mon–Fri. 🅿 ♿ 🌐
fundygeological.novascotia.ca

⓮ Windsor

🗺 3,800. 🚌 ℹ️ Hwy 101, exit 6, (902) 798 2275. 🌐 town.windsor.ns.ca

A quiet town whose elegant Victorian homes overlook the Avon River, Windsor was the home of Judge Thomas Chandler Haliburton, lawyer, historian, and the author of the Canadian "Sam Slick" stories, which achieved enormous popularity in the mid-1800s. Haliburton was one of the first widely recognized humorists in North America. His clever, fast-talking character Sam Slick was a Yankee clock peddler who coined idiomatic terms such as "the early bird gets the worm," and "raining cats and dogs." His elegant home is now the **Haliburton House Provincial Museum**. Set in gardens that Haliburton tended and loved, the house is furnished in Victorian antiques and contains many of his personal possessions, including his writing desk.

🏛 **Haliburton House Provincial Museum**
414 Clifton Ave. **Tel** (902) 798 2915. **Open** Jun–mid-Oct: daily. 🅿 ♿ limited. 🌐 haliburtonhouse.novascotia.ca

Two Island Beach in Parrsboro, famous for the two large rock outcrops known as the "Brothers Parrsboro"

⑮ Wolfville

🏔 4,200. ℹ Willow Park, (902) 542 7000. 🌐 wolfville.ca

The home of the acclaimed Acadia University, Wolfville and the surrounding countryside radiate a truly gracious charm. Here the green and fertile Annapolis Valley meets the shore of the Minas Basin, and keen visitors can follow country roads past lush farmlands, sun-warmed orchards, and gentle tidal flats.

Much of the valley's rich farmland was created by dikes built by the Acadians in the 1600s. After the Great Expulsion of 1755, the British offered the land to struggling New England villagers on the condition that the entire village would relocate. These hardworking settlers, known as Planters, proved so successful that the towns of the Annapolis Valley flourished.

Wolfville is a pretty town of tree-lined streets and inviting shops and restaurants. Nearby, the town's Visitor Information Center marks the start of a 5-km (3-mile) trail along the Acadian dikes to the graceful church at the **Grand Pré National Historic Site**. When the British marched into the Acadian village of Grand Pré in August 1755, it marked the beginning of the Great Uprooting, *Le Grand Dérangement*, which eventually forced thousands of Acadians from Nova Scotia *(see pp68–9)*. In 1921 a stone church modeled after French country churches was built on the site of the old village of Grand Pré as a memorial to this tragedy. The French Cross marks the spot where the Acadians boarded the ships. Visitors can also stroll around the garden grounds, where a statue of Evangeline, the heroine of Longfellow's epic poem about the Acadians, stands waiting for her lover, Gabriel. The site's information center features exhibits on the Acadians and their history. After the Great Expulsion,

Longfellow's Evangeline

many families hid locally, while some returned in later years.

🎫 **Grand Pré National Historic Site**
Hwy 101, exit 10. **Tel** (902) 542 3631. **Open** May–Oct: daily. 🅿 ♿ 🌐 pc.gc.ca

⑯ Annapolis Royal

🏔 550. 🚌 ℹ Prince Albert Rd., (902) 532 2562. 🌐 annapolisroyal.com

Toward the eastern end of the Annapolis Valley is the historic town of Annapolis Royal, the first capital of the colony of Nova Scotia. The British-built **Fort Anne National Historic Site** witnessed many battles between the English and the French for control of the area. The nearby fur-trading post of Port Royal *(see p51)*, the first European settlement in the New World north of Florida, was built in 1605 by Samuel de Champlain. The **Port Royal National Historic Site** is an exact replica of the original colony, based on French farms of the period, from plans drawn by Champlain.

Kejimkujik Park entrance sign

An hour's drive inland from Annapolis Royal lies **Kejimkujik National Park and National Historic Site**, which covers 381 sq km (147 sq miles) of inland wilderness laced with lakes and rivers. The park has paddling routes and hiking trails ranging from short walks to a 60-km (37-mile) perimeter wilderness and wildlife trail.

🎫 **Fort Anne National Historic Site**
St. George St. **Tel** (902) 532 2397. **Open** daily (Oct 16–May 14: by appt; call (902) 532 2321). 🅿 ♿ 🌐 pc.gc.ca

🎫 **Port Royal National Historic Site**
15 km W. of Annapolis Royal. **Tel** (902) 532 2898. **Open** May–Oct: 9am–5:30pm (to 6pm Jul & Aug). 🅿 ♿ 🌐 pc.gc.ca

🏞 **Kejimkujik National Park and National Historic Site**
Hwy 8. **Tel** (902) 682 2772. **Open** daily. 🅿 mid-May–Oct. ♿ 🌐 pc.gc.ca

⑰ Digby

🏔 2,600. 🚢 🚌 🚢 ℹ Shore Rd., (902) 245 5714. 🌐 digby.ca

This fishing town is synonymous with the plump scallops that are the prime quarry of its fishing fleet. The area around Digby also offers splendid scenery and is the starting place for a scenic trip along Digby Neck to the rocky coastal landscape of beautiful Long and Brier Islands.

The waters off these islands brim with finback, minke, and humpback whales, and whale-watching tours are one of the region's favorite pastimes. Some visitors may even glimpse the rare right whale, as about 200 of the 350 left in the world spend their summers in the Bay of Fundy.

Children having fun in a canoeing lake at Kejimkujik National Park

The Dory Shop Museum in Shelburne, center of local boat-building

⑱ Shelburne

🏛 1,700. 🚌 ℹ️ Dock St., (902) 875 4547. 🌐 town.shelburne.ns.ca

A quiet historic town nestled on the shore of a deep harbor, Shelburne was founded by 3,000 United Empire Loyalists fleeing persecution during the American Revolution of 1775. More loyalists followed over the next few years, and Shelburne's population swelled to 16,000, making it at the time the third-largest town in British North America. Over time, many of those settlers relocated to Halifax or returned to England, leaving behind the fine 18th-century homes they had built.

A walk along Water Street leads past some of the town's most attractive historic homes to the **Dory Shop Museum**. This two-storey structure has been a commercial dory (flat-bottomed) boat-building shop since its founding in 1880. During the days of the Grand Banks schooner fleet, Shelburne dories were famous for their strength and seaworthiness. The museum's first floor features displays on the industry and the salt-cod

fishery. Upstairs, skilled shipwrights demonstrate the techniques of dory building.

The 1995 film *The Scarlet Letter* was shot in Shelburne, with the whole main street becoming a movie set. The town is also home to the only active cooperage in Canada.

🏛 Dory Shop Museum
Dock St. **Tel** (902) 875 3219. **Open** Jun–Sep: daily. 🚗 🚻 limited. 🌐 shelburnemuseums.com/the-dory-shop

⑲ Lunenburg

🏛 2,600. 🚌 ℹ️ May–Sep: (902) 634 8100; Oct–Apr: (902) 634 3170. 🌐 explorelunenburg.ca

No town captures the seafaring romance of Nova Scotia as much as Lunenburg. In the mid-1700s the British, eager for another loyal settlement, laid out a town plan for Lunenburg. They then offered the land to Protestant settlers from Switzerland, Germany, and France. Although these were mainly farmers, they soon turned to shipbuilding and the town became a major center

for the trade. In 1996 the town was declared a UNESCO World Heritage Site, one of the best-preserved planned settlements in the New World. Lunenburg is also the home port of *Bluenose II*, a replica of Canada's most famous schooner.

The **Fisheries Museum of the Atlantic** fills several buildings along the waterfront. It is home to retired schooners, touch tanks, and daily sessions on how to shuck a scallop.

🏛 Fisheries Museum of the Atlantic
Bluenose Dr. **Tel** (902) 634 4794. **Open** mid-May–mid-Oct: daily; late Oct–May: Mon–Fri. 🚗 🚻 limited.

One of Mahone Bay's three waterfront churches

⑳ Mahone Bay

🏛 990. 🚌 ℹ️ Destination Southwest Nova Association, (902) 624 6151. 🌐 mahonebay.com

The small seaside town of Mahone Bay has been called the "prettiest town in Canada." Tucked into the shores of the bay that shares its name, the waterfront is lined with historic homes dating to the 1700s, and

The Lunenberg Fisheries Museum of the Atlantic along the town's romantic waterfront

at the back of the harbor three stately churches cast their reflection into the still waters.

The town has attracted some of Canada's finest artists and craftspeople, whose colorful shops line the main street. The small **Settlers Museum** offers exhibits and artifacts relating the town's settlement by foreign Protestants in 1754, and its prominence as a boat-building center. There is also a collection of 18th- and 19th-century ceramics and antiques.

🏛 **Settlers Museum**
578 Main St. **Tel** (902) 624 6263.
Open Jun–Sep: Tue–Sun.

㉑ Peggy's Cove

🗺 640. 🛈 Sou'wester Restaurant, (902) 823 2561.
🌐 peggyscoveregion.com

The still-operational **Peggy's Point Lighthouse** stands atop wave-worn granite rocks in Peggy's Cove and is one of the most photographed sights in Canada, a symbol of Nova Scotia's enduring bond with the sea. The village, with its colorful houses clinging to the rocks, and small harbor lined with weathered piers and fish sheds, has certainly earned its reputation as one of the province's most picturesque fishing villages. This is a delightful place to stroll through, with early morning and late afternoon being the most peaceful times.

The village was the home of well-known marine artist and sculptor, William E. deGarthe (1907–83). Just above the harbor, the deGarthe Gallery has a permanent exhibition of 65 of his paintings and sculptures.

Right outside the gallery, the Fishermen's Monument is a 30-m (98-ft) sculpture created by deGarthe as his memorial to Nova Scotian fishermen. Carved into an outcropping of native granite rock, the sculpture depicts 32 fishermen, and their wives and children. According to local legend, the large angel in the sculpture is the original Peggy, sole survivor of a terrible

The best-known symbol of Atlantic Canada, Peggy's Point Lighthouse

19th-century shipwreck, for whom the village was named.

Just outside the village, at the Whaleback promontory, is a memorial to the victims of the tragic Swissair 111 crash of 1998.

㉒ Halifax

See pp94–5.

㉓ The Eastern Shore

🚉 Halifax. 🚌 Antigonish. 🚢 Pictou.
🛈 Canso, (902) 366 2170.

A tour along the Eastern Shore is a trip through old-world Nova Scotia, through towns and villages where life has changed little since the turn of the 20th century. The tiny house and farm that comprise the **Fisherman's Life Museum** in Jeddore, Oyster Ponds (60 km/ 37 miles east of Halifax) was the home of an inshore fisherman, his wife, and their 13 daughters

around 1900. Today, the homestead is a living-history museum, where guides in period costume (many of them wives of local fishermen) re-enact the simple daily life of an inshore fishing family, still the heart of Nova Scotia culture. Visitors who arrive at midday may be invited to share lunch cooked over a woodburning stove. There are also daily demonstrations that include rug-hooking, quilting, and knitting, and visitors can tour the fishing stage, where salted fish were stored.

Sherbrooke Village is the largest living-history museum in Nova Scotia. Between 1860 and 1890, this was a gold and lumber boomtown. As the gold ran out, Sherbrooke once again became a sleepy rural village. In the early 1970s, some 25 of Sherbrooke's most historic buildings were restored. Within the village, scores of costumed guides bring 19th-century Nova Scotia to life. A ride on a horse-drawn wagon offers an overview of the town; the drivers share snippets of local history, as the horses trot along the village roads. At the Apothecary, visitors can watch the careful mixing of patent medicines, and those interested in the Ambrotype Studio can dress in period costumes, sitting very still while the vintage camera records their image on glass. Just outside town a massive waterwheel turns, powering the Lumber Mill.

🏛 **Sherbrooke Village**
Off Hwy 7. **Tel** (902) 522 2400.
Open Jun–Oct: daily. 🎫
🌐 sherbrookevillage.novascotia.ca

The Apothecary at the Sherbrooke Village living-history museum

㉒ Halifax

With its bustling waterfront, pretty parks, and unique blend of modern and historic architecture, Halifax is a fascinating city. Its cultured flavor belies its 250-year history as a brawling military town. Founded in 1749 by General Edward Cornwallis, Halifax was planned as Britain's military center north of Boston. The city has a long history of adventure, being the town where legalized pirates, or privateers, brought captured ships to be shared with the crown. On December 6, 1917, the city was devastated by an explosion caused by the collision of a Norwegian ship with a French munitions ship in the harbor. Today, Halifax is one of Canada's foremost centers of higher learning and has many colleges and seven universities.

Exploring Halifax

This is an easy town to explore on foot, as many of the better museums, historic sites, shops, and restaurants are located within the fairly contained historic core. Downtown, leading west from Brunswick Street, is hilly and green, ideal for a leisurely walk to appreciate the old-style architecture. Citadel Hill offers excellent views of the city, the harbor, and Dartmouth.

🏛 Historic Properties

1869 Upper Water St. **Tel** (902) 422-3077. **Open** daily. ♿

The Historic Properties are a wharfside collection of very old stone-and-timber-frame structures, which were originally built in the 19th century to hold the booty captured by privateers. Today, they house an intriguing collection of specialty and gift shops, pubs, and fine restaurants. This is one of the city's favorite gathering spots on warm summer nights, with crowds of strollers enjoying the lights of the harbor and music drifting from nearby pubs.

🏛 Maritime Museum of the Atlantic

1675 Lower Water St. **Tel** (902) 424 7490. **Open** May–Oct: daily; Nov–Apr: Tue–Sun. ♿ 🅿 on request.
w maritimemuseum.novascotia.ca

This harbourfront museum offers extensive displays on Nova Scotia's seafaring history, including small craft, a restored chandlery, and, at the dock outside, the elegantly refitted 1913 research vessel *Acadia*. The museum's most popular exhibit is the *Titanic* display, which offers artifacts recovered from the ship. There are fragments of the vessel's grand staircase, as well as a mural-sized photo showing the staircase in its original state. After the 1912 catastrophe, many of the bodies that were recovered were brought to Halifax, and 150 are buried at Fairview Lawn Cemetery.

🏛 Harbourfront

ℹ (902) 490 5946.

The Halifax Harbourwalk features interesting gift shops, cafés, and restaurants in historic settings along the boardwalk. This delightful promenade leads to the Halifax–Dartmouth Ferry Terminal, North America's oldest town ferry. A trip across the harbor is an inexpensive way to enjoy a panorama of Halifax.

🏛 Government House

1451 Barrington St. **Tel** (902) 424 7001. **Open** Jul–Aug: Mon, Fri–Sun. 🅿 compulsory.

The current home of Nova Scotia's Lieutenant Governor, this building has a Georgian façade that lends an urban grandeur. Completed in 1807, it cost over £30,000 (Can $59,200), a huge sum at the time for a humble fishing village. Tours last 30 minutes and cover several rooms.

A statue in Halifax Public Gardens, framed in flowers

🏛 Pier 21

1055 Marginal Road **Tel** (902) 425 7770. **Open** May–Oct: daily; Nov–Apr: variable. ♿ 🅿 **w** pier21.ca

Canada's entry point for more than a million immigrants and refugees, Pier 21 is now a National Historic Site. It offers powerful and emotional displays and fascinating images.

◆ Halifax Public Gardens

Spring Garden Rd. **Open** mid-Apr–late Nov: 8am–dusk daily. ♿
w halifaxpublicgardens.ca

Created in 1836, the Public Gardens are a beautiful 7-ha (17-acre) oasis of Victorian greenery and color in a bustling city. Tranquil paths wind past

The waterfront of Halifax, seen from the town ferry

For hotels and restaurants in this region see p351 and pp365–7. For transport information see p413

duck ponds, fountains, and a seemingly endless array of vivid flower beds. In the center of the gardens, an ornate bandstand is the site of Sunday concerts. On weekends (daily in summer), craftspeople gather outside the park's cast-iron fence to display their varied and colorful wares.

Halifax Citadel National Historic Site

5425 Sackville St./Citadel Hill. **Tel** (902) 426 5080. **Open** May–Oct: daily. Grounds: all year. 🎫 summer. ♿ 🌐
W pc.gc.ca

Overlooking the city, this huge star-shaped fortress has a commanding view of the world's second-largest natural harbor. Built between 1828 and 1856, the citadel and its fortifications provided a formidable defense. Visitors can stroll parade grounds where the kilted regiment of the 78th Highlanders perform with twice-daily musket drills. A cannon is fired daily at noon.

Halifax's famous town clock, built in 1803 as a gift from British royalty

Old Town Clock

Citadel Hill.

At the base of Citadel Hill stands the city's most recognized landmark, the Old Town Clock. The clock was a gift in 1803 from Edward, the British Duke of Kent and then military commander, who had a passion for punctuality. He designed the clock with four faces, so that both soldiers and citizens would arrive at their appointed destinations on time.

VISITORS' CHECKLIST

Practical Information
🗺 394,000. **i** 1595 Barrington St., (902) 490 5946. 🎫 Royal Nova Scotia International Tattoo (Jul); Atlantic Jazz Festival (Jul); International Busker's Festival (Aug).
W destinationhalifax.com

Transport
✈ 35 km (22 miles) N. of the city.
🚌 🚍 6040 Almon St.

Province House

1726 Hollis St. **Tel** (902) 424 4661.
🕐 Jul–Aug: 9am–5pm Mon–Fri, 10am–4pm Sat & Sun; Sep–Jun: 9am–4pm Mon–Fri. ♿

Built 1811–19, Province House is the oldest seat of government in Canada. In 1864 the Fathers of Confederation held two days of meetings here on the formation of Canada (see p54). Visitors can tour the rooms where these plans were laid.

Halifax City Center

① Historic Properties
② Maritime Museum of the Atlantic
③ Harbourfront
④ Government House
⑤ Pier 21
⑥ Halifax Public Gardens
⑦ Halifax Citadel National Historic Site
⑧ Old Town Clock
⑨ Province House

㉔ Cape Breton Island

The island of Cape Breton's irresistible draw for visitors is its wondrous natural beauty, best encountered on the 297-km (185-mile) Cabot Trail through Cape Breton Highlands National Park (see pp98–9). Every year thousands of hikers make the trek. From mountainous terrain with breathtaking ocean views to sandy beaches, dense forest, and fertile green highlands, the trail takes in a diversity of natural habitats. Whale, moose, and bald eagle sightings are common. When civilization beckons, the island is also rich in cultural sights, such as Canada's first single-malt distillery, Glenora, and the Alexander Graham Bell Museum. A steel swing bridge connects the island to the rest of Nova Scotia.

Saint Pierre Church at Chéticamp
Built in 1883, this striking Catholic church is at the center of the town of Chéticamp, which offers whale-watching opportunities and is the focus of the 3,000-strong local Acadian community.

Glenora Distillery
Located on the scenic Ceilidh Trail, Glenora was Canada's first single-malt distillery and is renowned for its Glen Breton Rare, a 10-year-old whisky. Visitors can also enjoy a pub, an inn, and a gift shop.

Lake Ainslee
This tranquil lake, encircled by scenic roads, attracts many bird species, such as ospreys and loons, which feed on its shores.

KEY

① **The Alexander Graham Bell Museum** sits on the shores of Bras d'Or Lake, Bell's summer home for 30 years. Prototypes of many of his famous inventions can be seen here.

② **Bird Islands** can be toured by boat to see seabirds, seals and eagles.

③ **Sydney Mines coastal town** dates back to the 1700s, with mining shafts that reach 5 km (3 miles) out to sea.

Key

▬ Major road
▭ Minor road
▬ Scenic route
— River
— National Park boundary

Margaree Harbour

Mabou

105

Port Hastings

St.

104

Isle Madame

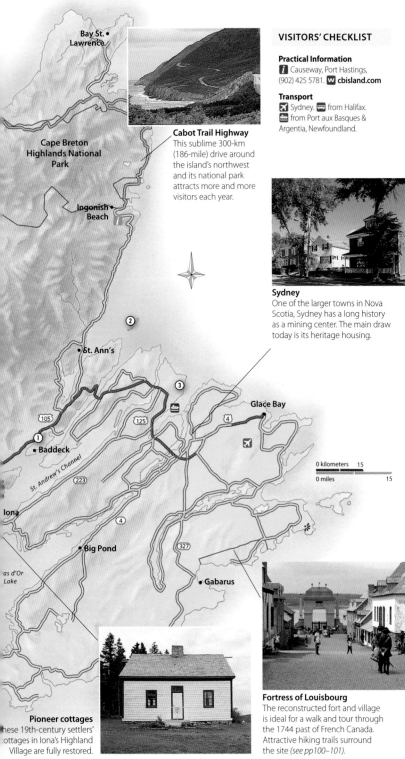

Bay St. Lawrence

Cape Breton Highlands National Park

Ingonish Beach

Cabot Trail Highway
This sublime 300-km (186-mile) drive around the island's northwest and its national park attracts more and more visitors each year.

St. Ann's

Glace Bay

Sydney
One of the larger towns in Nova Scotia, Sydney has a long history as a mining center. The main draw today is its heritage housing.

105

125

4

Baddeck

St. Andrew's Channel

223

Iona

4

Big Pond

327

as d'Or Lake

Gabarus

0 kilometers 15

0 miles 15

Pioneer cottages
hese 19th-century settlers' ottages in Iona's Highland Village are fully restored.

Fortress of Louisbourg
The reconstructed fort and village is ideal for a walk and tour through the 1744 past of French Canada. Attractive hiking trails surround the site (see pp100–101).

For map symbols see back flap

Exploring Cape Breton Island

The largest island in Nova Scotia, Cape Breton has a wild beauty and grandeur that makes for some of the most impressive scenery in Canada. From the rolling highlands, sprinkled with sparkling streams, to fine sandy beaches, the island's 300-km (186-mile) Cabot Trail provides one of the most memorable tours in Canada. Other inviting country roads lead to the stunning Mabou Hills, surrounding Lake Ainslee, and to romantic little towns including Baddeck, with its connection to Alexander Graham Bell, and the Acadian settlement of Chéticamp near the Margaree River Valley.

Lobster fishing boats in the Main à Dieu harbor on Cape Breton Island

Cape Breton Highlands National Park

In 1936 the Canadian Government set aside the 950 sq km (367 sq miles) of magnificent highlands in the northern tip of Cape Breton Island to form Cape Breton Highlands National Park. The park contains some of Canada's most famous scenery, with its mountains, green wilderness, and windswept coastal beauty. The best-known feature of the park is the spectacular 106-km (66-mile) section of the Cabot Trail highway, which traces much of the park's boundary in a loop from Chéticamp to Ingonish.

The Cabot Trail is the only route through the park, and most attractions are found along it. Entering the park from the west, the trail ascends along the flanks of the coastal mountains. The 24 look-out points along the trail present far-reaching views of the highlands rising from the sea. Continuing inland, the trail travels across the highland plateau. Just past French Lake, the short Bog Walk is a boardwalk trail through a highland fen,

with educational panels that describe this unique bog ecosystem, which is home to rare orchids. Visitors may even catch a glimpse of the park's many moose grazing here in a wetland marsh.

Crossing the French and Mackenzie Mountains, the trail descends dramatically to the charming old community of Pleasant Bay. It then reenters the highlands, crossing North Mountain, which, at 457-m (1,500-ft), is the highest point in the park. The trail descends into the Aspy River Valley, where

Picturesque Ingonish Beach on Cape Breton Island

a gravel road leads to the base of the 30-m (98-ft) high Beulach Ban Falls.

At Cape North, another side road leads to the scenic whale-watching destination of Bay St. Lawrence just outside the park. Farther on, the Scenic Loop breaks away from the Cabot Trail and follows the coast, offering awesome views as it descends to White Point. This road rejoins the Cabot Trail to the east, where it reaches the resort town of Ingonish. The Highland Links Golf Course here is ranked among the top public golf courses in Canada.

🅲 Cape Breton Highlands National Park

🛈 Chéticamp. **Tel** (902) 224 2306. **Open** mid-May–mid-Oct; Cabot Trail open daily throughout year. 🅿 👤 limited. 🆆 pc.gc.ca

Baddeck

Across the lake from the estate of Alexander Graham Bell, who loved the little town, Baddeck lies in rich farmland and is very much the island's premier resort destination. Set on the northwest side of Bras d'Or Lake, Baddeck is still the small, friendly town that charmed visitors in the 19th century. All amenities are within walking distance. The town's main street follows the waterfront and is lined with shops, cafés, and restaurants. Boat cruises around the lake are available from several places on Water Street by the shore.

The town's top attraction is the **Alexander Graham Bell National Historic Site**. The museum here contains the world's largest collection of photographs, artifacts, and documents about the life of this famous humanitarian and inventor. There are early telephones and several of his later inventions, including a copy of his HD-4 Hydrofoil.

Baddeck
🛈 454 Chebucto St, (902) 295 1911.

🏛 Alexander Graham Bell National Historic Site

559 Chebucto St, (Hwy 205). **Tel** (902) 295 2069. **Open** May–Oct: daily; Nov–Apr: by appt. 🅿 👤 🆆 pc.gc.ca

A fly-fisher tries his hand in the salmon- and trout-filled waters of the Margaree River

Margaree River Valley

Small and emerald green, the Margaree River Valley is a favorite with hikers, antique-hunters, and sightseers. The river has attracted salmon and trout anglers in large numbers since the mid-19th century.

In the little town of North East Margaree, the tiny but elegant **Margaree Salmon Museum** should fascinate even non-anglers with its beautiful historic rods and reels.

Paved and gravel roads follow the Margaree River upstream to the scenic spot of Big Intervale, where the headwaters come tumbling out of the highlands. For a taste of Gaelic culture, follow the Ceilidh Trail all the way to the **Glenora Distillery**, Canada's first single-malt distillery.

Margaree Valley
Margaree Fork, (902) 248 2803.

Margaree Salmon Museum
60 E. Big Interval Rd. **Tel** (902) 248 2848. **Open** mid-Jun–mid-Oct: 9am–5pm daily. limited.

Glenora Distillery
Route 19/Ceilidh Trail. **Tel** (902) 258 2662. **Open** daily May–Oct.
glenoradistillery.com

Chéticamp

This vibrant town is the largest Acadian community in Nova Scotia. Its beautiful Saint Pierre Church is visible from miles out at sea. The Acadians of Cape Breton are skilled craftspeople, and the town's seven co-ops produce pottery and hooked rugs. Chéticamp's best-known rug hooker was Elizabeth LeFort, whose large and intricate works depicting prominent moments in history have hung in the Vatican and in the White House. Several of her finest rugs are on display at the **Dr. Elizabeth LeFort Museum** at Les Trois Pignons.

Chéticamp is also a popular whale-watching destination; tours are available for seeing many varieties.

Dr. Elizabeth LeFort Museum
15584 Main St. **Tel** (902) 224 2642. **Open** May–Oct: daily. lestrois pignons.com/elizabeth-lefort-rugs/

Sydney

The only city on Cape Breton Island, Sydney is the second-largest town in Nova Scotia. Once the location of the biggest steel plant in North America, the town's main industries are now customer-support centers and tourism. Sydney has a small, attractive historic district around the Esplanade, with several restored buildings, such as Cossit House and Jost House, both dating from the 1870s. Downtown, boutiques, stores, and restaurants can be found along the town's main drag, Charlotte Street.

Sydney
Sydney, (902) 539 9876.

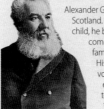

Alexander Graham Bell

Alexander Graham Bell was born in 1847 in Scotland. Bell's mother was deaf, and, as a child, he became fascinated by speech and communication. In 1870, Bell and his family moved to Ontario (see p222). His work involved transmitting the voice electronically, and he began experimenting with variations of the technology used by the telegraph. In 1876 he transmitted the world's first telephone message, "Watson, come here, I want to see you." With the

Alexander Graham Bell

patenting of his invention, Bell secured his role as one of the men who changed the world. In 1877, Bell married Mabel Hubbard, one of his deaf students. In 1885, the couple visited Cape Breton, where Bell later built his beautiful estate, Beinn Bhreagh, by Bras d'Or Lake. He lived and worked there each summer until he died in 1922. In Baddeck, the Alexander Graham Bell Museum focuses on his life and varied work.

Fortress of Louisbourg

Built between 1713 and 1758, the magnificent
Fortress of Louisbourg was France's bastion of
military strength in the New World. Today, it is
the largest military reconstruction in North
America. Inside, scores of historically costumed
guides bring the excitement of an 18th-century
French trading town to life. The streets and
buildings are peopled with merchants, soldiers,
fishmongers, and washerwomen, all going about
the daily business of the 1700s. From the lowliest
fisherman's cottage to the elegant home of the
Chief Military Engineer, attention to detail
throughout is superb. The costumed interpreters
offer information about the fortress, its history,
and the lives of people they portray.

Overview of the Fortress
A seat of government and a well-garrisoned
military stronghold for New France, the
Fortress of Louisbourg was home to
a town of thousands.

0 meters   50

0 yards   50

**The Quay and
Frederic Gate**
The Quay was the center of
commercial activity in the
town. It is still central to the
fort, as many activities now
take place at the Gate's
imposing yellow arch.

KEY

① Officers' rooms

② **The Icehouse** was used to store
fresh food for the Governor's table.

③ **The Guardhouse** held the vital
human line of defense; guards were
stationed here while on duty.

★ **The Engineer's
Residence**
Responsible for all public
construction projects at
the fortress, the engineer
was one of the most
important and powerful
men in the community.

★ King's Bastion
The largest building in the Citadel, the King's Bastion
Barracks housed the 500 French soldiers who
lived, ate, and slept here.

VISITORS' CHECKLIST

Practical Information
Rte. 22 SW. of Louisbourg.
Tel (902) 733 2280.
Open Victoria Day–Thanksgiving:
9:30am–5pm daily; check website
for other times of the year.

W parkscanada.gc.ca/
louisbourg

King's Bakery
Visitors can buy warm bread from this
working bakery that produced the
soldiers' daily rations.

The Forge
Traditional skills are
in evidence here, with
costumed workers
demonstrating exactly
the carefully learned craft
of the 18th century.

The Dauphin Gate
Soldiers in historic uniforms at the gate challenge visitors,
just as they would have in the 18th century. The gate's artistic
details are based on archeological relics from the original gate
recovered in the 1960s and drawings found in French archives.

Village and Saint Lawrence River, Bas-Saint-Laurent, Quebec ▶

QUEBEC

Introducing Quebec

Quebec is the largest of Canada's provinces and the biggest French-speaking territory in the world, with many of its eight million citizens holding firm to the language and culture inherited from their French ancestors. Landscapes range from pastoral valleys and villages along the American border, to vast expanses of tundra on the shores of Hudson Bay. At Quebec's heart is the Saint Lawrence River. Its north shore begins with the scenic Charlevoix region edging a wilderness of lakes, forest, and tundra that stretches to the Hudson Strait, past one of the world's largest power projects at James Bay. To the south lies the mountainous Gaspé Peninsula. There are two major cities: multi-ethnic Montreal, and Quebec City, the provincial capital and North America's only walled city.

The picturesque lakeside resort of Saint-Jovite in the Laurentian Mountains, set amid a backdrop of magnificent fall colors

Quebec's largest city, Montreal, has a vibrant downtown area that comes to life after dark

For map symbols *see back flap*

Key

- Expressway
- Divided highway
- Highway
- Other road
- Main railway
- Minor railway
- International border
- Regional border
- △ Summit

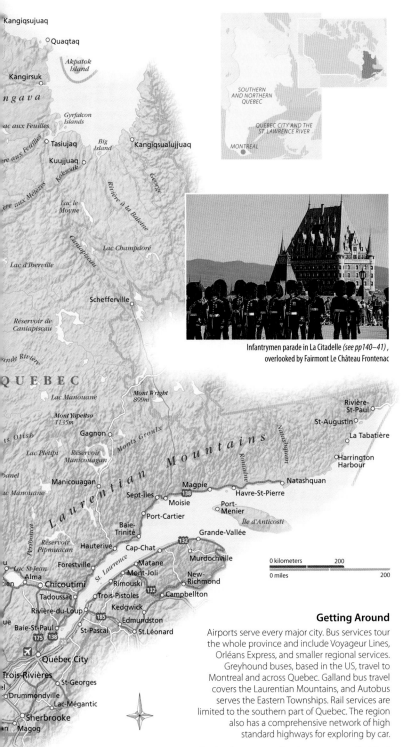

Kangiqsujuaq

Quaqtaq

Akpatok Island

Kangirsuk

n g a v a

Gyrfalcon Islands

ac aux Feuilles

ère aux Feuilles Tasiujaq

Big Island Kangiqsualujjuaq

Kuujjuaq

Koksoak

Rivière à la Baleine

George

ère aux Mélèzes

Lac le Moyne

Caniapiscau

Lac Champdoré

Lac d'Iberville

Schefferville

Réservoir de Caniapiscau

ande Rivière

Q U E B E C

Lac Manouane

Mont Wright 899m

Rivière-St-Paul

Mont Yapeitso 1135m

St-Augustin

La Tabatière

ts Otish

Gagnon

Monts Groulx

Lac Plétipi

Réservoir Manicouagan

Harrington Harbour

panel

Manicouagan

L a u r e n t i a n   M o u n t a i n s

Natashquan

Natashquan

ac Manouane

Magpie

Havre-St-Pierre

Sept-Îles

Moisie

Port-Menier

Romaine

Port-Cartier

Île d'Anticosti

Péribonca

Baie-Trinité

Grande-Vallée

Réservoir Pipmuacan

Hauterive

Cap-Chat

Murdochville

132

Lac St-Jean

Forestville

Matane

Alma

u Chicoutimi

St. Lawrence

Mont-Joli

New-Richmond

cien Tadoussac

Rimouski

132

Trois-Pistoles

Campbellton

Rivière-du-Loup

Kedgwick

185

Edmundston

ue Baie-St-Paul

St-Pascal

St-Léonard

175 138

Québec City

Trois-Rivières

St-Georges

el

Drummondville

Lac-Mégantic

Sherbrooke

an Magog

Infantrymen parade in La Citadelle *(see pp140–41)*, overlooked by Fairmont Le Château Frontenac

SOUTHERN AND NORTHERN QUEBEC

QUEBEC CITY AND THE ST. LAWRENCE RIVER

MONTREAL

0 kilometers — 200

0 miles — 200

Getting Around

Airports serve every major city. Bus services tour the whole province and include Voyageur Lines, Orléans Express, and smaller regional services. Greyhound buses, based in the US, travel to Montreal and across Quebec. Galland bus travel covers the Laurentian Mountains, and Autobus serves the Eastern Townships. Rail services are limited to the southern part of Quebec. The region also has a comprehensive network of high standard highways for exploring by car.

For hotels and restaurants in this region see pp351–4 and pp367–72

Maple Forests

There is more to Canada's ancient maple forests – long the pride of Quebec and Ontario – than their annual display of beauty. Every fall, turning leaves splash crimson and orange across the south, but it is in springtime that the trees give up their most famous product: maple syrup. Extracting techniques that were developed by Aboriginal Peoples were passed to Europeans in the 17th century. Traditional methods changed little until the 1940s, when part of the process was mechanized. Many age-old methods remain, however, including the final hand-stirring of the syrup.

Maple trees, either red maple *(Acer rubrum)* or sugar maple *(Acer saccharum)*, grow to heights of well over 30 m (100 ft), with thick trunks a meter (3 ft) in diameter. While their main product is the syrup, the hard wood is used for furniture and, of course, the leaf itself is the national symbol of Canada, officially established on the flag in 1965.

Collecting sap from trees by tapping maple trunks is the first step. Cuts are made low in the wood in spring as sap rises.

Transporting the sap in large barrels on a horse-drawn sleigh through the snowy forests is traditional. In the 1970s this was largely replaced by a network of plastic tubing that takes the sap directly from tree trunks to the sugar shacks.

Sugar shacks are built in the forest in the center of the "sugar bush", the cluster of maple trees that are producing sap. Men and women alike work long hours at slowly evaporating the sap, reducing it to syrup. Quebecois have their own rite of spring: when the first syrup is ready, it is poured onto the crisp snow outside the shacks to make *tire sur la neige*, a tasty frozen taffy.

Maple Syrup Products

Although 80 percent of Canada's annual maple harvest eventually becomes maple syrup, there is more to the industry than simply a sweet sauce. Boiled for longer, the syrup hardens into a pale golden sugar that can be used to sweeten coffee or eaten like candy. Maple butter, which is whipped with sugar, is also popular. Savory products benefit too; ham and bacon can be cured in syrup, which is delicious. The sweet-toothed people of Quebec use the syrup to make sugar pie, a tart with a sweet, fudge filling. Syrup is graded according to quality; clear golden fluid, produced at the start of the season, is the most prized, and is generally bottled. Later, darker syrup is used in cooking, and the final, even darker, batch makes a base for synthetic flavors or syrups. More than Can $100 million is spent annually on maple products.

Maple products are used in a variety of foods, both sweet and savory

The Story of Maple Syrup

The first maple-sugar farmers were Aboriginal Peoples. Long before European settlers arrived in the 16th century, tribes all over Northeast America sweetened savory dishes with syrup. An Iroquois legend tells the story of a chief in ancient times who, hurling an ax at a tree, found it stuck in the trunk at the end of the next day, dripping sweet fluid. That night the chief's wife boiled the day's hunt in the sap, and the syrup was born. Folk tales apart, it is certain that native people discovered the sap and techniques for refining it, few of which have changed, and passed their knowledge to Europeans freely.

Boiling maple sap involves 40 liters (84 pts) of sap to create one liter (2.2 pts) of syrup. The gold color and maple flavor develop as distillation takes place. The paler first syrup of the season is the most valuable.

Transforming sap into maple syrup takes place very slowly. The sap bubbles over a wood fire (maple wood is preferred) until about 98 percent of its water content evaporates. Modern processes use mechanized evaporators to boil the sap and draw off the steam, but even hi-tech methods still require a final hand-stirred simmering.

The Saint Lawrence Seaway

Extending from the Gulf of Saint Lawrence on the Atlantic coast to Duluth at the western end of Lake Superior in Minnesota, the Saint Lawrence Seaway and Great Lakes System flows across North America for over 3,700 km (2,300 miles). The Saint Lawrence Seaway itself stretches 553 km (344 miles) from Montreal to Lake Erie and covers 245,750 square km (95,000 sq miles) of navigable water. Open from March to December, it is the world's longest deep-draft inland waterway. Ships carry a huge quantity of domestic traffic, but over 60 percent of the total freight travels to and from overseas ports, mainly from Europe, the Middle East, and Africa. Traffic varies, with cargoes of grain traveling in superships alongside pleasure boats.

Locator Map

▨ The Saint Lawrence Seaway

The History of the Seaway

The Seaway has ancient beginnings: in 1680, French monk François Dollier de Casson started a campaign to build a mile-long canal linking Lac St. Louis and Montreal, which was finally opened in 1824 as the Lachine Canal. In 1833, the first Welland Canal (from Lake Ontario to Lake Erie) opened. The fourth Welland Canal was the first modern part of the Seaway to be built in 1932. 1951 brought US and Canadian cooperation to bear on a new seaway, which began in Canada in 1954. On April 25, 1959, the Seaway opened, linking the Great Lakes to the world.

Pleasure boats cruise the Seaway near the Thousand Islands by Kingston, Ontario. Each summer, small craft take advantage of the excellent sailing and waterskiing available in this section of the Seaway.

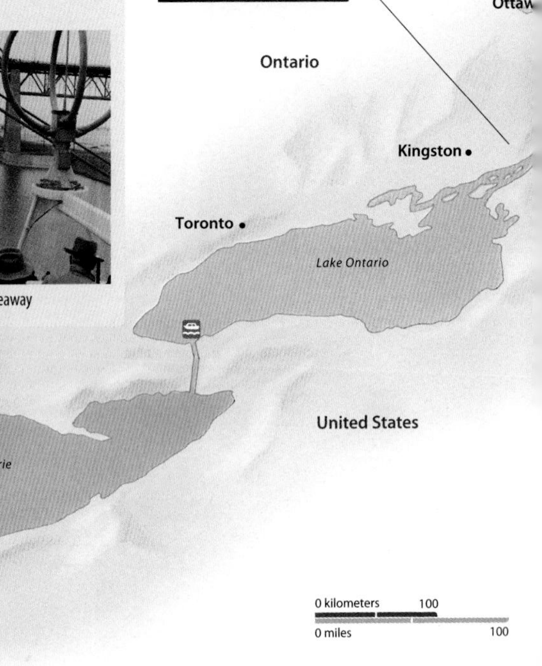

The *D'Iberville*, first ship to cross the Seaway

Ottawa

Ontario

Kingston •

Toronto •

Lake Ontario

↑ Lake Huron

United States

Lake Erie

0 kilometers   100

0 miles   100

Montreal is the historic beginning of the Seaway. It was here that the first link was built to the lakes during the 18th century, opening up pathways to the center of North America. The Seaway is open for nine months each year, despite much freezing weather.

Gulf of St. Lawrence

Quebec City

Quebec

Cargo ships carry iron ore, grain, coal, and other bulk commodities through the waterway: more than 2 billion tons of cargo have been shipped since 1959. Canada's heavy industry could not continue without the Seaway.

Montreal

St. Lambert Lock bypasses the Lachine Rapids west of Montreal. The Seaway is a watery staircase to America's heartland. The process involves raising and lowering the ships the height of a 60-story building.

Construction of the Seaway

In 1895, the US and Canadian governments appointed a Deep Waterways Commission to study the feasibility of what was to become today's Saint Lawrence Seaway; it reported in favor of the project two years later. After 50 years of intercountry wrangling, the jointly financed project was begun on August 10, 1954 – in the words of Canadian Prime Minister Louis St. Laurent "a bond rather than a barrier between Americans and Canadians." The massive undertaking was beset with problems not previously encountered, especially the discovery of ancient rock formations so hard that new machinery had to be created to dig through them. All work, including relocating villages and dredging the existing canals, had to be carried out with minimum disruption to the daily boat, rail, and car traffic of major cities. Nonetheless, the four-year construction was completed almost to the day.

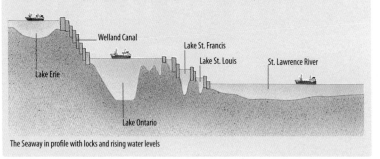

Welland Canal

Lake St. Francis

Lake St. Louis

St. Lawrence River

Lake Erie

Lake Ontario

The Seaway in profile with locks and rising water levels

For map symbols *see back flap*

MONTREAL

Montreal is the second-largest city in Canada. The pious 17th-century French founders of this vibrant island metropolis might be a little surprised to have produced a place that revels so much in its reputation for joie de vivre, but at least their edifices remain; the spires of some of Canada's finest churches still rise above the skyline.

Montreal's location at the convergence of the Saint Lawrence and Ottawa rivers made it Canada's first great trading center. It was founded in 1642 by a group of French Catholics as a Christian community and port. Much of its economic power has now moved west to Toronto, and what makes Montreal interesting today is a cultural, rather than a geographical, confluence. About 70 percent of its 1.75 million residents are of French descent, another 15 percent have British origins, and the rest represent nearly every major ethnic group. Many of its residents speak two or more languages. The communities form a kind of mosaic, with the anglophones in the west, the francophones in the east, and other ethnic communities in pockets all over the island. There is nothing rigid about these divisions: Anglophones eat and drink in the restaurants and bistros of the historic French district, and francophones visit the traditionally English area. The most interesting neighborhoods sprawl along the southern slopes of Mont-Royal – the 234-m (767-ft) hill from which the city derives its name. Vieux-Montréal's network of narrow, cobblestone streets huddles near the waterfront, while the main shopping area is farther north along Rue Sainte-Catherine. It extends below the city's surface in the maze of tunnels that connect the Underground City, the complex of homes, stores, and leisure venues that spreads out beneath the bustling city. Other modern attractions include the Tyrolienne MTL Zip Line, which gives visitors an aerial view of the Old Port, and the 360° Observation Deck, opened in 2016.

Montreal seen from the Parc du Mont-Royal, with the Saint Lawrence river in the background

◀ The grand, colorful ceiling of Basilique Notre-Dame-de-Montréal

Exploring Montreal

Montreal occupies a 50-km (31-mile) long island at the confluence of the Saint Lawrence River and the Ottawa River. The city core, where many sights are found, is fairly compact and lies to the south and east of Montreal's main landmark, Plateau Mont-Royal. Vieux-Montréal, the old city, is nestled on the shore of the Saint Lawrence, while the modern downtown lies between it and Plateau Mont-Royal. Streets follow a fairly consistent grid pattern making the city easy to navigate.

The skyscrapers of downtown Montreal at dusk

Key

— Highway
— Major road
  Pedestrian walkway
— Railway
▨ Major sight
▨ Sight

Sights at a Glance

Historic Buildings and Areas

1 Vieux-Port
3 Château Ramezay
4 Sir George-Etienne Cartier National Historic Site
7 Chinatown
8 Plateau Mont-Royal
9 Place des Arts
13 McGill University
15 Underground City
16 Square Dorchester and Place du Canada
19 Rue Sherbrooke
26 Lachine

Parks and Gardens

20 Parc du Mont-Royal
22 *Olympic Park pp128–9*
23 *Jardin botanique de Montréal*

Islands

24 Parc Jean-Drapeau

Churches and Cathedrals

2 *Basilique Notre-Dame-de-Montréal pp116–17*
11 Christ Church Cathedral
17 Cathédrale Marie-Reine-du-Monde
21 Oratoire Saint-Joseph

Museums and Galleries

5 Centre des sciences de Montréal
6 Centre d'histoire de Montréal
10 *Musée d'art contemporain de Montréal pp120–21*
12 McCord Museum
14 *Musée des Beaux-Arts pp122–3*
18 Centre Canadien d'Architecture
25 Maison Saint-Gabriel

For map symbols *see back flap*

Getting Around

A tunnel and 15 bridges link Montreal island to the mainland, and the Ville-Marie Expressway carries road traffic right into its heart. The most convenient way to get around within the city is on the métro and bus system, which service most sites of interest.

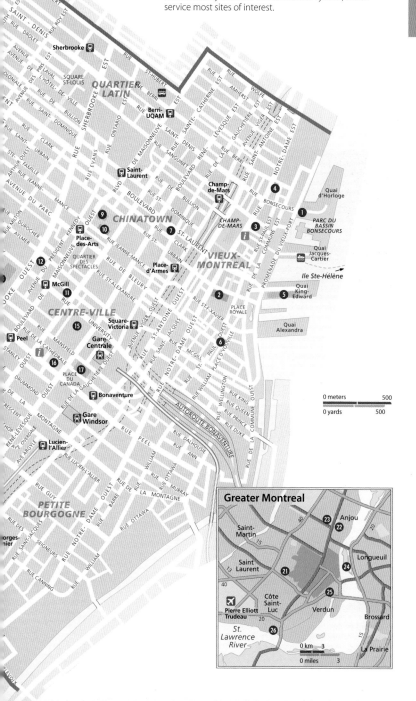

Sherbrooke

SAINT - DENIS

QUARTIER LATIN

SQUARE ST-LOUIS

Berri-UQAM

Saint-Laurent

Champ-de-Mars

CHAMP-DE-MARS

9

CHINATOWN

10

Place-des-Arts

7

QUARTIER DES SPECTACLES

Place-d'Armes

VIEUX-MONTREAL

12

McGill

11

CENTRE-VILLE

2

Square-Victoria

PLACE ROYALE

15

Peel

Gare Centrale

16

17

PLACE DU CANADA

Bonaventure

Gare Windsor

Lucien-l'Allier

PETITE BOURGOGNE

6

1

3

4

5

Quai d'Horloge

PARC DU BASSIN BONSECOURS

BONSECOURS

Quai Jacques-Cartier

Île Ste-Hélène

Quai King-Edward

Quai Alexandra

AUTOROUTE BONAVENTURE

| 0 meters | 500 |
| 0 yards | 500 |

Greater Montreal

Saint-Martin

23 Anjou

22

Saint Laurent

21

24 Longueuil

Pierre Elliott Trudeau

Côte Saint-Luc

25

Verdun

Brossard

26

St. Lawrence River

| 0 km | 3 |
| 0 miles | 3 |

La Prairie

Street-by-Street: Vieux-Montréal

Montreal's founders, led by Paul de Chomedey, Sieur de Maisonneuve, built the Catholic village of Ville Marie, which was to become Montréal, on the Saint Lawrence River in 1642. Missionary efforts failed to flourish, but the settlement blossomed into a prosperous fur-trading town with fine homes and a stone stockade. As Montreal expanded in the mid-20th century, the old city, Vieux-Montréal, fell into decline. In 1980, however, the district underwent a renaissance. The remaining 18th-century buildings were transformed into the restaurants, bistros, and boutiques that are so fashionable today, especially those of Rue Notre-Dame and Rue Saint-Paul.

View from the river
This clutch of historic streets leading down to the great Saint Lawrence River is a district of romance and charm in the midst of this modern city.

❷ ★ Basilique Notre-Dame de Montréal
One of the most splendid churches in North America, the city's 1829 Catholic showpiece has a spectacularly decorated and colorful interior.

**Pointe-à-Callière
Archeological Museum**
An underground tour here leads visitors past excavated ruins and early water systems dating from the 17th century.

For hotels and restaurants in this region see pp351–2 and pp367–9. For transport information see p410

Hôtel de Ville
The city hall was created in French Second Empire style in 1872–78, and restored to its glory in 1926. The marble hall features a statue of Montreal's first mayor.

Locator Map
See Montreal Map pp112–113

RUE BONSECOURS

RUE NOTRE-DAME

RUE SAINT-CLAUDE

PLACE JACQUES CARTIER

NT-VINCENT

S AINT-PAUL

UE DE LA COMMUNE

PROMENADE DES ARTISTES

Chapelle Notre Dame-de-Bonsecours
Long the spiritual home of Quebec's sailors, this church has fine views of the river from its tower.

Marché Bonsecours
The neo-Renaissance façade of this elegant building conceals its lively history, from its early 19th-century days as Canada's Parliament to a thriving time as a vegetable market.

❸ ★ Château Ramezay
Once the home of Montreal's governing city council, this 18th-century building pays tribute to the settling of Quebec with its fine museum of early tools and artifacts.

| 0 metres | 100 |
| 0 yards | 100 |

Key

— Suggested route

❶ Vieux-Port

333 Rue de la Commune. **Tel** (514) 496 7678. 🚇 Central Station. 🚌 55, 515, Terminus Voyager. 🚇 Square Victoria.
W oldportofmontreal.com

In its glory days of the 19th century, the Vieux-Port of Montreal was one of the most important inland harbors in North America, but it declined in the early 20th century. By the late 1980s, the Canadian government had begun to transform it into one of the most popular parks in Montreal. Its waterside walkways and open grassy fields blend almost seamlessly into the lovely streets of Vieux-Montréal, giving the old city a wide window onto the river.

Cyclists enjoying the waterfront promenade, Vieux-Port

The port has a bustling, recreational atmosphere. On summer afternoons, visitors and Montrealers alike stroll, cycle, or in-line skate along the Promenade du Vieux-Port.

❸ Château Ramezay

280 Rue Notre Dame E. **Tel** (514) 861 3708. 🚇 VIA Rail. 🚌 14, 55, 515, Terminus Voyager. 🚇 Champ-de-Mars. **Open** Jun–Sep: 9:30am–6pm daily; Oct–May: 10am–4:30pm Tue–Sun. **Closed** Jan 1, Dec 25. 🏛 ♿ 🅿
W chateauramezay.qc.ca

When Montreal's 11th governor, Claude de Ramezay, arrived in the city in 1702, he was homesick for Normandy and decided to build a residence that was reminiscent of the châteaux back home, with stone walls, dormer windows, and copper roof. The squat round towers, added in the 19th century, reinforce the effect.

❷ Basilique Notre-Dame-de-Montréal

In the center of Place d'Armes sits the Basilique, Montreal's grandest Catholic church. It was originally built in the 17th century, with a new building completed in 1829. American architect James O'Donnell excelled himself by building a vast vaulted cavern that was Canada's first Neo-Gothic church; it has 3,000 seats in the nave and two tiers of balconies. The church was splendidly redecorated in the 1870s with the intricate woodcarvings of craftsman Victor Bourgeau.

The main altar is surrounded by delicate pine and walnut woodcarving.

The nave is illuminated by a rose window under an azure ceiling.

★ Reredos
The focus of the nave is backed by azure, beneath a golden starry sky.

★ Pulpit
This ornate construction was sculpted by Philippe Hébert. The prophets Ezekiel and Jeremiah stand at its base.

Many of de Ramezay's governor successors lived here, and the building also housed the West India Company. This is one of the most impressive remnants of the French regime open to the public in Montreal.

The château has been restored to its original style. Of particular interest is the Nantes Salon, with its 18th-century carved paneling by the French architect Germain Boffrand.

Uniforms, documents, and furniture on the main floor reflect the life of New France's ruling classes, while the cellars depict the doings of humbler colonists. The scarlet automobile, made for the city's first motorist, is an interesting sight.

❹ Sir George-Etienne Cartier National Historic Site

458 Rue Notre Dame E. **Tel** (514) 283 2282. 🚇 Central Station. 🚌 14, 515, Terminus Voyager. 🚇 Champ-de-Mars. **Open** May–mid-Jun & Sep–Oct: 10am–5pm Fri–Sun; mid-Jun–Aug: 10am–5pm Wed–Sun. **Closed** Jan–Apr. ♿ 🛗 📷 **W** pc.gc.ca

George-Etienne Cartier (1814–73) was a Father of Confederation (see p54) and one of the most important French-Canadian politicians of his day. This national historic site comprises two adjoining graystone

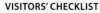

Ormolu clock at the Cartier site

houses owned by the Cartiers on the eastern edge of the old town. One is dedicated to Cartier's career as a lawyer, politician, and railroad-builder. In this house, you can sit at a round table and listen in either French or English to a very good summary of the political founding of modern Canada.

The second house focuses on the Cartiers' domestic life and the functioning of a Victorian upper middle-class family. Visitors can wander through formal rooms full of rich furniture and listen to snatches of taped conversation from "servants" talking about their lives.

The twin towers rise 69 m (226 ft) above the basilica and are visible across the old city.

The Vieux Séminaire dates from 1685 and still belongs to the Sulpician Fathers, the priests who also run the basilica. It is the oldest building in Montreal.

VISITORS' CHECKLIST

Practical Information
110 Rue Notre Dame W. **Tel** (514) 842 2925. **Open** 8am–4:30pm Mon–Fri (4pm Sat), 12:30–4pm Sun. ♿ 🛗 📷 🅿 daily.
W notredamebasilica.ca

Transport
🚇 Place d'Armes.

Pipe Organ
The renowned maker Casavant built the organ above the north door in 1891. Recitals are still held frequently.

Stained-glass windows
The basilica's beautiful windows were imported from Limoges in 1930. Each tells a story of Montreal's past; this shows New World pioneer Maisonneuve climbing Mont Royal in 1643.

Children playing outside the Centre des sciences de Montréal

❺ Centre des sciences de Montréal

King Edward Pier. **Tel** (514) 496 4724.
🚇 Central Station. 🚌 Terminus Voyager. 🚇 Champ-de-Mars.
Open 9am–4pm Mon–Fri, 10am–5pm Sat & Sun. 🌐 montrealscience centre.com

Dominating the Vieux-Port's King Edward Pier, this huge, airy building is home to a number of permanent and temporary exhibitions that focus on technology, engineering, and science, as well as other subjects. Among the permanent exhibitions, "Cargo" shows visitors how cargo transits through a large port like Montreal. The experience includes games, films, and cutaway containers. The exhibits were produced in collaboration with Quebec's Ministry of Education and are designed to appeal to children.

Attached to the Centre des sciences de Montréal is the IMAX Telus Theater that shows educational documentaries in 3-D on its immense screen.

❻ Centre d'histoire de Montréal

335 Place d'Youville. **Tel** (514) 872 3207. 🚌 61. 🚇 Square Victoria.
Open 10am–5pm Wed–Sun.
Closed mid-Dec–mid-Jan. 🏛
🌐 ville.montreal.qc.ca

The exhibits in this museum trace the history of Montreal from the earliest indigenous settlements to the modern age, with the focus on everyday life. The museum is housed in a handsome, red-brick fire station with a gracefully gabled roof built in 1903. There are three floors of exhibits. On the first floor, "Montreal, 5 Times," the museum's permanent exhibition, traces five passages in Montreal's history, beginning in 1535 with the meeting of First Nations peoples and European explorers and ending with the cultural boom of the 1960s. The museum's second and third floors are devoted to year-round changing exhibitions showcasing the city's advancements, its people, and their experiences, while a third-floor observation deck offers a scenic view of the Vieux-Port and Vieux-Montréal.

Centre d'histoire de Montréal

❼ Chinatown

🚇 Champ-de-Mars; Place des Arts.

The name has become a little anachronistic, as many of the restaurants and shops in this 18-block district just northeast of the Old City are now owned by Vietnamese and Thai immigrants. Most arrived in Montreal in the wake of 20th-century upheavals in Southeast Asia. The Chinese, however, were here first. They began arriving in large numbers after 1880, along with many European immigrants. The Chinese community stuck together in this corner of the city in an attempt to avoid discrimination from some of the town's residents. As they grew more prosperous, many of the descendants of the first immigrants moved to the wealthier areas of Montreal, leaving Chinatown to the elderly and to the newer arrivals. Many thousands of them now return during the weekends, making the narrow streets busy and full of people shopping for silk, souvenirs, vegetables, records, and barbecued meat.

Restaurants specialize in a range of delicious cuisines, serving Szechuan, Cantonese, Thai, Vietnamese, and Korean food, fragrantly filling the air with the smell of hot barbecued pork and aromatic noodles.

For those seeking respite from the bustle of the streets and their vibrant market stalls, there is a lovely little garden dedicated to the charismatic Chinese leader Sun Yat-sen on Clarke Street. Other features of the area include two large, Chinese-style arches, which span Rue de la Gauchetière, and, strangely enough, a pair of authentic pagodas on the roof of the modern Holiday Inn hotel.

A brightly colored market stall in vibrant Chinatown

Parc Lafontaine, a popular spot with a leisurely atmosphere in Plateau Mont-Royal

❽ Plateau Mont-Royal

Tel Tourisme Montréal: (514) 844 5400.
🚇 Sherbrooke; Mont-Royal.

No neighborhood captures the essence of Montreal more fully than the Plateau. Its main thoroughfares are lined with bistros, bookstores, boutiques, and sidewalk cafés. Nightclubs veer from the eccentric to the classic, and eateries from snack bars and sandwich shops to some of the best dining locations in the city. Jazz bars, too, are popular in this area.

The area's residents are a mix of students, working-class French-speakers, trendy young professionals, and ethnic families with roots in Europe and Latin America. They gather either in Parc Lafontaine, a neighborly expanse of green with an outdoor theater, or in "Balconville," a distinctly Montrealer institution linked to the duplexes and triplexes that many residents live in. To save interior space, these stacks of single-floor flats are studded with balconies linked to the street by fanciful, wrought-iron stairways. In summer they become centers for parties, family gatherings, and picnics.

The large working-class families for whom these homes were built in the early part of the 20th century lived very modestly, but they managed to amass enough money to build large, beautiful parish churches, notably the Eglise Saint-Jean-Baptiste. The Catholic bourgeoisie lived a little farther south, in gracious Second-Empire homes on Rue Saint-Denis or Carré Saint-Louis.

Mile End, an area that stretches roughly northeast from Mont Royal to St. Laurent Boulevard, is one of the city's trendiest districts. The ambiance is relaxed, with plenty of cafés, art galleries, and boutiques. Be sure to try the famous Montreal bagels at one of the St. Viateur bagel shops.

❾ Place des Arts

260 Blvd. de Maisonneuve W. **Tel** (514) 842 2112. 🚇 Place des Arts.
🌐 **placedesarts.com**

This complex of halls and theaters sits at the heart of the Quartier des Spectacles entertainment district and is Montreal's prime center for the performing arts. Both the Opéra de Montréal (Montreal Opera) and the Orchéstre Symphonique de Montréal (Montreal Symphony Orchestra) make their home here. The buildings of Place des Arts share a spacious central plaza with the outstanding Musée d'art contemporain (see pp120–21).

Place des Arts, Montreal's top entertainment venue

❿ Musée d'art contemporain de Montréal

Opened in 1964, the Montreal Museum of Contemporary Art is the only institution in Canada dedicated exclusively to modern art. Located in downtown Montreal, more than 60 percent of the approximately 7,600 paintings, drawings, photographs, videos, and installations in the permanent collection are by Quebec artists. Works date from 1939, but the emphasis is on the contemporary. There are also works by innovative international talents, such as the controversial Bill Viola, Louise Bourgeois, and Andrès Serrano. The exhibits are in wide, well-lit galleries, whose elegance helped to earn the museum a Grand Prix from Montreal Council.

Casier pour objet du désir
(2000)
Francine Savard's sculpture is a magnified 3D grid constructed with linden wood.

First Floor

★ **Sans titre** (1988)
Quebec-born artist Richard Mill's colorful abstract painting is is one of many of the museum's striking examples of abstraction from the perspective of Quebec artists from the 1940s to the present day.

Street Level

Key

- ▢ Permanent exhibition space
- ▢ Temporary exhibition space
- ▢ Pierre Granche sculpture
- ▢ Movie theater
- ▢ Video gallery
- ▢ Multimedia gallery
- ▢ Theater/seminar hall
- ▢ Art workshops
- ▢ Non-exhibition space

Entrance Hall
The museum uses this airy modern space, hung in places with pieces from its collection, for special events and receptions. A pleasant first-floor restaurant overlooks the hall.

Museum Guide

Only a small proportion of the artworks in the museum are on permanent display. They occupy the upper floor space along with rotating and visiting items. There is also a sculpture garden, accessible from the main museum building, that has rotating exhibits and is a good spot to rest during a tour of the galleries.

★ **Comme si le temps …
de la rue** (1991–2)
Pierre Granche's permanent
installation within the Place des
Arts complex is based on Egyptian
mythological figures, whose shapes
symbolize Montreal. Created to
contrast with the museum's
urban milieu, the work
exudes humor and poetry.

Main Entrance

Museum façade
Built in the 1990s, the MAC
building shows 320 artworks,
taken from their much larger
rotating collection.

⓫ Christ Church Cathedral

635 Rue Sainte-Catherine O. **Tel** (514)
843 6577. Central Station. 15.
McGill. **Open** 8am–5:30pm daily.
montrealcathedral.ca

Architect Frank Wills completed
Christ Church in 1859 as
the seat of the Anglican
bishop of Montreal. This
graceful Gothic
limestone building,
with a triple portal and
a tall slender spire, has
exterior walls studded
with gargoyles. The
church was too heavy
for the land, and the
stone spire was replaced in 1940
with a treated aluminum steeple.
Noon concerts are often held in
the cathedral's cool, dim interior
with its pointed arched nave
and magnificent stained-glass
windows, some from the William
Morris studio in London.

**Inuit slippers at the
Musée McCord**

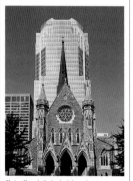
Christ Church Cathedral, based on
a 14th-century English design

⓬ Musée McCord

690 Rue Sherbrooke O. **Tel** (514) 398
7100. Central Station. 24.
McGill. **Open** 10am–6pm Tue, Thu
& Fri, 10am–9pm Wed, 10am–5pm
Sat & Sun. **Closed** Mon (except Jul &
Aug). **mccord-museum.qc.ca**

Lawyer David Ross McCord
(1844–1930) was an avid
collector of virtually everything that had to do with life
in Canada, including books,
photographs, jewelry, furniture,
clothing, documents, papers,
paintings, toys, and porcelain.

In 1919, he gave his considerable
acquisitions to McGill University
with a view to establishing a
museum of Canadian social
history. That collection, now
more than 1,500,000 artifacts,
is housed in a stately limestone
building that was once a social
center for McGill students.

The museum has a
good section of early
history, as well as
exceptional folk art.
A particularly fine
collection of
aboriginal and
Inuit items features
clothing, weapons,
jewelry, furs, and
pottery. A separate
room is devoted to the social
history of Montreal. The
museum's most celebrated
possession is a vast collection
of photographs that chronicle
every detail of daily life in
19th-century Montreal.

⓭ McGill University

845 Rue Sherbrooke O. **Tel** (514) 398
4455. Central Station. 24.
McGill. **Open** 9am–6pm Mon–Fri.
book in advance.
mcgill.ca

When it was founded in 1821,
Canada's best-known university
was set on land left for the
purpose by fur trader and land
speculator James McGill
(1744–1813). The university's
main entrance is guarded by
the Classical Roddick Gates.
Behind them an avenue leads
to the domed Neo-Classical Arts
Building, which is the oldest
structure on campus.

The rest of the 70 or so buildings range from the ornately
Victorian to the starkly concrete.
One of the loveliest is the
Redpath Museum, which holds
one of the city's most eclectic
and eccentric collections. A
huge number of fossils, including
a dinosaur skeleton, sit alongside African art, Roman coins,
and a shrunken head.

Redpath Museum
859 Rue Sherbrooke O. **Tel** (514) 398
4086. **Open** 9am–5pm Mon–Fri,
11am–5pm Sun. **Closed** Sat.

⑩ Musée des Beaux-Arts

The oldest and largest art collection in Quebec contains almost 36,000 objects, including paintings, sculptures, prints, drawings, photographs, and decorative objects, housed in five pavilions. The Michal and Renata Hornstein Pavilion focuses on world cultures, with theme-based areas that include African, Asian, and Islamic arts. The galleries in the Jean-Noël Desmarais Pavilion, shown below, focus on European art from the Middle Ages to the 20th century. In the Claire and Marc Bourgie Pavilion works include Inuit art and paintings from the colonial period to the 1960s, while the Liliane and David M. Stewart Pavilion is devoted to decorative arts and design. The newest building, the Michal and Renata Pavilion for Peace, displays international art from the medieval period through to the year 2000.

Façade of the Michal and Renata Pavilion for Peace
Opened in 2016 to celebrate Montreal's 375th anniversary, this pavilion is dedicated to international art and education.

★ **Portrait of a Young Woman (c.1665)**
This famous work originated in Rembrandt's native Holland. Painted in characteristically realist style, the sitter's pensive concentration is thrown into sharper relief by the deep black background.

Michal and Renata Hornstein Pavilion

Connected to the Desmarais Pavilion by an underground tunnel that contains an exhibition on ancient cultures, this gallery is dedicated to pre-1960 America, and includes Meso-American, Inuit, and First Nations art, as well as early European-style furniture, domestic silver, and decorative art. Later galleries follow the history of Canadian painting, from sacred church art to early Aboriginal studies by wandering artist Paul Kane and the impressionism of James Wilson Morrice. The Group of Seven and Paul-Emile Borduas are among those representing the 20th century.

18th-century silver teapot

Level 3

Access to the
Michal and Renata
Hornstein Pavilion

Level S2

A street-level entrance to the labyrinthine Underground City

Level 4

★ **Man of the House of Leiva (1590)**
El Greco's haunting portrayals of the Spanish aristocracy are a Renaissance highlight.

Gallery Guide

The exceptional painting collections are contained on levels 3 and 4 of the Desmarais Pavilion. Level 2 offers a fine café. The museum shop and main entrance are on level 1. Lower level S2 has contemporary art galleries and tunnel access to the Michal and Renata Hornstein Pavilion.

Key

▢ Contemporary art
▢ Art of ancient cultures
▢ 19th-century European art
▣ African art
▢ Old Masters
▢ Temporary exhibitions
▣ Non-exhibition space

into a vast network of over 30 km (19 miles) of well-lit, boutique-lined passages, housing more than 1,600 shops, 200 restaurants, hotels, film theaters, and concert halls.

⑯ Square Dorchester and Place du Canada

ℹ 1001 Rue du Square Dorchester.
Tel (514) 873 2015. Central Station.
Terminus Voyager. Peel, Bonaventure, Lucien-L'Allier.

These two open squares create a green oasis in downtown Montreal. On the north side of Boulevard René-Lévesque, statues including Canada's first French-Canadian prime minister, Sir Wilfrid Laurier, share Square Dorchester with a war memorial. On Place du Canada a statue of the country's first prime minister, Sir John A. Macdonald, looks out over the stately Boulevard René-Lévesque.

The buildings surrounding the park are eclectic. The mix includes a Gothic church, a shiny, black bank tower and the Sun Life Building (1933), a huge stone fortress that housed the British Crown Jewels during World War II.

⑮ Underground City

Central Station. Terminus Voyager. Peel, McGill, Bonaventure.

When Montreal opened its first métro (or subway) lines in 1966, it inadvertently created a whole new layer of urban life – the Underground City. It is theoretically possible to lead a rich life in Montreal without once stepping outside.
The first métro stations had underground links to just the two main train stations, a few hotels, and the shopping mall under the Place Ville-Marie office tower. This has turned

Varied architecture, from historic to Post-Modern, in Square Dorchester

Place du Canada, Square Dorchester, and the Cathédrale Marie-Reine-du-Monde ▶

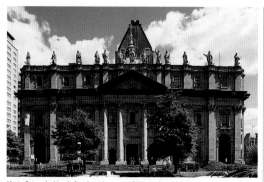

Marie-Reine-du-Monde façade with statues of Montreal's patron saints

⑰ Cathédrale Marie-Reine-du-Monde

1085 Rue Cathédrale. **Tel** (514) 866 1661. 🚇 Central Station. 🚌 Terminus Voyager. 🚇 Bonaventure. **Open** 7am–7pm Mon–Fri, 7:30am–7pm Sat & Sun. ♿ 🌐 cathedralecatholique demontreal.org

When Montreal's first Catholic cathedral burned down in 1852, Bishop Ignace Bourget decided to demonstrate the importance of the Catholic Church in Canada by building a new one in a district dominated at the time by the English Protestant commercial elite. To show his flock's loyalty to the Pope, he modeled his new church on St. Peter's Basilica in Rome.

The cathedral, which was completed in 1894, has dimensions that are a quarter of those

The altar canopy in the cathedral

of St. Peter's. The statues on the roof represent the patron saints of all the parishes that constituted the Montreal diocese in 1890. The magnificent altar canopy, a replica of the one Bernini made for St. Peter's, was cast in copper and gold leaf. Another reminder of Bourget's loyalty to Rome can be found on the pillar in the northeast corner of the church. Here lies a marble plaque listing the names of all the Montrealers who served in the Papal armies during the Italian war of independence in the 1850s.

⑱ Centre Canadien d'Architecture

1920 Rue Baille. **Tel** (514) 939 7000. 🚇 Central. 🚌 Terminus Voyager. 🚇 Guy Concordia. **Open** 11am–6pm Wed & Fri, 11am–9pm Thu, 11am–5pm Sat–Sun. **Closed** Mon & Tue. ♿ 🌐 book ahead. 🌐 cca.qc.ca

Visitors enter this museum and international research center through an unobtrusive glass door in an almost windowless façade of gray limestone that fronts this large U-shaped building. Well-lit exhibition rooms house a series of regular exhibits in rotation. The primary exhibits focus on architecture, design, and land-scape architecture. The two arms of the modern building embrace the ornate Shaughnessy House, which faces Boulevard René-Lévesque Ouest. Now part of the Centre, the house was built in 1874 for the president of the Canadian Pacific Railway, Sir Thomas Shaughnessy, and has an art-nouveau conservatory with an intricately decorated ceiling.

The facility is also a major scholarly institution. Its extensive collection of architectural plans, drawings, models, and photographs is the most important of its kind anywhere. The library alone has in excess of 215,000 volumes on the world's most significant buildings.

⑲ Rue Sherbrooke

🚇 Central Station. 🚌 Terminus Voyager. 🚇 Sherbrooke.

In the latter half of the 19th century, Montreal was one of the most important cities in the British Empire. Its traders and industrialists controlled about 70 percent of Canada's wealth, and many built themselves fine homes on the slopes of Mont Royal in an area that became known as the Golden, or Square, Mile. Rue Sherbrooke between Guy and University was their main street, and its shops, hotels, and churches were the most elegant in the country.

Some of that elegance survived the modernizing bulldozers of the 1960s. Holt Renfrew, Montreal's upscale department store, and the stately Ritz-Carlton Hotel still stand. So do two exquisite churches, the Presbyterian St. Andrew and St. Paul, and the Erskine American United at the corner of Avenue du Musée, which boasts stained-glass windows by Tiffany. Boutiques, bookstores, and galleries fill many of the rows of graystone townhouses. Millionaires not quite wealthy enough to make it into the Square Mile built graceful row homes on rues de la Montagne, Crescent, and Bishop nearby. Many of these now house trendy shops and bistros.

Farther west is the Grande Seminaire, where Montreal's Roman Catholic archdiocese still trains its priests.

Historic home on Rue Sherbrooke, the "Golden Square Mile"

Montreal's largest shrine, Oratoire Saint-Joseph, showing the steps climbed annually by pilgrims

⑳ Parc du Mont-Royal

Tel (514) 843 8240. 🚉 Central Station. 🚌 11. Ⓜ Mont-Royal. **Open** 6am–midnight daily. ♿

The steep green bump that rises above the city center is only 234 m (767 ft) high, but Montrealers call it simply "the mountain" or "la montagne." Jacques Cartier gave the peak its name when he visited in 1535, and it, in turn, gave its name to the city. The hill became a park in 1876, when the city bought the land and hired Frederick Law Olmsted, the man responsible for designing New York's Central Park, to landscape it. Olmsted tried to keep it natural, building a few lookouts linked by foot-paths. Succeeding generations have added Beaver Lake, a 30-m high (98-ft) cross made of steel girders, and the Voie Camillien-Houde, a thoroughfare that cuts through the park from east to west.

The mountain's 101 ha (250 acres) of meadows and hardwood forests still offer Montrealers a precious escape from urban life, as well as spectacular views of the city. The wide terrace in front of the Chalet du Mont-Royal pavilion looks out over the skyscrapers of the downtown core. The northern boundary of the park abuts two huge cemeteries, the Catholic Notre-Dame-des-Neiges and the old and stately Cimetière Mont-Royal (Mount Royal Cemetery), where many of Canada's finest rest.

㉑ Oratoire Saint-Joseph

3800 Chemin Queen Mary. **Tel** (514) 733 8211. 🚉 Central Station. 🚌 Terminus Voyager. Ⓜ Côte-des-Neiges. **Open** daily. ♿

Every year, two million pilgrims climb the 283 steps (99 of which can be climbed in prayer on the knees) to the entrance of this vast church. Their devotion would no doubt please Brother André (1845–1937), the truly remarkable man responsible for building this shrine to the husband of the Virgin Mary. It began when he built a hillside chapel to St. Joseph in his spare time. Montreal's sick and disabled joined him at his prayers, and soon there were reports of miraculous cures. Brother André began to draw pilgrims, and the present oratory was built to receive them. Pilgrims can pray on his tomb. He was beatified in 1982 and canonized in 2010.

The church's octagonal copper dome is one of the biggest in the world – 44.5 m (146 ft) high and 38 m (125 ft) wide. The interior is starkly modern; the elongated wooden statues of the apostles in the transepts are the work of Henri Charlier, who was also responsible for the main altar and the huge crucifix. The striking stained-glass windows were made by Marius Plamondon. The main building houses a museum depicting André's life. Beside the crypt church, a votive chapel is ablaze with flickering candles that have been lit by hopeful pilgrims.

A view of Montreal from the lofty Parc du Mont-Royal

㉒ Parc Olympique

Designed for the 1976 Olympic Games, Montreal's Parc Olympique showcases a number of stunning buildings and is a popular modern leisure attraction in this historic city. French architect Roger Taillibert created the 56,000-seat Stadium, used today for concerts by international stars as well as for big exhibitions. The circular stadium entrance, nicknamed "The Big O", has been reclaimed as a prestigious skateboarding venue. Arching up the side of the stadium is the Montreal Tower, with its fine views. Nearby, the Biodôme environmental museum replicates four world climates, while the Esplanade Financière Sun Life offers free outdoor activities for all the family on weekends.

Tennis Courts and the Stadium
An exceptional tourist attraction, the park can be toured fully during the day. Another popular way to visit is for a concert or sporting event.

★ Biodôme
Here are stunning re-creations of climate zones: a steamy rainforest, the freezing Polar World, the fertile forests of the Laurentian Mountains, and the fish-filled Saint Lawrence ecosystem.

KEY

① **The Rio Tinto Alcan Planetarium** offers a fresh approach to astronomy with two shows: one scientific, the other more whimsical.

② **The Biodôme** was first used as a velodrome for the 1976 Olympics – hence the unusual cycling-helmet design of its roof.

③ **A cable car** shoots up the side of the tower at speed; tickets can be combined with a guided tour of the Stadium or Biodôme.

④ **The stadium roof** was originally intended to be retractable. However, due to structural problems, it was replaced in 1998 by a detached, permanently closed roof.

⑤ **The Esplanade Financière Sun Life** presents a program of free outdoor activities for all, from mini-tennis to skateboarding events.

★ Montreal Tower
At 175 m (574 ft) this is the world's tallest inclined tower, arching over the stadium in a graceful sweep. A cable car takes visitors up the side of the tower to its large viewing deck in less than two minutes.

★ Inside the Stadium
The first event to take place in this cavernous space was the spectacular opening ceremonies of the 1976 Summer Olympic Games.

Viewing Deck
This glass platform provides some stunning views of the city. Signs point out sights of interest that can be as far as 80 km (50 miles) away.

Sports Centre
Reopened in 2015 after extensive renovation, this fully equipped center offers unbeatable facilities, including a 15-m (50-ft) deep scuba diving pool.

Plan of the Parc Olympique Area

1. Saputo Stadium
2. Pierre-Charbonneau Centre
3. Maurice-Richard Arena
4. Biodôme
5. Olympic Stadium
6. Sports Centre/Montreal Tower
7. Botanical Gardens
8. Esplanade Financière Sun Life
9. Rio Tinto Alcan Planetarium

0 meters 50
0 yards 50

The Jardin botanique is an oasis of calm away from the rush of the city

㉓ Jardin botanique de Montréal

4101 Rue Sherbrooke E. **Tel** (514) 872 1400. 🚇 Pie-IX. **Open** times vary throughout the year, so check website before visiting. 🅿️🌳♿ 🌐 **espacepourlavie.ca**

Montreal's botanical garden is among the largest in the world, a fine accomplishment for this northern city with a cold winter climate. Its 75-ha (185-acre) enclose 30 outdoor gardens, 10 green-houses, a "courtyard of the senses," in which blind interpreters help visitors discover the touch and smell of exotic flowers, and a bug-shaped Insectarium full of creepy-crawlies, both preserved and living. Its most peaceful havens are the 2.5-ha (6-acre) Chinese Garden, a delightful replica of a 14th-century Ming garden, and the exquisite Japanese Garden.

㉔ Parc Jean-Drapeau

20 Chemin Tour de Lille. **Tel** (514) 872 6120. 🚇 Jean Drapeau. ⛴️ Vieux-Port. **Open** 6am–midnight daily. ♿

Encompassing both Ile-Sainte-Hélène and Ile-Notre-Dame, Parc Jean-Drapeau is a popular visitor's attraction and a hub for major events, such as Piknic Electronik, which is held every Sunday throughout the summer.

The small forested Ile-Sainte-Hélène, sitting in the middle of the Saint Lawrence River, has played a major role in Montreal's emergence as a modern city. Originally named after Samuel de Champlain's wife (*see p51*), it was the site of Expo '67, the world fair that brought millions of visitors to the city that year.

Several reminders of those days remain – most notably La Ronde, the fair's amusement park, and the dome that served as the United States Pavilion. This is now the Biosphere, an interpretive center that examines the Great Lakes and Saint Lawrence River system. Between the dome and the roller coasters is the Fort de l'Ile-Sainte-Hélène, built in 1825 to protect Montreal from a potential American attack.

Bonsai tree at the Jardin botanique

Its red-stone walls enclose a grassy parade square that is used today by members of the Olde 78th Fraser Highlanders and the Compagnie Franche de la Marine, re-creations of two 18th-century regimental military formations that fought each other over the future of New France until 1759. The fort also houses the **Musée David M. Stewart**, a small and excellent museum of social and military history with educational activities for schools and younger visitors.

The Ile-Notre-Dame, a 116-ha (286-acre) wedge of land encircled by the Saint Lawrence Seaway, did not exist until 1967, when it was created with rock excavated for the Montreal métro system. It shared Expo '67 with Ile-Sainte-Hélène, and today the two islands constitute the Parc Jean-Drapeau.

Ile-Notre-Dame's most popular attraction by far is the monumental Casino de Montréal, a province-owned gambling hall housed in the old French and Quebec pavilions. Every day, thousands line up at its tables and slot machines. The casino never closes.

There are more refined entertainments – a rowing basin, excavated for the 1976 Olympics, superb floral gardens, and a carefully filtered body of water, which is the site of the city's only swimming beach. Ile-Notre-Dame's Circuit Gilles-Villeneuve, named for the Canadian champion, plays host to Formula 1 races.

Built for Expo '67, the Biosphere has displays on Canadian river systems

The province-owned Casino on Ile-Notre-Dame is open to the hopeful 24 hours a day

Musée David M. Stewart

20 Chemin Tour de Lille. **Tel** (514) 861 6701. **Open** 10am–5pm Wed–Mon. **Closed** Jan 1, Dec 25.

② Maison Saint-Gabriel

2146 Place de Dublin. **Tel** (514) 935 8136. Charlevoix. 57. **Open** late Jun–Sep: 1–5pm Mon–Sat; Sep–mid-Jun: 11am–6pm Tue–Sun. obligatory.
w maisonsaint-gabriel.qc.ca

This isolated fragment of New France at first appears lost among the apartment buildings of working-class Pointe-Saint-Charles. It was a farm when the formidable Marguerite Bourgeoys, Montreal's first schoolteacher and now a canonized saint, bought it in 1668 as a residence for the religious order she had founded in 1655.

The house, rebuilt in 1698 after a fire, is a fine example of 17th-century architecture, with thick stone walls and a steeply pitched roof built on an intricate frame of original heavy wooden timbers.

Marguerite Bourgeoys and her tireless sisters worked the farm and ran a school on the property for aboriginal and colonial children. They also housed and trained the *filles du roy* (the "king's daughters"), orphaned young girls sent abroad to be the women of his new colony. The house's chapel, kitchen, dormitory, and drawing rooms are full of artifacts dating from the 17th century. These include a writing desk the saint used herself and a magnificent vestment and cope, embroidered in silk, silver, and gold by a wealthy hermit who lived in a hut on the property.

② Lachine

Blvd. St. Joseph. **Tel** (514) 873 2015. Lionel Groulx. 191.

Lachine comprises a suburb of southwest Montreal and includes a small island of the same name west of the Lachine Rapids, where the Saint Lawrence River widens to form Lac-Saint-Louis. Lachine is now part of Montreal, but has a long history of its own. The old town along Blvd. Saint-Joseph is charming. Many of its fine old homes have become restaurants and bistros with outdoor terraces that overlook Parc René-Lévesque and the lake. One of the oldest houses, built by merchants in 1670, is now the **Musée de Lachine**, a historical museum and art gallery. The **Fur Trade at Lachine National Historic Site** is a building dedicated to the fur trade, which for years was Montreal's main support.

The Canal de Lachine, built in the 19th century to bypass the rapids, links the town directly to the Vieux-Port. The canal itself is now blocked to shipping, but the land along its banks has been turned into parkland with a bicycle trail.

Musée de Lachine

1 Chemin du Musée. **Tel** (514) 634 3478. **Open** Apr–Nov: noon–5pm Wed–Sun. reserve.

Fur Trade at Lachine National Historic Site

1255 Blvd. St. Joseph. **Tel** (514) 637 7433. **Open** mid-Jun–early Sep: 10am–5pm daily.

A view of the historical Musée de Lachine from the reclaimed canal

QUEBEC CITY AND THE SAINT LAWRENCE RIVER

The heart and soul of French Canada, Quebec City sits overlooking the Saint Lawrence River on the cliffs of Cap Diamant. As provincial capital, the city is the seat of regional government, and nowadays is the heart of French-Canadian nationalism. Parisian in atmosphere, with every tiny street worth visiting, Quebec City is almost entirely French-speaking. The European ambiance and architecture, and the city's crucial historical importance all contributed to the Historic District of Old Quebec being named as a UNESCO World Heritage Site in 1985. One of the world's great waterways, the Saint Lawrence River is home to rare marine wildlife. Right and minke whales swim as far upstream as Tadoussac and feed at the mouth of the Saguenay River. The Laurentian Mountains rise up above the Saint Lawrence on the north shore, and are a year-round natural playground. Nearer Quebec City, the rich scenery of the Charlevoix region is among the most beautiful in the country, contrasting with the soaring cliffs and wilderness of the Gaspé Peninsula. Offshore, the Ile d'Anticosti is a stunning nature preserve.

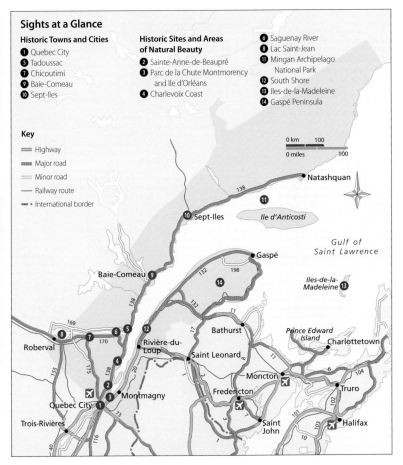

Sights at a Glance

Historic Towns and Cities
1 Quebec City
5 Tadoussac
7 Chicoutimi
9 Baie-Comeau
10 Sept-Iles

Historic Sites and Areas of Natural Beauty
2 Sainte-Anne-de-Beaupré
3 Parc de la Chute Montmorency and Ile d'Orléans
4 Charlevoix Coast

6 Saguenay River
8 Lac Saint-Jean
11 Mingan Archipelago National Park
12 South Shore
13 Iles-de-la-Madeleine
14 Gaspé Peninsula

Key
═══ Highway
▬▬ Major road
═══ Minor road
— Railway route
▬ ▪ International border

0 km   100
0 miles   100

Natashquan
138
11
10 Sept-Iles   Ile d'Anticosti
                    Gulf of Saint Lawrence
                    Gaspé
132   198
Baie-Comeau 9
            14
138   132
169   11
8   7   6   5   12   17   Bathurst   Prince Edward Island   Charlottetown
Roberval 170 Rivière-du-   Saint Leonard   8   11
          4   Loup   8   6   104
155 175 138 20   1   Moncton   Truro
        2   Fredericton   102
Quebec City 1 3 Montmagny   101   Halifax
Trois-Rivières   73   1   Saint   103
40   116   John   10

◄ Fairmont Le Château Frontenac rising behind buildings in Old Quebec

For map symbols *see back flap*

❶ Street-by-Street: Quebec City

One of the oldest communities on the American continent, Quebec City was discovered as an Iroquois village by the French explorer Jacques Cartier and founded as a city in 1608 by explorer Samuel de Champlain *(see p51)*. The British gained dominance over the city and the rest of the province at the Plains of Abraham battle just outside the city walls in 1759. Today the town is renowned as the heart of French Canada. The oldest part of the city is Basse-Ville, or Lower Town, which was renovated in the 1970s. With its winding staircases and cafés, it is a charming destination.

Musée du Fort
Military history is brought to life here in sound-and-light shows reenacting six Quebec sieges and battles, and numerous war relics.

★ Basilique Notre-Dame-de-Québec
This 1647 cathedral provides a rich setting for relics from early French rule in Quebec, and Old Master paintings.

Holy Trinity Anglican Cathedral
An elegant 1804 stone Neo-Classical façade conceals an English oak interior.

Fairmont Le Château Frontenac
Quebec City's best-known landmark has risen over the city since 1893, and has 611 luxurious guest rooms.

Key
— Suggested route

Musée de la civilisation
Human history through the ages is explored in this airy modern building linked to historic houses in the rest of the town, including Maison historique Chevalier.

VISITORS' CHECKLIST

Practical Information
🔳 517,000. *i* 12 rue Sainte-Anne, (418) 641 6290. 🎿 Winter Carnival (Jan–Feb); Summer Festival (Jul). 🆆 **quebecregion.com**

Transport
✈ 16 km (10 miles) west of the city. 🚍 450 Rue de Gare-du-Palais. 🚌 320 Rue Abraham-Martin. ⛴ 10 Rue des Traversiers.

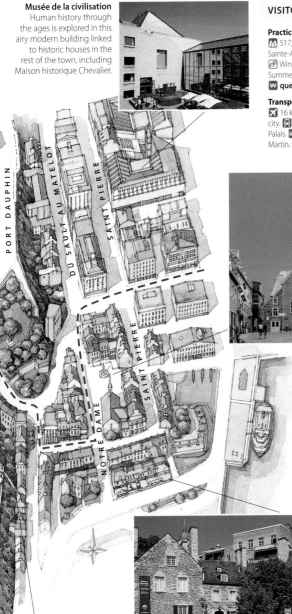

★ **Place Royale**
A virtual microcosm of Canadian history, Place Royale has experienced a renaissance, and the surrounding streets, with their 18th- and 19th-century architecture, have been sandblasted back to their original glory.

The funicular travels from Terrasse Dufferin to the Lower Town, providing excellent aerial views of the historic city center.

Maison historique Chevalier
Linked with the Musée de la civilisation, this home built for an 18th-century merchant showcases the decorative arts. Quebec furniture and the famous Quebec silverware feature in every room, as well as exhibits showing how well-to-do families lived in the 18th and 19th centuries.

0 meters   100
0 yards   100

Quebec City

Containing the only walled city north of the Rio Grande, Quebec City has narrow cobblestone streets and 18th-century buildings that lend a European air to this small provincial capital, just 55 square km (21 square miles). Most of the sights are packed into one accessible corner, above and below the Cap Diamant cliffs, with the Citadel rising up protectively at the top of the cliff. As Quebec's capital, the city is home to the provincial parliament, the Assemblée Nationale, which conducts its debates almost entirely in French in splendid chambers behind the ornate 19th-century façade of the grandiose Hôtel du Parlement.

Fairmont Le Château Frontenac dominates the skyline of Quebec City

Exploring Quebec City

Most of the main sights are easily reached on foot. The city can conveniently be divided into three parts. Basse-Ville, or Lower Town, is the oldest part, and rambles along the Saint Lawrence River at the foot of Cap Diamant. Above lies the walled city, Haute-Ville, or Upper Town. This area is full of shops and restaurants, similar to the Basse-Ville, but both Catholic and Protestant cathedrals are here, as is the imposing Fairmont Le Château Frontenac. Beyond the walls stretches Grande Allée, with the Hôtel du Parlement, where the parliament of Quebec sits.

Terrasse Dufferin

Sweeping along the top of Cap Diamant from Fairmont Le Château Frontenac to the edge of the Citadel, this boardwalk is well equiped with benches and kiosks, and offers unmatched views of the Saint Lawrence River, the Laurentian Mountains, and Ile d'Orléans. During winter, Les Glissades de la Terrasse, an ice slide for toboggans, is installed on the terrace.

Parc des Champs-de-Bataille

835 Ave. Wilfrid Laurier. **Tel** (418) 649 6157. **Open** daily.

Once a battlefield where the future of Canada was decided, the Battlefields Park is now a delightful grassy recreation ground, with grand monuments and a dedicated fountain –the only clues to the area's bloody and dramatic history. On September 13, 1759, British regulars under General James Wolfe defeated the French army on this clifftop field, the Plains of Abraham, just outside the walls of Quebec (*see pp52–3*), establishing permanent British rule in Canada. In 1908, the 103-ha (254-acre) battlefield was turned into one of the largest urban parks in North America.

Joan of Arc at Parc des Champs-de-Bataille

Assemblée Nationale

Ave. Honoré-Mercier & Grande Allée E. **Tel** (418) 643 7239. daily.
assemblee-nationale.fr

The Assemblée Nationale, Quebec's provincial parliament, meets just outside the walls of the Old City in this graceful Second-Empire building, completed in 1886 as a showcase of provincial history. Niches along the imposing façade and up the sides of the tall central tower display 22 bronze figures, each representing a person who played a vital role in Quebec's development. The first inhabitants of the territory are honored in a bronze rendition of a First Nations family by the main door. Inside, the blue chamber is the hub of Quebec's political activity.

Fortifications de Québec

Tel (418) 648 7016. **Open** mid-May–Oct: 10am–5pm daily.
parkscanada.gc.ca/fortifications

After a century of peace, the French-built fortifications that had secured Quebec since 1759 were transformed in the 1870s from a grim military necessity into this popular attraction. On the city's northern and eastern edges, low and high ramparts studded with cannons defend the clifftop and the plains, with the walls on the western side reaching 9 m (30 ft) at some points. Three elegant gates, the Saint-Jean, Kent, and Saint-Louis, pierce the western stretch. A

Quebec's 18th-century fortifications in the Parc d'Artillerie

Abundant produce stalls draw crowds at the market in Vieux Port

fourth, Prescott Gate, sits on the city's eastern side. Visitors can walk along the top of the walls for almost 5 km (3 miles).

 Vieux Port

i 100 Rue Quai Saint-André. **Tel** (418) 648 3300. &

This delightful area has its focus around the old harbor northeast of the walled city. In contrast to the crammed heritage of much of the Lower Town, Vieux Port is

an airy riverside walking site, full of new and restored modern attractions. Boat cruises downriver to the Chute Montmorency waterfalls *(see p143)* are available. Waterfront walkways pass chic boutiques, apartment blocks, the city's open-air theatre, and an extensive regional food market, the Marché du Vieux-Port.

🏛 Musée de la civilisation

85 Rue Dalhousie. **Tel** (418) 643 2158. **Open** late Jun–early Sep: 10am–5pm daily; late Sep–early Jun: 10am–5pm Tue–Sun. 🅿 🖼 & 🔲 **mcq.org**

Renowned Canadian architect Moshe Safdie designed this contemporary limestone-and-glass building in Basse-Ville to house Quebec's museum of history and culture. Although highly up-to-date in feel, the construction has won several prizes for blending in well with its historic surroundings. Three heritage buildings are part of the museum's structure including

Maison d'Estèbe, an 18th-century merchant's house. The museum also uses another nearby 18th-century house, Maison historique Chevalier, for displaying Quebec architecture and furniture in period setting.

Museum exhibits include "This is Our Story," which reflects on the city's First Nation and Inuit history, and the remains of a 250-year-old French flat-bottomed boat. Many exhibits are hands-on, and, during workshops for families, participants are encouraged to try on costumes from different eras.

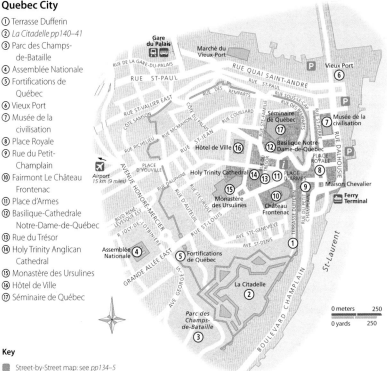

Antique and modern architecture at the Musée de la civilisation

Quebec City

① Terrasse Dufferin
② *La Citadelle pp140–41*
③ Parc des Champs-de-Bataille
④ Assemblée Nationale
⑤ Fortifications de Québec
⑥ Vieux Port
⑦ Musée de la civilisation
⑧ Place Royale
⑨ Rue du Petit-Champlain
⑩ Fairmont Le Château Frontenac
⑪ Place d'Armes
⑫ Basilique-Cathédrale Notre-Dame-de-Québec
⑬ Rue du Trésor
⑭ Holy Trinity Anglican Cathedral
⑮ Monastère des Ursulines
⑯ Hôtel de Ville
⑰ Séminaire de Québec

Key

▪ Street-by-Street map: see *pp134–5*

Place Royale

Rue Saint Pierre. **Tel** (418) 646 3167.

Of all the squares in Canada, Place Royale has undoubtedly the most history. Samuel de Champlain, the founder of Quebec, planted his garden on this site, and the French colonial governor Frontenac turned it into a market in 1673. A bust of Louis XIV was installed in 1686, and the square was named Place Royale.

Today it remains much as it did in the 18th century, exuding an air of elegance and delicate grandeur. A cobblestone court in the center of Basse-Ville, Place Royale is surrounded by steep-roofed early 18th-century buildings with pastel-colored shutters that were once the homes of wealthy traders. The square declined in the 19th century but is now fully restored and a favorite for street performers.

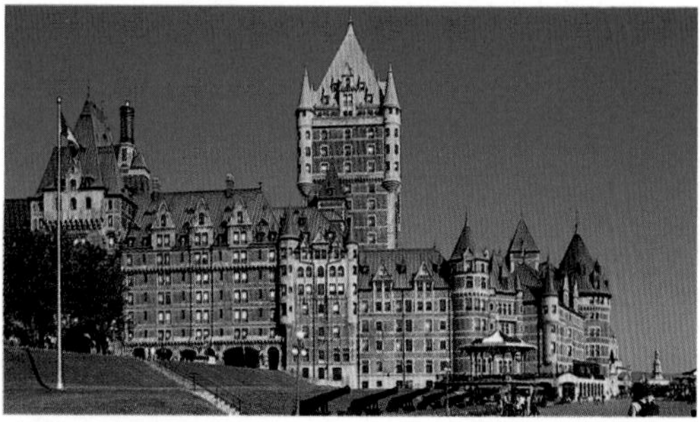

A familiar landmark of the city, the 611-room Fairmont Le Château Frontenac hotel

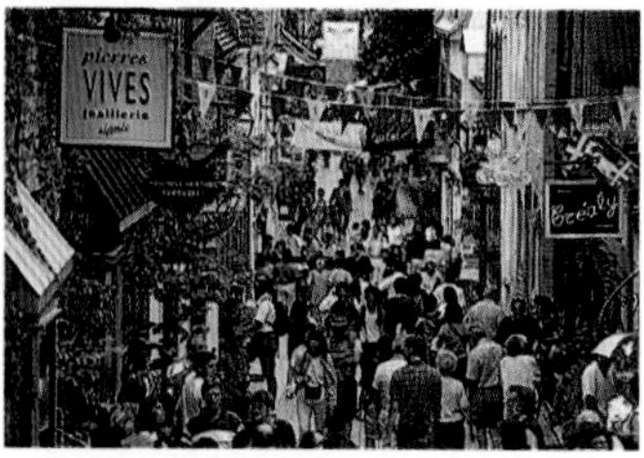

Rue du Petit-Champlain bustling with shoppers

Rue du Petit-Champlain

Below Dufferin Terrace in Old City. partial. quartierpetit champlain.com

The aptly named Escalier Casse-Cou, or Breakneck Stairs, descends from Haute-Ville past several levels of gift shops to end on this narrow little walkway in the oldest part of the town. French artisans built homes here as early as the 1680s, and Irish dockworkers moved to the area in the 19th century. Much of the historic architecture remained, but the area fell into decline early in the 20th century. The workers' homes have been transformed into 50 art and speciality shops and restaurants, and the short pedestrian walkway has become one of the liveliest spots in old Quebec City. While often crowded, some interesting boutiques can be found.

Place d'Armes

French colonial soldiers once used this attractive, grassy square just north of Château Frontenac as a parade ground, but its uses today are more congenial. Open horse-drawn carriages wait here to offer visitors a journey that reveals the square in all its charm. In the center, the Monument de la Foi commemorates the 300th anniversary of the 1615 arrival of Catholic Recollet missionaries. On the southwest corner next to the fine Anglican cathedral, lies the grand early 19th-century former Palais de Justice. The Musée du Fort opposite contains a large scale model of Quebec City in the 19th century.

Fairmont Le Château Frontenac

1 Rue des Carrières. **Tel** (418) 692 3861. *(see p353)*

The steep, copper-roofed landmark that dominates the skyline of Old Quebec is a luxury hotel, built by the Canadian Pacific Railway on the heights overlooking the Saint Lawrence River. In the 19th century, US architect Bruce Price designed the hotel as a French-style château on a huge scale, with dozens of turrets, towers, and a high copper roof studded with rows of dormer windows. Building continued for almost a century after the first section of the hotel was opened in 1893, with a final part completed in 1993. Made from brick and stone, the hotel now has 611 guest rooms and three upscale restaurants. The public areas are sumptuous and elegant.

Basilique-Cathédrale Notre-Dame de Québec

Place de l'Hôtel de Ville. **Tel** (418) 694 0665. **Open** 7am–4pm Mon–Fri, 7am–6pm Sat, 8am–6pm Sun.
notre-dame-de-quebec.org

This magnificent cathedral is the principal seat of the Roman Catholic archbishop of Quebec, whose diocese once stretched from here to Mexico. Fire destroyed the first two churches on the site before 1640, and the first cathedral built here was torn down by the British in 1759. A fourth version burned down in 1922. The present cathedral replaced it in the style of the 1647 original. Some modern materials have been used, but sensitively, to re-create the light feel; glowing stained glass, richly gilded decoration, and the graceful baldachin over the main altar add to the effect.

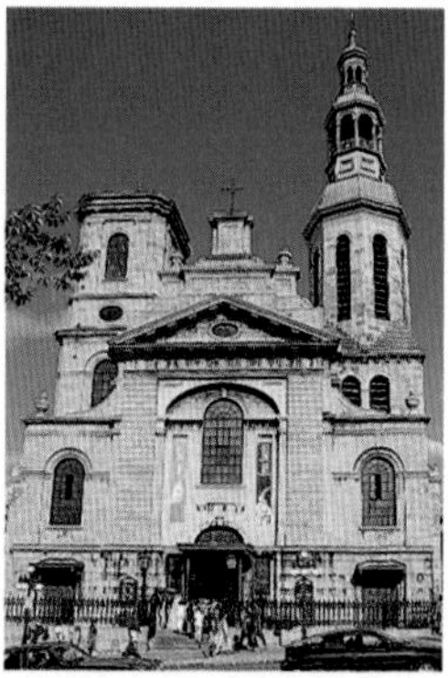

Imposing façade of the Basilique-cathédrale Notre-Dame de Québec

🚇 Rue du Trésor

Off Place d'Armes.

This tiny alley just across Rue de Buade from Holy Trinity cathedral is something of a Quebecois institution. Closed to cars, the little street is packed in summer with visitors eager to have their portraits drawn, painted, or caricatured by the dozens of street artists who gather here. Browsing for sketches and watercolors of Quebec scenes can be fun.

🏛 Holy Trinity Anglican Cathedral

31 Rue des Jardins.
Tel (418) 692 2193.
Open daily. ♿

After worshiping for nearly a century in the city's Catholic churches, in 1804 the Anglicans of Quebec finally had their own cathedral built at state expense. Their new mother church was the first Anglican cathedral outside Britain and is modeled on London's Neo-Classical Saint Martin's-in-the-Fields. To this day, gifts from England remain, including the prayer book and Bible donated by the British King George III. Cut from the King's Windsor Forest in England, the pews are of oak, and the eight-bell peal is the oldest in Canada. In the summer artists and artisans fill the verdant church grounds.

Reliquary from the Ursuline Convent

🏛 Monastère des Ursulines

Rue Donnacona. **Tel** (418) 694 0694.
Open daily. ♿

In 1639, Mère Marie de l'Incarnation brought the Ursuline order of nuns to Quebec and oversaw the construction in 1641 of the nunnery, which later burned down. Today, visitors can see the Saint-Augustin and Sainte-Famille wings, which date from a period of rebuilding between 1686 and 1721. Surrounded by fruit orchards, the charming complex has gradually evolved over the past four centuries. One of the buildings is North America's oldest girls' school (boys have been admitted since 2010).

The Hôtel de Ville seen from the small park in its grounds

Nearly a hundred nuns still live and work here, so access is limited. The beautifully decorated chapel and French antiques, including Louis XIII furniture, scientific instruments, paintings, and embroideries, are displayed in the Musée des Ursulines within the monastery. The museum also tells the story of the nuns' educational and missionary achievements. Mère Marie completed the first Huron, Algonquin, and Iroquois dictionaries. Copies are on display, along with embroidery and liturgical clothes from the 17th to 19th centuries.

🚇 Hôtel de Ville

2 Rue des Jardins. **Tel** (418) 641 6010.
Open 8:30am–4:30pm daily. ♿

This imposing building stands at the western end of the Rue de Buade, a popular gathering place for Quebec artists offering their wares. Built in 1833, and still the town hall to the city, its grounds are the focus for both locals and visitors. The small park here holds theater performances in the summertime.

🚇 Séminaire de Québec

2 Côte de la Fabrique. **Tel** (418) 692 2843. **Open** summer. 📷 obligatory. ♿ 🌐 **seminairedequebec.org**

In 1663, the first bishop of Quebec, François de Laval, built a seminary next to his cathedral to train Catholic priests for his huge diocese. Over the centuries it has been added to and now forms a graceful complex of 17th-, 18th-, and 19th-century buildings centered on a peaceful courtyard.

Within the seminary, visitors can admire the excellent 18th-century paneling that covers the walls of the chapel. The Musée de l'Amérique francophone is part of the complex and has a wonderfully eclectic collection, including a converted chapel decorated with fascinating wooden *trompe l'oeils*.

The 19th-century interior of the chapel at the Séminaire de Québec

La Citadelle

Both the French and British armies contributed to the building of this magnificent fort. The French started construction in 1693, with work completed in 1831 by the British. The purpose of the fort was to defend Quebec against an American attack that never came. Today the fortifications are a pleasant walkway that provides a tour around the star-shaped fortress. The Citadelle is home to the famous Royal 22e Régiment, a French-Canadian squad also known as the Vandoos. Because the Citadelle is still a working military barracks, visitors can see the regiment perform their daily tasks as well as their parade drill.

The Fortifications
From the mid-19th century, the Citadelle served as the eastern flank of Quebec City's defenses.

Governor-General's Residence
This splendid mansion with its double central staircase and marble hall has been the official home of Canada's governors-general since the 19th century.

Cape Diamond Redoubt
The oldest building in the Citadelle, the Redoubt dates back to 1693 when it was built under the leadership of the French Count Frontenac as a first citadel for Quebec. The Redoubt offers fine views of the Saint Lawrence River.

KEY

① **Cap Diamant** is the highest point of the Cape Diamond cliffs, from which the Lower Town descends.

② **Old Military Prison**

③ **Trenches** around the Citadelle were key defensive structures.

④ **The Vimy Cross** was erected in memory of the Canadians who fell at the Battle of Vimy Ridge in 1917 in World War I.

⑤ **The Prince of Wales Bastion** is the highest natural point in old Quebec. Nearby is a now-disused French powder magazine.

Chapel
A key part of the fortress, this private chapel used to be a British powder magazine and is now used for ceremonial purposes.

★ Changing of the Guard, Parade Square
Every day at 10am from June 24 to Labour Day, the Changing of
the Guard takes place. The ceremonial dress of the Vandoos –
scarlet tunic and blue trousers – is of British design.

VISITORS' CHECKLIST

Practical Information
1 Côte de la Citadelle.
Tel (418) 694 2815. **Open** May–
Oct: 9am–5pm daily; Nov–Apr:
10am–4pm daily. 🅿️ ♿ 🚻 in
museum. 📷 📱 📹 obligatory.
🆆 lacitadelle.qc.ca

The Barracks
As a fully operational military site,
the barracks is home to Canada's
most dashing regiment, the
Vandoos, who fought with
bravery in both world wars.

→ Plains of
Abraham

Entrance to the Citadelle

Ticket booth

0 meters   25
0 yards   25

★ Dalhousie Gate
One of the original structures remaining from the 19th century,
Dalhousie Gate is surrounded by portholes and gun fittings. These
helped the four-pointed fortress to cover its north, south, and west
flanks with defensive fire.

❷ Sainte-Anne-de-Beaupré

One of Canada's most sacred places, the shrine to the mother of the Virgin Mary was originally built in the 17th century. In 1650 a group of sailors who landed here after surviving a shipwreck vowed to build a chapel in honor of Saint Anne, the patron saint of those in shipwrecks. Over 800,000 visitors now come every year, including an annual pilgrimage on Saint Anne's Feast Day on July 26. This Neo-Romanesque basilica was built in the 1920s, and was the fifth church to be built on this site. In the entrance stand two columns of crutches, testimony to the many healings attributed to Saint Anne. The dome-vaulted ceiling is decorated with gold mosaics portraying the life of the saint. She is represented in a large gilt statue in the transept, cradling the Virgin Mary.

Statue of Saint Anne
The focus of the upper floor, the richly decorated statue sits in front of the relic of Saint Anne, presented to the shrine by Pope John XXIII in 1960.

Plan of the Shrine

1. Basilica
2. Monastery
3. Church Store
4. Museum
5. Blessing Office

The Basilica

In 1876, Saint Anne was proclaimed patron saint of Quebec, and in 1887 the existing church was granted basilica status. The Redemptorist order became the guardians of the shrine in 1878.

Entrance to Basilica's upper floor

KEY

① **Stained-glass windows** show the progress of pilgrims through the shrine, with the rose window as the centerpiece.

② **Bright mosaic floor tiles** echo ceiling patterns.

★ **The Basilica**
There has been a church on this site since 1658. In 1922, the previous basilica burned down. Today's version was built in 1923 and consecrated in 1976.

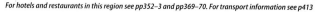

★ Pietà
A faithful copy of Michelangelo's
original in St. Peter's,
Rome, sits at the
ambulatory's
north end.

Montmorency Falls at Ile d'Orléans, Quebec's most dramatic waterfall

❸ Parc de la Chute Montmorency and Ile d'Orléans

🛈 Montmorency Falls, (418) 663 3330.
🚹 🛈 Ile d'Orléans Tourist Centre, 490
Côté du Pont, Saint Pierre, (418) 828 9411.
🆆 sepaq.com/montmorencyfalls

Located 13 km (8 miles) northeast of Quebec City, Montmorency Falls is Quebec's most celebrated waterfall. Higher than Niagara Falls, the cascade is created as the Montmorency River empties out into the Saint Lawrence River – a total of 30 m (98 ft) higher than the 56-m (184-ft) plunge of Niagara Falls from the Niagara River to Lake Ontario. The park surrounding the Falls offers a suspension bridge, an aerial cable car, a 300-m (980-ft) zipline and a series of trails that climb the surrounding cliffs.

A bridge nearby crosses the river to the Ile d'Orléans, which is covered with flowers, strawberry fields, and farmland. Its villages give a fascinating look at rural life in Quebec.

❹ Charlevoix Coast

🛈 495 Blvd. de Comporte, La Malbaie, (418) 665 4454.
🆆 tourisme-charlevoix.com

The Charlevoix Coast runs 200 km (124 miles) along the north shore of the Saint Lawrence River, from Sainte-Anne-de-Beaupré in the west to the mouth of the Saguenay Fjord. A UNESCO Biosphere Reserve because of its fine examples of boreal forest, the area is a slim band of flowery rural beauty on the southern edge of tundra that stretches northward. Gentle valleys protect old towns reaching to the river, with coastal villages sheltering beneath tall cliffs. Lying in a fertile valley is the exceptionally pretty Baie-Saint-Paul, whose streets are lined with historic houses and inns.

Just 35 km (22 miles) north of Baie-Saint-Paul lies the **Parc des Grands Jardins**, a vast expanse of lakes and black-spruce taiga forest with a herd of caribou. Small mountains offer walking and hiking. Farther downstream is the tiny and tranquil Isle-aux-Coudres. The lush, green farmland of this island is sprinkled with historic farms and a windmill.

🏛 **Parc des Grands Jardins**
Rte. 381. **Tel** (418) 439 1227. 🚹
🆆 sepaq.com/pq/grj

Moulin de l'isle-aux-Coudres, in the Charlevoix region

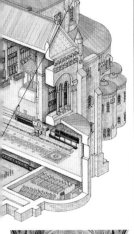

Basilica interior
Lit by sun streaming in through the stained-glass windows, the cream-and-gold interior is decorated in every corner.

The town of Tadoussac at the confluence of the Saint Lawrence and Saguenay rivers

❺ Tadoussac

🏘 850. 🚌 🚢 ℹ 197 Rue des Pionniers, (418) 235 4744.

Lined with boutiques, the old streets of this little town make a gentle start to exploring the local stretch of the Saint Lawrence River. In 1600, French traders picked this site to establish the first fur-trading post in Canada, noticing that for generations First Nations people had held meetings here to trade and parley. In the 19th century, the first Hôtel Tadoussac was built, and steamships began to transport well-heeled tourists to the village for a taste of its wilderness beauty.

Justifying two centuries of tourism, the scenery here is magnificent. Backed by rocky cliffs and towering sand dunes, the waterfront faces over the estuary where the Saint Lawrence and Saguenay rivers meet. In the town, the re-creation of the 17th-century fur-trading post and the oldest wooden church in Canada, the Petite Chapelle built in 1747, are popular.

However, the main attraction in Tadoussac can be found offshore. Whale-watching tours offer trips into the estuary to see many species in their natural environment. The thriving natural conditions in the estuary support a permanent colony of white beluga whales, which are joined in summer by minke, humpback, fin, and blue whales.

❻ Saguenay River

🚉 Jonquière. 🚌 Chicoutimi. ℹ 412 Blvd. Saguenay E., Bureau 100, Chicoutimi, (418) 543 9778. 🌐 **saguenaylacsaintjean.ca**

The Saguenay River flows through North America's southern-most natural fjord. This was formed from a retreating glacier splitting a deep crack in the Earth's crust during the last Ice Age, 10,000 years ago. Inky waters, 300m (985-ft) deep in places, run for 155 km (95 miles) beneath cliffs that average 300 m (985 ft) in height. Due to the exceptional depth, ocean liners can travel up to La Baie, a borough of Saguenay.

Running from Lac Saint-Jean to the Saint Lawrence estuary, the Saguenay is best known for its lush river banks and the wildlife that thrives in its lower reaches. Much of the pretty Bas Saguenay, the southern half of the river, is a national marine park with a healthy population of whales.

Beautiful views of the length of the fjord are available on the western shore at Cap Trinité, a cliff that rises 320 m (1,050 ft) over the channel, with a well-known 10-m (33-ft) statue of the Virgin Mary surveying the scenery from the lowest ledge.

❼ Chicoutimi

🏘 66,000. 🚉 Jonquière. 🚌 Chicoutimi. ℹ 412 Blvd. Saguenay E., Bureau 100, (418) 543 9778.

Snug in the crook of mountains on the western shore of the Saguenay, Chicoutimi is one of northern Quebec's most expansive towns, despite its modest population. The cultural and economic center of the Saguenay region, Chicoutimi's waterfront district has now been restored. A stroll along the riverside offers good views of the surrounding mountains and the confluence of the Chicoutimi, Du-Moulin, and Saguenay rivers.

Once a center for paper manufacturing, Chicoutimi still features a large pulp mill, the **Pulperie de Chicoutimi**. Though no longer operational, the plant can be toured, and an adjacent museum shows visitors the intricacies of this once important Quebecois industry.

🏭 **Pulperie de Chicoutimi**
300 Dubuc. **Tel** (418) 698 3100.
Open late Jun–Aug: 9am–6pm daily; Sep–mid-Jun: 10am–4pm Wed–Sun.
♿ 🌐 **pulperie.com**

Waterside view of a section of the deep Saguenay fjord

❽ A Tour of Lac-Saint-Jean

In the midst of the rocky, spruce-covered wilderness that characterizes central Quebec, Lac-Saint-Jean is an oasis of tranquility. Dairy farms, charming villages such as Chambord, and warm sandy beaches border the lake itself, which covers 1,000 sq km (386 sq miles). The lake and its rolling green landscape fill a crater-sized basin left by advancing glaciers at the end of the last Ice Age. Rivers and streams flow to the lake and tumble dramatically down the basin's steep walls into the blue waters, to be reborn as the source of the Saguenay River.

Tips for Drivers

Starting point: Chambord.
Length: 230 km (143 miles).
Getting around: This is a long, though relaxed, drive, and the road is well maintained. Inns and restaurants offer rest on the way in most towns and villages, including Mashteuiatsh. Small side roads make peaceful diversions.

⑥ **Parc National de la Pointe-Taillon**
Stretching into a peninsula, this park is excellent for cycling and hiking, but is best known for its fine, long beaches.

0 kilometers   10
0 miles   10

Key

▬ Tour route
═ Other roads

Chicoutimi

① **Chambord**
Sailing and swimming are top activities here, especially for children and families.

⑤ **Dolbeau**
Most visitors to Dolbeau arrive in July for the ten-day Western Festival, which features a rodeo and Western-style entertainment.

④ **Mashteuiatsh, Pointe-Bleu**
This village of the Montagnais people is open to visitors who can see at first hand age-old methods of carving, hunting, weaving, and cooking.

② **Village Historique de Val-Jalbert**
This outdoor museum is dominated by the 70-m (230-ft) Ouiatchouan Falls, which once acted as power for a pulp mill here in the 1920s.

③ **Roberval**
This town has a charming waterfront, from which spectators can see the finish of a swimming contest across the lake, which has taken place each July since 1946.

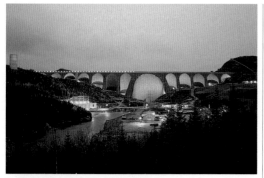
Daniel-Johnson Hydroelectric Dam, north of Baie-Comeau

❾ Baie-Comeau

🏘 23,000. ✈ 🚌 🚢 🛈 337 La Salle, (418) 294 2876.
Ⓦ ville.baie-comeau.qc.ca

This midsize town owes its entire existence to the US newspaper, the *Chicago Tribune*, which in 1936 built a mill near the mouth of the Manicougan River to supply its newspaper presses with paper. Declared a historic district in 1985, Baie-Comeau's oldest area is the Quartier Amélie, with rows of fine homes and an impressive hotel dating from the 1930s.

Paper production remains a vital industry here, but Baie-Comeau is most important today as a gateway to the enormous Manic-Outardes hydroelectric power complex, situated along Hwy 389, from 22 km (14 miles) to 200 km (124 miles) north of town. The most spectacular example is Manic-5, 212 km (132 miles) from Baie-Comeau. Its gracefully arched Daniel-Johnson Dam holds back a vast reservoir that fills a crater geophysicists believe might have been created by a meteorite millennia ago.

❿ Sept-Iles

🏘 26,000. 🚉 🚌 🚢 🛈 1401 Blvd. Laure, (418) 962 1238.
Ⓦ tourismeseptiles.ca/en

Until the 1950s, Sept-Iles led a quiet existence as a historic, sleepy fishing village. However, after World War II, the little settlement, located on the shores of a large, circular bay, drew the attention of large companies to use as a base for expanding the iron-mining industry in northern Quebec. Now the largest town along the north shore of the Gulf of Saint Lawrence, Sept-Iles has turned into Canada's second largest port as part of the Saint Lawrence Seaway. A boardwalk along the waterfront offers visitors the chance to see the large ships up close in action, and to observe the workings of a busy modern dock.

Although boasting the best of modern marine technology, the town also offers a reminder of its long-standing history. Vieux Poste near the center of the town is a fine reconstruction of a trading post, where the original inhabitants of the area met to barter furs with French merchants. A small museum with First Nations art and artifacts sells handmade crafts.

Despite its industrial importance, Sept-Iles is an area of

Sept-Iles from the air, showing the bustling dock in action

considerable natural beauty. Miles of sandy beaches rim the nearby coastline, and the salmon-rich Moisie River flows into the Gulf of Saint Lawrence just 20 km (12 miles) east of the town. The seven rocky islands that gave the city its name make up the Sept-Iles Archipelago Park.

Ideal for campers and hikers with its beaches and nature trails, one of the seven islands, Ile Grand-Basque, is a popular local camping spot. Another small island, Ile du Corossol, has been turned into a bird sanctuary that teems with gulls, terns, and puffins, and can be toured with a guide. Cruises are available for guided trips between islands.

⓫ Mingan Archipelago National Park

🚌 Sept-Iles. 🚢 Sept-Iles. 🛈 1401 Blvd. l'Aure, (418) 962 1238. Ⓦ pc.gc.ca

Located along the north shore of the Gulf of Saint Lawrence, the Mingan Archipelago National Park protects more than 1,000 islands and islets. This unspoiled northern wilderness is popular with outdoor enthusiasts, who visit this place for its harsh landscape, rich wildlife, and untouched ecosystems. Puffins, terns, and several gull species find refuge here. Gray, harbor, and harp seals all cluster along the tiny coves and bays, and finback whales are occasional visitors. As well as the abundant wildlife, the islands are home to the largest concentration of monoliths in Canada. Eroded over many centuries by the sea, these limestone carvings have surreal shapes. The best-known rocks look like flowerpots, with grasses sprouting from their peaks. Visitors can book a trip to admire the monoliths by boat.

Until 1974, the Ile d'Anticosti, east of the archipelago, was private property – all 8,000 sq km (3,090 sq miles) of it. The past owner, French chocolate tycoon Henri Menier, bought the island in 1895 and stocked it with a herd of white-tailed deer for his

"Flowerpot" limestone monoliths at the Mingan Archipelago National Park

friends to hunt. Now numbering 150,000, the deer herd is firmly ensconced but can still be hunted. Wildlife abounds; over 150 species of bird live in the relatively unspoiled forest and on the beaches. The village of Port Menier has 300 residents and acts as the local ferry terminus and lodging center. The island is separate from the Mingan Archipelago National Park, so there is no admittance fee.

Seal at Ile d'Anticosti

⑫ South Shore

🚉 Rivière-du-Loup. 🚌 Rivière-du-Loup. 🚢 Rivière-du-Loup.
ℹ️ 148 Rue Fraser, Rivière-du-Loup, (418) 867 1272, 1 888 825 1981.
🅦 **bassaintlaurent.ca**

Communities here can trace their roots back to the old 18th-century settlers of New France. Dotted along the flat, fertile farmland of the south shore of the Saint Lawrence River west of Gaspé and inland toward Montreal, the villages cover the area between the region's largest towns of Montmagny and Rimouski. Rivière-du-Loup, a seemingly unremarkable town in this stretch, provides for many people a taste of true Quebec. Featuring a historic stone church

that rears above the skyline, the old town rambles along hilly streets, and its 18th-century cottages have a French atmosphere. From the peak of the old town, views across the river valley are lovely. Other villages in this area feature unusual attractions. Farther along the main Route 132, Trois-Pistoles boasts a history that goes back to 1580, when Basque whalers arrived. The offshore Ile-aux-Basques was a whaling station in the 16th century, and today is protected as a bird sanctuary. Toward the region's commercial center, Rimouski, lies the Parc National du Bic, a small preserve of 33 sq km (13 sq miles) dedicated to the two forest zones – deciduous and boreal – that it encloses, and its varied coastal wildlife.

⑬ Iles-de-la-Madeleine

ℹ️ 128 Chemin Principal, Cap-aux-Meules, (418) 986 2245, 1 877 624 4437. 🅦 **tourismeilesdela madeleine.com**

Linked to the mainland by scheduled flights and ferries, many of the 12,000 residents of these remote islands in the Gulf of Saint Lawrence have taken to painting their homes in an assortment of mauves, yellows, and reds. Whether by sea or air, the approach gives striking views of the little communities on their low-lying, windswept islands, but the islands themselves have much to offer any visitor who makes the effort to see them. As well as having charming ancient villages, they are home to what are reputed to be some of the best beaches in the country, celebrated for their fine sand and their sheltered position.

Painted fisherman's cottage on the Ile-du-Havre-Aubert, Iles-de-la-Madeleine

⑭ Gaspé Peninsula Tour

Known in French as La Gaspésie, the Gaspé Peninsula stretches out north of New Brunswick to offer Quebec's wildest and most appealing scenery. As the peninsula spreads east, clumps of trees become dense pine forests, and the landscape becomes rough and rocky; cliffs along the northern coast reach 500 m (1,500 ft). The Chic-Choc mountains reach heights of 1,300 m (4,000 ft) and provide some of the province's best hiking. Shielded by the mountains, the southern coast harbors 18th-century fishing villages, inland fruit farms, exotic gardens, and wilderness national parks.

③ Parc National de la Gaspésie
Over 800 sq km (300 sq miles) of rough terrain mark a change from boreal to subalpine forest.

② Cap Chat
Named for a nearby cat-shaped rock, Cap Chat boasts the tallest windmill in the world at 110 m (360 ft).

① Grand Métis
This small town is home to one of Canada's most beautiful gardens, an exotic haven of 3,000 species, cultivars, and varieties of plants.

Réserve Faunique des Matane

Matane

Quebec City
Sainte-Flavie

Amqui

Causapscal

Routhierville

0 kilometres   20
0 miles   20

⑧ Carleton-sur-Mer
Founded in 1756 by Acadians fleeing the Great Expulsion in Nova Scotia (*see pp68–9*), today Carleton-sur-Mer is a pleasant, relaxed resort town, where visitors enjoy the mild coastal climate. Quality hotels and restaurants line the airy streets.

⑨ Vallée de la Matapédia
Starting at the confluence of two excellent salmon-fishing rivers, the picturesque Matapédia Valley is crisscrossed by covered bridges. Concealing long-established fruit farms, the valley's elm and maple trees show stunning fall colors.

④ **Sainte-Anne-des-Monts**

The entrance to the Parc National de la Gaspésie and the wildlife reserves of the Chic-Chocs, this 19th-century village has fine restaurants, and good salmon fishing nearby.

Tips for Drivers

The main road on this tour is Hwy 132, which follows the coastline from Grand Métis along the peninsula in a round trip. While too long to complete in a day, the journey can be broken in many of the local villages. Trips into the interior on the secondary road 299 are ideal for seeing the rocky wilderness.

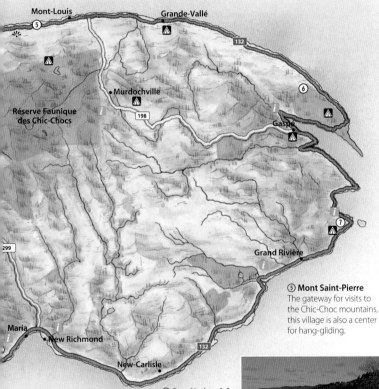

Mont-Louis

Grande-Vallé

Murdochville

Réserve Faunique des Chic-Chocs

Gaspé

⑥

299

Grand Rivière

⑦

Maria

New Richmond

New-Carlisle

⑤ **Mont Saint-Pierre**

The gateway for visits to the Chic-Choc mountains, this village is also a center for hang-gliding.

⑥ **Parc National du Canada Forillon**

The park contains the tail end of the Appalachian Mountains, now cliffs worn into rugged formations by the sea.

⑦ **Rocher Percé**

Situated out to sea south of the small town of Percé, this famous pierced landmark is the result of tidal erosion. In the 1930s, Percé became a popular spot for Canadian artists and still contains many galleries.

Key

▦ Tour route

═ Other roads

SOUTHERN AND NORTHERN QUEBEC

The vast area of land that stretches across Quebec from the Ontario boundary to historic Quebec City is rewarding in its diversity. In the south, the rich hilly farmland of the Appalachians and scarlet forests of maple trees attract many visitors each year, while the stark beauty of Nunavik's icy northern coniferous forests bursts into a profusion of wildflowers in spring, alongside the largest hydroelectric projects in the world. The center of the region is Quebec's natural playground, the Laurentian Mountains, a pristine lake-filled landscape offering fine skiing on ancient mountains. Populated by First Peoples until the Europeans arrived in the 16th century, the area was fought over by the French and British until the British gained power in 1759. Today French-speakers dominate.

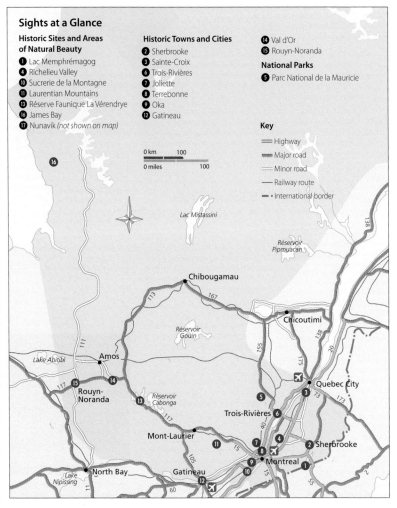

Sights at a Glance

Historic Sites and Areas of Natural Beauty
1 Lac Memphrémagog
4 Richelieu Valley
10 Sucrerie de la Montagne
11 Laurentian Mountains
13 Réserve Faunique La Vérendrye
16 James Bay
17 Nunavik (not shown on map)

Historic Towns and Cities
2 Sherbrooke
3 Sainte-Croix
6 Trois-Rivières
7 Joliette
8 Terrebonne
9 Oka
12 Gatineau
14 Val d'Or
15 Rouyn-Noranda

National Parks
5 Parc National de la Mauricie

Key
▭▭▭ Highway
▬▬▬ Major road
▭▭▭ Minor road
──── Railway route
━ ▪ ━ International border

0 km   100
0 miles   100

Lac Mistassini
Réservoir Pipmuacan
Chibougamau
Chicoutimi
Réservoir Gouin
Lake Abitibi
Amos
Rouyn-Noranda
Réservoir Cabonga
Trois-Rivières
Mont-Laurier
Quebec City
Sherbrooke
North Bay
Gatineau
Montreal
Lake Nipissing

◀ Fall colors reflecting in Lac Sauvage, the Laurentian Mountains, Quebec

For map symbols see back flap

Church by Lac Memphrémagog

❶ Lac Memphrémagog

🚌 Magog. ⛴ Magog. 🛈 2911
Milletta (Hwy 10, exit 115), Magog,
(800) 267 2744. 🅦 **tourisme-
memphremagog.com**

This area belongs to the Eastern
Townships, or the "Garden of
Quebec" that stretches from the
Richelieu River valley to the
Maine, New Hampshire, and
Vermont borders in the US. Set
among rolling hills, farmland,
woods, and lakes in a landscape
that is part of the Appalachians,
the Townships are among
Canada's top maple-syrup
producers (see pp106–7).

Lac Memphrémagog itself is
long, narrow, and surrounded
by mountains. It even boasts its
own monster, a creature named
Memphré, first spotted in 1798.
The lake's southern quarter dips
into the state of Vermont, so it
is no surprise that the British
Loyalists fleeing the American
Revolution were this region's
first settlers. Their influence can
be seen in the late 19th-century
red-brick-and-wood-frame
homes of lakeside villages such
as Georgeville and North Hatley,
and in the resort city of Magog
at the northern end of the lake.

Benedictine monks from
France bought one of the lake's
most beautiful sites in 1912
and established the Abbaye
Saint-Benoît-du-Lac. Today the
monks produce cider and a
celebrated blue cheese called
l'Ermite. They are also renowned
for Gregorian chant, and visitors
can hear them sing mass in the
abbey church.

❷ Sherbrooke

🏘 154,000. ✈ 🚌 ⛴ 🛈 785 Rue
King. **Tel** 1 (800) 561 8331, (819) 821
1919. 🅦 **destinationsherbrooke.com**

The self-styled "Queen of the
Eastern Townships," Sherbrooke
is this region's industrial,
commercial, and cultural
center. The city lies in a steep-
sided valley, with the historic
quarter delightfully situated
among the rolling farmlands
of the Saint-François and
Magog rivers. The first settlers
were British Loyalists from
the New England states.
Although their
heritage survives in
the fine old homes
and gardens of
Sherbrooke's
North Ward, and
in street names,
today the city is
overwhelmingly
French-speaking.
From the town
center runs the
Promenade du Lac-des-
Nations, a lovely waterfront
park with 20 km (12 miles) of
attractive cycling and walking
trails along the banks of the
Magog River.

❸ Sainte-Croix

🏘 2,500. 🛈 6375 Rue Garneau (418)
926 2620.

A charming, wooden manor
house with bold sweeping
front steps, pillars, and carved
curlicues is the centerpiece of
Domaine Joly-De Lotbinière.
This stunning estate was built
in 1851 by the local squire
(seigneur), according to the
Picturesque style. The house
is surrounded by banks of
geraniums and terraces of
walnut trees stretching down
to the river. Rare plant finds
include 20 red oaks estimated
to be over 250 years old. The
gardens were formerly known
for cultivating blue potatoes.

🏛 Domaine Joly-De Lotbinière
Rte. de Pointe-Platon. **Tel** (418) 926
2462. **Open** mid-May–mid-Oct:
10am–5pm daily. 🐾 ♿ partial.
🅦 **domainejoly.com**

❹ Richelieu Valley

🛈 1080 Chemin des Patriotes
Nord, Mont Saint-Hilaire, (450) 536
0395, 1 888 736 0395.
🅦 **vallee-du-richelieu.ca**

This fertile valley follows the
171-km (106-mile) Richelieu
River from Lake Champlain to
the confluence with the Saint
Lawrence River. **Fort Chambly**,
also known as Fort Saint Louis, in
the industrial town of Chambly
along the valley on the Montreal
Plain, is the best preserved of a
series of ancient buildings that
the French erected
to defend this vital
waterway from
Dutch and British
attack. Built from
solid stone in 1711
to replace the
original wooden
fortifications set up in
1675, the fort is well
preserved.
A sign to Fort Chambly in
the Richelieu Valley
in Saint-Denis-sur–
Richelieu commem-
orates Quebecois patriots who
fought in the failed 1837
rebellion against British rule.

Today the river flows past
attractive villages surrounded
by orchards and vineyards;
Mont Saint-Hilaire affords fine
views of Montreal, and is famed
for its apple plantations. Its
19th-century church was
declared a historic site in 1965
and features paintings by
Canadian Ozias Leduc (see p38).

🏛 Fort Chambly
2 Rue de Richelieu, Chambly.
Tel 1 (888) 773 8888 or (450) 658 1585.
Open mid-May–Jun & Sep–mid-Oct:
10am–5pm Wed–Sun; Jul–Aug:
10am–6pm daily. 🐾 🅦 **pc.gc.ca**

The 19th-century church at Mont Saint-
Hilaire, Richelieu Valley

Canoeists on Lac Wapizagonke in Parc National de la Mauricie

❺ Parc National de la Mauricie

Off Hwy 55 N. Shawinigan. **Tel** (819) 538 3232. 🚆 Shawinigan. **Open** daily. 🅿️ ♿ partial. 🅿️ For a fee. 🌐 **pc.gc.ca/mauricie**

Campers, hikers, canoeists, and cross-country skiers love this 536-sq km (207-sq mile) stretch of forest, lakes, and pink Precambrian granite. The park includes part of the Laurentian Mountains *(see p155)*, which are part of the Canadian Shield, and were formed between 950 and 1,400 million years ago. La Mauricie's rugged beauty is also accessible to motorists, who can take the winding 63-km (39-mile) road between Saint-Mathieu and Saint-Jean-des-Piles.

Another great drive starts at Saint-Jean-des-Piles and has good views of the narrow Lac Wapizagonke valley. With trout and pike in the lake, the area is an angler's delight. Moose and bear roam wild in the park.

❻ Trois-Rivières

🔺 132,000. ✈️ 🚌 🚍 🚢 ℹ️ 1457 Rue Notre Dame, (819) 375 1122, 1 800 313 1123. 🌐 **tourismetroisrivieres.com**

Quebec is one of the major paper producers in North America, and Trois-Rivières, a pulp and

paper town, is a main center of that industry. This fact often hides the rich historical interest that Trois-Rivières has to offer. The first colonists arrived here from France well before the city was founded in 1634. Although not many colonial dwellings remain, the city's charming old section has a number of 18th- and 19th-century houses and shops, many now cafés and bars.

Ursuline nuns have been working in the city since 1697, and the core of the old city is the **Monastère des Ursulines**, a rambling complex with a museum that traces the history of this teaching order, the oldest in the province. Tours of the chapel and, in summer, the gardens and old schoolrooms are offered. Rue des Ursulines features several little old houses with varying

The church of the Monastère des Ursulines in Trois-Rivières

architectural styles. Also here is an 18th-century manor house, the Manoir Boucher-de-Niverville. This cultural and historical site hosts displays on the rich history of the Mauricie region.

🏛️ Monastère des Ursulines

734 Rue des Ursulines. **Tel** (819) 375 7922. Museum: **Open** Mar & Apr: 1–5pm Wed–Sun; May–Jun & Sep–Nov: 10am–5pm Tue–Sun; Jul–Aug: 10am–5pm daily; Nov–Feb: by appt. 🅿️ 🎥 🌐 **musee-ursulines.qc.ca**

❼ Joliette

🔺 19,700. 🚌 ℹ️ 500 Rue Dollard, (450) 759 5013.

Two Catholic priests are responsible for turning this industrial town on L'Assomption River into a cultural center. In the 1920s, Father Wilfrid Corbeil founded the Musée d'Art de Joliette, whose collection ranges from medieval religious art to modern works. In 1978, Father Fernand Lindsay started the Festival International de Lanaudière, a series of summer concerts by some of the world's best-known musicians.

The nearby town of Rawdon, 18 km (11 miles) west, has a deserved reputation as a place of great natural beauty. Trails wind away from the small town along the Ouareau River, leading to the picturesque Dorwin Falls.

❽ Terrebonne

🗺 106,322. 🚌 🚲 🚃 ℹ 3645 Queen Street, 1 800 363 2788.

In 2001, three communities northwest of Montreal – Lachenaie, La Plaine, and Terrebonne – officially merged to form the city of Terrebonne. Lachenaie and Terrebonne itself are the oldest sectors, both founded in the 1670s, but a fire in 1922 engulfed many of the original buildings. Some graceful 19th-century homes remain, on Rue Saint-François-Xavier and Rue Sainte-Marie, many converted into restaurants.

The real gem here is the **Ile-des-Moulins**, a pre-industrial complex of living history in the middle of the Mille-Iles River, with water-powered mills for grinding grain, carding wool, and sawing lumber. One of the biggest buildings is the three-floor factory that was the first large-scale bakery in Canada. Built by the Northwest Company in 1803, it made the ship's biscuits that sustained the *voyageurs* who paddled west every year to trade for furs for the company.

Terrebonne is also the center of Quebec's horse-riding culture, and rodeo and ranching events take place regularly.

🏛 Ile-des-Moulins

866 Rue St-Pierre. **Tel** (450) 471 0619. **Open** Jun–Sep: 1–9 pm daily. 🚻 🅦 iledesmoulins.com

The Oka ferry as it travels across the Lake of Two Mountains

❾ Oka

🗺 5,000. 🚌 🚲 ℹ 183 rue des Anges, (450) 479 8389.

The prettiest way to approach this village north of Montreal is on the small ferry that chugs across the Lake of Two Mountains from Hudson. Framed by mountains and orchards, from the water the small Neo-Romanesque 1878 church is visible through the trees. Oka's **Abbaye Cistercienne** was founded by a group of monks who moved to Canada in 1881. The decor of the church is somewhat stark, in the Cistercian tradition, but the Neo-Romanesque architecture is gracefully simple and the gardens peaceful. Although the abbey is now closed, a shop in the nearby **Abbaye Notre-Dame du Lac** sells the Oka cheese that the monks developed. Nearby, the Parc d'Oka covers about 20 sq km (7 sq miles) of ponds and forests. It features the best beach and campground in the Montreal area, attracting sports lovers and visitors year-round.

🏛 Abbaye Notre-Dame du Lac

220 Chemin de la Montagne-Coupe, Saint-Jean-de-Matha. **Tel** (450) 460 1902. **Open** 8am–8pm Mon–Sat (store open daily). **Closed** lunchtimes. 🅦 abbayeval notredame.com

❿ Sucrerie de la Montagne

10 km (6 miles) south of Rigaud. 🚉 **Tel** (450) 451 0831. **Open** year round but call ahead. 🚻 🎫 obligatory. 🅦 sucreriedelamontagne.com

This Quebec Heritage site is set in a 50-ha (123-acre) maple forest on top of Rigaud Mountain near Rang Saint-Georges, Rigaud. It is entirely devoted to the many delights of Quebec's most famous commodity, the maple tree and its produce (*see pp106–7*). The site features a reconstructed 19th-century sugar shack, where collected maple sap is distilled and boiled in large kettles to produce the internationally renowned syrup. Over 20 rustic buildings house a fine bakery, a general store, and comfortable cabins for overnight guests. The heart of the complex is a huge 500-seat restaurant that serves traditional banquets of ham, pea soup, baked beans, pork rinds (called *Oreilles de Crisse*, or Christ's ears), and pickles, and dozens of maple-based products, including syrup, sugar, candies, taffy, muffins, and bread. Folk music accompanies the nightly feast. The tour includes an explanation of the maple syrup-making process, which is generally thought to have originated with the Aboriginal Peoples. They later imparted their secrets to European settlers, whose traditional methods are still in use today.

Quebecois Maple Syrup

Rue Saint-Louis in Terrebonne

⓫ Laurentian Mountains Tour

This whole region, from the lively resort of Saint-Sauveur-des-Monts in the south to north of Sainte-Jovite (also known as Tremblant), is nature's own amusement park, full of lakes, rivers, hiking and cycling trails, and ski runs visited all through the year. The mountains are part of the ancient Laurentian Shield, and are over a billion years old. Dotted with appealing, old French-style towns, this is a superb area to relax in or indulge in some vigorous sports in the national parks.

Tips for Drivers

Although the 175-km (108-mile) round tour of the Laurentian Mountains can be made from Montreal in a day on Hwy 15, the region is best seen and enjoyed by taking advantage of the slower, but more scenic, Hwy 117. There may be traffic congestion at the peak times of July through August and from December to March.

④ Sainte-Jovite
Full of historic architecture, this village lies in a wooded valley.

⑤ La Conception
Plenty of tiny hotels and street cafés add to the charm of this old village.

⑥ Mont Tremblant
The tallest of the Laurentian range with a vertical rise of about 645 m (2,116 ft), this is a popular international four-season resort.

③ Saint-Faustin-Lac-Carré
Saint-Faustin–Lac-Carré has an important role as the starting-off point for trips around the area. Local woods contain an interpretive center with flora and fauna trails.

② Sainte-Agathe-des-Monts
The largest town in the Laurentians provides busy café society all year round. Lac des Sables in town offers beaches and lake cruises.

① Val-Morin
This enchanting village is a charming introduction to the area, with traditional French homes and churches.

Key

▬▬▬ Tour route
═══ Other roads

0 kilometers 3
0 miles 3

⑫ Gatineau

Gatineau (known as Hull until 1992) is based just across the river from Ottawa in the province of Quebec, and, as a result, many federal bureaucracies have their headquarters here. For years, Gatineau has been a more relaxed and fun-loving counterpart to the national capital, an attitude that reveals itself even in its officialdom – City Hall, for instance, boasts a meditation center. From Hull's establishment in 1800, the city's liquor laws were far more lenient than Ottawa's, and so this was where Ottawa politicians came to party (the city still has a lower drinking age). Gatineau contains Canada's most-visited museum, the Canadian Museum of History, which provides a fascinating tour of the country over the past 1,000 years.

VISITORS' CHECKLIST

Practical Information
🏛 245,000. ℹ 103 Rue Laurier, (819) 778 2222, 1 800 265 7822.
🎭 Fall Rhapsody (Sep/Oct).
🌐 tourismeoutaouais.com

Transport
✈ Ottawa International 12 km (7 miles) south of the city. 🚌 200 Tremblay Rd, Ottawa.

🏞 Parc de la Gatineau

Hwy 5. **Tel** (819) 827 2020, 1 800 465 1867. **Open** daily. 🌐 ncc-ccn.gc.ca

This 360 sq km (140 sq miles) oasis of lakes and rolling hills between the Gatineau and Ottawa rivers is a weekend playground for city residents. The park contains fragments of Gothic buildings, collected by the former Prime Minister, William Lyon MacKenzie-King.

Casino du Lac-Leamy

1 Casino Blvd. **Tel** (819) 772 2100, 1 800 665 2274. **Open** 24 hours daily. ♿ 🌐 casinos.lotoquebec.com

Three million visitors a year are lured to this glittering casino, which is equipped with 1,800 slot machines and 64 gaming

Gaming room in the Casino du Lac-Leamy

tables. Owned by the Quebec Government, the casino opened in 1996 and is set in a park full of flowers and fountains.

🏛 Alexandra Bridge

Built in 1900, this handsome steel-framed bridge spans the Ottawa River and links Ontario to Quebec. From footpaths, drivers' lanes, and cycle routes, the bridge offers fine views of the

river, the Canadian Museum of History, and the Parliament Buildings in Ottawa.

🏛 Maison du Citoyen

25 Laurier St. **Tel** (819) 243 2345. **Open** 8:30am–4:30pm Mon–Fri. **Closed** public hols. ♿ 🌐 maisonducitoyen.fr

The heart of this complex is a vast atrium, the Agora, meant to serve as an all-weather gathering place for Gatineau's citizens, as well as an airy meditation center for the city's workers. Opening from it are City Hall, a library, a theater, and an art gallery.

🏛 Promenade du Portage

Linked with the city bridges, this main route downtown is full of lively cafés, restaurants, and a microbrewery. After dark the area and nearby Place Aubry become the focus of the city's excellent nightlife.

Gatineau City Center

① Alexandra Bridge
② Canadian Museum of History
③ Maison du Citoyen
④ Promenade du Portage

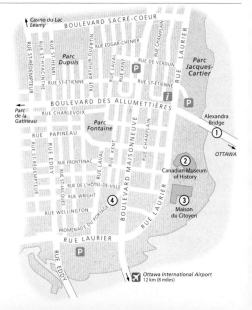

Canadian Museum of History

This museum was built in the 1980s to be the storehouse of Canada's human history. The architect, Douglas Cardinal, wanted the undulating façades of both buildings to reflect the Canadian landscape. The more curved hall is the Canadian Shield Wing, home to the museum's offices. The Glacier Wing displays the exhibits. Its entry is stunning; the dramatic interior of the Grand Hall contains the world's largest collection of totem poles. The Children's Museum is delightfully diverting, while the CINÉ+ Theatre offers the ultimate cinema experience. The fourth level holds an archive, which is open to the public.

VISITORS' CHECKLIST

Practical Information
100 Laurier St. Tel (819) 776 7000,
1 800 555 5621. **Open** 9:30am–
5pm daily (to 8pm Thu); check
website for longer summer hours.

W **historymuseum.ca**

The museum façade echoes the rolling Canadian landscape

Level Three

David M.
Stewart Salon

The Canadian History Hall is the largest ever exhibition on the history of Canada, from the end of the last Ice Age to the present day.

The Children's Museum
This extremely popular space contains the "Great Adventure," with interactive exhibits, a busy world market, and this brightly decorated Pakistani trolleybus.

Level Two

Main Entrance

Group Entrance

Level One

Library

★ **The Grand Hall**
The museum is home to the world's largest collection of totem poles, many of which are displayed in the Grand Hall.

Key to Floor Plan

- Canadian History Hall
- Children's Museum
- First Peoples Hall
- First Peoples of the Northwest Coast Exhibition
- W. E. Taylor Salon
- Grand Hall
- CINÉ+ Theater
- Special Exhibitions
- Non-Exhibition Space

For hotels and restaurants in this region see pp353–4 and pp370–72

The wildlife preserve of La Vérendrye, seen from the air

⑬ Réserve Faunique La Vérendrye

Tel (819) 736 7431. 🚌 Maniwaki. **Open** summer. ♿ partial. 🅦 **sepaq.com**

This wildlife preserve is situated approximately 471 km (292 miles) to the northwest of Montreal on Hwy 117. It is celebrated for long, meandering waterways and streams and, with hundreds of kilometers of canoe trails, is a legend among canoeists. Its rivers are usually gentle, and the 13,000 sq km (5,020 sq miles) of wilderness are home to large numbers of moose, bear, deer, and beaver. The land is practically untouched, but there are several campgrounds here for those who seek a truly peaceful break. In season, anglers can try for walleye, pike, lake trout, and bass. Hwy 117 traverses the park, providing access to many of its lakes and rivers, and is the starting point of hiking trails.

A moose at La Vérendrye

⑭ Val d'Or

🏘 36,000. 🚌 🛈 1070 3rd Ave. E., (819) 824 9646, 1 877 582 5367.

Val d'Or is principally a mining town and is a major center in the northwestern part of Quebec. The town sights here are not architectural but vivid living-history attractions of mines and historic villages from the area's heritage of lumber trade and mining. Miners have been digging gold, silver, and copper out of the ground around Val d'Or since the 1920s. A climb to the top of the 18-m (60-ft) Tour Rotary on the edge of town shows many still-active mineheads.

La Cité de l'Or is built around the abandoned Lamaque Goldmine, formerly one of the richest sources of gold in the area. In its heyday of the early 20th century, the mine had its very own small town site with a hospital, a boarding house for all single workers, and neat streets lined with little log cabins for married men and their families. The mine managers had more elaborate homes nearby, and there was a sumptuous guesthouse for visiting executives. Much of the Village Minier de Bourlamaque remains intact and was declared a historic site in 1979. Visitors can tour the village, the old analysis office and laboratories, and the minehead. For an extra fee, fascinating tours in coveralls and helmets are available down the 90 m (295 ft) mine shaft.

🏛 La Cité de l'Or

90 Ave. Perrault. **Tel** (819) 825 1274, 1 855 825 1274. **Open** late Jun–early Sep: 9am–6pm daily. 🅿 ♿ partial 🅦 **citedelor.com**.

⑮ Rouyn-Noranda

🏘 41,000. 🚌 🛈 1675 Lariviere Ave., (819) 797 3195, 1 888 797 3195. 🅦 **ville.rouyn-noranda.qc.ca**

As with all developed areas in the north of Quebec, towns here are based on heavy industry. Rouyn and Noranda sprang up virtually overnight in the 1920s, when prospectors found copper in the region. They merged into one city covering 6,600 sq km (2,548 sq miles) in 1986. Noranda, on the north shore of Lake Osisko, is a carefully planned company town, built to house the employees of the now-defunct Noranda copper mine. The lawns and tree-lined streets have an almost English air. Some residents are still employed in surrounding mines. The Glencore Smelter, one of the biggest and most efficient in the world, is based just outside the center of town and can be visited by arrangement.

Rouyn, on the south shore of the lake, is less structured and more commercial. It is also where Noranda residents often go for recreation, and it is useful as a refreshment and fuel center for those traveling to the northern wilderness. The **Maison Dumulon**, a reconstruction of Rouyn's first post office and general store, celebrates its pioneer spirit with displays on the first settlers.

🏛 Maison Dumulon

191 Ave. du Lac. **Tel** (819) 797 7125. **Open** Jun–Sep: daily; Oct–Jun: Wed–Sun. 🅿 ♿ 🅦 **maison-dumulon.ca**

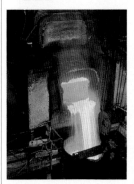

Copper being smelted into huge nuggets for export, Noranda

Canada geese fly over the tundra on the Ungava Peninsula that is Nunavik

⑯ James Bay

ℹ Tourisme Quebec, (877) 266 5687.

The thinly populated municipality of James Bay is roughly the size of Germany, which makes it much larger than most other municipalities in the region – about 350,000 sq km (135,000 sq miles). Its landscape, lakes, scrubby trees, and early pre-Cambrian rock are hardly urban, changing from forest to taiga to tundra and becoming gradually more inaccessible in the frozen northern parts.

However, what the region lacks in infrastructure it amply makes up for in power capacity. Its six major rivers, which all flow into the Bay, can produce enough electricity to light up the whole of North America. So far, the Quebec government has spent over Can $20 billion in building a third of the number of dams for what is already one of the biggest hydroelectric projects in the world. Five power plants produce nearly 16,000 megawatts of electricity to power much of Quebec and parts of the northeastern US. Le Grand 2 (known as LG-2) is the biggest dam and underground generating station in the world.

The main town in the area is the small settlement of Radisson. A functional but useful tourist center, Radisson also offers good views of the surrounding country. Not all of the Bay's dams and dikes can be seen, but the massive dams and series of reservoirs, especially LG-2, which is just east of town, are visible from above.

One of the vast power stations at James Bay

⑰ Nunavik

ℹ Nunavik Tourism Association, (819) 964 2876, 1 888 594 3424.
🌐 nunavik-tourism.com

In the far north of Quebec, the pristine Nunavik territory covers an area slightly larger than continental Spain. Its inhabitants number about 12,000, nearly all of them Inuit, who live in 14 communities along the shores of Hudson Bay, the Hudson Strait, and Ungava Bay. Nunavik is Quebec's last frontier, a wild and beautiful land that is virtually inaccessible except by airplane. Caribou herds, polar bears, and musk oxen roam the taiga coniferous forest and frozen Arctic tundra that covers this region. Seals and beluga whales can be found swimming in its icy waters.

Kuujjuaq, near Ungava Bay, is Nunavik's largest district, with a population of 2,400. This is a good jumping-off point for expeditions to the valley of Kangiqsujuaq near Wakeham Bay and the rugged mountains around Salluit.

Visitors come to Nunavik and Kuujjuaq to appreciate the many varieties of wildlife that roam freely in their natural setting. Summer is the best time for a trip; temperatures rise, but the ground remains frozen all year round.

The region has no railroads (and hardly any roads) and should be explored only in the company of a seasoned and reliable guide. Many Inuit groups and communities offer guide services and the opportunity to experience life on the land with Inuit families. Visitors should be prepared for a very warm welcome and the chance to sample traditional Inuit foods and hospitality.

ONTARIO

Introducing Ontario

The sheer size of Ontario is daunting. It is Canada's second-largest province, covering over one million sq km (416,000 miles) and stretching all the way from the Great Lakes on the US border to the frozen shores of Hudson Bay. Northern Ontario is relatively inaccessible, but this wild and stunningly beautiful region of turbulent rivers, deep forests, and Arctic tundra can be reached by air, and by the occasional scenic road and railroad. Much of the north is also sparsely populated, in striking contrast to the fertile lands farther south, and bordering Lake Ontario, which have attracted many thousands of immigrants. Both Toronto, Canada's biggest city, and Niagara Falls, the country's leading tourist destination, are here.

The tallest free-standing structure in the western hemisphere, Toronto's CN Tower, at night

0 kilometers   200

0 miles   200

A tour boat approaches the spectacular Horseshoe Falls at Niagara

Getting Around

Among several highways skirting the northern shore of Lake Ontario, the main ones are Hwy 401, from Toronto to Montreal in the east and Windsor in the west, and the Queen Elizabeth Way (QEW), from Toronto south to Niagara Falls. Niagara Falls, Toronto, and Ottawa are linked by bus and rail. Hwy 400 runs north from Toronto to Parry Sound, where it becomes Hwy 69 up to the Trans-Canada Highway. Buses cover northerly routes.

For map symbols *see back flap*

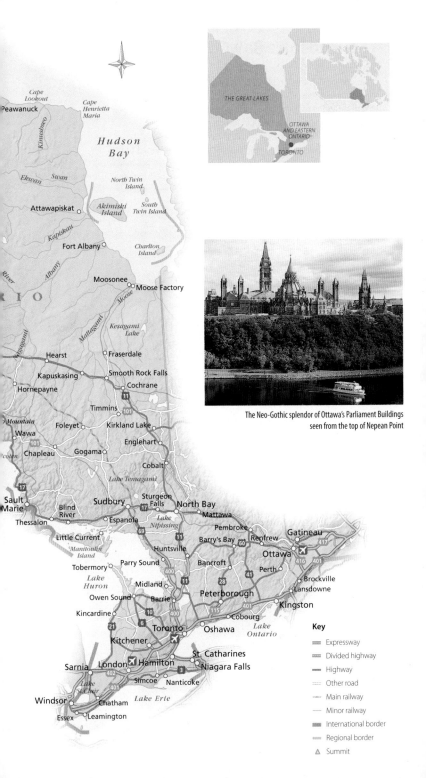

Cape
Lookout
Peawanuck
Cape
Henrietta
Maria

Kinushseo

*Hudson
Bay*

Ekwan
Swan

North Twin
Island

Attawapiskat
*Akimiski
Island*
South
Twin Island

Kapiskau

Fort Albany
Charlton
Island

Albany
River

Moosonee
Moose Factory

Mattagami
Moose

RIO

*Kesagami
Lake*

Wenagami

Hearst
Fraserdale

Kapuskasing
Smooth Rock Falls

Hornepayne
Cochrane

11

Timmins
101

Mountain
Foleyet
Kirkland Lake

Wawa
Englehart

101

coten
Chapleau
Gogama

Cobalt

Lake Temagami

17

Sault
Marie
Blind
River
Sudbury
Sturgeon
Falls
North Bay

17

Thessalon
Espanola
*Lake
Nipissing*
Mattawa

69

Pembroke
Renfrew
Gatineau

Little Current
Huntsville
Barry's Bay
60

417

*Manitoulin
Island*
Parry Sound
Bancroft
Ottawa

Tobermory
11
Perth
416
401

*Lake
Huron*
400
Midland
28
41
Brockville

Owen Sound
Barrie
Peterborough
Lansdowne

Kincardine
11
115
401
Kingston

10
400
Cobourg
*Lake
Ontario*

21
6
Toronto
Oshawa

Kitchener

Sarnia
London
Hamilton
St. Catharines

402
3
Niagara Falls

Simcoe
Nanticoke

Windsor
*Lake
St. Clair*
Lake Erie

Essex
Chatham

Leamington

THE GREAT LAKES

OTTAWA
AND EASTERN
ONTARIO

TORONTO

The Neo-Gothic splendor of Ottawa's Parliament Buildings
seen from the top of Nepean Point

Key

▬▬ Expressway

▬▬ Divided highway

▬ Highway

▭▭ Other road

▬▪▬ Main railway

▬ Minor railway

▬▬ International border

▬▬ Regional border

△ Summit

The Hudson's Bay Company

The Hudson's Bay Company (HBC) played a pivotal role in establishing England's presence in Ontario through the fur trade. It was incorporated on May 2, 1670, by King Charles II of England, who granted the new company wide powers, including a monopoly of trading rights to a huge block of territory bordering the Bay, then known as Rupert's Land. His decision was prompted by the successful voyage of the British ship *Nonsuch*, which returned from the recently discovered Hudson's Bay crammed with precious beaver furs. The Company was ordered to develop links with the Aboriginal Peoples of Rupert's Land, and trade took off swiftly. Here fashion played a part: the ladies and gentlemen of 18th-century Europe were gripped by a passion for the beaver hat, and the demand for beaver pelts became almost insatiable.

European fur couriers rapidly built up a roaring trade with Aboriginal fur trappers, which came to follow a seasonal pattern.

Lands and Trading Posts

From 1670 onward, trading goods were dispatched from England to the Company's main trading sites around Hudson Bay, modest stockaded settlements with safe stores for the merchandise. Larger outposts gradually became self-sufficient, catering to newer, smaller posts as the Company moved ever westward. By 1750, HBC camps were established at the mouths of all the major rivers flowing into Hudson Bay. James Bay's Fort Albany had a jail, a hospital, a smithy, a cooperage, a canoe-building jetty, and sheep and cattle barns, while gallant efforts were made to grow crops. Main trading posts serviced a network of smaller seasonal outposts. They continued their expansion west until the transfer of land rights to the new country of Canada in 1870.

Fort Yukon
1846–1869

Fort Good
Hope 1821

Fort Simpson
1821

Fort St. James
1821

Edmonton
1795

Cumberland
House 1774

Fort Victoria
1843

Key

🛶 Trading post

– – Trading route

〰〰 1670 boundary of Rupert's Land

The Seven Oaks Massacre of June 1816 in Manitoba occurred when HBC workers clashed with the rival North West Company, and 20 men were killed. The two companies agreed in 1821 to join territories and increased in power.

English traders assembled a variety of goods to trade with local tribes in return for the winter's supply of pelts. Transported by ship in spring, the merchandise ranged from trinkets to more substantial items including blankets, knives, and guns.

The Changing Fortunes of HBC

HBC reigned supreme in Canada until the 1840s, but civil disobedience led the British to relinquish claims to Washington State and Oregon in 1846, establishing the US border. No longer able to enforce its monopoly, HBC sold its land to Canada in 1869, retaining only areas around the trading posts. They were in key locations, which boosted HBC's expansion into real estate and retail in the 20th century. Today HBC is one of Canada's top companies, but it is majority-owned by a US firm.

The Bay in Vancouver, one of HBC's modern department stores

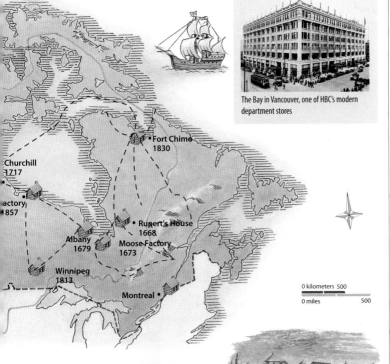

Churchill 1717

actory 857

Albany 1679

Winnipeg 1813

Fort Chimo 1830

Rupert's House 1668

Moose Factory 1673

Montreal

0 kilometers 500
0 miles 500

The beaver's coat is at its thickest and most valuable in winter, when the Aboriginal Peoples ventured out into the ice and snow to trap the animal. In spring, Aboriginal trappers delivered bundles of soft pelts to the Company's trading posts, in exchange for goods.

Company sailboats first carried materials to trade with Aboriginal Peoples. As the Company grew, it transported building materials, food, and seeds to set up what became sizeable settlements. Ships returned with up to 16,000 beaver pelts.

The Group of Seven

Formed in 1920, the Group of Seven revolutionized Canadian art. Mostly commercial artists working in an Ontario art firm, this small band of painters was inspired by a colleague, Tom Thomson. An avid outdoorsman, Thomson started making trips in 1912 into the wilderness of northern Ontario to produce dozens of brightly colored, impressionistic sketches. His friends realized that he was taking Canadian art in a new direction – these landscapes of their country were largely free of the rigid European focus that had characterized painting until then, and a nationalist movement had begun. After World War I and the death of Thomson in 1917, these same friends started the Group and held their first exhibition in Toronto in 1920. Many of the paintings shown depicted Nova Scotian, Ontarian, and Quebec wildernesses; a new art was born that forged a sense of national pride between the people and their land in this young country.

The Red Maple is A. Y. Jackson's vibrant landmark of 1914. Inspired by a fall visit to Algonquin Park, it embodied the Group aim of creating a national consciousness.

Edge of the Forest (1919) by Frank Johnston is just one of the Group's works that illustrates their statement: "Art must grow and flower in the land before the country will be a real home for its people." Using the impressive surroundings of their homeland, the Group painters developed a spontaneous style that broke away from European tradition.

Above Lake Superior was painted by Lawren Harris in 1922. Known for his simple, heroic images, Harris captures the harsh, exhilarating climate of the Great Lakes region in winter, known as "the mystic north." Harris believed that spiritual fulfillment could best be obtained by studying landscape. The Group also held the ethos that truly meaningful expression was accomplished only when the the subject of the work was one the viewer shared with the artist, in this case local landscape.

Falls, Montreal River (1920) was painted by J. E. H. MacDonald, who chose Algoma as his work base. Each of the Group had a preferred individual region in which they found most inspiration, mostly in Ontario. Sketching trips regularly took place in summer, with painters showing each other favorite areas.

Autumn, Algoma (1920)

This richly decorated canvas shows the extraordinary evening colors of the fall in Ontario. Algoma was J. E. H. MacDonald's chosen region, a Canadian Eden in northern Ontario that acted as his inspiration and where he regularly made sketching trips. MacDonald records uniquely Canadian subjects in this painting; the blazing foliage and looming pines serve to record and thus establish a Canadian identity. Influenced by the stark landscapes produced in Scandinavia from around 1900, MacDonald focuses on the chill drama in this scene to add a grandeur to his beloved landscape.

The Group of Seven

Based in a converted railway boxcar, the members hiked and boated to favorite places in Algonquin Park, Georgian Bay, Algoma, and Lake Superior to produce new art for their country. Following the 1920 exhibition, entitled The Group of Seven, their striking paintings immediately became popular, and the Group went on to exhibit together almost every year. Native inspiration was vital to the Group's subject and technique. The apparently raw and coarse methods were a rejection of the heavy, Realist oils produced in Europe at the time. Luminous colors and visible brushstrokes led one critic to remark that the Group had "thrown [their] paint pots in the face of the public." The Group held their final show in 1931 and disbanded the following year to make way for a wider group of painters from across Canada, the Canadian Group of Painters. Founders of a distinctive Canadian art movement based on a love of their country's natural beauty, the Group of Seven painters remain particularly celebrated in Canada and are still given prominence in top galleries across Ontario and the rest of the country today.

The photograph below, taken at Toronto's Arts & Letters Club in 1920, shows, from left to right: Varley, Jackson, Harris, Barker Fairley (a friend and writer), Johnston, Lismer, and MacDonald. Carmichael was not present.

The Group of Seven in 1920

TORONTO

Toronto has shed its prim, colonial image to become one of North America's most dynamic cities, a cosmopolitan mix of almost three million inhabitants drawn from more than 200 ethnic groups. Reveling in its position as the financial and commercial center of Canada, Toronto also boasts fine art museums, suave café-bars, and luxury stores.

Located on the northwest shore of Lake Ontario, the area of Toronto was originally settled by the Iroquois during the 17th century, and, after 1720, a French fur-trading post. Fought over by the US and Britain in the War of 1812 *(see pp52–53)*, Toronto has since been a peaceful city, growing dramatically after World War II, with the arrival of over 500,000 immigrants, especially Italians and, more recently, Asians.

The first place to start a visit is the CN Tower, formerly the world's tallest tower and the city's most famous tourist attraction. From the top, it is easy to pick out the sights of the city, and from the bottom a short stroll leads to Harbourfront or the financial district. To the north of downtown is the boisterous street-life of Chinatown and the superb paintings of the Art Gallery of Ontario. Nearby sits the University of Toronto, on whose perimeters lie the fine Royal Ontario Museum and two delightful specialty collections, the Gardiner Museum of Ceramic Art and the Bata Shoe Museum. A quick subway ride takes the visitor north to Casa Loma, an eccentric Edwardian mansion, and Spadina House, the elegant Victorian villa nearby. Many more attractions are scattered around the periphery, including Toronto Zoo and the Ontario Science Centre. The McMichael Canadian Art Collection, in nearby Kleinburg, contains an outstanding collection of paintings by the Group of Seven, among many others, in a pastoral setting.

Toronto's café society in the downtown area

◄ Toronto financial district at dusk

Exploring Toronto

Toronto is a large, sprawling city that covers over
640 sq km (247 sq miles) on the northwestern side of
Lake Ontario. The center offers a pleasant mix of office
blocks, leafy residential streets, and shopping areas,
while the suburbs, such as North York and Scarborough,
are more residential and spread out. The downtown core,
encompassing the financial district and Chinatown, is
bordered by College and Front on the north and south,
and Jarvis and Spadina on the east and west.

Sights at a Glance

Historic Areas and Buildings
❹ Fairmont Royal York Hotel
❽ Royal Alexandra Theatre
❿ First Post Office
⓭ Toronto City Hall
⓮ Chinatown
⓰ University of Toronto
⓱ Ontario Parliament Building
⓲ Spadina Museum, Historic
   House & Gardens
㉓ Fort York
㉔ Casa Loma
㉖ Distillery District

Parks and Gardens
㉗ The Toronto Islands
㉘ The Beaches and
   Scarborough Bluffs
㉙ Toronto Zoo

Modern Architecture
❶ *CN Tower p176*
❸ Rogers Centre

Museums, Galleries, and Concert Halls
❷ Ripley's Aquarium of Canada
❺ Hockey Hall of Fame
❻ Four Seasons Centre for
   the Performing Arts
❼ TD Gallery of Inuit Art
❾ TIFF Bell Lightbox
⓬ *Art Gallery of Ontario pp182–3*
⓳ Gardiner Museum
⓴ *Royal Ontario Museum pp188–9*
㉑ Bata Shoe Museum
㉚ Aga Khan Museum
㉛ Ontario Science Centre
㉜ Black Creek Pioneer Village
㉝ McMichael Canadian
   Art Collection
㉞ Museum of Contemporary Art

Shopping Areas
⓫ Queen Street West
⓯ Kensington Market
㉒ Yorkville
㉕ St. Lawrence Market

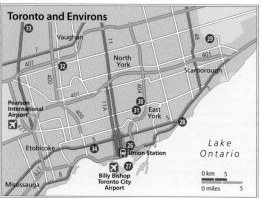

The city skyline over Ontario Lake at sunrise

Getting Around

Toronto's public transportation is excellent. The subway lines follow the main arteries: Bloor/Danforth (east–west) and Yonge/University (north–south). Buses and streetcars serve the areas around each subway station. The UP Express runs every 15 minutes between Pearson International Airport and Union Station.

Key

- Major sight
- Other sight
- Highway
- Major roads
- Minor roads
- Pedestrian walkway
- Railway

Street-by-Street: Harbourfront

Toronto's Harbourfront has had a varied history. Lake Ontario once lapped against Front Street, but the Victorians reclaimed 3 km (2 miles) of land to accommodate their railroad yards and warehouses. Ontario's exports and imports were funneled through this industrial strip until the 1960s, when trade declined. In the 1980s the area was given a new lease on life, when planners orchestrated the redevelopment of what has now become 10 sq km (4 sq miles) of reclaimed land. Harbourfront now boasts grassy parks, walkways, smart apartments, and a cluster of tourist sights in and around the Harbourfront Centre.

❶ ★ CN Tower
Once the world's tallest building, the CN Tower offers views of up to 160 km (100 miles) over Ontario, and a glass floor for those with iron nerves.

Ripley's Aquarium of Canada
This aquarium showcases over 16,000 marine creatures, from salmon and sawfish to sea nettles. Take the tunnel through the Dangerous Lagoon to be surrounded by 2.5 million liters of shark-infested water.

FRONT ST. W

BRE

LAKE SHORE

❷ ★ Rogers Centre
Using enough electricity to light the province of Prince Edward Island, a performance at the vast Rogers Centre stadium is an unforgettable experience.

Charter Boats
Sailing out onto Lake Ontario and around the three Toronto Islands provides fine views of the city. Small sailboats, motorboats, and tours are available.

Harbourfront Centre
A huge cultural complex, Harbourfront Centre offers a diverse selection of activities and cultural events, such as an ice rink, studios where visitors can watch glassblowers in action, art galleries, and dance, music and theatre performances.

Locator Map
See pp172–3

The Roundhouse
Steam locomotives sit around the still-operational turntable at the Roundhouse, home to the Toronto Railway Museum.

Steam Whistle Brewing at the Roundhouse is a working brewery in a historic former steam train repair facility. Tasting tours are available.

The Gardiner Expressway divides the city center from the waterfront and leads west to Niagara Falls *(see pp216–19)*.

The Power Plant
Contemporary Art Gallery hosts changing exhibitions of major international artists.

SIMCOE STREET

VD. W. GARDINER EXPRESSWAY

QUEEN'S QUAY

Docks for ferries to the island

0 meters 150
0 yards 150

Key
— Suggested route

Harbourfront Waterside
The waterside is a lively place for visitors, especially in summer. Private vessels are berthed in the basins at the water's edge and the walkways offer lake views.

Bill Boyle Artport
The hub of the Harbourfront Centre, where most of the activity takes place. There is a performance space and a contemporary gallery.

❶ CN Tower

At 553 m (1,814 ft) high, Canada's National Tower was the tallest free-standing structure in world for over three decades, and remains the tallest tower in the western hemisphere. The CN Tower was not originally designed as the world's tallest spire, but it so overwhelmed the city's visitors that it soon became one of Canada's prime tourist attractions. The tower houses one of the largest revolving restaurants in the world, which takes 72 minutes to make a full rotation. Open seasonally, EdgeWalk at the CN Tower offers the world's highest hands-free walk on a building at 356 m (1,168 ft).

VISITORS' CHECKLIST

Practical Information
301 Front St. W. **Tel** 416 868 6937.
Open 10am–10:30pm daily.
Closed Dec 25. 🅿 ♿ 🗹 ⊘
🖵 📷 🅦 cntower.ca

The SkyPod is reached by its own elevator and is the highest accessible point on the tower at 447 m (1,467 ft).

The 360 Restaurant at the CN Tower
Spectacular views combine with award-winning cuisine and wines from the world's highest cellar.

The LookOut Level offers visitors the chance to observe the city in comfort, away from the wind; signs identify main Toronto landmarks.

The Outdoor SkyTerrace is protected by steel grilles and illustrates how exposed the tower is, especially in windy weather.

The CN Tower from the Lake
The tower offers fantastic views of Toronto and Lake Ontario. On a clear day it is possible to see as far south as Niagara Falls *(see pp216–19)*.

Glass Floor
The ground is 342 m (1,122 ft) beneath this thick layer of reinforced glass, and even the courageous may feel a little daunted.

The outside elevators, featuring glass fronts and floors, take visitors shooting up the outside of the tower to the upper levels. Speeds take your breath away and make your ears pop; the elevators can reach the top in under a minute.

The inside staircase has 1,776 steps. Climbing the steps as part of a charity event is a popular fund-raising activity in Toronto.

View of the City from the LookOut Level
At 346 m (1,135 ft) above the city, the LookOut Level provides panoramas of Toronto from interior galleries. Horizons offers upscale bistro dining on this level.

❷ Ripley's Aquarium of Canada

288 Bremner Blvd. **Tel** 647 351 3474.
🚇 Union, St. Andrew. **Open** 9am–
11pm daily (to 6pm occasionally). 📷
♿ 📷 🖥 🅦 ripleyaquariums.
com/canada

Opened in 2013, this state-of-
the-art aquarium houses over
16,000 sea creatures. The display
of marine life from around the
world, starts with Ontario's Fishes
of the Great Lake Basin, and is
followed by the beautiful two-
storey Pacific Kelp Viewing Tank.
Deep below the Dangerous
Lagoon, a travelator ferries visitors
through a tunnel where tooth
sawfish and sand tiger sharks
swim overhead. To get even
closer, head to the tanks filled with
bamboo sharks, horseshoe crabs,
and stingrays. In Planet Jellies,
sea nettles appear to change
color in their back-lit tanks.

❸ Rogers Centre

1 Blue Jay Way. **Tel** 416 341 3000.
🚇 Union, St. Andrew. **Open** daily. 📷
♿ 📷 🅦 rogerscentre.com

Opened in 1989, the Rogers
Centre was the first sports
stadium in the world to have a
fully rectractable roof. In good
weather, the stadium is open to
the elements, but in poor
conditions the roof moves into
position, protecting the players
and crowd. Four gigantic roof
panels are mounted on rails and

Lavish interior lobby of the Fairmont Royal York

take 20 minutes to cover the
playing area. The end result looks
sort of like a giant hazelnut.
However, the building's looks are
partially redeemed by a pair of
giant-sized cartoon-sculptures
on the outside wall, the creation
of a popular contemporary artist,
Michael Snow.

The stadium is home to two
major sports teams, the Toronto
Argonauts from the Canadian
Football League, and the Toronto
Blue Jays of Major League
Baseball. The centre is also used
for special events and concerts.

❹ Fairmont Royal York

100 Front St. W. **Tel** 416 368 2511.
🚇 Union. ♿ 📷 🅦 fairmont.com/
royal-york-toronto

Dating from 1929, the Fairmont
Royal York has long been one of
Toronto's preeminent hotels, and

is renowned for its plush luxury.
It was built opposite the city's
main train station for the convenience of visiting dignitaries, but
for thousands of immigrants,
the hotel was the first thing
they saw of their new city.
The hotel was designed by the
Montreal architects Ross and
Macdonald in contemporary
Beaux-Arts style.

Having undergone multi-
million-dollar renovations in
2015, the Fairmont offers
11 floors of luxury rooms, an
updated pool and a health spa.
It remains a favorite with high-
powered visitors, which have
included visiting royalty.

Union Station, across the
street from the Fairmont Royal
York, was also designed by Ross
and Macdonald and shares a
similar Beaux-Arts style. Inside,
the cavernous main hall has a
grand coffered ceiling supported
by 22 sturdy marble pillars.

The retractable roof of the Rogers Centre rears above the playing field, the site of many football and baseball games

For hotels and restaurants in this region see p354 and pp372–4. For transport information see pp410–11

Modern exterior of the Four Seasons Centre for the Performing Arts

❼ TD Gallery of Inuit Art

79 Wellington St. West. **Tel** 416 982 4051. 🚇 Union, St. Andrew. **Open** 8am–6pm Mon–Fri, (10am–4pm Sat & Sun). ♿

The TD (Toronto Dominion) Centre consists of five jet-black skyscrapers, a modern tribute to the Toronto Dominion Bank by the architect and designer Mies van der Rohe. The southern tower displays a strong collection of Inuit Art on two levels of its foyer. The exhibits were assembled as a centennial project in the 1960s. They bought over 100 pieces in a variety of materials, including caribou antler and walrus tusk, but the kernel of the collection is the stone carving. Soapstone sculptures show mythological beasts and spirits, and scenes from everyday life. Some of the finest were carved by Johnny Inukpuk (1911–2007), whose *Mother Feeding Child* (1962) and *Tattooed Woman* (1958) have a raw, elemental force.

❺ Hockey Hall of Fame

Brookfield Place, 30 Yonge St. **Tel** 416 360 7765. 🚇 Union Station, King Station. **Open** Jul, Aug & Mar break: 9:30am–6pm Mon–Sat, 10am–6pm Sun; Sep–Jun: 10am– 5pm Mon–Fri, 9:30am–6pm Sat, 10:30am–5pm Sun. **Closed** Jan 1, Dec 25, Induction Day. 🎬 ♿ 🅆 hhof.com

The Hockey Hall of Fame is a lavish tribute to Canada's national sport, ice hockey (see p42. From its simple winter beginnings on frozen lakes and ponds, the game now ignites Canadian passions like no other. The Hall of Fame's ultra-modern exhibition area is inventive and resourceful, with different sections devoted to particular aspects of the game. There are displays on everything from the jerseys of the great players, including Wayne Gretzky and Mario Lemieux, to a replica of the Montréal Canadiens' locker room in the old Forum.

The original Stanley Cup

Another section traces the development of the goalie's mask from its humble start to the elaborately ainted versions of today. Interactive displays abound, and visitors can stop pucks fired by virtual players. A 3D film that mixes archival footage with computer animation plays every 30 minutes. Another area displays a collection of trophies, including the Stanley Cup, hockey's premier award.

❻ Four Seasons Centre for the Performing Arts

145 Queen St. W. **Tel** 416 363 8231; 416 345 9595 (National Ballet of Canada). 🚇 Osgoode. ⏰ 10:30am Sun. 🎵 free concerts: noon Mon & Wed. ♿ 🅆 coc.ca; national.ballet.ca

The Four Seasons Centre for the Performing Arts is Canada's first purpose-built opera and ballet house. Completed in 2006, it is home to both the Canadian Opera Company and the National Ballet of Canada. With the world's longest freespan glass staircase and a horseshoe-shaped auditorium featuring phenomenal advancements in modern engineering and acoustical design, it stages a full range of operatic repertoires, from chamber pieces by Mozart and Handel, to some of the monumental 19th- and 20th-century works, such as Wagner's *Ring Cycle*, which require an orchestra of over 100 musicians.

The world-class Canadian Opera Company, under the directorship of Alexander Neef, is the largest producer of opera in Canada. The National Ballet of Canada, with Karen Kain as Artistic Director, is the country's premiere dance company, with more than 60 dancers.

❾ Royal Alexandra Theatre

260 King St. W. **Tel** 416 872 1212; 1 800 461 3333. 🚇 St. Andrew. ♿ 🅆 mirvish.com/theatres/ royalalexandratheatre

In the 1960s, the Royal Alexandra Theatre was about to be flattened by bulldozers, when the flamboyant "Honest Ed" Mirvish, the king of the bargain store, came to the rescue.

Façade of the Royal Alexandra Theatre, built in 1907

For hotels and restaurants in this region see p354 and pp372–4. For transport information see pp410–11

The patio at the Black Bull on Queen Street West – one of the sunniest spots for a beer in the city

Mirvish saved a fine Edwardian theater, whose luxurious interior of red velvet, green marble, and flowing scrollwork once made it the most fashionable place in Toronto. It is now one of the four Mirvish theatres. Nowadays, the "Royal Alex," as it is commonly called, stages well-known plays and big-hit Broadway musicals. Evening performances are extremely popular, and booking ahead is required. Early arrivals can enjoy the Edwardian features in the bar before the show. One block west is the Princess of Wales Theatre, which is used for Broadway-style musicals. Across the street from the Royal Alex is the striking rotunda, Roy Thomson Hall *(see p389)*, home of the Toronto Symphony Orchestra.

❾ TIFF Bell Lightbox

350 King St. West. **Tel** 416 599 8433. St. Andrew. **Open** 10am–10pm daily. For films and exhibits. 10am–7pm Sun–Thu, 10am–9pm Fri & Sat. **tiff.net**

Besides featuring an outstanding playbill of international films in its five cinemas, TIFF Bell Lightbox has grown past being only a movie theater. The venue is the main event space for the world-renowned Toronto International Film Festival and has two galleries with notable movie-related exhibitions.

❿ First Post Office

260 Adelaide St. E. **Tel** 416 865 1833. King, Queen. 501, 504. **Open** 9am–5:30pm Mon–Fri, 10am–4pm Sat, noon–4pm Sun. Donation.

In 1829, the British House of Commons founded their colonial postal service and five years later established a post office in a far-flung outpost of the newly created town of Toronto. Remarkably, Toronto's First Post Office has survived, weathering many attempts by the city to have it demolished. The only remaining example in the world of a post office dating from the British North American postal era still in operation, the First Post Office functions fully. Visitors make the trip to write a letter with a quill pen and seal it themselves with hot wax. Today's mail, however, is processed by the national service, Canada Post. The First Post Office museum houses a permanent exhibit on the early postal system and a model of the early city of Toronto.

Young visitors on Queen Street West

⓫ Queen Street West

Osgoode. Queen 501.

Through the day and into the early morning hours, Queen Street West buzzes. Students and trendsetters reinvigorated this old warehouse area in the 1980s, but nowadays the street between University and Spadina is more varied, with chic designer stores and stylish restaurants mixed in with more mainstream chain stores. Between Spadina and Bathurst, boutiques, downbeat bars, and a few second-hand stores and fabric shops remain, while most stores go progressively upmarket.

A worker at Toronto's First Post Office stamping mail by hand

Street-by-Street: Downtown

Throughout the 19th century, Yonge Street was the commercial focus of Toronto, lined with scores of shops and suppliers. It also separated the city ethnically. In 1964, with the building of the new City Hall and Nathan Phillips Square, just across from Old City Hall, Toronto's center of gravity shifted to Queen Street. South of Queen Street lies the Financial District. Gleaming concrete-and-glass tower blocks started replacing Victorian buildings in the 1960s, and today the area is packed with skyscrapers – from Mies van der Rohe's classic black Toronto Dominion Centre to the 65-story Trump Tower, which was built in 2012 and is the country's tallest mixed-use skyscraper.

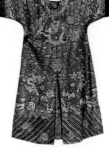

Textile Museum of Canada
This international collection features over 12,000 examples of fabrics, embroidery, and clothing through the ages.

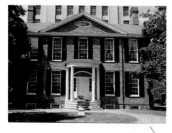

Campbell House Museum
This 19th-century home is a period piece from the days of the Victorian bourgeoisie.

Key

— Suggested route

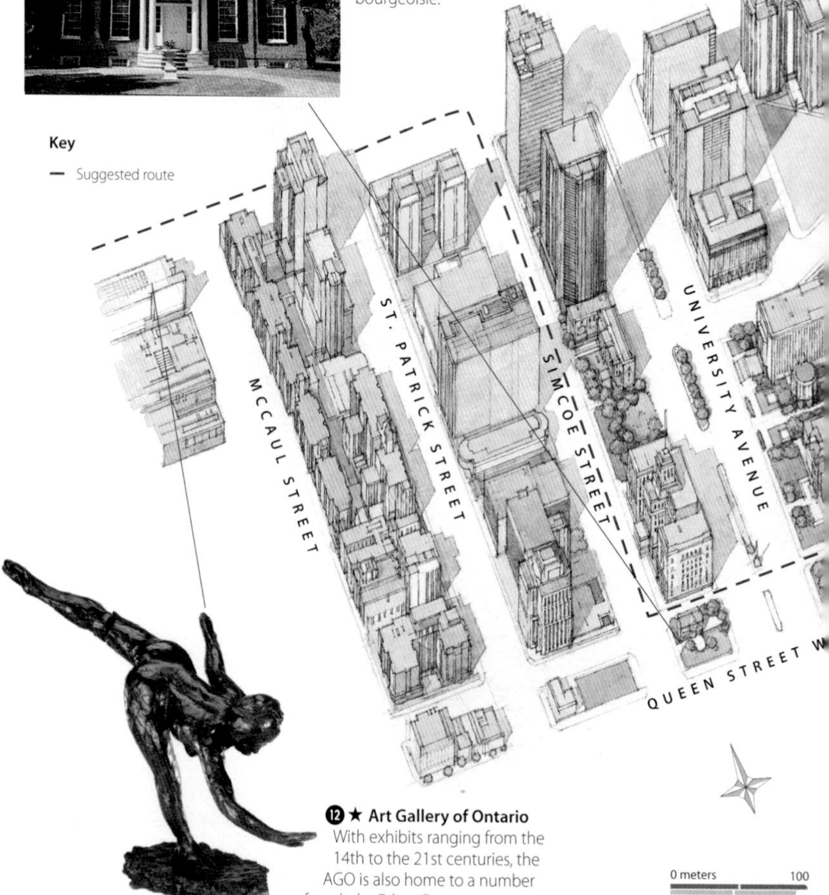

MCCAUL STREET
ST. PATRICK STREET
SIMCOE STREET
UNIVERSITY AVENUE
QUEEN STREET W

⓬ ★ Art Gallery of Ontario
With exhibits ranging from the 14th to the 21st centuries, the AGO is also home to a number of works by Edgar Degas.

0 meters 100
0 yards 100

For hotels and restaurants in this region see p354 and pp372–4. For transport information see pp410–11

Toronto Eaton Centre
Running a full block from Queen to Dundas, the Eaton Centre is downtown's largest mall. Outside its northern end, lively Yonge-Dundas Square sometimes hosts free concerts.

Locator Map
See Toronto Map pp172–3

Yonge Street is the main north–south thoroughfare of the city.

DUNDAS STREET WEST

BAY STREET

Church of the Holy Trinity
This charming Anglican church was built in the 19th century and features an elegant interior.

Nathan Phillips Square
is a lively gathering place for concerts, festivals, and civic celebrations.

⓭ ★ **Toronto City Hall**
Open since 1965, this controversial development slowly became popular with locals, who use the plaza as a skating rink in winter.

Old City Hall
Now operating as a provincial courthouse, the 19th-century Romanesque Revival-style Old City Hall sits in sharp contrast to its modern replacement across the street.

⑫ Art Gallery of Ontario

Founded in 1900 as the Art Museum of Toronto, the Art Gallery of Ontario holds one of Canada's most extensive collections of fine art and modern sculpture. This modern structure houses European works by Rembrandt, Bernini, Monet, Chagall, van Gogh, and Picasso; a superb collection of Canadian art, including the Group of Seven work *(see pp168–9)*; Inuit art; and the world's largest public collection of works by British sculptor Henry Moore. In 2008 the gallery reopened after a major expansion, designed by Toronto-born architect Frank Gehry, to accommodate an unprecedented gift of art and funding from art collector Ken Thomson.

★ African Art Collection
This late 18th-/early 19th-century reliquary figure from Gabon is just one of many exhibits in the African Collection that aim to show the relationships between art and culture in Africa.

★ Henry Moore Sculpture
The museum houses the world's largest public collection of works by Henry Moore, including *Draped Reclining Figure* (1952–3).

Tickets and information

Main entrance

The Massacre of the Innocents (c.1609)
Peter Paul Rubens's early 17th-century masterpiece, discovered in 2001, is a highlight of the Thomson Collection of European Art.

Café

Dundas Street

Key

- ▢ Contemporary art
- ▢ European art
- ▢ Temporary exhibitions
- ▢ Canadian art
- ▢ African art
- ▢ Prints, drawings, and photographs
- ▢ Non-exhibition space

Gallery Guide

The second floor houses collections of Canadian painting, with works by the "Group of Seven" (see pp168–9), and Inuit art. It also houses a significant collection of African and Oceanic art and the Henry Moore Sculpture Centre, which is home to Moore's sculptures, bronzes, and plaster casts. European art and photography are found mainly on the first floor. The Thomson Collection of Ship Models can be found on the Concourse level.

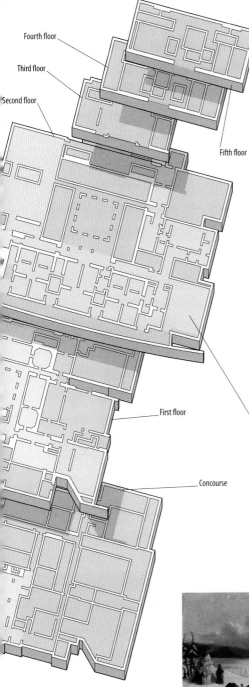

Fourth floor

Third floor

Second floor

Fifth floor

First floor

Concourse

Revamped Façade
The modern extension of the Art
Gallery of Ontario was designed
by Toronto-born, California-based
architect Frank Gehry. It was his
first building in Canada.

★ **The West Wind** (1916–17)
Tom Thomson's painting inspired a
distinctive Canadian style exemplified
by the "Group of Seven."

Scene in the Northwest (c.1845–46)
This painting by Canadian artist Paul
Kane shows British soldier and scientist
Captain John Henry Lefroy. It is part of
the Thomson Collection of Canadian Art
from the middle of the 19th century.

Built in the 1960s, the ultra-modern design of Toronto City Hall is internationally renowned

🔟 Toronto City Hall

100 Queen St. W. & Bay St.
🚇 Queen, Osgoode. 🚋 Queen 501.
Open 8:30am–4:30pm Mon–Fri. ♿

Completed in 1964, Toronto's City Hall was designed by the award-winning Finnish architect Viljo Revell. At the official opening, the Prime Minister Lester Pearson announced, "It is an edifice as modern as tomorrow," but for many cityfolk tomorrow had come too soon, and there were howls of protests from several quarters. Even now, after more than 50 years, the building appears uncompromisingly modern. It is the epitome of 1960s' urban planning, with two curved concrete-and-glass towers framing a central circular building where the Toronto councils meet. Nearby, the Old City Hall (see p181) is a grand 19th-century Neo-Romanesque edifice, whose towers and columns are carved with intricate curling patterns.

🔟 Chinatown

🚋 Queen 501, Dundas 505, College 506, Spadina 510.

The Chinese community in Toronto numbers around 531,600, over 12 percent of the city's total population. There have been several waves of Chinese migration to Canada,

the first to British Columbia in the late 1850s during the Gold Rush. The first Chinese to arrive in Toronto came at the end of the 19th century as workers on the Canadian Pacific Railway, settling in towns along the rail route. The Chinese found work in the Toronto laundries, factories, and on the railways. The last immigration wave saw prosperous Hong Kong Chinese come to live in Toronto in the 1990s.

Chinese Canadians inhabit every part of the city but are concentrated in four Chinatowns, the largest and liveliest of which is focused on Spadina Avenue, between Queen and College streets, and along Dundas Street, west of the Art Gallery of Ontario. These few city blocks are immediately different from their surroundings. The sights, sounds, and smells of the neighborhood

Vivid restaurant signs in Chinatown

are reminiscent not of Toronto but of Hong Kong. Stores and stalls spill over the sidewalks, offering a bewildering variety of Chinese delicacies, and at night bright neon signs advertise dozens of delicious restaurants.

🔟 Kensington Market

Baldwin St. & Augusta Ave. 🚋 Dundas 505, College 506, Spadina 510.
🌐 kensington-market.ca

Kensington Market is one of Toronto's most distinctive and ethnically diverse residential areas. It was founded at the turn of the 20th century by East European immigrants, who crowded into the patchwork of modest houses near the junction of Spadina Avenue and Dundas Street, and then spilled out into the narrow streets to sell their wares. The bazaar they established in their small 1930s houses has been the main feature of the area ever since.

Today, Portuguese, Jamaican, Mexican, and Vietnamese stall owners and shopkeepers rub shoulders with specialty cheese shops and high-end butchers. The lower half of Kensington Avenue, just off Dundas, is crammed with vintage clothing shops selling all manner of retro bargains, from original punk gear to flares. Baldwin is packed with grocery shops, butchers, and fishmongers, and the crazy, busy corner of Augusta and Baldwin is the epicenter of the "market." Augusta is lined with everything from empanada stalls to construction-clothing retailers.

A Torontonian samples exotic nuts in the bazaar of Kensington Market

Façade of the Ontario Parliament Building, home of the provincial legislature since 1893

⑯ University of Toronto

25 King's College Circle. **Tel** 416 978 5000. 🚇 St. George, Queen's Park. 🚋 College 506. ♿ 🚻 11am & 2pm Mon–Fri, 11am Sat. 🌐 **utoronto.ca**

The University of Toronto grew out of a Royal Charter granted in 1827 by King George IV to Toronto's King's College. Seen by the church as challenging its control of education, the new institution weathered accusations of godlessness and proceeded to swallow its rivals, becoming in the process one of Canada's most prestigious universities.

This unusual history explains the rambling layout of the present campus, a leafy area sprinkled with colleges. The best-looking university buildings are near the west end of Wellesley Street. Here, on Hart House Circle, lie the delightful quadrangles and ivy-clad walls of Hart House (1919), built in imitation of some of the colleges of Oxford and Cambridge universities in Britain. Nearby, King's College Circle contains University College, an imposing Neo-Romanesque edifice dating from 1859, Knox College with its rough gray sandstone masonry, and the fine rotunda of the university's Convocation Hall. UTAC, the University of Toronto Art Centre, has a permanent exhibition of Byzantine icons and other contemporary exhibitions. A visit to the campus can be rounded off by a short stroll along Philosophers' Walk, where the manicured lawns lead behind the Royal Ontario Museum and up to Bloor Street West.

Reminiscent of old British universities, Trinity College, University of Toronto

⑰ Ontario Parliament Building

Queen's Park. **Tel** 416 325 7500. 🚇 Queen's Park. 🚋 College 506. **Open** 8am–6pm Mon–Fri (daily from Victoria Day to Labour Day). Photo ID required except for under-16s. ♿ 🚻 🌐 **educationportal.ontla.on.ca**

There is nothing modest about the Ontario Parliament Building, a vast pink sandstone edifice that opened in 1893 and dominates the end of University Avenue. Ontario's elected representatives had a point to make. The province was a small but exceedingly loyal part of the British Empire and clamored to make its mark and had the money to do so. Consequently, the Members of Provincial Parliament (MPPs) commissioned this immensely expensive structure in the Romanesque Revival style. Finished in 1892, its main façade is a panoply of towers, arches, and rose windows decorated with relief carvings set beneath a series of high-pitched roofs.

The interior is of matching grandeur. Gilded Neo-Classical columns frame the main staircase, and enormous stained-glass windows illuminate long and richly timbered galleries. The chamber is a lavish affair, with a wealth of fine wooden carving that carries epithets urging good behavior, such as "Boldly and Rightly," and "By Courage, not by Craft."

In 1909, a fire razed the west wing, which was rebuilt in Italian marble. The stone was very expensive, so the MPPs were annoyed to find that a large amount of the marble was blemished by dinosaur fossils, which can still be seen today in the west hallway. Visitors can sometimes watch the parliament in session.

The front door of Spadina House with garlanded Victorian columns

⓲ Spadina Museum, Historic House & Gardens

285 Spadina Rd. **Tel** 416 392 6910.
🚇 Dupont. **Open** Jan–Mar: noon–5pm, Sat & Sun; Apr–Aug: noon–5pm, Tue–Sun; Sep–Dec: noon–4pm, Tue–Fri, noon–5pm, Sat & Sun.
Closed Mon; Good Fri, Dec 25, 26, Jan 1. 🅿 ♿ 🅒 Obligatory.

James Austin, first president of the Toronto Dominion Bank, had this elegant Victorian family home built on the bluff overlooking the city in 1866. The last of the Austins moved out in 1982, and the building, its contents, and gardens were acquired by the City of Toronto and the Province of Ontario. Spadina Museum has been restored to accurately reflect how the Austin family lived during the 1920s and 1930s. The general ambience appeals, but there are several enjoyable features, notably the Art Nouveau frieze in the Billiard Room and a trap door in the Palm Room that allowed gardeners to tend to the plants unseen by the family.

⓳ Gardiner Museum

111 Queen's Park. **Tel** 416 586 8080.
🚇 Museum. **Open** 10am–6pm Mon–Thu, 10am–9pm Fri, 10am–5pm Sat & Sun. **Closed** Jan 1, Dec 25. 🅿 ♿
🆆 gardinermuseum.on.ca

Opened in 1984, the Gardiner Museum is dedicated solely to ceramic art. It is the only museum of its kind in North America, and is considered one of the world's great specialty museums. Skillfully displayed, the collection traces the history of ceramics, with a detailed focus on its principal developmental stages. These start with Pre-Columbian pottery and the museum's fascinating displays of ancient pieces from Peru and Mexico that incorporate several grimacing fertility gods.

Examples of brightly colored *maiolica* (glazed, porous pottery) include painted pots made in Italy from the 15th and 16th centuries. Cheerfully decorated everyday wares are complemented by later Renaissance pieces relating classical myths and history. English delftware (tin-glazed earthenware) is also well represented in the collection. The 18th-century pieces gathered from France, Austria, Germany, and England are superb – particularly the

The Greeting Harlequin Meissen ceramic figure

collection of *commedia dell'arte* figures. These are derived from the Italian theatrical tradition of comic improvisation with a set of stock characters, notably the joker Harlequin. Intricately decorated in rainbow colors, these figurines were placed on dinner tables by the aristocracy to delight, impress, or even to woo their special guests.

The porcelain here is stunning, with many examples of exquisite Meissen from the 18th century. Packed in its own specially made leather carrying case to accompany a fine lady owner on her travels, a special feature is the embellished tea and chocolate service dating from the mid-18th century. Each tiny cup has intricate scenes of a harbor or of merchants and travelers surrounded in gold. The porcelain collection also contains over 100 finely decorated scent bottles from all over Europe.

⓴ Royal Ontario Museum

See pp188–9.

㉑ Bata Shoe Museum

327 Bloor St. W. **Tel** 416 979 7799.
🚇 St. George. **Open** 10am–5pm Mon–Wed, Fri & Sat, 10am–8pm Thu, noon–5pm Sun. **Closed** Good Friday, Dec 25. 🅿 ♿
🆆 batashoemuseum.ca

The Bata Shoe Museum was opened in 1995 to display the extraordinary range of footwear collected by Sonja Bata, a member of the eponymous shoe manufacturing family, a worldwide concern that sells footwear in 60 countries. To be sure her collection was seen to best effect, Sonja had the prestigious contemporary Canadian architect Raymond

The modern exterior of the Bata Shoe Museum

Moriyama design the building – an angular, contemporary affair complete with unlikely nooks and crannies created to look like a chic shoebox.

The collection is spread over several small floors and features three changing exhibitions developing a particular theme, as well as regularly rotated items selected from the museum's substantial permanent collection. More than a temple to fashion, the museum treats shoes as important ethnological pieces, illustrating not only changes in technology, but also shifting values and attitudes. Entire ways of life can be gleaned from the design of these beautiful objects, from climate and profession to gender and religion.

One fixed feature in the museum is the exhibition entitled "All About Shoes," which provides the visitor with an overview of the functions and evolution of footwear. It begins with a plaster cast of the earliest-known footprint, discovered four million years after it was made in Tanzania, and has an interesting section on medieval pointed shoes. A second permanent feature is the section on celebrity footwear. This rotating display could include Marilyn Monroe's red stiletto heels, a pair of Elton John's platforms, or Michael Johnson's gold lamé sprinting shoes. A fashion section, called Fashion Afoot, includes *haute-*

Traditional *Paduka* footwear, the Bata Shoe Museum

A lazy Sunday afternoon at Trattoria Nervosa in upscale Yorkville

couture shoes by Roger Vivier and Christian Louboutin. There is also a display of unusual and improbable footwear including unique French chestnut-crushing boots and a pair of US army boots made for use in the Vietnam War, the sole of these is shaped to imitate the footprint of a Viet Cong irregular.

㉒ Yorkville

🚇 Bay.

In the 1960s, tiny Yorkville, in the center of the city, was the favorite haunt of Toronto's hippies. With regular appearances by counter-cultural figures such as Joni Mitchell, it was similar to New York's Greenwich Village. The hippies then moved on, and Yorkville's brick-and-timber townhouses were colonized by upscale shops and fashionable restaurants.

Luxury hotels, designer boutiques, private art galleries, fine jewelers, and quality shoe stores all jammed into the neighborhood. Yorkville and Cumberland Avenues became the center of all this big spending, as did the elegant and discreet shopping complexes that lead off them.

The area has seen considerable reconstruction and redevelopment in recent years. Condos and the luxurious Four Seasons Hotel on Bay have risen up at its edges. To experience the lifestyle, pop into Pusateri's Fine Foods at the corner of Yorkville Avenue and Bay. For the international luxury brands such as Prada, Versace, and Tiffany's, walk down to Mink Mile on Bloor, which has a line of expensive chain stores running from Avenue Road to Yonge Street.

⑳ Royal Ontario Museum

Founded in 1912, the Royal Ontario Museum (ROM) is one
of the largest museums in North America. It holds a vast and
extraordinarily wide-ranging collection drawn from the fields
of fine and applied art, the natural sciences, and archaeology.
Special highlights include the dinosaur gallery, and an Asian
Arts gallery featuring Chinese sculpture and architecture and
Japanese art and culture. Opened in 2007, the ROM's building
is perhaps the most controversial in the city. The Michael Lee-
Chin Crystal addition is a bold crystalline formation designed
by architect Daniel Libeskind, which seems to burst out of the
original Edwardian edifice.

Key

▨ Asian arts and architecture
▨ Natural history
▢ Textiles and costume
▨ Canada galleries
▢ World cultures
▨ ROM Kids Boutique
▨ Temporary exhibitions
▨ Special exhibitions
▨ Non-exhibition space

The futuristic-looking Royal Ontario Museum

Gallery Guide

*Each floor of the ROM has two distinct
sections: the galleries in the original
building, and those in the stark,
angular Michael Lee-Chin Crystal.
The Totem Pole Stairs lead to the
original building, and the Stair of
Wonders to the Crystal. Ramps and
catwalks link the two sections.*

Hands-on
Biodiversity

The Green Room
This elegant English parlour dates from the 1750s.
One of several room settings featured in the
European galleries, it boasts the original green,
paneled walls, which were popular among the
gentry of the time.

Canada Gallery: First Peoples
This spacious gallery celebrates
Canadian culture, with a dynamic
approach to the country's
aboriginal traditions.

Tickets and
information

ROM Boutique

Level 1
(street level)

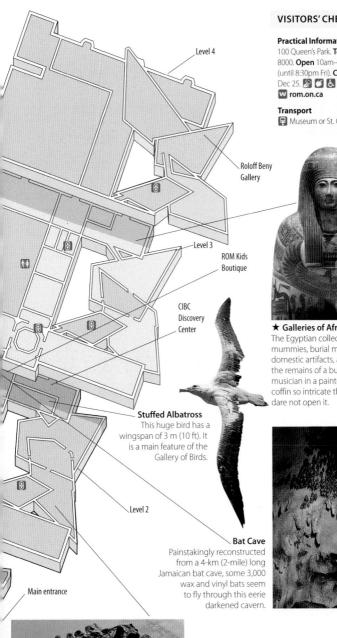

Level 4

Roloff Beny
Gallery

Level 3

ROM Kids
Boutique

CIBC
Discovery
Center

Stuffed Albatross
This huge bird has a
wingspan of 3 m (10 ft). It
is a main feature of the
Gallery of Birds.

Level 2

Main entrance

★ **Galleries of Africa: Egypt**
The Egyptian collection includes
mummies, burial masks, and
domestic artifacts, and contains
the remains of a buried court
musician in a painted golden
coffin so intricate that scholars
dare not open it.

Bat Cave
Painstakingly reconstructed
from a 4-km (2-mile) long
Jamaican bat cave, some 3,000
wax and vinyl bats seem
to fly through this eerie
darkened cavern.

★ **Dinosaur Gallery**
The most popular gallery in the ROM is
on the second floor of the Michael
Lee-Chin Crystal, with hundreds of
iconic and unusual dinosaur skeletons,
fossilized plants, insects, and marine life.

❷❸ Fort York

250 Fort York Blvd. **Tel** 416 392 7500.
🚋 511, 509. **Open** 10am–5pm daily
(Sep–mid-May: 10am–4pm Sat & Sun).
Closed Good Fri, Dec 25–26, Jan 1.
🅿️ ♿ 🅿️ 🆆 fortyork.ca

The British originally established
Fort York in 1793 to maintain
a military and naval presence
on Lake Ontario in the
turbulent years that followed
the American Revolution.
The fort was attacked and
largely destroyed by US forces
during the War of 1812
(see p52). The British rebuilt
the fort after the battle, and
their presence helped fuel the
growth of the Town of York,
now Toronto.
    The Fort has been
restored to its late wartime
appearance, with soldiers'

Bustling crowd at the St. Lawrence Market in downtown Toronto

barracks, officers' quarters
and fortifications. Today,
its defensive walls enclose
Canada's largest collection
of original buildings from
the War of 1812.
    The fort's visually striking
Visitor Centre displays exhibits

on varying themes that
explore the site's history
spanning 200 years. In
addition, Fort York attracts
thousands of visitors
during the festivals and
special events held here
throughout the year.

❷❹ Casa Loma

This unusual Edwardian house was designed
by E. J. Lennox, the man responsible for
Toronto's Old City Hall. With its combination
of architectural elements, the house is a
remarkable tribute to Sir Henry Pellatt (1859–
1939), one of the most influential industrialists
of early 20th century Canada. He made a
fortune in hydroelectric power during
the early 1900s, harnessing the
strength of Niagara Falls for
electricity. In 1906, Pellatt decided
to build himself a castle. Three
years and Can $3.5 million later,
construction was halted due to
the outbreak of World War I.

The Study hid secret
doors in its wooden
panels, one leading to
Sir Henry's
wine cellar.

★ **The Great Hall**
Oak beams support a ceiling
18-m (60-ft) high, in a hall featuring
a 12-m (40-ft) tall bay window.

The Terrace looks over
delightful formal gardens
and a fountain against a
backdrop of hills and
rhododendron forest.

The Bathroom was designed for
Sir Henry's personal use. It contains a
free-standing shower with six heads
and features lavish decoration.

㉕ St. Lawrence Market

91 Front St. E. ⊕ King. **Open** 8am–6pm Tue–Thu, 8am–7pm Fri, 5am–5pm Sat. North Market building: Farmers' Market 5am–5pm Sat, Antiques Market dawn–5pm Sun. 🔲 stlawrencemarket.com

Arrive with an appetite and join the crowds queuing for peameal bacon sandwiches, wood-oven baked bagels, and the most succulent Portuguese *churrasco* chicken rolls in the city. With over 100 vendors, the main market building, called the South Market, is the city's go-to spot for fresh seafood, fine meats, exotic cheeses, and top-quality fruits and vegetables. The complex's North Market building is being rebuilt. The weekend farmers' and antiques markets are held in a temporary structure at the Esplanade, just south of the main market building.

㉖ Distillery District

Mill St., between Parliament & Cherry sts. **Tel** 416 364 1177. 🚋 504 to Parliament, then 5-min walk south. **Open** daily. 🔲 thedistillerydistrict.com

The cobbled lanes and preserved Victorian industrial buildings of the pedestrianised shopping and entertainment area, the Distillery District, were once the home of the whisky distillery of Gooderham and Worts. The area consists of shops, studios, art galleries, bars, and restaurants spread out through 47 redeveloped buildings. Many of the distillery's original features have been retained, such as the pipes and trellises that crisscross above the red-brick alleys. The area is anchored by the Mill Street Brewery, a fitting landmark, and great place to sample locally made beer. Craft shops and fine art galleries abound, and packed patios with choice restaurants and cafés seem to be on every corner.

Pedestrians walking on the cobbled streets of the historic Distillery District

Façade of house and formal gardens
Two ha (5 acres) of garden add to the charm of the estate with perennial borders, roses, lawns, and woodland.

VISITORS' CHECKLIST

Practical Information
1 Austin Terrace. **Tel** 416 923 11 71. **Open** 9:30am–5pm daily. **Closed** Dec 25. 🎫 🎧 ♿ 🚫 📷 🔲 casaloma.ca

Transport
⊕ Dupont.

★ **Conservatory**
White walls offset the stained-glass dome. The marble flower beds conceal steam pipes for the rare plants.

Children learning to canoe and exploring the lagoons of the Toronto Islands

㉗ The Toronto Islands

🚇 Spadina 510 from Union, then 🚌 Queen's Quay. ℹ️ 416 392 8193 (ferry). 🅦 **torontoisland.com**

In Lake Ontario, just offshore from the city, the low-lying Toronto Islands, connected by footbridges, shelter Toronto's harbor and provide easy-going recreation in a car-free environment. Here, amid the cool lake breezes, visitors can escape the extremes of the summer heat, which can reach up to 35°C (95°F). Whatever the weather, there are views of the CN Tower (see p176).

It takes about an hour to walk from one end of the islands to the other. In the east is Ward's Island, a sleepy residential area; Centre Island, home to the Centreville Amusement Park for children, is in the middle, and to the west lies Hanlan's Point, which has one of the country's few public clothing-optional beaches.

㉘ The Beaches and Scarborough Bluffs

Beaches: 🚋 Queen 501.

The Beaches is one of Toronto's most beguiling neighborhoods, its leafy streets running up from the lakeshore. The area lies to the east of downtown, between Woodbine Avenue and Victoria Park Avenue. Queen Street East, the main thoroughfare, is liberally sprinkled with excellent cafés and shops. The Beaches was a restrained and quiet neighbor-

hood, but its long, sandy beach and boardwalk have made it extremely desirable. Rollerblading and cycling are popular here – a 3-km (2-mile) boardwalk runs along the beach and is very busy in summer. Many of Toronto's beaches have been approved for swimming; call 416 392 7161 for water-quality reports.

At its eastern end, the Beaches borders Scarborough, the large suburb whose principal attraction is also along the rocky lakeshore. Here, the striking Scarborough Bluffs, outcrops of rock made from ancient sands and clay, track along Lake Ontario for 16 km (10 miles). A series of parks provides access: Scarborough Bluffs and the Cathedral Bluffs parks offer great views of jagged cliffs, and Bluffers Park is ideal for picnics.

㉙ Toronto Zoo

361A Old Finch Ave., Scarborough. **Tel** 416 392 5900. 🚇 Kennedy, then 🚌 86A (weekdays all year plus weekends in summer). **Open** Mar 23–Apr 30 & Sep 8–Oct 31: 9:30am–4:30pm Mon–Fri (to 6pm Sat & Sun); May 1–Sep 7: 9am–7pm daily; Nov 1–Dec 31: 9:30am–4:30pm daily. **Closed** Dec 25. 🅿️ 🚹 🅦 **torontozoo.com**

Toronto has one of the world's best zoos, occupying a large slice of the Rouge River Valley.

The animals are grouped according to their natural habitats, both outside, amid the mixed forest and flatlands of the river valley, and inside large, climate-controlled pavilions.

Visitors can tour the zoo by choosing one of the marked

trails, or hop aboard the Zoo-mobile, a 30-minute ride with commentary that gives an excellent overview. It takes about four hours to see a good selection of animals, including such Canadian species as moose, caribou, and grizzly bear. There is also a pair of giant pandas and a polar bear enclosure. Splash Island provides a spot for young visitors to cool off in the water, amid walrus and beaver sculptures.

㉚ Aga Khan Museum

77 Wynford Dr. 🚇 Eglinton, then 🚌 100 Flemingdon Park east to Wynford Dr. **Tel** 416 646 4677. **Open** 10am–6pm Tue–Sun (to 8pm Wed). **Closed** Dec 25. 🎟️ free 4–8pm Wed. 🚹 📷 🅦 **agakhanmuseum.org**

The first North American museum dedicated to the arts of Muslim civilization, the Aga Khan Museum connects visual and live arts from the Iberian Peninsula to China through exhibitions, education programs, and a full roster of performances in its 350-seat auditorium. The museum's main floor includes a Persian-style salon and rotating displays of the permanent collection, whose exquisite manuscripts, drawings, paintings, decorated ceramics, metalwork, and architectural ornamentation date from the 8th to the 19th centuries. Four temporary exhibitions are

A mother and baby orangutan at Toronto Zoo

A hands-on exhibit at the Ontario Science Center

displayed on the second floor every year, highlighting the continuum of artistic traditions from early Muslim civilizations to the present day.

Designed by Japanese architect Fumihiko Maki, the museum shares a beautiful 6.8-ha site, complete with a landscaped park and formal garden, with the Ismaili Centre in Toronto, designed by Charles Correa.

Collection and architecture tours are offered from Tuesday to Sunday; Garden Tours are offered seasonally.

31 Ontario Science Centre

770 Don Mills Rd. **Tel** 416 696 3177. ▣ Eglinton or Pape, then ▥ Eglinton 100 or Don Mills 25. **Open** 10am–4pm Mon–Fri, 10am– 8pm Sat, 10am–5pm Sun. **Closed** Dec 25. ▨ ▧ ▥ ontariosciencecentre.ca

One of Toronto's most popular sights, the Ontario Science Centre attracts children in droves. They come for the center's interactive displays and hands-on exhibits exploring and investigating all manner of phenomena, from the Solar System to the human brain. At KidSpark children aged eight and under can make music, experiment with tracks, balls, and cogs, and join a construction team to build a house, while older kids will appreciate the AstraZeneca Human Edge gallery.

32 Black Creek Pioneer Village

1000 Murray Ross Parkway, Cnr Steeles Ave. W. & Jane St. **Tel** 416 736 1733. ▣ Finch, then ▥ 60. **Open** May & Jun: 9:30am–4:30pm Mon–Fri, 11am–5pm Sat & Sun; Jul–Aug: 10am–5pm Mon–Fri, 11am–5pm Sat & Sun; Sep–Dec 23: 9:30–4pm Mon–Fri, 11am–4:30pm Sat & Sun. **Closed** Jan–Apr (except March break). ▨ ▧ ▥ blackcreek.ca

Over the years, some 40 19th-century buildings have been moved to historic Black Creek Pioneer Village in the northwest of the city from other parts of Ontario. Inevitably, the end result is not entirely realistic – no Ontario village ever looked quite like this – but this living history showpiece is still great fun. Staff in period costume demonstrate traditional skills such as candle-making, baking, and printing. Among the more interesting buildings are the Doctor's House from 1860, and the Laskay Emporium general store, which shows the array of goods that could be bought. The Tinsmith Shop is manned by skilled craftsmen, and there is a Masonic Lodge meeting room. Five buildings are credited to Daniel Stong, a 19th-century pioneer; his pig house, smoke house, grain barn, and two contrasting homes – the first a crude log shack, the second a civilized house with a brick fireplace and a garden planted with herbs.

33 McMichael Canadian Art Collection

10365 Islington Ave., Kleinburg. **Tel** (905) 893 1121. **Open** May–Oct: 10am–5pm daily; Nov–Apr: 10am–4pm Tue–Sun. **Closed** Dec 25. ▨ ▧ ▥ mcmichael.com

In Kleinburg, about 30 minutes' drive north of downtown Toronto, Robert and Signe McMichael built themselves a fine log-and-stone dwelling overlooking the Humber River Valley. The McMichaels were also avid collectors of Canadian art, and in 1965 they donated their house and paintings to the province of Ontario. The art collection has greatly increased since then and, with more than 6,000 pieces, is now one of the most extensive collections of Canadian art in the province.

The focus of the McMichael is the work of the Group of Seven (*see pp168–9*), with the permanent galleries dedicated to displaying a selection of their works. The keynote paintings are characteristically raw and forceful landscapes illustrating the wonders of the Canadian wilderness. Both Tom Thomson (a famous precursor of the Group) and Lawren Harris are well represented. There are also exhibitions of contemporary, Aboriginal, and Inuit art.

34 Museum of Contemporary Art

158 Sterling Rd. **Tel** (416) 395 0067. **Open** see website for details. ▨ ▧ ▥ museumofcontemporaryart.ca

Previously located on arty Queen Street, this collection of Canadian contemporary art has found a new home in the Tower Automotive Building, an icon of Toronto's industrial heritage in the emerging Lower Junction district. The new design is based around the concept of the "agora": a communal space for the exchange and discussion of ideas, surrounded by not only the best and most innovative Canadian 21st-century art, but also guest exhibitions of international standard.

OTTAWA AND EASTERN ONTARIO

Eastern Ontario is justly famous for its history and natural beauty. The myriad lakes and waterways that dominate the landscape here once served as trade highways through the wilderness for First Nations people and explorers. Today they form a beautiful natural playground, with spectacular opportunities for outdoor activities such as boating, fishing, hiking, and skiing. The Saint Lawrence is one of the world's great waterways and begins near the small, historic city of Kingston. North of Lake Ontario lies the Canadian Shield, with the ancient lakes, rocks, and forest that epitomize Canada. A favorite with many Canadian vacationers, Algonquin Provincial Park is one of the country's most famous wilderness areas. Also popular is the picturesque Kawartha Lakes region. Rising majestically over the Ottawa River, Canada's capital is a storehouse of national history and stately architecture that attracts over 7.7 million visitors each year.

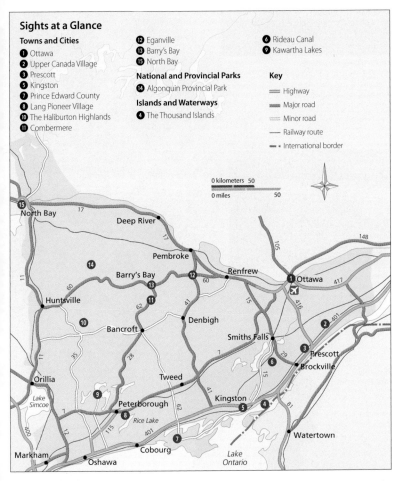

Sights at a Glance

Towns and Cities
1. Ottawa
2. Upper Canada Village
3. Prescott
5. Kingston
7. Prince Edward County
8. Lang Pioneer Village
10. The Haliburton Highlands
11. Combermere
12. Eganville
13. Barry's Bay
15. North Bay

National and Provincial Parks
14. Algonquin Provincial Park

Islands and Waterways
4. The Thousand Islands

6. Rideau Canal
9. Kawartha Lakes

Key

≡≡ Highway

▬▬ Major road

═══ Minor road

— Railway route

—‧— International border

◀ Aerial view of Parliament Hill, Ottawa   **For map symbols** *see back flap*

❶ Street-by-Street: Ottawa

Ottawa was a compromise choice for Canada's capital, picked in part because of the rivalry between the English and French and the cities that grew into today's urban giants, Toronto and Montreal. This compromise has, from its foundation in 1826, grown into a city with an identity all its own. Named capital of the Dominion of Canada in 1857, Ottawa has a fine setting on the banks of the Ottawa and Rideau rivers. Far more than just the political capital, the city has grown into a mix of English- and French-speaking residents and historic and modern buildings with plenty of attractions to keep its six million annual visitors busy.

A Mountie leading his horse by the Parliament buildings

The **Centennial Flame** was first lit in 1967 to commemorate a century of Confederation. It burns continually.

★ **Parliament Buildings**
The Changing of the Guard takes place outside at 10am daily from late June to late August. The ceremony adds to the grandeur of this seat of government.

Rideau Canal
Built in the mid-19th century, the Canal is now a playground for visitors, its banks lined with grassy cycling and walking paths.

WELLINGTON STREET

National War Memorial
Annually, on November 11, a memorial service takes place here to honor Canada's war veterans.

Fairmont Château Laurier is a luxury hotel, and arguably Canada's most famous. It has offered sumptuous accommodation to Canada's great and good since it was built in 1912.

Major's Hill Park
This peaceful, open-air space in the heart of the busy capital is marked by a statue of an Anishinabe scout, in honor of the First Nations' role in the development of Canada.

Nepean Point is a spot from which the whole of central Ottawa can be seen.

VISITORS' CHECKLIST

Practical Information

🗺 883,000. ℹ️ Capital Information Centre, 90 Wellington St., (613) 239 5000. 🎿 Winterlude (Feb), Canadian Tulip Festival (May). 🅦 **ottawatourism.ca**

Transport

✈ 18 km (11 miles) south of the city. 🚌 265 Catherine St., 200 Tremblay Rd. 🚆 200 Tremblay Rd., 3347 Fallowfield Rd.

0 meters 100
0 yards 100

Key

— Suggested route

Royal Canadian Mint
This Can $20 Olympic skiing coin was created by the Mint as a souvenir for the 1988 Winter Olympic Games in Calgary. The mint produces only special-edition and investment pieces.

MACKENZIE AVENUE

SUSSEX DRIVE

★ **National Gallery of Canada**
Featuring more than 25,000 artworks, this is the country's premier collection of the fine arts, housed in this outstanding granite and glass building.

Exploring Ottawa

The core of the capital is relatively contained, and many of the top sights can be easily accessed on foot. Running south through the city, the Rideau Canal is Ottawa's recreation ground year round, from boating and strolling during summer to skating across its icy surface in the freezing Canadian winter. The National Arts Centre is a focus for theater, music, and dance; history and art buffs can spend days visiting museums and galleries, both large and small. Just across the river, in the city of Gatineau, is one of the country's best museums, the Canadian Museum of History. Ottawa is a city with many festivals too; notably Winterlude, a three-weekend February celebration, while in spring the Canadian Tulip Festival transforms the city into a sea of flowers.

Away from downtown, the suburban National Capital Region is overflowing with museums for every enthusiast. Attractions include the Canada Agriculture and Food Museum and the Canada Aviation and Space Museum.

Cash register from a 19th-century shop at the Bytown Museum

Ottawa's majestic Neo-Gothic Parliament Buildings

🏛 Parliament Buildings

Parliament Hill, 111 Wellington St. **Tel** (613) 992 4793. **Open** Jul–Apr: 9am–4:30pm daily; May & Jun: 9am–7:30pm daily. **Closed** Jan 1, Jul 1, Dec 25. 🔲 parl.gc.ca

Dominating the skyline, the country's government buildings overlook downtown Ottawa in a stately manner. Undaunted by the tall buildings that have crept up around them in the 150 years since they became Ottawa's center of power, the East and West blocks glow green above the city because of their copper roofing. The Gothic-Revival sandstone buildings were completed in 1860. Located on a 50-m (164-ft) hill, the Parliament offers

a view of the Ottawa River. The Parliament Buildings are distinctly reminiscent of London's Westminster, both in their Victorian Neo-Gothic style and in their position. Largely destroyed in a fire in 1916, all the buildings are now restored to their former grandeur.

The Parliament Buildings can be toured year round. Visitors can climb the Peace Tower for glorious views of the city, and watch proceedings of the Senate and House of Commons whenever they are in session. Hand-carved sandstone and limestone character-ize the interior of the government chambers. In the summertime, Mounties patrol the neat, grassy grounds outside the Parliament. On July 1, which is Canada Day, Parliament Hill is the site of a large outdoor concert and celebration.

🏛 Bytown Museum

Ottawa Locks. **Tel** (613) 234 4570. **Open** mid-May–mid-Oct: 10am–5pm daily (to 8pm Thu; to 7pm mid-Jun–Aug); mid-Oct–mid-Dec & Feb–mid-May: 11am–4pm Thu–Mon. 🔲 bytownmuseum.com

Housed in Ottawa's oldest stone building (1827), the Bytown Museum traces the history of Ottawa's early years from the

Canada Aviation & Space Mu[...]

Macdonald-Cartier Bridge

GATINEAU

Ottawa River

BOTELER
BOLTO[...]

Royal Canadian Mint ⑤

CA[...]

Champlain Statue

No[...]
C[...]

④ National Gallery of Canada

Alexandra Bridge

Major' Hill Par[...]

Bytown Museum ②

Fair
Ch[...]
Laurier

Centre Block

①
Parliament Buildings

West Block

Supreme Court of Canada 🅿

STREET

SPARKS

O'CONNOR ST

Library and Archives Canada

WELLINGTON

BANK

Canadian War Museum

QUEEN STREET
ALBERT STREET
SLATER STREET
KENT STREET

LAURIER

BAY STREET

AVENUE

GLOU[...]

LYON ST

LAURIER STREET

Bus S[...]
2 km

🛫
Ottawa International Airport 15 km (9 miles)

Canada Agriculture & Food Museum 5 km (3 miles)

| 0 meters | | 500 |
| 0 yards | | 500 |

Key

▨ Street-by-Street map: see pp196–7

construction of the Rideau Canal through the rough and tumble days of Bytown, to the city's emergence as Canada's capital and beyond. The British Royal Engineer in charge of building the Rideau Canal, Lt. Colonel John By, set up his headquarters on this location in 1826. While work was underway, the building was used as a storehouse for military supplies and silver coins. The museum hosts exhibitions, guided tours, and family events.

The elegant Wilfrid's Restaurant at the Château Laurier

⊞ Fairmont Château Laurier

1 Rideau St. **Tel** (613) 241 1414. ♿
🆆 fairmont.com/laurier-ottawa

This wonderful stone replica of a French château is a fine example of the establishments built by railroad companies in the early 1900s. It has attracted both the great and the good since it opened as a hotel in 1912. Centrally located next door to Parliament Hill, its interior features large rooms with high ceilings. The hotel attracts an upscale clientele, including celebrities, government mandarins, and politicians. Zoé's Lounge, a restaurant with soaring columns, chandeliers, and palms, lit by an atrium, is a wonderful place for lunch, as is the hotel's larger restaurant, Wilfrid's.

⊞ Canadian War Museum

1 Vimy Pl. **Tel** (819) 776 7000, 1 800 555 5621. **Open** mid-May–mid-Oct: 9:30am–6pm daily (to 8pm Thu); mid-Oct–mid-May: 9:30am–5pm daily (to 8pm Thu). 🎟 Free Jul 1, Nov 11. ♿
🆆 warmuseum.ca

Canadians may have a reputation as a peaceful people but they have seen their share of the world's battlefields. This museum, housed in a stunning modern building close to Parliament Hill, looks at the country's military history and at how this history has shaped the nation and its people. Exhibits range from the earliest wars fought on Canadian soil between the French and the British to the present day. The LeBreton Gallery houses an extensive collection of military technology including vehicles, artillery, and other artifacts. The Beaverbrook Collection of War Art contains 13,000 works and is one of the largest collections of military art in the world. The Memorial Hall offers a space for quiet reflection. Its concrete walls are reminiscent of the rows of gravestones in Allied war cemeteries. The hall's sole artifact is the headstone from the grave of Canada's Unknown Soldier. The museum's Regeneration Hall, with its view of the Peace Tower on Parliament Hill, represents hope for a better future.

Demobilization sign at the War Museum

Sights at a Glance

Bordeleau Park

ROSE STREET
KING STREET
ST. PATRICK ST.
ST. PATRICK STREET
JULES AVENUE
MURRAY STREET
CLARENCE STREET
DALHOUSIE STREET
YORK STREET
GEORGE STREET
KING EDWARD AVENUE
NELSON STREET
CHAPEL STREET
FRIEL STREET
RIDEAU STREET
BESSERER STREET
STEWART STREET
CUMBERLAND STREET
WALLER ST.
NICHOLAS STREET
WILBROD STREET
OSGOODE STREET

⑦ ByWard Market
⑧ Laurier House

LAURIER AVENUE EAST

Conference Centre
National Centre

⑨
QUEEN
COLONEL BY DRIVE
Rideau Canal
ELIZABETH DR.
Confederation Park

Canada Science & Technology Museum
🚉 Train Station
3 km (2 miles)

Canadian Museum of Nature

🏛 Royal Canadian Mint

320 Sussex Dr. **Tel** (613) 993 8990,
1 800 276 7714. **Open** daily. 🚗 👍
📷 Obligatory, book ahead. **W** mint.ca

Founded in 1908 as a branch
of the British Royal Mint, this
one no longer produces regular
Canadian cash currency. Instead,
it strikes many special-edition
coins and Maple Leaf bullion
investment coins. The mint also
processes about 70 percent of
the country's gold in its refinery,
which is among the largest in
North America.

Tours take place throughout
the day; book to ensure you see
the process that turns sheets
of metal into bags of shiny gold
coins. Weekend tours may be
less interesting, as the production
lines are unlikely to be running.

The façade of Ottawa's imposing Cathédrale
Notre-Dame

🏠 Cathédrale Notre-Dame

Cnr Sussex Dr. & St. Patrick St.
Tel (613) 241 7496. **Open** 11:30am–
6pm Mon, 10am–6pm Tue–Sat,
8am–8:30pm Sun. 👍 🏠

Built between 1841 and 1865,
La Cathédrale Notre-Dame,
with its twin spires, is Ottawa's
best-known Catholic church.
It is situated in the ByWard
Market area and features a
spectacular Gothic-style
ceiling. The windows, carvings,
and the huge pipe organ are
also well worth seeing. Philippe
Parizeau (1852–1938) carved
the woodwork in mahogany.
In niches around the sanctuary,
there are wooden etchings of
prophets and apostles, crafted
by Louis-Philippe Hébert (1850–
1917), now painted to look like
stone. Joseph-Eugène Guigues,
the first bishop of Ottawa,

ByWard Market is known as a lively
area of Ottawa

oversaw the completion of
Notre-Dame, and his statue
is outside the basilica.

🏛 ByWard Market

Bounded by Cumberland, Sussex,
George, and St. Patrick sts. **Tel** (613)
562 3325. **W** byward-market.com

This neighborhood bustles
all year round; outdoors in
the summer, inside in winter.
The area is located just east
of Parliament Hill, across the
Rideau Canal, and offers a
colorful collection of craft
shops, cafés, boutiques, bistros,
nightclubs, and farmers' market
stalls. Special attractions include
the food market in the ByWard
Market Building on George
Street, and the cobblestoned
Sussex Courtyards. The cafés are
among Ottawa's most popular
places to dine.

🏠 Laurier House

335 Laurier Ave. E. **Tel** (613) 992 8142.
Open mid-May–Jun & Sep–mid-Oct:
10am–5pm Thu–Mon; July & Aug:
10am–5pm daily. 🚗 **W** pc.gc.ca/
laurierhouse

A national historic site, Laurier
House, a Victorian town house
built in 1878, served as the
chief residence of two notable
Canadian prime ministers,
Sir Wilfrid Laurier and William
Lyon Mackenzie King. Beautifully
furnished throughout, it houses
memorabilia, papers, and
personal possessions of both
former national leaders.

Rideau Canal

W pc.gc.ca/rideaucanal

Built in the mid-19th century,
the Rideau Canal, a UNESCO
World Heritage Site, travels
through lakes and canals from
Ottawa to the city of Kingston
(see p204). The canal flows
through the capital, providing
an attractive pastoral sight,
with its walking and cycling
paths bordering the water.
Once used for shipping, the
canal is now a recreational area.
In summer, visitors stroll along
its banks, while through
Ottawa's freezing winter the
canal, at 7.8 km (4.8 miles)
long, turns into the world's
largest skating rink. It is popular
with locals during the winter
festival, and also as a means
of commuting to work.

🏛 Canada Agriculture
and Food Museum

Experimental Farm Dr, just off Prince
of Wales Dr. **Tel** (613) 991 3044.
Open Mar–Oct: 9am–5pm daily;
Nov–Feb: 9am–5pm Wed–Sun.
Closed Dec 25. 🚗 👍 📷
W cafmuseum.techno-science.ca

This museum at the Central
Experimental Farm, a crop
research station and National
Historic Site, allows visitors to

Children can get close to animals at the Canada Agriculture and Food Museum

The National Arts Centre, at the heart of the city skyline

explore the sights and sounds of farm life through animals, exhibitions, hands-on demonstrations, and delicious foods. The farm's livestock barns and show cattle herds are especially popular with children, and everybody loves to discover what's cooking in the demo kitchen.

⛭ National Arts Centre
53 Elgin St. **Tel** (613) 947 7000. **Open** daily. 🅿 🅲 ♿
🆆 nac-cna.ca

Completed in 1969, the National Arts Centre (NAC) has four stages, an elegant canal-side restaurant, and a summer terrace. The original building, designed by noted Canadian architect Fred Lebensold, expanded in 2017 to include a dramatic windowed Elgin Street entrance with stellar views of the capital. Many Canadian and international artists in dance, theater, and music, including the National Arts Centre Orchestra, perform here regularly. Reserving tickets well in advance is recommended.

⛭ Canadian Museum of Nature
240 McLeod St. **Tel** (613) 566 4700, 1 800 263 4433. **Open** Jun–Aug: 9am–6pm Sat–Wed, 9am–8pm Thu & Fri; Sep–May: 9am–5pm Tue–Sun (to 8pm Thu). 🅿 🆆 nature.ca

Canada's national natural history museum entertains with its well thought-out

galleries highlighting birds, mammals, aquatic creatures, fossils and dinosaurs. The Vale Earth Gallery has beautiful geological specimens, and kids will enjoy the Arctic marine exhibit, where they can captain a research vessel. In the Animalium, visitors get a close up look at giant snails, tarantulas, and scorpions.

⛭ Canada Science and Technology Museum
1867 St. Laurent Blvd. **Tel** (613) 991 3044. **Open** check website for opening hours. 🅿 🆆 cstmuseum. techno-science.ca

Following extensive refurbishment this museum reopened in 2017, to coincide with Canada's 150th birthday celebrations. Exhibits include a wide range of fascinating displays exploring Canada's space history, transportation through the ages, and modern and industrial technology, with an immersive Children's Gallery.

⛭ Canada Aviation and Space Museum
Aviation & Rockcliffe Parkways. **Tel** (613) 993 2010. **Open** May–early Sep: 9am–5pm daily; early Sep–Apr: 10am–5pm Wed–Mon. 🅿
🆆 casmuseum.techno-science.ca

This huge building near Rockcliffe Airport houses over 130 aircraft, which have flown both in war and peace. A replica of the famous 1909 *Silver Dart*, the first aircraft to fly in Canada, is here, as is the nose cone from the *Avro Arrow*, the supersonic superfighter that created a political crisis in Canada, when the government halted its development in the 1950s. The *Spitfire*, valiant friend of the Allies in World War II, features alongside historic bush planes such as the *Beaver* and early passenger carrier jets. Displays detail the exploits of Canadian war heroes, while the Walkway of Time traces the history of world aviation.

The glassy exterior of the Canadian Aviation and Space Museum

National Gallery of Canada

Opened in 1988, the National Gallery of Canada provides a
spectacular home for the country's impressive collections
of art. Located near the heart of the capital, architect
Moshe Safdie's memorable pink granite-and-glass
edifice is architecture as art in its own right.
The National Gallery is one of the three largest
museums in the country, and is Canada's top
art gallery, with excellent collections of
both national and international exhibits.
The museum is a short stroll from
the Rideau Canal and Major's Hill Park.

Library

No. 29 (1950)
A vivid example of Jackson Pollock's
idiosyncratic "drip" technique, this was part of
an enormous canvas carefully cut into sections,
hence its title, *No. 29*.

★ Rideau Street Chapel
Set in a peaceful inner courtyard,
this 1888 chapel was saved from
bulldozers nearby and moved
here for safety.

Key

- [ ] Special exhibition space
- [ ] Canadian and Indigenous galleries
- [ ] Contemporary art
- [ ] International galleries
- [ ] Prints, drawings, and photographs
- [ ] Canadian Photography Institute
- [ ] Non-exhibition space

Gallery Guide

*On its first level the gallery houses the world's largest
collection of Canadian art. It also features international
displays and major traveling exhibitions. The second level
contains the European and American galleries and the
Canadian Photo Institute Galleries. Visitors can relax in the
two courtyards of the establishment.*

Inuit sculpture
This is represented in ancient
and modern forms; *Aurora Borealis
decapitating a young man*, shown
here, dates from 1965.

National Gallery Plaza
Measuring 9 m (30 ft) high, the giant spider "Maman" by sculptor Louise Bourgeois (1911–2010) towers over the plaza. Designed in 1999 and cast in 2003, the bronze sculpture features a pouch of 26 white marble eggs.

VISITORS' CHECKLIST

Practical Information
380 Sussex Dr. **Tel** (613) 990 1985.
Open May–Sep: 9:30am–6pm daily (to 8pm Thu); Oct–Apr: 9:30am–5pm Tue–Sun (to 8pm Thu). **Closed** Jan 1, Good Friday, Dec 25. 🏛 For special exhibitions. 🎫 📷 📱
w gallery.ca

Transport
🚌 1, 3, 9.

Level 2

Virgin and Child with an Angel (c.1535–39)
Francesco Salviati (1510–63) was taught by painter Andrea del Sarto in Florence. The placement of the divine group in a grotto, with a landscape in the distance, recalls del Sarto's work.

Level 1

★ **The Jack Pine** (1916)
In many ways the father of Canada's nationalist art movement of the early 20th century, Tom Thomson of the Group of Seven first attracted notice with his vivid, sketchy, impressionist paintings of the Ontario landscape, here shown with a brightly colored oil of a provincial tree framed in wilderness.

Ground level

Auditorium

Michael and Sonja Koerner Family Atrium
This delightful airy space is a sharp contemporary contrast to the treasures of yesteryear that abound in most of the rest of the gallery. Water Court is used as a contemplative gallery for sculpture.

Lecture hall

Main entrance

❷ Upper Canada Village

13740 County Road 2, Morrisburg. Exit 758 off Hwy 401, then drive south to County Road 2. **Tel** (613) 543 4328. **Open** early May–Labour Day: 9:30am–5pm daily; Labour Day onwards for two weeks: 9:30am–5pm Wed–Sun. 🅿️ 🎫 ♿ 🆆 uppercanadavillage.com

This recreated 19th-century town, in eastern Ontario, is made up of 40 authentic pre-Confederation (1867) buildings, relocated from the surrounding area to save them from flooding during construction of the Saint Lawrence Seaway in the 1950s. Today, it is preserved as a tourist attraction and is a colorful reminder of the province's social history. Costumed villagers work in the blacksmith's forge and the sawmill, while tinsmiths and cabinetmakers employ the tools and skills of the 1860s. A bakery, cheese factory, and general store are in operation. Special events include themed weekends and battle re-enactments. Adjacent to Upper Canada Village, the **Battle of Crysler's Farm Memorial** commemorates those who died in the War of 1812.

❸ Prescott

🏙️ 4,300. 🚌 ℹ️ 360 Dibble St. W. (613) 925 2812. 🆆 **prescott.ca**

The major attractions in this 19th-century town are its architecture and access to the Saint Lawrence River. Prescott's refurbished waterfront area and its busy marina make for a pleasant waterside stroll. Some

visitors come for the excellent scuba diving. There are 22 wrecks that sank between the late 19th- and mid-20th-centuries within an hour's drive.

Fort Wellington National Historic Site, east from the center of town, attracts many visitors. Originally built during the War of 1812 and rebuilt in 1838, four walls and some buildings remain. These include a stone block-house, which is now a military museum, incorporating refurbished officers' quarters.

🏛️ Fort Wellington
Prescott. **Tel** (613) 925 2896. **Open** mid-May–Jun & Sep–mid-Oct: 10am–5pm Thu–Mon; Jul & Aug: 10am–5pm daily. ♿ 🆆 **pc.gc.ca/fortwellington**

❹ The Thousand Islands

ℹ️ 10 King St. E., Gananoque, (613) 381 8427.
🆆 **1000islandstourism.com**

The Saint Lawrence River, one of the world's great waterways, is a gateway for ocean-going vessels traveling through the Great Lakes. Few stretches of the trip compare in charm or beauty to the Thousand Islands, an area that contains a scattering of over a thousand tiny islands, stretching from just below Kingston downriver to the waterside towns and cities of Gananoque, Brockville, Ivy Lea, and Rockport. Cruises of different lengths, including some full-day cruises that go to the curious Boldt's Castle, leave from Gananoque, Rockport, and Brockville.

Boldt's Castle, on Heart Island across the US border in the state of New York, was a folly built by millionaire hotelier George Boldt and abandoned in grief when his wife died in 1904. It was Oscar, Boldt's head chef at

A sailing vessel travels the Thousand Islands

the Waldorf Astoria in New York City, who, entertaining summer guests at the castle, concocted Thousand Island salad dressing.

❺ Kingston

🏙️ 123,000. 🚆 🚉 🚌 ⛴️ ℹ️ 209 Ontario St., (613) 548 4415; 1 888 855 4555. 🆆 **visitkingston.ca**

Once a center for ship building and the fur trade, Kingston was briefly (1841–44) the capital of the United Province of Canada (see p54). Constructed by generations of shipbuilders, the city's handsome limestone buildings reflect a dignified lineage. Kingston is still one of the freshwater sailing capitals of North America and the embarkation point for many local cruises. It is also home to more museums than any other town in Ontario. The restored British bastion **Fort Henry National Historic Site of Canada** is a living military museum brought to life by guards in bright scarlet period uniforms who are trained in drills, artillery exercises, and traditional fife and drum music of the 1860s. Canada's top military training university, the Royal Military College of Canada (RMCC), is also based in the city and the RMCC Museum, housed in an 1846

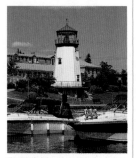

The 1838 lighthouse overlooks the pleasure boats of Prescott's marina

Guard at Fort Henry

Martello Tower, tells the story of today's cadets and their fore-bears (open in summer only).

A short walk away from the Visitor Information Centre and City Hall lies the **Marine Museum of the Great Lakes**. There are displays on the history of the Great Lakes and the ships that sailed on them, including the first ship built for the Lakes here in 1678. The museum also contains a 3,000-ton icebreaker, a fine example of shipbuilding in the last century. Boats are lifted 4 m (13 ft) at Kingston Mills lock station. Located about 7 km (4 miles) north of downtown Kingston, it is a great spot for walking, boat watching and picnicing.

🎫 **Fort Henry**
Kingston. **Tel** (613) 542 7388.
Open mid-May–Aug: 9:30am–5pm daily. 🅿 ♿ 🅆 forthenry.com

🏛 **Marine Museum of the Great Lakes**
55 Ontario St. **Tel** (613) 542 2261.
Open Mar–mid-May & Sep–Nov: 10am–4pm Mon–Fri; mid-May–Aug: 10am–4pm daily. 🅿 ♿
🅆 marmuseum.ca

❻ Rideau Canal

🅆 pc.gc.ca/rideaucanal

The Rideau Canal, originally a defensive barrier protecting Canada against the Americans and finished in 1832, stretches for 200 km (124 miles). The best way to enjoy this sparkling necklace of scenic waterway is by boat. A great feat of 19th-century engineering, which includes 47 locks and 24 dams, the system – a UNESCO World Heritage destination – allows boaters to float through tranquil woods and farmland, scenic lakes, and to stop in quaint villages, as well as visit the **Rideau Canal Visitor Centre** at Smith's Falls. The canal north of Kingston also contains a number of provincial parks which offer canoe routes. Also popular is the 400-km (249-mile) Rideau Trail, a hiking system linking Kingston and Canada's capital city, Ottawa.

🏛 **Rideau Canal Visitor Centre**
34 Beckwith St. S., Smiths Falls.
Tel (613) 283 5170. **Open** mid-May–Labour Day daily. 🅿 donation. ♿

❼ Prince Edward County

ℹ 116 Main St., Picton. **Tel** (613) 476 2421. 🅆 prince-edward-county.com

Loved by foodies, the once-quiet Prince Edward County is a burgeoning getaway destination. There are now dozens of vineyards squeezed onto the island. It is surrounded by Lake Ontario and the Bay of Quinte, and is sometimes referred to as Quinte's Isle. The island is also home to two camping and sunbathing beaches in Sandbanks Provincial Park. There, mountains of fine sand reach 25 m (82 ft) and are considered one of the most significant fresh-water dune systems in the world.

United Empire Loyalists *(see p52)* settled in the County following the American Revolution (1775), founding engaging small towns and a strong farming industry. Visitors can absorb the local historic architecture by traveling along the country roads and the Loyalist Parkway, either cycling or by car.

Historic house along the main street of Picton in peaceful Prince Edward County

❽ Lang Pioneer Village

104 Lang Rd., Keene (10 km/6 miles east of Peterborough). **Tel** (705) 295 6694. **Open** mid-May–mid-Jun: 10am–3pm Mon–Fri; mid-Jun–Labour Day: 10am–4pm daily. 🅿 ♿
🅆 langpioneervillage.ca

Located on the tiny Indian River 4 km (2 miles) north of Keene, Lang Pioneer Village is a traditional representation of Canada's past, featuring 20 restored 19th-century buildings, heritage gardens, and farmyard animals. Visitors can watch an ancient restored grist mill in action, and workers in period costumes display ancient skills while telling stories of what life was once like. Blacksmiths ply their trade in an authentic smithy. Villagers also demonstrate traditional methods of keeping the home clean, mending clothing, and cooking meals over open fires. Throughout the summer season, visitors can enjoy traditional afternoon teas at the Keene Hotel (1–3pm, for an additonal cost). Special events across the year focus on how the pioneers celebrated the various harvests and Christmas. There are also regular music workshops.

A view of the Rideau Canal passing through Westport village

Lush bullrushes surround a pond in Petroglyphs Provincial Park

❾ Kawartha Lakes

🛈 1400 Crawford Dr., Peterborough. **Tel** (705) 742 2201, 1 800 461 6424. 🌐 thekawarthas.ca

The Kawartha Lakes are part of the 386-km (240-mile) Trent–Severn Waterway that runs from Lake Ontario to Georgian Bay and was originally built in the 19th century. Today the area is a playground for vacationers, with water-based activities including cruises and superb fishing. Renting a houseboat from one of the riverside towns is a popular way of exploring the locality. At the center of the region lies the friendly city of Peterborough, notable for its university, pleasing waterfront parks, and the world's largest hydraulic liftlock. Thirty-four km (21 miles) north lies the Curve Lake Reserve's Whetung Ojibway Centre, one of the best places locally for aboriginal arts and crafts.

Petroglyphs Provincial Park, 55 km (34 miles) to the north of Peterborough, is better known to locals as the "teaching rocks" for the 900-plus aboriginal rock carvings cut into the park's white marble outcrops. Rediscovered in 1954, these preserved symbols and figures of animals, boats, spirits, and people were made by spiritual leaders to record their dreams and visions. Today the stones are housed in a huge glass building, built around them in 1984 to protect them from frost. The stones remain respectfully regarded to this day as a sacred site of the Aboriginal Peoples.

🏞 Petroglyphs Provincial Park
2249 Northey's Bay Rd, Woodview, off Hwy 28. **Tel** (705) 877 2552. **Open** mid-May–mid-Jun & Sep–mid-Oct: Wed–Sun; mid-Jun–Sep: 10am–5pm daily. 🚫 ♿ ♿

❿ The Haliburton Highlands

🛈 12340 Hwy 35, Minden. **Tel** (705) 286 1777, 1 800 461 7677. 🌐 myhaliburtonhighlands.com

The Haliburton Highlands are one of Ontario's year-round outdoor destinations, renowned for their forests, lakes, and spectacular scenery. In the summer, visitors enjoy boating, fishing, and swimming in this region. In fall, busloads of tourists travel to appreciate the celebrated seasonal colors; others come for the deer hunting. Winter brings snowmobilers, dog-sledders, and cross country skiers to the area's pristine forests and provincial parks.

The arty village of Haliburton is packed with cottage owners and vacationers in the summer. Head up Skyline Park Road for stunning views over the area, especially in autumn. Scenic Highway 35 winds its way through exceptional scenery from Minden north to the considerable charms of Dorset. The fire tower atop a rock cliff overlooking the village gives spectacular views of the Lake of Bays and the surrounding area. This spot is a fantastic viewing point for the myriad colors of Ontario's fall trees.

⓫ Combermere

🏠 250. 🛈 Ottawa Valley Tourist Association, (613) 732 4364. 🌐 ottawavalley.travel

The village of Combermere is a central point for people heading to a number of provincial parks in Eastern Ontario, including Algonquin (*see pp208–9*), Carson Lake, and Opeongo River. Along with Wilno and Barry's Bay, Combermere is one of three Madawaska Valley townships, and is a good tourist center for fuel and refreshments. A few kilometers (2 miles) south of Combermere lies the **Madonna House Pioneer Museum**. Founded by Catherine Doherty, this Catholic lay community has grown to have mission outposts around the world. It is managed by volunteers, who live on its cooperative farm. Since 1963, a recycling program has been raising money for the world's poor.

The Madonna at the Pioneer Museum

🏛 Madonna House Pioneer Museum
Hwy 517. **Tel** (613) 756 3713. **Open** mid-May–mid-Oct: 10am–5pm Tue–Sat. 🌐 madonnahouse.org

The breathtaking foliage of Lake Haliburton, Ontario

Cottages outside Barry's Bay, a popular spot for vacationers

⑫ Eganville

🗺 1,300. ℹ Ottawa Valley Tourist Association (613) 732 4364.
ⓦ ottawavalley.travel

This Highway 60 village with its little restaurants and gas station provides a handy tourist center for visitors to this picturesque region. Local attractions include the **Bonnechere Caves**, 8 km (5 miles) away. The caves were at the bottom of a tropical sea 500 million years ago. Gradually raised over millennia from the ocean bed, they are covered with fossils of primitive life forms. The privately owned site is open for tours in summer.

🏠 **Bonnechere Caves**
Tel (613) 628 2283. **Open** mid-May– mid-Oct: daily. 🗺 🖼
ⓦ bonnecherecaves.com

⑬ Barry's Bay

🗺 1,250. ℹ Ottawa Valley Tourist Association, (613) 732 4364.
ⓦ ottawavalley.travel

An attractive little town, Barry's Bay has a sizeable Polish population, as does its neighbor Wilno, site of the first Polish settlement in Canada. The area is home to many craftspeople and artisans, who sell their wares in the local villages. Barry's Bay has a meticulously restored railway station, originally built in the 1890s and now housing a collection of railway memorabilia. It also acts as a visitor information and community arts center, South of 60. Year-round sports

facilities can be found at nearby Kamaniskeg Lake and Redcliffe Point, both of which are popular places for renting cottages. Perched high on a hill, nearby Wilno overlooks scenic river valleys and boasts the fine church and grotto of St. Mary's.

🚂 **Barry's Bay Railway Station**
19503 Opeongo Line (Highway 60).
Tel (613) 756 5885. **Open** May–Jun & Sep–mid-Oct: 10am–4pm Thu–Mon; Jul–Aug: 10am–6pm daily; mid-Oct–Dec: 10am–4pm Wed–Sat.

⑭ Algonquin Provincial Park

See pp208–9.

⑮ North Bay

🗺 54,000. ✈ 🚂 🚌 ℹ 1375 Seymour St., (705) 472 8480.

Billing itself as the Gateway to the Near North, North Bay sits at the eastern end of Lake Nippissing, 350 km (217 miles) north of Toronto. The region's most famous natives are undoubtedly the Dionne quintuplets, born in 1934 (see below).

Lake Nippissing nearby is famous for its fishing and wilderness scenery. Boat cruises across the lake follow the old French explorers route. North Bay makes a good starting-point for trips to the area's many vacation spots.

The Dionne Quints

The hamlet of Corbeil experienced a natural miracle on May 28, 1934: the birth of the Dionne quintuplets. Annette, Emilie, Yvonne, Cecile, and Marie were the five identical girls born to Oliva and Elzire Dionne. The Quints' combined weight at birth was only 6.1 kg (13 lbs 5 oz), and the babies' lungs were so tiny that small doses of rum were required daily to help them breathe. Experts put the chances of giving birth to identical quintuplets at 1 in 57 million. The girls became international stars, attracting countless visitors to North Bay during the 1930s. A Quint industry sprang up with curiosity-seekers flocking to watch the young girls at play. The Dionne homestead, a traditional small farmhouse, became a museum dedicated to the quints, and while it moved to North Bay in 1985, it remained a popular attraction for many years.

⑭ Algonquin Provincial Park

To many Canadians, Algonquin, with its lush maple and pine woods, sparkling lakes, and plentiful wildlife, is as familiar a symbol of Canada as is Niagara Falls.

Founded in 1893, this is the oldest and most famous park in Ontario, stretching across 7,635 sq km (2,948 sq miles) of wilderness. Wildlife abounds; visitors have a chance to see beavers, moose, and bears in their natural habitats, and the park echoes with the hauntingly beautiful call of the loon, heard often in northern Ontario. Every August, on Thursday evenings, "wolf howls" are organized; park staff give a lecture on wolf ecology followed by imitation howls to encourage a nearby pack to respond. Opportunities for outdoor activities are plentiful; most visitors like to try one of the 2,000 km (1,243 miles) of canoe routes through the forested interior.

Killarney Lodge
This is one of the park's rental lodges, rustic buildings that are popular during the spring, summer, and fall.

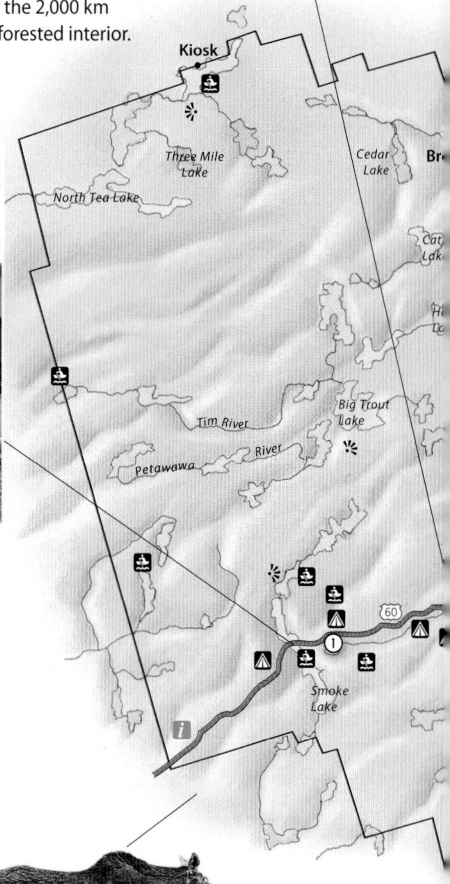

Canoe Lake
Two thousand km (1,243 miles) of canoe trails surround the park. They range from beginner and family routes, some as short as 6 km (4 miles), to 70-km (43-mile) treks for the experienced. Routes are well planned and marked.

KEY

① The **Algonquin Art Centre** exhibits international art displays, with a focus on nature and wildlife. It has both an indoor and outdoor gallery, with a gazebo, where art activities are conducted.

② The **Algonquin Logging Museum** tells the story of this traditional local trade, illustrated by a river dam and log-moving "alligator."

Moose near Highway 60
Visitors can usually spot a few moose in spring, especially near lakes and salty puddles by roadsides, which these huge animals seem to love.

Map labels: Kiosk, Three Mile Lake, North Tea Lake, Cedar Lake, Br, Ca, Lake, B, Le, Big Trout Lake, Tim River, River, Petawawa, 60, Smoke Lake

Lake Opeongo
With over 2,400 lakes, Algonquin is justly celebrated for its matchless fishing opportunities. Lake Opeongo, one of the largest in the park, is famous for its abundance of lake trout and smallmouth bass.

Park Visitor Centre
Opened in 1993 to celebrate Algonquin's centenary, the center contains a museum with displays on the park's wildlife, and natural and cultural history.

(map)

Radiant Lake
Petawawa
River
Lake Travers
Lake Lavielle

0 km 10
0 miles 10

②
ℹ
Whitney

Brewer Lake
This scenic fishing lake is situated on the Highway 60 corridor. A 56-km (35-mile) journey through the park, this beautiful route is popular with daytrippers and those wishing to catch the major sights in limited time.

Key
▬ Major road
▬ Minor road
— Provincial Park boundary

For map symbols *see back flap*

THE GREAT LAKES

The varied charms of the Canadian Great Lakes region, from the sleepy little farming towns bordering Lake Erie to the island-studded bays of Lake Huron and the wilderness encircling Lake Superior, tend to be obscured by the fame of Niagara Falls. One of the world's most famous sights, the falls occur where the Niagara River tumbles 50 m (164 ft) between Lakes Erie and Ontario. First Nations tribes once lived on the fertile land around the area's lakes and rivers, and fur traders used the lakes as a vital waterway. The War of 1812 resulted in British Canada securing trade rights to the northern lakeshores. Between 1820 and 1850 settlers established farms, and mining and forestry flourished in Canada's then-richest province. Today, the Trans-Canada Highway follows the untamed northern shores of Lakes Huron and Superior for over 1,000 km (620 miles), eventually reaching the bustling port of Thunder Bay. The Agawa Valley Tour Train, which leaves from Sault Ste. Marie, offers popular day-long rail tours into the wilderness.

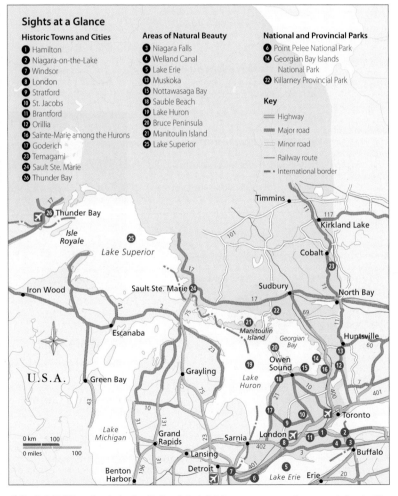

Sights at a Glance

Historic Towns and Cities
1. Hamilton
2. Niagara-on-the-Lake
7. Windsor
8. London
9. Stratford
10. St. Jacobs
11. Brantford
12. Orillia
16. Sainte-Marie among the Hurons
17. Goderich
23. Temagami
24. Sault Ste. Marie
26. Thunder Bay

Areas of Natural Beauty
3. Niagara Falls
4. Welland Canal
5. Lake Erie
13. Muskoka
15. Nottawasaga Bay
18. Sauble Beach
19. Lake Huron
20. Bruce Peninsula
21. Manitoulin Island
25. Lake Superior

National and Provincial Parks
6. Point Pelee National Park
14. Georgian Bay Islands National Park
22. Killarney Provincial Park

Key
=== Highway
▬▬ Major road
=== Minor road
— Railway route
--- International border

◄ Morning light shining on the rocky shoreline of the Bruce Peninsula, Ontario   **For map symbols** *see back flap*

The imposing façade of Dundurn Castle in Hamilton

❶ Hamilton

🏙 520,000. ✈ 🚉 🚌 📧 ℹ 28
James St., N. (905) 546 2666.
🌐 tourismhamilton.com

The city of Hamilton sits at the
extreme western end of Lake
Ontario, some 70 km (43 miles)
from Toronto. It was known as
a steel town, and the city's mills
used to churn out around
60 percent of Canada's total
production. Despite the town's
industrial roots, is a likeable place.
Dundurn Castle is a Regency-
style villa dating from the 1830s,
whose interior holds a fine
collection of period furnishings.
It was built for the MacNabs,
one of the most influential
families in Ontario, who
included in their number Sir
Allan Napier MacNab, a Premier
of Canada from 1854–6.

Another sight is the **Royal
Botanical Gardens**, comprising
forests, marshes, and small
lakes over some 1,093 ha
(2,700 acres) on the
north side of Hamilton
harbor. Among the
notable gardens here
are a fine Rose Garden;
the Laking Garden
with its peonies and
irises; and the heavily
perfumed Lilac
Arboretum. The Rock Garden,
built in 1935, contains an
amphitheater, conifers, tulips,
and cherry trees.

Also in town, the Canadian
Warplane Heritage Museum
has a display of more than 40
operational aircraft dating from
World War II to the jet age.

Rose in the Royal
Botanical Gardens

🏛 **Dundurn Castle**
610 York Blvd. **Tel** (905) 546 2872.
Open noon–4pm Tue–Sun. 🎫
🎥 obligatory. ♿ partial.

🌹 **Royal Botanical Gardens**
680 Plains Rd. West. **Tel** (905) 527
1158. **Open** daily. 🎫 ♿ 🌐 rbg.ca

❷ Niagara-on-the-Lake

🏙 15,000. 🚌 ℹ 26 Queen St., (905)
468 4263. 🌐 niagaraonthelake.com

Niagara-on-the-Lake is a
charming little town of elegant
clapboard mansions and leafy
streets, set where the mouth of
the Niagara River empties into
Lake Ontario. The town was
originally known as Newark and
under this name it became the
capital of Upper Canada (as
Ontario was then known) in
1792. Just four years later, the
British decided to move the
capital farther away from the US
border, and chose York (now
Toronto) instead. It was
a wise decision. The
Americans crossed
the Niagara River and
destroyed Newark in
the War of 1812 *(see
pp52–3)*. The British
returned after the war
to rebuild their
homes, and the Georgian town
they constructed has survived
pretty much intact.

Today, visitors take pleasure
in exploring the town's lovely
streets, but there is one major
attraction, **Fort George National
Historic Site**, a carefully restored
British stockade built in the

1790s just southeast of town.
The earth and timber palisade
encircles ten replica buildings
including three blockhouses,
the barracks, a guard house, and
the officers' quarters. There is also
a powder magazine store, where
all the fittings were wood or brass,
and the men donned special
shoes without buckles to reduce
the chance of an unwanted
explosion. Guides in old-style
British military uniforms describe
life in the fort in the 19th century.

Niagara-on-the-Lake is also
home to the annual Shaw
Festival, a prestigious theatrical
season featuring the plays of
George Bernard Shaw and other
playwrights; it runs from April
to October.

🏛 **Fort George National
Historic Site**
51 Queen's Parade, Niagara Pkwy.
Tel (905) 468 6614. **Open** May–Oct:
10am–5pm daily (weekends only Apr
& Nov); Dec–Mar: noon–4pm Sat &
Sun. 🎫 ♿ 🌐 pc.gc.ca/fortgeorge

Gardens in front of an early-19th-century
inn at Niagara-on-the-Lake

❸ Niagara Falls

See pp216–19.

❹ Welland Canal

ℹ 1932 Welland Canals Parkway,
St. Catharines, (905) 984 8880.
Open daily. 🌐 wellandcanal.com

Welland Canal was built to
solve the problem of Niagara
Falls. The Falls presented an

Aerial view of the small village of Long Point on the shore of Lake Erie

obstacle that made it impossible for boats to pass between lakes Ontario and Erie. Goods had to be unloaded on one side of the Falls and then carted to the other, a time-consuming and expensive process. To solve the problem, local entrepreneurs dug a canal across the 45-km (28-mile) isthmus separating the lakes early in the 19th century, choosing a route to the west of the Niagara River.

The first Welland Canal was a crude affair, but subsequent improvements have created today's version, which has eight giant locks adjusting the water level by no less than 99 m (324 feet). A remarkable feat of engineering, the canal is capable of accommodating the largest of ships. You can drive alongside the northerly half of the canal, on Government Road from Lake Ontario to Thorold, where seven of the eight locks are situated. The viewing platform at the Welland Canals Centre at Lock No. 3 in St. Catharines provides a great vantage point and has an information center detailing the canal's history. Ships sail the canal from April to December.

❺ Lake Erie

ℹ️ 660 Garrison Rd., Fort Erie, (905) 871 1332. 🆆 **forterie.ca**

Lake Erie is named after the First Nations people who once lived along its shores. The Erie were renowned for their skills as fishermen. Some 400 km (249 miles) long and an average of 60 km (37 miles) wide, Lake Erie is the shallowest of the Great Lakes and separates Canada from the US. Its northern shore is one of the most peaceful parts of Ontario, with a string of quiet country towns and small ports set in rolling countryside. Reaching out from the Canadian shoreline are three peninsulas, one of which has been conserved as the Point Pelee National Park *(see p214)*, home to a virgin forest and, during spring and summer, thousands of migrating birds.

About 30 km (19 miles) south of Niagara Falls, the small town of Fort Erie lies where the Niagara River meets Lake Erie, facing its sprawling US neighbor, Buffalo. The massive Peace Bridge links the two, and most people cross the border without giving Fort Erie a second look. They miss one of the more impressive of the reconstructed British forts that dot the Canada-US border. **Old Fort Erie** is a replica of the stronghold, destroyed by the Americans in the War of 1812. Entry is across a drawbridge, and the interior holds barracks, a powder magazine, and officers' quarters. The fort's battlefield is the site of one of the War of 1812's bloodiest battles, fought here during the siege of the fort in 1814.

🏛️ **Old Fort Erie**
350 Lakeshore Rd. **Tel** (905) 871 0540. **Open** mid-May–Oct: daily. 🅿️ ♿ partial. 🆆 **niagaraparks.com**

A merchant ship on the Welland Canal near the town of Welland

❻ Point Pelee National Park

Tel (519) 322 2365. **Open** daily. 🏕️
♿ 🚻 🅦 pc.gc.ca /pointpelee

A long, fingerlike isthmus, Point Pelee National Park sticks out into Lake Erie for 20 km (12 miles) and forms the southernmost tip of Canada's mainland. The park has a wide variety of habitats including marshlands, open fields, and ancient deciduous forest. These woods are a rarity, as they are one of the few places in North America's Carolinian Life Zone where many of the trees have never been logged. The profusion of species creates a junglelike atmosphere, with red cedar, black walnut, white sassafras, hickory, sycamore, and sumac, all struggling to reach the light.

This varied vegetation attracts thousands of birds, which visit on their spring and fall migrations. Over 370 species have been sighted here, and they can be observed from lookout points and forest trails. Every fall, hosts of orange-and-black monarch butterflies can also be seen here.

Contemporary painting at Windsor Art Gallery

A marshland boardwalk trail winds through Point Pelee and has good observation spots along the way. Bikes and canoes can be rented at the start of the boardwalk, and there is a concession stand here. Farther into the park, the visitor center features displays of local flora and fauna.

Water cascades at the main entrance of Windsor's Casino

❼ Windsor

🏙️ 211,000. ✈️ 🚗 🚆 🚌 🛈 333 Riverside Drive W., (519) 255 6530.
🅦 visitwindsoressex.com

A car-manufacturing town, just like its American neighbor Detroit, Windsor and its factories produce hundreds of US-badged vehicles every day. Windsor has clean, tree-lined streets and a riverside walkway, but its most noted attraction is a riverside Casino that draws thousands of visitors. The city has many lively bars and cafés, the best of which are along the first three blocks of the main street, Ouellette. Also of interest, the nearby **Art Gallery of Windsor**, also on the riverside, is noted for its excellent visiting, exhibitions.

During Prohibition, millions of bottles of alcohol were smuggled from Windsor into the US across the Detroit River. Visitors can tour the Italiante Canadian Club Brand Center, which includes whisky tasting.

From Windsor, it is an easy 20-km (12-mile) drive south along the Detroit River to the British-built Fort Malden at Amherstburg. Not much is left of the fort, but there is a neatly restored barracks dating from 1819, and the old laundry now holds an interpretation center. This relates the fort's role in the War of 1812 *(see pp52–3)*, where the English plotted with the Shawnee to invade the US.

🏛️ **Art Gallery of Windsor**
401 Riverside Dr. W. **Tel** (519) 977 0013.
Open Wed–Sun. ♿ 🅦 agw.ca

❽ London

🏙️ 370,000. ✈️ 🚗 🚆 🚌 🛈 267 Dundas St., (519) 661 5000, 1 800 265 2602. 🅦 londontourism.ca

Likeable London sits in the middle of one of the most fertile parts of Ontario and is the area's most important town. It is home to the respected University of Western Ontario, which has a striking modern art gallery and a campus with dozens of Victorian mansions. In addition, the few blocks that make up the town center are notably refined and well tended. The finest buildings in the center are the two 19th-century cathedrals, Saint Paul's, a red-brick Gothic-Revival edifice, built for the Anglicans in 1846, and the more ornate, Saint Peter's Catholic Cathedral, erected a few years later. In the

Kayakers alongside the boardwalk at Point Pelee National Park

northwest of the city, the Museum of Ontario Archaeology focuses on the 1,100-year history of the settlement of the area. The Lawson Iroquoian Village here is a reconstruction of a 500-year-old one, once occupied by the Neutral peoples, with elm longhouses and cedarwood palisades.

Reconstruction of a 500-year-old longhouse at Lawson Village

❾ Stratford

🚹 31,000. 🚌 ℹ️ 47 Downie St., 1 800 561 7926.
🌐 **visitstratford.ca**

In 1830, an innkeeper called William Sargint opened the "Shakespeare Inn" beside one of the rough agricultural tracks that then crisscrossed southern Ontario. The farmers who

The Underground Railroad

Neither underground nor a railroad, the name "Underground Railroad" (UGRR) was founded by abolitionists in the 1820s. The UGRR helped slaves from the southern United States to escape to both Canada and the free northern states. It was a secretive organization, especially in the South where the penalties for helping a slave to escape were severe. Slaves were moved north from safe house to safe house right up to the end of the American Civil War in 1865. Reverend Josiah Henson was one of those who escaped on the UGRR, and later founded a school for ex-slaves. Harriet Beecher Stowe's 1851 abolitionist novel *Uncle Tom's Cabin* was based on his life story.

Reverend Josiah Henson

settled nearby called the local river the "Avon" and named the town that grew up here "Stratford," after William Shakespeare's home town.

In 1952, local journalist Tom Patterson (1920–2005) organized a Shakespeare Festival. This first event was a humble affair held in a tent, but since then the festival has grown into one of Canada's most important theatrical seasons, lasting from May to early November (www.stratfordfestival.ca). The leading plays are still Shakespearean, but other playwrights are showcased too, including modern works.

Stratford is an attractive town with plenty of green lawns, riverside parks, and swans. The town is geared toward visitors, offering countless guesthouses and several good restaurants. The visitor center produces a book with information and photographs of all the town's bed-and-breakfasts. They also organize heritage walks, which pass by the town's many historic buildings. One architectural highlight is the Victorian town hall, with its turrets. Stratford has a plethora of art galleries, as well as craft boutiques and other stores.

Stratford's River Avon and Huron Street bridge, overlooked by the distinctive Victorian courthouse

❸ Niagara Falls

Although the majestic rumble of the falls can be heard from miles away, there is no preparation for the sight itself, a great arc of hissing, frothing water crashing over a 57-m (187-ft) cliff amid dense clouds of drifting spray. There are actually three cataracts to gaze at, as the speeding river is divided into twin channels by Goat Island, a tiny spray-soaked parcel of land. On one side of Goat Island is the Canadian Horseshoe Falls, and, on the far side, across the border, is the smaller American Falls, along with the comparatively narrow Bridal Veil Falls. Stunning close-up views are available from the vantage point of the Maid of the Mist or Hornblower Niagara Cruises boat trips. Even better is the walk down through a series of rocky tunnels that lead behind Horseshoe Falls, where the noise from the crashing waters is deafening.

American Falls
The Niagara River tumbles over the 260-m (850-ft) wide American Falls.

Rainbow Bridge
From the elegant span of the Rainbow Bridge there are panoramic views over the falls. The bridge itself crosses the gorge between Canada and the US. Here, on sunny days, rainbows rise through the spray.

KEY

① **Customs**

② **Bird Kingdom** is Canada's only indoor aviary and features over 400 exotic birds.

③ **The Table Rock Welcome Centre** is packed with amenities and offers access to the 4D immersive experience, Niagara's Fury.

Clifton Hill
This street boasts a range of attractions. Ripley's Believe it or Not Museum features a dog with human teeth as just one of its offerings.

★ Horseshoe Falls
Shaped like a horseshoe, this is the larger set of falls at Niagara, being some 670 m (2,200 ft) wide and 57 m (187 ft) high.

Journey Behind the Falls
An elevator from the Horseshoe Falls leads to the Journey Behind the Falls, where a series of tunnels take visitors behind a wall of water so thick it that blocks out daylight.

★ Hornblower Niagara Cruises boats
These intrepid vessels gets very close to the foot of the falls. Raincoats are supplied as passengers can expect to get wet on this thrilling trip.

Skylon Tower
The tower has an observation deck, which gives a bird's-eye view of the falls. It is also open at night, so visitors can see the floodlit waters.

Exploring Niagara Falls

Niagara Falls is a welcoming town that stretches along the Niagara River for about 3 km (2 miles). Renowned as a honeymoon destination, the town is well equipped to satisfy the needs of the 14 million people who visit the falls each year. It is divided into three main sections: to the south are the falls themselves; these are flanked by a thin strip of parkland that stretches out along the river bank as far as Clifton Hill, the glitziest street in Ontario, lined with garish amusement park attractions. To the west is the main motel strip, Lundy's Lane. To the north, on Bridge Street, lie the business district and the train and bus stations.

Horseshoe Falls

Named for their shape, the 670-m- (2,200-ft-) wide and 57-m- (187-ft-) high Horseshoe Falls are formed by the turbulent waters of the Niagara River roaring over a semicircular cliff to plunge into the bubbling cauldron below. By these means the Niagara River adjusts to the differential between the water levels of lakes Erie and Ontario, which it connects. The falls remain an awe-inspiring sight, despite the fact that the flow of the river is regulated by hydroelectric companies, which siphon off a substantial part of the river to drive their turbines. One result has been a change in the rate of erosion. By the 1900s, the falls were eroding the cliff beneath them at a rate of 1 m (3 ft) a year. Today, the rate is down to 30 cm (1 ft) a year.

The Hornblower boat at Horseshoe Falls

🚢 Hornblower Niagara Cruises

5920 Niagara Parkway. **Tel** (905) 642 4272. **Open** Apr–Oct: daily. 🎁 ♿
W niagaracruises.com

The best way to appreciate the full force of the falls is to take the Hornblower boat trip. Boats depart from the jetty at the

bottom of Clifton Hill and head upriver to the crashing waters under the falls. Raincoats are provided on this invigorating trip.

A wax museum and an array of other attractions at Clifton Hill

Clifton Hill

This short, steep street runs up from the edge of the Niagara River gorge and is lined with a string of fast-food restaurants and tourist attractions. The flashing lights and giant advertising billboards point the way to the Niagara Skywheel and such sights as the Guinness Book of World Records, House of Frankenstein, and Ripley's Believe it or Not! Museum, where visitors can speak to a genie in a crystal bottle and see oddities such as a man with a greater-than-usual number of pupils in his eyes.

White Water Walk

4330 Niagara Pkwy. **Tel** (905) 374 1221. **Open** mid-Apr–mid-Nov: daily. 🎁 ♿

Another way to admire the great force of the Niagara River's torrent is from down at the bottom of the canyon. The White Water Walk provides this

The dramatic arc of thundering waters at Horseshoe Falls

For hotels and restaurants in this region see pp355–6 and pp375–6

Wooden boardwalk along the Niagara River at the White Water Walk

close-up view by means of a tunnel and an elevator, which lead from the top of the gorge to a riverside boardwalk. The whirlpools and rapids here are some of the most spectacular, yet treacherous, in the world.

The Old Scow

Just above the falls, stranded on the rocks in the middle of the river, is the Old Scow, a flat-bottomed steel barge that was shipwrecked in August 1918. It was being towed across the Niagara River by a tugboat when the lines snapped. The scow hurtled towards the falls, getting within 767 m (2,516 ft), of the brink, and the two-man crew appeared to be doomed. Luckily the boat grounded itself on this rocky ledge just in time. The crew's ordeal was, however, far from over: they had to wait another 29 hours before being finally winched to safety. The Old Scow has been rusting away on the rocks ever since.

Niagara Glen Nature Reserve

3050 River Road. **Open** daily.
The small Niagara Glen Nature Reserve lies 7 km (4 miles) downriver from the falls. This segment of the gorge has been preserved in pristine condition, with bushes and low trees tumbling down the rocky cliffside. This is how it may have looked before the coming of the Europeans. Seven different hiking trails lead past boulders,

caves, and wildflowers. The walks are easy on the way down but a steep climb on the way up.

Whirlpool Aerocar

3850 Niagara Pkwy. **Tel** (905) 354 5711. **Open** Apr–Oct: daily. **Closed** during high winds.
The Niagara River makes a dramatically sharp turn about 4.5 km (3 miles) downstream from the falls, generating a vicious, raging whirlpool, one of the most lethal stretches of water in the whole of North America. The effect is created when the river pushes against the northwest side of the canyon, only to be forced to turn around in the opposite direction. The most stunning view of the whirlpool rapids is from the century-old Aerocar, a cable car of Spanish design that crosses the gorge,

high above the river. A different perspective of the falls can be seen from here.

Niagara Parks Botanical Gardens and Butterfly Conservatory

2565 Niagara Pkwy. **Tel** (905) 358 0025. **Open** daily. for conservatory.
The Niagara Parks Botanical Gardens are located 9 km (6 miles) downstream from the falls and comprise over 40 ha (99 acres) of beautifully maintained gardens divided into several different zones. One of the prettiest areas in summer is the rose garden, which displays over 2,400 different varieties. The extensive annual garden, which houses many rare species imported from all parts of the globe, puts on a year-round show. The gardens also include an arboretum that has examples of many different types of trees from beech and mulberry to magnolia and yew.

The butterfly conservatory is even more popular. At the beginning of a visit, a video is shown in the theater. The film explains the life cycle of a butterfly, from egg and larvae through to the emergence of the adult. Over 2,000 butterflies are housed in a huge heated dome, where they fly free – one of the largest collections in the world. A series of pathways pass through the dome, leading past the lush tropical flora on which the butterflies make their homes.

Butterfly at the Botanic Gardens and Conservatory

The Whirlpool Rapids are best seen from the Whirlpool Aerocar

A boat trip takes visitors up close to the spectacular Horseshoe Falls ▶

Alexander Graham Bell's library at the Bell Homestead in Brantford

❿ St. Jacobs

🏘 2,000. 🚌 ℹ 1406 King St. N.,
(519) 664 3518. 🅦 stjacobs.com

The main street of the charming village St. Jacobs is lined with craft shops selling quilts, brooms, baked goods, and furniture. Many of the goods are made by the members of the local Mennonite community, who run farms in the countryside. Visit the Mennonite Story, located in the village's visitor centre, to gain some insight into the Mennonite's and Amish sects' life. Just 3 km (2 miles) down the road, north of Waterloo, is **St. Jacobs Farmers' Market**. Housed in two cavernous buildings, many stalls here sell pork, and Bratwurst sausages with sauerkraut, hinting at the German heritage of the area.

⓫ Brantford

🏘 100,000. 🚆 🚌 ℹ 399 Wayne Gretzky Pkwy, (519) 751 9900.

Brantford is an unassuming manufacturing town that takes its name from Joseph Brant (1742–1807), the leader of a confederacy of tribes called the Six Nations. An Iroquois chief himself, Brant settled here in 1784. He soon decided that the interests of his people lay with the British, and his braves fought alongside the Redcoats during the American War of Independence (1775–83). Sadly, he had chosen the losing side and, after the war, his band was forced to move north to Canada, where the British ceded the First Nations people a piece of land at Brantford. The Iroquois (Six Nations) still live in this area, and host the Grand River Pow Wow, featuring traditional dances and crafts, every summer. Brantford is also known for its association with the telephone. In 1876, the first ever long-distance call was made from Brantford to the neighboring village of Paris by Alexander Graham Bell (1847–1922), who had emigrated from Britain to Ontario in 1870. Bell's old home, conserved as the **Bell Homestead National Historic Site**, is also located on the town's outskirts. The site has two buildings: Bell's homestead, furnished with many original family pieces; the other housing Canada's first telephone business office, moved here from downtown Brantford in 1969.

Fruit seller in Brantford

🚹 Bell Homestead National Historic Site
94 Tutela Heights Rd. **Tel** (519) 756 6220. **Open** 9:30am–4:30pm Tue–Sun. **Closed** Dec 24–Jan 1. 🅿 ♿ 📷 🅦 bellhomestead.ca

⓬ Orillia

🏘 32,000. 🚌 ℹ 50 Andrew St. S., (705) 325 1311. 🅦 orillia.ca

Orillia is a pleasant country town that was the home of the novelist and humorist Stephen Leacock (1869–1944). Leacock's tremendously popular *Sunshine Sketches of a Little Town* poked fun at the vanities of provincial Ontario life in the fictional town of Mariposa.

His old lakeshore home has been conserved as the **Stephen Leacock Museum**, containing original furnishings as well as details of his life.

Orillia lies along a narrow strip of water linking Lake Couchiching to Lake Simcoe and is a good base from which to cruise both lakes. On the shore, Orillia's Centennial Park has a marina and a long boardwalk that stretches all the way to Couchiching beach.

🏛 Stephen Leacock Museum
50 Museum Dr., Old Brewery Bay. **Tel** (705) 329 1908. **Open** 10am–4pm Wed–Sun. 🅿 ♿ 🅦 leacockmuseum.com

Bethune Memorial House in the town of Gravenhurst, Muskoka

⓭ Muskoka

🚌 Gravenhurst, Huntsville. ℹ 1342 Hwy 11 North RR #2, Kilworthy, (705) 689 0660. 🅦 discovermuskoka.ca

Muskoka comprises an area north of Orillia between the towns of Huntsville and Gravenhurst. The center of this lake country is Gravenhurst, a resort at the south end of Lake Muskoka. Here, a national historic site is devoted to the life and work of Doctor Norman Bethune (1890–1939), who pioneered mobile blood transfusion units during the Spanish

Civil War. **Bethune Memorial House**, his birthplace, has been restored in late-19th-century style.

🏛 **Bethune Memorial House**
235 John St. N. **Tel** (705) 687 4261.
Open Jun & late Oct: 10am–4pm Wed–Sat; Jul–mid-Oct: 10am–4pm daily. 🅿 🅦 pc.gc.ca/bethune

A trawler in the lake near Georgian Bay Islands, Ontario

⑭ Georgian Bay Islands National Park

Beausoleil Island. **Tel** (705) 527 7200, (705) 427 2532. **Open** daily.
🚤 DayTripper: Honey Harbor, (705) 526 8907. **Open** mid-May–mid-Jun & mid-Sep–mid-Oct: Fri–Tue; mid-Jun–mid-Sep: daily. 🅿
🅦 pc.gc.ca/georgianbay

The waters of Georgian Bay are dotted with thousands of little islands, often no more than a chunk of rock guarded by a windblown pine. The bay is large, beautiful, and flows into Lake Huron. Sixty of its islands have been incorporated into the Georgian Bay Islands National Park. The park's center is Beausoleil Island, the hub of the area's wide range of facilities.

The Mennonite Religious Community

The Mennonite Christian sect was founded in Europe in the early 16th century. The Mennonites were persecuted because they refused to swear any oath of loyalty to the state or take any part in war. In the 17th century, a group split off to form its own, even stricter, sect. These Ammanites (or Amish) emigrated to the US and then to Ontario in 1799. The old-order Amish own property communally and shun modern machinery and clothes, traveling around the highways in distinctive horse-drawn buggies and dressed in traditional clothes.

Amish couple driving a buggy

Beausoleil is also crossed by scenic hiking trails, but it is important to come properly equipped since it is a remote spot. The only way to reach the island is by the DayTripper water taxi from the hamlet of Honey Harbour. The journey takes about 40 minutes. Cruises through the islands aboard the Miss Midland depart from the town of Midland from mid-May through mid-October.

In Penetanguishene, east of Nottawasaga Bay, Discovery Harbour is a superb reconstruction of the British naval base that was established here in 1814. There are replicas of the barracks, blacksmith's shop, houses, and the original Officers' Quarters. Two replica schooners, HMS *Tecumseth* and HMS *Bee*, are moored at the King's Wharf. The below-decks area of the former is furnished as per the ship's 1815 log. The remains of its original hull are also on exhibit in the HMS *Tecumseth* Centre.

⑮ Nottawasaga Bay

🚌 Wasaga Beach or Collingwood.
ℹ 45 St. Paul St., Collingwood, (705) 445 7722, 1 888 227 8667.
🅦 visitsouthgeorgianbay.ca

Part of scenic Georgian Bay, Nottawasaga Bay is one of the region's most popular vacation destinations. Wasaga Beach has miles of golden, sandy beach and many chalets and cottages. As well as swimming and sunbathing, there is the curious Nancy Island Historic Site, behind Beach Area 2. The site has a museum which houses the preserved HMS *Nancy*: one of few British boats to survive the War of 1812 (see pp52–3).

Located on the southern shores of Georgian Bay, Collingwood and the Blue Mountains make an excellent location for hiking, cycling, and paddling in summer. In winter, the resort town of Blue Mountain is one of Ontario's top destinations for downhill skiing and snowboarding.

Discovery Harbour, Penetanguishene's restored British naval base

⓰ Sainte-Marie among the Hurons

Sainte-Marie among the Hurons is one of Ontario's most compelling attractions. Located 5 km (3 miles) east of the town of Midland, the site is a reconstruction of the settlement founded here among the indigenous Huron peoples by Jesuit priests in 1639. The village is divided into two main sections, one for Europeans (complete with a chapel and workshops), the other for Hurons, with a pair of bark-covered longhouses. Marking the boundary between the two is the small church of Saint Joseph, a simple wooden building where the Jesuits set about trying to convert the Hurons. Their efforts met with a variety of reactions, and the complex relationship between the two cultures is explored here in detail.

Exterior of Longhouse
The exterior of the longhouse had bark-covered walls built over a cedar pole frame that was bent to form an arch.

★ **Fireside Gathering**
Inside the longhouse, fish, skins, and tobacco were hung from the ceiling to dry. An open fire burned through the winter.

Church of Saint Joseph
This is the grave site of two Jesuit priests, Jean de Brébeuf and Gabriel Lalement, who were captured and put to death by the Iroquois.

KEY

① **In the hospital** the Jesuits used French medicines with limited success. The Hurons had no resistance to European diseases such as influenza and measles.

② **The blacksmith's shop** was important, as Sainte-Marie needed essential items such as hinges and nails, often made using recycled iron.

③ **The carpenter's shop** had an abundant supply of local wood, and craftsmen from France were employed by the priests to build the mission.

④ **Bastions** helped to defend the mission from attack. Built of local stone to ward off arrows and musket balls, they also served as observation towers.

Wigwam by the Palisades
This wigwam is built to traditional Ojibway design and lies next to the wooden palisade that encloses the mission. It was built to make visiting First Nations people feel at home.

★ Traditional Crafts
The costumed guides here have been trained in the traditional crafts employed by both the Huron and the French, including 17th-century cooking and blacksmith's work.

VISITORS' CHECKLIST

Practical Information
Hwy 12 (5 km/3 miles east of Midland).
Tel (705) 526 7838.
Open May–Oct: 10am–5pm daily.
🅿 ♿ 🅗 🅘 ✎ 🖥
Ⓦ hhp.on.ca

Chapel interior
The old chapel has been carefully re-created, and, with the light filtering in through its timbers, it is easy to imagine what it was like for the priests, as they gathered to say mass each day before dawn.

Entrance

0 meters	25
0 yards	25

The Cookhouse Garden
At Sainte-Marie, care is taken to grow crops the Huron way, with corn, beans, and squash planted in rotation. This system provided a year-round food supply, which was supplemented with meat and fish.

⑰ Goderich

📇 7,600. 🚉 ℹ️ Cnr Hamilton St. & Hwy 21. **Tel** (519) 524 6600, 1 800 280 7637. 🌐 **goderich.ca**

Goderich is a charming town overlooking Lake Huron at the mouth of the Maitland River. It was founded in 1825 by the British-owned Canada Company, which had persuaded the Ontario government to part with 1 million ha (2.5 million acres) of fertile land in their province for just 12 cents an acre, a bargain of such proportions that there was talk of corruption. Eager to attract settlers, the company built the Huron Road from Cambridge, in the east, to Goderich. The town was laid out with the main streets radiating out from the striking, octagon-shaped center.

Goderich possesses two excellent museums. The first, the **Huron County Museum**, houses a large collection of antique farm implements, as well as a military gallery and a reconstruction of a 19th-century town street. There is also a huge, steam-driven thresher. The **Huron Historic Gaol National Historic Site**, built between 1839 and 1842, is a preserved Victorian prison. Fascinating tours are available of its dank cells, the jailers' rooms, and the Governor's 19th-century house. The town is also renowned for its sunsets, particularly as viewed from the shore of Lake Huron.

🏛️ Huron Historic Gaol National Historic Site
181 Victoria St. N. **Tel** (519) 524 2686. **Open** May–Aug: 10am–4:30pm

Historic storefront in the charming town of Goderich

The golden sands of Sauble Beach on the shore of Lake Huron

Mon–Sat, 1–4:30pm Sun; Sep & Oct: 1–4pm Mon–Fri, 10am–4:30 pm Sat, 1–4:30pm Sun. 🖼️

🏛️ Huron County Museum
110 North St. **Tel** (519) 524 2686. **Open** Jan–Apr: 10am–4:30pm Mon–Fri, 1–4:30pm Sat; May–Dec: 10am–4:30pm Mon–Sat, 1–4:30pm Sun. 🖼️
♿ 🌐 **huroncountymuseum.ca**

⑱ Sauble Beach

🚌 Owen Sound. ℹ️ RR1, Sauble Beach (519), 422 1262.
🌐 **saublebeach.com**

One of the finest sandy beaches in Ontario, Sauble Beach stretches for 11 km (7 miles) along the shores of Lake Huron. Running behind this beach is a long, narrow band of campsites, cabins, and cottages. The center of the resort is at the pocket-sized village of Sauble Beach, which has a population of only 500. The quiet back streets of the village also offer friendly guesthouses and B&Bs. The most attractive and tranquil camping is found at Sauble Falls Provincial Park, north of the beach.

⑲ Lake Huron

ℹ️ Sarnia, Southern shore, (519) 344 7403. ℹ️ Barrie, Georgian Bay, (705) 725 7280 ℹ️ Sault Ste. Marie, North shore, (705) 945 6941.
🌐 **ontariotravel.net**

Of all the Great Lakes, Lake Huron has the most varied landscapes along its shoreline. To the south, the lake narrows to funnel past the largely industrial towns of Sarnia and Windsor on its way to Lake Erie, while its southeast shore is bounded by a gentle bluff, marking the limit of one of Ontario's most productive agricultural regions. Farther north, the long, thin isthmus of Bruce Peninsula stretches out into Lake Huron, signaling a dramatic change in the character of the lakeshore. This is where the southern flatlands are left behind for the more rugged, glacier-scraped country of the Canadian Shield. This transition can be seen clearly in the area of Georgian Bay. This is an impressive shoreline of lakes, forests, beaches, and villages that attracts large numbers of visitors. The lake's island-sprinkled waters are a popular area for water sports. Outdoor activities here include swimming, hiking, and fishing.

⑳ Bruce Peninsula Tour

The 100-km (62-mile) Bruce Peninsula divides the main body of Lake Huron from Georgian Bay and also contains some of the area's most scenic terrain. Bruce Peninsula National Park lies along the eastern shore and boasts craggy headlands and limestone cliffs with several hiking paths. Beyond the port of Tobermory, at the peninsula's tip, Fathom Five Marine National Park, comprises 19 uninhabited islands. The park is popular with divers because of its clear waters and amazing rock formations.

Tips for Drivers

Tour Route: The route follows Route 9 and Hwy 6. It can be reached from Owen Sound in the south, or Tobermory in the north.
Length: 100 km (62 miles).
Stopping-off points: Diving trips and tours to Flowerpot Island leave from Tobermory, which also has good accommodation.

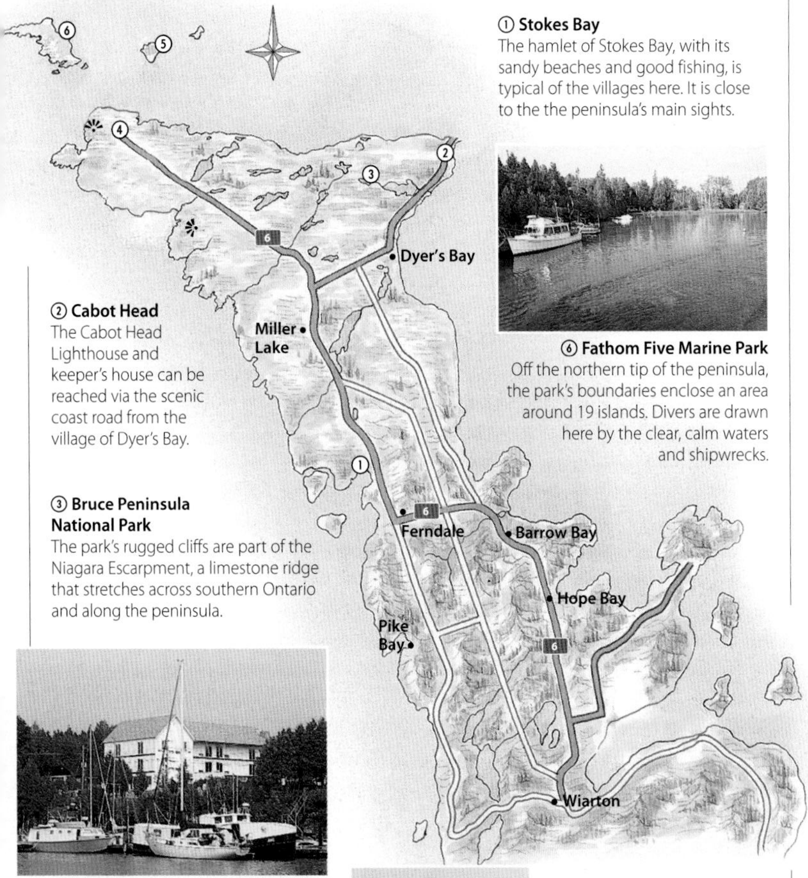

① Stokes Bay

The hamlet of Stokes Bay, with its sandy beaches and good fishing, is typical of the villages here. It is close to the the peninsula's main sights.

② Cabot Head

The Cabot Head Lighthouse and keeper's house can be reached via the scenic coast road from the village of Dyer's Bay.

⑥ Fathom Five Marine Park

Off the northern tip of the peninsula, the park's boundaries enclose an area around 19 islands. Divers are drawn here by the clear, calm waters and shipwrecks.

③ Bruce Peninsula National Park

The park's rugged cliffs are part of the Niagara Escarpment, a limestone ridge that stretches across southern Ontario and along the peninsula.

④ Tobermory

At the northern tip of the peninsula, this small fishing village is a hub for tourist acitivties in the area. Ferries to Flowerpot Island leave from here.

⑤ Flowerpot Island

The only island in Fathom Five Marine Park with basic facilities, it is noted for the rock columns that dot the coastline.

0 meters	500
0 yards	500

Key

▬ Tour route

═ Other roads

Map labels: Dyer's Bay, Miller Lake, Ferndale, Barrow Bay, Hope Bay, Pike Bay, Wiarton

㉑ Manitoulin Island

🏛 12,600. ℹ 70 Meredith St,
Little Current, (705) 368 3021.
Ⓦ **manitoulintourism.com**

Hugging the northern shores of
Lake Huron, Manitoulin Island
is, at 2,800 sq km (1,100 sq
miles), the world's largest freshwater island. A quiet place of
small villages, farmland, woodland, and lakes, its edges are
fringed by deserted beaches.
The lake's North Channel
separates Manitoulin from the
mainland, its waters attracting
summer sailors, while hikers
come to explore the island's trails.
   The Ojibway people first
occupied the island more than
10,000 years ago, naming it after
the Great Spirit – Manitou. First
Nations peoples still constitute
over a quarter of the island's
population. Every August, on Civic
Holiday weekend, they celebrate
their culture in one of Canada's
largest powwows, the Wikwemikong Cultural Festival
(Bay of the Beaver).
   On the north shore,
Gore Bay houses five
tiny museums that
focus on the island's
early settlers. Nearby,
the island's largest
settlement is Little
Current, a quiet town
with a handful of
motels and restaurants.
From May to October
the Chi Cheemaun car
ferry connects Tobermory on
the Bruce Peninsula to Manitoulin
Island. Reserve ahead.

Reflections in George Lake, Killarney Provincial Park

㉒ Killarney Provincial Park

Tel (705) 287 2900. 🚌 Sudbury.
Open daily. 🚻 for some facilities.
Ⓦ **ontarioparks.com/park/killarney**

Killarney Provincial Park is a
beautiful tract of wilderness
with crystal-blue lakes, pine
and hardwood forests, boggy
lowlands, and the spectacular
La Cloche Mountains,
known for their striking
white quartzite ridges.
This magnificent
scenery has inspired
many artists,
particularly members
of the Group of Seven
(see pp168–9), one of
whom – Franklin
Carmichael – saw the
park as Ontario's most
"challenging and
gratifying landscape."
The park's 100-km (62-mile) La
Cloche Silhouette Trail takes
between a week and ten days

Gore Bay on Manitoulin Island

to complete and attracts many
serious hikers to its stunning
views of the mountains and of
Georgian Bay. Canoeists can
paddle on the park's many lakes
and rivers by following a network
of well-marked canoe routes.

㉓ Temagami

🏛 900. 🚌 ℹ Chamber of Commerce,
Lakeshore Rd., (705) 569 3344.
Ⓦ **temagami.ca**

The tiny resort of Temagami and
its wild surroundings have long
attracted fur traders and trappers,
painters, and writers, most
famously Grey Owl (see p254),
the remarkable Englishman
who posed as an Aboriginal
Canadian and achieved celebrity
status as a naturalist and
conservationist in the 1930s.
The resort sits on the
distinctively shaped Lake
Temagami, a deep lake with
long fjords and bays as well
as 1,400 islands, which are

One of Lake Temagami's numerous canoe routes

crisscrossed by numerous scenic canoe routes and hiking and mountain-bike trails.

Even more remote is the Lady Evelyn Smoothwater Wilderness Park, farther to the west. The only way in is by canoe or float plane from Temagami, but the reward is some of Ontario's most stunning scenery. Much more accessible is the 30-m (98-ft) high Temagami Fire Tower lookout point, which provides panoramic views of the surrounding pine forests, and the charming Finlayson Provincial Park, a popular place to picnic and camp; both are located on Temagami's outskirts.

❷❹ Sault Ste. Marie

🏔 75,000. ✈ 🚌 ℹ 99 Foster Dr., (705) 759 5442. 🌐 saulttourism.com

Where the rapids of St. Mary's River link Lake Superior to Lake Huron sits the attractive town of Sault Ste. Marie, one of Ontario's oldest European communities.

The area was originally called "Baawitigong," meaning "place of the rapids," by the Ojibway people, who used the site as a meeting place during the whitefish season. It remains a strong First Nations area today.

The town itself was founded as a Jesuit mission and fur-trading post by the French in 1688. Called the "Sault" (pronounced "Soo"), after the French word for "rapids," the trading station prospered after 1798, when the rapids were bypassed by a canal. Since then, the canal has been upgraded time and again, and today transports the largest of container ships to the interior, thereby maintaining a thriving local economy.

Although there are regular boat trips along the canal, visitors are drawn to Sault Ste. Marie's main tourist attraction, the **Agawa Canyon Tour Train**, which offers day-long rail tours from the city into the surrounding wilderness. The train weaves north through dense forest, past secluded lakes and over yawning ravines

Canal locks at Sault Ste. Marie

to reach the spectacular scenery of Agawa Canyon where there is a 90-minute break for lunch.

🚂 **Agawa Canyon Tour Train**
129 Bay St. **Tel** (705) 946 7300.
Open mid-Jun–mid-Oct: once daily. ♿
♿ 🌐 agawatrain.com

❷❺ Lake Superior

ℹ Ontario Travel Information Centre, Sault Ste. Marie, (705) 945 6941.
🌐 ontariotravel.net

The least polluted and most westerly of the Great Lakes, Lake Superior is the world's largest body of freshwater, with a surface area of 82,000 sq km (31,700 sq miles). It is known for sudden violent storms, long a source of dread to local sailors. The lake's northern coast is a vast weather-swept stretch of wilderness,

dominated by granite outcrops and seemingly limitless forest. This challenging area is best experienced in Pukaskwa National Park and Lake Superior Provincial Park, both reached via the Trans-Canada Highway (Hwy 17), as it cuts a dramatic route along the lake's north shore.

❷❻ Thunder Bay

🏔 109,000. ✈ 🚗 🚌 ℹ Terry Fox Information Centre, Hwy 11/17 E., (807) 983 2041, 1 800 667 8386.
🌐 thunderbay.ca

On the northern shore of Lake Superior, Thunder Bay is Canada's third-largest freshwater port, its massive grain elevators dominating the city's water-front. Grain is brought to Thunder Bay from the prairies farther west, before being shipped to the rest of the world via the Great Lakes.

The town was originally established as a French trading post in 1679. These early days are celebrated at **Fort William Historical Park**, a replica of the old fur trading post, with costumed traders, French explorers, and First Nations' peoples. Fort William was amalgamated with the adjacent town of Port Arthur to form Thunder Bay in 1970.

🏰 **Fort William Historical Park**
Off Broadway Ave. **Tel** (807) 473 2333.
Open mid-May–mid-Sep: 10am–5pm daily. ♿ ♿ 🌐 fwhp.ca

Lake Superior, the world's largest freshwater lake

An abandoned farm in a durum wheat field near Assiniboia, Saskatchewan ▶

CENTRAL CANADA

Introducing Central Canada

Known locally as the Prairies, Central Canada covers the provinces of Manitoba, Saskatchewan, and eastern Alberta and encompasses the most productive agricultural and energy-rich part of the country. The region is dominated by prairie (often associated with borderless fields that stretch to the horizon) and covers a vast area of the western interior, which is the size of Mexico. The region is not all prairie, but has a variety of landscapes, from the forested aspen parkland to the west and north of the plains to the tundra of northern Manitoba and the rocky desert of the badlands in the southwest.

The Broadway Bridge and central Saskatoon overlooking the South Saskatchewan River

Grain elevators and wheat cars punctuate the vast fields of the Canadian prairies

For additional map symbols see back flap

Getting Around

Winnipeg, Edmonton, Regina, and Saskatoon, the four main cities of the region, are well served by public transportation, with regular air, train, and bus connections from British Columbia and other provinces. All four cities also have international airports. From Winnipeg, the Trans-Canada Highway follows the route established in the 19th century by the Canadian Pacific Railway, going 1,333 km (828 miles) west to Calgary. The more scenic Yellowhead Highway starts at the Forks in Winnipeg and runs through Yorkton and Saskatoon, reaching Edmonton at 1,301 km (808 miles), continuing on through Jasper National Park and British Columbia.

Key

▬▬ Expressway

▬▬ Divided highway

▬▬ Highway

:::: Other road

▬▪▬ Main railway

— Minor railway

▬▬ International border

▬▬ Regional border

△ Summit

The prairies of Manitoba, one of Canada's richest agricultural areas

Dinosaurs and Prehistoric Canada

It is easier to imagine gunslingers and coyotes in the desert-like badlands of the Red Deer River Valley in Alberta than it is to envisage the dinosaurs who once lived in this region. Over 75 million years ago the area was a tropical swamp, similar to the Florida Everglades, and the favored habitat of these huge reptiles, which dominated the Earth for some 160 million years. All the dinosaur specimens found here originate from the Cretaceous period (144–65 million years ago). Dramatic changes in the region's weather patterns, from wet and tropical to dry desert, helped to preserve an incredible number of dinosaur remains in the area. Today, the Dinosaur Provincial Park is a UNESCO World Heritage Site.

Locator Map

This Triceratops skull shows the dinosaur's flaring bony frill, which was used primarily for courtship and display. Its two horns were an awesome 1 m (3 ft) long. More types of horned dinosaurs have been found here in Alberta than anywhere else.

Trained staff carefully dig out a groove around the bone while it is still in the ground. Once removed, it will be matched to its adjoining bone.

The magnolia is thought to be one of Earth's first flowering plants, or angiosperms, and became widespread during the Cretaceous period.

Joseph Burr Tyrrell found the first important dinosaur skeleton sections in the Red Deer River Valley, Alberta, in 1884. A geologist, Tyrrell stumbled across the skull of a 71.5 million-year-old Albertosaurus while surveying coal deposits. Subsequently, palaeontologists rushed here to search for fossils. Drumheller's Royal Tyrrell Museum of Palaeontology is named after him (see p252).

An artist's re-creation of the Cretaceous landscape depicts the types of flora living at the time. Tree ferns dominated the country, and grew in large forests to heights of 18 m (60 ft). Similar species still grow in the tropics.

Horseshoe Canyon lies along the Red Deer River, its high, worn hills visibly layered with ancient sediments. Ice Age glaciers eroded the layers of mud and sand that buried the remains of dinosaurs and plants. Erosion continues to form this barren, lunar landscape, exposing more bones, petrified wood, and other fossils.

This dinosaur nest on display at the Royal Tyrrell Museum was discovered at Devil's Coulee, Alberta, in 1987, and contains several embryos and eggs of the plant-eating Hadrosaur.

The Field Station is home to the Dinosaur Visitor Centre, where displays describe locally found fossils. The tours head out into the badlands.

Simulated Dinosaur Dig

The Royal Tyrrell Museum offers the chance to experience the thrill of excavation on a realistic dinosaur dig in Midland Provincial Park. There are digging programs designed for all ages, including a kids-only session for 7–12s. Using the real tools and techniques of palaeontology, and with museum educators as guides, visitors can uncover casts of dinosaur bones, map the quarry, make a field jacket, and learn how to read fossils. There is also a hike through the badlands, where visitors can investigate real dinosaur remains.

The leg bone of a duck-billed dinosaur is revealed to be complete. Beneath it another piece of bone has been covered with strips of plaster of Paris to protect it during transportation to a laboratory.

The reconstructed skeleton of a Gorgosaurus towers over the Dinosaur Hall at the Royal Tyrrell Museum. The first dinosaur discovered in the area, Gorgosaurus was a fierce meat-eating predator. Despite being 8 m (26 ft) long and weighing some 2,032 kg (two tons), this dinosaur was capable of reaching speeds of 20 km/h (12 mph).

Canadian Mounties

The Royal Canadian Mounted Police are a symbol of national pride. Canada's first Prime Minister, Sir John A. Macdonald, founded the North West Mounted Police in 1873 in Ontario after violence in the west of the country (between illicit liquor dealers and First Nations peoples) reached a climax with the Cypress Hills Massacre *(see p251)*. Marching west, the Mounties reached the Oldman River, Alberta, 70 km (43 miles) west of the Cypress Hills, where they built Fort Macleod in 1874. The principal aims of the Mounties were to establish good relations with the Aboriginal Peoples of the Prairies and to maintain order over new settlers in the late 1800s. The Mounties won respect for their diplomacy, policing the Canadian Pacific Railway workers and the Klondike Gold Rush in the Yukon during the 1890s. In recognition of their service, they gained the Royal prefix in 1904.

The lush Cypress Hills were the site of a gruesome massacre, which led to the founding of the North West Mounted Police.

The march west covered 3,135 km (1,948 miles) from Fort Dufferin, Manitoba to southern Alberta. A force of 275 men, 310 horses, and cattle, was sent to catch the illicit whisky traders operating in the west. Battling with extreme temperatures, plagues of insects, and lack of supplies, the Mounties arrived at the Oldman River in 1874.

The Long March

Inspector James M. Walsh sealed the Mounties' reputation for bravery when he took only six men on a parley with Sioux Chief Sitting Bull. The Sioux had retreated to the area after their defeat of US General Custer at the Battle of the Little Big Horn in 1876. Although the Sioux were the traditional enemies of the local Blackfoot and Cree peoples, there was no fighting after the arrival of the Mounties. Walsh's force succeeded in enforcing law and order across mid-west Canada, winning respect for their diplomacy. Blackfoot chief Crowfoot praised their fairness saying, "They have protected us as the feathers of a bird protect it from winter."

Sioux Chief Sitting Bull

James M. Walsh

The adventures of the pioneering Mounties have long been a source of inspiration to countless authors and filmmakers. Square-jawed and scarlet clad, the Mountie was the perfect hero. Perhaps the best-known "Mountie" film was the 1936 *Rose Marie* starring crooner Nelson Eddy and Jeanette MacDonald.

The skilled horsemen of the Musical Ride are selected after two years on the force. The officers then begin seven months of intensive training.

The Musical Ride

The Musical Ride is a thrilling spectacle of 32 riders and horses performing a series of traditional cavalry drills set to music. The drills have not changed since their original use in the British army over a century ago. Staying in tight formation, the horses do the trot, the canter, the rally, and the charge. Every summer the Ride is performed in different venues across Canada and the US.

As an enduring symbol of Canada the image of the Mounties has adorned everything from postage stamps and currency to this 1940s promotional tourist poster for Lake Louise in Banff National Park.

32 specially bred horses take part in the Musical Ride. A mixture of thoroughbred stallion crossed with black Hanoverian mare, the horses train for two years.

Today's Mounties are a 28,000-strong police force responsible for the enforcement of federal law across Canada. Their duties range from counting migratory birds to exposing foreign espionage. Jets, helicopters, and cars are all used by modern Mounties.

CENTRAL CANADA

Central Canada covers a vast region of boreal forest and fertile grasslands, often known as the Prairies, which traverses Manitoba, Saskatchewan, and part of Alberta. Originally, First Nations peoples lived here, and depended on the herds of buffalo that provided them with food, shelter, and tools. However, by the end of the 19th century the buffalo were hunted almost to extinction. European settlers built towns and farms, some taking Aboriginal wives and forming a new cultural grouping, the Métis. By the 20th century the area's economy came to rely on gas, oil, and grain. Today the Prairies, punctuated by striking, tall grain elevators, are known for the flatness of their landscape and the intriguing history of their towns.

Sights at a Glance

Historic Towns and Cities
1 Winnipeg
2 Steinbach
3 Selkirk
5 Gimli
6 Portage la Prairie
8 Dauphin
9 Yorkton
10 Fort Qu'Appelle
11 Regina
12 Moose Jaw
13 Saskatoon
16 Maple Creek
17 Medicine Hat
18 Lethbridge

21 Red Deer
23 Edmonton
24 Vegreville
27 North Battleford and Battleford
28 Batoche National Historic Site
29 Duck Lake
30 The Pas
31 Flin Flon
32 Churchill

Rivers and Lakes
4 Lake Winnipeg

National and Provincial Parks
7 Riding Mountain National Park
14 Grasslands National Park

15 Cypress Hills Interprovincial Park
20 Dinosaur Provincial Park
22 Elk Island National Park
25 Wood Buffalo National Park
26 Prince Albert National Park

Museums
19 Royal Tyrrell Museum

Key
Highway
Major road
Minor road
Railway route
International border

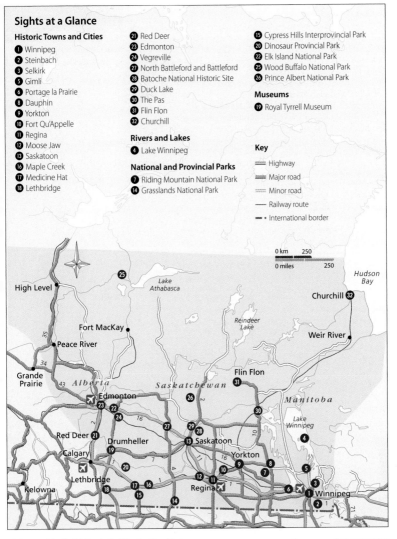

◄ Prairie and farmlands below the foothills of southern Alberta

For map symbols see back flap

❶ Winnipeg

Winnipeg is a cosmopolitan city located at the geographic heart of Canada. Over half of Manitoba's population live here, mostly in suburbs that reflect the city's broad mix of cultures. Winnipeg's position, at the confluence of the Red and Assiniboine rivers, made it an important trading center for First Nations people going back some 6,000 years. From the 1600s Europeans settled here to trade fur. During the 1880s grain became the principal industry of the west, aided by a railroad network routed through Winnipeg. Today, this attractive city, with its museums, historic buildings, and excellent restaurants, makes for an enjoyable stay.

Exploring Winnipeg

Most of Winnipeg's sights are within easy walking distance of the downtown area. The excellent Manitoba Museum of Man and Nature and the Ukrainian Cultural Centre lie east of the Exchange District. At the junction of the Red and Assiniboine rivers is The Forks, a family entertainment center devoted to the city's history. At the junction of Portage and Main streets lie the city's financial and shopping districts with their banks and malls.

🚌 St. Boniface

Riel Tourism, 219 Provencher Blvd.
Tel 1 (866) 808 8338. **Open** Mon–Fri (daily in summer). 🚻 🅿️
w tourismeriel.com

Canada's second-largest French-speaking community outside of Quebec lives in the historic district of St. Boniface. This quiet suburb faces The Forks across the Red River and was founded by priests in 1818 to care for the Métis (see p55) and the French living here. In 1844 the Grey Nuns built a convent that now houses

the St. Boniface Museum. Priests built the Basilica of St. Boniface in 1818. Although the building was destroyed by fire in 1968, its elegant white façade is one of the city's best-loved landmarks. Métis leader Louis Riel was buried here after his execution following the rebellion at Batoche in 1885.

🏛 Manitoba Children's Museum

45 Forks Market Rd. **Tel** (204) 924 4000. **Open** daily. 🚻 🅿️
w childrensmuseum.com

Located within The Forks complex, this popular museum provides a series of enticing hands-on exhibits aimed at children from the ages of 3 to 11. Kids can get creative in the Pop m'Art exhibit or experiment with water in the Splash Lab. In the Engine House youngsters can play at being train drivers on a reconstructed 1952 diesel engine while learning the history of Canada's railroad.

Sunset over The Forks Market and marina, Winnipeg

Airport
10 km (6 miles)

⑤ Winnipeg Art Gallery

④ Legislative Building

Assiniboine Park

| 0 meters | | 500 |
| 0 yards | | 500 |

The brightly colored building housing the Manitoba Children's Museum

The Forks
National Historic Site
Forks Market Rd. **Tel** (204) 983 6757.
Open daily. 🚶 some attractions
and special events. ♿
w theforks.com

The historic riverside parkland
of The Forks stretches along the
west shore of the Red River from
the Esplanade Riel Pedestrian
Bridge to the confluence with
the Assiniboine River. The
riverside walkway offers fine
views of the city center and
St. Boniface cathedral, and you
can access the French Quarter
via the pedestrian bridge.

For more great views, head to
the observation Tower at The
Forks Market and Johnston
Terminal. This once bustling
railroad terminus is now filled
with shoppers searching out
crafts, folk art, and specialty
food. Kids will enjoy the Variety
Heritage Adventure Park, a
playground with a pretend
train, tipi, and fort, just north
of the Children's Museum.

Legislative Building
Cnr Broadway & Osborne. **Tel** (204)
945 5813. **Open** daily. ♿ 🎧 Jul–Sep.

The Legislative Building is built
of a rare and valuable limestone
complete with the remains of
fossils threaded through its
façade. The building is set in
12 ha (30 acres) of beautifully
kept gardens dotted with statues
of poets such as Robert Burns
of Scotland, and Ukrainian
Taras Shevchenko, which
celebrate the province's
ethnic diversity.

The Golden Boy statue adorns the dome
of the Legislative Building

Winnipeg Art Gallery
300 Memorial Blvd. **Tel** (204) 786 6641.
Open 11am–5pm Tue–Sun (to 9pm
Fri). 🎫 ♿ 📷 📸

Designed by local architect
Gustavo da Roza, the jagged,
modernist design of this gallery
has made it a well-known
downtown landmark. Along
with late Gothic and Early
Renaissance works, ceramics,
and 19th-century Canadian art,
the WAG boasts the largest
collection of contemporary Inuit
art in the world, with over 13,000
sculptures, prints, drawings, and
textiles. Works by women Inuit
artists are particularly well
represented, and there are
some wonderful monochrome
drawings and prints depicting
hunting and magical scenes.

A new Inuit Art Centre, set
to open in 2020, is being
constructed next to the existing
building of the WAG in order to
showcase a much larger portion
of this fantastic collection.

Winnipeg Town Center
① St. Boniface suburb
② Manitoba Children's Museum
③ The Forks National
　Historic Site
④ Legislative Building
⑤ Winnipeg Art Gallery
⑥ Exchange District and
　Old Market Square
⑦ Manitoba Museum (see p243)
⑧ Canadian Museum for
　Human Rights

Exchange District and Market Square

492 Main St. **Tel** (204) 942 6716.
May–Sep: call to book.
exchangedistrict.org

When the Canadian Pacific Railway built its transcontinental line through Winnipeg in 1881, the city experienced a boom that led to the setting up of several commodity exchanges. Named after the Winnipeg Grain Exchange, this district was soon populated with a solid array of handsome terracotta and cut stone hotels, banks, warehouses, and theaters. The Exchange District is now a National Historic Site and has been restored to its former glory. It now houses boutiques, craft stores, furniture and antique stores, galleries, artists' studios, and residential lofts.

The center of the district is Old Market Square, a popular site for staging local festivals and outdoor concerts.

Canadian Museum for Human Rights

85 Israel Asper Way. **Tel** (204) 289 2000.
Open 10am–5pm Tue–Sun (to 9pm Wed). **humanrights.ca**

In a daring glass and limestone structure designed by Antoine Predock, the Canadian Museum for Human Rights sits at the forks of the Red and Assiniboine rivers, a historic meeting place for over 5,000 years. It dominates the Winnipeg skyline.

The museum's goal is to increase awareness of human rights in Canada and around the world through interactive exhibitions, learning programs, and daily tours. It has ten themed galleries and a wonderful bistro.

The striking building housing the Canadian Museum for Human Rights

Lower Fort Garry National Historic Site

5925 Hwy 9. **Tel** (204) 785 6050. **Open** mid-May–Jun: 9:30am–5pm Mon–Fri; July & Aug: 9:30am–5pm daily.
partial. **pc.gc.ca/garry**

Located 32 km (20 miles) north of Winnipeg on the banks of the Red River, Lower Fort Garry National Historic Site is North America's only restored stone fort from the fur-trading era. Walls and buildings that have stood on the bank of the Red River for over 180 years tell inspiring tales of discovery and struggle.

Costumed interpreters bring to life the history of the setting to the sounds of metal being hammered and aromas from the campfire.

Sculpture in the Leo Mol garden, Assiniboine park

Royal Canadian Mint

520 Lagimodière Blvd. **Tel** (204) 984 1144. **Open** 9am–5pm Tue–Sat (daily May–Labour Day). **Closed** Jan 1, Dec 25. **mint.ca**

The Royal Canadian Mint is housed in a striking building of rose-colored glass. The mint produces more than four billion coins annually for Canadian circulation, as well as for 75 other countries including Thailand and Iceland.

Assiniboine Park

2355 Corydon Ave. **Tel** (204) 927 6000.
Open daily. **assiniboinepark.ca**

Stretching for 153 ha (378 acres) along the south side of the Assiniboine River, Assiniboine Park is one of the largest urban parks in central Canada.

One of the park's best-loved attractions is the Leo Mol Sculpture Garden, which has some 50 bronze sculptures by the Ukrainian artist, who lived in Winnipeg from 1948 until his death in 2009. The park's Conservatory offers a tropical palm house, which has seasonal displays of a wide range of flowers and shrubs. The park also features an English garden, a miniature railroad, and a fine French formal garden. The Pavilion Gallery showcases art from the province and also has a permanent exhibition on Winnie-the-Pooh. In summer, the Lyric Theatre hosts live music.

The Assiniboine Park Zoo specializes in cold-hardy animals from the northern latitudes and mountain ranges such as polar bears, cougars, elk, and bald eagles. A large statue of Winnie the Bear is thought to be modeled on the Winnie-the-Pooh of the A. A. Milne books.

The park's numerous cycling and walking trails are popular in summer, as is cross-country skiing, skating, and tobogganing in winter.

A pink glass pyramid houses the Royal Canadian Mint

For hotels and restaurants in this region see pp356–7 and pp376–7. For transport information see pp412–13

The Manitoba Museum

Outstanding displays of the region's geography and people are imaginatively presented at this excellent museum, which also includes a planetarium. The visitor proceeds through chronologically organized galleries with displays that range from pre-history to the present day. Each geographical area also has its own gallery: from the Earth History Gallery, which contains fossils up to 500 million years old, to the re-creation of Winnipeg in the 1920s, including a cinema, and a dentist's office. One of the museum's biggest draws is a full-size replica of the *Nonsuch*, a 17th-century ketch.

Key

- Orientation Gallery
- Earth History Gallery
- Arctic/Sub-Arctic Gallery
- Boreal Forest Gallery
- Grasslands Gallery
- Discovery Room
- Urban Gallery
- Nonsuch Gallery
- Hudson's Bay Company Gallery
- Parklands/Mixed Woods Gallery
- Temporary exhibits
- Non-exhibition space

Moose Diorama
A moose and her calf among the conifers of the boreal forest are part of a display that includes a group of Cree people rock painting and gathering food before the harsh winter sets in.

Boreal Forest Mezzanine

Earth History Mezzanine

Nonsuch Gallery
This two-masted ketch, built in England in 1968, is a replica of the *Nonsuch* that arrived in Hudson Bay in 1688 in search of furs.

Main entrance

Gallery Guide
The galleries are arranged on two levels, with steps connecting to mezzanines in the Earth History and Boreal Forest galleries. Part of a three-story addition houses the museum's Hudson's Bay Company collection.

Buffalo Hunt
A Métis hunter chasing buffalo symbolizes the museum's focus on man's relationship with his environment.

Big horn steer at the Mennonite Heritage Village, Steinbach, Manitoba ▶

Ploughing with horses at the Mennonite Heritage Village, Steinbach

❷ Steinbach

🗺 15,800. 🚌

About an hour's drive southeast of Winnipeg, Steinbach is a closely knit community with impressive businesses in trucking, manufacturing, and especially car dealerships. These are run largely by the Mennonites, members of a Protestant religious sect who are noted for their fair dealing.

Steam Engine at the Mennonite Heritage Village

The Mennonites came to Steinbach on ox-drawn carts in 1874, having fled from religious persecution in Russia. Despite not having a rail link, the town thrived, as the Mennonites were good farmers and, later, car dealers. The nearby **Mennonite Heritage Village** re-creates a 19th-century Mennonite settlement, with some buildings dating from the 1870s, and a church and school furnished to the period. Its restaurant serves home-made meals such as borscht, a soup produced with red cabbage and cream. In mid-May, the village hosts Spring on the Farm, featuring a tractor show and traditional food.

🏠 **Mennonite Heritage Village**
Hwy 12 North. **Tel** (204) 326 9661.
Open May, Jun, & Sep: 9am–5pm
Mon–Sat, 11:30am–5pm Sun;
Jul & Aug: 9am–6pm Mon–Sat,
11:30am–6pm Sun; Oct–Apr:
9am–5pm Mon–Fri. 🚾 ♿ 🖊 🏠
🆆 mennoniteheritagevillage.com

❸ Selkirk

🗺 10,000. 🚌 ℹ Red River North Tourism, 18 Main St., (204) 485 4881.
🆆 redrivernorthtourism.com

Named after the fifth Earl of Selkirk, Thomas Douglas, whose family had an interest in the Hudson's Bay Company, Selkirk was established in 1882, when settlers arrived along the shores of the Red River. Today, on Main Street, a 7.5-m (25-ft) high statue of a catfish proclaims Selkirk as the "Catfish capital of North America." Sport fishing is a year-round activity, attracting enthusiasts from across North America.

The city's Marine Museum of Manitoba on Eveline St. displays six restored historic ships, including the 1897 S.S. *Keenora*, Manitoba's oldest steamship.

❹ Lake Winnipeg

🚉 Winnipeg. 🚌 Winnipeg. ℹ Travel Manitoba, (204) 927 7800, 1 800 665 0040. 🆆 travelmanitoba.com

Lake Winnipeg is a huge stretch of water some 430 km (270 miles) long that dominates the province of Manitoba, connecting the south of the province to the north at Hudson Bay via the Nelson River. Today, the resorts that line the lake are popular with locals and visitors alike.

Numerous beaches line the southeastern coast of the lake, including Winnipeg Beach, one of the province's most popular summer resort areas. A wood carving of a head by Hungarian artist Peter "Wolf" Toth stands in the local park. Called *Whispering Giant*, the sculpture honors the Ojibway, Cree, and Assiniboine First Nations people of Manitoba.

Grand Beach in the **Grand Beach Provincial Park** has long powdery-white sand beaches and huge grass-topped dunes over 12 m (39 ft) high. Stretching back from the beach, the marsh, which is also known as the lagoon, is one of the park's treasures, and supports many species of birds, such as the rare and endangered piping plover.

Moving west from the lake, **Oak Hammock Marsh** provides an important habitat for over 300 species of birds and animals. The marsh's tall grass prairie, meadows, and aspen-oak bluffs house birds such

Historic ships outside the Marine Museum of Manitoba in Selkirk

Carved cedar sculpture in the park at Winnipeg Beach

as the ruff (a shorebird), the garganey (a duck), and the sharp-tailed sparrow.

Hecla/Grindstone Provincial Park occupies a number of islands in the lake. A causeway links the mainland to Hecla Island, originally inhabited by the Anishinabe (Ojibwa) people. The first European settlers here were Icelanders, who arrived in 1875. Today, the lakeside village of Hecla is a pretty open-air museum featuring several restored 19th-century buildings. From Hecla there are hiking and biking trails that lead to view-points for sightings of waterfowl such as great blue herons and the rare western grebe.

Grand Beach Provincial Park
Hwy 12, nr Grand Marais. **Tel** (204) 754 5040. **Open** daily. partial.
gov.mb.ca

Hecla/Grindstone Provincial Park
Hwy 8, nr Riverton. **Tel** (204) 378 2261. **Open** daily. **gov.mb.ca**

❺ Gimli

2,200. 108–94 First Ave., (204) 642 6697. **gimli.ca**

Located on the western shores of Lake Winnipeg, Gimli is the largest Icelandic community outside Iceland. The settlers arrived, having gained the rights to land, at nearby Willow Creek in 1875. They soon proclaimed an independent state, which lasted until 1897, when the government insisted that other immigrants be allowed to settle in Gimli. Today, the **New Iceland Heritage Museum** tells the story of the town's unusual history.

Gimli has a distinctly nautical atmosphere, with cobbled sidewalks leading down to a picturesque harbor and a wooden pier. At the Icelandic Festival of Manitoba, held every August, visitors can play at being Vikings, listen to folk music, and eat Icelandic specialties.

About 25 km (16 miles) west of Gimli, Narcisse Snake Dens protect the habitat of thousands of red-sided garter snakes that can be seen here during early spring and early fall, on a specially designated short trail.

New Iceland Heritage Museum
108–94 First Ave. **Tel** (204) 642 4001.
Open May–Aug: 9am–4pm daily; Sep–Apr: 10am–4pm Mon–Fri, 1–4pm Sat & Sun. **nihm.ca**

❻ Portage la Prairie

13,000. 97 Saskatchewan Ave. E, (204) 239 8334. **city-plap.com**

Portage la Prairie lies at the center of a rich agricultural area growing wheat, barley, canola, and vegetables. The town is named after the French term for an overland detour, as Portage la Prairie lies between Lake Manitoba and the Assiniboine River, which formed a popular waterway for early travelers.

Statue of a Viking in the village of Gimli

Today, this thriving farming community contains the Fort La Reine Museum and Pioneer Village, on the site of the original fort built by the French explorer, La Vérendrye, in 1738. The museum offers exhibits of tools and photographs detailing 19th-century prairie life. The popular railroad display features a caboose, a watchman's shack, and the cigar-stained business car of Sir William Van Horne, founder of the Canadian Pacific Railroad. Pioneer Village successfully re-creates a 19th-century settlement with authentic stores and a church.

Pioneer Village, part of the Fort La Reine complex at Portage la Prairie

❼ Riding Mountain National Park

Hwys 10 & 19. **Tel** (204) 848 7275.
Open daily. 🚫 **W** pc.gc.ca

One of Manitoba's most popular natural attractions, Riding Mountain National Park is a vast 3,000 sq km (1,158 sq miles) wilderness. The best hiking trails and some of Manitoba's most beautiful scenery are to be found in the center of the park, where a highland plateau is covered by forests and lakes. To the east, a ridge of evergreen forest houses moose and elk. A small herd of bison can also be found in the park near Lake Audy. Bison were reintroduced here in the 1930s after they had been hunted out at the end of the 19th century. The most developed area here is around the small settlement of Wasagaming, where information on the park's network of trails for cycling, hiking, and horseback riding is available. Canoes can also be hired for exploring Clear Lake.

For a unique camping experience, yurts and oTENTiks (a cross between a tent and a cabin) at Wasagaming Campground can be booked through Parks Canada.

❽ Dauphin

🏙 8,400. ✈ 🚌 🚆 🛈 100 Main St. S., (204), 622 3216.
W tourismdauphin.ca

A pleasant tree-lined town, Dauphin was named after the King of France's eldest son by the French explorer La Vérendrye. Located north of Riding Mountain National Park, Dauphin is a distribution-and-supply center for the farms of the fertile Vermilion River valley. The **Fort Dauphin Museum** in town is a replica of an 18th-century trading post. Exhibits include a trapper's birchbark canoe and several early pioneer buildings, including a school, church, and a blacksmith's store.

Today, the onion-shaped dome of the town's Church of the Resurrection is a tribute to Dauphin's Ukrainian immigrants, who began to arrive in 1891.

🏛 Fort Dauphin Museum
140 Jackson St. **Tel** (204) 638 6630. **Open** May–Sep: daily; Oct–Apr: by appointment. 🚫 🎦

❾ Yorkton

🏙 16,000. 🚌 🛈 Jct Hwy 9 & Hwy 16 (306), 783 8707.
W tourismyorkton.com

Founded as a farming community in 1882, Yorkton is located in central Saskatchewan. The striking architecture of its churches, especially St. Mary's, reflects the town's Ukrainian heritage. The church was built in 1914. Its 21-m (69-ft) high dome, icons and paintings are stunning. The **Western Development Museum** (one of four in the province) tells the story of immigrants to the region.

🏛 Western Development Museum
Hwy 16A. **Tel** (306) 783 8361. **Open** 9am–5pm Mon–Fri, noon–5pm Sat & Sun (closed Mon Jan–Mar). 🚫 🅿
W wdm.ca

The magnificent dome at St. Mary's Church, Yorkton

The elegant façade of Motherwell Homestead

❿ Fort Qu'Appelle

🏙 2,000. 🛈 160 Company Ave. S., (306) 332 5266. **W** fortquappelle.com

Named after an 1864 Hudson's Bay Company fur-trading post, the picturesque town of Fort Qu'Appelle is located between Regina and Yorkton on Highway 10. The **Fort Qu'Appelle Museum** is built on the site of the old fort and incorporates a small out-building that was part of the original structure. The museum houses Aboriginal artifacts such as antique beadwork and a collection of pioneer photographs.

The 430-km (267-mile) long Qu'Appelle River stretches across two-thirds of southern Saskatchewan. At Fort Qu'Appelle the river widens into a string of eight lakes bordered by several provincial parks. Scenic drives through the countryside are one of the attractions of the valley.

About 30 km (19 miles) east of Fort Qu'Appelle is the **Motherwell Homestead National Historic Site**. This gracious house with ornamental gardens was built by politician William R. Motherwell. He introduced many agricultural improvements to the area and was so successful that he became Saskatchewan's agriculture minister from 1905 to 1918.

🏛 Fort Qu'Appelle Museum
198 Bay Ave N. **Tel** (306) 332 5751.
Open Jun–Aug: 1–5pm daily. 🚫
🅿 limited.

🏠 Motherwell Homestead
Off Hwy 22. **Tel** (306) 333 2116.
Open mid-May–Jun: 10am–4pm Mon–Fri; Jul & Aug: 10am–4pm daily.
🚫 🅿 limited. **W** pc.gc.ca

One of a small herd of bison at Riding Mountain National Park

⓫ Regina

215,000. ✈ 🚂 🚌 ℹ 1925 Rose St., (306) 789 5099, 1 800 661 5099.
w tourismregina.com

Regina is a friendly, bustling city and the capital of Saskatchewan. The city was named for Queen Victoria by her daughter, Princess Louise, who was married to the Governor General of Canada. Regina was established in 1882, after starting life as a tent settlement called Pile O'Bones. This is a derivation of "oskana" (a Cree word meaning buffalo bones), from the piles of bones left behind after hunting.

Today, Regina is a thriving modern city, whose highrise skyline contrasts with the 350,000 trees of the man-made Wascana Centre, a 9-sq-km (3.5-sq-mile) park containing a vast lake. The lake's Willow Island is a popular site for picnics and can be reached by ferry. The park is also a haven for some 60 species of waterfowl, including Canada geese. The **Royal Saskatchewan Museum** borders beautiful Wascana Park. Its Earth Sciences Gallery depicts 3.5 billion years of geological history of Saskatchewan, while the First Nations Gallery traces 10,000 years of aboriginal culture in the province. The Life Sciences Gallery shows Saskatchewan's eco-regions and the impact of the "human factor." The original

Canadian goose in Wascana Centre Park

headquarters for the North West Mounted Police lies west of the city center.

Today, the Royal Canadian Mounted Police Depot Division trains all Canada's Mounties and is also the site of the **RCMP Heritage Centre**. Here, the story of the Mounties is told from their beginnings following the Cyprus Hills Massacre in 1873 (see p251). Among the highlights are the ceremonies and drills that are regularly performed by special trained groups of Mounties, including the Sergeant Major's Parade and Sunset Retreat Ceremonies.

🏛 **Royal Saskatchewan Museum**
2445 Albert St. **Tel** (306) 787 2815.
Open daily. **Closed** Dec 25. ♿ ♻ (donation). w royalsaskmuseum.ca

🏛 **RCMP Heritage Centre**
5907 Dewdney Ave. W. **Tel** (306) 522 7333. **Open** daily. ♻ 🎥 ♿
w rcmphc.com

One of several murals on downtown buildings in Moose Jaw

⓬ Moose Jaw

35,000. 🚂 🚌 ℹ Jct Thatcher Drive E & Hwy 1, (306) 693 8097.
w tourismmoosejaw.ca

The quiet town of Moose Jaw was established as a railway terminus by the Canadian Pacific Railroad in 1882. A terminus for the American Soo Line from Minneapolis, Minnesota soon followed. Today, 46 murals celebrate the lives of the early railroad pioneers and homesteaders, decorating buildings around 1st Avenue. Nearby, River Street has 1920s hotels and warehouses that reflect Moose Jaw's time as "sin city" during the 1920s – when Prohibition in the United States meant that illegally produced liquor was smuggled from Canada to Chicago, by gangsters such as the infamous Al Capone.

The Moose Jaw branch of the Western Development Museum focuses on transportation and has a gallery on the Snowbirds, Canada's top aerobatic team.

Cadets of the Royal Canadian Mounted Police Academy in Regina are put through their paces

Traditional powwow dancer in Wanuskewin Heritage Park, Saskatoon

⓭ Saskatoon

🏠 250,000. ✈ ⊒ 🚇 🚌
ℹ 101–202 Fourth Ave. N., (306) 242 1206, 1 800 567 2444.
Ⓦ **tourismsaskatoon.com**

Founded in 1882 by Ontario Methodist John Lake as a temperance colony, Saskatoon is located in the middle of prairie country. Today, the city is an agricultural and commercial hub for cattle ranchers and wheat farmers from surrounding communities. The region's history is told just south of downtown in Saskatoon's branch of the Western Development Museum, which focuses on the town's boom years in the early 1900s, re-creating the bustling main street of a typical prairie town, including its railroad station and a hotel. The town center houses The Ukrainian Museum of Canada, with its brightly colored traditional textiles, and the Remai Modern Art Gallery, with a permanent art collection and changing exhibitions of international, national, and regional artwork.

The South Saskatchewan River meanders through the city and is bounded by many lush parks, including the outstanding 307-ha (759-acre) **Wanuskewin Heritage Park**. The park is devoted to Northern Plains First Nations history, with arch-aeological sites that confirm the existence of hunter-gatherer communities some 6,000 years ago. Some of the digs are open to the public in the summer. The park's wooded hills and marshy creeks are still held to be sacred lands by the Northern Plains peoples, who act as interpretive guides. Easy-to-follow trails lead past tipi rings, an ancient medicine wheel, buffalo trails, and a buffalo jump *(see p300)*.

🏛 **Wanuskewin Heritage Park**
Off Hwy 11. **Tel** (306) 931 6767. **Open** 9am–4:30pm Mon–Fri, 11am–4pm Sat. **Closed** Sun, holidays 🅿 🅰 limited.
📷 🚫 🅿 Ⓦ **wanuskewin.com**

⓮ Grasslands National Park

Jct Hwys 4 & 18. ℹ Val Marie, (306) 298 2257. **Open** daily; check website for opening hours of visitor centers.
Ⓦ **pc.gc.ca**

Situated in the southwest corner of Saskatchewan, Grasslands National Park was set up in 1988 to preserve one of the last original prairie grasslands in North America. The park is an area of climatic extremes, where summer temperatures can be as high as 40 °C (104 °F), and winter ones as low as -40 °C (-40 °F). This environment supports a range of rare wildlife, including short-horned lizards and ferruginous hawks. The rugged landscape along the Frenchman River valley is the only remaining habitat of the black-

Black-tailed prairie dog

tailed prairie dog in Canada. Visitors may hike and camp in the park, but facilities are basic.

East of the park is the striking, glacially formed landscape of the **Big Muddy Badlands**. In the early 1900s, caves of eroded sandstone and deep ravines provided hideouts for cattle thieves such as Butch Cassidy.

🏛 **Big Muddy Badlands**
Off Hwy 34. **Tel** (306) 267 3312. Tours in summer from Coronach. 🅿

Buttes (isolated flat-topped hills) in the Big Muddy Badlands seen from Grasslands National Park

For hotels and restaurants in this region see pp356–7 and pp376–7

⓯ Cypress Hills Interprovincial Park

Hwy 41. 🛈 (403) 893 3833.
Open daily. 🆆 cypresshills.com

Straddling the border between Saskatchewan and Alberta, the Cypress Hills Interprovincial Park offers fine views of the plains from its 1,400-m (4,593-ft) high peaks. The park's landscape is similar to the foothills of the Rocky Mountains, with its lodgepole pine forests and abundant wildflowers. Walking trails through the park offer the visitor the chance to see moose, elk, and white-tailed deer, as well as the 220 or more species of bird that stop here during migration, such as the rare trumpeter swan and mountain chickadee.

In the eastern section of the park, in Saskatchewan, **Fort Walsh National Historic Site** houses a reconstruction of Fort Walsh, which was built in 1875 by the Mounties to keep out the illicit whisky traders who were causing trouble among the aboriginal population. Costumed guides relate the history of the North West Mounted Police.

🖰 **Fort Walsh National Historic Site**
Cypress Hills Interprovincial Park.
Tel (306) 662 2645. **Open** mid-May–Jun & Sep: 9:30am–5pm Tue–Sat; Jul & Aug: 9:30am–5pm daily. 🚹
🆆 pc.gc.ca

⓰ Maple Creek

🏙 2,200. 🚌 🛈 114 Jasper St., (306) 662 4005. 🆆 maplecreek.ca

Located on the eastern edge of the Cypress Hills and affectionately known as "Old Cow Town," Maple Creek was established as a ranching center in 1882. The town still has a look of the Old West with trucks and Stetson-wearing ranchers filling the downtown streets. Maple Creek's many original 19th-century storefronts include the elegantly refurbished Commercial Hotel with its marble-floored lobby.

High Level Bridge over the Oldman River, Lethbridge

⓱ Medicine Hat

🏙 62,000. ✈ 🚌 🛈 330 Gehring Rd. SW. (403) 527 6422, 1 800 481 2822. 🆆 tourismmedicinehat.com

The south Saskatchewan River Valley is the picturesque setting for the town of Medicine Hat, which was founded in 1883 as a center for natural gas extraction. Medicine Hat also became a center for the manufacture of clay products, such as pottery, due to the natural abundance of clay along the banks of the South Saskatchewan River. Today, the **Medalta Potteries National Historic Site** in the 150-acre (60-ha) Historic Clay District is a living, working museum dedicated to telling the stories of the industry and the people who worked there.

🖰 **Medalta Potteries National Historic Site**
713 Medalta Ave. SE. **Tel** (403) 529 1070. **Open** daily. 🚹 ▣
🆆 medalta.org

⓲ Lethbridge

🏙 90,000. ✈ 🚌 🛈 2805 Scenic Dr. S., (403) 320 1222, 1800 661 1222.
🆆 exploresouthwestalberta.ca

Coal, oil, and gas are the basis of Lethbridge's success. Alberta's third-largest city was named after mine-owner William Lethbridge in 1885, but First Nations peoples, such as the Blackfoot, have inhabited the area since prehistoric times.

Lying on the banks of the Oldman River, Lethbridge is home to the notorious Fort Whoop-up, established in 1869 by whisky traders John Healy and Alfred Hamilton for the sole purpose of profiting from the sale of illicit, and often deadly, whisky. Many First Nations peoples, drawn by the lure of the drink, were poisoned or killed by the brew, which was made with substances such as tobacco and red ink. Today, a reconstruction of Fort Whoop-up and three galleries conjure up life at the fort in the 1870s.

Cypress Hills Massacre

On June 1, 1873 a group of whisky traders attacked an Assiniboine camp, killing several women, children, and braves in retaliation for the alleged theft of their horses. Many Aboriginal Peoples had already died from drinking the traders' liquor, which was doctored with substances such as ink and strychnine. The massacre led to the formation of the North West Mounted Police. Their first post at Fort Macleod in 1874, and another at Fort Walsh in 1875, marked the end of the whisky trade and earned the Mounties the Aboriginal Peoples' trust.

Two Assiniboine people from an engraving made in 1844

⑩ Royal Tyrrell Museum

The outstanding Royal Tyrrell Museum was opened in 1985 and is the only museum in Canada devoted to 4.5 billion years of the Earth's history. The layout of the exhibits enables visitors to follow the course of evolution through displays of dinosaurs and fossils from different ages. The museum uses interactive displays, videos, and three-dimensional dioramas to re-create distinct prehistoric landscapes, bringing the age of the dinosaurs and the study of palaeontology to life.

VISITORS' CHECKLIST

Practical Information
Hwy 838, 6 km NW of Drumheller.
Tel (403) 823 7707, 1 888 440 4240.
Open May 15–Aug: 9am–9pm daily; Sep: 10am–5pm daily; Oct–May 14: 10am–5pm Tues–Sun (except for public hols). 🚻 ♿
✏ 📷 🌐 tyrrellmuseum.com

Transport
🚌 Calgary.

Key

- 🟫 Cretaceous Alberta Gallery
- 🟫 Preparation Lab
- ⬜ Lords of the Land
- ⬜ Burgess Shale
- 🟫 Devonian Reef
- ⬜ Dinosaur Hall
- 🟫 Bearpaw Sea
- ⬜ Age of Mammals
- 🟫 Cretaceous Garden
- ⬜ Terrestrial Palaeozoic
- ⬜ Palynology Playroom
- ⬜ Ice Ages Gallery
- 🟫 Non-exhibition space

Dinosaur Hall
In Dinosaur Hall, a T-rex towers over a display of some 35 complete dinosaur skeletons.

The Ice Ages Gallery
displays skeletons of woolly mammoths and sabre-toothed tigers that inhabited North America.

Gallery Guide

The collection is housed on several levels reached by a series of ramps. Each area contains a display on an era of geological time. Introductory exhibits on fossils and dinosaurs are followed by displays on prehistoric mammals and the Ice Ages. The largest and most popular part of the museum is the Dinosaur Hall.

Organized Treks

Visitors on a trek through the badlands

The Royal Tyrrell Museum has a Field Centre within Dinosaur Provincial Park *(see opposite)*. As well as interesting displays on the park's history, the Field Centre is the starting point for guided tours run by the park (by bus or on foot). These allow participants to learn more about the creatures that populated ancient Alberta. There is also a self-guided walking tour.

Auditorium

Black Beauty Skull
This T-rex was found in the Crowsnest Pass area of south-western Alberta. The black discoloration was the result of a chemical reaction as the skeleton fossilized.

Elk Island National Park's largest lake, Astotin Lake, is skirted by a popular hiking trail

⓴ Dinosaur Provincial Park

Rte 544. **Tel** (403) 378 4342.
Open daily. 🅿 🅆 **albertaparks.ca**

Two hours' drive southeast of the town of Drumheller, the UNESCO World Heritage Site of Dinosaur Provincial Park, established in 1955, contains some of the world's richest fossil beds. Located along the Red Deer River Valley, the park includes dinosaur skeletons mostly from the late Cretaceous Period, about 75 million years ago (see pp234–5). More than 300 mostly intact skeletons have been discovered here, and over 30 institutions worldwide have specimens from this valley on display.

From Drumheller it is possible to drive the 48-km (30-mile) loop **Dinosaur Trail** through the "Valley of the Dinosaurs." The trail passes the Royal Tyrrell Museum, takes in stunning views of the badlands landscape from highpoints such as Horseshoe Canyon, and leads to intriguing rock hoodoos.

🏕 **Dinosaur Trail**
ℹ Drumheller, (403) 823 1331.
🅆 **traveldrumheller.com**

⓵ Red Deer

🏙 98,000. 🚌 ℹ 101–4200 Hwy 2 (403) 346 0180.
🅆 **visitreddeer.com**

Located midway between Calgary and Edmonton, this bustling city was founded in 1882 by Scottish settlers as a stopover point for travelers. A modern city with good cultural and recreational facilities, Red Deer is the hub of central Alberta's rolling parkland district. The city has some interesting buildings, such as the award-winning St. Mary's Parish, and the landmark Water Tower, known as the "Green Onion." The city's beautiful reserve of Waskasoo Park is located along the Red River.

⓶ Elk Island National Park

Hwy 16. **Tel** (780) 922 5790. **Open** daily. 🅿 🅆 **pc.gc.ca**

Established in 1906 as Canada's first animal sanctuary, Elk Island became a national park in 1913. It offers a wilderness retreat only half-an-hour's drive from Edmonton. This 194 sq km (75 sq miles) park provides a habitat for large mammals such as elk, the plains bison, the rarer, threatened wood bison, and moose. The park's landscape of transitional aspen parkland (an area of rolling meadows, woodlands, and wetlands) is, according to the World Wildlife Fund for Nature, one of the most threatened habitats in North America.

Aspen trees grow mostly on dry ridges, while balsam, poplar, and white birch grow near wet areas. Plants such as sedges and willows also thrive in the wetlands alongside a host of birds such as the swamp sparrow and yellow warbler.

Elk Island is a popular day trip from Edmonton as well as being a draw for wildlife photographers. There are 13 hiking trails of varying lengths. During the summer a wide range of activities is available in the park including swimming, kayaking, canoeing, and camping. Cross-country skiing is the most popular winter activity.

Hoodoos, towers of rock sculpted by erosion, near Drumheller

Ice Palace at West Edmonton Mall

㉓ Edmonton

930,000. ✈ ✛ 🚗 🚋
i 9797 Jasper Ave., (780) 401 7696.
w exploreedmonton.com

Edmonton spans the valley of the North Saskatchewan River and sits in the center of Alberta province, of which it is the capital. Established as a series of Hudson's Bay Company trading posts in the 1790s, this city is now the focus of Canada's thriving oil industry.

Edmonton's downtown area is centered on Jasper Avenue and Sir Winston Churchill Square, where modern high-rises sit among shops and restaurants. The gigantic **West Edmonton Mall** contains over 800 stores, an amusement and water park, over 100 restaurants, a bowling center, an ice rink, an aquarium, and a movie theater. In contrast is one of Alberta's oldest buildings, the delightful Alberta Legislature, opened in 1913. Overlooking the river, on the site of the old Fort Edmonton, the building has beautiful landscaped grounds. There is also the Royal Alberta Museum, with its natural history displays.

Southwest of downtown, Fort Edmonton Park re-creates the original Hudson's Bay Company fort with reconstructions of street areas in 1885 and 1920. Here visitors can experience past times, wandering around original shops and businesses, as well as taking rides on a horse-drawn wagon, steam train, or street car.

Northwest of downtown is the Telus World of Science, which boasts an IMAX theatre, Observatory, and Star Theatre.

🎠 **West Edmonton Mall**
170th St. & 87th Ave. **Tel** (780) 444 5200. **Open** daily. ♿

㉔ Vegreville

5,500. 🚌 *i* at the giant Pysanka, (780) 632 6800.

Along the Yellowhead Hwy, heading eastward from Edmonton, lies the predominantly Ukrainian town of Vegreville. Its community is famous for producing traditionally Ukrainian, highly decorated Easter eggs (or *pysanky*). Visible from the road is a giant pysanka covered with intricate bronze, gold, and silver designs that tell the story of the region's Ukrainian settlers, and celebrates their religious faith, bountiful harvests, and the protection they received from the RCMP. The egg is 7 m (23 ft) high, and is made of over 3,500 pieces of aluminum.

A giant decorated Easter egg, or pysanka, celebrates Vegreville's heritage

㉕ Wood Buffalo National Park

Main access: Fort Smith, NWT.
Tel (867) 872 7900. **Open** daily. 🏞
w pc.gc.ca

The largest national park in Canada, Wood Buffalo is about the size of Denmark, covering an area of 44,807 sq km (17,300 sq miles). The park was made a UNESCO World Heritage Site in 1983 because of the range of habitat it offers for such rare species of animal as the wood bison.

There are three different environments here: fire-scarred forest uplands; a large, poorly drained plateau filled with streams and bogs; and the Peace-Athabasca Delta, full of sedge meadows, marshes, and shallow lakes. Sightings of bald eagles and peregrine falcons are common, and the park is the only remaining natural nesting site of the rare whooping crane in the world.

The Grey Owl Story

Long before conservation became popular, the renowned naturalist by the name of Grey Owl, took up the cause. Inspired by his Mohawk wife, Anahareo, he wrote the first of several best-selling books, *Men of the Last Frontier*, in 1931, the same year he became the official naturalist of Prince Albert National Park. He built a cabin on the peaceful shores of Lake Ajawaan from where he ran a beaver protection program. When Grey Owl died of pneumonia in 1938, there was uproar when a newspaper discovered that he was really an Englishman. Born in Hastings in 1888, Archibald Stansfield Belaney took on the identity of Grey Owl when he returned to Canada after World War I. He wore buckskins and wore his hair in Apache-style braids. A generation later Grey Owl's legacy remains the protection of Canada's wildlife.

Grey Owl feeding a beaver

⓴ Prince Albert National Park

Established in 1927, Prince Albert National Park covers 3,875 sq km (1,500 sq miles) of wilderness, from the gently rolling terrain of aspen parkland in the south to the spruce and fir trees of the northern boreal forest. These distinct environments house different wildlife populations, with moose, wolf, and caribou in the forests, and elk, bison, and badger in the parkland. The center of the park, and the most accessible areas for visitors, are the hiking and canoeing trails around the Kingsmere and Waskesiu Lakes. The townsite of Waskesiu is the best place from which to begin exploring the park.

VISITORS' CHECKLIST

Practical Information
Off Hwy 2. **Tel** (306) 663 4522.
Open daily. Nature center open Jul–Aug only.
W pc.gc.ca
W waskesiuwildernessregion.com

Key

▬ Major road

═ Minor road

▪▪ Hiking route

— Rivers

Grey Owl's cabin by Ajawaan Lake
A 20-km (12-mile) hiking trail leads to Grey Owl's log cabin, "Beaver Lodge."

Beach resort at Waskesiu Lake
The village of Waskesiu offers visitors a wide range of facilities, including stores, hotels, and a sandy beach.

Kingsmere Lake

Crean Lake

The Hanging Heart Lakes form a waterway that leads to Lake Crean – one of the popular canoe trips in the park.

The Nature Centre explains the park's ecology.

0 km 3

0 miles 3

Waskesiu Lake

• Waskesiu

Prince Albert

Mud Creek Trail is a 2-km (1-mile) loop that skirts the lake then follows Mud Creek. In spring, spawning fish attract bears.

View over Waskesiu Lake
Fall foliage across the boreal forest seen around the lake from Kingsmere Road.

For map symbols *see back flap*

Gun with carriage at Fort Battleford National Historic Site

㉗ North Battleford and Battleford

👥 18,500. 🚌 ℹ️ Jct Hwys 16 & 40, (306) 445 2000, 1 800 243 0394. 🌐 battlefords.ca

North Battleford and Battleford, together known as The Battlefords, face each other across the North Saskatchewan River. Named after a ford in the Battle River, the area was the site of age-old conflicts between the Blackfoot and Cree. An important early settlement in the West, it was the seat of the North-West Territories government from 1876 to 1882. Today, the communities are thriving industrial centers, although the North Battleford branch of the Western Development Museum focuses on rural life.

The **Allen Sapp Gallery** displays works by one of Canada's best-loved contemporary artists, who died in 2015. Sapp's delicately colored paintings and drawings celebrate the traditions of the Northern Plains Cree community.

Between the Saskatchewan and Battle rivers is the **Fort Battleford National Historic Site** containing a well-restored North-West Mounted Police post. The stockade has original buildings, including the look-out point in the commander's residence, officers' quarters, and restored barracks now housing a museum. Costumed guides tell the story of when 500 settlers took refuge in the stockade during the North-West Rebellion.

🏛 Allen Sapp Gallery
1 Railway Ave. E. **Tel** (306) 445 1760. **Open** Jun–Sep: 11am–5pm daily; Oct–May: noon–4pm Wed–Sun. 🖼 donation. ♿ 🌐 allensapp.com

🏛 Fort Battleford National Historic Site
Off Hwy 4. **Tel** (306) 937 2621. **Open** mid-May–Jun: 10am–4pm Mon–Fri; Jul–Aug: 10am–4pm daily. 🖼 ♿ 🌐 pc.gc.ca

㉘ Batoche National Historic Site

Rte 225 off Hwy 312. **Tel** (306) 423 6227. **Open** mid-May–Jun & Sep–mid-Oct: 9am–5pm Mon–Fri; Jul & Aug: 9am–5pm daily. 🖼 ♿ 🌐 pc.gc.ca

The original village of Batoche was the site of the Métis's last stand against the Canadian Militia, led by Louis Riel and Gabriel Dumont in 1885 *(see p55)*.

From the 17th century, white fur traders in the west had married aboriginal wives and adopted tribal languages and customs. The resulting mixed raced peoples, the Métis, had originally rebeled in 1869 in the Winnipeg area in defense of their land rights. When history began to repeat itself in 1885, Métis rebels recalled Riel from exile in Montana to declare a provisional government at Batoche. Violence erupted on May 9, 1885 into what was to become known as the North-West Rebellion. Riel surrendered, was tried for treason, and hanged in Regina.

Today, the Batoche National Historic Site of Canada occupies the site of the village and battlefield. The 6-sq-km (2.5-sq-miles) park houses the bullet-ridden St. Antoine de Padoue Church and Rectory, as well as the cemetery, where the Métis leaders are buried. An interpretive center features an audio-visual presentation telling the history of Batoche and the rebellion through the eyes of the Métis.

St. Antoine de Padoue Church and Rectory at Batoche National Historic Site

For hotels and restaurants in this region see pp356–7 and pp376–7

Polar Bears

Known as the "Lord of the Arctic," the magnificent polar bear can weigh as much as 650 kg (1,433 lb). In the fall the bears begin to congregate along the bay east of Churchill waiting for ice to form in order to hunt seals. Their acute sense of smell can detect a scent up to 32 km (20 miles) away and pick up the presence of seals under 1 m (3 ft) of snow and ice.

Between 900 and 1,000 bears pass by and through Churchill during the season. The best way to view them is in a tundra buggy, a large buslike vehicle that is warm, safe, and elevated over 2 m (6.5 ft) from the ground.

The majestic polar bear

for centuries, used by both Aboriginal Peoples and, later, European explorers and fur traders, to travel from the northern forests to the prairies. Today, visitors may follow the historic route on guided canoe tours as well as fishing for northern pike, lake trout, walleye, and perch.

❷ Churchill

🏠 800. ✈ 🚂 🛈 Off Kelsey Blvd. (204) 675 8863. 🅦 churchill.ca

Located at the mouth of the Churchill River on Hudson Bay, the town retains the look of an industrial town, with no luxury hotels, few paved roads, and few trees. This vast Arctic landscape is snow-free only from June through to the end of September. Churchill has no road access and can be reached only by plane or train from Winnipeg, Thompson, and The Pas. Despite its remote situation, Churchill was an important point of entry into Canada for early European explorers and fur traders arriving by boat in the 18th century. The Hudson's Bay Company established an outpost for fur-trading here in 1717.

Today, visitors come to see the polar bears, beluga whales, and the splendid tundra flora in this region. In the spring and fall the tundra's covering of moss, lichens, and tiny flowers bursts into an array of colors. In the summer beluga whales move upriver and can be seen from boat trips or on scuba dives. Churchill is also one of the best places to see the Northern Lights.

❷ Duck Lake

🏠 670. 🚌 🛈 (306) 467 227. 🅦 ducklake.ca

A little to the west of the small farming village of Duck Lake lies a plaque commemorating the first shots fired in the North-West Rebellion. On March 26, 1885, a police interpreter and a Cree emissary scuffled during a parley, and the officer was killed. During the ensuing battle, 12 NWMP officers and six Métis died. The Battle of Duck Lake is depicted in a series of murals at the town's interpretive center.

❸ The Pas

🏠 5,500. ✈ 🚂 🚌 🛈 1559 Gordon Ave., (204) 623 7256.
🅦 townofthepas.com

Once a key fur-trading post dating back some 300 years, The Pas is now a major industrial distribution and transportation center for Manitoba's northwest. Nearby Clearwater Lake Provincial Park is named for the lake itself, which is said to be so clear that it is possible to see the bottom at 11 m (36 ft). The park offers a walking trail through "the caves," a geological phenomenon, where rock masses split away from cliffs to create huge crevices that provide shelter for a number of animals, including black bears, moose, wolves, and foxes.

❹ Flin Flon

🏠 5,100. ✈ 🚌 🛈 Hwy 10A, (204) 687 7674. 🅦 cityofflinflon.ca

Steep hilly streets reflect the fact that Flin Flon lies on Precambrian rock (as old as the formation of the Earth's crust itself, roughly 3.8 billion years ago), and the area is famous for its distinctive greenstone. The town bears the name of a fictional character of a popular novel, *The Sunless City* by J. E. P. Muddock. The book was read by a prospector at the time he staked his claim here in 1915. Copper and gold are still mined in Flin Flon, but visitors mostly come to experience the vast wilderness of the nearby Grass River Provincial Park.

The distinctive Grass River, where strings of islands dot the countless lakes of the river system, has been a trade route

Polar bear warning sign near Churchill

Winter sunset, Mount Seymour Provincial Park, British Columbia ▶

BRITISH COLUMBIA AND THE ROCKIES

Introducing British Columbia and the Rockies

The dramatic beauty of British Columbia (BC) and the Rockies' lakes, forests, and mountain ranges – which stretch across the border into Alberta – make it a much-visited area. There is a wide variety of landscapes available here, from the northern Rockies with their bare peaks, to the south's Okanagan Valley with its orchards and vineyards. The region's temperate climate means that BC has more species of plants and animals than anywhere else in the country.

Millions of visitors come here every year, drawn by a wide range of outdoor activities. To the west, Vancouver Island offers ancient rainforest and the impressive coastal scenery of the Pacific Rim National Park Reserve. Vancouver is a stunningly attractive city, with good transportation links to the rest of the region, including Calgary in the east.

Rainforest in Gwaii Haanas National Park Reserve and Haida Heritage Site on Haida Gwaii

Illuminated by over 3,300 lights, Victoria's Parliament Buildings are reflected in the waters of Inner Harbour on Vancouver Island

Key

- ━━ Expressway
- ━━ Divided highway
- ━━ Highway
- ⋯⋯ Other road
- ⋯⋯ Main railway
- ⎯ Minor railway
- ━━ International border
- ⋯⋯ Regional border
- △ Summit

For map symbols see back flap

Snow-covered peaks reflected in the waters of
Emerald Lake in the Rockies' Yoho National Park

Getting Around

The Trans-Canada Highway (Hwy 1) is the major highway
that leads to the rest of the province from Vancouver, passing
through the gold rush route along the Fraser Canyon, then
on to Alberta. From Hope, there are two more roads leading
to the interior: the Coquihalla Highway (Hwy 5) travels to
Kamloops and beyond, until it connects to Hwy 16, which
cuts through Jasper National Park; Hwy 3, meanwhile, runs
east and west through BC. VIA Rail runs a scenic route from
Vancouver to Jasper. Bus routes cover most destinations.

The Rocky Mountains

The Canadian Rocky Mountains are a younger section of the Western Cordillera, a wide band of mountain ranges that stretch from Mexico to Canada. Formed between 120 and 20 million years ago, they include some of Canada's highest peaks, the 325-sq-km (125-sq-mile) Columbia Icefield, and glacial lakes. In summer wild flowers carpet the alpine meadows; in winter both visitors and locals take advantage of the snow-covered slopes to indulge in winter sports. The flora and fauna of the Canadian Rockies are protected within several National Parks; the most noted being Banff, Jasper, and Yoho *(see pp304–315)*, which houses the renowned Burgess Shale fossil beds.

Locator Map

The Canadian Rockies

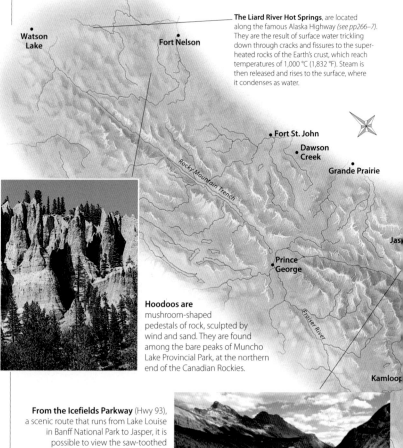

Watson Lake

Fort Nelson

The Liard River Hot Springs, are located along the famous Alaska Highway *(see pp266–7)*. They are the result of surface water trickling down through cracks and fissures to the super-heated rocks of the Earth's crust, which reach temperatures of 1,000 °C (1,832 °F). Steam is then released and rises to the surface, where it condenses as water.

Fort St. John

Dawson Creek

Grande Prairie

Rocky Mountain Trench

Jas

Prince George

Fraser River

Hoodoos are mushroom-shaped pedestals of rock, sculpted by wind and sand. They are found among the bare peaks of Muncho Lake Provincial Park, at the northern end of the Canadian Rockies.

Kamloop

From the Icefields Parkway (Hwy 93), a scenic route that runs from Lake Louise in Banff National Park to Jasper, it is possible to view the saw-toothed appearance of the youngest peaks in the range. These were formed during the last episode of uplift, about 20 to 15 million years ago. Older ranges such as the Appalachians *(see p29)* have rounded tops formed by long-term erosion.

Maligne Canyon is a 50-m deep (164-ft), limestone gorge in Jasper National Park. The canyon was formed by the meltwaters of a glacier that once covered the valley. Today, the Maligne River rushes through this narrow channel, which also drains a series of underground caves.

The Lewis Overthrust in Waterton Lakes National Park is a geological phenomenon. When rocks were moving east during the formation of the Rockies, a single mass composed of the lowest sedimentary layer of the Rockies – known as the Lewis Thrust – came to rest on top of the prairies.

The Burgess Shale fossil beds in Yoho National Park are a UNESCO World Heritage Site and contain fossils dating from the Cambrian to the Permian ages some 570–290 million years ago. There are two main fossil beds; Walcott's Quarry, and Mt. Stephen, known for its wealth of trilobite (Cambrian marine animal) fossils.

The Formation of the Rocky Mountains

There are three main forces responsible for the formation of the Rocky Mountains. First, large areas of the Earth's crust (known as tectonic plates), constantly moving together and apart, created uplift. Second, the North American plate was subducted by the Pacific plate, which caused a chain of volcanoes to form from the molten rock of the oceanic crust. Third, erosion caused by the Ice Ages, as well as rivers and wind, deposited sedimentary rocks on the North American plate, which was then folded by more plate movement between 50 and 25 million years ago. The Rockies' jagged peaks reflect their recent formation.

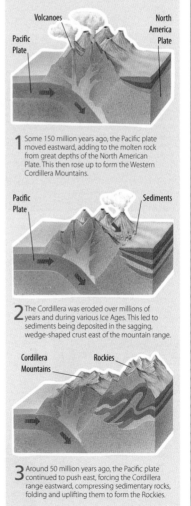

1 Some 150 million years ago, the Pacific plate moved eastward, adding to the molten rock from great depths of the North American Plate. This then rose up to form the Western Cordillera Mountains.

2 The Cordillera was eroded over millions of years and during various Ice Ages. This led to sediments being deposited in the sagging, wedge-shaped crust east of the mountain range.

3 Around 50 million years ago, the Pacific plate continued to push east, forcing the Cordillera range eastward, compressing sedimentary rocks, folding and uplifting them to form the Rockies.

Forestry and Wildlife of Coastal British Columbia

From its southern border with the United States to the northern tip of Haida Gwaii, the coastal region of British Columbia ranks as the richest ecological region in Canada. The warm waters of the north Pacific Ocean moderate the climate, creating a temperate rainforest teeming with life such as the black-tailed deer, black bear, and cougar. Dense forest still covers many islands, bays, and inlets along the coast, and is home to a large number of plant and animal species, including some of the tallest trees in Canada. Douglas Fir and Sitka Spruce can grow as high as 91 m (300 ft).

Trumpeter swans are so-called for their distinctive, brassy call. They are found on marshes, lakes, and rivers.

Temperate Rainforest Habitat

High rainfall and a mild climate have created these lush forests of cedar, spruce, and pine, with their towering Douglas Firs and Sitka Spruces. Housed beneath the dripping forest canopy is a huge variety of ferns, mosses, and wildflowers, including orchids. Today, environmentalists campaign to protect these ancient forests from the threat of logging.

Bald eagles, with their distinctive white heads, can be seen in large numbers diving for fish in the ocean near Haida Gwaii. This area is noted for having one of the largest bald-eagle populations in BC.

The white black bear, also known as the kermode or "spirit bear," is unique to coastal British Columbia. It is related to the black bear, and is an agile salmon catcher.

Black-tailed deer are found only on the north Pacific coast. They are the smallest member of the mule deer family and are preyed on by cougars in the area.

Harlequin ducks are small and shy, and the males have striking markings. A good swimmer, the harlequin enjoys fast-flowing rivers and the strong surf of the Pacific.

Salmon

BC's coastal waters are home to five Pacific salmon species: pink, coho, chinook, sockeye, and chum. Together they support one of the main commercial food fisheries in the world, though numbers are declining in some parts of BC. Pacific salmon spawn in freshwater streams only once in their life, then die.

Their offspring migrate downstream and out to sea, where they grow to adults ranging in size from 7 kg (15 lb) to over 45 kg (100 lb). At maturity they swim long distances upstream in order to return to the waters of their birth.

Chinook Salmon leaping while swimming upstream to spawn.

Sockeye Salmon are highly prized in BC's fishing industry for their firm, tasty flesh.

Coastline Habitat

The warm waters of the north Pacific Ocean provide a habitat for more species of wildlife than any other temperate coastline. This distinctive region is characterized by having thousands of islands and inlets, which provide a home for a range of animals. Mammals such as gray, humpback, and killer whales can be seen here, as can sea otters, seals, and sea lions.

Northern sea lions live in colonies along the rocky BC coast. Large, lumbering animals, they have short "forearms" that enable them to move on land.

The glaucous gull is a large, gray-backed sea gull, which nests along coastal cliffs, and on the numerous small islands here.

Sea otters were hunted, almost to extinction, for their thick fur coats. Today, these playful creatures are numerous off the coast of mainland BC and Vancouver Island.

Killer whales (or orcas) are found off the sheltered eastern coast of Vancouver Island and up BC's mainland coast. They are known as "killer" because they feed on other mammals.

The Alaska Highway

The building of the Alaska Highway was an extraordinary achievement. Winding through 2,451 km (1,523 miles) of wilderness, mountains, muskeg (moss-covered bog), and forest, the first road was completed in 1942, only eight months and twelve days after construction began. Linking the United States to Alaska through British Columbia, it was built after the Japanese attacked Pearl Harbor in 1941, as a military supply route and to defend the northwest coast of Alaska.

Today, the original gravel road has been replaced by a two-lane, mostly asphalt highway. The highway's many curves are gradually being straightened, shortening its total length, and the present road now covers 2,394 km (1,488 miles).

Locator Map

▨ Map area

Kluane National Park and Reserve contains some of the most dramatic scenery to be seen along the highway. The Kluane Mountains are among the highest in Canada, and icefields cover around half of the park's area.

Whitehorse is the capital of the Yukon and the center of the province's forestry and mining industries. The town, at mile 910 of the highway, retains a frontier atmosphere, and it is still possible to hear coyotes at night.

Historical Mile 836 marks the site of the Canol Project. This oil pipeline was built alongside the highway, to aid the military effort. The pipe ran an incredible 965 km (600 miles) to an oil refinery in Whitehorse.

Teslin Lake derives its name from the Tlingit language, meaning "long and narrow waters." The highway follows the 130-km long (80-mile) stretch of water, lined by snow-capped peaks. Today, the area attracts anglers eager to catch the plentiful trout, grayling, and pike, and hunters looking for game.

YUKON

Fairbanks

Destruction Bay ②

Haines Junction

Kluane National Park

Johnson's Crossing

Llewellyn Glacier Provincial Park

The Alaska Highway in winter is often covered in snow and affected by frost heave. Since it was opened to the public in 1949, teams of maintenance workers have ensured that the road is open year round.

Construction of the Highway

The Alaska Highway was built in under nine months by US army engineers and Canadian construction workers. The recruiting poster for workers warned: "This is no picnic… Men will have to fight swamps, rivers, ice, and cold. Mosquitoes, flies, and gnats will not only be annoying but will cause bodily harm. If you are not prepared to work under these […] conditions, DO NOT APPLY."

The workers shared mobile army camps that were moved along the route as construction progressed. If a company got stuck in one of many dismal swamps, they employed such techniques as laying corduroy – where whole trees were laid side by side, then spread with gravel. In some places en route as many as five layers were required.

Bogged-down truck waits for corduroy to be laid

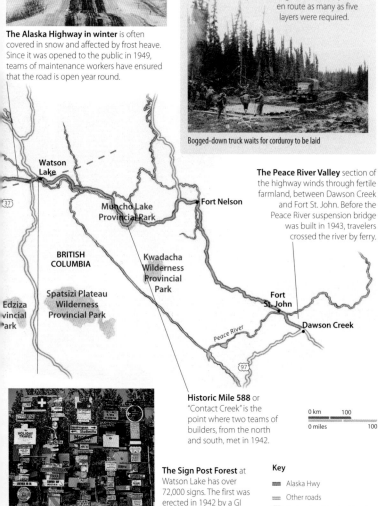

Watson Lake

37

Muncho Lake Provincial Park

Fort Nelson

BRITISH COLUMBIA

Kwadacha Wilderness Provincial Park

Spatsizi Plateau Wilderness Provincial Park

Edziza vincial ark

Fort St. John

Dawson Creek

Peace River

97

The Peace River Valley section of the highway winds through fertile farmland, between Dawson Creek and Fort St. John. Before the Peace River suspension bridge was built in 1943, travelers crossed the river by ferry.

Historic Mile 588 or "Contact Creek" is the point where two teams of builders, from the north and south, met in 1942.

0 km   100
0 miles   100

The Sign Post Forest at Watson Lake has over 72,000 signs. The first was erected in 1942 by a GI missing his hometown of Danville, Illinois.

Key

▪▪▪ Alaska Hwy

═══ Other roads

National and Provincial parks

- - Provincial boundaries

VANCOUVER AND VANCOUVER ISLAND

Looking out toward the waters of the Georgia Strait, Vancouver occupies one of the most beautiful settings of any world city. The coastal mountains form a majestic backdrop for the glass towers and copper-topped skyscrapers of the city. It was Captain James Cook who claimed the area for the British when he stepped ashore at Nootka Sound, Vancouver Island, in 1778. Until then the area had been inhabited for more than 10,000 years by the First Nations peoples, whose cultural heritage is celebrated in two of Canada's best museums: the UBC Museum of Anthropology in Vancouver and Victoria's Royal BC Museum. Established as a city after a fire destroyed the fledgling town of Granville in 1886, Vancouver offers historic districts, lush gardens, and wilderness parks within its environs. A short ferry ride away, Vancouver Island's world-famous Pacific Rim National Park Reserve is a major whale-watching center.

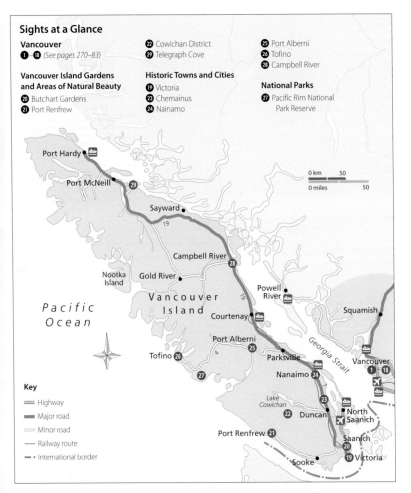

Sights at a Glance

Vancouver
1 – **18** *(See pages 270–83)*

Vancouver Island Gardens and Areas of Natural Beauty
20 Butchart Gardens
21 Port Renfrew

22 Cowichan District
29 Telegraph Cove

Historic Towns and Cities
19 Victoria
23 Chemainus
24 Nainamo

25 Port Alberni
26 Tofino
28 Campbell River

National Parks
27 Pacific Rim National Park Reserve

Key
- ▬▬ Highway
- ▬▬ Major road
- ▬▬ Minor road
- ── Railway route
- ▬·▬ International border

◀ Partial view of Ga'akstalas and Sky chief totem poles in Stanley Park, Vancouver

For map symbols *see back flap*

Exploring Vancouver

The heart of Vancouver is its downtown area, a finger of land bounded by the waters of English Bay. The city center radiates from Robson Square. The 405-ha (1,000-acre) Stanley Park occupies the tip of the peninsula, next to the West End. The historic Chinatown and Gastown districts are close to Main Street, the city's south to north axis.

Sights at a Glance

Historic Streets and Buildings
❷ Chinatown
⓬ Old Hastings Mill Store Museum

Parks and Gardens
❶ Dr. Sun Yat-Sen Classical
   Chinese Garden
❾ Queen Elizabeth Park and
   Bloedel Conservatory
⓾ VanDusen Botanical Garden
⓭ Stanley Park
⓯ Lynn Canyon Park and
   Ecology Centre
⓰ Grouse Mountain
⓱ Capilano Suspension Bridge
⓲ Lighthouse Park

Modern Architecture
❹ BC Place Stadium

Museums and Galleries
❸ Science World
❺ Vancouver Art Gallery
❻ Vancouver Maritime Museum
❼ Museum of Vancouver and
   H. R. MacMillan Space Centre
⓫ *University of British Columbia*
   Museum of Anthropology pp280–81

Shopping Areas
❽ Granville Island
⓮ Lonsdale Quay Market

Key
- ▨ Sight
- ━ Highway
- ━ Major road
- ┄┄ Minor road
- Pedestrian walkway
- ═══ Railway
- ── Skytrain

For map symbols *see back flap*

WEST CORDOVA STREET

HARBOUR GREEN PARK

WEST HASTINGS STREET

ST PENDER STREET

ELVILLE STREET

CANADA PLACE

Canada Place

North Vancouver

Vancouver Harbour

Waterfront Station

SeaBus Terminal

WATERFRONT ROAD W

CRAB PARK AT PORTSIDE

Burrard

WEST HASTINGS STREET

HORNBY STREET

BURRARD STREET

PENDER STREET

WEST PENDER

GASTOWN

WATER ST

MAPLE TREE SQUARE

POWELL STREET

DOWNTOWN

Granville

HOWE STREET

VICTORY SQUARE

ABBOTT ST

CAMBIE ST

EAST CORDOVA STREET

MAIN STREET

5

ROBSON SQUARE

Vancouver City Centre

GRANVILLE STREET

RICHARDS STREET

DUNSMUIR STREET

WEST PENDER ST

EAST HASTINGS STREET

COLUMBIA STREET

GORE AVENUE

2

1

KEEFER STREET

GEORGIA STREET

ROBSON STREET

LIBRARY SQUARE

CAMBIE STREET

BEATTY STREET

Stadium-Chinatown

CHINATOWN

UNION STREET

SMITHE STREET

YMOUR STREET

SEYMOUR STREET

NELSON STREET

YALETOWN

HELMCKEN STREET

HAMILTON STREET

EXPO BOULEVARD

4

DUNSMUIR VIADUCT

GEORGIA VIADUCT

PACIFIC BOULEVARD

STATION ST

Yaletown-Roundhouse

DRAKE STREET

BOULEVARD

COOPERS PARK

CREEKSIDE PARK

Plaza of Nations

Pacific Central Station

AVID LAM PARK

MARINASIDE CRESCENT

Yaletown

Cambie Bridge

3

Main Street-Science World

TERMINAL AVENUE

Spyglass Place

The Village

QUEBEC STREET

e Creek

Stamps Landing

SPYGLASS PLACE

CAMBIE STREET

WEST 1ST AVENUE

2ND AVENUE

MILLBANK

ARLESON PARK

STREET

6TH AVENUE

Olympic Village

CAMBIE STREET

WEST

0 meters		400
0 yards		400

Getting Around

Vancouver's transportation system includes the SeaBus, bus, and SkyTrain, one of the longest automated light rapid transit systems in the world. The Canada Line is a tunnel connecting the waterfront to Richmond and the airport. The SeaBus runs between Lonsdale Quay in North Vancouver and Waterfront Station downtown, where it is possible to connect with the bus and SkyTrain system. Many Vancouverites commute by car, and rush-hour traffic is to be avoided because access to downtown is limited to a few bridges, including the hectic Lions Gate Bridge.

Vancouver's stunning harbor with mountains as a backdrop

Street-by-Street: Waterfront and Gastown

One of Vancouver's oldest areas, Gastown faces the waters of Burrard Inlet and lies between Columbia Street in the east and Burrard Street in the west. The district grew up around a saloon, opened in 1867 by John "Gassy Jack" Deighton whose statue can be seen on Maple Tree Square. Today, Gastown is a charming mix of cobblestone streets, restored 19th-century buildings, and storefronts. Chic boutiques and galleries line Powell, Carrall, and Cordova streets. Restaurants and cafés fill the mews, courtyards, and passages. Several eateries open onto Blood Alley, named for the city's first slaughterhouses. On the corner of Water and Cambie streets, visitors can hear the musical chimes of the steam clock every 15 minutes, and be entertained by street performers.

★ **Canada Place**
Canada Place is a waterside architectural marvel of white sails and glass that houses a hotel, a convention center, a trade center, a cruise ship terminal, and FlyOver Canada, which is a breathtaking flight simulator attraction.

The SeaBus
Stunning views of the harbor can be seen from the SeaBus, a catamaran that ferries passengers across Burrard Inlet between the central Waterfront Station and Lonsdale Quay in North Vancouver.

The Waterfront Station occupies the imposing 19th-century Canadian Pacific Railroad building.

★ **Harbour Centre Tower**
The Harbour Centre is a modern high-rise building best known for its tower, which rises 177 m (581 ft) above the city. On a clear day it is possible to see as far as Victoria on Vancouver Island from it.

Water Street
Much of the quaint charm of Gastown can be seen here. Water Street boasts gas lamps and cobblestones, as well as shops, cafés, and the famous steam clock.

Locator Map
See map pp270–71

Steam Clock
The world's first steam clock is still maintained by the man who built it in the 1970s. It toots every 15 minutes on the corner of Water and Cambie streets.

"Gassy" Jack Statue
Gastown is named after John "Gassy Jack" Deighton, an English sailor noted both for his endless chatter and for the saloon he opened here for the local sawmill workers in 1867.

The Inuit Gallery on Cambie Street offers a variety of original Inuit art such as jewelry and paintings.

WATERFRONT ROAD EAST

0 meters 100
0 yards 100

WATER STREET

OVA STREET WEST

WEST

T WEST

CAMBIE STREET

ABBOTT STREET

CARRALL STREET

Shopping on Cordova St. West is a delightful experience with its range of small galleries and trendy boutiques.

Triangular Building
Reminiscent of New York's Flatiron Building, this striking structure was built in 1908–9 as a hotel and forms the corner of Alexander and Powell streets. It is now an apartment building.

Key

— Suggested route

Peaceful pavilion in the Dr. Sun Yat-Sen Classical Chinese Garden

❶ Dr. Sun Yat-Sen Classical Chinese Garden

578 Carrall St. **Tel** (604) 662 3207.
🚉 & 🚌 Central Station, 19, 22. 🚌
Downtown terminal. **Open** variable
hours, so check website before visiting.
Closed Jan 1, Dec 25. ♿ 🅿 ♿
🅦 **vancouverchinesegarden.com**

Opened in 1986, the first full-sized Ming Dynasty-style classical Chinese garden built outside of China offers a refuge from Vancouver's bustling city center. The garden owes its tranquility to ancient Taoist principles, which aimed to create a healthy balance between the contrasting forces of man and nature.

Over 50 skilled craftsmen came from Suzhou, China's Garden City, to construct the garden, using traditional tools and techniques. Pavilions and walkways were all built with materials from China. Many of the plants and trees symbolize different virtues. Willow is a symbol of feminine grace, and the plum and bamboo represent masculine strength. Complimentary Chinese tea rounds out the soothing atmosphere.

❷ Chinatown

Pender St. 🚌 East Hastings & East
Pender sts routes.
🅦 **vancouver-chinatown.com**

Vancouver's Chinatown, the second-largest in North America, is older than the city itself. In 1858 the first wave of Chinese immigrants was drawn to Canada by the promise of gold. The Canadian Pacific Railroad attracted even more Chinese workers in the 1880s with jobs to build the new railroad. Today Chinatown stretches from Carrall to Gore streets and still provides a warm welcome for more recent Asian immigrants.

Declared an historic area in 1970, Chinatown has restored many of its notable houses with their elaborately decorated roofs and covered balconies. The main drag, Pender Street, is the best place to view the architectural details that decorate the upper stories of the buildings, such as highly painted wooden balconies.

Bilingual sign in Chinatown

Street signs with colorful Chinese characters add to the authentic atmosphere.

Whether buying mouth-watering duck, or watching the spicy dumplings known as won tons being made at top speed, or settling down to taste the myriad dishes available in numerous fine restaurants, the main attraction for the visitor is food. There is also a fascinating range of stores, from bakeries selling savory and sweet buns to traditional herbalists, and jewelers specializing in jade. In contrast to the bustling markets there are also several relaxing tearooms, as well as the nearby Dr. Sun Yat-Sen Chinese Garden, which also offers tea and cakes and has weekly evening concerts of Chinese music under the soft light of lanterns throughout the summer.

❸ Science World

1455 Quebec St. **Tel** (604) 443 7440.
🚉 Central Station. 🚌 Central Station.
Open 10am–5pm Mon–Fri,
10am–6pm Sat & Sun. **Closed** Dec 25.
♿ ♿ 🅦 **scienceworld.ca**

Overlooking the waters of False Creek, near the Main Street Railway Station, stands the 47-m- (154-ft-) high steel geodesic dome that houses Vancouver's science museum, Science World. The dome was

The striking geodesic dome housing Vancouver's interactive Science World

For hotels and restaurants in this region see pp357–8 and pp377–80. For transport information see p411

designed for Expo '86 and inspired by American inventor R. Buckminster Fuller. It is now one of the city's most striking landmarks and home to the highly interactive science museum.

In the Eureka! Gallery, visitors can design their own inventions. The Sara Stern Gallery lets visitors touch the furs and bones of animals, while the Puzzles and Illusions Gallery boggles the mind with its optical tricks and displays. For 2- to 6-year-olds, the Kidspace Gallery provides a safe and colorful environment for learning and play. The outdoor Ken Spencer Science Park features interactive environmental exhibits.

The museum is renowned for its OMNIMAX® Theatre, where a huge screen shows films that feature space exploration, journeys to exotic locations, and fun animation.

❹ BC Place Stadium

777 Pacific Blvd. **Tel** (604) 669 2300.
🚇 Stadium. **Open** varies, depending on scheduled events. 🦽
📷 May–Oct: Tue–Fri. 🦽
Ⓦ bcplacestadium.com

Standing out from the city's skyline, the state-of-the-art, retractable roof of the BC Place Stadium was unveiled in 2011. When the arena opened in 1983, it had a white fabric roof and was the first covered stadium in Canada and the largest air-supported dome in the world. The versatile stadium is able to convert in a matter of hours from a football field seating 60,000 people to a more intimate concert bowl seating up to 30,000.

Among the famous guests who have visited the dome are Queen Elizabeth II and Pope John Paul II. Visitors hoping to catch a glimpse of a celebrity or two can take behind-the-scenes tours to the locker rooms, playing fields, and media lounges. The stadium also houses the **BC Sports Hall of Fame and Museum**, which chronicles the history of the region's sporting heroes.

The state-of-the-art BC Place Stadium

🏛 **BC Sports Hall of Fame and Museum**
BC Place Stadium. **Tel** (604) 687 5520.
Open 10am–5pm daily. 🦽 🦽
Ⓦ bcsportshalloffame.com

❺ Vancouver Art Gallery

750 Hornby St. **Tel** (604) 662 4719.
🚇 Central Station. 🚌 Central Station.
🚌 3. **Open** 10am–5pm daily (to 9pm Tue; admission by donation). 🦽 🦽
Ⓦ vanartgallery.bc.ca

What was once British Columbia's imposing provincial courthouse now houses the Vancouver Art Gallery. The building was designed in 1906 by Francis Rattenbury, an architect known for the Gothic style of Victoria's Parliament building and the Empress Hotel (see pp284–85). The interior was modernized in 1983 by Arthur Erickson, another noted architect,

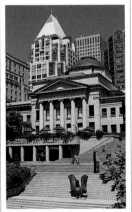

Decorative Victorian features on the Vancouver Art Gallery façade

who designed the UBC Museum of Anthropology (see pp280–81).

The Vancouver Art Gallery presents a full range of national and international art by groundbreaking contemporary artists and major historical figures, including the most significant body of work by British Columbian artist Emily Carr. The gallery also houses a permanent collection of 10,000 works of art. Visitors can take part in talks and tours, or visit interpretive sites and learning centers, as well as the Gallery Café and the Gallery Store.

❻ Vancouver Maritime Museum

1905 Ogden Ave. **Tel** (604) 257 8300. 🚇 & 🚌 Central Station. **Open** Mon–Sun 10am–5pm (to 8pm Thu; admission by donation). **Closed** Mon mid-Sep–mid-May, Dec 25. 📷 (entry by donation 5–8pm Thu). 🦽
Ⓦ vancouvermaritimemuseum.com

Celebrating Vancouver's history as a port and trading center, this museum's star feature is the schooner, St. Roch. Built as a supply ship for the Mounties in 1928, in 1940–42 it was the first ship to navigate the Northwest Passage in both directions.

Other displays include Map the Coast, which tells the story of British Captain George Vancouver and the crews of the Chatham and the Discovery, who charted the inlets of the coast of BC in 1792. The Children's Maritime Discovery Centre has a powerful telescope, through which the busy port can be viewed.

Steel sculpture in front of the Museum of Vancouver's distinctive façade

❼ Museum of Vancouver and H. R. MacMillan Space Centre

1100 Chestnut St., Vanier Park. **Tel** (604) 736 4431; Space Centre (604) 738 7827. 🚇 Central Station. 🚌 Central Station. 🚌 22. **Open** Museum: 10am–5pm Tue–Sun & holiday Mon; until 8pm Thu. Space Centre: 10am–3pm Mon–Fri, 10am–5pm Sat & hols, noon–5pm Sun. 📷 Museum: 5–8pm Thu by donation. ♿ 🅆 **museumof vancouver.ca**, 🅆 **spacecentre.ca**

Located in Vanier Park near the Vancouver Maritime Museum *(see p275)*, the Museum of Vancouver is a distinctive addition to the city's skyline. Built in 1967, the museum's curved, white, concrete roof is based on a First Nations hat. Outside, a stunning sculpture, which looks like a giant steel crab, sits in a fountain on the museum's south side.

Displays here include the Orientation Gallery, which re-creates British Columbia's rocky coastline and mountainous interior. Vancouver's history is explored from the culture of the First Nations of the area to the city's pioneering days. The museum is also noted for its depiction of everyday life, with exhibits such as an 1880s Canadian Pacific Railroad car, and the 1950s gallery, with a vintage Ford Thunderbird and a working jukebox.

At the same location, the H. R. MacMillan Space Centre is popular with both children and adults, who can explore the universe in the Planetarium and in the GroundStation Canada Theatre.

❽ Granville Island

1661 Duranleau St. **Tel** (604) 666 5784. 🚇 Central Station. 🚌 Central Station. 🚌 50. **Open** Market: 9am–7pm daily; other stores: 10am–7pm daily. ♿ 🅆 **granvilleisland.com**

Today, this once-down-trodden industrial district has a glorious array of stores, galleries, and artists' studios in its brightly painted warehouses and tin sheds. The Great Fire of 1886 destroyed almost all of fledgling Vancouver and drove people south across the water to Granville Island and beyond. Many of the early buildings were constructed on land reclaimed in 1915 to cope

Granville Island Brewing Company sign

with the burgeoning lumber and iron industries. There are very few chain stores on the island, and the smaller stores are known for their variety, originality, and quality, displaying a range of local arts and crafts such as rugs, jewelry, and textiles.

The island is also a center for the performing arts and boasts several music, dance, and theater companies.

A daily public market offers a cornucopia of foods that reflect Vancouver's ethnic diversity. Waterside cafés and restaurants occupy the False Creek Shore, where there was once a string of sawmills.

❾ Queen Elizabeth Park and Bloedel Conservatory

4600 Cambie St. **Tel** Conservatory: (604) 257 8584. 🚌 15. **Open** Conservatory: 10am–5pm daily (May–mid-Sep: 9am–8pm Mon–Fri, 10am–8pm Sat & Sun). 📷 for Conservatory. ♿

Queen Elizabeth Park is located on Little Mountain, Vancouver's highest hill (152-m/499-ft), and has fine views of the city. Despite being built on the site of two former stone quarries, the park's gardens are continually in bloom from early spring.

The plastic-domed Bloedel Conservatory is perched on top of the hill, and grows plants from many climactic zones in the world, from rainforest plants and trees to desert cacti. There are also free-flying colorful tropical birds and fishponds filled with Japanese carp.

The plastic dome of the Bloedel Conservatory in Queen Elizabeth Park

A dazzling fall display of reds and oranges, one of many attractions in Stanley Park

⑩ VanDusen Botanical Garden

5251 Oak St. **Tel** (604) 257 8463.
🚇 Central Station. 🚌 Central Station, 17. **Open** daily (hours vary). **Closed** Dec 25. 🅿 ♿
🌐 vandusengarden.org

This 22-ha (54-acre) garden was opened in 1975. In 1960 the land was under threat from its original owners, the Canadian Pacific Railroad, who wanted to build high-rise apartments. It took a campaign by local people and a donation from Mr W. J. VanDusen, a wealthy local businessman, to save the site.

Marble statue at the Botanical Gardens

Today, visitors enjoy a spectacular display of over 7,500 families of plants from six continents, set among lakes and marble sculptures. The Perennial Garden is filled with roses in summer, while September heralds the blazing reds and oranges of fall. The Visitor Center is leading the Garden's green initiatives: the roof uses solar panels and collects rainwater to be used throughout the gardens.

⑪ University of British Columbia Museum of Anthropology

See pp280–81.

⑫ Old Hastings Mill Store Museum

1575 Alma Rd. **Tel** (604) 734 1212.
🚌 4th Ave. route. **Open** Jun 15–Sep 15: 1–4pm Tue–Sun; Sep 16–Dec 1 & Feb 14–Jun 14: 1–4pm Sat & Sun. **Closed** Dec & Jan. 🅿 donation.
♿ 🌐 hastings-mill-museum.ca

The Old Hastings Mill Store Museum was Vancouver's first general store and post office and one of the few wooden buildings to survive the Great Fire of 1886. Built in 1865, it was moved from its original site at Gastown in 1930 to the shores of Jericho Beach and then to its present home on Alma Street, at the corner of Point Grey Road. Starting in the 1940s, local people contributed a variety of historic artifacts, and today it is an interesting small museum. Behind the pretty clapboard exterior, the museum's exhibits include a range of Victorian artifacts such as a horse-drawn cab, antique sewing machines, and an

The Old Hastings Mill Store Museum, one of Vancouver's oldest buildings

extensive collection of aboriginal artifacts including impressive hand-woven baskets.

⑬ Stanley Park

2099 Beach Ave. **Tel** (604) 257 8400.
🚇 Central Station. 🚌 Central Station, 123, 135. ⛴ Horseshoe Bay.
Open daily. ♿

This is a magnificent 404-ha (1,000-acre) park of tamed wilderness, just a few blocks from downtown, that was originally home to the Musqueam and Squamish Canadians. Named after Lord Stanley, Governor General of Canada, the land was made into a park by the local council in 1886. It offers visitors the opportunity to experience a range of typical Vancouver attractions. There are beaches, hiking trails, and fir and cedar woods, as well as wonderful views of the harbor, English Bay, and the coastal mountains. Bicycles can be rented for the popular ride around the 10-km (6-mile) perimeter seawall. The park is also home to the **Vancouver Aquarium** where visitors can watch incredible marine life, including dolphins and playful sea otters. The African penguins at Penguin Point are a popular exhibit.

🐋 **Vancouver Aquarium** Stanley Park. **Tel** (604) 659 3474. **Open** Jul & Aug: 9:30am–6pm daily; Sep–Jun: 10am–5pm daily. 🅿 🍴 ♿
🌐 vanaqua.org

⓫ University of British Columbia Museum of Anthropology

Founded in 1947, this outstanding museum houses one of the world's finest collections of Northwest coast First Nations' art. Designed by Canadian architect Arthur Erickson in 1976, the museum is housed in a stunning building overlooking mountains and sea. The tall posts and huge windows of the Great Hall were inspired by the post-and-beam architecture of Haida houses and are a fitting home for a display of full-size totem poles, canoes, and feast dishes. Through the windows of the Great Hall, the visitor can see the magnificent outdoor sculpture complex, which includes two houses designed by Haida artist Bill Reid and 'Namgis artist Doug Cranmer.

★ **The Great Hall**
The imposing glass-and-concrete structure of the Great Hall is the perfect setting for totem poles, canoes, and sculptures.

Outdoor Haida Houses and Totem Poles

Set overlooking the water, these two Haida houses and collection of totem poles are faithful to the artistic tradition of the Haida and other tribes of the Pacific Northwest, such as the Salish, Tsimshan, and Kwakiutl. Animals and mythic creatures representing various clans are carved in cedar on these poles and houses, made between 1959 and 1963 by Vancouver's favorite contemporary Haida artist Bill Reid and 'Namgis artist Doug Cranmer.

Carved red cedar totem poles

Climbing Figures
These climbing figures are thought to have decorated the interior of First Nations family houses. Carved from cedar planks, the spare style is typical of Coast Salish sculpture.

Ceramic Jug
This beautifully decorated jug was made in Central Europe in 1674 by members of the Anabaptist religious sect. The foliage motifs are in contrast to the freely sketched animals that run around the base.

**★ The Raven and
the First Men** (1980)
Carved in laminated yellow
cedar by Bill Reid, this modern
interpretation of a Haida creation
myth depicts the raven, a wise
and wily trickster, trying to
coax mankind out into
the world from a
giant clamshell.

VISITORS' CHECKLIST

Practical Information
6393 NW Marine Drive.
Tel (604) 822 5087.
Open 10am–5pm daily
(to 9pm Tue).
Closed Dec 25 & 26.
🎫 ♿ 📷 🏪 🅦 moa.ubc.ca

Transport
🚌 4 UBC, 84 UBC.

Gallery Guide

*The museum's collections are arranged on
one level. The Ramp gallery leads to the Great
Hall, featuring the cultures of Northwest-
coast First Nations peoples. The Multiversity
Galleries contain artifacts from other
cultures, and a range of 15th- to
19th-century European ceramics
is housed in the Koerner
European Ceramics Gallery.*

Wooden Frontlet
Decorated with abalone shell, this
wooden frontlet was a ceremonial
head-dress worn only on important
occasions such as births
and marriages.

**Red Cedar Carved
Front Doors**
This detail comes from the
set of stunning carved red
cedar doors that guard the
entrance to the museum.
Created in 1976 by a group
of First Nations artists from
the 'Ksan cultural center
near Hazelton, the doors
show the history of the first
people of the Skeena River
region in British Columbia.

Key
- ☐ The Great Hall
- ☐ Bill Reid Rotunda
- ☐ Multiversity Galleries
- ☐ Koerner European
  Ceramics Gallery
- ◼ The O'Brian & Audain Gallery
- ◼ Michael M. Ames Theatre
- ◼ Non-exhibition space

⑭ Lonsdale Quay Market

123 Carrie Cates Ct., North Vancouver.
Tel (604) 985 6261. 🚊 Lonsdale.
Open 9am–7pm daily. ♿
Ⓦ lonsdalequay.com

The striking concrete-and-glass building housing the Lonsdale Quay Market forms part of the North Shore SeaBus terminal. The market has a floor devoted to food – everything from fresh-baked bread to blueberries – as well as an array of cafés and restaurants that serve a variety of ethnic cuisines. On the second floor, visitors will find specialty shops offering a wide choice of hand-crafted products and gift items from local designers, as well as Kid's Alley, a row of child-oriented shops. The complex includes a hotel and spa, and a pub.

The modern fountain at Lonsdale Quay

⑮ Lynn Canyon Park and Ecology Centre

3663 Park Rd. **Tel** (604) 990 3755.
🚌 Hastings. 🚊 Lonsdale Quay, then bus 228 or 229. **Open** daily. Ecology Centre Jun–Sep: 10am–5pm daily; Oct–May: 10am–5pm Mon–Fri, noon–4pm Sat & Sun. **Closed** some hols, varies. 🎥 donation. 🎬 💻
Ⓦ dnv.org/ecology

Located between Mount Seymour and Grouse Mountain, Lynn Canyon Park is a popular hiking destination, noted for its lush second-growth temperate

rain forest. The original 90-m (295-ft) trees were logged in the early 20th century and a few of the huge stumps with circumferences of up to 11 m (36 ft) can still be seen lying on the forest floor. Some of the stumps have springboard notches left by lumberjacks of the time.

Several marked trails, some of them steep and rugged, lead through the canyon, with longer hikes heading into surrounding park land. Many of the trails, however, are gentle strolls through Douglas fir, western hemlock, and western red cedar. If you venture far enough into the forest, it is possible to see black bears, cougars, and black-tailed deer, but most visitors keep to the main trails where they are more likely to see squirrels, jays, woodpeckers, and banana slugs, which can grow to lengths of 26 cm (10 in). There are wonderful views from the 50-m (164-ft) high suspension bridge that crosses the canyon. From here, it's a short walk to 30 Foot Pool, a popular summer spot for sunbathing and swimming. A 40-minute walk takes hikers to the beautiful Twin Falls.

The nearby Ecology Centre offers guided walks, shows natural history films, and features interesting displays on the flora, fauna, and ecology of the area. Global environmental concerns are also covered.

Panoramic view of Vancouver's skyline from Grouse Mountain

⑯ Grouse Mountain

6400 Nancy Greene Way. **Tel** (604) 980 9311. 🚊 Lonsdale Quay. 🚌 236.
Open 9am–10pm daily. 🎿 ♿ 🚠
🖥 Ⓦ grousemountain.com

From the summit of Grouse Mountain visitors experience the grandeur of BC's dramatic landscape and stunning views of Vancouver. On a clear day it is possible to see as far as Vancouver Island in the west, the Coastal Mountains to the north and toward the Columbia Mountains in the east.

The famous "Grouse Grind" is a tough 3-km (2-mile) trail to the 1,127-m (3,700-ft) peak, but most visitors choose to take the Skyride aerial tramway. In the summer there are many activities, including mountain-bike tours, nature walks, and hang-gliding competitions, plus logger sports such as chain-saw sculpture.

In the winter, the summit has all the amenities of a ski resort, including ski schools, 26 ski runs, equipment rental, snowboarding, snowshoeing, an ice rink, and 13 illuminated slopes for night skiing.

At the Refuge for Endangered Wildlife, an enclosed natural habitat that is home to two orphaned grizzly bears and one timber wolf, wildlife rangers give daily talks. The Theatre in the Sky presents videos that take viewers on an aerial tour of BC and tell the tale of the orphaned bears.

The Skyride aerial tramway, Grouse Mountain

⓱ Capilano Suspension Bridge

3735 Capilano Rd., North Vancouver.
Tel (604) 985 7474. 🚌 Highlands 236.
Open daily (hours vary according to season). **Closed** Dec 25. 🅿 🛈 May–
Oct. 🅿 🛈 🅦 capbridge.com

The Capilano Suspension Bridge has been popular since it was built in 1889. Pioneering Scotsman George Grant Mackay, drawn by the wild beauty of the place, had already built a small cabin overlooking the Capilano Canyon. Access to the river below was almost impossible from the cabin, and it is said that Mackay built the bridge so that his son, who loved fishing, could easily reach the Capilano River.

The present bridge, which dates from 1956 and is the fourth to be constructed here, hangs 70 m (230 ft) above the canyon and spans 137 m (450 ft), making it one of the longest such bridges in the world. Nature lovers are drawn by the views and the chance to wander through old-growth woods (old trees that have never been felled) past trout ponds and a 61-m (200-ft) waterfall. The Treetops Adventure includes seven suspension bridges through evergreens, built 30 m (100 ft) above the forest floor. Not for the faint-hearted, the Cliffwalk has a series of narrow cliffside walkways jutting out above the Capilano River.

Point Atkinson Lighthouse

⓲ Lighthouse Park

Off Beacon Lane, West Vancouver.
Open 6am–10pm daily.
🅦 lighthousepark.ca

Named after the hexagonal lighthouse built at the mouth of Burrard Inlet in 1910 to guide ships through the foggy channel, Lighthouse Park is an unspoiled area with 75 ha (185 acres) of old growth forest and wild, rocky coast. The trees here have never been logged, and some of the majestic Douglas firs are over 500 years old.

There is a variety of hiking trails in the park, some leading to a viewpoint near the 18-m (60-ft) **Point Atkinson Lighthouse**. On a clear day one can see stunning vistas across the Strait of Georgia all the way to Vancouver Island. A 2-hour hike leads through about 5 km (3 miles) of old-growth forest, taking walkers through the fairly rugged terrain of moss-covered gullies and steep rocky outcrops with breathtaking views of the sea and surrounding area. Wear good walking shoes or boots, stay on the trails, and be prepared for inclement weather.

The drive to the park itself is spectacular. Scenic **Marine Drive** winds along the West Vancouver coastline edging past beaches, clinging to rocky shoreline and passing some of Canada's priciest real estate. On the way, there are a couple of towns that are worth a stop. **Ambleside** has a long beach, which is a favorite with families and dogs but packed on sunny summer weekends. From here there are great views of Stanley Park and the Lions Gate Bridge. A seawall walkway leads to Dundarave Pier, with panoramic views sweeping from Vancouver right around to the Strait of Georgia. **Dundarave** itself is a small village with a pleasing cluster of shops, cafés, and restaurants, as well as a beach that is not so busy as the beach at Ambleside.

The Capilano Suspension Bridge crossing the dramatic tree-covered Capilano Canyon

⑲ Victoria

A quiet, attractive city, Victoria enjoys a reputation for having an old-fashioned, seaside-town atmosphere. This is enhanced in the summer by the abundance of flowers in hanging baskets and window boxes that decorate every lamppost, balcony, and storefront. Established as a Hudson's Bay Company fur-trading post in 1843 by James Douglas, Victoria had its risqué moments during its gold rush years (1858–63), when thousands of prospectors drank in 60 or more saloons on Market Square. Victoria was established as the provincial capital of British Columbia in 1871, but was soon outgrown by Vancouver, now BC's largest city. Today, Victoria is still the province's political center as well as one of its most popular attractions for visitors.

Fishing boats and pleasure craft moored in Victoria's Inner Harbour

Octagonal main dome in the Parliament Buildings

Exploring Victoria

A stroll along Victoria's Inner Harbour takes in many of the city's main attractions, such as the Royal British Columbia Museum with its dramatic depictions of the geology and indigenous cultures of the region. Dominating the area are two late 19th-century buildings: the Fairmont Empress Hotel and the Parliament Buildings, designed by noted architect,

and Victoria's adopted son, Francis Rattenbury. Between Fort and View streets is the four-story shopping mall, the Bay Centre. Bastion Square, with its restaurants and boutiques, lies to the south of Market Square and its restored 1850s buildings.

🏛 Parliament Buildings

501 Belleville St. **Tel** (250) 387 3046. **Open** 9am–5pm Mon–Fri. **Closed** Jan 1, Dec 25. ♿ 📷 Mon–Fri (summer: 6pm Mon–Fri, weekends). 🌐 **leg.bc.ca**

Victoria's many-domed Parliament Buildings are an impressive sight, particularly at night, when the façades are illuminated by thousands of lights. Designed by Francis Rattenbury, the buildings were completed in 1897. Rattenbury, a 25-year-old British architect who had arrived in British Columbia only the year before, won a provincial competition to design the new Parliament Buildings. He went on to design several of the province's structures, including the nearby Fairmont Empress Hotel.

The Parliament Buildings illuminate the waters of the Inner Harbour

The history of British Columbia is depicted throughout the Parliament Buildings. A statue of explorer Captain George Vancouver is perched on top of the main dome. Inside, large murals show scenes from the past.

Sights at a Glance

① Market Square
② Bastion Square
③ The Bay Centre
④ Fairmont Empress Hotel
⑤ Maritime Museum
of British Columbia
⑥ Parliament Buildings

⑦ Royal BC Museum
See pp288–9
⑧ Thunderbird Park
⑨ Helmcken House
⑩ Beacon Hill Park
⑪ Emily Carr House

[Map of Victoria downtown]

City Hall
CENTENNIAL SQUARE
CORMORANT STREET
STREET
PANDORA AVENUE
JOHNSON STREET
STREET
YATES STREET
③ The Bay Centre
VIEW STREET
FORT STREET
BLANSHARD STREET
QUADRA STREET
DOUGLAS STREET
BROAD STREET
Craigdarroch Castle
BROUGHTON STREET
Art Gallery of Greater Victoria, Government House
COURTNEY STREET
BURDETT AVE
airmont mpress Hotel
WNTOWN
FAIRFIELD ROAD
Terminal
HUMBOLDT STREET
Royal BC Museum
⑨ Helmcken House
ACADEMY CLOSE
rbird
SOUTHGATE STREET
QUADRA ST
South Park
⑩ Beacon Hill Park
BEACON HILL STREET
DOUGLAS STREET
AMES BAY

↑ ✈ Victoria Airport 25 km (15 miles)

0 meters 250
0 yards 250

🏨 Fairmont Empress Hotel
721 Government St. **Tel**
(250) 384 8111. **Open** daily.
♿ W fairmont.com/empress-victoria

Completed in 1908 to a Francis Rattenbury design, the Empress is one of Victoria's best-loved sights. Close to the Parliament Buildings, the hotel overlooks the Inner Harbour and dominates the skyline with its ivy-covered Edwardian splendor. Visitors can sample the luxurious decor of the hotel's public bars and lounges, such as the Q at the Empress, and the Palm Court with its lovely Tiffany-glass dome.

🏛 Bastion Square
Government St. **Tel** (250) 885 1387.
Open daily. ♿ W bastionsquare.ca
This beautifully restored square faces Victoria's picturesque harbor and contains some of the city's oldest 19th-century buildings. What were once luxury hotels and offices, built during the boom era of the late 1800s, now house several eclectic restaurants. Restoration began in 1963, when it was discovered that the Hudson's Bay Company's fur-trading post Fort Victoria, established in 1843, once stood on this site. Today, this pedestrian square includes the MacDonald Block building, built in 1863 in Italianate style,

Bastion Square is a popular lunch spot for locals and visitors

with elegant cast-iron columns and arched windows. The old courthouse, built in 1889, houses the Maritime Museum of British Columbia. In summer, both visitors and workers lunch in the courtyard cafés.

🏛 Market Square
560 Johnson St. **Tel** (250) 386 2441.
Open 10am–5pm Mon–Fri,
11am–4pm Sun & public hols.
Closed Jan 1, Dec 25. ♿ limited.
W marketsquare.ca

Two blocks north of Bastion Square on the corner of Johnson Street, Market Square has some of the finest Victorian saloon, hotel, and store façades in Victoria. Most of the buildings were built in the 1880s and 1890s, during the boom period of the Klondike Gold Rush. After decades of neglect, the area received a face-lift in 1975. The square is now a shoppers' paradise, with a variety of stores selling everything from books and jewelry to musical instruments and other arts and crafts.

One of the giant totem poles on display at Thunderbird Park

🎴 Thunderbird Park

Cnr Belleville & Douglas streets.

This compact park lies at the entrance to the Royal British Columbia Museum *(see pp288–89)* and is home to an imposing collection of plain and painted giant totem poles. During the summer months it is possible to watch aboriginal artists in the Thunderbird Park Carving Studio producing these handsome carved totems. The poles show and preserve the legends of many different tribes from the Aboriginal Peoples of the Northwest Coast.

🏛 Helmcken House

10 Elliot St. Square. **Tel** (250) 356 7226. **Open** 10am–5pm Mon–Sat (to 9pm Thu), 1–5pm Sun. **Closed** Mon Sep–May. 🚫 ♿ 📷

Located in Elliot Square in the Inner Harbour area, the home of Hudson's Bay Company employee Dr. John Sebastian Helmcken was built in 1852 and is thought to be one of the oldest houses in British Columbia. The young doctor built his house with Douglas fir trees felled in the surrounding forest. This simple but elegantly designed clapboard dwelling contains many of the original furnishings, including

the piano, which visitors are permitted to play. Among other exhibits are a collection of antique dolls and the family's personal belongings, such as clothes, shoes, and toiletries.

🏛 Maritime Museum of British Columbia

470 Belleville St. **Tel** (250) 385 4222. **Open** 10am–5pm daily. 🚫
🌐 mmbc.bc.ca

At this fascinating three-story museum of coastal history, exhibits tell the stories of the giant canoes of the Coast Salish First Nations Peoples. It is located inside the landmark CPR Steamship Terminal building, built in 1924 on the Inner Harbour. The museum's collection spans from 1775 to the present and includes over 35,000 nautical artifacts such as ship records, photographs, charts, and models. Several life-size vessels are a part of the collection as well.

🏬 The Bay Centre

1150 Douglas St. **Tel** (250) 952 5690. **Open** 10am–6pm Mon–Wed & Sat, 10am–9pm Thu–Fri, 11am–6pm Sun. ♿ 🌐 thebaycentre.ca

The Bay Centre is a shopping mall within walking distance of the Inner Harbour and was initially built behind the façades of several historic buildings on Government Street. The Driard Hotel, designed in 1892 by John Wright, was saved from demolition by a public campaign,

as were the fronts of the 1910 Times Building and the fine, 19th-century Lettice and Sears Building. Behind these elegant façades, there are three floors of stores selling everything from fashion and gifts to handmade chocolates and gourmet food.

🏠 Emily Carr House

207 Government St. **Tel** (250) 383 5843. **Open** May–Oct: 11am–4pm Tue–Sat. 🚫 ♿ 📷 🌐 emilycarr.com

Emily Carr, one of Canada's best-known artists *(see pp38–39)*, was born in 1871 in this charming, yellow clapboard house. It was built in 1864 by prominent architects Wright and Saunders, under instruction from Emily's father, Richard Carr. Located just a few minutes walk from Inner Harbour, both the house and its English-style garden are open to visitors. All the rooms are appropriately furnished in late 19th-century period style, with some original family pieces. Visitors can see the dining room where Emily taught her first art classes to local children. Emily's drawing of her father still sits upon the mantel in the sitting room, where, as an eight-year-old, she made her first sketches.

🎴 Beacon Hill Park

Douglas St. **Tel** (250) 361 0600. **Open** daily. ♿

In the late 19th century this delightful park was used for stabling horses, but in 1888 John

Emily Carr House, where renowned painter Emily Carr was born

Blair, a Scottish landscape gardener, redesigned the park to include two lakes and initiated extensive tree planting. Once a favorite haunt of artist Emily Carr, this peaceful 74.5-ha (184-acre) park is now renowned for its lofty old trees (including the rare Garry oaks, some of which are over 400 years old), picturesque duck ponds, and a 100-year-old cricket pitch.

🏛 Art Gallery of Greater Victoria

1040 Moss St. **Tel** (250) 384 4171. **Open** 10am–5pm Tue–Sat; 10am–9pm Thu, noon–5pm Sun. 🖼 **W** aggv.ca

This popular gallery's contemporary facilities are located in the heritage neighborhood of Rockland, a few blocks west of Craigdarroch Castle. Inside, visitors will find a diverse presentation of exhibitions, including contemporary, Canadian, heritage, and national touring exhibitions.

On permanent exhibition is the work of British Columbia's premier artist, Emily Carr, featuring her paintings of the British Columbian coastal forests and depictions of the lives of First Nations peoples, as well as excerpts from her writings and archival photographs.

Shinto shrine detail at the Art Gallery

In its quaint courtyard garden, the gallery also houses the only original Japanese Shinto shrine in North America.

🏠 Craigdarroch Castle

1050 Joan Cres. **Tel** (250) 592 5323. **Open** Jun–Sep: 9am–7pm daily; Oct–May: 10am–4:30pm daily. **Closed** Jan 1, Dec 25, 26. 🖼 **W** thecastle.ca

Completed in 1890, Craig-darroch Castle was the pet project of respected local coal millionaire Robert Dunsmuir. Although not a real castle, the design of this manor home was based on that of his ancestral home in Scotland and mixes several architectural styles such as Roman and French Gothic.

When the castle was threatened with demolition in 1959, a group of local citizens formed a society that successfully battled for its preservation. Today, the restored interior of the castle is a museum that offers an insight into the lifestyle of a wealthy Canadian entrepreneur.

The castle is noted for having one of the finest collections of Art Nouveau lead-glass windows in North America, and many of the rooms and hallways retain their patterned-wood parquet floors and intricately carved paneling in white oak, cedar, and mahogany. Every room is filled with opulent Victorian furnishings from the late 19th century and dec-orated in original colors such as deep greens, pinks, and rusts. Several layers of the paint have been painstakingly removed from the drawing room ceiling to reveal the original hand-painted and stenciled decorations beneath, including wonderfully detailed butterflies and lions.

📷 Government House

1401 Rockland Ave. **Tel** (250) 387 2080. **Open** daily (gardens only). ♿ **W** ltgov.bc.ca

A tower at Craigdarroch Castle in the elaborate French Gothic style

The present Government House building was completed in 1959 after fire destroyed the 1903 building, which was designed by renowned architect Francis Rattenbury.

As the official residence of the Lieutenant-Governor of British Columbia, the Queen's representative to the province, the house is not open to the public, but visitors can view 5.5 ha (14 acres) of stunning public gardens with beautiful lawns, ponds, an English country garden, and a Victorian rose garden. From Pearke's Peak, a mount formed from the rocky outcrops that surround the property, there are marvelous views of the grounds.

The 1959 Government House, built with blue and pink granite

The Royal British Columbia Museum

The Royal British Columbia Museum tells the story of this region through its natural and human history. The museum is regarded as one of the best in Canada for the striking way it presents its exhibits. A series of imaginative dioramas re-create the sights, sounds, and even smells of areas such as the seashore, the ocean, and the coast forest, all of which occupy the second floor Natural History Gallery.

   The region's history is presented on the third floor, including a reconstruction of an early 20th-century town. Visitors can experience the street life of the time in a cinema showing silent films and a saloon. The collection of aboriginal art and culture in the First Peoples Gallery includes a ceremonial Big House.

Third
Floor

19th-century Chinatown
As part of an 1875 street scene, this Chinese herbalist's store displays a variety of herbs used in traditional Chinese medicine.

★ First Peoples Gallery
Made of cedar bark and spruce root in around 1897, this hat bears the mountain goat crest of the raven clan.

First Nations' Ceremonial Masks
The mouse, raccoon, and kingfisher are carved on these masks belonging to the Martin family, who wore them to dance on ceremonial occasions.

Key

☐ First Peoples Gallery

☐ Modern History Gallery

☐ Feature exhibits

☐ Natural History Gallery

☐ IMAX Victoria Theater

☐ Non-exhibition space

Exterior of the Museum
The museum's main exhibits building was opened in 1968, after years of having to occupy several sites in and around the Legislative Buildings. The museum also houses provincial archives and a cultural precinct.

Modern History Gallery
A variety of streets, stores, and public buildings, from the 1700s to 1990s, are re-created in this gallery. Here, the Grand Hotel occupies an authentic wooden sidewalk.

Second Floor

★ **Natural History Gallery**
A full-size prehistoric tusked mammoth guards the entrance to the Natural History Gallery, which includes several lifelike dioramas that re-create British Columbia's coastal forests and ocean life since the last Ice Age.

VISITORS' CHECKLIST

Practical Information
675 Belleville St.
Tel (250) 356 7226. **Open** 10am–5pm daily (late May–late Sep: to 10pm). **Closed** Jan 1, Dec 25.
w royalbcmuseum.bc.ca

Transport
3, 4, 28, 30.

★ **Seashore Diorama**
This diorama uses sound, film, lighting, and realistic models of animals such as this northern sea lion.

First Floor

Gallery Guide
The main exhibits of the museum are housed on the second and third floors. The Natural History Gallery, on the second floor, reconstructs a range of environments from the Coast Seashore to the Old Growth Forest displays. The third floor has the First Peoples and Modern History galleries.

Main Entrance

The lily pond in the formal Italian garden at Butchart Gardens

⓴ Butchart Gardens

800 Benvenuto Ave., Brentwood Bay. **Tel** (250) 652 4422, 1 866 652 4422. 🚆 Victoria. 🚌 Victoria. **Open** 9am daily; closing times vary by season. ♿ 🅿 🌐 **butchartgardens.com**

These beautiful gardens were begun in 1904 by Mrs. Jennie Butchart, the wife of a cement manufacturer. When her husband moved west to quarry limestone near Victoria, Mrs. Butchart began to design a new garden, which would stretch down to the water at Tod Inlet. When the limestone deposits ran out, Mrs. Butchart decided to add to her burgeoning garden by landscaping the quarry site into a sunken garden, which now boasts a lake overhung by willow and other trees laden with blossom in spring. A huge rock left in the quarry was turned into a towering rock garden. Today, visitors can climb stone steps to see stunning views from the top. As their popularity grew, so the gardens were filled with thousands of rare plants collected from around the world by Mrs. Butchart.

Nowadays, the gardens are arranged into distinct areas. There is a formal Italian garden with a lily pond that features a fountain bought in Italy by the Butcharts in 1924. The rose garden is filled with the scent of hundreds of different blooms in summer. During the summer the gardens are illuminated and play host to evening musical performances.

㉑ Port Renfrew

🏔 200. 🛈 2070 Phillips Rd., Sooke, (250) 642 6351.

Port Renfrew is a small, friendly fishing village and ex-logging town. A popular daytrip from Victoria, the town offers visitors access to Botanical Beach, where a unique sandstone shelf leaves rock pools filled with marine life such as starfish at low tide.

Port Renfrew is famed for its hiking along old logging roads: the Sandbar Trail goes through a Douglas fir plantation to a large river sandbar where it is possible to swim at low tide. A more serious hike is the 47-km (29-mile) Juan de Fuca Marine Trail from Port Renfrew to China Beach. This trail offers a range of hikes, from treks lasting several days to short beach walks. The town is one of two starting points for the West Coast Trail in Pacific Rim National Park Reserve *(see pp292–3)*.

㉒ Cowichan District

🚆 & 🚌 from Duncan. 🛈 2896 Drinkwater Rd., (250) 746 4636, 1 888 303 3337. 🌐 **cvrd.bc.ca**

Located on the south central coast of Vancouver Island, about 60 km (37 miles) north of Victoria, the Cowichan District incorporates both the Chemainus and Cowichan valleys. Cowichan means "warm land" in the language of the Cowichan, one of British Columbia's largest First Nations groups; the area's mild climate means the waters of Cowichan Lake are warm enough to swim in during the summer months. The largest freshwater lake on the island,

Lake Cowichan offers excellent fishing, canoeing, and hiking. The warm climate here also favors grape-growing, and the Cowichan Valley is BC's second-highest wine-producing region. Self-guided or escorted wine tasting tours along country back roads are popular.

Between the town of Duncan and the lake lies the Valley Demonstration Forest, which has scenic lookouts and signs explaining forest management. Duncan is known as the City of Totems, as it displays more than 40 poles in the downtown area. Yellow-painted footprints on the sidewalks guide visitors on the "Totem Trail".

Stunning vista over Lake Cowichan in the Cowichan Valley

㉓ Chemainus

🏔 4,100. 🚆 🚌 🛳 🛈 9796 Willow St., (250) 246 3944. 🌐 **chemainus.bc.ca**

When the local sawmill closed in the late 1970s, picturesque Chemainus transformed itself into a major attraction with the painting of giant murals around the town that depict the history of the region. Local artists continued the project, and today there are more than 40 murals on the outside walls of local buildings, based on real events in the town's past. Larger-than-

First Nations' faces looking down from a Chemainus town mural

Pleasure craft and fishing boats moored in Nanaimo harbor

life images of indigenous Cowichan people, pioneers, and loggers have revitalized the town. Visitors enjoy browsing in the town's various antiques stores and relaxing in the many pleasant sidewalk cafés.

Environs

Some 70 km (43 miles) south of Chemainus, Swartz Bay is the departure point on Vancouver Island for ferries to the Southern Gulf Islands and the mainland. Visitors are drawn to the 200 mostly uninhabited islands by their tranquility and natural beauty. It is possible to stroll along empty beaches, where sightings of eagles and turkey vultures are common. There are fishing charters for visitors who enjoy catching salmon and cod, and kayaking tours offering stops on isolated shores to view otters, seals, and marine birds.

Salt Spring is the most-populated Gulf island, with about 10,500 inhabitants. In the summer, visitors come to wander around the pretty village of Ganges, where a busy marina surrounds the wooden pier. The village offers stores, cafés, galleries, and colorful markets.

㉔ Nanaimo

🚹 82,000. ✈ 🚌 🚢 ⛴ 🚆 ℹ 2450 Northfield Rd., (250) 751 1556, 1 800 663 7337. 🆆 tourismnanaimo.com

Originally the site of five villages of the indigenous Coast Salish peoples, Nanaimo was established as a coal-mining town in the 1850s. As the second-largest city on Vancouver Island, Nanaimo has plenty of malls and businesses along the Island Highway, but it is the Old City Quarter on the waterfront in the heart of downtown Nanaimo that visitors enjoy most.

The Old City Quarter has many 19th-century buildings, including the Nanaimo Court House, designed by Francis Rattenbury in 1895. The **Nanaimo Museum** includes a re-creation of an old schoolroom, a First Nations exhibit, and a Sports Hall of Fame. Other exhibits include aboriginal artifacts in a village diorama.

🏛 Nanaimo Museum
100 Museum Way. **Tel** (250) 753 1821. **Open** 10am–5pm Mon–Sat (daily in summer). 💲 donation to a local charity. ♿ 📷 book in advance.

㉕ Port Alberni

🚹 25,000. ✈ 🚌 🚢 ℹ 2533 Port Alberni Hwy., (250) 724 6535.

Port Alberni sits at the head of Alberni Inlet, which stretches 48 km (30 miles) from the interior of Vancouver Island to the Pacific Ocean in the west. The town now depends upon hikers, kayakers, and wildlife watchers, and it is a popular haunt for salmon fishers. Every year the Salmon Derby and Festival offers thousands of Canadian dollars for the biggest fish caught during the last weekend in August. The town's other attractions include a 1929 locomotive offering train rides along the waterfront during the summer from the 1912 Port Alberni Railway Station to the steam operated MacLean Sawmill. Many visitors also come to cruise on the freighter *M.V. Frances Barkley*. The ship delivers mail down the inlet, as well as offering trips to Ucluelet, Bamfield, and other waypoints near the Pacific Rim National Park Reserve. It also carries kayaks and canoes for those hoping to sail around the Broken Group Islands *(see p292)*.

A carved eagle soars over Port Alberni Pier

Just east of Port Alberni, it is possible to hike among awe-inspiring old growth Douglas firs and red cedars in the outstanding Cathedral Grove, located in the MacMillan Provincial Park.

A 1929 steam locomotive offering rides along Port Alberni's waterfront

🐋 Tofino

🏠 1,700. 🛈 1426 Pacific Rim Hwy., 1 888 720 3414. 🆆 tourismtofino.com

Once a timber town, Tofino is now a busy tourist center for the Pacific Rim National Park Reserve *(see below)*. Its sandy beaches and woodland trails attract visitors all year round; in the summer, surfing, hiking, kayaking, and whale watching also draw the crowds. The Pacific Rim National Park Reserve begins just past the junction of Tofino/Ucluelet.

In Tofino, the **Eagle Aerie Gallery** displays works by First Nations artist Roy Vickers, while The **Whale Centre Maritime Museum**

Sunset at Chesterman Beach, Tofino

showcases artifacts from local shipwrecks and First Nations history. It also organizes whale-watching excursions.

Just north of Tofino, the UNESCO Biosphere Reserve of Clayoquot Sound features a diverse range of ecosystems, including islands, mountains, and temperate rainforests. Boating and paddling day trips can be arranged through several

tour operators in Tofino, and hiking trails are easily accessible on a few islands.

🏛 **Eagle Aerie Gallery**
350 Campbell St. **Tel** (250) 725 3235.
Open 10am–5pm daily. 🆆 royhenry
vickers.com/the_gallery

🏛 **The Whale Centre Maritime Museum**
411 Campbell St. **Tel** (250) 725 2132.
Open 9am–8pm daily.
🆆 tofinowhalecentre.com

🐋 Campbell River

🏠 32,000. 🛈 1235 Shoppers Row, (250) 286 6901.
🆆 campbellrivertourism.com

Located on the northeast shore of Vancouver Island, Campbell River is renowned as a center for

🐋 Pacific Rim National Park Reserve

The Pacific Rim National Park Reserve is composed of three distinct areas: Long Beach, the West Coast Trail, and the Broken Group Islands, all of which occupy a 130-km (80-mile) strip of Vancouver Island's west coast. The park is a world famous area for whale-watching, and the Kwistis Visitor Centre off Hwy 4 has the latest information on their movements. Long Beach offers a range of hiking trails, with parking at all trail heads and beach accesses. The most challenging hike is the 75-km (47-miles) West Coast Trail, between Port Renfrew and Bamfield. The Broken Group Islands are popular with kayakers.

The Broken Group Islands
This is an archipelago of some 100 islets popular with kayakers and scuba divers.

The **Schooner Cove Trail** is one of nine scenic and easy-to-follow trails along the sands of Long Beach.

The **Kwistis Visitor Centre** has viewing platforms for whale watching.

Long Beach
The rugged, windswept sands of Long Beach are renowned for their wild beauty, with crashing Pacific rollers, unbeatable surfing opportunities, rock pools filled with marine life, and scattered driftwood.

Tofino

Long Beach

Port Albion

Ucluelet

DODD ISLAND

TURRET ISLAND

EFFINGHAM ISLAND

The crashing waters of Elk Falls near the Campbell River

salmon fishing. The waters of Discovery Passage are on the migration route for five major species of salmon, including the giant Chinook. There are boat tours, which follow the fish up river. Visitors can rent a fishing boat or try their luck catching fish from the 183-m (600-ft) Discovery Pier in the town.

Just 2 km (1 mile) northwest of Campbell River, Elk Falls Provincial Park houses large Douglas fir forests and several waterfalls; there are terrific views of Elk Falls itself from the new suspension bridge.

㉙ Telegraph Cove

🚌 Port McNeill. 🛈 1594 Beach Drive, Port McNeill, (250) 956 3881.

Located on the northern end of Vancouver Island, Telegraph Cove is a small, picturesque boardwalk village, with distinctive high wooden houses built on stilts that look over the waters of Johnstone Strait. In summer, the Northern resident orcas, drawn by the migrating salmon, come to cavort on the gravel beds in the shallow waters of Robson Bight, an ecological reserve established in 1982. Visitors may view the whales' antics from tour boats or from Port McNeill.

Orcas in the waters of Johnstone Strait, Vancouver Island

Whale Watching

Migrating gray whales

More than 20 species of whale are found in British Columbia's coastal waters. Around 22,000 gray whales migrate annually from their feeding grounds in the Arctic Ocean to breed off the coast of Mexico. The whales tend to stay near to the coast and often move close enough to Vancouver Island's west shore to be sighted from land. From March to August there are daily whale-watching trips from Tofino and Ucluelet.

VISITORS' CHECKLIST

Practical Information
Hwy 4.
Tel (250) 726 3500.
Open daily. 🚻 🛈 Mar–Sep.
🚫 🅿 🅦 pc.gc.ca

Transport
🚌 from Port Alberni.

West Coast Trail
This trail passes stunning scenery, including moss-draped rainforest and deep, rocky gullies.

Key

▬ Major road

▭ Minor road

▪▪ West Coast Trail

— National Park boundary

━ Rivers

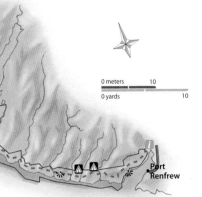

Bamfield

0 meters 10
0 yards 10

At the Nitinat Narrows hikers on the West Coast Trail must take a short ferry ride across this pretty waterway. The trail is open from May to September.

Port Renfrew

THE ROCKY MOUNTAINS

The Canadian Rockies occupy a band of the provinces of British Columbia and Alberta nearly 805 km (500 miles) wide, and are part of the range that extends from Mexico through the US into Canada. Between 65 and 100 million years ago, a slow but massive upheaval of the Earth's crust caused the rise of the Rocky Mountains and the dramatic, jagged appearance of their peaks, 50 of which are over 3,048 m (10,000 ft) high. A region of spectacular beauty, the landscape of the Rockies is dominated by snow-topped peaks, luminous glaciers, and iridescent glacial lakes, now protected in a series of national parks. The discovery of natural hot springs at Banff in 1883 prompted the federal government to create Canada's first national park. Since 1984 Banff, Jasper, Kootenay, and Yoho parks have become UNESCO World Heritage sites.

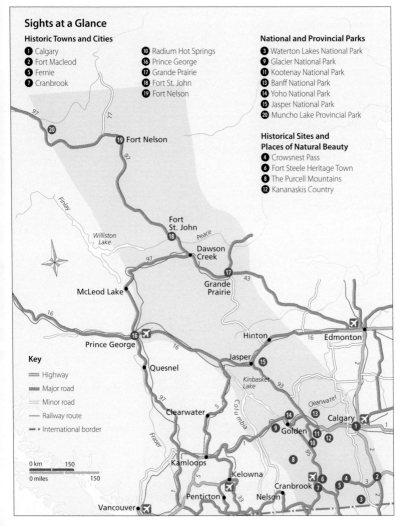

Sights at a Glance

Historic Towns and Cities

1. Calgary
2. Fort Macleod
5. Fernie
7. Cranbrook
10. Radium Hot Springs
16. Prince George
17. Grande Prairie
18. Fort St. John
19. Fort Nelson

National and Provincial Parks

3. Waterton Lakes National Park
9. Glacier National Park
11. Kootenay National Park
13. Banff National Park
14. Yoho National Park
15. Jasper National Park
20. Muncho Lake Provincial Park

Historical Sites and Places of Natural Beauty

4. Crowsnest Pass
6. Fort Steele Heritage Town
8. The Purcell Mountains
12. Kananaskis Country

Key

- Highway
- Major road
- Minor road
- Railway route
- International border

0 km   150
0 miles   150

◀ Mount Edith Cavell's Angel Glacier and meltwater lake, Jasper National Park, Alberta   **For map symbols** *see back flap*

❶ Calgary

Established in 1875, Calgary is famous for hosting the Winter Olympics of 1988, and for the city's Stampede. Calgary covers the largest area of any city in Alberta, and lies between the eastern foothills of the Rockies and the Prairies. It is a sophisticated place, a culinary hub with skyscrapers, galleries, and theaters, but it is also a basecamp to adventure. The city's western atmosphere, still redolent at times of the frontier, belies the fact that its modern skyline has grown since the oil boom of the 1960s. Noted for its proximity to Banff National Park, Calgary's center, with its offices and stores, is 128 km (79 miles) east of the town of Banff *(see p307)*.

The colorful façade of Eau Claire Market, Calgary, Alberta

Calgary Tower

101 9th Ave. SW. **Tel** (403) 266 7171. **Open** daily. 🅿 ♿ 🆆 calgarytower.com

The Calgary Tower is one of the city's tallest structures, with two elevators that hurtle to the top in 62 seconds, and two emergency staircases composed of 802 steps apiece. From street level to the top, Calgary Tower measures 191 m (627 ft). At the top there is a restaurant and a glass-floored observation deck, both of which offer incredible views across to the Rockies.

Studio Bell, National Music Centre

9th Ave. SE at 4th St. SE. **Tel** (403) 543 5115. **Open** daily. 🅿 ♿ 🆆 nmc.ca
The NMC (National Music Centre) is housed in an award-winning building inspired by the Canadian landscape and instrument designs, to the delight of Calgary's East Village neighborhood. As the home for music in Canada, NMC is known for its collection of over 2,000 rare instruments, artifacts,

sound equipments and Canadian music memorabilia. It also hosts a wide variety of live music events.

Eau Claire Market

200 Barclay Parade SW. **Tel** (403) 264 6450. **Open** daily. ♿
Housed in a brightly colored warehouse, this market provides a welcome contrast to the surrounding office blocks downtown. Located on the Bow River, opposite Prince's Island Park, it offers specialty stores selling a fine variety of gourmet foods, contemporary arts, craft markets, cinemas, cafés, and restaurants. Walkways connect to a footbridge that leads to Prince's Island Park.

❓ Prince's Island Park

The pretty Prince's Island Park lies close to the city center on the banks of the Bow River. This tiny island is connected to the city via several bridges, including a pedestrian bridge at the end of 4th Street SW.

Calgary Tower surrounded by the skyscrapers of the city's skyline

Sights at a Glance

① Saint George's Island
② Fort Calgary
③ Studio Bell, National Music Centre
④ Arts Commons
⑤ Glenbow Museum
⑥ Calgary Tower
⑦ Calgary Chinese Cultural Centre
⑧ Eau Claire Market
⑨ Prince's Island Park

During hot summers, visitors and locals picnic under the cool shade of the park's plentiful trees, and many outdoor festivals are held here.

Calgary Chinese Cultural Centre

197 1st St. SW. **Tel** (403) 262 5071.
Open daily. for museum.
W culturalcentre.ca

Located in downtown Calgary, the Chinese Cultural Centre was completed in 1992. It is modeled on the 1420 Temple of Heaven in Beijing, which was used exclusively by emperors. The center was built by artisans from China using traditional skills. The Dr. Henry Fok Cultural Hall is the highlight of the building with its 21-m-high (70-ft) ceiling and an impressive dome adorned with dragons and phoenixes.

Blue tiles inside the dome of the Calgary Chinese Cultural Centre

Each of the dome's four supporting columns is decorated with lavish gold designs, which represent the four seasons.

Glenbow Museum

130 9th Ave. SE. **Tel** (403) 268 4100.
Open variable hours, so check website before visiting.
W glenbow.org

Located in the heart of downtown Calgary, the Glenbow Museum is one of western Canada's largest museums, hosting three major temporary exhibitions annually, in addition to having over 20 permanent galleries. The museum houses an excellent collection of Canadian and contemporary art, as well as a wide range of objects that chronicle the history of the Canadian West through First Nations and pioneer artifacts. An extensive military collection includes medieval armor and Samurai swords. Glenbow's gallery, Niitsitapiisini, traces the story of the Blackfoot people of the northwestern plains of Alberta and Montana.

Arts Commons

205 8th Ave. SE. **Tel** (403) 294 9494.
Open daily. **W** artscommons.ca

Opened in 1985, this large complex houses four theaters and a concert hall, as well as five rental boardrooms. Located in the heart of the city on Olympic Plaza, the center has staged events as diverse as jazz and blues concerts to rodeos, festivals, and live theater.

VISITORS' CHECKLIST

Practical Information
1,095,000. **i** Tourism Calgary 200, 238–11 Ave. S.E., (403) 263-8510, 1 800 661 1678.
Calgary Stampede (Jul); Folk Music Festival (Jul); Taste of Calgary (Aug); Calgary Fringe Festival (Aug).
W visitcalgary.com

Transport
17 km (11 miles) NE. of city.
Greyhound Bus Station, 850 16th St. SW.

The lobby of the Arts Commons

Mountie's cabin in the Interpretive Centre at Fort Calgary Historic Park

🏠 Hunt House and Deane House

806 9th Ave. SE. **Tel** (403) 269 7747.
Open Deane House: daily. 🅿️

The restored Hunt House lies across the Elbow River from the Fort Calgary Interpretive Centre. This small log house is one of the few buildings left from the original settlement of Calgary in the early 1880s.

Nearby Deane House, also restored, was built for the Superintendent of Fort Calgary, Captain Richard Burton Deane, in 1906. Today, the house is a restaurant, where visitors can enjoy a meal in a delightful period setting.

🏠 Fort Calgary Historic Park

750 9th Ave. SE. **Tel** (403) 290 1875.
Open daily. 🅿️ ♿ 🌐 fortcalgary.com

Fort Calgary was built by the North West Mounted Police in 1875 at the confluence of the Bow and Elbow rivers. The Grand Trunk Pacific Railway arrived in 1883, and the tiny fort town grew to over 400 residents in a year. In 1887, a fire destroyed several of the settlement's key buildings and a new town was built out of the more fire-resistant sandstone. In 1914 the land was bought by the Grand Trunk Pacific Railway, and the fort was leveled. Pieces of the fort were discovered during an archeological dig in 1970, and the well-restored site was opened to the public in 1978.

Today, the reconstructed fort offers an Interpretive Centre, which tells of Calgary's colorful past through exhibits such as a re-created quartermaster's store and carpenter's workshop. There are also delightful walks along the river.

🌳 St. George's Island

St. George's Island sits on the edge of the Bow River, near downtown Calgary. The island houses part of Calgary Zoo, including the Canadian Wilds, Botanical Gardens, Penguin Plunge, and Prehistoric Park.

The zoo prides itself on the presentation of its animals, which can be seen in their appropriate habitats. Canadian Wilds is a series of environments that highlights the diversity of the Canadian landscape and its wildlife. There are aspen woodlands where it is possible to see the endangered woodland caribou, and visitors can wander the boreal forest environment, maybe spotting the rare whooping crane in the shallow wetlands area. Penguin Plunge features more than 40 birds housed in a shoreline landscape.

The zoo is surrounded by the Botanical Gardens, which has a vast greenhouse displaying plants from around the world.

The Prehistoric Park offers a reconstructed Mesozoic landscape, where visitors can picnic among 29 life-size dinosaurs.

The stately whooping crane at Calgary Zoo, St. George's Island

🌳 Stampede Park

1410 Olympic Way SE. **Tel** (403) 261 0101. **Open** daily. 🅿️ some events. ♿ 🌐 calgarystampede.com

Famous as the site of the Calgary Stampede, the park offers year-round leisure and conference facilities. There is a permanent horse racetrack, as well as two ice-hockey stadiums, one of which is housed inside the

Calgary Stampede

An exuberant ten-day festival of all things western, the Calgary Stampede is held every July in Stampede Park. Originally established as an agricultural fair in 1886, the Stampede of 1912 attracted 14,000 people. In the 1920s one of its still-popular highlights, the risky but exciting covered wagon races, became part of the show.

Today's festival has an array of spectacular entertainments that dramatize scenes from western history. They can be seen both on site and in Calgary itself. The fair starts with a dazzling parade through the city, and then features bull riding, tie-down roping, and steer wrestling. The main events are *Showdown Sunday – Rodeo's Richest Afternoon*, and chuckwagon racing, which have combined prize money of over Can $2 million.

Heritage Park Historical Village houses some 70 historic buildings

striking Saddledome, named for its saddle-shaped roof. Trade shows, such as antiques and home improvements, and concerts are also held here.

Fish Creek Provincial Park
Bow Bottom Trail SE. **Tel** (403) 297 5293. **Open** daily. partial.
albertaparks.ca

Established in 1975, Fish Creek Provincial Park is one of North America's largest urban parks, covering 13 sq km (5 sq miles) of forest along the Fish Creek valley. Park guides hold slide shows on both the ecology and history of the region, detailing the park's many archeological sites, such as buffalo jumps dated between 750 BC and 1800 AD.

The park's forest is a mix of white spruce, aspen, and balsam poplar. In winter, many of the hiking trails become cross-country ski trails, popular with locals and visitors alike. The Canada goose, the great blue heron, and the bald eagle are among a variety of birds that visit the park during both summer and winter.

Heritage Park Historical Village
1900 Heritage Drive SW. **Tel** (403) 268 8500. **Open** Village: May–Oct; museum and café: all year. **Closed** Nov–Apr.
heritagepark.ca

Heritage Park Historical Village sits on the shore of Glenmore Reservoir, and contains over 70 historic buildings, from outhouses to a 2-story hotel that have been brought here from sites all over western Canada. The buildings have been organized into time periods, which range from an 1880s fur-trading post to the shops and homes of a small town

between 1900 and 1914. Most of the 45,000 artifacts that furnish and decorate the village have been donated by residents of Calgary and the surrounding towns, and vary from teacups to steam trains.

Among the most thrilling of the exhibits, a working 19th-century amusement park has several rides, and three original, operating steam locomotives. A replica of the SS *Moyie*, a charming sternwheeler paddle boat, takes visitors on 30-minute cruises around the Glenmore Reservoir. Ride one of two vintage electric streetcars to the park's front gates and walk down a 1930s–1940s urban streetscape. The sense of stepping back in time is enhanced by the clip-clopping of horse-drawn carriages, and by the smells and sounds of shops such as the working bakery and the blacksmith's, which are all staffed by costumed guides.

Victorian drink container at Heritage Park

Canada Olympic Park
88 Canada Olympic Rd. SW. **Tel** (403) 247 5452. **Open** daily (hours vary according to season).

WinSport's Canada Olympic Park was the site of the 1988 XV Olympic Winter Games. Today, both locals and visitors can enjoy the facilities all year round, including riding on the bobsleds and luge tracks, mountain biking, and zip-lining. The views toward the Rockies and over Calgary from the 90-m (295-ft) high Olympic Ski Jump Tower are truly stunning. The Park is home to Canada's Sports Hall of Fame, with 12 interactive galleries and some 100,000 artifacts.

Telus Spark
220 St. George's Drive NE. **Tel** (403) 817 6800. **Open** daily; hours vary, so check before visiting.
sparkscience.ca

Relocated and redesigned in 2011, the Telus Spark is a popular interactive museum. It offers such exhibits as Being Human, Earth & Sky, and the Creative Kids Museum. Live theater programs and science demonstrations take place in the Presentation Theatre. The latest technology allows for a memorable experience for both kids and adults alike. There is also an interactive outdoor park.

The Military Museums
4520 Crowchild Trail SW. **Tel** (403) 974 2850. **Open** 9am–5pm Mon–Fri, 9:30am–4pm Sat & Sun.
themilitarymuseums.ca

The Military Museums include naval, air force, and army museums under one roof. The focus is on the history of the Canadian Forces, from the North-west Rebellion in 1885 to today.

Sherman tank on display outside the Military Museums

The mountain-ringed Waterton Lake in Waterton Lakes National Park

❷ Fort Macleod

🏠 3,100. 🚌 *i* The Fort – Museum of the North West Mounted Police, 219 Jerry Potts Blvd., (403) 553 4703. **W** fortmacleod.com

Alberta's oldest settlement, Fort Macleod was established in 1874 as the first North West Mounted Police outpost in the west. Sent to control lawless whisky traders at the Fort Whoop-up trading post, the Mounties *(see p236)* set up Fort Macleod nearby.

Today's town retains many of its historic buildings, and the reconstructed fort palisades house the fort's museum, which tells the story of the Mounties' journey.

The world's oldest and best-preserved buffalo jump lies just 16 km (10 miles) northwest of Fort Macleod. **Head-Smashed-In Buffalo Jump** is a UNESCO World Heritage site. This way of hunting buffalo, in which aboriginal people wearing buffalo skins stampede herds of the animals to their deaths over a cliff, was perfected by the Blackfoot tribe. The site takes its name from the brave whose head was smashed in when watching the kill from under the cliff.

🏛 Head-Smashed-In Buffalo Jump
Hwy 785, off Hwy 2. **Tel** (403) 553 2731. **Open** daily. 🅿 ♿

❸ Waterton Lakes National Park

🚗 Calgary. *i* Park Info Centre, open mid-May–Oct, (403) 859 5133. **Open** daily. 🅿 ♿ partial. **W** pc.gc.ca

Scenery as amazing as any of that found in the Rockies' other national parks characterizes the less-known Waterton Lakes National Park. Located in the southwest corner of Alberta along the US border, the park is an International Peace Park and manages a shared ecosystem with Glacier National Park in the US.

The park owes its unique beauty to the geological phenomenon of the Lewis Overthrust, which was forged over a billion years ago (before the formation of the Rockies), when ancient rock was pushed over newer deposits. Thus, the peaks of the mountains rise up sharply out of the flat prairies.

Waterton's mix of lowland and alpine habitats means it has the widest variety of wildlife of any of Canada's parks, from bears to bighorn sheep, and from waterfowl to nesting species such as sapsuckers.

❹ Crowsnest Pass

i Frank Slide Interpretive Centre, (403) 562 7388. **Open** daily. **Closed** public holidays. 🅿 **W** history.alberta.ca

Crowsnest Pass is located 1.5 km (1 mile) off Highway 3, in Alberta close to the border with BC. Like

Visitors on an underground tour of Bellevue Mine at Crowsnest Pass

most Rocky Mountain passes, it is enclosed by snowcapped mountains. In the early 1900s this area was dominated by the coal-mining industry and was the site of Canada's worst mine disaster. In 1903, a huge mass of rock slid off Turtle Mountain into the valley below, hitting the town of Frank and killing 70 people. The Frank Slide Interpretive Centre offers two award-winning audio-visual presentations about this tragic event. A trail through the valley is marked with numbered stops and leads hikers to the debris left by the disaster. Visitors can learn more about the history of local mining communities at the Bellevue Mine, which offers tours through the same narrow tunnels that working miners took daily between 1903 and 1961. Tours are available of Leitch Collieries, a fascinating early mining complex.

The Rocky Mountains tower over houses in the town of Fernie

❺ Fernie

🏠 4,800. 🚌 *i* 102 Commerce Rd, off Hwy 3., (250) 423 6868.
🌐 **tourismfernie.com**

Fernie is an attractive, tree-lined town set amid a circle of pointed peaks on the British Columbia side of Crowsnest Pass. The town owes its handsome appearance to a fire that burned it to the ground in 1904 and again in 1908, since when all buildings have been constructed from brick and stone. Among several historic buildings, the 1911 courthouse stands out as the only château-style courthouse in BC. Fernie is known for its winter sports, and boasts the best powder snow in the Rockies. The skiing season runs from November to April. The nearby Fernie Alpine Resort is huge and capable of taking over 13,000 skiers and riders up the mountain every hour.During the summer, the Mount Fernie Provincial Park offers a broad range of hiking trails through its magnificent mountain scenery. Boat trips on the many nearby lakes and rivers are popular, as is the fishing.

Helicopter trips take visitors close to the mountains to see the formations and granite cliffs particular to this region of the Rockies.

❻ Fort Steele Heritage Town

9851 Hwy 95. **Tel** (250) 417 6000. **Open** daily. 🅿 ♿ 🌐 **fortsteele.ca**

A re-creation of a 19th-century pioneering supply town, this settlement was established in 1864, when gold was discovered at Wild Horse River. Thousands of prospectors and entrepreneurs arrived by the Dewdney Trail, which linked Hope to the gold fields. The town was named after the North West Mounted Police Superintendent, Samuel Steele,

Re-creation of a 19th-century barber's shop at Fort Steele Heritage Town

who arrived in 1887 to restore peace between warring groups of Ktunaxa peoples and European settlers. The town underwent a brief boom with the discovery of lead and silver, but the mainline railroad was routed through nearby Cranbrook instead, and by the early 1900s Fort Steele was a ghost town.

Today, there are over 60 reconstructed or restored buildings, staffed by guides in period costume, including the general store, livery stable, and Mountie officers' quarters, with personal items such as family photographs, swords, and uniforms. Demonstrations of traditional crafts such as quilt- and ice cream-making are also held here. Tours at the nearby Wild Horse River Historic Site include the chance to pan for gold.

The Buffalo

The large, shaggy-headed type of cattle known as buffalo is really a North American bison. These apparently cumbersome beasts (a mature bull can weigh as much as 900 kg/1,980 lbs) are agile, fast, and unpredictable.

Before European settlers began moving west to the plains in the 18th and 19th centuries, the buffalo lived in immense herds of hundreds of thousands. It is estimated that as many as 60 million roamed here. Initially hunted only by the Plains peoples, who respected the beasts as a source of food, shelter, and tools, the buffalo were subsequently hunted almost to extinction by Europeans. By 1900 less than 1,000 animals remained. In 1874 a rancher called Walking Coyote bred a small herd of just 716 plains bison whose descendants now roam several Canadian national parks.

A North American plains bison

The luxurious dining car on a restored train at Cranbrook's rail museum

❼ Cranbrook

🏔 19,000. ✈ 🚌 ℹ 2279 Cranbrook St. N., (250) 426 5914. 🅦 cranbrooktourism.ca

Cranbrook is the largest town in southeast BC and lies between the Purcell and the Rocky Mountain ranges. A major transportation hub for the Rocky Mountain region, Cranbrook is within easy reach of a variety of scenic delights, including alpine forest and the lush, green valleys of the mountain foothills. A range of wildlife such as elk, wolves, cougar, and the highest density of grizzlies in the Rockies may be spotted on one of many hikes available here.

The town's main attraction is the **Cranbrook History Centre**, a rail museum which includes a collection of deluxe "hotels on wheels," dating from between the 1880s and the 1950s, that can be used for touring the facilities.

🏛 **Cranbrook History Centre**
57 Van Horne St. S. **Tel** (250) 489 3918. **Open** Apr–mid-Oct: daily; late Oct–Apr: Tue–Sat. 🏞 ♿

❽ The Purcell Mountains

🚌 Kamloops. ℹ 500 10th Ave. N./Hwy 95, Golden, (250) 344 7125.

The rugged and beautiful Purcell Mountains face the Rockies across the broad Columbia River Valley. The region is one of the most remote in the Rockies and attracts hunters and skiers from across the globe. A high range

of granite spires, called the Bugaboos, also draws mountain climbers. In the north of the Purcell range, and in one of its few accessible areas, the Purcell Wilderness Conservancy, covers a vast 21 sq km (8 sq miles). Carefully regulated hunting expeditions for bear, mountain goats, and elk are permitted here.

From the nearby pretty town of Invermere, it is possible to access one of the most difficult trails in Canada; the Earl Grey Pass Trail extends some 56 km (35 miles) over the Purcell Mountains. It is named after Earl Grey, Canada's Governor General from 1904 to 1911, who chose the Purcell range as the place to build a vacation cabin for his family in 1909. The trail he traveled followed an established route used by the Kinbasket peoples of the Shuswap First Nations. Today the trail is notoriously dangerous; bears, avalanches, and fallen trees are often hazards along the way. Hiking along it requires skill and experience and should not be attempted by a novice.

❾ Glacier National Park

🚌 Revelstoke/Golden. ℹ Revelstoke, (250) 837 7500. **Open** daily. 🏞 ♿ 🅦 pc.gc.ca

Glacier National Park covers 1,350 sq km (520 sq miles) of wilderness in the Selkirk Range of the Columbia Mountains. The park was established in 1886, and its growth was linked to the growth of the railroad, which was

The remote Purcell Mountains are noted for hunting and skiing

For hotels and restaurants in this region see p358 and pp380–81

The Illecillewaet Glacier is one of 420 glaciers in Glacier National Park

routed through Roger's Pass in 1885. Today, many of the park's most accessible walking trails follow abandoned railroad lines. Other trails offer visitors stunning views of the park's 150 glaciers, including the Great Glacier, now known as the Illecillewaet Glacier.

The park is known for its very wet weather in summer and almost daily snowfalls in winter, when as much as 23 m (75 ft) of snow may fall in one season. The threat of avalanche is serious here, and visitors should stop at the Roger's Pass Center for up-to-date information.

The Roger's Pass line was abandoned by the Canadian Pacific Railway due to avalanches, and a tunnel was built underneath it instead. The Trans-Canada Highway (Hwy 1) follows the route of the pass as it bisects the park, en route to the lovely town of Revelstoke. From here visitors may access the forests and jagged peaks of Mount Revelstoke National Park.

Taking the waters at Radium Hot Springs

❿ Radium Hot Springs

🏔 1,000. 🛈 Chamber of Commerce, 7556 Main St. E., (250) 347 9331, 888 347 9331. 🅦 **radiumhotsprings.com**

This small town is famous for its mineral springs and is a good base for exploring the nearby Kootenay National Park. In the summer, flower-filled pots decorate the storefronts of the many coffee shops and pubs along the main street, and the town has more motel rooms than residents.

Many of the 1.2 million annual visitors come to bathe in the healing waters of the springs. There are two pools, a hot soaking pool for relaxing in, and a cooler swimming pool. Locker rooms, swimsuits, showers, and towels can all be rented, and massages are readily available.

Visitors can explore the nearby Columbia Valley Wetlands too. Fed by glacial waters from the Purcell and Rocky mountains, the Columbia River meanders through these extensive marsh lands, which provide an important habitat for over 250 migratory waterfowl such as Canada geese and tundra swans.

⓫ Kootenay National Park

🚌 Banff. 🛈 Park Info Centre, open mid-May–Sep, (250) 347 9505. **Open** daily. 🐾 ♿ 🅒 🅦 **pc.gc.ca**

Kootenay National Park covers 1,406 sq km (543 sq miles) and is known for its ecology, climate, and diversity of landscape. The 94-km (58-mile) Kootenay Parkway (Hwy 93S) bisects the park from north to south. It winds through the narrow gorge of Sinclair Canyon, past the world-famous Radium Hot Springs Pools, along the deep red cliffs of the Redwall Fault, and up over the Sinclair Pass. The road continues into the Kootenay River Valley, past Hector Gorge, and into the Vermilion Valley. Short nature trails introduce you to magical Paint Pots, iron-rich mineral springs with rust-colored clay banks. Visitors will see the Marble Canyon, whose 35-m (115-ft) deep dolomite walls are carved by the glacial waters of Tokumm Creek. The Fireweed Trail at Vermilion Pass features vibrant regenerating forests growing along the Continental Divide, in the wake of old forest fires.

The ochre-colored Paint Pot pools in Kootenay National Park

⓬ Kananaskis Country

🚌 Canmore. 🛈 907 7th Ave., Canmore., (403) 678 0760. 🅦 **albertaparks.ca**

Kananaskis Country is a verdant region of the Rocky Mountain foothills, with mountain peaks, lakes, rivers, and alpine meadows. Located southwest of Calgary on the boundary of Banff National Park, this 4,000 sq km (1,544 sq miles) of wilderness is popular for hiking and viewing wildlife such as eagles, wolves, and bears. The town of Canmore serves as the center of this large recreational area, and has plenty of accommodations, as well as information on outdoor activities such as wildlife tours.

⑬ Banff National Park

The best known of the Rockies' national parks, Banff was also Canada's first. The park was established in 1885, after the discovery of natural hot springs by three Canadian Pacific Railroad workers in 1883. Centuries before the arrival of the railroad, Blackfoot, Stoney, and Kootenay peoples lived in the valleys around Banff. Today, Banff National Park covers an area of 6,641 sq km (2,564 sq miles) of some of the most sublime scenery in the country. The park encompasses impressive mountain peaks, forests, glacial lakes, and mighty rivers. Some four million visitors a year enjoy a range of activities, from hiking and canoeing in summer, to skiing in winter.

Peyto Lake
One of the most rewarding walks in Banff is a short stroll from the Icefields Parkway, near Bow Summit, which leads to a vista over the ice-blue waters of Peyto Lake.

Parker Ridge

Jasper

Saskatchewan River

93

0 km   5
0 miles   5

Mistaya Lake

93

Bow Lake

Bow River

1

View from Icefields Parkway
Renowned for its stunning views of high peaks, forests, lakes, and glaciers, this 230-km (143-mile) road runs between Lake Louise and Jasper.

Saskatchewan River Crossing lies at the junction of three rivers, along the route used by explorer David Thompson, who first came here in the late 1700s and began mapmaking.

Bear Safety

Both grizzly and black bears are found in the Rockies' national parks. Although sightings are rare, visitors should observe *The Mountain Guide*, a Parks Canada publication that is free to all park visitors and provides wildlife safety tips. The fundamental rules are: don't approach the animals; never feed them; don't run; and stay calm. Bears have an excellent sense of smell, so if you are camping be sure to lock food or trash inside a car or in the bear-proof boxes provided.

Grizzly bear in Banff

Valley of the Ten Peaks
A scenic road from Lake Louise winds to Moraine Lake, which is ringed by ten peaks each over 3,000 m (10,000 ft) high.

Johnston Canyon
This spectacular gorge boasts two impressive waterfalls, and is one of the most popular trails in the park. The walk can be reached from the Bow Valley Parkway (see p306), and has walkways close to the falls. Displays along the way explain the canyon's geology.

Key

═══ Highway
▬▬▬ Major road
─── Rivers

Lake Minnewanka
is Banff's largest lake and is a popular place for picnics and boat trips.

Bankhead
An interpretive hiking trail displaying historic photographs leads visitors around this coal mine and ghost town.

Vermilion Range

Diamond Glacier

Banff

Shadow Lake

Sundance Range

Yoho NP Vancouver

Lake Louise
The turquoise waters of Lake Louise are an abiding symbol of the beauty of the Rockies. It was here that one of the first resorts was established in Banff, with visitors beginning to arrive in 1885.

For map symbols see back flap

Exploring Banff National Park

It is impossible to travel through Banff National Park and not be filled with awe. It has some 25 peaks that rise over 3,000 m (10,000 ft) and are magically reflected in the turquoise waters of the park's many lakes. Banff townsite offers visitors a full range of facilities, including the therapeutic hot springs that inspired the founding of the park, and is an excellent base for exploring the surrounding country. Even the highway is counted an attraction here. The Icefields Parkway (Hwy 93) winds through stunning mountain vistas and connects Banff to Jasper National Park, beginning at the renowned Lake Louise.

Icefields Parkway (Highway 93)

The Icefields Parkway is a 230-km (143-mile) scenic mountain highway that twists and turns through the jagged spines of the Rocky Mountains. The road is a wonder in itself, where every turn offers yet another incredible view, as it climbs through high passes from Lake Louise to Jasper.

The road was built during the Depression of the 1930s, as a work-creation project. Designed for sightseeing, the highway was extended to its present length in 1960, with plenty of pull-offs to allow visitors to take in the views.

Bow Summit is the highest point on the highway, at 2,068 m (6,785 ft), and has a side road that leads to the **Peyto Lake** viewpoint, which looks over snow-topped peaks mirrored in the brilliant blue of the lake. In summer, Bow Summit's mountain meadows are covered with alpine flowers. From here, it is also possible to see the Crowfoot Glacier, a striking chunk of ice in the shape of a crow's foot, hanging over a cliff-face.

Farther north a trail leads down from a parking lot to **Mistaya Canyon** with its sheer-sided walls, potholes, and an impressive natural arch. The highway passes close by the Icefields (which cross the park boundaries into Jasper National Park), and the Athabasca Glacier is clearly visible from the road. Mountain goats and bighorn sheep are drawn to the mineral deposits by the roadside.

The Bow Valley Parkway passing scenic country along the river

The Bow Valley Parkway

This parkway, running between Banff and Lake Louise, is a 55-km (34-mile-) long scenic alternative to the Trans-Canada Highway. The road follows the Bow River Valley and offers visitors the chance to explore the gentle country of the valley with many interpretive signs and viewpoints along the way. From the road it is possible to see the abundant wildlife such as bears, elk, and coyotes.

About 19 km (12 miles) west of Banff, one of the best short walks leads from the roadside to the **Johnston Canyon** trail. A paved path leads to the canyon and two impressive waterfalls. The path to the lower falls is wheelchair accessible, and the upper falls are a slightly longer 2.7-km (1.7-mile) hike. A boardwalk along the rock wall leads to the floor of the canyon, offering valley views close to the railroad crossing through the mountains.

Among the most striking natural phenomena in the canyon are the Ink Pots, a series of pools where vivid blue-green water bubbles up from underground springs. Interpretive signs explain how this fascinating canyon took shape, and how the water created its unique rock formations.

Lake Minnewanka Drive

This narrow, winding 14-km (9-mile) loop road begins at the Minnewanka interchange on the Trans-Canada Highway. From here it is a pleasant drive to picnic sites, hiking trails, and three lakes. Lake Minnewanka is Banff's biggest lake, almost 28 km (17 miles) long.

A popular short trail leads to **Bankhead**, the site of an abandoned coal mine that was the first settlement in Banff and whose heyday was in the first half of the 19th century. The footpath displays old photographs and notices that depict the life of the miners.

Lake Minnewanka, the largest lake in Banff National Park

Banff Springs Hotel, styled after the baronial castles of Scotland

Banff

The town of Banff grew up around the hot springs that were discovered here in the 1880s. The Canadian Pacific Railway manager, Sir William Cornelius Van Horne, realized the springs would attract visitors, so he built the grand Banff Springs Hotel in 1888. The resort was very popular, and the town expanded to accommodate the influx.

Located at the foot of Sulphur Mountain, The **Cave and Basin National Historic Site** is the site of the original spring found by the railroad workers in 1883 and is now a museum telling the story of Banff's development. The **Upper Hot Springs Pool**, also at the base of Sulphur Mountain, is a popular resort where visitors can relieve their aches in the mineral-rich, healing waters.

At 2,281 m (7,484 ft) above sea level, Sulphur Mountain provides a spectacular view of the surrounding area. Although there is a 5-km (3-mile) trail to the top, a glass-enclosed gondola (cable car) carries visitors to the summit in eight minutes. Here the viewing platforms offer beautiful vistas of the Rockies.

Banff is busy all year round. In winter, snow sports from skiing to dog-sledding are available, while summer visitors include hikers, cyclists, and mountaineers. The **Banff Park Museum** was built in 1903 and houses specimens of animals, plants, and mineral samples.

🏛 Banff Park Museum
91 Banff Ave. **Tel** (403) 762 1558. **Open** seasonal. **Closed** Jan 1, Dec 25. 🅿 ♿ Ⓦ **pc.gc.ca**

Gondolas or cable cars take visitors up Sulphur Mountain in eight minutes

Lake Louise
ℹ by Samson Mall, (403) 522 3833.
One of Banff National Park's major draws, the beauty of Lake Louise is an enduring image of the Rockies. Famed for the blueness of its water and the snow-capped peaks that surround it, Lake Louise also boasts the Victoria Glacier, which stretches almost to the water's edge. Trails around the lake offer exhibits that explain the lake's formation some 10,000 years ago, at the end of the last Ice Age. The amazing color of the water of this and other lakes in the park comes from deposits of glacial silt, known as rock flour, suspended just beneath the surface. Dominating the landscape at one end of the lake is the imposing hotel Château Lake Louise, built in 1894.

During the summer, a gondola carries visitors up to Mount Whitehorn for stunning views of the glacier and the lake. In winter, the area attracts large numbers of skiers, ice-climbers, and snowboarders.

In Lake Louise village visitors can stock up on supplies, such as food, clothes, and gas.

Moraine Lake
Less well known than Lake Louise, Moraine Lake is every bit as beautiful, with its shimmering turquoise color. The lake has a pretty waterside lodge that offers accommodations, meals, and canoe rentals. There are several trails that all start at the lake: one lakeside path follows the north shore for 1.5 km (1 mile), while the climb, which leads up Larch Valley-Sentinel Pass trail, offers more stunning vistas, ending at one of the park's highest passes.

⓮ Yoho National Park

Inspired by the beauty of the park's mountains, lakes, waterfalls, and distinctive rock formations, this area was named Yoho, for the Cree word meaning "awe and wonder." Yoho National Park lies on the western side of the Rockies range in BC, next to Banff and Kootenay national parks.

The park offers a wide range of activities, from climbing and hiking to boating or skiing. The park also houses the Burgess Shale fossil beds, an extraordinary find of perfectly preserved marine creatures from the prehistoric Cambrian period, over 500 million years ago. Access to the fossil beds is by guided hike and is limited to a maximum of 12 people each trip.

WAPTA ICEFIELD

Emerald Lake
The rustic Emerald Lake Lodge (see p358) provides facilities at this quiet, secluded place in the middle of the park. The lake, which is named for the intense color of its waters, is a popular spot for canoeing, walking, and riding horses.

Natural Bridge
Found in the center of the park, over the waters of the Kicking Horse River, Natural Bridge is a rock bridge formed by centuries of erosion, which have worn a channel through solid rock.

Vancouver Glacier National Park

0 km   3
0 miles   3

Key

— Highway

— Major road

— Rivers

Hoodoo Creek
These fabulous, mushroom-like towers of rock have been created by erosion and can be accessed from a short, but very steep, trail.

The Yoho Valley is noted for its stunning scenery, including the Takakkaw Falls.

Takakkaw Falls
Takakkaw means "it is wonderful" in the language of the Aboriginal Peoples, and these are among the most impressive falls in Canada, with a drop of 254 m (833 ft). The cascade can be accessed along the Yoho Valley Road, which is open seasonally.

Burgess Shale is a UNESCO World Heritage Site set up to protect two fossil beds. Day-long guided hikes here are by reservation only.

Kicking Horse River
This wild river rushes through Yoho alongside the original 1880s railroad. Today the tracks carry freight and the "Rocky Mountaineer" tourist train (see pp414–415).

Lake O'Hara
Shadowed by the majestic peaks of Mounts Victoria and Lefroy, Lake O'Hara is astonishingly beautiful. However, guests wishing to use the area's excellent hiking trails must book in advance as access is limited to protect this fragile environment.

Lake O'Hara nestled amongst the peaks of Yoho National Park ▶

⑮ Jasper National Park

The most northerly of the four Rocky Mountain national parks, Jasper is also the most rugged and the largest, covering an area of 10,878 sq km (4,200 sq miles) of high peaks and valleys dotted with glacial lakes. The Columbia Icefield (see p314), a vast area of 400-year-old ice that is 365 m (1,198 ft) thick in places, is part of the national park. From the icefield, fingers of ice reach down through many of Jasper's valleys.

Some of the most accessible hiking trails in the park start from the Maligne Lake and Canyon, and the town of Jasper. The town is located roughly in the park's center and is the starting point for many of the most popular walks and sights here.

Pyramid Lake
Ringed by jagged peaks, both Pyramid and nearby Patricia Lake lie close to Jasper town.

The Jasper Tramway
Only a few kilometers out of Jasper town is the popular Jasper Tramway, which takes visitors to a viewing platform near the summit of The Whistlers at 2,277 m (7,470 ft). Panoramic vistas take in the park's mountains, forests, and lakes.

Snake Indian River

Jasp Lak

Victoria Cross Range

Prince George ◀─── Jasper ●

16

93

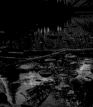

Mount Edith Cavell
It is possible to drive up this mountain as far as Cavell Lake, from where the trail leads to Angel Glacier and to the flower-strewn Cavell Meadows.

0 km 20
0 miles 20

Key

▬ Major road

═ Minor road

▬ Rivers

Maligne Canyon

One of the most beautiful canyons in the Rockies, Maligne's sheer limestone walls and several impressive waterfalls can be seen from the many footbridges that are built both along and across its walls.

Miette Hot Springs

Visitors here enjoy relaxing in the warmest spring waters in the Rockies. The springs are said to have healing effects because of their high mineral content.

Edmonton

16

Medicine Lake

Renowned for its varying water levels, Medicine Lake is drained by a series of underground tunnels and caves. It is also one of Jasper's prettiest lakes.

Miette Range

Rocky River

Maligne Range

Maligne Lake

Athabasca River

93

Banff National Park
Yoho National Park
Calgary

Columbia Icefield

Sunwapta River offers white-water rafters a choice of conditions, from calm to turbulent.

Athabasca Falls

The dramatic, rushing waters of these falls are the result of the Athabasca River being forced through a narrow gorge.

For map symbols *see back flap*

Exploring Jasper

Established in 1907, Jasper National Park is as staggeringly beautiful as anywhere in the Rockies, but it is distinguished by having more remote wilderness than the other national parks. These areas can be reached only on foot, horseback, or by canoe, and backpackers need passes from the Park Trail Office for hikes that last more than one day. Jasper also has a reputation for more sightings of wildlife such as bear, moose, and elk than any of the other Rockies' parks.

Although most of the park services are closed between October and Easter, visitors who brave the winter season have an opportunity to cross-country ski on breathtaking trails that skirt frozen lakes. In addition, they can go ice fishing, downhill skiing, or on guided walking tours on frozen rivers. In the summertime there are a range of daytrips that are easily accessible from the park's main town of Jasper.

Downhill skiing is just one of the outdoor activities around Jasper

Columbia Icefield and Icefield Centre

Icefields Parkway. **Tel** (780) 852 6288. **Open** May–Oct: daily. ♿ 🅦 pc.gc.ca

The Columbia Icefield straddles both Banff and Jasper national parks and forms the largest area of ice south of Alaska. The Icefield, which covers 325 sq km (125 sq miles) and can be as thick as 365 m (1,198 ft), was created during the last Ice Age.

Around 10,000 years ago, ice filled the region, sculpting out wide valleys, sheer mountain faces, and sharp ridges. Although the glaciers have retreated over the last few hundred years, during the early years of the 20th century ice covered the area where the Icefields Parkway now passes. An interpretive center explains the Ice Age and the impact of the glaciers on the landscape of the Rockies. Tours of the Athabasca Glacier, in four-wheel drive Ice Explorers, are available from the center, which also has information on local trails.

Athabasca Falls

Located at the junction of highways 93 and 93A, where the Athabasca River plunges 23 m (75 ft) to the river bed below, these are among the most dramatic waterfalls in the park. Despite being a short drop compared with other falls in the Rockies, the force of the waters of the Athabasca River being pushed through a narrow, quartz-rich gorge transforms these waters into a powerful, foaming torrent.

Jasper

The town of Jasper was established in 1911 as a settlement for Grand Trunk Pacific Railroad workers, who were laying track along the Athabasca River Valley. As with Banff, the coming of the railroad and the growth of the parks as resorts went hand-in-hand, and the town expanded to include hotels, restaurants, and a visitor center. Today, many of the park's main attractions are close to the town, which is located at the center of the park, on both Highway 16 and Icefields Parkway (Hwy 93).

Just 7 km (4.4 miles) out of town is the Jasper Tramway station, from where visitors may take a brisk, 7-minute ride up **The Whistlers**. The trip whisks visitors up to the upper terminal at 2,277 m (7,470 ft), where there is a clearly marked trail

The wild waters of Athabasca River make it a popular venue for white-water rafting

leading to the summit at 2,470 m (8,100 ft). On a clear day the view is incomparable. For those who would rather walk than ride the tram, there is a 2.8-km (1.7-mile) trail to the top of the mountain. The trail winds upward, offering panoramic views of both the Miette and Athabasca valleys, and, in July, the lush meadows are blanketed with colorful wildflowers.

A boat cruise on Maligne Lake, the largest natural lake in the Rockies

Patricia and Pyramid Lakes
North of Jasper townsite, the attractive Patricia and Pyramid lakes nestle beneath the 2,763-m (9,065-ft) high Pyramid Mountain. Forming a popular daytrip from the town, the lakes are noted for windsurfing and sailing. Equipment rental is available from two lakeside lodges.

The deep blue waters of Pyramid Lake beneath Pyramid Mountain

Maligne Lake Drive
Maligne Lake Drive begins 5 km (3 miles) east of Jasper townsite and leads off Hwy 16, following the valley floor between the Maligne and the Queen Elizabeth ranges. This scenic road travels past many magnificent sights, with viewpoints along the way offering panoramas of Maligne Valley. Among the route's most spectacular sights is the Maligne Canyon, reached by a 4-km (2-mile) interpretive hiking trail that explains the special geological features behind the gorge's formation. One of the most beautiful in the Rockies, Maligne Canyon has sheer limestone walls as high as 50 m (164 ft) and many waterfalls, which can be seen from several foot bridges. The road ends at

Maligne Lake, which is surrounded by snow-capped mountains and, at 22 km (14 miles) long, is the largest natural lake in the Rockies. There are several scenic trails around it, one of which leads to the Opal Hills and amazing views of the area. Guided walks around here can be organized from Jasper, and it is possible to rent fishing tackle and canoes and kayaks to go out on the lake.

Medicine Lake
Medicine Lake is also reached from a side road off Maligne Lake Drive. The lake is noted for its widely varying water levels. In autumn the lake is reduced to a trickle, but in springtime the waters rise, fed by the fast-flowing Maligne River. A vast network of underground caves and channels are responsible for this event.

Miette Hot Springs
Tel (780) 866 3939, 1 800 767 1611.
Open May–Oct: daily. 🚻 🚽
Located 61 km (38 miles) north of Jasper along the attractive Miette Springs Road, these springs are

the hottest in the Rockies, reaching temperatures as high as 54°C (129°F). However, the thermal baths are cooled to a more reasonable 40°C (104°F) for bathers. The waters are held to be both relaxing and healthy – they are rich in minerals, such as calcium, sulfates, and small amounts of hydrogen sulfide (which smells like rotten eggs).

The resort of Miette Springs houses two pools, including one suitable for children. The springs are part of a leisure complex that offers both restaurants and hotels.

Mount Edith Cavell
Named after a World War I heroine nurse, this mountain is located 30 km (19 miles) south of Jasper townsite. The scenic road that climbs it is paved but has some rough sections and narrow switchbacks. The road ends at Cavell Lake by the north face of the mountain. From here, a guided trail leads to a small lake beneath the Angel Glacier. A three-hour walk across the flower strewn Cavell meadows has views of the glacier's icy tongue.

A peninsula of ice from Angel Glacier seen from Mount Edith Cavell

Typical kitchen of the late 1900s at the Grande Prairie Museum & Heritage Village

⑯ Prince George

🏔 72,000. ✈ 🚉 🚌 ℹ 101–1300 First Ave., (250) 562 3700. 🌐 **tourismpg.com**

The largest town in Northern British Columbia, Prince George is a bustling supply-and-transportation center for the region. Two major highways pass through here, the Yellowhead (Hwy 16) and Highway 97, which becomes the Alaska Highway at Dawson Creek. Established in 1807 as Fort George, a fur-trading post at the confluence of the Nechako and Fraser rivers, the town is well placed for exploring the province.

Today, Prince George has all the facilities of a larger city, including a university specializing in First Nations history and culture, as well as its own symphony orchestra and several art galleries. The **Exploration Place Museum and Science Centre** lies on the site of the original Fort, within the 26-ha (64-acre) Fort George Park, and has a collection of artifacts from aboriginal cultures, European pioneers, and early settlers.

Over 1,600 lakes and rivers are within an hour's drive of the community, making Prince George an ideal location for angling enthusiasts.

🏛 **The Exploration Place Museum and Science Centre**
333 Becott Place. **Tel** (250) 562 1612. **Open** 9am–5pm daily. **Closed** Jan 1, Dec 25. 🅿 ♿ 🌐 **theexploration place.com**

⑰ Grande Prairie

🏔 55,000. ✈ 🚌 ℹ 11330 106th St., (780) 539 7688. 🌐 **gptourism.ca**

Grande Prairie is a large, modern city in the northwest corner of Alberta. Surrounded by fertile farming country, the city is a popular stop for travelers heading north toward Dawson Creek and the Alaska Highway (*see pp266–7*). The city is the hub of the Peace River region; it offers extensive opportunities for shopping in its giant malls and many downtown specialty stores, with the added draw of having no provincial sales tax (*see p384*).

Running through the city center is the attractive wilderness of Muskoseepi Park. Covering 405 ha (1,000 acres), the park offers a variety of outdoor activities including walking and biking trails, and cross-country skiing.

The **Grande Prairie Museum & Heritage Village** is also housed in the park and has

15 buildings containing over 55,000 historical artifacts. There are several reconstructions, including a 1911 schoolhouse, a rural post office, and a church. A renowned display of dinosaur bones recovered from the Peace River Valley are also on display at the museum.

Bear Creek, which runs through Muskoseepi Park, has become a magnet for bird-watchers, as sightings of eagles are common. The Grand River wetlands, particularly those at Crystal Lake, located in the northeast corner of the city, contain one of the few breeding grounds for the rare trumpeter swan.

🏛 **Grande Prairie Museum & Heritage Village**
Cnr 102nd St. & 102nd Ave. **Tel** (780) 830 7090. **Open** daily. **Closed** Jan 1, Dec 25. ♿ 🌐 **cityofgp.com**

⑱ Fort St. John

🏔 20,000. ✈ 🚌 ℹ 9324 96th St., (250) 785 3033. 🌐 **fortstjohn.ca**

Fort St. John is located at Mile 47 of the Alaska Highway, among the rolling hills of the Peace River Valley. During the construction of the Highway in 1942, the tiny town dramatically expanded from a population of about 800 to 6,000. When completed, the highway turned Fort St. John into a busy supply center that caters to visitors exploring the area, as well as supporting the growth of agriculture in the surrounding countryside. However, the town boomed when oil was found

Lush farmland along the Peace River in northern British Columbia

The green waters of Muncho Lake framed by mountains in Muncho Lake Provincial Park

here in the 1950s, in what proved to be the largest oil field in the province. Today, Fort St. John's pride in its industrial and pioneering heritage is reflected in the local museum, which has a 41-m (136-ft) high oil derrick at its entrance and a range of exhibits that tell the story of the local oil industry.

⓲ Fort Nelson

🏔 4,000. 🚌 🚏 ℹ 5319 50th Ave. S., (250) 774 2541.
🌐 **northernrockies.ca**

Despite the growth of the oil, gas, and lumber industries in the 1960s and 1970s, Fort Nelson retains the atmosphere of a northern frontier town. Before the building of the Alaska Highway in the 1940s, Fort Nelson was an important stop on route for the Yukon and Alaska, and until the 1950s was without running water or electricity. Fur trading was the main activity until the energy boom; even today both aboriginal and white trappers hunt wolf, beaver, and lynx, for both their fur and their meat.

Today, the town has an air and bus service, a hospital, and good visitor facilities such as motels, restaurants, and gas stations. Local people are famous for their friendliness, and during the busy summer months run a program of free talks describing life in the north to visitors. A small museum displays photographs and artifacts that tell the story of the building of the 2,451-km (1,523-mile) Alaska Highway.

⓴ Muncho Lake Provincial Park

Off Hwy 97. **Tel** (250) 776 7000.
Open daily.

One of three provincial parks (including Stone Mountain and Liard River Hot Springs) that were established after the building of the Alaska Highway, Muncho Lake occupies the most scenic section of the road. The park encompasses the bare

peaks of the northern Rockies, whose stark limestone slopes incorporate the faults, alluvial fans, and hoodoos that are a testament to thousands of years of glacial erosion. The Highway skirts the eastern shoreline of the 12-km (7-mile) long Muncho Lake before crossing the Liard River, where the Mackenzie Mountain range begins. In early summer, passing motorists are likely to see moose grazing among meadows filled with colorful wildflowers. The park's bogs are popular with botanists eager to see the rare yellow Lady's Slipper orchid. The roadside also attracts goats, sheep, and caribou, drawn by delicious deposits of sodium, known as mineral licks.

Lynx near Fort Nelson

Visitors may stay in the park at one of the campgrounds or lodges in order to explore its 861 sq km (332 sq miles) of wilderness. The deep waters of Muncho Lake house a good supply of trout for anglers.

SOUTHERN AND NORTHERN BRITISH COLUMBIA

Southern British Columbia covers the region south of Prince George, down to the US border. There is a vast variety of natural beauty here, including the forests and waterfalls of Wells Gray Provincial Park, and the lush valleys, wineries, and lake resorts of the Okanagan Valley. One of the most stunning wildernesses in North America, northern British Columbia spreads north of Prince Rupert, between the Coast Mountains in the west, the Rockies in the east, and the Yukon. Its dramatic landscape ranges from the volcanic terrain around Mount Edziza, with its lava flows and cinder cones, to the frozen forests of Atlin Provincial Park. Haida Gwaii can be accessed by plane or ferry, and much of the trip is across open ocean. For 10,000 years the archipelago has been home to the Haida people, who are famous for their totem-carving.

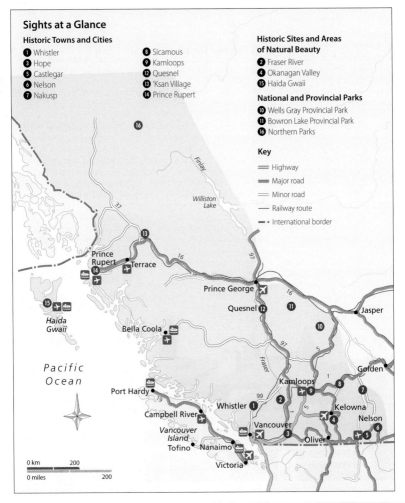

Sights at a Glance

Historic Towns and Cities

1 Whistler
3 Hope
5 Castlegar
6 Nelson
7 Nakusp
8 Sicamous
9 Kamloops
12 Quesnel
13 'Ksan Village
14 Prince Rupert

Historic Sites and Areas of Natural Beauty

2 Fraser River
4 Okanagan Valley
15 Haida Gwaii

National and Provincial Parks

10 Wells Gray Provincial Park
11 Bowron Lake Provincial Park
16 Northern Parks

Key

═══ Highway
▬▬ Major road
═══ Minor road
——— Railway route
■ ■ International border

0 km   200
0 miles   200

◀ Grapevines of Blue Mountain Vineyards & Cellars overlooking Vaseux Lake, Okanagan Valley   **For map symbols** *see back flap*

The Trans-Canada Highway overlooking the Fraser Canyon along the Fraser River

❶ Whistler

🏔 10,000. ✉ ℹ 4230 Gateway Drive, (604) 935 3357. 🆆 whistler.com

Whistler is home to the largest ski resort in North America, Whistler Blackcomb. Set among the Coast Mountains, 125 km (78 miles) north of Vancouver, Whistler Blackcomb is divided into five distinct areas: Whistler Village, Village North, Upper Village, Blueberry Hill, and Whistler Creekside. Whistler and Blackcomb mountains have one of the greatest vertical rises of any ski runs in North America. The skiing and snowboarding here is among the best in the world, with mild Pacific weather and reliable winter snow. In summer, there is snowboarding and skiing on Blackcomb's Horstman Glacier, and mountain biking.

Whistler Village offers visitors a full range of facilities, from comfortable B&Bs to luxurious five-star hotels. Café-lined cobbled squares and cozy bars and restaurants cater to all tastes, while a range of stores sells everything from ski-wear to indigenous arts and crafts. Whistler was also the 2010 Winter Olympics venue for most snow sports.

❷ Fraser River

ℹ Vancouver, 1 800 667 3306.

The majestic Fraser River travels 1,375 km (854 miles) through some of BC's most stunning scenery. The river flows from its source in the Yellowhead Lake, near Jasper, to the Strait of Georgia, near Vancouver. Along the way, it heads north through the Rocky Mountain trench before turning south near the town of Prince George. It continues by the Coast Mountains, then west to the town of Hope through the steep walls of the Fraser Canyon, and on toward Yale.

It was Fraser Canyon that legendary explorer Simon Fraser found the most daunting when he followed the river's course in 1808.

However, when gold was discovered near the town of Yale 50 years later, thousands of prospectors swarmed up the valley. Today, Yale is a small town with a population of 200 and the delightful **Yale Museum**, where exhibits focus on the history of the gold rush, as well as telling the epic story of the building of the Canadian Pacific Railroad through the canyon. This section of river is also a popular white-water rafting area, and trips can be arranged from the small town of Boston Bar. At Hell's Gate the river thunders through the Canyon's narrow walls, which are only 34 m (112 ft) apart.

🏛 **Yale Museum**
31187 Douglas St. **Tel** (604) 863 2324. **Open** May–Sep: daily. 🅿 ♿
🆆 historicyale.ca

❸ Hope

🏔 6,100. ✉ ℹ 919 Water Ave., (604) 869 2021. 🆆 hopebc.ca

Located at the southern end of the Fraser Canyon, Hope is crossed by several highways, including Hwy 1 (the Trans-Canada) and Hwy 3. It is an excellent base for exploring the Fraser Canyon and southern BC, as well as being within easy reach of several provincial parks. The beautiful country of Manning Provincial Park, with its lakes, mountains, and rivers, is noted for its outdoor activities – swimming, hiking, fishing, and sailing in summer, and downhill and cross-country skiing in winter.

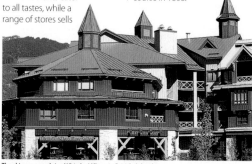

The ski resort at alpine Whistler Village in British Columbia

❹ Okanagan Valley Tour

The Okanagan Valley is actually a series of valleys, linked by a string of lakes, that stretches for 250 km (155 miles) from Osoyoos in the south, to Sicamous in the north. The main towns here are connected by Highway 97, which passes through the desert landscape near Osoyoos, and on to the lush green orchards and vineyards for which the valley is most noted. Mild winters and hot summers have made the Okanagan one of Canada's favorite vacation destinations.

Tips for Drivers

Starting point: On Highway 97 from Vernon in the north; Osoyoos in the south.
Length: 175 km (109 miles).
Highlights: Blossom and fruit festivals are held in spring and summer, when roadside stalls offer a cornucopia of fruit. Wine tours are available year-round.

④ Kelowna
The biggest city in the Okanagan, Kelowna lies on the shores of Lake Okanagan between Penticton and Vernon, and is the center of the wine-and-fruit-growing industries.

⑤ Vernon
Surrounded by farms and orchards, Vernon owes its lush look to the growth of irrigation in 1908. Several small resorts are set around the nearby lakes.

③ Summerland
This small but charming lakeside resort boasts several 19th-century buildings and stunning views from the top of Giant's Head Mountain.

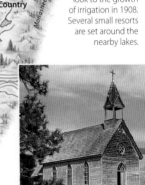

② Penticton
This sunny lakeside town is known for Okanagan Lake Beach, windsurfing, and local winery tours, as well as for its Peach Festival, held every August.

⑥ Historic O'Keefe Ranch
Founded by the O'Keefe family in 1867, this historic ranch displays original artifacts belonging to the family who lived here until 1977. The original log cabin remains, as do the church and store.

① Osoyoos
Visitors are drawn here by hot summers, the warm waters and sandy beaches of Lake Osoyoos, and the nearby pocket desert.

Key

━━ Tour route
══ Other roads

0 km   25
0 miles   25

Impressive historic stone buildings in the attractive town of Nelson

❺ Castlegar

🏠 8,000. ✈ 🚌 ℹ 1995 6th Ave., (250) 365 6313. 🌐 **castlegar.com**

Located in southeastern BC, Castlegar is a busy transportation hub. The town is crossed by two major highways, Hwy 3 and Hwy 22, and lies at the junction of the important Kootenay and Columbia rivers.

In the early 1900s, a steady influx of Doukhobors (Russian religious dissenters fleeing persecution) began arriving here. The **Doukhobor Discovery Centre** reflects the group's heritage and houses a variety of traditional clothes and tools, and antique farm machinery.

Traditional Doukhobor tunic

🏛 **Doukhobor Discovery Centre** 112 Heritage Way. **Tel** (250) 365 5327. **Open** May–Sep: daily. 🅿 ♿ 🌐 **doukhobor-museum.org**

❻ Nelson

🏠 10,500. 🚌 ℹ 91 Baker St., (250) 352 3433. 🌐 **discovernelson.com**

One of the most attractive towns in southern British Columbia, Nelson overlooks Kootenay Lake. Established in the 1880s as a mining town, with the coming of the railroad in the 1890s, Nelson flourished as a center for transporting ore and timber. The town owes its good looks to its location on the shores of the lake and to the large number of public buildings and houses that were constructed between 1895 and 1920. British Columbia's best-known architect, Francis Rattenbury (*see p284*), played a part in the design of some of the town's most prestigious and beautiful structures, such as the elegant Burns building, which was built in 1899 for millionaire cattle rancher and meat packer, Patrick Burns.

In 1908, Rattenbury also designed the Nelson Court House, a stately stone building with towers and gables.

Today, the town has a thriving cultural scene, with an art walk during the summer, as well as numerous cafés, book, and craft shops. Visitors also enjoy the short ride on Car 23, a 1906 streetcar that operated in the town between 1924 and 1949 (it was restored in 1992), and which today travels along Nelson's delightful waterfront. The infocenter provides visitors with a map and guide for the heritage walking tour of the town's historic buildings.

❼ Nakusp

🏠 1,500. ℹ 92 6th Ave. NW., (250) 265 4234. 🌐 **nakusparrowlakes.com**

With the snow-topped Selkirk Mountains as a backdrop, and overlooking the waters of Upper Arrow Lake, Nakusp is a charming town. Originally developed as a mining settlement, the town is now known for its mineral hot springs. There are two resorts close to town; the Nakusp and Halcyon Hot Springs, both of which provide therapeutic bathing in hot waters, rich in sulfates, calcium, and hydrogen sulfide, said to be good for everyday aches, as well as arthritis and rheumatism. Roughly 40 km (25 miles) to

The town of Nakusp, overlooking picturesque Upper Arrow Lake

the south of Nakusp, in the Slocan Valley, are two fascinating abandoned silver mining towns, New Denver and Sandon. Sandon had 5,000 inhabitants at the height of the mining boom in 1892. It also had 29 hotels, 28 saloons, and several brothels and gambling halls. A fire in 1900, poor metal prices, and dwindling ore reserves crippled the mines, and Sandon became a ghost town. Today, the town has been declared an historic site, and its homes and businesses are being carefully restored.

The nearby town of New Denver suffered a fate similar to Sandon's, but is also noted as the site of an internment camp for the Japanese during World War II. The Nikkei Internment Memorial Centre on Josephine Street is the only center in Canada devoted to telling the story of the internment of over 20,000 Japanese Canadians. The center is surrounded by a formal Japanese garden.

Houseboats moored along the waterfront at Sicamous

❽ Sicamous

🏚 3,200. 🚌 ℹ 446 Main St., (250) 836 2477. 🌐 sicamouschamber.bc.ca

Sicamous is an appealing waterfront village with charming streets hung with flower-filled planters. Located between Mara and Shuswap lakes, at the junction of the Trans- Canada Highway and Highway 97A, the town is ideally placed for touring the lakes, and the town of Salmon Arm, at the northern end of the Okanagan Valley (see p321). Over 200 houseboats are available for renting in the summer, and there are numerous marinas and watersport rental companies. The lakes have over 1,000 km (620 miles) of shoreline to explore. From a boat it is possible to view the inlets and forested landscape of Lake Shuswap, where black bears, deer, moose, coyotes, and bobcats have all been spotted along the shore. In summer, visitors and locals enjoy

A horse's snow shoe on display at Kamloops

the good public beach on the lake, as well as the pleasant walk along a marked waterfront trail.

❾ Kamloops

🏚 90,000. ✈ 🚌 🚌 ℹ 1290 West Trans-Canada Hwy, (250) 372 8000. 🌐 tourismkamloops.com

Kamloops means "where the rivers meet" in the language of the Secwepemc First Nations. The largest town by area in BC's southern interior, it lies at the crossroads of the north and south Thompson Rivers. Three major highways also meet here – the Trans-Canada, Hwy 5, and Hwy 97 to the Okanagan Valley – as do the Canadian Pacific and Canadian National railroad.

European settlement began in 1812, when fur traders started doing business with First Nations peoples. The **Secwepemc Museum and Heritage Park** focuses on the cultural history of the Secwepemc First Nations and has a wide variety of artifacts, including a birch-bark canoe, hunting equipment, traditional clothing and cooking utensils. Outside, in the Heritage Park, short trails lead visitors through the archeological remains of a 2,000-year-old Shuswap winter village site, which includes four authentically reconstructed winter pit houses and a summer camp. The village has a hunting shack, a fish-drying rack, and a smoke house.

The museum store sells pine-needle and birch-bark baskets, moccasins, and a wide variety of beaded and silver jewelry.

In the town center, the Art Gallery has a small but striking collection that features landscape sketches by A. Y. Jackson, one of the renowned Group of Seven painters (see pp168–69).

🏛 **Secwepemc Museum and Heritage Park**
200–330 Chief Alex Thomas Way. **Tel** (250) 828 9749. **Open** Jun–Sep: daily; Sep–May: 8:30am–4:30pm Mon–Fri.
📷 ♿

❿ Wells Gray Provincial Park

Tel (250) 674 3334. 🚌 Clearwater. 🚌 Clearwater. **Open** May–Sep. 🌐 wellsgray.ca

Wells Gray Provincial Park is one of the most beautiful wildernesses in British Columbia, and offers wonders comparable to the Rockies in the east. The park was opened in 1939 and is distinguished by alpine meadows, thundering waterfalls, and glacier-topped peaks that rise as high as 2,575 m (8,450 ft). The Canadian National Railroad and Hwy 5 follow the Thompson River along the park's western edge, offering stunning views.

From the Clearwater Valley Road, off Hwy 5, there are several trails, from easy walks to arduous overnight hikes in remote country. A selection of small trails, just a few minutes from the road, lead to the spectacular sight of Dawson Falls.

⓫ Bowron Lake Provincial Park

Tel (250) 377 8888. 🚌 Quesnel. 🚐 Quesnel. **Open** May–Sep. 🛶 (canoe trip) ♿ partial.

Bowron Lake Provincial Park is located about 120 km (76 miles) east of Quesnel on Highway 26 in the Cariboo Mountains. The park is renowned for having a 112-km (70-mile) rectangular waterway composed of nine lakes, three rivers, streams, small lakes, and many portages (trails linking the waterways). There is a week-long canoe trip here, but it is limited to 50 canoeists at a time, and must be booked ahead, either by phone or online. It is a special trip that allows visitors to come quietly upon wildlife such as moose or beaver. In late summer, bears come to feed on the spawning sockeye salmon in the Bowron River.

A grizzly bear rearing up

⓬ Quesnel

🗺 9,500. ✈ 🚌 🚐 ℹ 703 Carson Ave., (250) 992 8716. 🌐 tourismquesnel.com

Quesnel is a busy logging town that started life as a gold-rush settlement between 1858 and 1861. The town was the last along the Gold Rush Trail, or Cariboo Road (now Hwy 97), which was lined with mining

A 19th-century horse and carriage in the streets of Barkerville

towns between here and Kamloops. Quesnel occupies an attractive position in a triangle formed by the Fraser and Quesnel rivers. The town's sights include the Riverfront Trail System, a tree-lined 12-km (7-mile) path that runs along the banks of both rivers. Just outside the town's limits, Pinnacles Provincial Park features the geological wonder of hoodoos, rocky columns formed 12 million years ago, when the volcanic surface was eroded by Ice Age meltwaters.

From Quesnel, 87 km (54 miles) east on Hwy 26, lies the historic mining town of **Barkerville**. It was born when Englishman Billy Barker dug up a handful of gold nuggets in 1862. Today, it is a good example of a perfectly preserved 19th-century mining town, with over 120 restored or reconstructed buildings and costumed guides. Visitors can see a blacksmith at work in his forge, watch showgirls put on the kind of display the miners would have seen at the theater, or take a ride on a stagecoach.

🎪 **Barkerville Historic Town** 87 km E. of Quesnel, Hwy 26. **Tel** (250) 994 3332, 1 888 994 3332. **Open** daily. 🛶 ♿ 🌐 **bakerville.ca**

⓭ 'Ksan Village

Tel (250) 842 5544, 1 877 842 5518. **Open** grounds: year round; houses: Apr–Sep: daily. 🛶 ♿ 🌐 **ksan.org**

Some 290 km (180 miles) east of Prince Rupert, 'Ksan Village is a re-creation of an 1870 aboriginal settlement, established in the 1950s to preserve the culture of the Gitxsan First Nations. Gitxsan people have lived in the area for thousands of years, particularly along the beautiful Skeena River valley. Their way of life was under threat from an influx of white settlers, who arrived in the 1850s at Prince Rupert to work their way up river to mine or farm.

Noted for their skill in carving and painting masks, totems, and

Gitxsan carved cedarwood totem pole in 'Ksan Village

canoes, Gitxsan elders are now schooling new generations in these skills at 'Ksan Village. Within the complex are seven traditional longhouses containing a carving school, museum, and gift shop.

⓮ Prince Rupert

🗺 13,000. ✈ 🚌 🚐 ⛴ ℹ 200–215 Cowbay Rd., (250) 624 5637, 1 800 667 1994. 🌐 **visitprincerupert.com**

Prince Rupert is a vibrant port city, and the second-largest on BC's coast. Located on Kaien Island, at the mouth of the Skeena River, the city is circled by forests and mountains, and overlooks the beautiful fjord-studded coastline. The busy harbor is the main access point for Haida Gwaii and Alaska.

Like many of BC's major towns, Prince Rupert's development is linked to the growth of the railroad. Housed in the 1914 Grand Trunk Railroad Station, the Kwinitsa Railway Museum tells the story of businessman Charles Hay's big plans for the town, which were largely unfulfilled: he went down with the *Titanic* in 1912.

Tsimshian First Nations were the first occupants of the area, and as recently as 150 years ago the harbor was lined with their large cedar houses and carved totems. The **Museum of Northern British Columbia** focuses on northwest coast First Nations culture and history. Tsimshian dance, song, and drama are performed in a traditional longhouse, and there are archaeological tours.

🏛 **Museum of Northern British Columbia**
100 1st Ave. W. **Tel** (250) 624 3207.
Open Jun–Sep: daily; Oct–May: Tue–Sat. **Closed** Dec 25, 26. 🅿 ⬅ 🎦
🆆 museumofnorthernbc.com

⑮ Haida Gwaii

🚃 & 🚌 Prince Rupert. 🅸 3220 Wharf St., Queen Charlotte., (250) 559 8316 (open all year).
🆆 gohaidagwaii.ca

Shaped like a bent ice-cream cone, the Haida Gwaii (previously called Queen Charlotte Islands) are an archipelago of about 150 islands across from the city of Prince Rupert.

The islands were left untouched by the last Ice Age, and have an eco-system unique to Canada. The forests house distinctive species of mammal such as the dusky shrew and short-tailed weasel. There is also a large population of bald eagles, and the spring brings hundreds of migrating gray whales past the shores.

The islands have been the home of the Haida people for thousands of years. Today, the Haida are recognized for their artistic talents, particularly their carvings and sculptures from cedar wood and argillite (a black slatelike stone found only on these islands).

Atlin Lake in remote Atlin Provincial Park

It was the Haida who led environmental campaigns against logging companies in the 1980s, leading to the founding of the **Gwaii Haanas National Park Reserve and Haida Heritage Site** in 1988. The park has centuries-old rainforest, with 1,000-year-old Sitka spruce, red cedar, and western hemlock.

🌀 **Gwaii Haanas National Park Reserve and Haida Heritage Site**
Tel (250) 559 8818. **Open** daily. 🅿 (no fee in winter). 🆆 pc.gc.ca

⑯ Northern Parks

Mount Edziza, Spatsizi; Hwy 37. Atlin; Hwy 7. 🅸 (250) 771 4591.
🆆 hellobc.com

The provincial parks of northern British Columbia comprise Mount Edziza Provincial Park, Spatsizi Plateau Wilderness Provincial Park, and, farther north, Atlin Provincial Park. These offer remote landscapes, with high peaks, icefields, and tundra.

Established in 1972, Mount Edziza Provincial Park is distinguished by its volcanic landscape, which includes lava rivers, basalt plateau, and cinder cones. The park can be reached by boat or float plane. There is no vehicle access within the park, and only long, rugged overland trails or chartered float planes take visitors through open meadows, arctic birch woods, and over creeks.

Across the highway lies the even more rugged country of Spatsizi Plateau Wilderness Provincial Park, which includes the snow-capped peaks of the Skeena Mountains. Gladys Lake, a small lake in the center of the park, is an ecological reserve for the study of sheep and mountain goats. Access to the park is again limited to a small road leading from the village of Tatogga along Hwy 37. The village also offers guides and float plane hire.

The spectacular Atlin Provincial Park is only accessible from the Yukon on Hwy 7, off the Alaska Hwy. About one-third of the park is covered by large icefields and glaciers.

Masset, a small fishing village on Graham Island, Haida Gwaii

NORTHERN
CANADA

Introducing Northern Canada

Northern Canada covers the Yukon, Northwest Territories, and Nunavut, and stretches up to within 800 km (500 miles) of the North Pole, and from the Atlantic Ocean west to the Pacific, equating to 37 percent of Canada's total area. Much of the landscape is incredibly harsh: barren, treeless, frozen tundra dominates most of the year, with subarctic forest, mountains, glaciers, and icy lakes and rivers. Nonetheless, an abundance of wildlife flourishes, with musk ox, caribou, polar bears, and seals. At the height of the brief summer the "midnight sun" provides 24-hour days, while the Aurora Borealis *(see p341)* illuminates dark winters with ribbons of colored light. Development in the North has occurred only where conditions are hospitable, often where the land is most scenic and varied. Populated by First Nations people some 25,000 years ago and the Inuit about 3,000 BC, this uniquely dramatic land is enjoyed by 500,000 visitors a year.

Glorious flaming fall colors are studded with evergreens in the north of the Yukon

◀ A caribou herd, Dempster Highway, near Eagle Plains in the Yukon

Getting Around

The watchword when traveling in this region is cost; trips, accommodations, and even food are all far more expensive than in the rest of the country. In the Yukon all major towns are connected by bus, but the most flexible way to travel around is by car. Air is the best means of traveling in Nunavut and the Northwest Territories – there are 600 landing strips and small airports here. Visitors should be aware that accommodations are equally restricted. In many settlements only one hotel is available, but the Yukon towns are well equipped with places to stay.

NORTHERN
CANADA

Key

— Highway
=== Other road
--- Minor railway
▦ International border
▦ Regional border
△ Summit

Verdrup Islands

Ellesmere Island

Queen Elizabeth Islands

Baffin Bay

Devon Island

Resolute
(Qausuittuq)

Lancaster Sound

Bylot Island

Pond Inlet
(Mittimatalik)

Somerset Island

Borden Peninsula

ince of Vales sland

Brodeur Peninsula

Baffin Island

Qikiqtarjuak

Cumberland Peninsula

Igloolik

Pangnirtung

Committee Bay

Prince Charles Island

Nettilling Lake

King William Island

Kugaaruk
(Pelly Bay)

Melville Peninsula

Arctic Circle

Amadjuak Lake

Hall Peninsula

Gjoa Haven
(Uqsuqtuuq)

Iqaluit
(Frobisher Bay)

Repulse Bay

Foxe Basin

Foxe Peninsula

Kimmirut

N U N A V U T

Southampton Island

berdeen Lake

Coral Harbour
(Salliq)

Baker Lake
(Qamanittuaq)

Coats Island

Rankin Inlet

Whale Cove
(Tikirarjuaq)

Hudson Bay

Arviat

| 0 kilometers | | 400 | |
| 0 miles | | | 400 |

Inuit in the Northwest Territories using a dog sledge for transportation

For map symbols *see back flap*

Inuit Art and Culture

For centuries, the hunting and trapping lifestyle has created a distinct culture for the Inuit. Their customs have remained largely the same throughout the communities of eastern and central Northern Canada, although regional differences can be seen in the varied artforms. The Inuit have a limited written tradition, and much of 21st-century culture is still oral. It might seem surprising, given the outstandingly harsh environment and limited natural resources, that their communities offer a flourishing artistic output, but it is the hardship of northern life that has promoted artistic achievement. For example, the Inuit use their tool-making skills for sculpture. Inuit culture is closely tied to their lansdcape and environment, which has inspired many artists and mythmakers.

This woodblock print of a girl meeting a polar bear represents an artform developed in the 1950s. Stone cuts and stencils are also used to interpret drawings by older artists.

Warm clothing is both functional and decorative, and often painstakingly handwoven from scraps from the remains of a kill. Most clothing is made from fur or wool.

Inuit beadwork and jewelry was made in earlier times from bone and ivory; colored stones and beads are now used. Each piece shows birds, animals, or people, and is unique. Western influences include new designs in silver and gold.

This soapstone carving of an Inuk (Inuit person) with a seal reflects the vital role seals have always played in Inuit culture.

Inuit Women Preparing Char

The outdated, and now offensive, name for the Inuit people is "eskimo," a local Cree word meaning "eaters of raw meat." The Inuit traditionally eat their meat uncooked, as the Arctic has no trees for firewood. Much of the caribou, polar bear, and fish was sundried or mixed with sauces made from summer fruits and berries. The arrival of the stove and modern fuels has changed the menu somewhat, although tradition remains at the heart of the community's eating habits.

These dancing costume ornaments are carved from ivory or whalebone and worn by Inuit dancers to celebrate ceremonial events. As with clothing, Arctic bird feathers are used for decoration.

Inuit father and son in parkas, which are traditionally made by the women of the family. They use caribou, wolf, and polar bear fur. Today, imported Western fabrics are added for decoration.

Inuit fishermen have made the best possible use of their often-limited natural resources and still rely largely on small-scale fishing for food.

Inuit homes are no longer the traditional igloo. Most people have moved to camps or community housing.

Inuit Myth

Set on the very fringes of the habitable world, the Inuit guarded against the threat of starvation with a supernatural belief system based on the respect of the animals they hunted, being careful to guard against divine retribution. Their myths promote the belief that every living creature has a soul, and that the village shaman could travel between the upper and lower worlds to commune with, and appease, the spirits in control of the hunt and the weather. Since earliest times hunting tools and weapons have been carved with the representations of the appropriate guardian spirit, and singers and musicians are well versed in legends of sea spirits and human heroes.

Carving of an Inuk fighting his spirit

Traditional hunting and fishing remains at the core of Inuit culture, although in the 1960s the Ottawa government unsuccessfully tried to stop these ancient practices.

Drum dancing is one of the varied forms of traditional music, and plays an important part in most of life's great events: births, weddings, a successful hunt, and honoring a person who has died. Another form of music, throat singing, is usually performed by two women facing one another to recount a legend, life event, or myth.

NORTHERN CANADA

Still one of the most remote destinations on Earth, Northern Canada – renowned for its Arctic beauty – is now accessible to adventurous travelers in search of untouched terrain for superlative, challenging hiking and exploring. This vast landscape encompasses the Yukon, Northwest Territories, and Nunavut. Many of the settlements at this brink of the world were established only in the 20th century. Some of the first towns grew up around Mountie outposts, established to monitor trappers, explorers, and whalers; more recently defense outposts have developed settlements. Local Inuit communities have gradually given up their nomadic life, and many are now settled around these outposts. These small towns are bases for exploring the stunning surrounds. In the winter the north descends to -50°C (-58°F), yet in summer warm air sweeps in and the tundra bursts into bloom. The thaw acts in defiance of eight long months of winter, when everything is draped in a blanket of white. This is a startlingly beautiful land with deserted plains, icy trails, rare wildlife, and gentle people, and is ripe for discovery.

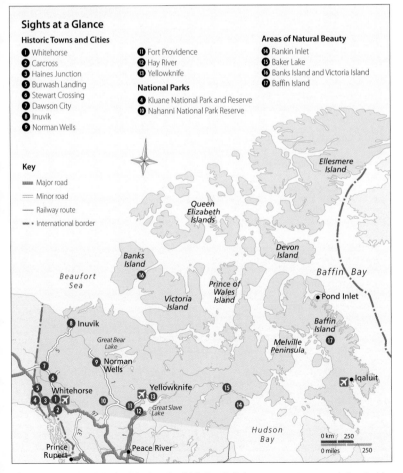

Sights at a Glance

Historic Towns and Cities
1 Whitehorse
2 Carcross
3 Haines Junction
5 Burwash Landing
6 Stewart Crossing
7 Dawson City
8 Inuvik
9 Norman Wells
11 Fort Providence
12 Hay River
13 Yellowknife

National Parks
4 Kluane National Park and Reserve
10 Nahanni National Park Reserve

Areas of Natural Beauty
14 Rankin Inlet
15 Baker Lake
16 Banks Island and Victoria Island
17 Baffin Island

Key
▪▪▪▪ Major road
=== Minor road
— Railway route
▪▪ ▪ International border

Ellesmere Island

Queen Elizabeth Islands

Banks Island 16

Beaufort Sea

Devon Island

Prince of Wales Island

Victoria Island

Baffin Bay

● Pond Inlet

8 Inuvik

Great Bear Lake

9 Norman Wells

7

6

5

4 3

Whitehorse

2

10

11

12

13 Yellowknife

Great Slave Lake

15

14

Baffin Island 17

Melville Peninsula

✈ Iqaluit

Hudson Bay

Prince Rupert

Peace River

0 km   250
0 miles   250

◀ Photographer capturing the Northern Lights (*aurora borealis*), Northwest Territories   **For map symbols** *see back flap*

● Whitehorse

Whitehorse takes its name from the local rapids on the Yukon River that reminded miners in the gold rush of "the flowing manes of albino Appaloosas." The town evolved when 2,500 stampeders on the hunt for gold braved the arduous Chilkoot and White Pass trails on foot in the winter of 1897–98 and set up camp here by the banks of Lindeman and Bennett lakes. Boatmen made over 7,000 trips through the rapids during the spring thaw of 1898, before a tramway was built around them. On the spot where gold miners could catch a boat downstream to the mines of the Klondike and the glittering nightlife of Dawson City in the Yukon, a tent town sprang up, and Whitehorse was born. This regional capital is the fastest-growing town in the northern territories, but despite all modern amenities, the wilderness is always only a few moments away.

▥ MacBride Museum of Yukon History

1124 Front St. **Tel** (867) 667 2709. **Open** mid-May–Sep: daily; Sep–mid-May: Tue–Sat. 🅿 ♿
W macbridemuseum.com

The MacBride Museum is housed in a log cabin along the Yukon River. From Gold Rush fever to the birth of Whitehorse, this is the place to learn about the history of the Yukon. Gold to Government – Yukon's Modern History is one of several fascinating galleries. Other galleries cover wildlife, archaeology, and the area's First Nations peoples. Among the special features are Engine 51 from the White Pass and Yukon Route railway, and a log cabin depicting fictional character Sam McGee. In the summer there are daily talks and skits.

▥ Log Skyscrapers

208 & 210 Lambert St.
Two blocks away from the Old Log Church Museum on Elliott Street are the unique log skyscrapers. Now several decades old, these log cabins have two or three floors. They are still lived in; one was home to a Yukon member of parliament. Worth a detour, the cabins offer a pleasing respite from the rather functional architecture that characterizes much of the rest of town.

▥ Old Log Church Museum

303 Elliott St. **Tel** (867) 668 2555 **Open** May–Aug: daily; Sep–Apr: by appointment. 🅿 ♿
W oldlogchurchmuseum.ca

In August 1900, Anglican missionary Rev. R. J. Bowen was sent to Whitehorse to build a church. He held services in one tent and lived in a second, as the log building took shape. The church opened on October 17 and the log rectory was built that winter. These buildings are among the few remaining here from the gold rush period. In 1953, the log church became the Diocese of Yukon cathedral and is said to be the only log cathedral in the world. Now, exhibits and interactive programs feature Inuit and First Nations cultures, missionaries, and the development of the Anglican church in the north.

The Old Log Church, constructed entirely from local timber

▥ S.S. *Klondike* National Historic Site

End Second Ave. **Tel** (867) 667 4511. **Open** mid-May–mid-Sep: 9:30am–5pm daily. 🅿 ♿
W pc.gc.ca

Originally built in 1929, the S.S. *Klondike* paddle-steamer sank in 1936. Rebuilt from its wreckage, the *Klondike* made ten supply trips each season to Dawson City. In the early 1950s, bridges along the road to Dawson were built too low, blocking the passage of the sternwheelers, so all journeys stopped. The

The city center of Whitehorse, sheltered in the Yukon River valley

For hotels and restaurants in this region see p359 and pp382–3

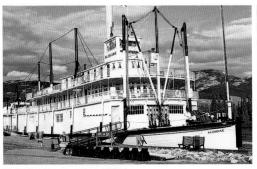
S.S. *Klondike* in its permanent home in Whitehorse

Klondike ceased operating in 1955 and was beached forever in Whitehorse. It is now restored to its heyday in every detail, right down to the 1937 *Life* magazines on the tables and authentic staff uniforms. Although no longer operational, the boat is a National Historic Site, with regular guided tours of the interior on offer.

Lake Laberge
Klondike Hwy. **Tel** (867) 667 3084.
Open daily, weather permitting.
Largest of the lakes in the area, Lake Laberge is 62 km (39 miles) from Whitehorse along the Klondike Hwy. Frozen for half of the year, with temperatures dropping below -30°C (-22°F), this popular summer swimming, fishing, and boating destination comes to life during the annual thaw. The lake is famous among locals as the site of the funeral pyre of Yukon poet Robert Service's *Cremation of Sam McGee*, which relates the demise of a fictional local hero. Trout fishing is excellent; fish were barged here by the ton during the Klondike gold rush to feed the hordes of hopeful miners.

Local mountain goat

Yukon Wildlife Preserve
Takhini Hot Springs Rd. **Tel** (867) 456 7300. **Open** varies according to season. **yukonwildlife.ca**
This sanctuary, set up in 1965 for research and breeding purposes, lies about 25 km (16 miles) from the town, off the Klondike Hwy. A beautiful reserve of forest, grassland, meadows, and water areas, it has 11 species of northern mammals in large enclosures. Moose, bison, hares, elk, caribou, mountain goats, mule deer, thinhorn sheep, musk oxen, Arctic foxes, and lynx can all be seen, protected in the 300-ha (740-acre) parkland of their natural roaming habitat.

Whitehorse City Center
① MacBride Museum of Yukon History
② Log Skyscrapers
③ Old Log Church Museum
④ S.S. *Klondike*

0 meters 250
0 yards 250

For map symbols see back flap

Male caribou resting near Carcross, as herds migrate across the Yukon

❷ Carcross

🗺 450. 🚆 🚌 ℹ (867) 821 4431.
Open mid-May–Sep daily.
🆆 travelyukon.com

Carcross is a small village that lies at the picturesque con-fluence of Bennett and Tagish lakes, an hour's drive south of the Yukon's regional capital, Whitehorse. Early miners crossing the arduous Chilkoot Pass on their journey to the bounty of the gold mines in the north named the site "Caribou Crossing" after herds of caribou stormed their way through the pass between Bennett and Nares lakes on their biannual migration. The town was estab-lished in 1899 in the height of the gold rush with the arrival of the White Pass and Yukon railroad. "Caribou Crossing" was

abbreviated officially to Carcross to avoid duplication of names in Alaska, British Colombia, and a town in the Klondike. Carcross has a strong aboriginal tradition, and was once an important caribou hunting ground for the Tagish tribe. Tagish guides worked for US Army surveyors during the building of the Alaska Highway in 1942 *(see pp266–7)*. Just 2 km (1 mile) north is the "smallest desert in the world", Carcross Desert. Blasted by strong winds, the sandy plain is barren, and the only remnant of a glacial lake that dried up after the last Ice Age. The strength of the winds allows little vegetation to grow, but the spot is memorable.

❸ Haines Junction

🗺 600. 🚌 ℹ Kluane National Park and Reserve Visitor Centre, 280 Alaska Hwy, (867) 634 7250.
🆆 hainesjunctionyukon.com

Haines Junction is a handy fuel and food stop for visitors on the way to the impressive Kluane National Park and Reserve. The town has a post office, several shops, restaurants, and a few motels and cabins. Trips into the park for rafting canoeing, and hiking excursions can be organ-ized from the town, at the park's administrative headquarters. For rafting, book well ahead. Haines Junction was once a base camp for the US Army engineers, who

in 1942 built much of the Alcan Highway (now Alaska Highway) that links Fairbanks in Alaska to the south of Canada. The St. Elias Mountains tower above the town, and air trips can be taken from here to admire the views of the frozen scenery, glaciers, and icy peaks of this wilderness.

Kaskawulsh Glacier rising over Kluane National Park and Reserve

❹ Kluane National Park and Reserve

Tel (867) 634 7250. 🚌 Haines Junction. **Open** year round. ♿ 🅿
📷 🆆 pc.gc.ca

This superb wilderness area is a UNESCO World Heritage Site. Covering 21,980 sq km (8,487 sq miles) of the southwest corner of the Yukon, the park shares the St. Elias mountain range, the highest in Canada, with Alaska. The whole park comprises one of the largest non-polar icefields in the world.

Two-thirds of the park is glacial, filled with valleys and lakes that are frozen year-round, broken up by alpine forests, meadows, and tundra. The landscape is one of the last surviving examples of an Ice Age environment, which disappeared in the rest of the world around 5,000–10,000 BC. Mount Logan, at 5,959 m (19,551 ft), is Canada's tallest peak. Numerous well-marked and established trails make for excellent hiking here, and several conveniently start from the main road. There are also

The St. Elias range dominates the small town of Haines Junction

Kluane National Park and Reserve displays radiant foliage in fall, as seen here in the Alsek River area

some less-defined routes, which follow the old mining trails. There are trails to suit both the novice and experienced hiker, ranging from a two-hour stroll to a ten-day guided trek.

Kluane's combination of striking scenery and an abundance of wildlife, including moose, Dall sheep, and grizzly bears, make it the Yukon's most attractive wilderness destination. Trips into the park are organized from nearby Haines Junction. Due to the hazardous weather, untamed wildlife, and isolated conditions, safety measures are mandatory here.

❺ Burwash Landing

🏚 100. 🚺 Whitehorse (867) 667 3084.

Northwest of Haines Junction by 124 km (77 miles), this little village at the western end of Kluane Lake lies just outside Kluane National Park on the Alaska Hwy. A community was established in 1905 after a gold strike, and Burwash Landing is now a service center. Visitors can also enjoy stunning panoramas of Kluane Lake to the south.

The village is noted for the **Kluane Museum of Natural History**, with many animal-related exhibits, including a mammoth's tooth and numerous displays on local

natural history. Focus is also given to the traditional lifestyle of the region's tribe of Southern Tutchone people.

🏛 **Kluane Museum of Natural History**
Burwash Landing. **Tel** (867) 841 5561. **Open** mid-May–mid-Sep: 9am–6:30pm daily. 🅿 ♿

❻ Stewart Crossing

🏚 35. 🚌 🚺 Whitehorse (867) 667 3084.

Approximately 180 km (112 miles) east of Dawson City *(see p340)*, Stewart Crossing is a small community at the junction of the Klondike Hwy and the Silver Trail, which leads to the small mining settlements of Mayo, Elsa, and Keno, once famous for their silver trade. During the gold rush in the late 19th century, the area was referred to as the "grubstake," because enough gold could be panned from the river sandbars

here during the summer to buy the following year's stake. Stewart Crossing is a modest service center that also operates as the starting-point for canoe trails on the Stewart River. Unusual for this wild terrain, these boat trips are suitable for children and beginners. Trips should be organized in Whitehorse or Dawson City.

About an hour's drive north, at Km 655.1, is the **Tintina Trench Rest Area**. Providing in a glance visible proof of the geological theory of plate tectonics, the trench itself stretches for several hundred kilometers across the Yukon, with layers of millennia-old rock gaping open to the skies. "Tintina" means "chief" in the local language, and this is one of the largest geological faults in the Yukon system. This area is an ideal place to view the trench, which runs up to here along the route of the Klondike Hwy, from a course parallel with the Yukon River that begins at Fortymile village.

Broad Valley by Stewart Crossing near the Yukon River

Winter at Kluane National Park and Reserve, Yukon Territory ▶

The Palace Grand Theatre in Dawson City

❼ Dawson City

🏠 1,350. ✈ 🚌 ℹ Cnr Front & King sts., (867) 993 5575. 🌐 dawsoncity.ca

The town of Dawson City, in the Yukon, came into prominence during the Klondike gold rush of 1898 (see pp56–7), when the population boomed and the city grew from a moose pasture into a bustling metropolis of some 30,000 people, all seeking their fortune in the new "Paris of the North." The town continues to mine gold, but tourism is now one of Dawson City's key sources of income.

Dawson City Museum has displays on the gold rush and artifacts from that period. A popular attraction is Diamond Tooth Gerties, the gambling hall complete with a honky-tonk piano and can can girls.

🏛 **Dawson City Museum**
595 5th Ave. **Tel** (867) 993 5291.
Open mid-May–late-Sep: 10am–6pm daily; late Sep–mid-May: by appointment. 🅿 ♿
🌐 dawsonmuseum.ca

🎰 **Diamond Tooth Gerties**
Cnr 4th Ave. & Queen St. **Tel** (867) 993 5525. **Open** May–mid-Sep: daily; variable in winter. 🅿 ♿

❽ Inuvik

🏠 3,200. ✈ ℹ 2 Firth St., (867) 777 8600. 🌐 trulyarctic.ca

About 770 km (480 miles) north of Dawson City, in the Northwest Territories (NWT), Inuvik lies at the tip of the Dempster Hwy, the most northerly road in Canada. Inuvik has only a very recent history. Founded in the 1950s as a supply center for military projects in the NWT, the town prospered in the oil boom of the 1970s. Full of functional contemporary architecture, Inuvik has a charm that lies more in its location as a good visitors' center for the region – there are a few hotels and several shops, which is no mean feat for a town that boasts just a single traffic light. It is, nonetheless, the most-visited town in the northern Arctic, and popular as a craft center for the Inuit and as a starting point for a tour of the far north.

Inuvik welcomes its visitors

Environs
The settlement of Paulatuk lies 400 km (250 miles) east of Inuvik and is one of the smallest communities in the NWT. It is well placed for hunting, fishing, and trapping game; these activities remain its staple support after many centuries. Its location is also useful as a stepping-stone to the wilderness of the territory. Tourism is becoming popular, and trips into Tuktut Nogait National Park with Inuit guides are available.

❾ Norman Wells

🏠 700. ✈ ℹ Visitor Information Center and Museum, 23 MacKenzie Drive, (867) 587 2415. **Open** daily.
🌐 normanwells.com

In 1920 crude oil discoveries were made here near a small Dene settlement. Oil production surged in World War II, when the US established a pipeline to supply oil to the Alaska Highway while it was being built, and the town grew.

Today, Norman Wells, which is in the NWT, is the starting point for the Canol Heritage Trail, a long-distance path of wilderness trail through the Canol Road above the Ross River in the Yukon Territory, which links up with the Yukon Highway system. There are few facilities along the trail, making it one of the toughest trekking paths in the world. Despite the difficulties, this is a popular destination with experienced hikers.

❿ Nahanni National Park Reserve

✈ Fort Simpson. **Open** year round.
🅿 ℹ Nahanni National Park Reserve, 10002-100 Street, Fort Simpson.
Tel (867) 695 7750. 🌐 pc.gc.ca

Nahanni National Park Reserve, in the NWT, sits astride the South Nahanni River between the border with the Yukon and the small settlement of Fort Simpson. In 1978, it was one

Inuvik's town church and hall, shaped like an igloo

The vast expanses of Nahanni National Park Reserve in summer

of the first places in the world to be designated a UNESCO World Heritage Site to protect its geological history. The park is a great wilderness, with four vast river canyons, hot springs, and a spectacular undeveloped waterfall, Virginia Falls. The falls, at 90 m (295 ft), are twice the height of Niagara but have less volume. They boast excellent flora and fauna: at least 16 species of fish enjoy the cascades, and more than 180 varieties of bird live overhead. Wolves, grizzly bears, and woodland caribou also move freely in the park.

The park's main activities are whitewater rafting and canoeing. In summer, water-sports take precedence over walking tours, as the rivers thaw, and the landscape bursts into bloom with wildflowers. The park is usually reached by float plane.

⓫ Fort Providence

🏠 750. 🚌 ℹ️ Northern Frontier Visitors Association, 4–4807 49th St., Yellowknife, (867) 873 4262.

The Dene people call this village "zhahti koe," which means mission house in their indigenous language. Fort Providence began life as a Catholic mission and was later enlarged by the Hudson's Bay Company (see pp166–7), which set up an outpost here in the late 19th century. Attracted by

this and the prospect of employment, the local Dene First Nations people settled here permanently. Today the town is a Dene handicrafts center.

Just north of the village lies the Mackenzie Bison Sanctuary. The sanctuary is home to the world's largest herd of 3,000 rare pure wood bison. The park stretches for 100 km (60 miles) north along the banks of Great Slave Lake, and bison can be seen along the road.

⓬ Hay River

🏠 3,700. ✈️ 🚌 ℹ️ Hay River Hwy, (867) 874 3180. **Open** Jun–Sep.

Set on the banks of Great Slave Lake, the small community of Hay River is the major port in the Northwest Territories. A lifeline, the town supplies the High Arctic settlements and the northernmost towns in the country, particularly Inuvik, with essentials. When the river thaws in spring, it supplies freight. The town looks designed for the purpose it serves – the wharves are lined with barges and tugs, as well as the local fishing fleet.

Unusually for this area, Hay River's history stretches back over a millennium. The Dene moved here centuries ago, lured by the town's strategic position at the southern shore of the Great Slave Lake, for its hunting and fishing. Attractions here are based on local industry; as a shipping center, the harbor is a bustling place to spot barges. The original Dene settlement, now a village of 300 people, sits across the river north from the Old Town and welcomes visitors.

The Northern Lights

The Northern Lights, or *aurora borealis*, are believed to be the result of solar winds entering the Earth's ionosphere some 160 km (100 miles) above the surface of the planet. Emanating from the sun, these winds collide with the gases present in the Earth's upper atmosphere, releasing energy that becomes visible in the night sky. The stunning consequences are visible in the Yukon and the NWT, most often from August to October. Some aboriginal groups attach religious significance to the Lights, believing them to be the spirits of dead hunters, while 19th-century gold prospectors mistook them for vapors given off by ore deposits. Whatever one's beliefs, the sparkling ribbons of light are an awesome sight.

⑱ Yellowknife

Originally an aboriginal Dene settlement, Yellowknife is named after the yellow-bladed copper hunting knives used by its first residents. The Hudson's Bay Company closed its outpost here in 1823 due to failing profits, but the Old Town thrived again with gold mining in the 1930s, and again after 1945. With improved road communications, the city became the regional capital of the Northwest Territories in 1967. Growing bureaucratic needs and three diamond mines 300 km (186 miles) north of Yellowknife have helped it flourish.

VISITORS' CHECKLIST

Practical Information
🏙 20,000. ℹ Northern Frontier Visitors Association, 4–4807 49th St., (867) 873 4262, 1 877 881 4262. 🎉 Long John Jamboree, Snowking Winter Festival (Mar); Folk on the Rocks (Jul).
🌐 visityellowknife.com

Transport
✈

Makeshift houseboats on the Great Slave Lake, Northwest Territories

The Old Town

Just 1 km (0.5 mile) north of downtown, the Old Town is situated on an island and a rocky peninsula on Great Slave Lake. By 1947 Yellowknife had outgrown itself, and the New Town rose from the sandy plain southward. An unusual community thrives here on Yellowknife Bay, many living on makeshift houseboats. Also interesting is the variety of older architecture that can be seen from a stroll around this now-residential area. Shops and accomodations are found farther south in the New Town. A good vantage point from which to survey the area is the Bush Pilots Monument at the north end of Franklin Avenue.

Wildcat Café

3904 Wiley Road. **Tel** (867) 873 4004. **Open** May–Sep: 11:30am–10pm Mon–Fri, 10:30am–9pm Sat & Sun. ♿
🌐 wildcatcafe.ca

The oldest restaurant in Yellowknife, this institution is open only during the summer. A true frontier stop, and one of Yellowknife's earliest permanent buildings, the log cabin is set

Yellowknife City Center

① Old Town
② Wildcat Café
③ Prince of Wales Northern Heritage Centre
④ Legislative Assembly

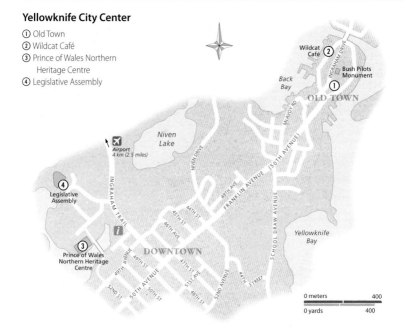

under the hill of the Old Town and has been refurbished in 1930s style. Its atmospheric interior is reminiscent of the pioneer days even after renovations. This establishment is the most-photographed building in Yellowknife.

Prince of Wales Northern Heritage Centre, Yellowknife, Northwest Territories

🏛 Prince of Wales Northern Heritage Centre

4750 48th Street. **Tel** (867) 767 9347. **Open** daily. **Closed** public hols. 🚻 🍴 🖥 🅦 pwnhc.ca

This local museum's displays feature typically northern artifacts such as a mooseskin boat, as well as items illustrating the history of flying in the north. Changing exhibits explain life in the subarctic and Beaufort Delta regions.

🏛 Legislative Assembly

Frame Lake. **Tel** (867) 767 9010, 1 800 661 0784. **Open** daily. 🚻 🍴 🅦 assembly.gov.nt.ca

Built in 1993, this headquarters of local government has a tall domed roof. Signifying equal rights for all ethnic groups, the government chamber is the only round one of its kind in the country, with a large oval table to give all delegates equal responsibility, in the manner practiced by aboriginals. Decorated with paintings and Inuit art, the chamber also features a large polar bear rug. The official public government rooms can be toured when the council is not in session.

⓮ Rankin Inlet

🏔 2,800. 🛈 Kivalliq Regional Visitor Centre (867), 645 3838. 🛬

Founded in 1955, when North Rankin Nickel Mine opened, Nunavut's Rankin Inlet is the largest community in the stony plateau of Kivalliq, which stretches east of the Canadian Shield to Hudson Bay. This small town is the government center for the Kivalliq Region, whose population, now 85 percent aboriginal, has settled mainly on the coast.

This region is characterized by its rural way of life and stunning scenery. **Iqalugaarjuup Nunanga Territorial Park**, 10 km (6 miles) from the town center, contains a traditional Thule (ancestor of the Inuit) restored site with stone tent rings, meat stores, and semi-subterranean winter houses.

🏕 Iqalugaarjuup Nunanga Territorial Park

10 km (6 miles) NW. of Rankin Inlet, on the Meliadine River. **Tel** (867) 975 7700. **Open** daily, weather permitting.

⓯ Baker Lake

🏔 2,000. 🛬 🛈 (867) 793 2456. 🅦 bakerlake.ca

Baker Lake is geographically at the center of Canada and is the country's only inland Inuit community. Located at the source of the Thelon River, in Nunavut, the area has always been a traditional summer gathering place for the Inuit. Today it is an important center

for Inuit art, especially textiles. Heading westward, at the **Thelon Wildlife Sanctuary** visitors can see herds of musk ox in their natural habitat and glimpse other indigenous animals and birds.

🦌 Thelon Wildlife Sanctuary

300 km (186 miles) w. of Baker Lake. **Tel** (867) 975 7700. **Open** daily.

⓰ Banks Island and Victoria Island

🛈 (867) 979 4636.

Located in the Arctic Ocean, Banks Island is home to the largest herds of musk ox in the world. The animals dwell in **Aulavik National Park**, on the remote northern tip of the island. This numbers among the world's most remote wildlife destinations, and is accessible only by plane. Note that the park is best accessed from the Northwest Territories.

Split between the Northwest Territories and Nunavut, Victoria Island has a town in each – Ulukhaktok in NWT and the Inuit Cambridge Bay in Nunavut, where local aboriginal people traveled each summer for char fishing and caribou and seal hunting. The town today is a service center for locals and visitors along the Arctic coast. Polar bears, musk ox, wolves, and Arctic birds live nearby.

🏕 Aulavik National Park

Sachs Harbour. **Tel** (867) 777 8800. **Open** daily, weather permitting. 🅦 pc.gc.ca

An Inuit igloo builder near Baker Lake, in Nunavut, practicing this traditional skill

For hotels and restaurants in this region see p359 and pp382–3

⑰ Baffin Island

Part of Nunavut, Baffin Island is one of the most remote places in North America. At 500,000 sq km (193,000 sq miles), the island is the fifth largest on the planet, with more than 60 percent of its landmass lying above the Arctic Circle. Sparsely populated, the island is inhabited by just 11,000 people, 9,000 of whom are Inuit. Most people live in one of eight settlements scattered throughout the island, the chief of which is Iqaluit, capital of the territory of Nunavut.

With its spectacular fjords and knife-edged mountains sparkling with glaciers, Baffin Island offers a chance to experience all the outdoor activities of the Arctic. Canoeing, kayaking, trekking, and thrilling walks are all unbeatable here. Many of the activities often take place in close proximity to abundant wildlife, including polar bears and whales.

Bylot Island

Sirmilik National Park

Arctic Bay

Brodeur Peninsula

Borden Peninsula

Pond Inlet
A jewel in Nunavut's twinkling crown, Pond Inlet is blessed with stunning scenery of mountains, glaciers, and icebergs, and is surrounded by abundant Arctic marine life. Snowmobiling and dogsledding to the floe edge are popular.

Pri
Cha
Isl

Auyuittuq National Park

Auyuittuq is the third-largest national park in Canada at 19,089 sq km (7,370 sq miles). It is one of the few national parks with land above the Arctic Circle. A spectacular destination, the park displays a pristine wilderness of mountains, valleys, and fjords. In spring the meadows thaw out from under their snowy coverlets, and wildflowers burst into bloom. Within the park, wildlife abounds, with animals ranging from snow geese and arctic foxes to polar bears sharing the territory. Even in the brief summer, the weather can be tricky, with the risk of snow. Be prepared for cool weather, though temperatures can rise. The nearby town of Pangnirtung is a craft center.

Wildflowers flourish beneath Auyuittuq's frozen peaks

Cape Dorset is of interest archeologically because predecessors of the modern Inuit, the Thule and Dorset peoples, lived in this area. Cape Dorset is also known for its print-making tradition.

Key
— River
— National Park boundary

Pangnirtung
This little town of 1,400 residents sits at the southern end of the Pangnirtung Fjord, around which is a 100-km (62-mile) hiking trail that is the most popular on Baffin. Some of the cliff faces here are more than 1,500 m (4,921 ft) high.

ACCESSING CANADA'S NORTH

While tourism to Nunavut increases every year, the only access to these remote settlements is by air, which is very expensive compared to mainland routes. Despite the cost, however, every community has its own airport.

Iqaluit
Iqaluit is the gateway to exploring Baffin Island. The little town, selected as the capital for the territory of Nunavut *(see p61)*, is about 60 percent Inuit and a useful service center.

Kimmirut
This hamlet is well known as an art colony, particularly for its Inuit stone-carvers. It is slightly warmer than the rest of the island, and the meadows here burst into flower during the short summer.

For map symbols *see back flap*

TRAVELERS' NEEDS

WHERE TO STAY

As expected in a country of its size, Canada has a wide range of lodgings, from stately, world-famous hotels, such as Quebec City's Fairmont Le Château Frontenac, to family-run, intimate bed-and-breakfasts (B&Bs). There is also a variety of excellent middle-range accommodations, including rural inns, cabins to rent in scenic spots, elegant town apartments, hostels, houseboats, and convenient motels. Whether visitors need a mid-journey bed for the night or a seasonal rental, there is ample choice, and advance booking may not always be necessary. The listings on pages 350–59 describe a selection of venues for every taste and budget.

Contemporary room with a Jacuzzi in Château Montebello, Outaouais *(see p353)*

Grading and Facilities

There is no government-sponsored hotel grading system in Canada, but the voluntary "Canada Select," where places are rated by numbers of stars, is usually accurate. Note, however, that a four-star establishment in Canada's Far North or in the countryside may not have the same facilities as one with the same rating in a major city.

The Canadian Automobile Association (CAA) also operates an assessment system, mostly for hotels and motels along main highways, and this is widely recognized as consistent and accurate. Look into CAA membership (or affiliated memberships) for discounts.

Air-conditioning is usually standard, except in national park lodges, some motels and B&Bs, as well as cooler coastal and northern regions. Central heating is efficient across the country. Cable TV, radio, irons and ironing boards, and coffee-making facilities are fairly standard. Private bathrooms are usual, but some exceptions exist. Specify if you want a bathtub or shower, and where relevant, remember to ask for double or twin beds when booking a double room.

Prices

With such a wide range of accommodations, prices vary immensely. In cities, the top hotel's presidential suite may command a daily rate in excess of Can $1,000, while a hiker's hostel provides a dormitory bed for under Can $40. Budget hotels and B&Bs usually charge below Can $100 a night per person – but check because prices tend to rise in high season and fall in low season. Note that high season can also mean winter due to skiing or polar-bear watching, although it generally refers to summer.

Reservations

Advance reservations are recommended in major cities year-round, as well as in resort towns during summer and winter *(see pp44–7)*. Provincial tourist offices *(see p401)* can assist in bookings.

Children

Traveling with children is relatively easy in Canada. Most properties supply cots or junior-sized beds in parents' rooms. Major hotels offer babysitting services, usually for a fee. They may require 24 hours' notice. A minor (child under 18) traveling to Canada with one parent may need written consent (or other documentation) from the second parent under the anti-abduction regulation.

Disabled Travelers

Most public buildings provide wheelchair facilities with ramps and wide doors. However, some lodgings in historic buildings may not have such facilities, so always check in advance.

Façade of the award-winning Le Priori hotel, Quebec City *(see p353)*

Luxury Hotels

Canada's major cities boast some world-class establishments. The railroad age of the late 19th century ushered in château-style hotels. Nowadays, most of these château-hotels, including

Rustic Clayoquot Wilderness Resort, surrounded by forested slopes *(see p357)*

Ottawa's Château Laurier *(see p355)*, are operated by Fairmont Hotels. Luxury chains are well represented: Relais & Châteaux, Four Seasons, Hilton, Radisson, Sheraton, and Westin chains operate in the major cities.

Chain Hotels

Canada has numerous franchise and chain hotels and motels. Reliable and comfortable, if occasionally a little bland, chains vary in style and price from grand resorts to the less-expensive but well-known Days Inn, Best Western, Choice Hotels, and Howard Johnson. Popular with families and business travelers, many such properties provide services including breakfast and Wi-Fi access.

Efficiency Apartments

In addition to traditional cottages for rent, there is a variety of other options available. Motorhomes or RVs (Recreational Vehicles) are popular and can be leased in major cities. Airbnb offers private rooms and other accommodations rented out by local residents.

Campgrounds are found throughout Canada. Those in provincial or national parks often have limited facilities, but private operations mostly provide Wi-Fi, laundry facilities, and a convenience store.

Cottages or cabins are quintessentially Canadian. Ontario is famous for its selection of well-equipped rural vacation homes, which are available weekly, monthly, or seasonally. National parks also rent lodges and offer campgrounds.

Accommodations Taxes

Remember that lodgings of almost every kind are subject to taxes on top of the basic tariff. Provincial Sales Tax (PST) must be paid on accommodations and on goods and other services. It varies from province to province and ranges up to 10 percent. Rules vary slightly between provinces.

For example, Alberta has no PST, but levies a 4 percent lodging tax on hotel and motel stays; campsites, B&Bs, and guesthouses are tax-free. The Goods and Services Tax (GST) is a standard national charge of 5 percent throughout the country; this affects most accommodation classes. In Nova Scotia, New Brunswick, Prince Edward Island, Newfoundland and Labrador, and Ontario, the GST and PST are combined as Harmonized Sales Tax (HST) of 12 to 15 percent.

Recommended Hotels

Within the listings given in this guidebook, accommodations fall into a variety of categories. "Luxury" describes lodgings of distinction, where impeccable service matches discerning design. "Boutique" refers to intimate, usually smaller, non-chain hotels. "Chain hotels" ranges from simple rooms to more upmarket options. "Motel" refers to standard yet comfortable lodgings.

"B&Bs" (known as *gîtes* in Quebec) denote smaller establishments with personal service, ranging from cozy inns to farmhouses. "Resort" refers to destination-type lodgings, which offer recreational activities such as swimming, skiing, horseback riding, and canoeing. "Historic" describes older establishments that have retained a traditional aesthetic. "Rural" relates to country lodgings in a tranquil setting, and "Room with a view" refers to places with noteworthy vistas. "Budget" describes value-for-money accommodation.

Outstanding lodgings have been highlighted as "DK Choice" entries. These may include a special B&B, funky boutique hotel with excellent service, or upscale tents in Canada's wilderness offering a memorable experience.

Plush interior of the Fairmont Château Laurier, Ottawa *(see p355)*

Where to Stay

Newfoundland and Labrador

CHANGE ISLANDS: Seven Oakes Island Inn and Cottages $
Historic
NL, A0G 1R0
Tel *(709) 621 3256*
W sevenoakesislandinn.com
A restored 19th-century home with a wraparound deck and sweeping ocean views.

CORNER BROOK: Marble Mountain Resort $$
Resort
Exit #8 TCH, NL, A2H 2N2
Tel *1 800 636 2725*
W skimarble.com
Rooms come with well-equipped kitchens and fireplaces.

GRAND-FALLS WINDSOR: Hill Road Manor B&B $$
Historic
1 Hill Rd, NL, A2A 1G9
Tel *1 866 489 5451*
W hillroadmanor.com
This 1939 B&B retains its original high ceilings and French doors. Breakfast menu changes daily.

NORRIS POINT: The Tides Inn $$
Motel
263 Main St, NL, A0K 3V0
Tel *1 877 350 3310*
W thetidesinn.ca
Spacious rooms at this quiet inn within Gros Morne National Park.

QUIRPON: Quirpon Lighthouse Inn $$$
Rooms with a view
NL, A0K 2X0
Tel *1 877 254 6586*
W linkumtours.com
Unique accommodation in a restored 1922 lighthouse-keeper's home. Located on the edge of Iceberg Alley.

The Great George, in picturesque Charlottetown

ST. JOHN'S: Blue on Water $$
Boutique
319 Water St., NL, A1C 1B9
Tel *1 877 431 2583*
W blueonwater.com
Premier boutique hotel on North America's oldest street. Modern design with great harbor views.

DK Choice

ST. JOHN'S: Doctor's House Inn & Spa $$$
Luxury
21 Old Hopeall Road, Green's Harbour, NL, A0B 1X0
Tel *(709) 582 2754*
W doctorshousenewfoundland. com
Oceanfront walks and Newfoundland ponies render a unique experience at this elegant Tudor mansion, transformed into a getaway. Jacuzzi available; book in advance for spa therapy.

TWILLINGATE: Hillside B&B $$
B&B
14 Blanfords Ln, NL, A0G 4M0
Tel *(709) 884 1666*
W bbcanada.com/nfhillside
Welcoming option in the center of Iceberg Alley. Breakfast gets good reviews. Hiking trails nearby.

New Brunswick, Prince Edward Island, and Nova Scotia

ANTIGONISH: Azelia Farmhouse B&B $$
309 Connors Rd, RR 2, NS, B2G 2K9
Tel *(902) 863 4262*
W azeliafarmhouse.com
Quaint rooms await at this cozy farmhouse. Alpacas graze in the surrounding pastures.

BAY FORTUNE: Inn at Bay Fortune $$$
Historic
Rte. 310, RR 4, PE, C0A 2B0
Tel *(902) 687 3745*
W innatbayfortune.com
Charming historical inn. Friendly owners and exceptional food.

BOUCTOUCHE: Auberge le Vieux Presbytère $$
Historic
157 Chemin du Couvent, NB, E4S 3B8
Tel *(506) 743 5568*
W vieuxpresbytere.nb.ca
Set in an old Catholic rectory with spacious rooms and beautiful gardens. Superb dining.

Price Guide
For a standard double room per night, including breakfast (where served), service charges, and taxes.

$	up to Can $100
$$	Can $100 to 200
$$$	over Can $200

CARAQUET: Hotel Paulin $$
Luxury
143 Blvd Saint-Pierre W, NB, E1W 1B6
Tel *(506) 727 9981*
W hotelpaulin.com
Antique furnishings and excellent fare made with local produce.

CHARLOTTETOWN: The Great George $$$
Luxury
58 Great George St., PE, C1A 4K3
Tel *(902) 892 0606*
W thegreatgeorge.com
Set in a heritage building with luxurious rooms and suites that include Jacuzzis and fireplaces.

DIGBY: The Digby Pines $$
Luxury
103 Shore Rd, NS, B0V 1A0
Tel *(902) 245 2511*
W digbypines.ca
Elegant accommodations with heated outdoor pool, nightly bonfires, and kids' playground.

EDMUNDSTON: Auberge Les Jardins Inn $$
Boutique
60 Rue Principale, NB, E7B 1V7
Tel *(506) 739 5514*
W lesjardinsinn.com
Inn with charming rooms and old-fashioned decor. Cheaper motel rooms available as well.

FREDERICTON: Delta Fredericton $$
Resort
225 Woodstock Rd, NB, E3B 2H8
Tel *(506) 457 7000*
W marriott.com
Family-friendly urban resort with pools and superb dining facilities.

GEORGETOWN: The Georgetown Inn $$
Boutique
62 Richmond St, PE, C0A 1L0
Tel *(902) 652 2511*
W peigeorgetownhistoricinn.com
Quaint rooms, some with ocean views and screened-in decks. Friendly hosts and fabulous dining.

GRAND TRACADIE: Dalvay by the Sea $$$
Rural
Rte. 6, Dalvay Beach, PE, C0A 1P0
Tel *(902) 672 2048*
W dalvaybythesea.com

Contemporary room at the Hilton Saint John

Designated National Historic Site in a charming but remote spot. Ample outdoor activities and a fine restaurant.

HALIFAX: Cambridge Suites $$
Chain hotel
1583 Brunswick St., NS, B3J 3P5
Tel *(902) 420 0555*
W cambridgesuiteshalifax.com
Contemporary rooms in the heart of downtown. Wonderful rooftop patio with harbor views.

INGONISH: Keltic Lodge Resort and Spa $$$
Resort
383 Middle Head Peninsula, NS, B0C 1L0
Tel *(902) 285 2880*
W kelticlodge.ca
Charming property in a breathtaking setting. Three restaurants with sweeping ocean views.

INVERNESS: Cabot Links Resort $$$
Resort
15933 Central Ave., NS, B0E 1N0
Tel *(855) 652 2268*
W cabotlinks.com
Luxurious rooms, all with beautiful views, modern furnishings, and spa-like bathrooms. Fabulous dining and a terrific golf course.

LIVERPOOL: White Point Beach Resort $$
Resort
75 White Point Beach Resort Rd, Hunts Point, NS, B0T 1G0
Tel *(902) 354 2711*
W whitepoint.com
Gorgeous family surf resort with a lodge as well as lakefront cabins. Dining, golf, and spa facilities.

LOUISBOURG: Point of View Suites $$
Rooms with a view
15 Commercial St. Ext, NS, B1C 2J4
Tel *(902) 733 2080*
W louisbourgpointofview.com
Modern suites with views over Fortress of Louisbourg. Fun, historic dining experience on site.

MONCTON: Amsterdam Inn and Suites $
Chain hotel
2550 Mountain Rd, NB, E1G 3V7
Tel *(506) 383 5050*
W amsterdaminns.com
Great-value hotel with big rooms, friendly staff, and good breakfasts. Close to casino and attractions.

DK Choice

PEGGY'S COVE: Oceanstone Seaside Resort $$
Resort
8650 Peggy's Cove Rd, Indian Harbour, NS, B3Z 3P4
Tel *(902) 823 2160*
W oceanstoneresort.com
Situated right by the ocean, these lavish accommodations come with Jacuzzis, vaulted ceilings, and postcard-pretty views. Conveniently located to Halifax and Peggy's Cove, yet in a beautiful remote setting right next to the crashing waves.

RUSTICO: Barachois Inn $$$
Luxury
2193 Church Rd, PE, C0A 1N0
Tel *(902) 963 2194*
W barachoisinn.com
Heritage buildings furnished with antiques. Welcoming hosts and great breakfasts.

SAINT ANDREWS: Europa Inn $$
Motel
48 King St., NB, E5B 1Y3
Tel *(506) 529 3818*
W europainn.com
Centrally located with comfortable rooms, gourmet breakfasts, and a good restaurant.

SAINT JOHN: Hilton Saint John $$
Chain hotel
1 Market Square, NB, E2L 4Z6
Tel *(506) 693 8484*
W 3.hilton.com
Spacious and modern rooms, some with amazing harbor views.

ST. PETER'S: The Inn at St. Peter's $$$
Rooms with a view
1668 Greenwich Rd, PE, C0A 2A0
Tel *(902) 961 2135*
W innatstpeters.com
Ocean-view rooms and cottages set in lovely grounds. Great restaurant and attentive owner.

SHEDIAC: Maison Tait House $$
Historic
293 Main St., NB, E4P 2A8
Tel *(506) 532 4233*
W maisontaithouse.com
A 1911 building featuring pretty rooms with modern amenities. Excellent restaurant.

SUMMERSIDE: Clark's Sunny Isle Motel $
Motel
720 Water St. East, PE, C1N 4J1
Tel *(902) 436 5665*
W sunnyislemotel.com
Great value for comfortable rooms and landscaped gardens. A walking trail along the waterfront.

WEST POINT: West Point Lighthouse Inn $$
Rooms with a view
364 Cedar Dunes Park Rd, O'Leary, PE, C0B 1V0
Tel *(902) 859 3605*
W westpointharmony.ca
Unique and beautifully appointed accommodations in a historic lighthouse.

Montreal

CHINATOWN: Holiday Inn Select Montréal Centreville $$$
Chain hotel
99 Ave. Viger Ouest, H2Z 1E9
Tel *(514) 878 9888*
W ihg.com
Reliable chain hotel with an indoor pool, restaurant, lounge, gym, and sauna.

DOWNTOWN: Auberge de Paris $
Budget
907 Rue Sherbrooke Ouest, H3B 1B4
Tel *(514) 522 6124*
W aubergemontreal.com
Modern hostel with comfortable rooms and secure lockers. Women's-only dorm with private bathrooms. On-site bistro.

DOWNTOWN: Hôtel Viger $
Budget
1001 Rue Saint-Hubert, H2L 3Y3
Tel *(514) 845 6058*
W hotel-viger.com
Basic, clean accommodations with bathrooms and TV sets.

For more information on types of hotels *see page 349*

DOWNTOWN: Delta Montréal $$
Chain hotel
475 Ave. du Président Kennedy, H3A 1J7
Tel *(514) 286 1986*
w deltamontreal.com
Reliable hotel with grand rooms, some with views of the sprawling city and Mont-Royal.

DOWNTOWN: Hotel Château Versailles $$
Boutique
1659 Rue Sherbrooke Ouest, H3H 1E3
Tel *(514) 933 3611*
w versailleshotels.com
Historic townhouses with period features and a French restaurant.

DOWNTOWN: Le Nouvel Hotel $$
Boutique
1740 René Lévesque Ouest, H3H 1R3
Tel *(514) 931 8841*
w lenouvelhotel.com
Bright, spacious, contemporary rooms. Good for families.

DOWNTOWN: Residence Inn $$
Chain hotel
2170 Lincoln Ave., H3H 2N5
Tel *(514) 935 9224*
w residencemontreal.com
Rooms have kitchenettes and a dining area. Breakfast buffet.

DOWNTOWN: Fairmont Le Reine Elizabeth $$$
Luxury
900 René-Lévesque Ouest, H3B 4A5
Tel *(514) 861 3511*
w fairmont.com
Distinguished hotel favored by celebrities, reopened in 2017 after a total refurbishment.

DOWNTOWN: Ritz-Carlton Montréal $$$
Luxury
1228 Rue Sherbrooke Ouest, H3G 1H6
Tel *(514) 842 4212*
w ritzmontreal.com
Plush rooms, exquisite dining, and magnificent grounds.

PLATEAU MONT-ROYAL: Auberge de la Fontaine $$
Boutique
1301 Rue Rachel Est, H2J 2K1
Tel *(514) 597 0166*
w aubergedelafontaine.com
Two Second-Empire homes converted into a stylish hotel close to downtown.

PLATEAU MONT-ROYAL: Le Jardin d'Antoine $$
Boutique
2024 Rue Saint-Denis, H2X 3K7
Tel *(514) 843 4506*
w aubergelejardindantoine.com
Located in the trendy Latin Quarter. Airy and deluxe rooms overlook a courtyard garden.

Indoor pool at the Delta Montréal, downtown Montreal

VIEUX-MONTREAL: Hotel InterContinental Montréal $$
Luxury
360 Rue Saint-Antoine Ouest, H2Y 3X4
Tel *(514) 987 9900*
w ihg.com
Modern high-rise in city's financial and entertainment district. Lap pool, sauna, and massage services.

DK Choice

VIEUX-MONTREAL: Hostellerie Pierre du Calvet $$$
Luxury
405 Rue Bonsecours, H2Y 3C3
Tel *(514) 282 1725*
w pierreducalvet.ca
Opulent elegance in a 1725 stone-built house. Rooms evoke history with original fireplaces, oak paneling, and window seats. Breakfast is served in the atrium where several parrots reside. Two superb restaurants feature outstanding service, cuisine, and decor.

VIEUX-MONTREAL: Hôtel Epik Montréal $$$
Boutique
171 Rue Saint-Paul Ouest, H2Y 1Z5
Tel *(514) 842 2634*
w epikmontreal.com
A 1723 home with 10 beautifully appointed rooms and suites. Luxurious breakfasts and an upscale Italian restaurant.

VIEUX-MONTREAL: Hotel Gault $$$
Boutique
449 Rue Saint-Hélène, H2Y 2K9
Tel *(514) 904 1616*
w hotelgault.com
Exemplary service and quirky design. Grand library in the lobby.

VIEUX-MONTREAL: Hotel le Saint-James $$$
Luxury
355 Rue Saint-Jacques St, H2Y 1N9
Tel *(514) 841 3111*
w hotellestjames.com
Plush rooms. Sweeping wrought-iron staircase from balconied mezzanine to the restaurant.

VIEUX-MONTREAL: Le Saint-Sulpice Hôtel Montréal $$$
Boutique
414 St. Sulpice St., H2Y 2V5
Tel *(514) 288 1000*
w lesaintsulpice.com
Steps from the Port, with 108 elegant rooms and and a popular in-house restaurant, Sinclair.

Quebec City and the St. Lawrence River

BAIE SAINT-PAUL: Auberge La Maison Otis $
Boutique
23 Rue St.-Jean-Baptiste, QC, G3Z 1M2
Tel *(418) 435 2255*
w maisonotis.com
Charming country inn with a spa, restaurant, and gardens. Salmon fishing, golf, and skiing nearby.

DK Choice

BAIE SAINT-PAUL: Le Germain Hotel Charlevoix $$
Luxury
50 Rue de la Ferme, QC, G3Z 0G2
Tel *(418) 657 5945*
w legermainhotels.com
Chic, contemporary rooms in a pastoral setting on a former farm once, owned by the Petites Franciscaines de Marie. Enjoy locavore dining and shop in the on-site pastry shop and, during summer, farmers' market.

GASPÉ: Gite du Mont-Albert $$
Resort
2001 Route du Parc, Sainte-Anne-des-Monts, QC, G4V 2E4
Tel *(418) 890 6527*
w sepaq.com
Stay in the lodge or rent a cabin in serene environs. Ample opportunities to hike and ski in the local national park.

Warm-toned interiors of the luxurious Hotel le Saint-James, Vieux-Montreal

**L'ILE VERT: Les Maisons du
Phare de l'Ile Verte** $$
Budget
2802 Route du Phare, QC, G0L 1K0
Tel *(418) 898 2730*
W phareileverte.com
Simple accommodations with
kitchens in an island lighthouse.
Breakfasts are served, but other
meals are self-catered.

**ILES-DE-LA-MADELEINE:
Domaine au Vieux Couvent** $$
Historic
*292 Rte 199, Havre-aux-Maisons, QC,
G4T 5A4*
Tel *(418) 969 2233*
W domaineduvieuxcouvent.com
This refurbished convent is a
heritage landmark. Ocean-view
rooms plus six apartments.

**LAC-SAINT-JEAN: Hôtel du
Jardin** $$
Motel
*1400 Blvd du Jardin, Saint-Félicien,
QC, G8K 2N8*
Tel *(418) 679 8422*
W hoteldujardin.com
Modern hotel with spacious
rooms. Some have whirlpool baths.
Restaurants and indoor pool.

**LA MALBAIE: Fairmont Le
Manoir Richelieu** $$$
Luxury
181 Rue Richelieu, QC, G5A 1X7
Tel *(418) 665 3703*
W fairmont.com
Resembles a castle perched on a
cliff. Beach, bike and ski pathways,
as well as golf course and six
restaurants at hand.

PERCÉ: Hôtel La Normandie $$$
Rooms with a view
221 Route 132 W, QC, G0C 2L0
Tel *(418) 782 2112*
W normandieperce.com
Clapboard inn overlooking
Percé Rock. Beautiful perennial
gardens and an excellent seafood
restaurant on site.

**QUEBEC CITY:
Hotel Clarendon** $$
Historic
57 Rue Sainte-Anne, QC, G1R 3X4
Tel *(418) 692 2480*
W hotelclarendon.com
Art Deco hotel offering old-
fashioned European luxury.
Restaurant and live jazz bar.

**QUEBEC CITY: Hotel Particulier
Belley** $$
Boutique
249 Rue Saint-Paul, QC, G1K 3W5
Tel *(418) 692 1694*
W hotelbelley.com
Former tavern sheltered beneath
old fortifications. Uniquely deco-
rated small rooms.

**QUEBEC CITY:
Le Priori** $$
Boutique
*15 Rue Sault-au-Matelot,
QC, G1K 3Y7*
Tel *(418) 692 3992*
W hotellepriori.com
Once architect Jean
Baillairgé's home.
Stone walls, modern
furniture and art.

**QUEBEC CITY:
Fairmont Le Château
Frontenac** $$$
Luxury
1 Rue des Carrières, QC, G1R 4P5
Tel *(418) 692 3861*
W fairmont.com
Century-old railway hotel with
river views and personalized ame-
nities. There is a cozy bar on site.

SEPT-ILES: Hôtel Sept-Iles $$
Budget
451 Arnaud Ave., QC, G4R 3B3
Tel *(418) 962 2581*
W hotelseptiles.com
Balconies overlook the river. Basic
rooms and an on-site restaurant.

**TROIS-RIVIÈRES: Delta Trois-
Rivières** $$
Chain hotel
*1620 Rue Notre-Dame Centre, QC,
G9A 6E5*
Tel *(819) 376 1991*
W deltahotels.com
Modern high-rise popular with
families. Sunday brunch buffet.

Southern and
Northern Quebec

**LAURENTIAN MOUNTAINS:
Auberge de la
Montagne-Coupée** $$
Rooms with a view
*1000 Ch. de la Montagne Coupée,
Saint-Jean-de-Matha, QC, J0K 2S0*
Tel *(450) 886 3891*
W montagnecoupee.com
Comfortable inn amid forested
hills. Breakfast and dinner included.

**LAURENTIAN MOUNTAINS:
Le Gite des Merveilles** $$
Resort
*3914, Chemin Doncaster,
Val David, QC, J0T 2N0*
Tel *(819) 322 7613*
W domainedesmerveilles.com
A beautiful lodge with comfort-
able rooms. Tranquil setting.

**MAGOG: Auberge
L'Étoile-sur-le-Lac** $$
Rooms with a view
1200 Principal Ouest, QC, J1X 2B8
Tel *(819) 843 6521*
W etoilesurlelac.ca

The designer Le Priori hotel, Quebec City

Some balconies overlook Lac
Memphremagog. Meals served
on terrace in summer. Spa on site.

**NORTH HATLEY: Manoir
Hovey** $$$
Luxury
575 Rue Hovey, QC, J0B 2C0
Tel *(819) 842 2421*
W manoirhovey.com
Romantic inn modeled on George
Washington's Virginia home.
Some rooms have fireplaces.
Award-winning restaurant.

**NUNAVIK: Auberge Kuujjuaq
Inn** $
Rural
550 Airport Rd, Kuujjuaq, QC, J0M 1C0
Tel *(819) 964 2903*
W nvkuujjuaq.ca
Basic accommodations amid
elemental Tundra wilderness.
Lodging in Quebec's north is
scarce, so book ahead.

DK Choice

**OUTAOUAIS:
Château Montebello** $$$
Luxury
*392 Rue Notre-Dame, Montebello,
QC, J0V 1L0*
Tel *(819) 423 6341 2*
W fairmont.com
This two-in-one property is
home to the world's largest log
hotel, plus the adjacent Kenauk,
a remote seigneury with
secluded lakeside cabins. Enjoy
drinks around the six-sided
fireplace before dining on
exquisite local cuisine. A range
of outdoor activities is on offer.

**RICHELIEU VALLEY: Les Trois
Tilleuls** $$
Luxury
*290 Rue Richelieu, Saint-Marc-sur-
Richelieu, QC, J0L 2E0*
Tel *(514) 856 7787*
W lestroistilleuls.com
Historic country inn bordering
the Richelieu River. Excellent spa,
art gallery, and beautiful gardens.
Marina with boat rentals.

For more information on types of hotels *see page 349*

ROUYN-NORANDA: Hotel Albert $$
Chain hotel
84 Principal, QC, J9X 4P2
Tel *(819) 762 3545*
W bestwesternquebec.com
An old-fashioned hotel with basic, comfortable rooms.

Toronto

AIRPORT: Hotel Indigo $$
Chain hotel
135 Carlingview Dr., M9W 5E7
Tel *(416) 637 7000*
W igh.com
Modern hotel near the airport. Serviceable rooms.

DOWNTOWN: bE Sixfifty Hotel $$
Boutique
650 Bay St., M5G 1M8
Tel *(416) 971 6500*
W besixfifty.com
Chic new pod-style hotel in a 100-year-old heritage building. Snug but bright, high-tech rooms.

DOWNTOWN: Omni King Edward Hotel $$
Luxury
37 King St. E., M5C 1E9
Tel *(416) 863 9700*
W omnihotels.com
Full amenities at this regal hotel. Elaborate afternoon tea.

DOWNTOWN: DoubleTree by Hilton Hotel $$$
Chain hotel
108 Chestnut St., M5G 1R3
Tel *(416) 977 5000*
W doubletree.com
Elegant, plush rooms. Cantonese fine dining at Lai Wah Heen.

DOWNTOWN: Eaton Chelsea $$$
Chain hotel
33 Gerrard St. W., M5G 1Z4
Tel *(416) 595 1975*
W chelsea.eatonhotels.com
Centrally located hotel, free for children under 17. Separate family pool with waterslide.

DOWNTOWN: Hilton Toronto Hotel $$$
Chain hotel
145 Richmond St. W., M5H 2L2
Tel *(416) 869 3456*
W 3.hilton.com
Great location in the city's financial district; only a few blocks from the shopping hub, Queen West.

DOWNTOWN: Hyatt Regency $$$
Boutique
370 King St. W., M5V 1J9
Tel *(416) 343 1234*
W toronto.regency.hyatt.com

Urban chic hotel at the heart of the entertainment district.

DOWNTOWN: Shangri-La Hotel $$$
Luxury
188 University Ave., M5H 0A3
Tel *(647) 788 8888*
W shangri-la.com
One of Toronto's most luxurious design hotels, with lush, Asia-inspired decor.

DOWNTOWN: Sheraton Centre Toronto $$$
Chain hotel
123 Queen St. W., M5H 2M9
Tel *(416) 361 1000*
W sheratontoronto.com
Located right across City Hall, this landmark high-rise has the largest indoor-outdoor pool in the city.

DK Choice

DOWNTOWN: Windsor Arms Hotel $$$
Luxury
18 St. Thomas St., M5S 3E7
Tel *(416) 971 9666*
W windsorarmshotel.com
This iconic Neo-Gothic institution boasts a stone-carved doorway and lobby. Rooms feature mahogany furnishings, fireplaces, and bathrooms with limestone floors. There are separate dining rooms for fine and casual dining, as well as for afternoon tea. Enjoy the splendid spa and saltwater pool.

SOUTH OF FRONT STREET: Delta Toronto Hotel $$
Chain hotel
75 Lower Simcoe St., M5J 3A6
Tel *(416) 849 1200*
W marriott.com
Located two blocks from the CN Tower, this 46-floor hotel has spacious rooms with great views over the South Core.

SOUTH OF FRONT STREET: Fairmont Royal York $$$
Luxury
100 Front St. W., M5J 1E3
Tel *(416) 368 2511*
W fairmont.com/royal-york-toronto
Iconic, landmark railway hotel with impeccable service.

SOUTH OF FRONT STREET: Radisson Hotel Admiral Toronto-Waterfront $$$
Chain hotel
249 Queen's Quay W., M5J 2N5
Tel *(416) 203 3333*
W radisson.com
Stylish waterfront hotel with stunning views. Outdoor pool.

SOUTH OF FRONT STREET: The Westin Harbour Castle $$$
Rooms with a view
1 Harbour Square, M5J 1A6
Tel *(416) 869 1600*
W westinharbourcastletoronto.com
Stunning lake views from many rooms at this waterfront hotel. Great rooftop terrace.

WEST END: Annex Garden $$$
B&B
Euclid Ave., M6G 2T1
Tel *(416) 258 1179*
W annexgarden.com
Beautifully restored historic home with two rooms and two suites. Fireplaces and underfloor heating.

WEST END: Drake Hotel $$$
Boutique
1150 Queen St. W., M6J 1J3
Tel *(416) 531 5042*
W thedrakehotel.ca
An 1890 hotel with ultra-hip digs in one of the six Bohemian rooms..

WEST END: Gladstone Hotel $$$
Boutique
1214 Queen St. W., M6J 1J6
Tel *(416) 531 4635*
W gladstonehotel.com
Inspired design in all 37 rooms of this imposing red-brick landmark.

Ottawa and Eastern Ontario

ALGONQUIN PARK: Arowhon Pines $$$
Resort
Arowhon Rd, Algonquin Park, ON, P1H 2G5
Tel *(705) 633 5795*
W arowhonpines.ca
Easily accessible lakeside log cabins for the perfect Algonquin experience. Canoeing available. Open from June to mid-October.

Opulent furnishings in the lobby at Fairmont Royal York, Toronto

Inviting room with a four-poster bed at the Swiss Hotel, Ottawa

COBURG: King George Inn $$
Historic
77 Albert St., ON, K9A 2L9
Tel (905) 373 4610
W thekinggeorgeinn.com
Housed in a former provincial jail with themed and non-themed rooms Family rooms with bunk beds are also available.

FENELON FALLS: Eganridge Inn & Spa $$
Resort
26 Country Club Drive, ON, K0M 1N0
Tel (705) 738 5111
W eganridge.com
Offers rooms with terraces, private cottages, and a lodge. Private dining room and an excellent spa.

HALIBURTON: Sir Sam's Inn & Waterspa $$$
Resort
1491 Sir Sam's Rd, Eagle Lake, ON, K0M 1N0
Tel (705) 754 2188
W sirsamsinn.com
Outdoor pool, indoor sauna, water spa at this lakeside inn. Ample opportunities to swim, windsurf, sail, or kayak.

KINGSTON: Rosemount Inn & Spa $$$
Historic
46 Sydenham St. S., ON, K7L 3H1
Tel (613) 531 8844
W rosemountinn.com
A mid-19th century property offering afternoon tea and wine-inspired spa treatments.

KINGSTON: Secret Garden Inn $$$
B&B
73 Sydenham St., ON, K7L 3H3
Tel (613) 531 9884
W thesecretgardeninn.com
Heritage home with antique furnishings and private baths. Friendly and informative owners. Located blocks away from the Lake Ontario waterfront.

NORTH BAY: Best Western North Bay $$
Motel
700 Lakeshore Dr., ON, P1A 2G4
Tel (705) 474 5800
W bestwesternnorthbay.com
Good location for lake and museums. Modern amenities.

OTTAWA: Delta Ottawa City Center $$
Chain hotel
101 Lyon St. N., ON, K1R 5T9
Tel (613) 237 3600
W marriott.com
Choose from bedroom suites or studios with kitchenettes and balconies. Indoor saltwater pool.

OTTAWA: Lord Elgin Hotel $$
Historic
100 Elgin St., ON, K1P 5K8
Tel (613) 235 3333
W lordelginhotel.ca
Historic landmark hotel in downtown Ottawa. Amenities include a lap pool, whirlpool, and sauna.

OTTAWA: Swiss Hotel $$
Boutique
89 Daly Ave., ON, K1N 6E6
Tel (613) 237 0335
W swisshotel.ca
Family-run hotel in a central neighborhood. Some rooms have fireplaces and Jacuzzis.

DK Choice

OTTAWA: Fairmont Château Laurier $$$
Luxury
1 Rideau St., ON, K1N 8S7
Tel (613) 241 1414
W fairmont.com/laurier-ottawa
Ottawa's 1912 landmark fairy-tale castle is a popular meeting place for afternoon tea or dinner. Spend the evening on old-style elegance while spotting celebrities in the lounge. Over 400 rooms, an indoor Art Deco pool, and spa services available. Exemplary service.

PRINCE EDWARD COUNTY: Merrill Inn $$$
Boutique
343 Main St. E., Picton, ON, K0K 2T0
Tel (613) 476 7451
W merrillinn.com
Red brick 1887 mansion boasts elegant, well-appointed rooms and a highly regarded restaurant.

RICE LAKE: Golden Beach Resort $$
Resort
7100 Northumberland County Rd. 18, ON, K0K 2X0
Tel (905) 342 5366
W goldenbeachresort.com
A family-run waterfront resort, with a variety of condos and cottages.

The Great Lakes

COLLINGWOOD: The Westin Trillium House, Blue Mountain $$
Resort
220 Gord Canning Dr., Blue Mountains, ON, L9Y 0V9
Tel (705) 443 8080
W westinbluemountain.com
At Blue Mountain ski resort. Kids' club, aquatic center, and golf courses. Kitchenettes available.

DK Choice

GODERICH: Benmiller Inn & Spa $$$
Resort
81175 Benmiller Line, ON, N7A 3Y1
Tel (519) 524 2192
W benmiller.ca
Set in a forested valley, this eco-friendly inn offers elegant accommodations in many buildings, including a historic mill. An excellent spa with river views awaits. Lake Huron's beaches and an extensive trail network are nearby.

HAMILTON: Sheraton Hotel Hamilton $$
Chain hotel
116 King St. W., ON, L8P 4V3
Tel (905) 529 5515
W sheratonhamilton.com
Geared mostly toward business travelers, but still a good base to explore local sights. Indoor pool.

JORDAN: Inn on the Twenty $$
Boutique
3845 Main St., ON, L0R 1S0
Tel (905) 562 5336
W innonthetwenty.com
Highly rated country inn set on the Wine Route. Features include fireplaces and whirlpools.

For more information on types of hotels see page 349

NIAGARA FALLS: Old Stone Inn Boutique Hotel $$
Historic
6080 Fallsview Blvd., ON, L2G 7L6
Tel *(905) 357 1234*
W oldstoneinnhotel.com
Boutique property housed in century-old flourmill. Easy access to attractions, but quiet location.

NIAGARA FALLS: Sheraton on the Falls $$
Rooms with a view
5875 Falls Ave., ON, L2G 3K7
Tel *(905) 374 4445*
W sheratononthefalls.com
Book here to sleep mere meters from the falls. Reasonable rates for incomparable views.

NIAGARA-ON-THE-LAKE: Harbour House $$
Boutique
85 Melville St., ON, L0S 1J0
Tel *(905) 468 4683*
W niagarasfinest.com
Highly rated hotel, perfectly located near the Niagara River. Perfect spot from which to set off on a wine tour.

PORT STANLEY: Inn on the Harbour $$
Boutique
202 Main St., ON, N5L 1H6
Tel *(519) 782 7623.*
W innontheharbour.ca
Rustic yet elegant inn next to a fishing wharf. Eclectic decor.

SAULT STE. MARIE: Delta Sault Ste. Marie Waterfront Hotel $$
Chain hotel
208 St. Mary's River Dr., ON, P6A 5V4
Tel *(705) 949 0611*
W marriott.com
A harborfront hotel overlooking the marina. Convenient location.

STRATFORD: Foster's Inn $$
Boutique
111 Downie St., ON, N5A 1X2
Tel *(519) 271 1119*
W fostersinn.com
Centrally located hotel with original maple hardwood floors.

THUNDER BAY: Best Western NorWester Hotel $$
Motel
2080 Hwy 61, ON, P7J 1B8
Tel *(807) 473 9123*
W bestwestern.com
Basic hotel with heated indoor pool. Golfing, fishing, and skiing options nearby.

TOBERMORY: Blue Bay Motel $$
Motel
32 Bay St., ON, N0H 2R0
Tel *(519) 596 2392*
W bluebay-motel.com

Hotel located near the docks and the ferry to Manitoulin Island. Close to diving, kayaking, and boat tours, plus hiking and skiing trails.

WINDSOR: Waterfront Hotel $$
Rooms with a view
277 Riverside Dr., ON, N9A 5K4
Tel *(519) 973 5555*
W bestwestern.com
Rooms with fantastic views of the Detroit skyline and the river. Short walk to the casino.

Central Canada

CHURCHILL: Lazy Bear Lodge $$$
Rural
313 Kelsey Blvd., MB, R0B 0E0
Tel *(204) 663 9377*
W lazybearlodge.com
This wooden lodge is a good base for polar-bear viewing. Packages include pick-ups, meals, and tours.

DRUMHELLER: Newcastle Country Inn $$
B&B
1130 Newcastle Trail, AB, T0J 0Y2
Tel *(403) 823 8356*
W newcastlecountryinn.net
Rooms in this comfortable, three-star inn include a continental breakfast.

DK Choice

EDMONTON: Mettera Hotel on Whyte $$$
Boutique
10454 82 Ave., AB, T6E 4Z7
Tel *(780) 465 8150*
W metterra.com
A contemporary hotel located in trendy Old Strathcona. Unique "fire and water" suites, 24-hour business and fitness centers, plus a restaurant and full-service spa. Price includes deluxe breakfasts and evening wine-tasting (Mon–Sat). Close to restaurants, entertainment, and nightlife.

EDMONTON: Union Bank Inn $$$
Boutique
10053 Jasper Ave., AB, T5J 1S5
Tel *(780) 423 3600*
W unionbankinn.com
Housed downtown in the 1911 Union Bank building. À-la-carte breakfast and nightly wine and cheese trays are included.

LETHBRIDGE: The Norland $$
B&B
5801 1st Ave. S., AB, T1J 4P4
Tel *(403) 795 3130*
W thenorland.com
A 1910 colonial-style Victorian mansion on a 10-acre estate by Gaol Lake. The seven luxury suites are grand and elegant.

MOOSE JAW: Grant Hall Hotel $$
Boutique
401 Main St. N., SK, S6H 0W5
Tel *(844) 885 4255*
W granthall.ca
A restored 1920s railway hotel, with spacious rooms and a rooftop terrace lounge.

REGINA: The Hotel Saskatchewan $$$
Chain hotel
2125 Victoria Ave., SK, S4P 0S3
Tel *(306) 522 7691*
W marriott.com
Historic hotel built in 1927 with park and city views. Spa, fitness center, and convention facilities.

RIDING MOUNTAIN NATIONAL PARK: Elkhorn Resort $$$
Resort
#3 Mooswa Dr. E., Onanole, MB, R0J 1N0
Tel *(204) 848 2802*
W elkhornresort.mb.ca
Year-round resort surrounded by boreal forest. Spa, horseback riding, golf, and winter sports.

SASKATOON: Delta Bessborough $$$
Historic
601 Spadina Crescent, SK, S7K 3G8
Tel *(306) 244 5521*
W marriott.com

Sheraton on the Falls, right next to Niagara Falls

Room at the Fairmont Waterfront in Vancouver

Iconic railway hotel with business and fitness centers, indoor pool, full-service spa, and restaurants.

SASKATOON: The James Hotel $$$
Luxury
620 Spadina Crescent E., SK, S7K 3T5
Tel (306) 244 6446
w thejameshotel.ca
Modern boutique hotel scenically located at the river's edge. Stylish lounge. Includes a full breakfast.

DK Choice

WINNIPEG: Fort Gary Hotel $$
Luxury
222 Broadway Ave., MB, R3C 0R3
Tel (204) 942 8251
w fortgarryhotel.com
This opulent hotel, built in 1913, is a National Historic Site, noted for its romantic interiors and plush amenities. There is an exceptional spa, fitness center with pool, conference center, and a revolving restaurant. Palm Lounge offers a lavish Sunday brunch and nightly music.

Vancouver and Vancouver Island

BARKLEY SOUND: Eagle Nook Resort & Spa $$$
Rural
Box 289, Ucluelet, BC, V0R 3A0
Tel (604) 357 3361, 1 800 760 2777
w eaglenook.com
Idyllic hideaway set in 28 ha (70 acres) of wilderness. Ideal for kayaking, wildlife viewing, and salmon fishing.

SOOKE : Sooke Harbour House $$$
Luxury
1528 Whiffin Spit Rd, BC, V9Z 0T4
Tel (250) 642 3421
w sookeharbourhouse.com
Oldest B&B on the island with ocean and mountain views. Biking, kayaking, and hiking nearby.

TOFINO: Middle Beach Lodge $$
Resort
400 Mackenzie Beach Rd, BC, V0R 2Z0
Tel (250) 725 2900
w middlebeach.com
Oceanfront, rustic log cabins with fireplaces and hot tubs. One lodge for families; others are adults only.

DK Choice

TOFINO: Clayoquot Wilderness Resort $$$
Resort
380 Main St., BC, V0R 2Z0
Tel (250) 726 8235, 1 888 333 5405
w wildretreat.com
Unique deluxe outpost with luxury en-suite tenting. Guests can try their hand at swift-water kayaking, surfing, fly fishing, bear watching, rock climbing, and hiking. A spa, yoga classes, and a gym are on-site. There is a ranch-style cookhouse with an open kitchen and stone fireplace. Guests are transferred from Tofino in a private seaplane. Open from May to September.

VANCOUVER: Georgian Court Hotel $$
Boutique
773 Beatty St., BC, V6B 2M4
Tel (604) 682 5555
w georgiancourthotelvancouver.com
Deluxe hotel with a women-only floor, on-site restaurants, and spa service. Jogging, walking, and cycling paths nearby.

VANCOUVER: Greystone B&B $$
Historic
2006 West 14th Ave., BC, V6J 2K4
Tel (604) 732 1375
w greystonebb.com
A 1910 Craftsman house with just two rooms plus a suite with two bedrooms, a full kitchen, and garden access.

VANCOUVER: Fairmont Hotel Vancouver $$$
Historic
900 West Georgia St., BC, V6C 2W6
Tel (604) 684 3131
w fairmont.com
Elegant, old-fashioned landmark. Relax at the fabulous spa after hiking or skiing. Disabled-friendly.

VANCOUVER: Fairmont Waterfront $$$
Rooms with a view
900 Canada Place Way, BC, V6C 3L5
Tel (604) 691 1991
w fairmont.com
Spectacular glass-and-steel design hotel located beside pretty walkways. Guests can enjoy mountain and ocean views from the pool.

VANCOUVER: Four Seasons $$$
Luxury
791 West Georgia St., BC, V6C 2T4
Tel (604) 689 9333
w fourseasons.com
Family-friendly hotel next to the Pacific Centre mall. An indoor-outdoor pool on site.

VANCOUVER: Granville Island Hotel $$$
Boutique
1253 Johnston St., BC, V6H 3R9
Tel (604) 683 7373
w granvilleislandhotel.com
Waterfront hotel with unique luxury rooms on Granville Island. Pet-friendly.

VANCOUVER: Metropolitan Hotel Vancouver $$$
Luxury
645 Howe St., BC, V6C 2Y9
Tel (604) 687 1122
w metropolitan.com
Popular with business travelers. Intimate rooms, a health center, a squash court, and an indoor lap pool.

VANCOUVER: O Canada House B&B $$$
Historic
1114 Barclay St., BC, V6E 1H1
Tel (604) 688 0555
w ocanadahouse.com
Home-made breakfasts and a guests' pantry at this 1897 home. Yoga gear available. Sherry served in the evenings.

VANCOUVER: Thistle Down House $$$
Historic
3910 Capilano Rd, BC, V7R 4J2
Tel (604) 986 7173
w thistle-down.com
A 1920 heritage-listed home with bright rooms. Some have fireplaces, balconies, and patios.

VICTORIA: Days Inn Victoria on the Harbour $$
Chain hotel
427 Belleville St., BC, V8V 1X3
Tel (250) 386 3451
w daysinnvictoria.com
A good-value hotel within walking distance of downtown. Outdoor pool (seasonal) and free parking.

VICTORIA: Inn at Laurel Point $$
Rooms with a view
680 Montreal St., BC, V8V 1Z8
Tel (250) 386 8721
w laurelpoint.com
A stunning contemporary waterfront hotel overlooking the Inner Harbour. Some glassed balconies allow harbor views from bed. Japanese gardens.

For more information on types of hotels *see page 349*

VICTORIA: Fairmont Empress $$$
Luxury
721 Government St., BC, V8W 1W5
Tel *(250) 384 8111*
W fairmont.com
This iconic ivy-clad landmark offers old-fashioned elegance. A deluxe refurbishment has added a spa and nail salon. Excellent service.

VICTORIA: Humboldt House Bed & Breakfast $$$
Boutique
867 Humboldt St., BC, V8V 2Z6
Tel *(250) 383 0152*
W humboldthouse.com
Old Victorian home in a quiet neighbourhood. Themed rooms and in-room champagne breakfasts. Short walk to downtown.

The Rocky Mountains

DK Choice

**BANFF:
Fairmont Banff Springs $$$**
Luxury
405 Spray Ave., AB, T1L 1J4
Tel *(403) 762 2211*
W fairmont.com
Iconic "Castle in the Rockies" in Banff National Park with un-paralleled views of Bow River and Mount Rundle. Watch the sunset while sipping cocktails. Enjoy the spa, mineral baths, golf course, and pools. Horseback rides and naturalist-guided hikes of the park available. Impeccable service.

CALGARY: Hotel Arts $$$
Boutique
119 12th Ave. SW., AB, T2R 0G8
Tel *(403) 266 4611*
W hotelarts.ca
Some rooms at this hip hotel have balconies, marble baths, and two-person Jacuzzis. The hotel bar's patio overlooks the pool.

CANMORE: Quality Resort Château Canmore $$
Rooms with a view
1718 Bow Valley Trail, AB, T1W 2X3
Tel *(403) 678 6699*
W chateaucanmore.com
Rooms at this all-suite hotel have fireplaces, kitchenettes, and mountain views. Children up to 18 can stay with adults for free.

CRANBROOK: Elizabeth Lake Lodge $$
Rooms with a view
590 Van Horne St. S., BC, V1C 4W7
Tel *(250) 426 6114*
W elizabethlakelodge.com

Rooms with views of the Elizabeth Lake Bird Sanctuary. Some have kitchenettes.

FIELD: Emerald Lake Lodge $$$
Rural
PO Box 10, BC, V0A 1G0
Tel *(403) 410 7417*
W crmr.com
Gorgeous, cozy lodge and superb dining surrounded by log cabins in mountainous Yoho National Park.

FORT NELSON: Woodlands Inn & Suites $$
Motel
3995 50th Ave. S., BC, V0C 1R0
Tel *(250) 774 6669*
W woodlandsinn.ca
Full-service hotel with fitness center, kitchenettes, coin laundry, and free airport shuttle.

GOLDEN: Vagabond Lodge $$
Resort
1581 Cache Close, BC, V0A 1H0
Tel *(250) 344 2622*
W vagabondlodge.ca
Luxurious boutique-style lodge at Kicking House Mountain Resort, with splendid mountain views from some balconies. No telephones or TVs in rooms.

LAKE LOUISE: Fairmont Château Lake Louise $$$
Resort
111 Lake Louise Dr., AB, T0L 1E0
Tel *(403) 522 3511*
W fairmont.com
Overlooks Lake Louise. Enjoy canoeing, hiking, and horseback riding. Children and pets welcome.

PRINCE GEORGE: Norton Ranch Cottages $$
Rural
6505 Lower Mud River Rd, BC, V2N 5C3
Tel *(250) 612 1361*
W nortonranch.com
Three Western-style cottages on a ranch. Horse- and pet-friendly.

Bright lobby of the Prince of Wales Hotel in Waterton Lakes

RADIUM HOT SPRINGS: Bighorn Meadows Resort $$
Resort
10 Bighorn Blvd., BC, V0A 1M0
Tel *(250) 347 2323*
W bighornmeadows.com
Golf resort with fully equipped suites. Mountain views, fireplaces, and decks with BBQs.

WATERTON LAKES: Prince of Wales Hotel $$$
Resort
Waterton Lakes National Park, AB, T0K 2M0
Tel *(403) 859 2231*
W glacierparkinc.com
Quirky summer-only inn on bluff overlooking lake. Good mountain views and wildlife watching.

Southern and Northern British Columbia

DK Choice

**108 MILE RANCH:
The Hills Health Ranch $$**
Resort
4871 Hwy 97, BC, V0K 2Z0
Tel *(250) 791 5225*
W spabc.com
Stay on a working ranch amid splendid mountain scenery. Trail riding through forested mountains, cowboy cookouts, yoga lessons, and a health and weight-loss center are some of the facilities offered. Cabins are available as well.

BARKERVILLE: Kelly and King House B&Bs $$
Historic
Main St., BC, V0K 2R0
Tel *(250) 994 3328, (866) 994 0004*
W kellyhouse.ca
Stay in a restored Gold Rush village. Book one of the en-suite rooms or the entire house.

CHASE: Quaaout Lodge & Spa $$
Resort
1663 Little Shuswap Rd, BC, V0E 1M2
Tel *(250) 679 3090*
W quaaoutlodge.com
Resort overlooking Little Shuswap Lake. Horseback riding, fishing, canoeing, hiking, and golfing.

HARRISON HOT SPRINGS: Harrison Hot Springs Resort & Spa $$$
Resort
100 Esplanade Ave., BC, V0M 1K0
Tel *(604) 796 2244*
W harrisonresort.com

Enjoy the five mineral hot-spring pools while gazing at stars and mountains. Peaceful lake views.

HOPE: Manning Park Resort $$
Resort
7500 Hwy 3, Manning Provincial Park, BC, V0X 1R0
Tel *(250) 840 8822*
w manningpark.com
Wide range of accommodations. Indoor and outdoor sports as well.

KAMLOOPS: Plaza Hotel $$
Historic
405 Victoria St., BC, VC2 2A9
Tel *(250) 377 8075*
w theplazahotel.ca
Boutique heritage hotel located downtown. Free acccess to nearby pool and fitness facilities.

KELOWNA: Hotel Eldorado $$$
Rooms with a view
500 Cook Rd, BC, V1W 3G9
Tel *(250) 763 7500*
w hoteleldoradokelowna.com
Lakeside 1920s' charm with modern luxuries. Lively bar and popular Sunday brunch.

OLIVER: Hester Creek Estate Winery Villa $$$
Luxury
877 Rd 8, BC, V0H 1T0
Tel *(250) 498 4435*
w hestercreek.com
Private Mediterranean-style suites with beautiful vineyard and orchard views. Breakfast included.

PRINCE RUPERT: Prince Rupert Crest Hotel $$
Rooms with a view
222 1st Ave. W., BC, V8J 1A8
Tel *(250) 624 6771*
w cresthotel.bc.ca
This charming property is located on a bluff near Cow Bay. Rooms offer harbor, city, mountain, and Kaien Island views.

WHISTLER: Fairmont Château Whistler $$$
Luxury
4599 Château Blvd., BC, V0N 1B4
Tel *(604) 938 8000*
w fairmont.com
Luxurious castle-like hotel with a golf course and spa on site, and hiking trails nearby. Pet- and kid-friendly.

WHISTLER: Whistler Peak Lodge $$$
Resort
4295 Blackcomb Way, BC, V0N 1B4
Tel *(604) 938 0878*
w whistlerhi.com
Rooms feature kitchenettes and fireplaces. Children are welcome. Short walk to the gondolas.

Warm and inviting interiors of the Fairmont Château Whistler, British Columbia

Northern Canada

DAWSON CITY: Downtown Hotel $$
Motel
1026 2nd Ave., YT, Y0B 1G0
Tel *(867) 993 5346*
w downtownhotel.ca
Decor reminiscent of the Klondike gold-rush era. Free airport shuttle and Jacuzzi.

DK Choice

DAWSON CITY: Bombay Peggy's Inn & Pub $$$
Historic
2nd Ave. & Princess St., YT, Y0B 1G0
Tel *(867) 993 6969*
w bombaypeggys.com
Built in 1900 and restored to its Victorian elegance, this small hotel has individually themed rooms. Serves croissants in the morning, and chocolate and port in the afternoon. Adjoining pub offers a selection of single-malt Scotch, Yukon-brewed beers, and Martinis.

HAINES JUNCTION: Dalton Trail Lodge $$$
Rural
Box 5331, YT, Y0B 1L0
Tel *(867) 634 2099*
w daltontrail.com
Family-owned wilderness lodge with comfy cabins and hearty food. Fishing and hiking packages.

HAY RIVER: Eileen's Bed & Breakfast $$
Motel
3 Wright Cr., NT, X0E 0R2
Tel *(867) 875 7607*
w eileensbnb.com
Centrally located, modern, and fully equipped suites with complimentary airport shuttle.

INUVIK: Capital Suites $$$
Motel
198 Mackenzie Rd, NT, X0E 0T0
Tel *(867) 678 6300*
w capitalsuites.ca

Studios and one-and two-bed-room suites. WiFi, snack shop, gym, laundry, and shuttle.

IQALUIT: Capital Suites $$$
Motel
807 Aviq St., NU, X0A 0H0
Tel *867 975 4000*
w capitalsuites.ca
Modern suites plus gym, laundry, mini market, and free WiFi.

IQALUIT: Frobisher Inn $$$
Hotel
Astro Hill, NU, X0A 0H0
Tel *(867) 979 2222*
w frobisherinn.com
Deluxe rooms feature Jacuzzis and fireplaces. Three restaurants and movie theater on site.

WHITEHORSE: Annie Lake Cabins $$
B&B
Km 2.1 Annie Lake Rd., YT, Y1A 5P7
Tel *(867) 456 4531*
w annielakecabins.com
Modern mountain-view ensuite cube cabins are private and comfortable. Open Apr–Dec.

WHITEHORSE: Skky Hotel $$
B&B
91622 Alaska Hwy, YT, Y1A 3E4
Tel *(867) 456 2400*
w skkyhotel.com
Refined inn, close to downtown. Free airport shuttle.

YELLOWKNIFE: Bayside Bed & Breakfast $$
Boutique
3505 McDonald Dr., NT, X1A 2H2
Tel *(867) 445 5003*
w baysidenorth.com
Located in scenic Old Town with lovely views of Yellowknife Bay. Good food at Dancing Moose Café.

YELLOWKNIFE: Explorer Hotel $$$
Motel
4825 49th Ave.., NT, X1A 2R3
Tel *(867) 873 3531*
w explorerhotel.ca
Enjoy cocktails in the Trapline Lounge and supper at Trader's Grill.

For more information on types of hotels *see page 349*

WHERE TO EAT AND DRINK

What makes Canadian cuisine unique is its regional specialties: Alberta beef, Arctic char fish from Canada's north, salmon from BC, Nova Scotia lobster, and Quebec French *tortières* (meat pies) to name a few. While these specialties can be sampled in their place of origin, many of the larger towns offer a choice of Canada's best regional produce, and in some areas this includes Canadian wines and beers *(see p363)*. In fact, the "locavore" and "100-mile diet" movements, where chefs take pride in featuring local produce, have swept the nation. Traditional game, including rabbit, caribou, and bison, are now gourmet dishes at cosmopolitan restaurants, while French haute cuisine is available in major cities. Since Canada is a nation of immigrants, ethnic restaurants are common everywhere. German, Greek, Chinese, Thai, Indian, Ukrainian, African, and Italian cuisines, along with other international favorites, provide a wide range of options at a price to suit every budget. The listings on pages 364–83 describe a selection of restaurants chosen for their variety, service, and good value.

White-linen tablecloths and intimate decor of Vancouver's CinCin *(see p378)*

Types of Restaurants

Eating out in Canada is surprisingly affordable, especially when compared to European prices. Restaurants are extremely varied, with the tearoom, bistro, brasserie, and theater café competing with the more usual family restaurant and fast-food outlet. Many pubs also serve excellent bar food at reasonable prices.

Lobster suppers are a unique Canadian dining experience. Held throughout the summer on Prince Edward Island, these lively gatherings often take place in basements of community halls on wooden tables, where fishermen have just brought in the catch. Equally unique, though by no means public, are Inuit dinners. Traveling through the Arctic north might result in an invitation to join an Inuit family for the evening meal of sundried caribou sweetened with berry sauces or smoked and dried local fish.

Vegetarian

Vegetarian options are on the increase throughout Canada. Expect to see at least one vegetarian or even vegan dish on the menu, and gluten-free items often feature too. "Healthy Eating" is a government initiative promoting heart-healthy eating. The menus of participating restaurants feature the heart symbol to denote low-fat dishes. Anyone on a special or weight-loss diet should ask the chef to leave out certain high-calorie ingredients.

Fresh fruit is easily obtained throughout the south of the country, and is abundant during summer and early autumn at roadside stalls in the primary growing areas of Ontario and British Columbia. Some of the best berries and peaches in the world are enjoyed here during summer. However, most food in the Northwest Territories and Nunavut is imported and mostly either canned or frozen. Fresh food in Canada's north is hard to obtain, and expensive.

Alcohol

The minimum age of public purchase and consumption of alcohol is 19 across most of the country, except in Quebec, Manitoba, and Alberta, where it is 18. Canada produces many award-winning wines *(see p363)*, which are increasingly available everywhere.

Open-air dining is popular in downtown Montreal

Classy decor at Bistro Le Coq, a French bistro in Halifax *(see p366)*

While alcohol is not sold in corner stores and supermarkets, liquor stores sell a range of quality wines and spirits. Separate government-run stores in Ontario sell only beer.

Eating Hours and Reservations

Lunch tables are usually available from noon to 2pm. Although dinner is usually served between 6pm and 9pm, later seatings, sometimes well into the night, are available in larger cities and resort areas. Reserving a table in advance is a good idea. Call ahead and cancel if your plans change.

Paying and Tipping

It is possible to eat well in Canada for a bargain price. A snack in a café seldom costs more than Can $10. In a good restaurant, a three-course meal with wine often costs Can $45–$70 per person. Even gourmet dinners can start at Can $45. Luncheon items are generally less expensive, with similar choices to the dinner menu. Restaurant tax includes the 5 percent GST (Goods and Services Tax) and the varying provincial sales tax, applicable everywhere except Alberta. Taxes are included on the final cheque. Service charges are rarely included, but might be added to the bill for a large group. Tipping is generally

expected, and should be about 15 percent of the net cheque. Normally, a tip should increase if you are bringing a larger party to a restaurant and for exceptional service. Tipping is also expected in bars and nightclubs.

Children

Most restaurants offer high chairs or booster seats, and some provide crayons and coloring books to keep kids amused. Note that a children's menu or half-portions might be available for those under eight years old. Parents are expected to keep children seated at the table and to take noisy or upset youngsters outside until they calm down.

Disabled Facilities

Most new restaurants, as well as existing establishments undergoing renovation, have made their sites wheelchair-accessible. However, many older and rural establishments may not have such facilities and should be checked out in advance.

Dress Code

Most restaurants operate a "smart-casual" dress policy, especially at lunchtime, but exceptions to this can include sneakers (trainers), cut-off jeans, and dirty or ripped clothes.

The rule generally runs as follows: the more expensive and exclusive the restaurant, the more formal the attire required. Evening dress is rarely necessary.

Smoking

More than 80 percent of Canadians do not smoke, and local by-laws restrict areas where people can legally smoke. Smoking is not allowed in any public places, including bars, cafés, restaurants, and some terraces and patios. Many parks also ban smoking, but if you do smoke, be sure to extinguish your cigarette to avoid starting a forest fire.

Recommended Restaurants

Within these listings, eating establishments reflect Canada's widely multicultural society, which extends into the far north, "backcountry" regions, as well as major cities. Hence, restaurant themes describe cuisine types: Chinese, Greek, Hungarian, Indian, and so on.

Restaurants that carry the "DK Choice" designation are specially recommended. They may feature a chef's table, exquisitely prepared regional specialties paired with a sommelier-recommended wine or beer, or offer exemplary service. Whatever the selection, it is bound to offer a nuanced understanding of Canadian cuisine.

Café-bars in cities are mostly inexpensive and popular options

The Flavors of Canada

With a rich history of multiculturalism, Canada's culinary heritage is diverse. *Poutine* (french fries topped with cheese curds and hot gravy) is the closest thing to a national dish, while regional specialties have their own strong identities. Seafood dominates Atlantic Canada and British Columbian menus, while steaks and burgers are best in the ranching areas of Alberta and Saskatchewan. Acadian cuisine is found in New Brunswick and Nova Scotia, and in Northern Canada age-old Inuit techniques produce a variety of sundried caribou and fish dishes. But the Canadian specialty that is famous the world over is maple syrup.

Vegetable squash

Pacific salmon, caught in the Khutzeymateen River, BC

Fish and Seafood

Bordered by oceans on three sides, Canada offers great seafood, particularly on its east and west coasts. Produce from here can easily make it from the ocean to the dinner plate within 24 hours. Oysters, clams, and scallops are a main feature of East Coast menus. Prince Edward Island is famous for its lobster and mussels; Pacific salmon,

Dungeness crab, and shellfish, notably shrimp (prawns), dominate British Columbian fare, along with albacore tuna and Arctic char. More unusual dishes, often incorporating historic preserving methods, include Solomon Grundy (Nova Scotia's marinated herring), and cod tongues, as well as smoked salmon from the east and west coast. Freshwater fish, both the farmed and wild versions, is caught in an estimated two million lakes dotted across Canada, and offers a delicate contrast to seafood. In the west of the country, the tender Winnipeg goldeye, trout, and pickerel, often cooked over open fires at informal summer outdoor shore lunches throughout the central region, are a uniquely Canadian treat.

Scallop · Crab · Mussels · Oysters · Sardines · Salmon · Lobster · Clams
Selection of superb seafood from the clear waters of Canada

French-Canadian Dishes and Specialties

The center of French-style gourmet cuisine in Canada is Quebec. Dishes here are reminiscent of the best European food. For some more traditional French-Canadian dishes, cities and towns in the province usually serve specialties. These include *creton*, *tourtière*, and many varieties of pâtisserie. Smoked beef is another popular local delicacy. The Maritime Provinces offer excellent, originally French, Acadian dishes from recipes that are hundreds of years old. As well as meat pies, patés, and stews, rich desserts and cakes feature in their filling menus. Vieux-Montréal's bistros offer many classic delights, such as *escargots à la bourguignonne*. French-Canadians are known for their rich desserts, such as *trempettes* (fried bread soaked in maple syrup) and caramel-soaked *pouding au chômeur*.

Maple syrup

Creton is a coarse, spicy pork pâté. It is delicious served on hunks of fresh baguette with cornichons (gherkins).

Baskets of rosy apples outside a Nova Scotia farm shop

Meat and Game

Alberta's cattle ranches are the source of Canada's finest beef. Most beef in rural areas is served simply, with salad and fries, but one much-loved local dish is cowboy-inspired beef hash – corned beef with baked beans and fried potatoes. Lamb and buffalo are also farmed, in smaller numbers. The Yukon, Northwest Territories, and Nunavut supply much of the country's game; caribou, musk ox, and moose are all sent south to be cooked in the European style. Local people, especially the Inuit, smoke meat for the winter months. Their smoked caribou is delicious and very popular. Famous for making the most of a kill, First Nations peoples use every part of the animal for either clothing or food – even moose fleas are something of a delicacy. Goose, duck, and fish are all smoked or sundried, providing staples for the very long, harsh winter. Caribou and birds are preserved by being hung out on lines to dry in the Arctic sun.

Fiddlehead fern shoots for sale in a New Brunswick market

Fruit and Vegetables

Ontario is the fruit bowl of Canada. In addition to its thriving wine industry, the area is famous for its strawberries and cranberries. Peaches and apples are also cultivated here in large quantities, as are blueberries, which also flourish in Nova Scotia and Quebec. Corn, black beans, and vegetable squash (collectively known as the "three sisters") are produced in Ontario alongside zucchini (courgettes), huge tomatoes, and fresh herbs. In New Brunswick, fiddleheads (fern shoots) and dulse (seaweed) are sautéed as a vegetable side dish.

WHAT TO DRINK

Molson "Canadian" and Labatt "Blue" are among the best-selling beers in Canada, but craft beers produced by such microbreweries as Ontario's Creemore Brewery and Quebec's Unibroue are also well respected. Canada produces some excellent wines from hybrid grapes, thanks largely to European winemakers, who have emigrated here. Most wine comes from three areas: the southern Okanagan Valley of BC (see p321), Nova Scotia's Annapolis Valley, and a narrow strip along the Niagara Peninsula of southern Ontario. Grape varieties include Chardonnay, Pinot Noir, and Riesling. Rye whisky is distilled in BC; Canadian Club is the most popular brand, but local distilleries produce specialties.

Escargots à la bourguignonne are snails cooked in garlic and parsley butter and served in their shells.

Tourtière, a pastry-topped pie filled with meat and vegetables flavored with spices, is country fare.

Pouding au chômeur (literally "pudding of the unemployed") is an upside-down cake with a rich caramel base.

Where to Eat and Drink

Newfoundland and Labrador

BONAVISTA: Bonavista Social Club $
International
Upper Amherst Cove, NL, A0C 2A0
Tel *(709) 445 5556* **Closed** *Mon–Wed*
Home to the only wood-fired bread oven in the province, this eatery makes everything from multigrain to sourdough bread. The handmade pizzas are particularly noteworthy. Locally sourced ingredients.

CORNER BROOK: Jennifer's The Upper Level Restaurant $
North American
48–50 Broadway, NL, A2H 4C4
Tel *(709) 632 7979*
Family-run for over two decades, Jennifer's is known for reliable service and some of the best gourmet dining in the area. Try the seafood chowder or the Newfoundland dish *cod au gratin* (flake cod, white sauce, Cheddar cheese, and breadcrumbs).

CORNER BROOK: Newfound Sushi $
Sushi
117 Broadway, NL, A2H 5B6
Tel *(709) 634 6666* **Closed** *Sun*
One of the few sushi spots on the West Coast. Sushi rolls are named after local landmarks: Humber River Roll or Blow Me Down Roll. Cozy, intimate atmosphere.

FERRYLAND: Ferryland Lighthouse Picnics $
North American
Lighthouse Rd, NL, A0A 2H0
Tel *(709) 363 7456* **Closed** *Sep–May; Mon–Tue*
Enjoy a unique picnic experience at this 19th-century lighthouse. After a 40-minute hike, guests are handed a basket filled with goodies and a blanket to spread out in the grass. Great home-made lemonade and cake. Watch for breaching whales in late spring. Reservations mandatory.

GRAND FALLS-WINDSOR: 48 High $
Fine Dining
48 High St, NL, A2A 1C6
Tel *(709) 489 9299*
Named for the street on which it stands, 48 High offers a gourmet dining experience. Try the zorba penne, the chicken pesto fusilli or the seafood medley platter. Quiet, relaxed ambience.

JOE BATT'S ARM: Nicole's Café $
Contemporary Canadian
159 Main Rd, Fogo Island, NL, A0G 2B0
Tel *(709) 658 3663*
An upscale culinary experience on Fogo Island where traditional Newfoundland dishes are modernized. Be sure to sample the famous Growlers home-made ice cream. Cozy interior with local artwork displayed.

LABRADOR CITY: Mes Amis Dining Room $$
North American
Two Seasons Inn, 96 Avalon Dr., NL, A2V 2L3
Tel *(709) 944 2661*
North American dishes with a Newfoundland twist. Try the *cod au gratin*. Space for business lunches as well. Wine list plus a separate bar area.

NORRIS POINT: Sugar Hill Inn's Chanterelles $$
Mediterranean
129 Sexton Ln, NL, A0K 3V0
Tel *(888) 299 2147* **Closed** *Nov–Apr*
Locally sourced ingredients are prepared with authentic olive oils and vinegars for the ultimate Mediterranean flair. The specialty is seafood, including halibut, cod, salmon, shrimp, and scallop. Offers more than 80 varieties of wine.

ROCKY HARBOUR: Java Jack's $
North American
88 Main St. N., NL, A0K 4N0
Tel *(709) 458 3004*
Closed *Oct–mid-May*
Java Jack's started out as a café and is now a trendy restaurant in a heritage home. Fresh fish, wild game, and vegetarian dishes

Beautifully served seafood at St. John's Raymonds Restaurant

Price Guide
Prices (in Canadian dollars) are based on a three-course meal for one, including half a bottle of house wine and service.

$	up to Can $45
$$	Can $45 to 70
$$$	over Can $70

are served with organic greens from the garden.

ST. JOHN'S: Piatto Pizzeria Enoteca $
Italian
377 Duckworth St., NL, A1C 1H8
Tel *(709) 726 0909*
This pizzeria strictly follows the traditions and processes of Neapolitan pizza-making. Calzone and pasta dishes are also served. Some ingredients are grown in the volcanic ash of Mount Vesuvius.

ST. JOHN'S: Adelaide Oyster House $$
Seafood
334 Water St., NL, A1C 1C1
Tel *(709) 722 7222* **Closed** *Mon*
A contemporary, upbeat restaurant specializing in oysters. Often packed with people, so show up before the opening time of 5pm to get a guaranteed seat. Sit at the common table to get to know the locals.

DK Choice

ST. JOHN'S: Raymonds Restaurant $$$
Contemporary Canadian
95 Water St., NL, A1C 1A4
Tel *(709) 579 5800* **Closed** *Sun & Mon*
Housed in a restored classical building overlooking the harbor and the Narrows, Raymonds features an award-winning menu inspired by rustic Atlantic Canadian cuisine. The focus here is on using the province's seafood, game, vegetables and berries. For the ultimate dining experience, try the seven-course wine-pairing taste menu.

TWILLINGATE: Canvas Cove Bistro $$
Seafood
52 Main St., NL, A0G 4M0
Tel *(709) 884 1888* **Closed** *Oct–Apr*
Sampling the exceptional lobster chowder at this bistro is an absolute must. The large wine menu features selections from nearby Auk Island Winery. Try the Newfie Screech banana flambé for dessert.

Stunning gardens and wraparound veranda at The Inn at Bay Fortune, Prince Edward Island

New Brunswick, Prince Edward Island, and Nova Scotia

ADVOCATE HARBOUR: Wild Caraway $$
Contemporary Canadian
3721 Highway 209, NS, B0M 1A0
Tel *(902) 392 2889*
Housed in a century-old home, the restaurant overlooks the beautiful Bay of Fundy. The chefs here add global flavors to the locally sourced food. The menu specializes in seafood and pork.

ANNAPOLIS ROYAL: German Bakery and Sachsen Café $
German Bakery
358 St. George St., NS, B0S 1A0
Tel *(902) 532 1990*
Friendly, family-owned place with great views over Fort Anne. Sample the authentic *schnitzel*, and *bratwurst* with *sauerkraut*. Excellent baked goods. Great German beers and wines.

ANTIGONISH: Gabrieau's Bistro $$
Contemporary Canadian
350 Main St., NS, B2G 2C5
Tel *(902) 863 1925* **Closed** *Sun*
Gabrieau's has a gorgeous dining room and bar serving delicious fare. Lots of locally sourced ingredients crafted into imaginative dishes. There is also a tapas menu. Good breakfasts, and exceptional desserts.

BADDECK: Herring Choker Deli $
Deli
10158 Hwy 105, Nyanza, NS, B0E 1B0
Tel *(902) 295 2275*
Great soups and sandwiches served in huge portions. Try the home-made bread and the cinnamon rolls. Ideal place to pick up a packed lunch.

BAY FORTUNE: The Inn at Bay Fortune $$$
Contemporary Canadian
758 Route 310, PE, C0A 2B0
Tel *(902) 687 3745*
Originally built for a Broadway playwright, The Inn is now home to farm-to-table fine dining and a custom-built wood-fired oven. The set menu includes seafood, homegrown salad, and wood-roasted meat. Fine wine selection.

BRACKLEY: The Dunes Café $$
Contemporary Canadian
3622 Brackley Point Rd., PE, C1E 1Z3
Tel *(902) 672 1883*
Spacious and airy café with beautiful gardens. The menu features a lot of locally sourced seafood used to prepare fresh and inventive dishes. Great wine list and cocktails. Fabulous desserts.

CARAQUET: Mitchan Sushi $
Japanese
49 A Blvd. Saint-Pierre W, NB, E1W 1B6
Tel *(506) 726 1103* **Closed** *Mon & Tue*
A local favorite with a friendly atmosphere. The menu features delicious and authentic Japanese food. Sushi and sashimi is made with fresh local fish and seafood.

CHARLOTTETOWN: Sim's Corner Steakhouse and Oyster Bar $$$
Steakhouse
86 Queen St., PE, C1A 4A7,
Tel *(902) 894 7467*
Choose oysters on display at the oyster bar, then dine on the large patio or in the intimate boudoir-like interior. Excellent food, with good drinks as well.

CHETICAMP: Restaurant Acadien $
Traditional Canadian
15067 Main St., NS, B0E 1H0
Tel *(902) 224 3207*
A cultural experience. Servers in traditional Acadian dress offer dishes such as chicken fricot, blood pudding, and meat pie served with cranberry sauce. Hearty meals and great desserts.

DIGBY: Fundy Restaurant $$
Seafood
34 Water St., NS, B0V 1A0
Tel *(902) 245 4950*
Located right on the waterfront, overlooking the Annapolis Basin. Fantastic seafood served in a fun atmosphere. Order the fat Digby scallops sautéed in garlic butter, or the fried clams. Wash it down with Keith's India Pale Ale.

FREDERICTON: The Schnitzel Parlour $
German
304 Union St., NB, E3A 3L9
Tel *(506) 450 2520* **Closed** *Sun–Tue*
Friendly owners serve up hearty portions of authentic German food in a welcoming environment. Awesome *schnitzel* as well as home-made chocolates.

FREDERICTON: Wolastoq Wharf $$
Contemporary Canadian
527 Union St., NB, E3A 3N3
Tel *(506) 449 0100*
A First Nations-run restaurant on Union Street near the waterfront. The menu features upmarket dishes prepared using the daily catch, including whole Atlantic lobster, diver-caught scallops and haddock four ways.

FREEPORT: Lavena's Catch Café $
Seafood
15 Hwy 217, NS, B0V 1B0
Tel *(902) 839 2517*
Not very fancy but considered one of the best seafood restaurants in Nova Scotia. Try the lobster dinner, halibut chowder, or scallops. Live music at weekends.

The unassuming exterior of Fundy Restaurant, Digby's popular seafood spot

For more information on types of restaurants *see page 361*

GEORGETOWN:
Clamdiggers Beach House
and Restaurant $
Seafood
7 West St., PE, C0A 1L0
Tel *(902) 652 2466*
Big portions of fresh seafood
served up at this beachside
eatery. Enjoy a pre-dinner drink
on the restaurant deck. Famous
for the fried scallops and clams.

HALIFAX: Bistro Le Coq $$
French
1584 Argyle St., NS, B3J 2B3
Tel *(902) 407 4564*
Casual yet elegant spot offering
French-style cooking. Enjoy
succulent oysters, light crepes,
juicy steak *frites*, old-fashioned
cocktails, and decadent desserts.

DK Choice

HALIFAX:
Chives Canadian Bistro $$$
Contemporary Canadian
1537 Barrington St., NS, B3J 1Z4
Tel *(902) 420 9626*
An unforgettable meal here
always starts with a brown paper
bag of biscuits served with
bowls of warm molasses to dip
them in. Sample some of the
best local charcuterie, cheeses,
seafood, meat, and vegetarian
dishes matched with Nova
Scotian wines. Chef Craig Finn
has also published three best-
selling cookbooks.

LA HAVE: LaHave Bakery $
Café
Hwy 331, NS, B0R 1G0
Tel *(902) 688 2908*
Take a quaint cable ferry to this
bakery café for great soups and
excellent sandwiches. Guests
can sit in the antique-furnished
interiors, on the sunny front
porch, or on the dock at the back.

LUNENBURG: Salt Shaker
Deli $
International
124 Montague St., NS, B0J 2C0
Tel *(902) 640 3434*
Serves award-winning smoked
seafood chowder, steaming
bowls of local mussels, and
fishcakes. Delicious thin-crust
pizzas, and Asian-inspired
dishes as well.

LUNEBERG: Fleur de Sel $$$
French
53 Montague St., NS, B0J 2C0
Tel *(902) 640 2121*
Beautiful and innovative food in
a relaxed setting. The changing
menu uses local produce with
high-end ingredients such as foie

gras, duck, and lobster. Limited
seating, so book ahead.

MABOU: Red Shoe Pub $
Pub
11533 Route 19, NS, B0E 1X0
Tel *(902) 945 2996*
Lively pub owned by famous
Canadian musicians The Rankin
Sisters. Delicious pub food
served by friendly staff. Live
music adds a Cape Breton
cultural experience.

MARGATE: Shipwright's Café $$
Contemporary Canadian
11869 Route 6, PE, C0B 1M0
Tel *(902) 836 3403*
A farm-to-table experience in
a country home with produce
grown on site. Savour delicious
food lovingly prepared by the
chef, who is also the owner. Save
room for the Enticing desserts.

MIRIMACHI: 1809 Restaurant &
Bar $$
Seafood
1809 Water St., NB, E1N 1B2
Tel *(506) 773 5651*
Enjoy fresh seafood on a huge
sunny deck overlooking scenic
Miramichi River. Salmon prepared
in 20 different ways, and plenty
more seafood and pasta besides.

MONCTON: Pump House
Brewery $$
Pub
5 Orange Ln, NB, E1C 4L6
Tel *(506) 855 2337*
This pub serves great food and a
range of microbrews. Particularly
excellent thin-crust pizzas. A local
favorite for weekend evenings.

MONTAGUE: Windows on
the Water Café $$
Seafood
106 Sackville St., PE, C0A 1R0
Tel *(902) 838 2080*
Well-prepared hearty meals in a
cozy setting. Great views over the
water. Delicious seafood dishes
are served in large portions. Save
room for the bread pudding.

Colourful interior of Halifax's Chives Canadian Bistro

NEW GLASGOW: New Glasgow
Lobster Suppers $$
Seafood
604 Route 258, Hunter River, PE,
C0A 1N0
Tel *(902) 964 2870*
Though a bit of a tourist trap,
Lobster Suppers is still worth a
visit for an authentic Maritimes
lobster experience. The lobster
meal comes with unlimited sides,
soft-drinks, and desserts. Try the
mile-high lemon meringue pie.

PEGGY'S COVE: Rhubarb
Restaurant $$
Contemporary Canadian
8650 Peggy's Cove Rd, Indian
Harbour, NS, B3Z 3P4
Tel *(902) 821 3013*
This gem amongst lots of tourist
traps serves excellent fresh, local
cuisine. The creative menu has
plenty of choice. Great service
and beautiful views.

QUISPAMSIS:
Smoking Pig BBQ $$
Barbecue
515 Hampton Rd., NB, E2E 3W8
Tel *(506) 847 7672* **Closed** *Mon &*
Tue
The house specialty at this
family-friendly place is wood-
smoked ribs, cooked over the
authentic pit barbecue, but there
are enough creative veggie sides
to satisfy non-carnivores.

RUSTICO: The Pearl Café $$$
Contemporary Canadian
7792 Cavendish Rd, PE, C0A 1X0
Tel *(902) 963 2111*
Considered by locals one of Prince
Edward Island's best restaurants,
Pearl serves delicious food in a
quaint setting. Fantastic decor
and prompt service. Book ahead.

SAINT ANDREWS: Rossmount
Inn $$$
Contemporary Canadian
4599 Route 127, NB, E5B3S7
Tel *(506) 529 3351*
Located in a grand mansion,
Rossmount Inn offers a great
fine-dining
experience with
an emphasis on
decadent, locally
sourced fresh food,
including lobster
and suckling pig.

SAINT JOHN:
Thandi's $$
Indian/International
33 Canterbury St., NB,
E2L 2C6
Tel *(506) 648 2377*
Housed in a
beautifully renovated
heritage building,

Thandi's primarily serves superb Indian food, but also fabulous steaks and seafood. Popular bar.

SHEDIAC: The Tait House $$
Contemporary Canadian
293 Main St., NB, E4P 2A8
Tel *(506) 532 4233*
Fine dining in a restored historic home. Relish seafood made with locally sourced ingredients. Extensive wine list, attentive service, and a buzzing atmosphere.

SHELBURNE: The Sea Dog Saloon $$
Seafood
1 Dock St., NS, B0T 1W0
Tel *(902) 875 1131*
Pub and restaurant with a big deck over the water that serves hearty portions of quintessential Nova Scotian food. Be sure to sample the salt cod dinner or the award-winning chowder.

SOURIS: 21 Breakwater $
Seafood
21 Breakwater St., PE, C0A 2B0
Tel *(902) 687 2556*
Situated on the far west of Prince Edward Island, where boats from the mainland dock, and serving local seafood, artisan burgers, and hearty sandwiches. Enjoy waterfront views. .

WOLFVILLE: Rosie's $$
Pub
460 Main St, NS, B4P 1E2
Tel *(902) 542 0059*
A homey spot where locals come to tuck into Canadian comfort food, from ribs to fried haddock. Pair your choice from the menu with a taster set of ales from adjacent brewpub Paddy's .

Montreal

CHINATOWN: Maison Kam Fung $
Chinese
11779 Blvd. de Pierrefonds, Pierrefonds, H8Z 3K8
Tel *(514) 878 2888*
Try delicious Peking Duck and some of the best dim sum in the city. Range of Szechwan and Cantonese dishes to choose from as well. Lavish decor.

DOWNTOWN: Boustan $
Middle Eastern
2020 Rue Crescent, H3G 2B8
Tel *(514) 843 3576*
Inexpensive Lebanese meals with takeout and late-night delivery. Try the tasty shawarma platters, kebabs, and couscous. Range of freshly squeezed juices.

Picturesque façade of the terraced-establishment housing The Pearl Café , Rustico

DOWNTOWN: L'Orchidée de Chine $
Chinese
2017 Rue Peel, H3A 1T6
Tel *(514) 287 1878*
Stylish restaurant serving reasonably priced Hunan, Pekinese, and Szechwan cuisine. Try the crispy duck in pastry or sautéed lamb with spicy sauce.

DOWNTOWN: Restaurant Phayathai $
Thai
1235 Rue Guy, H3H 2K5
Tel *(514) 933 9949*
Come to Phayathai for classic Thai dishes such as *pad thai* noodles and green curry. Try their fragrant soups featuring ginger, coriander, and lemon. Helpful staff.

DOWNTOWN: La Station des Sports $
Pub
862 Sainte-Catharine Est, H2L 2E3
Tel *(514) 903 8571*
Sprawling sports bar with afford-able food. Especially crowded when one of the city's professional sports teams is playing. Good selection of draft beers.

DOWNTOWN: Chez la Mère Michel $$
French
1209 Rue Guy, H3H 2L3
Tel *(514) 934 0473* **Closed** *Mon*
Traditional French restaurant serving splendid cuisine in a gorgeous Victorian house since 1965. Try their Dover sole *à la meunière* and *coq au vin*. Selection of over 7,000 wines.

DOWNTOWN: Restaurant Europea $$
French
1227 Rue de la Montagne, H3G 1Z2
Tel *(514) 398 9229*
Run by acclaimed chef Jerome Ferrer. Interesting taster menus and a chef's table feature a lot of local produce. Specialties include veal, lobster, bison, *bouillabaisse*, and scallops.

DOWNTOWN: Tiradito $$
Peruvian-Japanese
1076 Rue de Bleury, H2Z 1N1
Tel *(514) 866 6776* **Closed** *Sun & Mon*
Tiradito mixes up Peruvian and Japanese cuisine in a classy yet accessible way. Tiraditos are Peruvian-style sashimi; there's also ceviches, empanadas and other street snacks.

DOWNTOWN: Le Montréalais $$$
Fine Dining
900 René-Lévesque Blvd Ouest, H3B 4A5
Tel *(514) 861 3511*
The elegant Le Montréalais, located at the Fairmont Hôtel le Reine Elizabeth, focuses on dishes that highlight seasonal and regional ingredients. Also try what are considered Montreal's best martinis in the hotel's Les Voyageurs lounge.

DOWNTOWN: Queue de Cheval $$$
Steakhouse
1181 Rue de la Montagne, H3G 1Z2
Tel *(514) 390 0091*
This upscale steakhouse is a local favorite with great ambience and service. Try the sirloin, filet mignon, or wagyu beef. Outdoor seating in the summer. Reservations are essential.

OUTREMONT: Maïko Sushi $
Japanese
387 Rue Bernard Ouest, H2V 1T6
Tel *(514) 490 1225*
Guests at Maiko Sushi get to watch the amazing chefs at work at the sushi bar. Choose from a range of steaks, *tempura*, and *teriyaki*. Outside dining in summer.

For more information on types of restaurants *see page 361*

Original 1930s decor at family-run Wilensky's Light Lunch in Saint Urbain

OUTREMONT: Les Deux Singes de Montarvie $$
Bistro
176 Rue Saint-Viateur Ouest, H2T 2L3
Tel *(514) 278 6854*   **Closed** *Sun & Mon*
This lively French bistro has a varied menu featuring Arctic char, calamari, duck, and more. Intimate ambience. Fine French wines.

OUTREMONT: Faros $$
Seafood
362 Fairmount Ouest, H2V 2G5
Tel *(514) 270 8437*
This cozy restaurant is a Montreal favorite for traditional seafood dishes. A great place for a romantic meal for two. Try the Faros Feast, which features different pairs of appetizers and mains. Book ahead.

PLATEAU MONT-ROYAL: L'Anecdote $
North American
801 Rue Rachel Est, H2J 2H7
Tel *(514) 526 7967*
Arguably some of Montreal's best burgers and great home-made mayonnaise. Classic 1950s decor with movie posters and chrome fittings. Good wine list.

PLATEAU MONT-ROYAL: Au Pied de Cochon $
Bistro
536 Ave. Duluth Est, H2L 1A9
Tel *(514) 281 1114*   **Closed** *Mon & Tue*
Extremely popular bistro helmed by celebrity chef Martin Picard. Wonderful tender meat and *foie gras*. Try their signature dish, Duck in a Can.

PLATEAU MONT-ROYAL: Aux Vivres $
Vegetarian
4631 Blvd Saint-Laurent, H2T 1R2
Tel *(514) 842 3479*
What started as a tiny place in 1997 is now one of the city's best vegetarian eateries. Serves vegan and gluten-free fare. No alcohol.

PLATEAU MONT-ROYAL: Café Santropol $
Contemporary Canadian
3990 Rue Saint-Urbain, H2W 1K2
Tel *(514) 842 3110*
Trendy restaurant that makes the most of its Plateau setting with summer dining in a "secret" garden. Serves delicious soups, sandwiches, and desserts.

PLATEAU MONT-ROYAL: L'Express $
Bistro
3927 Rue Saint-Denis, H2W 2M4
Tel *(514) 845 5333*
Parisian-style bistro serving reasonably priced French fare. Specialties include fish soup with Gruyère croutons. Extensive wine cellar.

PLATEAU MONT-ROYAL: Pintxo $
Basque
256 Rue Roy Est, H2W 1M6
Tel *(514) 844 0222*
Experience a Basque journey of flavor at Pintxo, named after the traditional dish of slices of bread with different toppings: salmon tartar, charcuterie, and cheeses.

DK Choice

PLATEAU MONT-ROYAL: Schwartz's Montréal Hebrew Delicatessen $
Deli
3895 Blvd. Saint-Laurent, H2W 1L9
Tel *(514) 842 4813*
Romanian-Jewish immigrants made smoked brisket a staple Montreal meal in 1928, when they opened what is now a landmark deli. The food at the Hebrew Delicatessen is consistently good and popular. Choose from lean, medium, or fatty smoked meat. No alcohol. Long lines so expect to wait.

PLATEAU MONT-ROYAL: Thanjai Restaurant $
Indian
4759 Ave. Van Horne, H3W 1H8
Tel *(514) 419 9696*   **Closed** *Tue*
This popular spot grew from a small takeout place to the full restaurant it is today. Serves a range of flavorful, authentic south Indian dishes such as *dosa, idli,* and *pongal.* No alcohol.

PLATEAU MONT-ROYAL: Lawrence Restaurant $$
French
5201 Blvd. St.-Laurent, H2T 1S4
Tel *(514) 503 1070*   **Closed** *Mon*
This bustling restaurant serves great seafood – especially lobster – and tender meats. Mouth-watering home-smoked trout and popular brunches. Attentive, knowledgeable service.

PLATEAU MONT-ROYAL: Moishe's $$
Steakhouse
3961 Blvd Saint-Laurent, H2W 1Y4
Tel *(514) 845 3509*
A landmark of the boisterous Jewish Quarter, serving locally raised beef and twice-baked Monte Carlo potatoes.

PLATEAU MONT-ROYAL: Bistro L'Entrepont $$$
French
4622 Ave. de l'Hôtel de Ville, H2T 2B9
Tel *(514) 845 1369*
Small, unpretentious bistro with smart, friendly service and a small but varied menu. BYOB.

PLATEAU MONT-ROYAL: Provisions $$$
Contemporary Canadian
1268 Ave Van Horne, H2V 1K6
Tel *(514) 508 0828* **Closed** *Sun & Mon*
Elegant 30-seat spot for creative, exquisitely presented dishes. There's no menu: ingredients sourced from the markets each day are chalked up on a board to give an idea of what to expect in either the 5- or 7-course set menu.

SAINT URBAIN: Wilensky's Light Lunch $
Diner
34 Ave. Fairmount Ouest, H2T 2L9
Tel *(514) 271 0247*   **Closed** *Sun*
Inexpensive 1930s diner with great period decor. Don't miss the Wilensky's Special: a salami and bologna roll with mustard. Delicious home-made cherry cola.

VIEUX-MONTREAL: Le Cartet $
French
106 Rue McGill, H2Y 2E5
Tel *(514) 871 8887*
Trendy boutique restaurant known for its mimosa-accompanied

breakfasts and brunch. Generous servings and a salad-sandwich bar at front. Good duck *confit* salad and home-made soups.

VIEUX-MONTREAL: Olive et Gourmando $
Café
351 Rue Saint-Paul Ouest, H2Y 2A7
Tel *(514) 350 1083*   **Closed** *Sun & Mon*
Superb little café serving breakfast and lunch. Melt-in-your-mouth croissants and delicious home-made iced tea. Vegan options.

VIEUX-MONTREAL: Stash Café $
Polish
200 Rue Saint-Paul Ouest, H2Y 1Z9
Tel *(514) 845 6611*
A great introduction to home-style Polish cuisine. Delicious soul food such as hot borscht, *perogies* (dumplings), *nalesniki* (crepes), and an unusual sausage salad.

VIEUX-MONTREAL: Tuck Shop $$
Bistro
4662 Rue Notre-Dame Ouest, H4C 1S7
Tel *(514) 439 7432*   **Closed** *Sun & Mon*
Tuck Shop is a dinner-only bistro with a changing seasonal menu. Try the beef tartar, crispy pork belly, or home-made ravioli. Finish with the divine Quebec cheese plate.

VIEUX-MONTREAL: Le Club Chasse et Pêche $$$
Canadian
423 Rue Saint-Claude, H2Y 3B6
Tel *(514) 861 1112*   **Closed** *Sun & Mon*
Leather-bound menu featuring iconic Canadian fare – exceptional venison, duck, salmon, oysters, and scallops. Excellent dessert list.

Freshly made croissants and sandwiches on display at Montreal's Olive et Gourmando

VIEUX-MONTREAL: Toqué! $$$
French
900 Place Jean-Paul-Riopelle, H2Z 2B2
Tel *(514) 499 2084*   **Closed** *Sun & Mon*
The innovative chefs at this fine-dining French restaurant offer beautifully presented fusion meals featuring duck, venison, Arctic char, lamb, and salmon. Extensive list of French and other international wines.

Quebec City and the Saint Lawrence River

BAIE SAINT-PAUL: Le Saint-Pub $
Pub
2 Rue Racine, Baie-Saint-Paul, QC, G3Z 2P8
Tel *(418) 240 2332*
Popular English-style pub located in the heart of town. Excellent beer-tasting menu with many freshly brewed beers. Great pub food served in generous portions.

BAIE SAINT-PAUL: Le Mouton Noir $$
French
43 Rue Sainte-Anne, QC, G3Z 1N9
Tel *(418) 240 3030*   **Closed** *Mon & Tue*
"The Black Sheep" has a gorgeous summer patio overlooking the Gouffre River. Serves award-winning seafood; try the scallops and seared tuna with *ratatouille*. Romantic atmosphere and attentive staff.

BAIE-COMEAU: Restaurant La Cache d'Amélie $$$
French
37 Marquette, Baie-Comeau, QC, G4Z 1K4
Tel *(418) 296 3722*
Upscale restaurant serving what is considered some of the best food on the North Shore. Seasonal menu offering delicious regional fare. Great wine list.

BAS SAINT LAURENT, NOTRE-DAME-DU-LAC: Auberge Marie Blanc $$
Traditional Canadian
2629 Rue Commerciale Sud, Témiscouata-sur-le-Lac, QC, G0L 1X0
Tel *(418) 899 6747*   **Closed** *Oct–mid-May*
Located in a quaint summertime inn, the Auberge Marie Blanc restaurant has a beautiful patio overlooking Lake Temiscouta. Superb regional dishes that focus on locally grown produce – *pour votre santé* (for your health). No alcohol.

Stylish, colorful interior of Montreal's Tuck Shop bistro

CHARLEVOIX, SAINT-SIMEON: Auberge sur Mer $$
Seafood
109 Rue du Quai, QC, G0T 1X0
Tel *(418) 638 2674*   **Closed** *Nov–May*
Inn and restaurant with a panoramic view of the river. Basic but delicious meals including salads, sandwiches, and soups. The daily specials may include crab *bisque* and Matane shrimps. There is also a children's menu.

HAVRE-SAINT-PIERRE: Restaurant Chez Julie $
International
1023 Rue Dulcinée, QC, G0G 1P0
Tel *(418) 538 3070*
This unpretentious seafood restaurant is popular with locals. Try the smoked salmon pizza or seafood pizza with *béchamel* sauce. Friendly staff.

ILE D'ORLÉANS, SAINT PIERRE: Le Vieux-Presbytère $$
Traditional Canadian
1247 Rue Msgr. d'Esgly, QC, G0A 4E0
Tel *(418) 828 9723*
Housed in a presbytery converted to an inn. The cozy, casual dining room gorgeous views of the Saint Lawrence River. Venison, bison, and ostrich, and a range of seafood dishes are part of the daily *table d'hôte* specialties.

ILES-DE-LA-MADELEINE, L'ÉTANG-DU-NORD: La Table des Roy $$
French
1188 Chemin La Vernière, QC, G4T 3E6
Tel *(418) 986 3004*   **Closed** *Oct–May*
Enjoy a truly gastronomic experience at the former family home of chef Johanne Vigneault. Delicious lobster ravioli, island *bouillabaisse*, and lamb. Locally sourced ingredients, such as smoked herring, where possible. Reservations mandatory.

For more information on types of restaurants *see page 361*

LAC-SAINT-JEAN, SAINT-GEDEON: Microbrasserie du Lac-St-Jean $
Pub
120 Rue de la Plage, St.-Gédéon, QC, G0W 2P0
Tel *(418) 345 8758* **Closed** *Sep–May; Mon–Wed*
This microbrewery has a great selection of Quebec beers. Delicious regional pub food, including a trout platter, accompanies the drinks.

LA MALBAIE: Auberge des Peupliers $$
Traditional Canadian
381 Rue St.-Raphael, QC, G5A 2N8
Tel *(418) 665 4423*
A fine example of the *Route des Saveurs* (flavor trail) in Quebec's Charlevoix area. The daily local-food specials may include sturgeon and lamb. Fantastic farm-fresh salad.

MATANE: Belle Plage $$$
Seafood
1310 Matane-sur-Mer, QC, G4W 3M6
Tel *(418) 562 2323* **Closed** *Oct–Apr*
Hotel Belle Plage has a great seafood restaurant overlooking the Saint Lawrence River. Features an on-site smokehouse. Don't miss the delectable smoked salmon infused with cognac. Vegetarian and gluten-free options available.

PERCE: La Maison du Pêcheur $
Seafood
155 Place du Quai, QC, G0C 2L0
Tel *(418) 782 5331* **Closed** *mid-Oct–May*
Popular with locals, this Percé restaurant specializes in fresh salmon tartar with seaweed. Other seafood items on the menu include lobster, cod's tongues and cheeks, snow crab, ocean catfish, scallops, and halibut. Great ocean views.

QUEBEC CITY: Le Cochon Dingue Champlain $
Regional
46 Blvd. Champlain, QC, G1K 4H5
Tel *(418) 692 2013*
One of four branches in the city, Le Cochon Dingue is a popular Quebec restaurant. Great choice for families, with a children's menu and games. Try the steak *frites*, ribs, and mussel trios. Hearty breakfast menu. French wines.

QUEBEC CITY: Hobbit Bistro $$
Bistro
700 Rue Saint-Jean, QC, G1R 1R1
Tel *(418) 647 2677*
Featuring Hobbit-inspired artworks, this local hangout serves affordable, delicious bistro

A range of brews offered on tap at Les Brasseurs de Temps in Gatineau

fare. Menu changes regularly. Enjoy a refreshing Montreal McAuslan microbrew.

QUEBEC CITY: L'Improviste Restaurant $$
French
44 Rue des Jardins, G1R 4L7
Tel *(418) 692 1666*
Several intimate and elegant dining rooms, some private. Go for the *escargots*, Caesar salad, caribou with juniper berries, or deer stew. Delicious coffee and dessert. Reserve ahead.

DK Choice

QUEBEC CITY: Aux Anciens Canadiens $$$
Traditional Canadian
34 Rue Saint-Louis, QC, G1R 4P3
Tel *(418) 692 1627*
Located in the oldest house in Quebec, dating to 1675, Aux Anciens Canadiens takes guests on a culinary journey back in time. The staff, dressed in period costumes, serve authentic, traditional dishes from the region. Try the indulgent Quebec tasting meat platter for two. Children's menu available as well.

RIMOUSKI: Bistro L'Ardoise $$
Bistro
152 Rue Saint-Germain Est, QC, G5L 1A8
Tel *(418) 732 3131* **Closed** *Sun*
Trendy bistro serving regional produce. Try the special soups such as soubise, and mains such as stuffed rabbit and fresh lamb. Great foie gras and moussaka.

SAINTE-FLAVIE: Capitaine Homard $$
Seafood
180 Route de la Mer, QC, G0J 2L0
Tel *(418) 775 8046* **Closed** *mid-Sep–Apr*
Serving food since 1967, Capitaine Homard offers

0.5–2.2 kg (1–5 lb) fresh Gaspesian lobsters as well as crab, shrimp, and smoked salmon. Try their lobster *bisque*, and clam chowder.

Southern and Northern Quebec

CHAMBLY: Fourquet-Fourchette $$
Regional
1887 Ave. Bourgogne, QC, J3L 1Y8
Tel *(450) 447 6370*
Summertime terrace overlooking Fort Chambly. Traditional Quebec cuisine, featuring recipes dating to the early settlers' period. Food paired with delicious beer from the local brewery, Unibroue.

GATINEAU: Les Brasseurs de Temps $
Pub
170 Rue Montcalm, QC, J8X 2M2
Tel *(819) 205 4999*
Lively pub and brewery with excellent craft beers and 12 fresh brews on tap. "Museum of Beer" on site. Great upscale pub food, including duck burgers.

Beautiful table setting at Quebec's Aux Anciens Canadiens

GATINEAU: Soif $
Wine Bar
88 Rue Montcalm, QC, J8X 2L7
Tel *(819) 600 7643*
Popular local hangout for the creatively inclined. The mackerel fritters and bison tartare with croutons are perfect accompaniments to an extensive wine list.

GATINEAU: Le Pied de Cochon $$
French
248 Rue Montcalm, QC, J8Y 3C1
Tel *(819) 777 5808* **Closed** *Sun & Mon*
A local landmark, Le Pied de Cochon is an upscale, fine-dining restaurant serving traditional French cuisine. The *goût-du-jour* (taste of the day) is a special delight not to be missed.

GATINEAU: Sterling $$
French
835 Rue Jacques-Cartier, QC, J8T 2W3
Tel *(819) 568 8788* **Closed** *Sun*
Upscale steak and seafood restaurant in a historic building with a breathtaking view of the Gatineau River. Leave some room for the classic French desserts.

LAURENTIAN MOUNTAINS: Chocolaterie Marie-Claude $
Café
1090 Rue Valiquette, Sainte-Adele, QC, J8B 2M3
Tel *(450) 229 3991* **Closed** *Mon, Wed, Thu*
Choose from more than 30 varieties of delicious handmade chocolates. Great waffles, salads, and croissants. Gelato or chocolate fondue for dessert. Excellent espresso and *café au lait*.

LAURENTIAN MOUNTAINS: Kayak Café $
Canadian
2202 Chemin du Moulin, Labelle, QC, J0T 1H0
Tel *(819) 686 1111* **Closed** *Oct–Apr*
A summertime restaurant that is also a base for canoe, kayak, and SUP tours. Their versatile menu features soups, mushroom and brie on toast, steaks, mussels, and Queen Elizabeth cake.

LAURENTIAN MOUNTAINS: A L'Express Gourmand $$
French
31 Rue Morin, Sainte Adele, QC, J8B 2M3
Tel *(450) 229 1915*
Ensconced in a 100-year-old schoolhouse, this restaurant is renowned for simple yet delicious French dishes lovingly made from scratch.

Picturesque seating at the popular Outaouais restaurant, Les Fougères

LAURENTIAN MOUNTAINS: Restaurant Le Cheval de Jade $$$
French
688 Rue de Saint-Jovite, Mont Tremblant, QC, J8E 3J8
Tel *(819) 425 5233* **Closed** *Sun & Mon*
The chef at this fine dining spot is a *canardier* (duck) master, hence the duck dishes are a must, as is as their specialty, the Mediterranean *bouillabaisse*. Choose from the Discovery and Gastronomic menus. Reservations essential.

MONTEREGIE: L'Auberge des Gallants $$
Regional
1171 Chemin Saint-Henri, Sainte-Marthe, QC, J0P 1W0
Tel *(450) 459 4241*
Located inside a wildlife sanctuary, L'Auberge des Gallants is a spa, hotel, restaurant, and sugar shack all in one. Offers upscale dining amid tranquility. There is a generous Sunday brunch.

OUTAOUAIS: Café 349 $
Contemporary Canadian
349 Rue Main, Shawville, QC, J0X 2Y0
Tel *(819) 647 6424* **Closed** *Sun*
Owner Ruth Smiley-Hahn bakes mouthwatering muffins, and desserts, and serves tasty all-natural country-style meals seasoned with fresh herbs.

OUTAOUAIS: Le Hibou $$
Bistro
757 Riverside, Wakefield, QC, J0X 3G0
Tel *(819) 459 8883*
Casual bistro with outdoor, riverfront seating. Delicious home-made pescatarian (fish and vegetarian) food. Sample the beet salad and French onion soup. Friendly service.

OUTAOUAIS: L'Orée du Bois $$
French
15 Kingsmere Rd, Chelsea, QC, J9B 1A1
Tel *(819) 827 0332* **Closed** *Mon, Sun (Nov–Apr)*
Housed in a traditional farmhouse with cozy wooden interiors. Serves great seasonal fare: asparagus, mushrooms, raspberries, and regional meats. On-site smoke-house uses maple for flavoring.

DK Choice

OUTAOUAIS: Les Fougères $$$
Fine Dining
783 Route 105, Chelsea, QC, J9B 1P1
Tel *(819) 827 8942*
Experience country elegance in the forested Gatineau Hills. Les Fougères is extremely popular for its fresh regional dishes paired with fine wines selected by the resident sommelier. There is a fantastic 11-course tasting menu. The monthly *table d'hôte* features seasonal, organic local foods. Children's menu available as well.

RIGAUD: Sucrerie de la Montagne $$
Traditional Canadian
300 Rang Saint-Georges, QC, J0P IP0
Tel *(450) 451 0831*
Traditional sugar shack open year-round. In season, take a tour of the sap-gathering and syrup-production facilities. Stock up on maple-pancake mix, maple syrup, and maple candies from the shop.

ROUYN-NORANDA: Brochetterie La Maison Grecque $
Greek
152 Ave. Principale, QC, J9X 4P5
Tel *(819) 797 0086*
A welcoming atmosphere with Greek music in the background. Home-made locally smoked fish, grilled meats, and *baklava* are their specialty *brochettes* (meat on a skewer).

SAINT-DENIS-SUR-RICHELIEU: Les Chanterelles du Richelieu $$$
French
611 Chemin des Patriotes, QC, J0H 1K0
Tel *(450) 787 1167* **Closed** *Jan–mid-Mar*
Serves quality regional cuisine in a fine dining setting, with dishes featuring Richelieu products, wherever possible. Delicious bison osso-buco, foie gras, and filet mignon.

For more information on types of restaurants *see page 361*

SHERBROOKE: Auguste $$
French
82 Rue Wellington N., QC, J1H 5B8
Tel *(819) 565 9559*
Quintessential bistro fare at its finest, from duck breast to beef tartare. Don't skip the housemade desserts.

SHERBROOKE: Restaurant Le Chou-Bruxelles $$
Belgian
1461 Rue Galt Ouest, QC, J1H 2A9
Tel *(819) 564 1848* **Closed** *Mon*
This Belgian joint serves well-prepared rabbit, mussels, salmon, Brome duck, and other regional specialties. Choose from *table d'hôte* and gastronomic menus. Bring your own bottle.

TROIS RIVIERES: Le Manoir du Spaghetti $
Italian
1147 Rue Hart, QC, G9A 4S3
Tel *(819) 373 0204*
Enjoy simple pastas and a tasty pulled pork pizza in a casual, welcoming dining room.

Toronto

DOWNTOWN: Asian Legend $
Chinese
418 Dundas St. W., M5T 1G7
Tel *(416) 977 3909*
Traditional China dim sum and stir fry. Other specialties include crispy pancake, Szechuan smoked duck, and bean curd. Tsingtao beer and jasmine tea.

DOWNTOWN: Ethiopian House $
Ethiopian
4 Irwin Ave., M4Y 1K9
Tel *(416) 923 5438*
Serves authentic Ethiopian food meant to be eaten with one's hands. Scoop up spicy chickpeas, chard, or stewed meats with *injera* bread. Generous portions, but service can be slow.

DOWNTOWN: Karine's $
Vegan
109 McCaul, Unit 32, M5T 3K5
Tel *(416) 591 0863*
Home-made vegan food. The all-day breakfast sometimes features meat options. Wide selection of gluten-free desserts. Delicious soy-milk fruit shakes. No alcohol.

DOWNTOWN: Manpuku Modern Japanese Eatery $
Japanese
105 McCaul St., Unit 29–31, M5T 2X4
Tel *(416) 979 6763* **Closed** *Sun*
Basic but reliable noodle house. Try *takosen* (octopus) and *unatama*

don (barbecued eel and rice), both hard to find in Toronto, especially at such reasonable prices.

DOWNTOWN: Torteria San Cosme $
Spanish
181 Baldwin St., M5T 1L9
Tel *(416) 599 2855* **Closed** *Sun*
A vibrant spot serving Mexican street-style sandwiches on crusty telera bread rolls, with tasty fillings such as smoked ham with Oaxaca cheese, chicken mole, pulled pork, or huevos and chorizo.

DOWNTOWN: 309 Dhaba Indian Excellence $$
Indian
309 King St. W., M5V 1J5
Tel *(416) 740 6622*
Unpretentious Indian restaurant serving up scrumptious butter chicken, sizzling *tandoori* dishes, lamb aubergine, and okra chicken. Also has a grand 60-item luncheon buffet.

DOWNTOWN: Marben $$
Regional
488 Wellington St. W., M5V 1C9
Tel *(416) 979 1990*
Closed *Mon, Tue lunch*
Despite its industrial styling the interior is cozy, and there's a dining terrace outside. The menu features fresh, seasonal, regional fare. Meat-lovers will enjoy the charcuterie board appetizer. Good wine list.

DOWNTOWN: N'Awlins Jazz Bar & Grill $$
Cajun-Creole
299 King St. W., M5V 0C4
Tel *(416) 595 1958*
N'Awlins is a popular bar and grill featuring live jazz music. House specials here include southern-state specialties such as spicy seafood, surf 'n' turf, jambalaya, gumbo, and blackened catfish.

Friendly and knowledgeable staff enhance the experience.

DOWNTOWN: Rodney's Oyster House $$
Seafood
469 King St. W., M5V 1K4
Tel *(416) 363 8105* **Closed** *Sun*
As the name indicates, Rodney's specialty is oysters, both raw and pan-fried. Clams, mussels, crab, lobsters, scallops, and shrimp are also on the menu. Good range of salt and freshwater fish. Four types of chowder available.

DOWNTOWN: Le Sélect Bistro $$
French
432 Wellington St. W., M5V 1E3
Tel *(416) 596 6405*
Wonderfully authentic Parisian bistro in a bright, open space with curved banquettes. Expect the best of bistro cuisine – cassoulet, bouillabaisse, haunch of venison, and steak tartare. Endless wine list.

DOWNTOWN: Sultan's Tent and Café Moroc $$
Moroccan
49 Front St., M5E 1B3
Tel *(416) 961 0601*
Groups can sit down to a traditional *diffa* (lavish banquet) at Sultan's Tent or enjoy a meal at the café. Don't miss the *keskesu* Casablanca and rack of lamb. Evening entertainment includes belly dancing.

DOWNTOWN: Wildfire Steakhouse & Wine Bar $$
Steakhouse
8 Colborne St., M5E 1E1
Tel *(416) 350 8188*
Upscale steakhouse with a cozy, candlelit atmosphere. House specialties include sterling silver steaks spiced and aged for four weeks. Great *churrasco* (barbecue) ribs, chicken, and lamb.

Lil' Baci, a trendy Italian restaurant in Toronto's East End

DOWNTOWN: Alo $$$
Contemporary Canadian
163 Spadina Ave., M5V 2L6
Tel *(416) 260 2222* **Closed** *Sun & Mon*
French flavors married with modern techniques characterize the tasting menus prepared by top chef Patrick Kriss, an alumnus of the two-Michelin-starred Daniel Boulud.

DOWNTOWN: Benihana $$$
Japanese
Fairmont Royal York Hotel, 100 Front St. W., M5J 1E3
Tel *(416) 860 5002* **Closed** *Sun & Mon, lunch*
Part of the global Japanese chain known for its *hibachi* steaks and *teppanyaki*. Steak, chicken, seafood, fresh vegetables, and sushi prepared in front of guests.

DOWNTOWN: Biagio $$$
Italian
155 King St. E., M5C 1G9
Tel *(416) 366 4040* **Closed** *Sun, Sat lunch*
Located inside the Saint Lawrence Town Hall, Biagio has a formal dining room and a garden patio. Try the *risotto ai funghi* (risotto with mushrooms) and *sella di'agnello* (rack of lamb).

DOWNTOWN: Biff's Bistro $$$
French
4 Front St. E., M5E 1G4
Tel *(416) 860 0086*
Upscale, modern bistro. Tasty steak *frites*, beef *bourguignon*, and haddock chowder. Oysters available at the bar after 5pm. Exceptional baked-to-order madeleines.

DOWNTOWN: Buca $$$
Italian
604 King St. W., M5V 1M6
Tel *(416) 865 1600*
Basement *osteria* serving earthy Italian fare. It is a favorite with food critics. It offers quirky items such as bison prosciutto, and delicious *nodini* (garlic ball rolls).

DOWNTOWN: Bymark $$$
International
66 Wellington St. W., M5K 1J3
Tel *(416) 777 1144* **Closed** *Sun*
Upscale restaurant in the financial heart of the city. Courtyard bar with views of the Mies van der Rohe towers. Great veal *braciole* with braised beef cheeks, and tuna puttanesca.

DOWNTOWN: La Palette $$$
French
492 Queen St. W., M5V 2B2
Tel *(416) 929 4900*
Great spot for a romantic dinner, with a classic bistro ambience.

Snowy table linen at North 44°, one of Toronto's most upscale restaurants

Market-fresh ingredients are conjured into French standards such as cassoulet with confit duck leg and *moules frites*. International wines and beers.

EAST END: Kalyvia $
Greek
420 Danforth Ave., M4K 1P3
Tel *(416) 463 3333*
Home-style Mediterranean food served taverna-style. Patio seating that allows for people-watching in the Greek neighborhood. Fantastic seafood *pikilia* combos.

EAST END: Lady Marmalade $
Mexican
898 Queen St. E., M4M 1J3
Tel *(647) 351 7645*
Quirky breakfast, brunch, and lunch spot in hopping Leslieville. Delicious food with a tinge of Mexico and creative twists on eggs Benedict. Prepare to join the line on weekends. Cash only.

EAST END: Lil' Baci $
Italian
892 Queen St. E., M4M 1J2
Tel *(416) 465 4888*
Popular Italian joint dishing up delicious pizzas, pastas, and salads from southern Italy. Ontario craft beers available on tap along with Canadian and Italian wines.

EAST END: Off the Hook $
International
749 Broadview Ave., M4K 2P6
Tel *(416) 465 4356*
Fancy fish n' chips in a casual setting. Choose your fish, batter, and sauce to go with delicious fries and even better coleslaw. Decent local beers on tap.

EAST END: The Real Jerk $$
Jamaican
842 Gerrard St. E., M4M 1Y7
Tel *(416) 463 6055* **Closed** *Sun*
High-quality Jamaican food from jerk dishes to rotis is

complemented by an extensive rum selection. Busiest on lively karaoke nights.

EAST END: Rodeo Brazilian Steakhouse $$
Brazilian
95 Danforth Ave., M4K 1N2
Tel *(416) 465 0969* **Closed** *Mon*
Authentic *rodizio* (steakhouse) with an all-you-can-eat Brazilian menu. Choose from fried plantains, fish, roasted pineapple, and *churrascaria*. Live music.

EAST END: Tapas at Embrujo $$
Spanish
97 Danforth Ave., M4K 1N2
Tel *(416) 778 0007*
A lively place serving seafood, vegetarian tapas, and paella. Good selection of Spanish sherries and wines. Live flamenco shows on Sunday.

NORTH: North 44° $$$
Fine Dining
2537 Yonge St., M4P 2H7
Tel *(416) 487 4897*
Elegant Canadian fine dining in a contemporary setting. Popular with celebrities. Gourmet seared duck breast, crisp-skinned chicken, and halibut on the menu.

WEST END: Café 668 $
Vegetarian/Asian
885 Dundas St. W., M6J 1V9
Tel *(416) 703 0668*
Café 668 offers an extensive menu of Vietnamese, Chinese, and Thai vegetarian cuisine. Try their tempura platters, seaweed tofu soup, or the house special *lor-hon* (vegetable stir-fry). No alcohol.

WEST END: Fresh $
Vegan
894 Queen St. W., M6J 1G3
Tel *(416) 599 4442*
Starting as a tiny juice bar, Fresh has become a Toronto institution with many locations. With an extensive, fully vegan menu, it is a haven for Toronto non-meateaters, as well as anyone in search of a healthy meal.

WEST END: Terroni $
Italian
720 Queen St. W., M5C 1K6
Tel *(416) 504 0320*
Lively place popular with families who come to enjoy rustic Italian fare in a shabby-chic setting. Great pizzas and plenty of other dishes. There's a second branch on Victoria St. at Adelaide and another at 1095 Yonge St. between the Rosedale and Summerhill stations.

For more information on types of restaurants *see page 361*

DK Choice
WEST END: Boralia   **$$$**
Contemporary Canadian
59 Ossington Ave., M6J 2Y9
Tel *(647) 351 5100* **Closed** *Mon & Tue*
A refreshingly unusual menu featuring modern twists on historical Canadian cuisine. Pine needle-smoked mussels and grilled whelks with *beurre blanc* are some tempting examples. Impressive wine cellar.

WEST END: Chiado   **$$$**
Seafood
864 College St., M6H 1A3
Tel *(416) 538 1910*
Considered one of the best fish restaurants in the city, Chiado flies in fresh catch from the Azores daily. Formal, traditional service and an unusual wine list of Portuguese vintages.

Ottawa and Eastern Ontario

HALIBURTON HIGHLANDS: Wild Orchid Thai Bistro   **$**
Thai
3 North Water St., ON, K0M 2K0
Tel *(705) 286 1532*
This deservedly popular family-run restaurant serves exceptional cuisine at affordable prices. No website; call ahead for timings.

HALIBURTON HIGHLANDS: Bonnie View Inn   **$$**
Traditional
2713 Kashagawigamog Lake Road, ON, K0M 1S0
Tel *(705) 457 2350* **Closed** *Mon & Tue Nov–Apr*
Looking out on Kashagawigamog Lake, this small, family-run resort has a welcoming, pine-clad dining room with a huge fireplace. Meals are carefully presented.

HALIBURTON HIGHLANDS: Rhubarb   **$$$**
Fine Dining
9201 Hwy 118 (corner of Hwy 35), Carnarvon, ON
Tel *(705) 489 4449*
This sophisticated eatery on Mirror Lake serves delicious food in an airy, rustic space that is in keeping with its country locale. Dishes are beautifully presented.

KINGSTON: Chez Piggy   **$$**
Bistro
68-R Princess St., ON, K7L 1A5
Tel *(613) 549 7673*
This popular bistro is in a secluded courtyard within a former stable.

Tasteful dining area in Chiado, West End Toronto

Serves tasty fresh fare all day that keeps folks returning to what is locally known as "The Pig."

KINGSTON: Le Chien Noir Bistro   **$$**
Bistro
69 Brock St., ON, K7L 1R8
Tel *(613) 549 5635*
Trendy place with superb farm-to-table comfort food. Range of regional and international wines served by the glass. Attentive service. Good brunch.

KINGSTON: River Mill Restaurant   **$$**
Mediterranean
2 Cataraqui St., ON, K7K 1Z7
Tel *(613) 549 5759* **Closed** *Sun, afternoon Sat*
Located in a heritage wool mill. Elegant, relaxed ambience, with a waterfront location, an unusual feature in Kingston. Great sampler plate. Extensive wine selection, with vintage and private-order wines.

OTTAWA: Light of India   **$**
Indian
730 Bank St., ON, K1S 3V4
Tel *(613) 563 4411*
An intimate and busy favorite in trendy Glebe serving food from the northern parts of India. Fantastic luncheon buffet that changes daily. Great service.

OTTAWA: New Mee Fung   **$**
Vietnamese
350 Booth St., ON, K1R 7K1
Tel *(613) 567 8228* **Closed** *Tue*
This busy and noisy joint serves possibly the best Vietnamese cuisine in Ottawa. Delectable wraps, satay soup with beef, and barbecued meats. Generous servings and attentive service. Reserve ahead.

OTTAWA: The Table Restaurant   **$**
Vegetarian
1230 Wellington St., ON, K1Y 3A1
Tel *(613) 729 5973*
Popular vegetarian eatery with a constantly changing buffet menu of organic and gluten-free dishes. Dishes are priced by the weight of the plate. No alcohol.

OTTAWA: Yang Sheng   **$**
Chinese
662 Somerset St. W, ON, K1R 5K4
Tel *(613) 235 5794*
Popular Cantonese and Schezuan restaurant with specialties such as traditional dim sum, home-made rice and noodle dishes, and barbecued duck and pork. Great soups.

OTTAWA: The Fish Market   **$$**
Seafood
54 York St., Byward Market, ON, K1N 5T1
Tel *(613) 241 3474*
The Fish Market is popular for its fresh fish dinners, lobster, and oysters. Try the Cajun blackened catfish with Creole sauce. Extensive, eclectic wine list. The wine bar bistro in the basement plays host to local jazz bands on Sunday, Tuesday, and Wednesday evenings.

OTTAWA: Sidedoor   **$$**
Fusion
18B York St., ON, K1N 5T5
Tel *(613) 562 9331*
Inspired by Asian street food, this lively place is most lauded for its tacos, starters, and warm gourmet doughnuts for dessert. Also, adenturous main course dishes such as lobster with green curry. Tapas-style service.

DK Choice
OTTAWA: Beckta Dining & Wine   **$$$**
Fine Dining
150 Elgin St., ON, K2P 1L4
Tel *(613) 238 7063*
Closed *Sat & Sun lunch*
Cutting-edge cuisine is on offer in this beautiful and stately home built in 1875. Opt for the chef-inspired tasting menu with wine-and-cheese pairing options. A separate wine bar with a light-bite menu is also available. Reserve ahead.

OTTAWA: Wilfrid's   **$$$**
Contemporary Canadian
Fairmont Château Laurier, 1 Rideau St., ON, K1N 8S7
Tel *(613) 241 1414*
Located in the elegant Fairmont Château Laurier, Wilfrid's offers resplendent buffet breakfasts and

Sunday brunch, and lighter lunches and fine dining at dinner, in a room with views of Parliament Hill. Inspired takes on Canadian classic dishes. The maple crepes are a popular breakfast choice, or for lunch try the seafood chowder. Great service.

PRINCE EDWARD COUNTY: Blumen Garden Bistro $$
Fine Dining
647 Highway 49, Picton, ON, K0K 2T0
Tel *(613) 476 6841*
Sublime creations at this destination restaurant on the edge of Picton. The savory apple-and-onion-stuffed pork tenderloin and pulled braised rabbit over homemade gnocchi are unbeatable.

The Great Lakes

BAYFIELD: Black Dog Village Pub and Bistro $
Pub
5 Main St. N., ON, N0M 1G0
Tel *(519) 565 2326*
Black Dog is a pub in a historic building, with 20 drafts on tap and a multitude of Scotch to choose from. The pub food on offer is casual, but delicious.

BAYFIELD: Little Inn of Bayfield $$$
Fine Dining
26 Main St. N., ON, N0M 1G0
Tel *(519) 565 2611*
Located in an erstwhile stagecoach stop, this is an elegant place with lovely street views. Local produce features prominently.

BEAMSVILLE: Peninsula Ridge Estate Winery $$$
Fine Dining
5600 King St. W., ON, L0R 1B0
Tel *(905) 563 0900* **Closed** *Mon & Tue*
Dine in a beautiful Queen Ann-Revival farmhouse on a hill with views of the Niagara Escarpment and Lake Ontario. Fresh local dishes pair with the perfect wine from the estate. Try foraged mushroom salad; follow with beef-cheek ravioli with scallops; finish with a seasonally inspired sorbet.

GODERICH: Ivey Dining Room at Benmiller Inn & Spa $$
Fine Dining
81175 Benmiller Rd, ON, N7A 3Y1
Tel *(800) 265 1711*
Ivey Dining Room takes pride in using locally sourced produce to prepare seasonal Canadian cuisine. Gorgeous setting in a lush valley behind a millstream.

GODERICH: Thyme on 21 $$
Fine Dining
80 Hamilton St., ON, N7A 1P9
Tel *(519) 524 4171* **Closed** *Mon*
Though billed as casual cuisine, the award-winning food and Victorian home setting make this place more fine dining than casual. Try the sirloin steak and scallops.

HAMILTON: Wass Ethiopian Restaurant $
Ethiopian
207 James St. S., ON, L8P 3A8
Tel *(289) 389 5294*
Sample traditional Ethiopian food with separate meat and vegetarian options. Participate in a coffee ceremony and taste the signature honey wine.

MUSKOKA: Oar & Paddle $$
Pub
530 Muskoka Rd N., Gravenhurst, ON, P1P 1G3
Tel *(705) 687 8618*
This pub, with wooden pews to dine on and oars on the walls, has a relaxed, rustic vibe. Great food with an Ontarian twist. Try the wild boar and blueberry burger, and the peameal bacon sandwich with brie and cranberries.

MUSKOKA: Top of the Cove $$
International
375 South Bay Rd, Honey Harbour, ON, M5H 2G4
Tel *(705) 756 3399* **Closed** *mid-Sep–mid-May*
This late-spring and summertime waterside restaurant, overlooking the Georgian Bay marina, serves delicious seafood, pasta, burgers and prime steak.

MUSKOKA: Bartlett's Lodge $$$
Fine Dining
PO Box 10004, Algonquin Park, ON, P1H 2G8
Tel *(705) 633 5543* **Closed** *mid-Oct–mid-May*
The restaurant in this picturesque Canadian log resort in the renowned Algonquin Provincial Park ferries its diners in across the lake by motorized canoe or pontoon boat. Locally farmed produce and lake fish are used to create a delicious fine-dining experience. BYOB.

NIAGARA FALLS: Elements on the Falls $$
International
6650 Niagara Pkwy, ON, L2G
Tel *(905) 354 3631*
Amazing views over the falls right from Table Rock Welcome Centre at this casual restaurant, popular with tourists. Choose from lamb, steak, veggie pastas, burgers, or locally caught perch and pickerel. Plenty of options for kids as well.

NIAGARA FALLS: Revolving Dining Room at Skylon Tower $$$
Fine Dining
5200 Robinson St., ON, L2G 2A3
Tel *(905) 356 2651*
Dine more than 213 m (700 ft) above the falls, with an ever-changing vista. The menu highlights include steak and seafood, besides lobster tails. Children's menu. Good choice of wines.

DK Choice

NIAGARA-ON-THE-LAKE: Olde Angel Inn $$
Pub
224 Regent St., ON, L0S 1J0
Tel *(905) 468 3411*
History abounds at this pub housed in Ontario's longest-running inn. Great ambience with fieldstone fireplaces, hand-hewn beams, and plank flooring. Serves traditional British pub fare, including fish and chips, and bangers and mash. Range of savory pies, including fisherman's and steak and kidney. Choose from 25 different draft beers.

Brightly lit interiors of Le Chien Noir Bistro, Kingston

For more information on types of restaurants *see page 361*

NIAGARA-ON-THE-LAKE:
Tiara $$$
Fine Dining
155 Byron St., ON, L0S 1J0
Tel *1888 669 5566*
Elegant restaurant in the stately
Queen's Landing Hotel, with
beautiful views of the marina.
Superb Sunday brunch buffet.

ST. CATHARINE'S:
Murphy's Restaurant $
Seafood
*38 Lakeport Rd, Port Dalhousie,
ON, L2N 5B4*
Tel *(905) 934 1913* **Closed** *Mon &
Tue Nov–mid-Apr*
Good location beside the original
Welland Canal. Nautical theme,
with the bar made out of a boat
hull. Children's menu.

SAULT STE. MARIE:
Arturo Ristorante $$
Italian
515 Queen St. E., ON, P6A 2A2
Tel *(705) 253 0002* **Closed** *Sun &
Mon*
A family restaurant featuring
Italian decor and wines worthy
of a Tuscan eatery. Superb pasta.
Try the house specials: *gamberoni*
(tiger shrimp) and pepper steak.

**STRATFORD: Pazzo Taverna
and Pizzeria** $
Italian
70 Ontario St., ON, N5A 3H2
Tel *(519) 273 6666* **Closed** *Mon*
Casual but elegant decor.
Gourmet pizzas featuring local
ingredients. Gathering place for
theater-goers. Great lunch spot.

**STRATFORD: The Prune
Restaurant** $$$
Fine Dining
151 Albert St., ON, N5A 3K5
Tel *(519) 271 5052* **Closed** *lunch,
Sun & Mon*
Located in Stratford's historic
downtown district, the Prune has
been serving theatergoers for
over 40 years. Fixed-price menus
featuring local, seasonal cuisine.

**STRATFORD: Revival House
Restaurant** $$$
Contemporary Canadian
70 Brunswick St., ON, N5A 6V6
Tel *(519) 273 3424* **Closed** *Mon*
Locavore destination restaurant
housed in an old church. Great
ambience. Serves fantastic modern
Canadian cuisine sourced from
nearby producers. Live music.

**THUNDER BAY: The Sovereign
Room** $$
Gastropub
220 Red River Rd, ON, P7B 1A6
Tel *(807) 343 9277* **Closed** *Sat–
Wed lunch, Mon lunch*

Simple decor, but one of the
city's best eateries. Reasonably
priced gourmet food, including
duck *confit* poutine and pork
belly. Generous portions. Good
beer selection.

WINDSOR: Motor Burger $
Diner
888 Erie St. E., ON, N9A 3Y6
Tel *(519) 252 8004*
Dine in an industrial space
specializing in creative, award-
winning burgers and small
batch beers.

WINDSOR: Smoke and Spice $
American/Barbecue
7470 Tecumseh Rd E., ON, N8T 1E9
Tel *(519) 252 4999*
Not for the faint of heart or
vegetarians, Smoke and Spice
is where Canada meets the deep
south. Delicious pulled porks
and some of the best ribs in
the city.

Central Canada

DK Choice

EDMONTON: Corso 32 $$
Italian
10345 Jasper Ave. NW., AB, T5J 1Y7
Tel *(780) 421 4622*
Minimalist decor in this
downtown dining room belies
the lavish attention paid to
the cuisine at Corso 32. Chef
Daniel Costa's delectable
Italian dishes include handmade pasta, ravioli in black
truffle sauce, velvety chicken
liver tortellini, fish with anchovy
vinaigrette, and mouthwatering
gelato for dessert. Select wines
and liquors, including grappa.
With only 34 seats in this
intimate restaurant, be sure
to book ahead.

EDMONTON:
Tres Carnales $$
Mexican
10119 100A St., AB, T5J 0R5
Tel *(780) 429 0911* **Closed** *Sun*
Cheerful eatery serving authentic
Mexican food. Choose from fresh
tacos and salsa, tortillas, and spicy
chicken. Beer and Sangria.

EDMONTON: Hardware Grill $$$
Contemporary Canadian
9698 Jasper Ave. NW., AB, T5H 3V5
Tel *(780) 423 0969* **Closed** *Sun*
This modern restaurant has a
multiple award-winning wine list.
Savour delicacies such as porcini-
crusted sea bass, Angus steaks,
and Alberta lamb. There is also a
tasting menu.

**LETHBRIDGE: Two Guys and
a Pizza Place** $
Pizzeria
316 11 St. S., AB, T1J 2N8
Tel *(403) 331 2222*
The best pizza joint in town. Try
the Pulled Pork or Honey Almond
Chicken pizza. Excellent craft
beer selection, too.

REGINA: La Bodega $$$
Spanish/Latin American
2228 Albert St., SK, S4P 2V2
Tel *(306) 546 3660* **Closed** *Mon*
Stylish restaurant serving a
creative mix of Spanish and Latin
tapas, steaks, and seafood. Start
with their lobster guacamole,
and also try the *antipasti*, foie
gras, and falafel. Sunday brunch.

REGINA:
Diplomat Steakhouse $$$
Steakhouse
2032 Broad St., SK, S4P 1Y3
Tel *(306) 359 3366*
A plush interior and intimate
booths are the hallmarks of this
award-winning steakhouse.
Choose from a range of steaks
and seafood. Flambé desserts
plus wine cellar and rare Cognacs.

The welcoming dining room at Two Guys and a Pizza Place in Lethbridge

REGINA: Willow on Wascana **$$$**
Fine Dining
3000 Wascana Dr., SK, S4P 4W7
Tel *(306) 585 3663* **Closed** *Sun*
Savor delicious seasonal Prairie cuisine in a scenic lakeview setting. Innovative dishes on the menu include artisanal produce, roasted duck, bison, and boar.

SASKATOON: Ayden Kitchen & Bar **$**
Contemporary Canadian
265 3rd Ave. S., SK, S7K 1M3
Tel *(306) 954 2590* **Closed** *Sun*
Celebrity chef Dale MacKay dishes up decadent comfort foods in a casual and atmospheric setting. Ask for the off-menu Butcher Burger.

SASKATOON: The Berry Barn **$**
Traditional Canadian
830 Valley Rd., SK, S7K 3J6
Tel *(306) 931 6767* **Closed** *Jan & Feb*
Riverfront restaurant on a pretty Saskatoon berry farm. Home-style cooking plus a great gift shop. You can pick your own berries in season, or simply enjoy them made into pies and desserts in the restaurant.

SASKATOON: The Granary **$$**
Fine Dining
2806 8th St. E., SK, S7H 0V9
Tel *(306) 373 6655*
Designed to resemble a grain elevator. The fine-dining menu includes filet mignon, prime rib, salmon, and Saskatoon berry pie.

SASKATOON: Saskatoon Station Place **$$**
Mediterranean
221 Idylwyld Dr. N., SK S7L 6V6
Tel *(306) 244 7777*
Dine in a vintage rail car or in an elegant room amid historic memorabilia. There are Greek specialties on the menu as well as steaks and seafood.

SASKATOON: Saboroso Brazilian Steakhouse **$$$**
Brazilian
2600 8 St. E. #340, SK, S7H 0V7
Tel *(306) 249 4454*
Dining is a sensory experience in this traditional Brazilian steakhouse. *Rodizio*-style carvings at the table include beef, lamb, chicken, and pork.

SASKATOON: Truffles Bistro **$$$**
French
230 21st St. E., SK, S7K 0B9
Tel *(306) 373 7779*
Traditional French cuisine prepared using local ingredients. The long narrow dining room oozes European charm.

WATERTON PARK: Wieners of Waterton **$**
Fast Food
301 Windflower Ave., AB, T0K 2M0
Tel *(403) 339 1079*
At this little lodge nestled in the mountains of the National Park, hot dogs are taken to a wonderful new level, with buns baked fresh daily, home-made sauces, and great sides. There are vegetarian options, too.

WINNIPEG: Nuburger **$**
Burgers
472 Stradbrook Ave., MB, R3L 0J9
Tel *(204) 888 1001*
Creative burgers with healthy ingredients, made with locally sourced ingredients including natural Manitoba beef and chicken. Vegan options available.

WINNIPEG: Pizzeria Gusto **$**
Italian
404 Academy Rd, MB, R3N 0B8
Tel *(204) 944 8786* **Closed** *Sun*
Imaginative gourmet pizzas are topped with local produce and baked in a wood-burning oven. There are other classic Italian dishes too, including a lobster risotto, and a mouthwatering list of wines.

WINNIPEG: Resto Gare **$$**
French
630 Rue des Meurons, MB, R2H 2P9
Tel *(204) 237 7072*
Set in a former train station in the French Quarter, Resto Gare serves delightful French cuisine. Try the French onion soup or *tourtière* (meat pie). Extensive wine list.

WINNIPEG: Segovia Tapas Bar and Restaurant **$$**
Spanish
484 Stradbrook Ave., MB, R3L 0J9
Tel *(204) 477 6500*
Lively restaurant in trendy Osborne/Corydon Village. Tasty Spanish-style dishes include chorizo and apples, ceviche, risotto, and smoked char.

Vancouver and Vancouver Island

CAMPBELL RIVER: Harbour Grill **$$$**
Fine Dining
112–1334 Island Hwy, BC, V9W 1A7
Tel *(250) 287 4143* **Closed** *Sun*
Overlooking the harbor and marina, Harbour Grill has great views and upscale seafood, steak, and poultry dishes. Try roast duck and fresh halibut. Helpful staff.

Genoa Bay Café, located right next to the water near the city of Duncan

DUNCAN: Genoa Bay Café **$$**
Café
5000 Genoa Bay Rd, BC, V9L 5Y8
Tel *(250) 746 7621*
Romantic, casual café located on the water's edge overlooking Genoa Bay. Specialties include seafood chowder, calamari, halibut and chips. Delicious desserts, including heirloom carrot cake.

**NANAIMO:
Asteras Greek Taverna** **$$**
Greek
347 Wesley St., BC, V9R 3A7
Tel *(250) 716 0451*
Excellent prices for authentic Greek food. Varied menu, with dishes such as *avgolemono* soup, *spanokopita* (traditional savory pie), *souvlaki* (Greek kebabs), and *ekmek* custard (bread pudding).

PARKSVILLE: Pacific Prime Restaurant **$$$**
Steakhouse
181 Beachside Dr., BC, V9P 0B1
Tel *(250) 947 2109*
Located in the Beach Club Resort, this upscale steakhouse with views overlooking the beach and mountains is known for its extensive local wine list.

RICHMOND: Fisherman's Terrace Seafood Restaurant **$**
Chinese
4151 Hazelbridge Way, BC, V6X 4J7
Tel *(604) 303 9739*
Despite the name, this is a Chinese restaurant housed in the Aberdeen Centre mall. But don't be put off: it's fabulously popular and serves fantastic, authentic dim sum, right down to the chicken feet.

For more information on types of restaurants *see page 361*

The beautifully lit and lavishly decorated CinCin Restaurant & Bar, Vancouver

RICHMOND: Pajo's Fish and Chips $
Seafood
12351 3rd Ave., BC, V7E 2Z1
Tel *(604) 272 1588*
On the docks of the Steveston Wharf, this is a fun outdoors restaurant to take kids to. Serves the freshest cod, salmon, and hand-cut chips. No alcohol.

SALT SPRING ISLAND: Hastings House $$$
Contemporary Canadian
160 Upper Ganges Rd, BC, V8K 2S2
Tel *(250) 537 2362* **Closed** *Nov–Feb*
Hastings House is a hotel and restaurant set in an English manor overlooking Ganges' harbor. Uses homegrown herbs, fruit, and greens. Menu changes daily. Extensive wine list.

SOOKE: Sooke Harbour House $$$
Seafood
1528 Whiffen Spit Rd, BC, V9Z 0T4
Tel *(250) 642 3421* **Closed** *Tue & Wed in winter*
Savor innovative culinary delights and an excellent wine list. The daily set menu has a range of fish and seafood such as sea urchins and local shellfish. Beautiful gardens provide organic herbs and vegetables.

TOFINO: SoBo $$
International
311 Neill St., BC, V0R 2Z0
Tel *(250) 725 2341*
Sophisticated Bohemian, or SoBo, has delicious wood-stone oven pizzas, grilled elk kebab, and home-made ice cream and pies. Excellent local and world wines.

DK Choice

TOFINO: The Pointe Restaurant $$$
Fine Dining
The Wickaninnish Inn, 500 Osprey Ln., BC, V0R 2Z0
Tel *(250) 725 3106*
Housed in "The Wick's" cedar lodge, the Pointe has a gorgeous fireplace and stunning views of the Pacific Ocean. Local specialties on offer include fresh seafood, exquisite lamb, and great beef. Enjoy sommelier-picked Pacific Northwest wines. The ocean surges over rocks beside diners, making this a great place for storm-watching.

VANCOUVER: Planet Veg $
Indian
1941 Cornwall Ave., BC, V6J 1C8
Tel *(604) 734 1001*
Bustling cafeteria-style vegetarian restaurant. Superb *roti* rolls, rice pots, and some burgers as well. Patient staff helps guests with the menu. Great Indian sweets for dessert. No alcohol.

VANCOUVER: Sushi Bella $
Sushi
2059 West 4th Ave., BC, V6J 1N3
Tel *(604) 734 4990*
Great spot for traditional sushi and sashimi rolls along with fusion Bella rolls, where French is blended with Japanese. Try the *ahi* tuna poke and fresh *ahi* sashimi.

VANCOUVER: La Taqueria Pinche Taco Shop $
Mexican
322 W. Hastings St., BC, V8B 1K6
Tel *(604) 568 4406*
One of four branches, this tiny shop serves fresh and authentic tacos, mostly made using local and organic ingredients. Taste the *horchata* (sweet rice drink), too.

VANCOUVER: The Acorn Restaurant $$
Vegetarian
3995 Main St., BC, V5V 3P3
Tel *(604) 566 9001*
Even carnivores are repeat customers at this stylish "vegetable-forward" eatery. Really fresh, imaginative cooking and a trendsetting bar list.

VANCOUVER: CinCin Restaurant & Bar $$
Italian
1154 Robson St., BC, V6E 1B2
Tel *(604) 688 7338*
Pronounced chin-chin, this famous restaurant features great tasting menus. Watch the food being prepared on a rotisserie or in a wood-fired oven. Great wine list.

VANCOUVER: East is East $$
Middle Eastern
3243 West Broadway, BC, V6K 2H5
Tel *(604) 734 5881*
Exotic decor with low tables, decorative cushions, and live dancing. Try the Chai Feast tasting menu, Eastern Ecstasy dessert, and delicious spicy chai tea.

VANCOUVER: Havana $$
Cuban
1212 Commercial Dr., BC, V5L 3X4
Tel *(604) 253 9119*
Nuevo Latino cuisine with delicious Cuban cocktails. Daily breakfast spread, plus tapas, sandwiches, and entrées. Try the paella featuring West Coast mussels, house-made chorizo, and much more.

VANCOUVER: Kirin Restaurant City Centre $$
Chinese
201–555 West 12th Ave., BC, V5Z 3X7
Tel *(604) 879 8038*
One of four Kirins in Vancouver serving delicious home-made

Breathtaking views of the Pacific Ocean at Tofino's The Pointe Restaurant

dim sum and fresh seafood. Vegetarian options available. Sample the abalone with mushrooms in oyster sauce.

VANCOUVER: Maenam $$
Thai
1938 West 4th Ave., BC, V6J 1M5
Tel *(604) 730 5579* **Closed** *Sun lunch*
Traditional Thai style spot, with some dishes for sharing. Chef's menu available. Great wine pairings. Try the eight-spice fish.

VANCOUVER: Olive & Anchor Restaurant $$
International
6418 Bay St., BC, V7W 2H1
Tel *(604) 921 8848*
Overlooking the Horseshoe Bay ferry dock, Olive & Anchor has a solid presentation of multicultural favorites. Go for the chicken *tikka masala*, burgers (including tofu), and pasta bowls.

VANCOUVER: Stepho's Souvlaki Greek Taverna $$
Greek
1124 Davie St., BC, V6E 1N1
Tel *(604) 683 2555*
Popular local institution with a noisy but fun atmosphere and tasty food in huge portions. Excellent Greek salad.

VANCOUVER: Torafuku $$
Pan Asian
858 Main St., BC, V6A 2W1
Tel *(778) 903 2006*
Minimal decor but a hip, vibrant atmosphere, with funkily named, creative takes on Asian classics, from dim sum to sushi. The set menu to share takes away all the agony of choice for a good price.

VANCOUVER: Bishop's $$$
Contemporary Canadian
2183 West 4th Ave., BC, V6K 1N7
Tel *(604) 738 2025*
Bishop's has a regional menu that changes weekly. The three-course *prix fixe* menu is a great deal. The walls showcase a collection of First Nations' art.

DK Choice

VANCOUVER: The Blue Water Cafe $$$
Seafood
1095 Hamilton St., BC, V6B 5T4
Tel (604) 688 8078
Blue Water is internationally known for serving the freshest, sustainable coastal seafoods. Sidle up to the raw bar for sablefish sushi; in the dining room, seafood on ice is superbly presented. About 30 wines by the glass, mostly local.

VANCOUVER: Chambar $$$
Belgian
568 Beatty St., BC, V6B 2L3
Tel *(604) 879 7119*
Hip fine-dining restaurant with an European menu designed by three-starred Michelin chef and co-owner Nico Schuermans. As befits his Belgian origins, the beer menu is phenomenal.

VANCOUVER: Diva at the Met $$$
Fine Dining
645 Howe St., BC, V6C 2Y9
Tel *(604) 602 7788*
The open kitchen at Diva creates a welcoming experience, where flavors of regional fare, such as truffled sole or butter-toast ice cream, engage the senses. To round off, there's a superb selection of artisanal cheeses.

VANCOUVER: Gotham Steak House & Cocktail Bar $$$
Steakhouse
615 Seymour St., BC, V6B 3K3
Tel *(604) 605 8282*
Most steaks at the Art Deco Gotham are served with the bone still in. Delicious pork and lamb also on offer. Their Seafood Tower features Dungeness crab, Alaskan king crab, lobster, and more.

VANCOUVER: Lupo $$$
Italian
869 Hamilton St., BC, V6B 2R7
Tel *(604) 569 2535*
Cozy fine-dining restaurant with an open fireplace. Sample divine dishes such as local rack of lamb and wild salmon.

VANCOUVER: Tojo's Japanese $$$
Japanese
1133 West Broadway, BC, V6H 1G1
Tel *(604) 872 8050*
Chef Tojo, who invented the California Roll, serves some of the city's best sushi, sashimi, and nigiri. Sit at the sushi bar or in one of the romantic niches.

VANCOUVER: West $$$
Contemporary Canadian
2881 Granville St., BC, V6H 3J4
Tel *(604) 738 8938*
Trendy restaurant, where the West Coast takes on traditional Canadian cuisine. Try the lobster gnocchi or Fraser Valley Pork. Great cocktail selection, too.

VICTORIA: J & J Wonton Noodle House $
Chinese
1012 Fort St., BC, V8V 3Z9
Tel *(250) 383 0680* **Closed** *Sun & Mon*
Cozy and popular noodle house serving handmade noodles

Period decor at the Gotham Steak House & Cocktail Bar, Vancouver

made fresh every day. Go for the delicious wonton soups, green onion cake, and Hunan chicken.

VICTORIA: Brasserie L'Ecole $$
French
1715 Government St., BC, V8W 1Z4
Tel *(250) 475 6260*
Closed *Sun & Mon*
Small, romantic, and busy eatery in Chinatown. Wonderful French-country menu that uses local, seasonal ingredients.

VICTORIA: Fish Hook $$
Seafood
805 Fort St., BC, V8W 1H6
Tel *(250) 477 0470*
There's an Indian twist to many of the dishes, including chef Kunal Ghose's famous chowder, but there are also gourmet tartines, a kind of open sandwich filled with the local catch. Always busy.

VICTORIA: Spinnakers $$
Pub
308 Catherine St., BC, V9A 3S8
Tel *(250) 386 2739*
Superb brewpub with a very knowledgeable staff to help marry beer to food. Sip on their award-winning hand-crafted artisanal ales, and specialty beers on tap.

VICTORIA: Il Terrazzo $$
Italian
555 Johnson St., BC, V8W 1M2
Tel *(250) 361 0028*
In the Old Town, with a lovely courtyard patio, six fireplaces, and a wood-burning oven. Noteworthy homemade meatballs and thinnest-crust pizza from their open-flame oven. Excellent wine list.

For more information on types of restaurants *see page 361*

VICTORIA: Q at the Empress $$$
Fine Dining
721 Government St., BC, V8W 1W5
Tel *(250) 389 2727*
Located in the landmark
Empress Hotel, Q restaurant
and bar guarantees delicious
regional food and great service.
Unforgettable afternoon tea.

The Rocky Mountains

**BANFF: Coyotes
Southwestern Grill** $$
Southwestern
206 Caribou St., AB, T1L 1A2
Tel *(403) 762 3963*
Casual, with delicious home-made
food, from the pizzas and salads
to the barbecued flank steak and
spice-rubbed beef tenderloin.
Vegetarian options available.

BANFF: The Maple Leaf $$
Canadian
137 Banff Ave., AB, T1L 1C8
Tel *(403) 760 7680*
Warm and intimate setting. Menu
focused on local Alberta beef, bison,
and elk, and British Columbian
seafood. Extensive wine list.

**BANFF: The Bison
Restaurant & Terrace** $$$
Traditional Canadian
211 Bear St., AB, T1L 1E4
Tel *(403) 762 5550*
With great mountain views and a
seasonal patio, The Bison serves
organic, regional cuisine with an
emphasis on buffalo and game.
No dress code – those in hiking
boots are welcome.

**BANFF: Sleeping Buffalo
Restaurant & Lounge** $$$
Traditional Canadian
700 Tunnel Mountain Rd, AB, T1L 1B3
Tel *(403) 760 4484*
Serves delectable game such as
caribou, bison, and wild boar, all
raised at the Canadian Rocky
Mountain Resorts' ranch.

**CALGARY: Pfanntastic
Pannenkoek Haus** $
Dutch
2439 54th Ave. SW., AB, T3E 1M4
Tel *(403) 243 7757* **Closed** *Mon & Tue*
This pancake house, located
in a strip mall, is a great insider's
secret. There are over 80
varieties of sweet crepes and
savory pancakes to choose
from. Alternatively, "build your
own *pannenkoek*".

CALGARY: Silver Dragon $$
Chinese
106 3rd Ave. SE., AB, T2G 0B6
Tel *(403) 264 5326*
Don't miss this thriving
Cantonese and Schezuan place
in Chinatown. Come for the
trolley-service dim sum brunch.
Staff are helpful in identifying
choices. Make reservations.

**CALGARY:
Charcut** $$$
Steakhouse
899 Centre St. SW. #101, AB, T2G 1B8
Tel *(403) 984 2180*
Upscale steakhouse bringing the
country to the city with a rustic-
chic atmosphere and a farm-to-
table philosophy that includes a
beer steward and house-
butchered meats. Reservations
recommended.

CALGARY: River Café $$$
Fine Dining
25 Prince's Island Park, AB, T2P 0R1
Tel *(403) 261 7670*
Located in a tranquil island
setting with a gorgeous view of
the water from the patio.
Sample seasonal organic food,
made using regional fish, game,
and produce. Great weekend
brunches and daily vegetarian
options on offer.

CALGARY: Rouge $$$
Fine Dining
1240 8th Ave. SE., AB, T2G 0M7
Tel *(403) 531 2767*   **Closed** *Sun*
Located in a late 19th-century

building on the Bow River,
home-grown herbs, sustainable
seafoods, and locally reared
meats are used to prepare
delectable regional dishes.

**CANMORE: Beamer's
Coffee Bar** $
Café
120, 737 7th Ave., AB, T1W 3H8
Tel *(403) 609 0111*
Canmore favorite offering
over 40 types of gourmet,
custom-roasted coffee bean,
along with teas and delicious
home-made sandwiches
and cookies.

DK Choice

CANMORE: The Trough $$$
Contemporary Canadian
725 9 St., AB, T1W 2V7
Tel *(403) 678 2820*   **Closed** *Mon*
The Trough, deservingly
popular among foodies,
is known for its exquisitely
prepared and presented
food. Don't miss the
delicious Alberta beef
tenderloin and the scallops.
Fantastic wine pairings and
mouthwatering desserts, plus
a romantic atmosphere.
Family-owned, with friendly
and helpful staff. Book ahead.

**FIELD: Mount Burgess Dining
Room** $$$
Contemporary Canadian
1 Emerald Lake Drive, BC, V0A 1G0
Tel *(250) 343 6321*
Overlooking the spectacular
lake in Yoho Park, this restaurant
is well worth an hour's drive
from Banff. The seasonal menu
features free-range elk and bison,
plus an award-winning wine list.

**GOLDEN: Eagle's Eye
Restaurant** $$$
Traditional Canadian
1500 Kicking Horse Trail, BC, V0A 1H0
Tel *(250) 439 5553* **Closed** *Seasonal*
At 2,347 m (7,700 ft), this is
Canada's highest restaurant.
Enjoy Alberta lamb and wild
boar burgers while taking in
fantastic views. Reservations for
dinner are essential.

JASPER: Bear's Paw Bakery $
Café
*4 Pyramid Lake Rd, Jasper National
Park, AB, T0E 1E0*
Tel *(780) 852 3233*
This delightful café serves up
delicious home-made pastries,
sandwiches, and soups. Special
coffees and chai on offer. Eat in
or takeout options. Great place
to go with children.

Patio seats with gorgeous mountain views at The Bison Restaurant & Terrace, Banff

Ornate decor of the Emerald Lounge, located in the Fairmont Jasper Park Lodge

JASPER: The Emerald Lounge $$$
Traditional Canadian
1 Old Lodge Rd, Jasper National Park, AB, T0E 1E0
Tel (780) 852 3301
The patio seating at the Fairmont Jasper Park Lodge commands great views of Whistler's Mountain. Sample from a varied menu that includes a delicious range of grilled meats. Free meals for kids from the children's menu.

KIMBERLY: The Old Bauernhaus $$$
German
280 Norton Ave., AB, V1A 1X9
Tel (250) 427 5133 **Closed** Tue & Wed
Originally a 17th-century Bavarian barn, the Old Bauerhaus was disassembled, shipped, and rebuilt here in 1989. Experience old-world charm while sampling the Bavarian Feast and schnitzel. Children's menu available.

LAKE LOUISE: Lake Agnes Tea House $
Café
Access from Fairmont Château Lake Louise, 111 Lake Louise Dr., AB, T0L 1E0
Tel (403) 763 7242 **Closed** mid-Oct–May
Historic refuge that was built as a hikers' shelter. Choose from over 100 varieties of tea plus home-made soups and sandwiches. It's a hot climb up in the summer, so be sure to carry water.

LAKE LOUISE: Elkhorn Dining Room $$$
Traditional Canadian
Mile 22 Bow Lake, Icefield Parkway, AB, T0L 1E0
Tel (403) 522 2167 **Closed** Seasonal
Located within the quaint, historic Num-Ti-Jah Lodge, Elkhorn has a phenomenal view of Bow Lake and the surrounding mountains. Beautiful candlelit

three-course meals, with lots of game dishes.

LAKE LOUISE: Poppy Brasserie $$$
International
Fairmont Château Lake Louise, 111 Lake Louise Dr., AB, T0L 1E0
Tel (403) 522 1601 **Closed** Seasonal
Hotel-restaurant with stunning views of Lake Louise. The menu features a mix of regional Canadian and international dishes, including Japanese specials. Winter opening (Nov–Apr) depends on hotel occupancy: call ahead.

LAKE LOUISE: The Post Hotel Dining Room $$$
Fine Dining
200 Pipestone Rd, AB, T0L 1E0
Tel (403) 522 3989
Promises a memorable dining experience. Helpful staff assist in choosing the perfect wine from among 2,300 options. Exquisite regional and international cuisine. Try the caribou, beef stroganoff, and lobster salads.

NELSON: Outer Clove $$
Unique
536 Stanley St., V1L 1N2
Tel (250) 354 1667
This unusual restaurant serves exclusively garlic-themed dishes from appetizers and mains to desserts, including garlic chocolate-chip cookies and garlic ice cream. Chefs use 2.2 kg (5 lb) of garlic every day in deliciously inventive ways. A must-try.

REVELSTOKE: 112 Restaurant and Lounge $$$
Fine Dining
112 First St. E., BC, V0E 2S0
Tel (250) 837 2107
The Regent Hotel's 112 is a refined restaurant with

specialties such as rack of lamb, charbroiled steaks, and cioppino (fish stew). Sip on the delicious, locally brewed Mt. Begbie draft beer.

Southern and Northern British Columbia

FORT LANGLEY: Beatniks Bistro $
Bistro
9194 Glover Rd, BC, V1M 2S4
Tel (604) 888 4487
With a relaxed atmosphere and attentive staff, Beatniks serves everything from burgers to seafood linguine. Great Okanagan microbrewery beers, signature cocktails, and wines.

HARRISON HOT SPRINGS: Morgan's Bistro $$
Canadian
160 Esplanade Ave., BC, V0M 1K0
Tel (604) 491 1696
Morgan's has a great summertime patio with a view over Harrison Lake. Sample its diverse menu, with home-made focaccia to accompany salads, tenderloin, braised short ribs, and lamb chops.

KELOWNA: The Yellow House Restaurant $$
Canadian
526 Lawrence Ave., BC, V1Y 6L7
Tel (250) 763 5136
At this restaurant in a Victorian house everything is home-made: from the stock and soups to the sauces and desserts. Try the signature seafood pasta or oven-roasted duck breast. Great martinis.

Elkhorn Dining Room, found inside the quaint Num-Ti-Jah Lodge, Lake Louise

For more information on types of restaurants see page 361

DK Choice

KELOWNA:
Waterfront Wines $$
Canadian
1180 Sunset Dr., BC, V1Y 9W6
Tel *(250) 979 1222* **Closed** *Sun & holiday Mon*
Trendy, award-winning restaurant with minimal, airy interiors. Superb sommelier-advised pairings of fine Okanagan wines to some of the freshest regional fare. Delicacies include wild salmon, pork shoulder, and duck breast. Sharing plates are available too. In season, try their delectable wild mushrooms including morels. Sip one of the cocktails, wines, or craft beers on the summer patio.

OSOYOOS: The Diamond
Steak and Seafood House $$
Mediterranean
8903 Main St., BC, V0H 1V0
Tel *(250) 495 6223* **Closed** *Mon & Tue*
Family-run Greek-Italian place serving great calamari and Greek salad. Other popular dishes include steaks, seafood, and several kinds of pizzas. Try their specialty prime rib. Good choice of local wines available. Cozy fireplace in the winter.

PRINCE GEORGE: Spicy Greens
Restaurant $
Asian
6545 Hart Hwy, BC, V2K 3A4
Tel *(778) 415 5111*
Spicy Greens serves delicious home-made Asian fare, specifically South Indian, Sri Lankan, and Singapore cuisine. Sample the madras curries or *mee goreng* (spicy fried noodles).

PRINCE GEORGE: Shogun
Japanese Steakhouse $$
Japanese
770 Brunswick St., BC, V2L 2C2
Tel *(250) 563 0121*
Reserve seats at the Teppan grill, where chefs create meals in front of guests. Alternatively choose the private Shojii room. Great tempura and steaks, and generous portions.

PRINCE RUPERT: Cow Bay Café $
Café
205 Cow Bay Rd, BC, V8J 1A2
Tel *(250) 627 1212* **Closed** *Sun & Mon*
Cow Bay is a popular, laid-back café located on the docks overlooking the harbor. The daily whiteboard menu features vegetarian options and fish of the day. Dishes are wiped off the board when they run out, so arrive early for maximum choice. Great desserts.

PRINCE RUPERT: Opa Sushi $$
Japanese
34 Cow Bay Rd, BC, V8J 1A5
Tel *(250) 627 4560*
This unusual sushi joint is one of the last fishing-net lofts on the coast. Intimate ambience. Traditional and innovative West-Coast inspired sushi at this intimate eatery.

TERRACE: Don Diego's $
TexMex
3212 Kalum St., BC, V8G 2M9
Tel *(250) 635 2307* **Closed** *Sun*
With a daily changing menu of inexpensive TexMex food and a cozy ambience, Don Diego's is a rightly popular spot. Delicious *enchiladas*, generous helpings, and lots of gluten-free options.

WHISTLER: Blacks Pub &
Restaurant $$
Traditional Canadian
4270 Mountain Square, BC, V0N 1B4
Tel *(604) 932 6945*
Located at the base of Blackcomb and Whistler mountains, Blacks is one of Whistler's oldest establishments. The sports pub upstairs features a large selection of beers on tap.

WHISTLER: Bearfoot Bistro $$$
French
4121 Village Green, BC, V0N 1B4
Tel *(604) 932 3433*
Innovative restaurant, where tasting menus of regional French food are paired with a range of local and international wines.

Northern Canada

DAWSON CITY: Drunken
Goat Taverna $$
Greek
950 2nd Ave., YT, Y0B 1G0
Tel *(867) 993 5868*
Run by a Greek owner, the Drunken Goat is a picturesque restaurant serving Greek fare in generous portions. Get the sharing platters to sample the varied menu.

DAWSON CITY: Klondike
Kate's $$
Canadian
1102, 3rd Ave., YT, Y0B 1G0
Tel *(867) 993 6527* **Closed** *Oct–Mar*
This family restaurant with a friendly atmosphere is located in a gold rush-era building, dating from 1904. Great daily specials, all-day breakfasts, and weekend brunch. Also serves espressos, lattes, and fruit smoothies.

The dockside location of Cow Bay Café in Prince Rupert, British Columbia

Key to Price Guide *see page 364*

FORT PROVIDENCE:
Snowshoe Inn Café $
Diner
#1 Mackenzie Dr., NT, X0E 0L0
Tel *(867) 699 3511*
The Snowshoe is a family-run inn
serving typical diner fare, such as
burgers, fish and chips, chicken
wings, and shrimp. All-day
breakfasts and a full dessert menu.

HAY RIVER: Back Eddy Cocktail
Lounge & Restaurant $$
Contemporary Canadian
6 Courtoreille St., NT, X0E 0R0
Tel *(867) 874 6680*
One of Hay River's most popular
eateries, this is a combination of
restaurant, lounge, and sports
bar. The menu includes steak,
seafood, and local fish, such as
Great Slave Lake whitefish.
Relaxed atmosphere.

INUVIK: Alestine's $
Traditional Canadian
48 Franklin Rd., NT, X0E 0T0
Tel *(867) 777 3702*
Casual eatery serving local fish
and chips, fish tacos, reindeer
chili, and traditional donuts.
Weather permitting, check out
the views from the rooftop patio.

IQALUIT: The Frob $$$
Traditional Canadian
Astro Hill Complex, NU, X0A 0H0
Tel *(867) 979 2222*
Housed in the Frobisher Inn, The
Frob displays lovely prints from
the Pangnirtung Print Collection.
Local artists come in to sell their
wares in what amounts to
a dinner and art show. Regional
fare is on offer, including wild
muskox and Arctic char.
Popular Sunday brunch menu.

IQALUIT:
The Granite Room $$$
Fine Dining
1056 Mivvik St., NU, X0A 0H0
Tel *(867) 979 4433*
The Granite Room at the
Discovery Lodge hotel serves fine
cuisine in elegant surroundings.
A soup and salad bar, daily *table
d'hôte*, and Sunday brunch.
Try the caribou steak and
Pangnirtung halibut. Worth
booking ahead for groups of
more than four.

NORMAN WELLS:
Yamouri Inn $$
International
1 Town Square, NT, X0E 0V0
Tel *(867) 587 2744*
Yamouri Inn's dining room
has a relaxed, cozy atmosphere.
The menu is extensive and
varied, and a further takeout
option is available.

Lively outdoor seating area at the French restaurant Bearfoot Bistro, in Whistler

WHITEHORSE:
Klondike Rib & Salmon $
Traditional Canadian
2116 2nd Ave., YT, Y1A 1B9
Tel *(867) 667 7554*   **Closed** *Oct–
Apr*
Housed in turn-of-the-century
buildings, this popular barbecue
joint with its own traditional
smokehouse serves hearty
platefuls of local fish, smoked
meats, and wild game. Great
pies, too.

WHITEHORSE: Pickapeppa $
Caribbean
2074 2nd Ave., YT, Y1A 1B1
Tel *(867) 456 4990*
This bright green hole-in-the-
wall cannot be missed. Visit
for authentic Jamaican jerk
chicken, patties, and curried
goat. Warm yourself on a cold
day with a welcome bit of heat
in the North.

WHITEHORSE: Antoinette's $$
Diner
4121 4th Ave., YT, Y1A 1H7
Tel *(867) 668 3505*   **Closed** *Sun*
Antoinette's has a laid-back
atmosphere and warm Caribbean
feel, with bright tablecloths and
red walls. Food is well presented,
and the menu includes curries,
bison burgers, Trinidadian
halibut, and vegetarian options.
Desserts choices include rose-
petal-infused crème brûlée and
apple pie.

WHITEHORSE:
Burnt Toast Café $$
Contemporary Canadian
2112 2nd Ave., YT, Y1A 1B9
Tel *(867) 393 2605*
Burnt Toast is a casual restaurant
featuring contemporary decor.
Dinner menu includes tapas
and locally made elk-and-
blueberry sausage. Good Sunday
brunch with a variety of egg
dishes, home-made granola,
and mimosas.

YELLOWKNIFE: The Fat Fox $
Café
5008 50th St., NT, X1A 1R8
Tel *(867) 445 9438*   **Closed** *Sun*
Cozy, northern living-room
decor, offering excellent tea,
coffee, pastries, plus hearty
breakfasts and lunches, all
served with a warm smile.
Vegan options available.

YELLOWKNIFE:
Zehabesha $
Ethiopian
5030 50th St., NT, X1A 3R8
Tel *(867) 873 6400*   **Closed** *Sun*
Experience the warming flavours
of spice up north at this family-
run restaurant, with generous
portions of hearty meat and
vegetable curries ladled onto
soft injera flatbread.

YELLOWKNIFE: Bullocks
Bistro $$$
Traditional Canadian
3534 Weaver Dr., NT, X1A 2S9
Tel *(867) 873 3474*
This small place oozes frontier
character. Sit at the bar and
chat with the cook, as he
prepares muskox, caribou,
bison, and fresh fish from
Great Slave Lake.

DK Choice

YELLOWKNIFE: Thornton's
Wine & Tapas Room $$$
Tapas
5125 52nd Ave., NT, X1A 1S8
Tel *867 669 9463*   **Closed** *Mon*
The plain exterior and location
beside a bowling alley conceal
an elegant and classy
restaurant. Thornton's has a
modern interior with high
ceilings, an upscale ambience,
and excellent service. Choose
from a selection of tapas and
main courses. Good wine list
and a delicious Sunday brunch.
Reserve ahead.

For more information on types of restaurants *see page 361*

SHOPPING IN CANADA

Shopping in Canada offers more than the usual tourist fare of Mountie dolls and maple-leaf T-shirts. Visitors can choose from a wide range of products, and buy everything from electronic equipment to clothes and jewelry. There is also a variety of goods unique to the country – maple syrup from Quebec, smoked salmon from British Columbia, and cowboy boots from Alberta, to name a few. First Peoples art, inspired by centuries-old tradition, includes carvings by West-Coast peoples and Inuit paintings and tapestries. In each major city there are covered malls, chainstores, specialty shops, and galleries, as well as street markets to explore. In country areas, beautifully made crafts by local people can be found. Be aware that sales taxes are added to the price of many items.

Shopping Hours

Store hours vary, but in larger cities most stores are open by 9am and close between 5pm and 9pm. However, some grocery and variety stores are open 24 hours a day, and in major towns several pharmacies are also open for 24 hours. In most towns, stores have late opening until 9pm on Friday evening. However, in smaller towns and villages you should not expect any store, including the gas station, to be open after 6pm. Sunday openings are increasing: usually hours run from noon to 5pm but vary from province to province. Check first, as many places may be closed in rural areas. The opening of stores on public holidays also varies from province to province.

How to Pay

Most Canadian stores accept all major credit cards, with VISA and MasterCard being the most popular. Some stores require a minimum purchase in order to use the card. Many people prefer to use debit cards (bank cards) rather than cash, but ATM machines are available at most banks and corner stores so that you can withdraw cash from your bank account. In either case using your debit card should secure you a more favorable exchange rate than those offered by bureaux de change and hotels. Point-of-sale terminals for bank cards are available in most supermarkets and all but the smallest stores.

US dollars are the only non-Canadian currency accepted in department stores. Bear in mind, however, that the exchange rate is usually lower, sometimes as much as 15 percent, than a bank will give. Larger stores in resort towns may offer money-changing facilities within the store.

Sales Taxes

In Canada there are three types of sales taxes: Provincial Sales Taxes (PST), the federal Goods and Services Tax (GST), and the Harmonized Sales Tax (HST). HST is a combination of PST and GST, and varies between 13 and 15 percent. Ontario, Prince Edward Island, Nova Scotia, New Brunswick, and Newfoundland and Labrador all charge HST. The remaining provinces and territories charge 5 percent GST plus PST of between 7 and 10 percent. Alberta, Northwest Territories, Nunavut, and the Yukon do not charge PST.

Canadians love to curse the GST, which currently runs at 5 percent. It is added to most retail transactions; the major exception is basic food items.

Consumer Rights and Services

Smart shoppers always check a store's refund policy before buying an item. Policies vary; some stores will refund money on unwanted items, while others offer store vouchers, and many will not exchange or refund sale merchandise. Reputable stores will take back defective merchandise within one month of purchase, as long as it is accompanied by the original bill of sale.

Local art and craft work on display in a store in British Columbia

Canadian Goods

Products made in Canada offer shoppers a wide variety of choice. Although most specialty items are sold across the country, many goods are less expensive in their province of origin. Hand-knitted sweaters and pottery are particularly good value in Atlantic Canada, as is the much-praised Seagull pewter made in Nova Scotia. The Prairie provinces and Alberta specialize in cowboy attire: tooled belts, vests, cowboy hats, and boots. Farther west, British Columbian artisans produce elaborate carvings, including totem poles. Jade

The vast Eaton Centre on bustling Yonge Street, downtown Toronto

jewelry, from locally mined stone, is also reasonable here.

Local specialties from Quebec and Ontario include maple syrup and sugar-related products. Quebec artisans make beautiful wood carvings, too. In Ontario, First Nations basketwork is a good choice as a lasting souvenir.

Indigenous carvings can be found across the country, especially in the far north. Genuine Inuit carvings are inspected and stamped by the federal government. A sticker featuring an igloo marks a true piece, which will also be signed by the artist. Since the 1950s, the Inuit have been producing prints of traditional scenes, which are popular, as is traditional jewelry. Beautifully handmade parkas, embroidered panels, and soft deer-hide moccasins also make excellent souvenirs.

Contemporary Canadian art features highly in the various gift shops and galleries throughout the country. Photographs and prints are recommended for the budget-conscious shopper.

Modern sportswear and outerwear is both durable and beautifully designed. Camping, hiking, and boating equipment are fine buys, as is fishing tackle. With such a strong tradition of outdoor life, a wide range of products is usually available at well below European prices.

Pottery jar, Nova Scotia

And for those who need an extra suitcase to carry their finds home, the renowned Tilley travel cases and products are made and sold locally throughout Canada.

Department Stores

The Bay is the major middle-range department store chain across the country. Canadian department stores have suffered financially in recent decades. They are changing to meet the competition of US chains, such as Wal-Mart and discount stores, and membership stores including Costco. Chains such as Sears occupy the middle to lower end of the market place. Canadian Tire sells everything from auto parts to sporting goods and has become a national institution.

Malls and Shopping Centers

Suburbia may not offer the most culture in Canada, but some of the malls are fine destinations in themselves. The renowned modernist Eaton Centre, however, is in the heart of downtown Toronto and is enclosed by a glass-and-steel arched roof, with a wonderful sculpted flock of geese soaring over shoppers. Around 50 million visitors annually enjoy this showcase of modern architecture, though it has been derided as "brutalism" by conservative Torontonians. The West Edmonton Mall in Edmonton, Alberta is another attraction. Over 800 stores, more than 100 restaurants, 34 movie theaters, a huge water park, an amusement park, a theme hotel, a mini-golf course, an ice rink, and an aquarium with dolphins are some of the sights that draw Canadians and visitors alike to this retail paradise.

Exclusive stores are largely found in the country's retail capital, Toronto. Bloor Street and Yorkville Avenue are lined with status brands known the world over, such as Tiffany, Holt Renfrew, Ralph Lauren, and Gucci. Both Vancouver and Montreal have their own selection of world-class luxury stores. Montreal clothing boutiques are filled with high-end and street-stylish fashions, and many items crafted from local designers. For those unable to travel to the north, Inuit art features highly in craft shops here.

The Underground City, a vast network of boutiques beneath the streets of Montreal

Shopping in Montreal, Toronto, and Vancouver

Canada's three largest cities offer shopping experiences with one thing in common: international fare. Montreal's cosmopolitan edge complements its wide-ranging stores, from chic boutiques to antiques shops to an underground network of stores and services. Toronto's shop-'til-you-drop attitude includes the Bay/Bloor neighborhood and Yorkville as well as dozens of ethnic communities selling the wares of their home countries. Vancouver shows off with about ten great shopping areas, as befits a spreading coastal city, with *haute couture* alongside art, furniture, and much more.

Toronto's Eaton Centre is home to hundreds of stores

Department Stores and Malls

Canada's most well-known department store is **The Bay/ La Baie**, a modern moniker for the Hudson's Bay Company, which started here in the 17th century as a trading post between the early settlers and the Aboriginal Peoples. The Bay is found in all three cities, and its distinctive brand of rainbow-striped blankets, sweaters, and coats have always been a hit with visitors. In downtown Toronto, the mammoth **Eaton Centre** shopping complex is anchored at its north end at Yonge and Dundas by the department store Nordstrom, and stretches south to Queen, where The Bay is located. In between, shoppers will find a rich choice of chains, from the Apple Store and Indigo Books to Swedish retailer H&M, Roots, and AX Armani Exchange. Montreal's **Place Montréal Trust** is home to around 70 boutiques, including several major retailers. A good rendez-vous point is the mall's soaring 9-m (30-ft) fountain. In Vancouver, the **Pacific Centre** is arguably the city's premier shopping mall downtown, while in nearby Richmond, the **Aberdeen Centre** plays host to a bevy of Asian stores, restaurants, and services.

Markets

Vancouver's milder climate allows for longer seasons of the outdoor markets, but Canada's two other large cities do not shy away from this popular shopping experience. Montreal's **Jean-Talon Market**, with over 100 vendors, is mainly outdoors from May until October, although it is open year round and contains 20 indoor stores. In Toronto, the **Saint Lawrence Market**, with over 60 vendors, is much loved by locals for its excellent range of fresh produce and meats. Vancouver's **Granville Island** boasts an authentic farmer's market along with several galleries, boutiques, and artisans' stores.

Antiques and Crafts

Toronto's vintage shops are scattered across the city. Try the long stretch of Queen Street East for mid-century modern furniture and quirky shops. The large **Sunday Antique Market** sets up from dawn until 5pm across from the Saint Lawrence Market *(see p191)*. **Toronto Antiques on King's** showroom is bursting with higher-end pieces. **Craft Ontario Shop** in Yorkville features beautiful items from the Ontario Crafts Council. The shop in the **Textile Museum** is packed with bags, scarves, and all manner of hand-made materials. In Montreal, **L'Art des Artisans du Québec** is a perfect store for original gifts made of wood, pewter, and glass, designed by talented Quebec artists. Local crafts are also on sale in the 15 boutiques of **Marché Bonsecours**. In Vancouver, antiques shops are spread along Main Street, from Hastings to Marine Drive. The city's **Antique Warehouse** is an attractive stop for aficionados.

Designer Fashion and Jewelry

In Montreal, women's fashion by exclusively Quebec designers can be found at **Anne de Shalla**, while there is a wide variety of designer menswear at **L'Uomo Montréal**. **La Maison Ogilvy**, a respected fashion retailer in Montreal since 1866, stocks high-end items.

In Toronto, most designer stores, including **Tiffany & Co.**, **Royal de Versailles**, and **Gucci**, are centered in the Bloor-Yorkville

The market on Granville Island in Vancouver

area, including the flagship store for **Holt Renfrew**, a Canadian retailer known for its fine products, especially in cosmetics, fashion, and jewelry. Vancouver's Robson Street contains high-fashion stores, such as Armani and Canada's own **Roots**. Gastown offers high-end independent boutiques along Water Street.

Art, Books, Music, and Giftware

The largest bookstore chain in the country is Chapters/Indigo, and the large outlets in major centers also have excellent music offerings (and cafés). The **Canadian Guild of Crafts** in Montreal not only displays fine giftware in wood, ceramic, blown glass, metal, and handmade jewelry, but it also has a permanent collection of Inuit art worth perusing. In Vancouver, rare books or early titles on western Canadiana can be found at **MacLeod's Books**.

Specialty Stores

Canadian Maple Delights in Montreal is the quintessential homage to maple syrup: there's everything from gelati, pastries, mustards, vinaigrettes, and jams to around 100 other maple treats. In Toronto and Montreal, **La Casa del Habano** is the best place to enjoy a fine Havana cigar with a Cuban cocktail or coffee. And for those so inclined, **Héritage Fur** is a furrier as well as an art gallery in the heart of Vieux-Montréal. Vancouver's **Mountain Equipment Co-op** was started by climbers in the 1970s, and is now one of Canada's best outdoor outfitters and is found in all major cities. A Can $5 lifetime membership fee is payable before any purchases can be made there.

DIRECTORY

Department Stores and Malls

Aberdeen Centre
4151 Hazelbridge Way, Richmond, Vancouver.
Tel (604) 270 1234.
W aberdeencentre.com

The Bay/La Baie
585 Rue Sainte-Catherine O, Montreal; 176 Yonge St., Toronto; 674 Granville St., Vancouver.
W thebay.com

Eaton Centre
220 Yonge St., Toronto.
Tel 416 598 8560.
W torontoeatoncentre.com

Pacific Centre
700 W. Georgia St., Vancouver.
Tel (604) 688 7235.
W pacificcentre.com

Place Montréal Trust
1500 McGill College Ave., Montreal.
Tel (514) 843 8000.
W placemontrealtrust.com

Markets

Granville Island
South side of downtown, Vancouver. **Tel** (604) 666 6655. W granvilleisland.com

Jean-Talon Market
7070 Henri Julien Ave., Montreal. **Tel** (514) 277 1588. W marchepublics-mtl.com

Saint Lawrence Market
92 Front St. E., Toronto.
Tel 416 392 7219.
W stlawrencemarket.com

Antiques and Crafts

Antique Warehouse
226 S.W. Marine Dr., Vancouver. **Tel** (604) 324 3661. W antiqueware house.ca

L'Art des Artisans du Québec
Complexe Desjardins, 150 Rue Sainte-Catherine O., Montreal. **Tel** (514) 288 5379. W artdes artisansduquebec.com

Craft Ontario Shop
1106 Queen St. W., Toronto. **Tel** (416) 921 1721.
W craftontario.com

Marché Bonsecours
350 Rue Saint-Paul E., Montreal. **Tel** (514) 872 7730. W marche bonsecours.qc.ca

Sunday Antique Market
Saint Lawrence North Market, Toronto. **Tel** (416) 410 1310. W sunday antiquemarket.com

Textile Museum Shop
55 Centre Ave., Toronto.
Tel (416) 599 5321.
W textilemuseum.ca

Toronto Antiques on King
284 King St. W. at John St., Toronto. **Tel** 416 345 9941.

Designer Fashion and Jewelry

Anne de Shalla
Marché Bonsecours, 350 Rue Saint-Paul Est, Montreal.
Tel (514) 398 0761.
W productions annedeshalla.com

Gucci
130 Bloor St. W., Toronto.
Tel (416) 963 5127.

Holt Renfrew
1300 Rue Sherbrooke O., Montreal; 50 Bloor St. W., Toronto; Pacific Centre, 727 Dunsmuir St., Vancouver.
W holtrenfrew.com

La Maison Ogilvy
1307 Rue Sainte-Catherine O., Montreal.
Tel (514) 842 7711.
W ogilvycanada.com

Roots
1001 Robson St., Vancouver.
Tel (604) 683 4305

1025 Rue Sainte-Catherine O., Montreal.
Tel- (514) 845 7995

100 Bloor St. W., Toronto.
Tel 416 323 3289.
W roots.com

Royal de Versailles
101 Bloor St. W., Toronto.
Tel (416) 967 7201.
W royaldeversailles.com

Tiffany & Co.
85 Bloor St. W., Toronto.
W tiffany.ca

L'Uomo Montréal
1452 Rue Peel, Montreal.
Tel (514) 844 1008.

Art, Books, Music, and Giftware

Canadian Guild of Crafts
1460 B. Sherbrooke St. W., Montreal. **Tel** (514) 849 6091. W canadianguild.com

MacLeod's Books
455 West Pender St., Vancouver.
Tel (604) 681 7654.

Specialty Stores

Canadian Maple Delights
84 Rue Saint-Paul E., Montreal.
Tel (514) 765 3456.

385 Water St., Vancouver.
Tel (604) 682 6175.

La Casa del Habano
1434 Rue Sherbrooke O., Montreal.
Tel (514) 849 0037
114 Yorkville Ave., Toronto.
Tel 416 926 9066

Héritage Fur
30 Rue Saint-Paul E., Montreal.
Tel (514) 392 9272.

Mountain Equipment Co-op
130 W. Broadway, Vancouver.
Tel (604) 872 7858
400 King St. W., Toronto.
Tel (416) 340 266.
W mec.ca

ENTERTAINMENT IN CANADA

Entertainment in Canada boasts all the sophistication tourists have come to expect from a major North American country, coupled with delightful rural entertainments in relaxing local venues. Covering mainstream world-class productions in Ottawa and the country's other larger cities, Canada also offers the latest in alternative acts and traditional artforms, particularly in its exceptional folk music heritage. Music of the highest quality, both classical and modern, is offered throughout the country, and major cities provide first-rate theater, dance, and film, not to mention many musical shows and film festivals.

Information

Provincial daily newspapers are the most reliable sources of information about forthcoming events; the *Vancouver Sun*, *Montreal Gazette*, *Ottawa Citizen*, and *Toronto Star* are the most popular. Listings are usually published at least once a week. The *Globe and Mail* and *National Post* are produced in Toronto but are sold countrywide and have excellent arts sections. For more detailed local listings, pick up a free weekly, such as *Now* in Toronto and the *Georgia Straight* in Vancouver. Tourist offices *(see p401)* are helpful; some operators may assist in booking tickets. Visitor centers and hotel lobbies have weekly entertainment guides, such as *Where*, a magazine with editions for locations across Canada. In Quebec, French-language entertainment is chronicled by *La Presse* and *Le Devoir*. *Maclean's* is a national weekly magazine with arts coverage.

Booking

Ticketmaster outlets are found in many shopping malls and represent major halls across the country. Tickets to venues in Quebec are available from Admission Network. Different offices cater to different sports and artistic events in each city. Most venues, however, can be contacted directly for tickets.

Disabled Visitors

Major Canadian venues are well equipped to deal with wheelchair users. All interior halls contain ramps and restroom access. Parking lots will have designated disabled spaces nearby. A hearing loop system is available at Ottawa's National Arts Centre *(see p201)*, and at most other major venues. Call ahead to check their availability. Outside ramps and elevators are provided to reach concerts halls and theaters at most large centers.

Theater

Toronto, Ottawa, Vancouver, Montreal, Stratford, and Niagara-on-the-Lake are the top theater centers in Canada (most of their productions are in English). Homegrown talent mixes here with shows imported from Europe and the US. Musicals and classical theater are always popular, as is Shakespeare, but there is a wide spectrum of shows – for example, Toronto's Princess of Wales and Royal Alexandra Theatres mount Broadway productions, as well as world premieres, such as *Lord of the Rings*. The main theaters have a principal season from November to May, but summer attractions are on the rise. Musicals and historical reconstructions provide family entertainment; the best known is the musical *Anne of Green Gables*, performed every summer in Charlottetown.

Film

Hollywood blockbusters have no better chance of success than in Canada, where premieres are often parallel with the US, so visitors may well see films in advance of a showing in their own country. Huge IMAX™ and OMNIMAX™ movie theaters can be found in the center of major cities, particularly in Ottawa and Hull.

Canada has a fine history of filmmaking: the documentary genre was invented here, and more recently its art films have attracted a wider audience. The main centers to see the new trends are Montreal, Vancouver, and Toronto. Robert Lepage, Canada's own theater and movie impresario, has an international following among the cognoscenti. The Surrealist David Cronenberg, director of *Eastern Promises* (2007) *and Maps to the Stars* (2014), is also

Façade of The Royal George Theatre, Niagara-on-the-Lake, Ontario

Toronto International Film Festival, a must for avid moviegoers

Canadian. Quebec's Denys Arcand is admired for his intensely human dramas, such as *Jesus of Montreal* (1989), *Love and Human Remains* (1993) and *An Eye for Beauty* (2014). The National Film Board selects and releases a work by aboriginal talent each year, comprising feature films, animations, and documentaries. Ideal for spotting new talent, every year the Toronto International Film Festival is a magnet to moviegoers, as are parallel festivals held in Montreal and Vancouver.

Classical Music, Opera and Ballet

Classical music and opera draw large audiences in Canada, and this is reflected by the high quality of performers and venues. The Canadian Opera Company is based at the Four Seasons Centre for the Performing Arts *(see p178)* in Toronto, with a repertoire ranging from Mozart to cutting-edge pieces sung in English. The National Ballet of Canada, rival to the Royal Winnipeg Ballet, is also based here; both companies feature period pieces and experimental work in their seasonal run. Fringe theater takes off in Toronto each summer with hundreds of shows selected by lottery. Well over 100,000 people annually visit the state-of-the-art Jack Singer Concert Hall in the Arts Commons center to hear the celebrated Calgary

Philharmonic Orchestra. The Vancouver Symphony Orchestra plays at the Orpheum Theatre in Vancouver.

Rock, Folk, and Pop Music

During the last two decades, Canadian pop music acquired a credibility that even its kindest supporters would admit had previously been lacking. Quebec's Celine Dion is a superstar, and Shania Twain, rapper Drake and crooner Michael Bublé are international stars. Alanis Morissette and Sarah McLachlan are worthy successors to their country's heritage of folk rock. Modern-day icons Justin Bieber, Avril Lavigne, Nelly Furtado, and Carly Rae Jepson have been wooing teenagers worldwide with their pop anthems.

Canada is perhaps most famous for its folk music, with such stars as the late Leonard Cohen, Neil Young, and Joni Mitchell being the best-known

Celine Dion, one of Canada's best-selling international artists

faces from a centuries-old tradition. The product of an intensely musical rural people, the nature of Canadian song changes across the country, moving from the lonesome Celtic melodies on the east coast to the yodeling cowboys in the west. Atlantic Canada has numerous tiny, informal venues, where an excellent standard of music can be found. Quebec's French folksters include singer Gilles Vigneault *(see p34)* who is also admired in Europe. The Yukon's memories of the gold rush surface in 19th-century vaudeville, reenacted by dancing girls and a honky-tonk piano in Whitehorse.

Entertainment in Montreal, Toronto, and Vancouver

A visit to the three largest cities in the country will not disappoint when it comes to great entertainment. Each is rich in theater, film, and music venues. Montreal has spawned both French and English musical artists, and annual festivals abound, such as the Festival International de Jazz de Montréal. The renowned Toronto International Film Festival attracts the cream of Hollywood celebrities every September, and Vancouver is no slouch with its vibrant live music scene, dance clubs, and Irish pubs in numerous neighborhoods.

Giant flag in the parade at the annual Pride Toronto

Festivals

Festival fever hits Canada's three largest cities in the summer, but late spring and early fall can offer unique events too. Montreal's own **Cirque du Soleil** often premieres its new productions in its home city, and the **Festival International de Jazz de Montréal** is known for its hundreds of free concerts. Toronto's **Contact Photography Festival** enables new artists to exhibit alongside internationally famous photographers. Both the **Pride Toronto** and **Vancouver Gay Pride** festivals attract huge crowds. The **Toronto Caribbean Carnival**, commonly known as Caribana, bursts into colour and life over the first weekend in August. The **Vancouver International Film Festival** is fast becoming as popular as the **Toronto International Film Festival**. In July, Vancouver's **Dancing on the Edge Festival** showcases contemporary dance.

Theater

Montreal has an important theater for the anglophone enthusiast. The **Centaur Theatre Company** is housed in the former Montreal Stock Exchange building and stages high-quality English-language productions by both emerging and established playwrights. Both Canadian and international plays are performed regularly. Toronto's live theater community thrives, mainly due to the **Mirvish** production company and its theaters, and the city often showcases the continental premiere of large-scale productions, such as *Lord of the Rings*.

Vancouver's nonprofit **Arts Club Theatre Company** has produced more than 45 seasons of professional live theater. The city also hosts the **Bard on the Beach** – western Canada's largest professional Shakespeare festival, performed in Vancouver's Vanier Park.

Rock, Folk, and Pop Music

The main location for rock and pop concerts in Montreal is the **Bell Centre**, while folk music and up-and-coming artists can be found in the Quartier Latin (Latin Quarter) at any of the trendy bistros and bars along Saint-Denis and Ontario streets. Toronto's largest pop/rock concerts can be enjoyed at the **Rogers Centre** or the **Air Canada Centre**. There is also the **Sony Centre for the Performing Arts** for major shows. During the summer months, rock groups play at the **Molson Amphitheatre** and at **Echo Beach**, right on the waterfront. In Vancouver, **Rogers Arena** usually hosts the biggest rock and pop concerts, while the more intimate **Orpheum Theatre** hosts single or smaller groups of musicians.

Classical Music, Opera and Ballet

The **Opéra de Montréal**, founded in 1980, is the largest francophone opera company in North America. For dance lovers, **Les Grands Ballets Canadiens de Montréal** has a wide repertoire and invites prestigious international ballet companies each year to Place des Arts. Toronto is home to the **Toronto Symphony Orchestra**, whose main performance venue is the Roy Thomson Hall, and to the

The setting for Bard on the Beach – Vancouver's Shakespeare Festival

Performance by the Opéra de Montréal at the city's Place des Arts

Canadian Opera Company and the **National Ballet of Canada**, which are showcased at the **Four Seasons Centre for the Performing Arts**. In Vancouver, the **Queen Elizabeth Theatre** plays host to both the **Vancouver Opera** and **Ballet British Columbia**.

Bars and Clubs

Montreal has two main clubbing areas: Rue Crescent, a two-block area packed with patios and pubs between Rue de Maisonneuve and Rue Sainte-Catherine, and Rue Saint-Laurent, a predominantly French-speaking neighborhood with more upscale locations and most of the dance clubs. Toronto's Queen Street and King Street West neighborhoods (from University to Spadina avenues) are where big, brash dance clubs and comedy venues are located. The city's gay village and its nightclubs are in the Church-Wellesley Streets area. Vancouver's nightlife spreads all over: from Robson street downtown, to Gastown, where the artsy community owns galleries that double as bars. Kitsilano is the city's homage to California life, with pretty people and beachside bars and clubs.

DIRECTORY

Festivals

Cirque du Soleil
Tel 1 877 924 7783.
W cirquedusoleil.com

Contact Photography Festival
Toronto. May.
Tel 416 539 9595.
W contactphoto.com

Dancing on the Edge Festival
Vancouver. Jul.
W dancingontheedge.org

Festival International de Jazz de Montréal
Late Jun–early Jul.
Tel (514) 871 1881.
W montrealjazzfest.com

Pride Toronto
Jun. Tel 416 927 7433.
W pridetoronto.com

Toronto Caribbean Carnival (Caribana)
Aug. Tel 416 391 5608.
W torontocaribbeancarnival.com

Toronto International Film Festival
Early Sep. Tel (416) 599 8433. W tiff.net

Vancouver International Film Festival
Late Sep–early Oct.
Tel (604) 683 3456.
W viff.org

Vancouver Gay Pride
Aug. Tel (604) 687 0955.
W vancouverpride.ca

Theater

Arts Club Theatre Company
1585 Johnston St., Vancouver. Tel (604) 687 1644. W artsclub.com

Bard on the Beach
Vanier Park, Kits Point, Whyte Ave., Vancouver.
Tel (604) 739 0559.
W bardonthebeach.org

Centaur Theatre Company
453 Rue Saint-François-Xavier, Montreal.
Tel (514) 288 3161.
W centaurtheatre.com

Mirvish Theatres
Princess of Wales Theatre, 300 King St. W., Toronto
Royal Alexandra Theatre, 260 King St. W., Toronto
Ed Mirvish Theatre, 244 Victoria St., Toronto
Panasonic Theatre, 651 Yonge St., Toronto.
Tel 416 872 1212.
W mirvish.com

Theatre Passe Muraille
16 Ryerson Ave., Toronto.
Tel 416 504 7529.
W passmuraille.ca

Rock, Folk, and Pop Music

Air Canada Centre
40 Bay St., Toronto.
Tel 1 855 985 5000.
W theaircanadacentre.com

Bell Centre
1260 Rue de la Gauchetière O., Montreal.
Tel (514) 932 2582.
W centrebell.ca

Echo Beach
909 Lakeshore Blvd W., Toronto.
Tel 416 269 5700.
W echobeach.ca

Molson Amphitheatre
909 Lakeshore Blvd W., Toronto.
Tel 416 260 5600.
W livenation.com

Orpheum Theatre
884 Granville St., Vancouver. Tel (604) 665 3050. W vancouver.ca/theatres

Rogers Arena
800 Griffiths Way, Vancouver.
Tel 1 855 985 5000.
W rogersarena.com

Rogers Centre
Next to the CN Tower, Toronto.
Tel 1 855 985 5000.
W rogerscentre.com

Sony Centre for the Performing Arts
1 Front St. E., Toronto. Tel 1 855 872 7669.
W sonycentre.ca

Classical Music, Opera, and Ballet

Ballet British Columbia
Vancouver.
Tel (604) 732 5003.
W balletbc.com

Bell Centre

Canadian Opera Company
Toronto.
Tel 416 363 8231.
W coc.ca

Four Seasons Centre for the Performing Arts
145 Queen St. W., Toronto.
Tel 416 363 8231.
W fourseasonscentre.ca

Les Grands Ballets Canadiens de Montréal
Tel (514) 849 0269.
W grandsballets.com

National Ballet of Canada
Toronto.
Tel 416 345 9595.
W national.ballet.ca

Opéra de Montréal
Tel (514) 985 2258.
W operademontreal.com

Queen Elizabeth Theatre
649 Cambie St., Vancouver.
Tel (604) 665 3050.
W vancouver.ca/theatres

Toronto Symphony Orchestra
Tel 416 593 4828.
W tso.ca

Vancouver Opera
Tel (604) 683 0222.
W vancouveropera.ca

SPECIALTY VACATIONS AND ACTIVITIES

The sheer variety of the massive, unspoiled landscape is, in many ways, what attracts visitors to Canada. Taking advantage of the 45 national parks, several of which are UNESCO World Heritage sites, most specialty vacations tend to revolve around Canada's spacious natural playgrounds. The range of activities available in this single country is wide: sledding and snowmobiling with Inuit guides or cruising in the spring through the flower-filled Thousand Islands of Ontario are both possibilities. Other choices include scenic train rides through the Rockies, trout-fishing in pristine secluded lakes, and adventurous world-class hiking.

Hiking

Canada is one of the world's top hiking destinations, with excellent facilities and a wide variety of terrain for beginners and experts alike. Hiking trails range from leisurely nature walks to several days' physically demanding trek through starkly beautiful wilderness.

The preferred starting places for hiking trails in each national park are well marked. Accommodations for longer trips are often available in cabins or yurts within a park; alternatively you can bring your own tent or rent one in a nearby town. Large-scale maps of any area, including national and provincial parks, can be obtained from **World of Maps** in Ottawa.

Most of the more popular hikes require a level of fitness but little preparation before-hand. The best-known hiking areas are found in Alberta and British Columbia, in particular in and around the "big four parks" of Banff, Jasper, Kootenay, and Yoho, which straddle the Rocky Mountains. The variety of lands here, from the lush, gently rolling country near Calgary to craggy mountain peaks, reinforces the popularity of the area. More centrally, the prairie provinces offer a surprising variety of walking, from the arid badlands of Alberta's dinosaur country to the wilderness hiking in Prince Albert National Park. In the east, the mountains resume; the steep scenery of the Quebec park of Gatineau and the untamed wilds of the eastern and central Gaspé Peninsula both have wonderful scenery.

In northern Canada the hiking is less accessible but equally rewarding. Most walking and hiking takes place from July to August, when temperatures do rise slightly, although drops to -30°C (-22°F) are not unusual. At best, the weather remains unpredictable. The Chilkoot Pass is a 53-km

Turquoise Lake O'Hara in Yoho National Park

(33-mile) trail that follows the path of early gold prospectors in the late 19th century from Dyea in Alaska to Bennett in northern British Columbia. For the area, this is a relatively well-traveled path and gives a good taste of northern scenery. More arduous, not to say dangerous, is the memorable Pangnirtung Trail through the southeast of Baffin Island, which even in the summer has a permanently frozen ice cap. Inuit guides will take hikers through the frozen wastes by arrangement.

Occasionally wildlife-watching hikes are available, and teams of husky dogs carry visitors on sleds across ice paths in the wilderness to reach remote destinations. Such tours are worth researching as they tend to be expensive due to their remoteness and a lack of other modes of transportation.

Hikers near Weasel River, Auyuittuq National Park, Baffin Island

Safety Measures

Training and safety procedures must be followed for any hike. Always contact the local park or provincial tourist office for their advice and route maps before setting off. Remember, however unlikely a meeting may seem, wildlife can be aggressive; following instructions on bear safety is a must *(see p304)*. While less alarming, insects are a constant irritant: take all possible measures to repel blackflies and mosquitos. However clear and sparkling it may seem, do not drink stream or river water without thoroughly boiling it first, as it may contain an intestinal parasite, which can lead to "beaver fever" or giardiasis.

In the far north, freezing weather conditions place a premium on safety measures. Never go on a trip without telling someone your planned route and expected time of arrival. Consult local wardens about wildlife and routes, and take the proper equipment. Even in the summer, freezing weather changes can be sudden, so be prepared. Those venturing into little-known territory must be accompanied by a trained guide or seek local advice on dealing with the unexpected.

Equipment

Most hiking areas offer rental outlets for tents and cold-weather clothing. Nonetheless, sturdy walking boots, rain gear, and a change of clothing are essentials that hikers have to bring themselves, or buy in a nearby town. Appropriate medication and a first-aid kit

Emerald Lake Lodge in scenic Yoho National Park

should also be taken, in particular bug repellent, and antihistamine. Exposure, resulting in either sunstroke or hypothermia, can be guarded against by using appropriate clothes. On a long trip, carry energy-giving foods such as chocolate or trail mix.

National Parks

Canada's 40-plus national parks cover the country's most beautiful mountains, lakes, rivers, forests, and coastline. Areas of unspoiled wilderness, they are the ideal destination for those seeking an outdoor vacation filled with sports, activities, or even a natural spa. The most celebrated upland areas are the "big four" parks in Alberta and BC, Kluane in the Yukon, and

the arctic flower-filled tundra of Auyuittuq National Park in southern Baffin Island.

All national parks in Canada are administered by the government heritage body, **Parks Canada**, and each has a visitors' center or park office to welcome visitors. Here walking, hiking, canoeing, and fishing information is available, often from staff who know every detail of the terrain. These offices also issue permits for fishing, which are necessary in each park. Hunting of any kind and use of firearms are all strictly forbidden in national parks, as is feeding the wildlife and damaging any trees and plants. Most parks have camping facilities, or rustic lodges and cottages. The parks generally charge for these facilities, and most have a daily, weekly, or yearly entrance fee, but some are free. Annual passes are available from either the individual park or online on the Parks Canada website.

Swimmers at Radium Hot Springs in the Rockies

Canoeists on Wapizagonke Lake,
Parc National de la Mauricie

Canoeing

Aboriginal Canadians perfected
the canoe to maneuver around
the country's vast system of
waterways for food and survival;
today canoeing is a largely
recreational pursuit. In provincial
or national parks with many lakes
and rivers, canoeists can portage
(or trek) to the backwaters,
getting away from the most
populated areas at a gentle pace.

Over 250,000 lakes and 35,000
km (22,000 miles) of waterways
in Ontario make this the most
accessible canoeing destination.
Rivers and lakes making up
more than 25,000 km (16,000
miles) of canoe routes run
through the Algonquin,
Killarney, and Quetico parks.
The Rideau Canal, which travels

190 km (120 miles) from Ottawa
to Kingston is a favorite route
through the province, taking in
the capital, the sprinkling of tiny
islands near the historic town
of Kingston, and acres of fruit
orchards by the fertile
waterway. While traveling
through the islands, be careful
of the other marine traffic. The
Canal connects with the
Saint Lawrence Seaway, the
world's largest draft inland
waterway, and shipping
regulations are tight. Smaller
craft may have to make way
for tankers. Most towns near
canoeing routes will rent boats
by the day, week, or month, and
wetsuits, oars, and life jackets
are usually available. Because of
the popularity of watersports,
Canada is an extremely
reasonable place to buy fishing
and canoeing equipment; many
outfitters offer good-quality
products at considerably less
than European and US prices.

Whitewater Rafting

Whitewater rafting may be
attempted in the national
parks of British Columbia.
The Mackenzie River system,
which runs from BC backwaters
through the Northwest
Territories, provides occasionally
hair-raising rafting and canoeing.
Most routes in the far north are
for the experienced only. The
toughest trek of all is the 300-km

(180-mile) run of the South
Nahanni River near Fort Simpson
in the Northwest Territories.

Inexperienced boaters and
rafters can take advantage of
two-week basic training
courses offered all over the
country. Lake canoeing in
Wells Gray Provincial Park is
popular throughout the
province for those seeking
a more relaxing alternative.

Windsurfing in Georgian Bay Islands
National Park, Lake Ontario

Other Watersports

Although the season may be
short, sailing has always been a
popular summer pastime. Canada
contains a large proportion of the
world's fresh water, and there are
allegedly more boats per head
here than anywhere else in the
world. The Great Lakes are the
prime sailing and windsurfing

Whitewater rafting on the Athabasca River, Jasper National Park in the Rocky Mountains

Snowmobiling in Ontario across virgin powder snow

areas, as are both east and west coastal regions from May to September. Paddleboarding is popular throughout the country, with rentals available at coastal and resort areas. Swimming is also a favorite in warm weather; beaches on Prince Edward Island and Cape Breton off the east coast offer warm waters and sandy beaches, while lakes in Ontario, such as Lake Huron, provide inland swims. Torontonians sometimes swim in Lake Ontario in the summer, and surfers head to the west coast of Vancouver Island year-round.

Fishing

Almost 8 million sq km (3 million sq miles) of inland waters go partway to justifying Canada's reputation as a paradise for anglers. There are countless varieties of sports fish (see p31), not to mention the charterboat ocean fishing for salmon off the Pacific coast. Many parks offer fishing, often in secluded, pristine lakes and rivers. Be sure to contact the park's main office to obtain a fishing license. While most visitors fish in summer, a tiny wooden structure that sits on the frozen lake makes winter fishing more comfortable. These huts sit over a hole in the ice and are often heated. It may be worth buying rods and reels at your destination; Canadian fishing equipment is very high quality, with a good choice, and is usually very well priced.

A snowboard

Skiing, Snowboarding, and Snowmobiling

Not for nothing is Canada known as the Great White North, and its snowy terrain provides some of the world's best skiing and snowboarding. In the east, the Laurentian resorts of Mont Tremblant and Mont-Sainte-Anne offer excellent downhill skiing. Moving west, the resorts of Whistler, Lake Louise, and Banff provide unforgettably dramatic skiing. High in the Rockies, powder snow awaits the adventurous; heli-skiing (lifting skiers by helicopter to pristine slopes) takes place on the deserted British Columbia peaks. Many of the runs are higher than those in the European Alps, particularly in Banff and Lake Louise. These sites have held major competitions, including the Winter Olympics at Whistler in 2010. Another advantage to skiing in Canada is the proximity of the mountains to major cities; it is perfectly possible to spend the day zipping down slopes and then dine out in town.

Cross-country skiing is available across the country, but is particularly fine in southern and central Ontario's rolling terrain and Quebec's Laurentian mountain range and Eastern Townships. Many downhill ski resorts have a network of cross-country trails, but there are also dedicated cross-country ski areas and numerous parks with groomed trails.

Terrain parks have become increasingly popular in snowsports centers across the country. Most downhill resorts have an area with jumps and rails.

Snowmobiles are a necessity for many living in rural areas, but snowmobiling is also a popular winter sport. Ontario has almost 50,000 km (31,000 miles) of snowmobile trails. Seasoned riders can cover up to 500 km (300 miles) in two days. Traveling in groups is advised; there are many popular pitstops en route. These "snow inns" often offer package deals.

 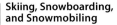

SURVIVAL GUIDE

PRACTICAL INFORMATION

Canada is one of the world's top tourist destinations, offering visitors a mix of urban sophistication and outdoor pleasures. Visitors' facilities are generally excellent. Accommodations and restaurants are of international standard *(see pp348–83)*, public transportation is efficient *(see pp406–19)*, and tourist information centers are found nearly everywhere. The following pages contain useful information for all visitors. Personal Security and Health *(see pp402–3)* details a number of recommended precautions, while Banking and Currency *(see p404)* answers the important financial queries, together with taxation details. There is also a section on how to use the Canadian telephone and postal services.

When to Go

Weather and geography dominate any visit to Canada. The vastness of the country means that most trips will be centered on one of the major cities, Montreal, Ottawa, Toronto and Vancouver, although it is possible to stay in remote areas such as the isolated Inuit settlements dotted around Hudson Bay. Depending on each visitor's interests, the best time to go will be dictated by local climate and the time of year.

In general, the climates on both the west and east coasts are temperate, while harsher weather occurs in the center of the country; in Alberta, Manitoba, and Saskatchewan, the summers are fine but the winters long and hard. Northern Canada is at its most welcoming during July and August when the land thaws, and the temperature is more likely to climb above freezing point.

In eastern Canada, New Brunswick, Nova Scotia, and Prince Edward Island, there are four distinct seasons, with snowy winters, mild springs, and crisp falls; summer is still the best time to visit the provinces' resorts. Ontario and Quebec have hot, humid summers and cold winters, with snow lingering until late March. Spring and fall are brief, although the latter in particular can be a rewarding time to make a visit.

The northeastern province of Newfoundland and coastal Labrador have the most extreme temperatures, ranging on a winter's day from 0°C (32°F) to -50°C (-58°F) in St. John's on Newfoundland's east coast. Winter visitors to British Columbia and the Rockies can enjoy some of the best skiing in the world. This region is also noted for its temperate weather but can be very wet in spring and fall, as Pacific depressions roll in over the mountains.

Entry Requirements

All visitors to Canada should have a passport valid for longer than the intended period of stay. Stricter US security regulations mean this now includes American citizens, who must show passports when entering Canada. Travelers from the UK, US, EU, and all British Commonwealth countries do not require a special visa to visit. Tourists are issued with a visitor's visa on arrival if they satisfy immigration officials that they have a valid return ticket and sufficient funds for the duration of their stay. Visitors can stay up to six months, but to extend their stay they

Visitors enjoying a ride on a swing carousel at the Canadian National Exhibition in Toronto

◀ A light rail train passing through the fall forest, Edmonton, near Alberta must apply to Citizenship and Immigration Canada in Ottawa before the expiration of their authorized visit. As visa regulations are subject to change, check with the nearest Canadian Consulate, Embassy, or High Commission before travel.

Anyone under the age of 18 traveling unaccompanied by an adult needs a letter of consent from a parent or guardian. The person meeting the child also needs to have full authorization and proof of permission.

Travel Safety Advice

Visitors can get up-to-date travel safety information from the Foreign and Commonwealth Office in the UK, the State Department in the US and the Department of Foreign Affairs and Trade in Australia.

Tourist Information

Canadian tourist offices are famous for the amount and quality of their information, offering everything from local maps to hotel, B&B, or camp-ground bookings. Special tours such as wilderness camping, archeological digs, and wildlife-watching can often be arranged through the local information centers. All major provincial and national parks have visitors' centers, which generally provide maps detailing hiking trails and canoe routes.

Destination Canada is the central tourism organization, and each province has its own tourism authority. Many smaller towns also have their own seasonal tourist offices. Accommodations can usually be booked at the booths found in airports and regional offices and online.

Opening Hours and Admission Prices

Most museums, parks, and other attractions throughout

Canadian Time Zones

Canada has six time zones spanning a four-and-a-half hour time difference from coast to coast. Between Vancouver and Halifax there are five zones; Pacific, Mountain, Central, Eastern, and Atlantic Standard Time, with an unusual half-hour difference between Newfoundland and Atlantic time. Every province except Saskatchewan uses Daylight Saving Time to give longer summer days from mid-March to October or November. Clocks go back an hour in October/November, and forward an hour in March.

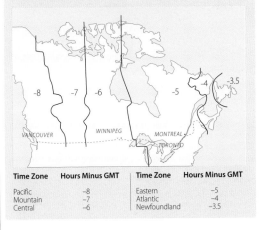

Time Zone	Hours Minus GMT	Time Zone	Hours Minus GMT
Pacific	–8	Eastern	–5
Mountain	–7	Atlantic	–4
Central	–6	Newfoundland	–3.5

Canada charge an admission fee. Many sights offer a range of discount packages for families, children, and seniors, with tourist office leaflets, brochures, and local newspapers often carrying discount coupons. Some galleries and museums have free-of-charge days or evenings, or a free hour daily before closing time. As a rule, most of the sights are open for longer through summer but may close completely during the winter months. Many museums and galleries close one day each week in winter, usually on a Monday or Tuesday, but not on weekends. Although many attractions are closed on major holidays, such as Christmas and New Year's Day, a surprising number are open all year round. School summer holidays in Canada are from late June to Labour Day Weekend, which ends on the first Monday in September. Labour Day

"The Small Apple" tourist booth in Ontario

Weekend generally signifies the end of summer, after which opening hours change to shorter winter hours of operation. Rural sights generally have shorter hours year round than those in cities.

Senior Travelers

In Canada people over 60 are generally referred to as "seniors," and are offered a wide range of discounts. Reduced rates frequently apply to the cost of movie tickets, public transportation, entrance fees, and some restaurant menus. When applicable, reductions range from 10 to 50 percent for people aged from 55, 60, or 65, depending on the province or attraction. If discounts are not advertised it is always a good idea to inquire.

Trips with a component of lifelong learning for older adults are organized by **Road Scholar**, a non-profit organization once known as Elderhostel Canada. A typical holiday comprises morning lectures, guided tours in the afternoon, and a communal dinner.

Tourists enjoying the scenery of Niagara Falls

Traveling with Children

Although Canada lacks the numbers of theme parks of the US, its beach resorts, parks, and city centers have much to offer children and families. Most types of accommodation state whether or not they welcome children. Those hotels that do often do not charge for a child sharing a parent's room. They will usually provide cribs and high chairs, and sometimes have baby-sitting services.

Restaurants generally welcome children, and many offer kids' menus and high chairs, or will warm up milk and baby food. Some fast-food outlets have play areas. It is best to check in advance with more upscale establishments.

Discounted airfares for children have mostly been phased out in North America, although infants under two years old who are not taking up a seat may travel for ten percent of the full fare. On public transportation, children under two travel free, and those under 12 have lower fares. If you are renting a car, you can reserve one or two car seats for children from your rental firm (see p419).

Etiquette

Canada is very much a multi-cultural nation (see pp32–3) that welcomes and respects people and customs from the rest of the world. Indigenous Canadians are never referred to as "Indians"; in general they are known as Canada's "First

Nations," "First Peoples," or "Aboriginal Peoples," while the term "eskimos" has been superceded by "Inuit" (see p37). In Quebec, be prepared to hear French spoken first. It is also appreciated if visitors show that they have tried to learn a few French words.

Canada's relaxed, informal atmosphere is evident in its dress codes, which tend to be practical and dependent on the climate. Canadians favor jeans and sweatshirts, and dress in layers, so they can add or subtract clothing, especially when moving between well-heated malls and winter streets. However, in the cities and larger towns more formal clothing is expected, particularly in more stylish restaurants, theaters, and other formal places. Even the more humble eateries insist on proper attire, and the sign "no shoes, no shirt, no service" is frequently seen in many tourist areas. Topless sunbathing is generally frowned upon in Canada.

Drinking in non-licenced public places, such as city parks, is illegal, and it is also illegal to have opened bottles of alcohol in the car when traveling. It is against the law to smoke in public places, such as on transport, in public buildings, and in restaurants and bars

throughout Canada. A service charge is seldom included in checks at Canadian restaurants. Unless it is included, the standard tip in Canada is 15 percent. Taxi drivers expect a similar tip, while barbers and hairdressers should receive about 10 percent of the total. It is customary to tip porters at airports and train stations, cloakroom attendants, bellhops, doormen, and hotel porters Can $1 per bag, and to leave something for the hotel maids. Tipping bar staff in bars and nightclubs is also expected. Anyone in charge of a large party of visitors should prepare to be generous.

Student Travelers

With an International Student Identity Card (ISIC), full-time students are entitled to discounts on travel as well as admission prices to movies, galleries, museums, and many other tourist attractions. The ISIC card should be purchased in the student's home country at a **Student Travel Association** (STA) office in the nearest city. There are also a wide range of bus and rail discounts available

International student I.D. card

to students, such as the "Go Canada" Accommodation and Coach Pass, which offers both reduced-cost travel and stays in youth hostels across the country. The pass can be booked through local agents specializing in student travel. VIA Rail also offers students the "Canrail Pass," which allows a period of unlimited travel on all routes. Reasonably priced accommodations are available on university campuses in the larger cities in July and August. There are also comfortable hostels throughout the country, most of which are affiliated with Hostelling International (HI). Eating out doesn't need to be expensive; it's possible to find great food on a budget.

Electricity

Canadian electrical appliances come with either a two- or three-prong plug, and most sockets will accept either. The system is a 110-volt, 60-cycle system. You will need an adaptor, if you are visiting from outside North America.

Batteries are universal and readily available for all appliances. Bear in mind that bargain electrical goods purchased here will probably need modification for use in Europe.

Disabled Travelers

Travelers with physical disabilities can expect some of the best facilities in the world in Canada. Overall, large towns and cities offer wheelchair access in most public buildings, as well as on public transportation. Most curbs are dropped at inter-sections, and a large number of subway staions have elevators. Check the Toronto Transit Commission (TTC) website for more information.

Formerly the Canadian Paraplegic Association, **Spinal Cord Injury (SCI) Canada** is a great resource for those with physical disabilities. With 40 offices across the country, SCI offers disabled travelers advice on accessing most attractions. Go to the main SCI Canada website for more information about the federation and its provincial offices.

There is a wide choice of hotels with disabled facilities in Canada. Most of the big chains such as Best Western and Holiday Inn are easily accessible, as are some luxury hotels and hostels. The Canadian Paraplegic Association (CPA) also has details on the most disabled-friendly attractions. Many of the national and provincial parks have interpretive centers, short nature trails, campsites and board-walks that are wheelchair accessible. Call the relevant park for more information.

Conversion Chart

Imperial to Metric
1 inch = 2.54 cm
1 ft = 30 cm
1 mile = 1.6 km
1 oz = 28 gm
1 lb = 454 gm
1 pint = 0.6 liters
1 gal = 4.6 liters

Metric to Imperial
1 cm = 0.4 inches
1 m = 3 ft, 3 inches
1 km = 0.6 miles
1 gm = 0.04 oz
1 kg = 2.2 lbs
1 liter = 1.8 pints

DIRECTORY

Immigration

Canadian High Commission
Trafalgar Square, London, SW1Y 5BJ, UK
Tel (020) 004 6000.

Citizenship and Immigration Canada
Operations Support Centre, Ottawa, ON, K1A 1L1. **Tel** 1 (888) 242 2100. **W** cic.gc.ca

Consulate General
1251 Avenue of the Americas, New York, NY, 10020-1175., US **Tel** (212) 596 1628. **W** canada international.gc.ca

Travel Safety Advice

Australia
Department of Foreign Affairs and Trade
W smartraveller.gov.au

UK
Foreign and Commonwealth Office
W www.gov.uk/ foreign-travel-advice

US
US Department of State
W travel.state.gov

Tourist Information

Destination Canada
Suite 800, 1045 Howe St., Vancouver, BC, V6Z2A9.
Tel (604) 638 8300.
W destinationcanada. com

Provincial Offices

British Columbia
Hello BC.
Tel 1 (800) 435 5622.
W hellobc.com

Newfoundland and Labrador
Tel 1 (800) 563 6353.
W newfoundland labrador.com

Northwest Territories
Tel 1 (800) 661 0788.
W spectacularnwt.com

Nova Scotia Tourism
Tel 1 (800) 565 0000.
W novascotia.com

Nunavut Tourism
Tel 1 (800) 491 7910.
W nunavuttourism.com

Ontario Tourism
10 Dundas St. E., Suite 900, Toronto, ON, M7A 2A1. **Tel** 1 (800) 668 2746.
W ontariotravel.net

Travel Alberta
400, 1601-9 Ave. SE., Calgary, AB, T2G 0H4.
Tel 1 (800) 252 3782.
W travelalberta.com

Travel Manitoba
21 Forks Market Rd., Winnipeg, MB, R3C 4T7.
Tel 1 (800) 665 0040.
W travelmanitoba.com

Tourism New Brunswick
Tel 1 (800) 561 0123.
W tourismnew brunswick.ca

Tourism Prince Edward Island
Tel 1 (800) 463 4734.
W tourismpei.com

Tourism Quebec
Suite 100, 1255 Peele St., Montreal, QC, H3B 4V4.
Tel 1 (877) 266 5687.
W quebecoriginal.com

Tourism Saskatchewan
189–1621 Albert St., Regina, SK, S4P 2S5. **Tel** 1 (877) 237 2273. **W** tourism saskatchewan.com

Tourism Yukon
Tel 1 (800) 661 0494.
W travelyukon.com

Senior Travelers

Road Scholar
11, Ave. de Lafayette, Boston, MA 02111, US.
Tel 1 (800) 454 5768
W roadscholar.org

Student Travelers

STA Travel
Tel 1 (800) 667 2887
W travelcuts.com.

Disabled Travelers

Access To Travel
Government of Canada.
W accesstotravel.gc.ca

Société de transport de Montréal
W stm.info/en/access

Spinal Cord Injury Canada
Tel (416) 200 5814.
W sci-can.ca

Toronto Transit Commission
W ttc.ca/TTC_ Accessibility

Translink Metro Vancouver
W translink.ca/en/Rider-Guide/Accessible-Transit. aspx

Personal Security and Health

With its comparatively low crime rate, Canada is a safe country to visit. In contrast to many US cities, there is little street crime in the city centers, perhaps because so many Canadians live downtown that the cities are never empty at night. However, it is wise to be careful and to find out which parts of town are safer than others. Avoid city parks after dark, and make sure that cars are left locked. In the country's more remote areas visitors must observe sensible safety measures. Wildlife and climatic dangers can be avoided by seeking — and heeding — local advice. If a serious problem does arise, contact one of the national emergency numbers in the telephone directory.

Personal Safety

There are few off-limit areas in Canadian cities. Even the seedier districts tend to have a visible police presence, making them safer than the average suburban area at night. Always ask your hotelier, the local tourist information center, or the police, which areas to avoid. Although theft is rare in hotel rooms, it is a good idea to store any valuables in the hotel safe, as hotels will not guarantee the security of property left in rooms. Make sure you leave your hotel room key at the front desk when you go out.

Pickpockets can be a hazard at large public gatherings and popular tourist attractions, so it is a good idea to wear cameras and bags over one shoulder with the strap across your body. Try not to be seen with large amounts of cash, and, if necessary use a coin purse and a wallet for larger bills. Keep your passport separate from your cash and credit cards. Never hang your purse over the back of your chair in restaurants; put it on the floor beside your feet with one foot over the strap, or pinned down by a chair leg. Travelers should not carry their wallets in their back pockets, as this makes a very easy target. Safe options for both sexes are zippered purse belts worn under clothing.

Law Enforcement

Canada is policed by a combination of forces. The Royal Canadian Mounted Police (RCMP) operate throughout most of the country, while Ontario, Quebec, and Newfoundland and Labrador are looked after by provincial forces. There are also city police in large urban areas, and some First Nations reserves have their own police forces. For the most part, the officers are noted for their helpful attitude, but it is unwise to comment on (or joke about) safety, bombs, guns, and terrorism in places such as airports, where it is possible to be arrested for off-the-cuff remarks. Drinking and driving is also taken seriously here, and remember that open alcohol containers in a car are illegal. Narcotics users face criminal charges often followed by moves for deportation.

Lost Property

As soon as something is lost, report it to the police. They will issue a report with a number that you will need in order to make a claim on your insurance policy. If a credit card is missing, call the company's toll-free number and report it immediately.

If you lose your passport, contact the nearest embassy or consulate. They will be able to issue a temporary replacement, as visitors do not generally need a new passport if they will be returning directly to their home country. However, if you are traveling on to another destination, you will need a full passport. It is also useful to take photocopies of your driver's license and birth certificate, as well as notarized passport photographs, if you are contemplating an extended visit or need additional I. D.

Travel Insurance

Travel insurance is essential in Canada to cover health problems, accidents, trip-cancellation, and interruption, as well as theft and loss of valuable possessions.

Canadian health services are excellent, but if you do not wish to pay you will need insurance. If you already have private health insurance you should check to see if the coverage includes all emergency hospital and medical expenses such as physician's care, prescription drugs, and private duty-nursing. In case of a serious illness, separate coverage is also required to send a relative to your bedside or return a rented vehicle. Emergency dental treatment, and out-of-pocket expenses or loss of vacation costs also need their own policies. Your insurance company or travel agent should recommend the

Toronto policemen on bicycles

right policy, but beware of exclusions for pre-existing medical conditions.

Medical Treatment

A comprehensive range of treatment centers are available in Canada. For minor problems pharmacies are often a good source of advice, and walk-in clinics in the cities will treat visitors relatively quickly. In smaller communities, or in more difficult cases, go straight to the emergency room of the closest hospital, but be prepared for a long wait. In a serious medical emergency dial 911 in most areas, or 0 for the operator, to summon an ambulance.

Anyone taking a prescription drug should ask their doctor for extra supplies when they travel, as well as a copy of the prescription, in case more medication is needed on the trip. It is also a good idea to have this copy, or a list of your prescribed medication, available at airport security. It is a sensible precaution to take a simple first-aid kit for longer trips in the more remote or Arctic areas of the country. Generally this should include aspirin (or paracetamol), antihistamine for bites or allergies, motion-sickness pills, antiseptic, bandages and band aids, calamine lotion, and bug repellent. Antibiotic creams are useful for intrepid wilderness hikers.

All cities and larger towns have dental clinics that will provide emergency treatment.

Natural Hazards

There are times when Canada's mosquitoes and black flies can be so troublesome that moose and deer leave the woods for relief. Insects are a major irritant for tourists in rural areas. They are at their worst during annual breeding periods from late spring to midsummer, and

until the temperatures drop in Northern Canada. There are precautions one can take to alleviate the misery, the most effective one being the regular application of insect repellant. Stick to light-colored clothes, as the bugs are drawn to dark ones, and cover as much skin as possible with long sleeves, and pants tucked into boots and socks. It might even be worth investing in a gauze mask for your head and neck if you plan to venture into deserted areas at peak breeding times. Canada is notorious for its cold winter weather, but tourists are not likely to suffer many serious problems. The media gives daily extensive coverage to the weather, and, on days when frostbite is possible they offer detailed reports. Dressing in layers and wearing a hat is necessary. Sunscreen is needed in summer, even on overcast days.

Warning sign for motorists

Bears

Canada's national parks service, particularly in the Rockies, supplies advice on bear safety (see p304), but unless you are camping or hiking in the woods it is unlikely that you will come across a bear. Encounters can be avoided by following a few basic rules: never leave food or garbage near your tent, car, or

RV, do not wear scent, and make a noise (many hikers blow whistles) as you walk, as bears are more likely to attack if surprised. If you do come across a bear, do not scream or run since bears are very fast, and do not try to escape by climbing a tree – they are even better at that. Instead, keep still, speak to them in a low voice, and put your luggage on the ground to try and distract them.

DIRECTORY

Emergency Services

Ambulance Fire, Police
In most of Canada and in large cities call 911; elsewhere dial 0.

Consulates and Embassies

United States
Montreal: 1155 Rue Saint-Alexandre., (514) 398 9695.
Ottawa: 490 Sussex Drive., (613) 238 5335.
Toronto: 360 University Ave., 416 595 1700.
Vancouver: 1075 West Pender St., (604) 685 4311.
W ca.usembassy.gov

UK
Montreal: Suite 1940, 2000 McGill College Ave., (514) 866 5863.
Ottawa: 80 Elgin St., (613) 237 1530.
Toronto: Suite 2800, 777 Bay St., 416 593 1290.
Vancouver: Suite 800, 1111 Melville St., (604) 683 4421.
W gov.uk/government/world/canada

A polar bear approaching a tourist Tundra Buggy, northern Manitoba

Banking and Currency

Canadian currency is based on the decimal system, and has 100 cents to the dollar. Two of the most useful coins are the 25-cent, otherwise known as the quarter, and $1 pieces, which operate pay telephones (becoming scarce), newspaper boxes, and vending machines. They are also handy for public transportation in the larger cities, where as a matter of policy bus drivers often do not carry any change. It is best to arrive with some Canadian currency, around Can $50–100, including small change for tipping and taxis. Exchange bureaux are readily available in airports and train stations.

DIRECTORY

Currency Exchange And Wiring Money

American Express
Check replacement, Canada
Tel 1 800 221 7282.

Travelex
Tel 1 855 270 0627.

Western Union
Wiring money, Canada
Tel 1 800 235 0000.

Sandstone façade of the Toronto Stock Exchange

Banks

Canada's main national banks are the Royal Bank of Canada, Bank of Montréal, TD Canada Trust, Canadian Imperial Bank of Commerce (CIBC), Scotiabank, and National Bank of Canada. These banks generally accept foreign ATM (automatic teller machine) cards, although it is wise to check with your bank first. ATMs can be found at bank branches.

Banks are usually open Monday to Friday, from 9am to 5pm; some stay open later on Fridays, and a few open on Saturday mornings. All banks are closed on Sundays and on statutory holidays.

 Scotiabank

Scotiabank logo

Traveler's Checks and Currency Cards

Traveler's checks are largely being phased out and it is growing harder to find hotels, restaurants, and stores that will accept them as direct payment. Their replacement is the preloaded currency card, a much safer alternative to carrying cash. Check carefully, however, for hidden charges (on daily withdrawal limits, for example), and remember that despite the issuers' claims, not all outlets will accept these cards exactly as they would a bank card; you may still have to locate an ATM to withdraw cash for your payments and purchases.

ATMS

Automated Teller Machines (ATMs) can be found in most bank lobbies across Canada, as well as grocery stores, shopping centers, gas stations, train and bus stations, and airports. Before you travel ask your bank which ATM systems will accept your bank card, and how much each transaction will cost, as a charge may apply. The popular systems Cirrus and Plus both accept Visa and MasterCard.

Credit Cards

Credit cards are used extensively in Canada; MasterCard and VISA are widely accepted, American Express and Diner's Club less so in smaller outlets. Credit cards are often asked for as a form of ID, and for placing large deposits – most car-rental companies in Canada insist on a credit card or require a substantial cash deposit. Some hotels also prefer prepayment by credit card. Credit cards can also be used to secure cash advances, but you will be charged interest from the date of withdrawal.

Wiring Money

If you run out of money or have an emergency, it is possible to have cash wired from home in minutes using an electronic money service. Both American Express and Travelex provide this service, as does Western Union, which has around 22,000 outlets all over North America.

Western Union's familiar sign

Coins and Bank Notes

Canadian coins are issued in denominations of five cents (the nickel), ten cents (the dime), 25 cents (the quarter), $1 (dubbed the "loonie," because it has an illustration of the bird, the Canadian loon on one side), and the $2 coin or "toonie". The copper penny was removed from circulation in 2013.

Bank notes are printed in denominations of $5, $10, $20, $50, and $100. However, $100 dollar bills are sometimes viewed with suspicion, as they are not used very often in small stores, or even in cafés and gas stations.

Media and Communications

Canada has some of the most sophisticated communication systems in the world. Despite the popularity of mobile phones, there are still public payphones everywhere – in cafés, bars, public buildings, gas stations, and post offices. Most operate with coins, and while local calls are a bargain, international calls can be expensive. Wi-Fi is also widely available in hotels and cafés.

Canada Post, the country's mail service is certainly reliable, but it is renowned for being slow. It can be quick however, if you are willing to pay an extra fee for priority handling and delivery.

Public Telephones

Public telephones operate on 25 cent coins, although there is an increasing number of phones that accept both credit and phone cards. Rates are generally cheaper between 6pm and 8am, and on weekends. All local calls cost at least 50 cents (private subscribers have free local calls). For any call outside the local area, including international calls, the operator will tell you how much to pay for the initial period and will then ask for more money, as your call progresses. It is usually easier to make long-distance calls using a phone card than to have the stacks of change required.

Public roadside telephones are found countrywide

Postal Services

All mail from Canada to outside North America is by air and can take between seven and ten days to arrive. If you are sending mail locally, it can also take days – not including the postal code will make the service even slower. To send mail, look for signs that say "Canada Post" since some post offices are located in malls and pharmacies.

Mobile Phones and E-mail

Check roaming charges with your network before you travel. It may be worth getting a pay-as-you go plan for your trip.

Almost every Canadian hotel and most motels and hostels offer free Wi-Fi. The exceptions are lodges in remote locations, such as the far north. Many cafés and visitor centers also have free Wi-Fi. Only the more expensive city hotels charge for Internet access.

Media

The only papers that see themselves as national publications are the *National Post* and *The Globe and Mail*, both based in Toronto. There is also a national news weekly called *Maclean's*. All cities have their own daily newspapers and some, such as Toronto, have several.

Many cities and regions have free weeklies *(see p388)* that provide excellent coverage of local events.

Canada has a national 24-hour public broadcasting corporation (CBC), 80 percent of whose programs are produced locally. CBC also provides an excellent radio service, and can be a good source of information on local happenings and weather for visitors. They also have a national service in French.

Useful Information

Canadian Post Customer Services line.
Tel 1 800 267 1177.

DIRECTORY

Provincial Codes

Alberta: 403, 587, & 780.
British Columbia: 236, 250, 604, & 778.
Manitoba: 204 & 431.
New Brunswick: 506.
Northwest Territories: 867 (Yukon & Nunavut).
Nova Scotia & PEI: 782 & 902.
Newfoundland & Labrador: 709.
Ontario: 416, 437, & 647 (Toronto).
705: (central and northeast).
226, 289, & 519: (southwest peninsula).
343 & 613: (Ottawa region).
807: (northwest).
Quebec: 438 & 514 (Montreal).
819 & 873: (north).
418 & 581: (east).
Saskatchewan: 306 & 639.

Reaching the Right Number

- The area code is needed for all local calls. For calls to another area code: dial **1** followed by the area code and the **7-digit local number**.
- For international calls: dial **011** then the **code of the country** (Australia 61, UK 44) followed by the **area/city code** (minus the first 0) and the number. To call the US from Canada dial **1**, the area code, then the number.
- For international operator assistance, dial **0**.
- For information on numbers within your local area, dial **411**.
- For information on long distance numbers, call **1**, followed by the area code then **555 1212**.
- An **800**, **855**, **866**, **877**, or **888** prefix means that the call is toll free.

TRAVEL INFORMATION

The majority of visitors to Canada arrive by air, usually at one of the country's three largest international airports – Vancouver, Toronto, or Montreal. It is also possible to fly direct to cities such as Halifax, Winnipeg, Edmonton, Calgary, and St. John's, Newfoundland.

The size of the country makes flying between locations popular with visitors who wish to see more than one part of the country. For example, on a short stay, it could prove difficult to see Toronto and Montreal in the east, as well as the Rocky Mountains in the west, without spending some time in the air. There are other transportation choices that allow visitors to see much of Canada. The national rail network, VIA Rail, links most major cities, while long-distance bus routes often provide a less-expensive way to see the country. There are short cruises and ferry rides that take in some spectacular scenery. Exploring Canada by car is also a popular choice, enabling visitors to get to locations that can be difficult to reach any other way.

Air Canada is the country's major air carrier

Arriving by Air

Canada is a destination for several international airlines, and the country's major carrier **Air Canada** is linked with national airlines around the world. All Europe's principal airlines fly into Toronto or Montreal, while Vancouver is a gateway for carriers such as Cathay Pacific, Air New Zealand, and national airlines from the Far East.

Visitors who intend to see parts of the US as well as Canada can find plenty of connecting flights to such principal US destinations as New York, Los Angeles, Dallas, Chicago, and Atlanta.

International Flights

Flights between Canada and Europe take from five to ten hours; from Asia or Australia, across the Pacific, you may be in transit for as long as 20 hours. Older travelers or those with children may wish to consider a stopover for the sake of comfort (Hawaii is a popular choice, and some stop over in Hong Kong, Shanghai, or even Tokyo). It is also a good idea to plan flights so that they account for international time differences.

Canada has 13 international airports, the busiest being at Toronto, Montreal, and Vancouver. It is also possible to fly direct into airports in cities such as Edmonton, Halifax, Ottawa, Winnipeg, and St. John's, Newfoundland. All the major cities are connected with airports in the US. Several leading airlines offer special deals that allow visitors to fly to one part of North America and leave from another.

Air Fares

Flights to Canada from Europe, Australia, and the US can be expensive during peak holiday periods such as Christmas, New Year, and between July and mid-September. Book as far ahead as possible and you will have a better chance of finding a competitive fare.

Airport	Information
Calgary (YYC)	(403) 735 1200
Edmonton (YEG)	(780) 890 8900
Halifax (YHZ)	(902) 873 4422
Montréal–Mirabel (YMX)	(514) 394 7377
Montréal–Trudeau (YUL)	(514) 394 7377
Ottawa (YOW)	(613) 248 2000
St. John's (YQB)	(709) 758 8500
Toronto (YYZ)	416 776 9892
Vancouver (YVR)	(604) 207 7077
Winnipeg (YWG)	(204) 987 9402

keep in mind though that the cheapest tickets generally impose such restrictions as a maximum (of 3–6 months) length of stay. It can also be expensive to alter dates of travel, and it is worth considering insuring yourself against last-minute, unforeseen delays or cancellations.

Charter flights with airlines such as Air Transat sometimes offer a cheaper alternative, with savings of 20 percent on some tickets. Round-the-world fares are popular with those looking for longer itineraries, as are package vacations, which provide a variety of choices. The kinds of deals available range from fly/drive vacations with a much-reduced car rental as part of the price of the ticket,

to a guided tour, including all accommodations, transportation, and meals.

On Arrival

Just before landing in Canada you will be given customs and immigration documents to fill in. On arrival you will be asked to present them, along with your passport, to the appropriate customs and immigration officials.

The larger airports offer a better range of services, but most airports have shops, medical and postal services, foreign-exchange bureaus, newsstands, and bookstores. The major car-rental companies have outlets at the airport, and buses, taxis, limousines, and shuttle buses into town are available. Most terminals offer facilities for disabled travelers.

Visitors hoping to catch a connecting flight to another part of the country will have to claim and clear their baggage through customs before checking in

Roads to and from airports are well sign-posted

with the connecting airline. Arrangements for transferring to domestic flights are usually made when you book your trip. Ask airline staff if you need more information; in large airports, such as Toronto's Pearson International, there are three separate terminals.

DIRECTORY

Airlines in Canada the UK, and US

Air Canada
Tel UK: (0990) 247 226.
Can and US: 1 888 247 2262.
Ⓦ aircanada.ca

Air Transat
Tel Can and US: (514) 636 3630,
1 877 872 6728.
Ⓦ airtransat.com

American Airlines
Tel UK: (020) 7660 2300. Can and US: 1 800 433 7300.
Ⓦ aa.com

British Airways
Tel UK: (0844) 493 0787. Can and US: 1 800 247 9297.
Ⓦ britishairways.com

...nce from Downtown	Average Taxi Fare to City	Bus or Train to City
16 km (10 miles)	CAN $40	30 mins
31 km (19 miles)	CAN $55	55 mins
42 km (26 miles)	CAN $63	45 mins
55 km (34 miles)	CAN $70	40–55 mins
22 km (14 miles)	CAN $40	45 mins
18 km (11 miles)	CAN $30	25 mins
8 km (5 miles)	CAN $25	No Service
24 km (15 miles)	CAN $63	45–55 mins
15 km (9 miles)	CAN $35	25 mins
10 km (6 miles)	CAN $22	45 mins

Domestic Air Travel

Because of the distances involved, flying around the country has become an accepted part of Canadian life. There is a complex network of domestic flights, with numerous local airlines, some of which are linked to Air Canada. The smaller operators fly within provinces, and to remote locations where they are often the only means of transportation. In all there are some 125 domestic destinations. It is possible to book domestic flights with a travel agent before departure or, once in Canada, through local agents or on the internet. Domestic flights along the busier routes are becoming cheaper, and discounts are often advertised in the local press. A range of pass deals are available exclusively for visitors from abroad. Light aircraft can also be chartered for fascinating but costly trips over far-flung landmarks such as Baffin Island.

A Dash-7 regional aircraft during a trip in Canada's far north

Air Routes and Airlines

The impressive array of domestic flights available here means that most of the nation's smaller urban areas are within reach of regular services. However, you will generally have to fly to the major city in the area, principally Toronto, Montreal, or Vancouver, and then take a connecting flight.

Some of the smaller airlines are connected with Canada's major carrier, **Air Canada**, and it is often possible to book your connection through the national airline. The majority of the country's long-haul domestic routes run east-to-west, connecting the cities: from Halifax on the east coast, through to Montreal, Toronto, Ottawa, Winnipeg, Calgary, and Edmonton to Vancouver in the west. North-to-south flights to places such as the Yukon and the Northwest Territories usually originate from Edmonton and Winnipeg. In the remote north, charter flights are the only way to reach isolated destinations such as Ellesmere Island, with the exception of Churchill, Manitoba, which is also connected by train.

Apex Fares and Other Discounts

Domestic air travel in Canada is reasonably priced, especially on popular routes, where low-cost airlines such as **WestJet** are giving competition to **Air Canada**. Ticket structuring is very streamlined. The most expensive fares offer more flexibility than the cheapest ones. To get the least-expensive fares, plan on booking at least seven days in advance and be flexible in your travel dates. Be aware that only the most-expensive fares allow for refunds and free changes.

Seat sales are another bargain option, whereby an airline will advertise discounted tickets to boost travel on popular routes during quiet times of the year. There is, however, very little flexibility on these deals, and you have to fly within a specific period of time.

Air Canada offers pass deals for visitors who want to travel all over the country, as well as to the US. Most of the offers involve paying for a number of coupons, each of which represents a single flight within either the continent or a specific region.

Fly-Drive Deals

A good way to make the most of a visit to Canada is to book a fly-drive vacation. The deal invariably involves a substantial cut in the cost of the car rental. Arrangements can also be made to pick up and drop off your vehicle in different places. It would be possible, for example, to pick up a car in Toronto, tour Ontario, dropping the car off in Ottawa before flying on to Vancouver on the west coast. Known as one-way car rental, these deals may involve large drop-off fees: from Toronto to Ottawa costs around Can \$200. Travel agents offer a wide range of such packages.

Baggage Restrictions

Passengers traveling economy on domestic flights should be aware that there are restrictions on the amount and weight of baggage that can be taken on board. The type of aircraft determines what can be carried, and light aircraft usually accept only hand-baggage.

In general, passengers are entitled to have two suitcases, each with an average weight of 32 kg (70 lb) per item. Hand-baggage must fit safely under aircraft seats or in overhead lockers, so check the permitted dimensions with the airline. Garment bags may be carried on board some aircraft, but must be soft-sided and comply with size restrictions – length 112 cm (45 in), depth 11 cm (4.5 in) – so remember to check with your airline or travel agent when puchasing your ticket.

WestJet logo

Checking In

Security is a necessity nowadays and can make the boarding procedure take longer. It is best to check with the airline, but generally for domestic flights you should arrive at the airport 90 minutes before your departure; for flights to the US and other international flights, allow at least 2 hours. If you check in online, you can usually arrive at the airport only an hour before departure, but keep in mind that long waits at security are unpredicatble and could slow you down. Visitors from other countries traveling within Canada should carry a passport to verify that he or she is the traveler named on the ticket.

It is also worth noting that the daily peak periods at the larger Canadian airports are usually from 7am to 9am and from 3pm to 8pm. Passenger volume also increases significantly during the winter holiday season, over Easter, and in summer, so it is wise to allow extra time for parking, check-in, and security screening during these periods.

DIRECTORY

Domestic Airlines

Air Canada
Tel (514) 393 3333, 1 888 247 2262. W aircanada.ca

Air North (Alberta, BC, NWT, and Yukon)
Tel (867) 668 2228, 1 800 661 0407. W flyairnorth.com

Bearskin Airlines (Manitoba and Ontario)
Tel 1 800 465 2327.
W bearskinairlines.com

Calm Air
(Manitoba, inc. Churchill and Nunavut)
Tel 1 800 839 2256.
W calmair.com

First Air
(Nunavut and NWT)
Tel 1 800 267 1247.
W firstair.ca

Porter Airlines (Atlantic Provinces, Ontario, Quebec, and the US)
Tel 1 888 619 8622.
W flyporter.com

WestJet
Tel (403) 444 2586, 1 800 538 5696.
W westjet.com

Principal Domestic Air Routes

Canada's major airline is Air Canada. It provides links to a number of regional carriers to form a comprehensive domestic air network, while WestJet specializes in western destinations.

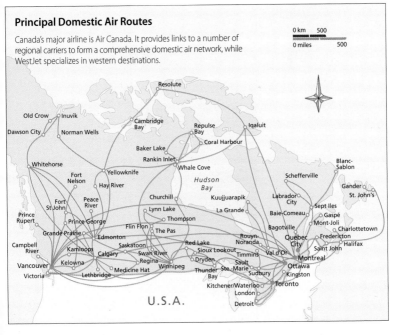

0 km 500
0 miles 500

Resolute
Old Crow   Inuvik
Dawson City   Norman Wells
Cambridge Bay
Repulse Bay   Iqaluit
Coral Harbour
Baker Lake
Rankin Inlet
Whitehorse
Yellowknife   Whale Cove
Fort Nelson   Hudson Bay   Blanc-Sablon
Hay River   Schefferville   Gander
Churchill   Kuujjuarapik   Labrador City   St. John's
Fort St John   Peace River   La Grande   Sept Iles
Prince Rupert   Lynn Lake   Baie-Comeau   Gaspé
Prince George   Thompson   Bagotville   Mont-Joli
Grande Prairie   Flin Flon   The Pas   Rouyn-Noranda   Quebec City   Charlottetown
Campbell River   Edmonton   Saskatoon   Red Lake   Sioux Lookout   Val d'Or   Fredericton
Kamloops   Swan River   Timmins   Saint John   Halifax
Vancouver   Calgary   Regina   Dryden   Sault Ste-Marie   Montreal
Kelowna   Winnipeg   Thunder Bay   Sudbury   Ottawa
Victoria   Lethbridge   Medicine Hat   Ste-Marie   Kingston
Kitchener/Waterloo   Toronto
London
Detroit

U.S.A.

GETTING AROUND CANADA'S CITIES

Although the car is a popular way to travel in Canada, the country is noted for the fast, frequent, and efficient public transit systems of its cities. In general, the best way for visitors to explore Canada's urban centers is primarily on foot, using public transportation as a back up. The streets are clean and safe, and strolling through different neighborhoods is a pleasant way to get to know them. Most cities are bike-friendly, too, with protected cycling lanes. Municipal transit systems are reasonably priced, with discounted multi-

ticket deals and day passes. Driving around downtown areas can be daunting, particularly during the rush hour, and parking tends to be both difficult and expensive.

Most transit systems offer free maps, available at stations or tourist information centers. The following pages detail how to get around Canada's three largest cities, Vancouver, Toronto, and Montreal *(see endpaper for detailed transit maps)*, as well as other provincial capitals and the most visited towns and communities.

Montreal

Montreal's bus and subway network is integrated, so that the stations connect with bus routes, and tickets can be used on either (the fare is Can $3.25 per sector). Be sure to get a transfer ticket, which should take you anywhere in the city for one fare. Known as the Métro, Montreal's subway is clean, safe, and air-conditioned in summer and heated in the winter. It is by far the fastest and cheapest way to get around town *(see endpaper)*. Free maps are available at any of the ticket booths. Visitors can buy a Tourist Pass for one or three days at major hotels and at the Visitor Information Office downtown.

Driving is not recommended here, as the roads are busy and parking is severely restricted, especially in the old town. It is best to use the city's park-and-ride system. Cabs can be hailed in the street. They have a white or orange sign on the roof; the sign is lit up, when the cab is available.

Many streets in Montreal have bike lanes. The Great Montreal Bike Path-Guide is available free at the tourist office. Bikes can be taken on the Métro anytime except during rush hour, from about 7am to 10am and 5pm to 7pm on weekdays. There are some lovely bike paths, such as the waterfront trail on the historic Canal de Lachine, and those that lead through Cité du

Havre and across Pont de la Concorde to the islands. There are a number of bicycle shops offering daily or weekly rental; they generally require a deposit in addition to the daily rate.

Toronto

The Toronto Transit Commission (TTC) operates a huge system of connecting subway, bus, and streetcar lines that serves the entire city. It is one of the safest and cleanest systems of its kind anywhere in the world. There are two major subway lines, with 66 stations along the way *(see endpaper)*. The "Ride Guide" shows every major place of interest and how to reach it by public transit, and is available at most subway ticket offices.

Picturesque riverside cyling route in Quebec City

To ride buses and streetcars, you must have exact change, a ticket, or a token. These are available at subway ticket booths and some convenience stores.

Toronto does not have a zone system, meaning a single, flat-fare ticket can be used for one trip, using any public transportation in the city. If you plan to connect from the subway to a streecar or bus, or if taking several connecting buses, be sure to collect a transfer pass once you have paid the fare.

A single fare for an adult is Can $3.25, while children under 12 travel free. Savings can be made when buying multiple tokens, and a day pass costs Can $12.50, which lasts until 5:30 am the following morning. Visit TTC's website for more information on fares, maps, and schedules.

It is easy to catch a cab in Toronto; they can be hailed in the street, called in advance, or found outside hotels. Bikes are a popular mode of transport, particularly during warmer months. Some roads have cycle lanes, but most don't. As a result, cyclists should take care, particularly on roads busy with pedestrians and streetcars. **Bike Share Toronto**, a public rental-bike system, is popular with cycling commuters. Alternatively, the Martin Goodman Trail is a well-marked scenic bicycle route along the scenic waterfront.

Toronto cabs gather at a taxi stand

Vancouver

This city's well-organized network of light rail (called SkyTrain), bus, and ferry services is run by Translink. An inexpensive Transit Guide is available from newsstands and information centers. It includes a map of the city showing all routes. Driving is not the best way to see the city, as congestion is heavy, and downtown parking is expensive, with metered parking limited to just two hours. There is a park-and-ride system, where cars can be left at certain points around the city center.

The SkyTrain is a light rail system of driverless trains that connects downtown Vancouver with the suburbs of Burnaby, New Westminster, Surrey, Port Moody, and Coquitlam. It travels partially beneath ground and partially overground on a raised track. The main terminal is at Waterfront Station at the bottom of Seymour Street. An alternative to the SkyTrain is to use the city's downtown bus routes. These offer delightful tours past the city's top attractions, although it is advisable to avoid rush-hour traffic. Bus services end around midnight, but there is a scaled-down "Night Owl" service.

Many people commute from downtown Vancouver to the North Shore by boat. The SeaBus is a 400-seat catamaran that shuttles between Lonsdale Quay in North Vancouver and the downtown terminal at Waterfront Station. The trip takes around 15 minutes and includes wonderful views of the mountains and Vancouver skyline. Aquabus Ferries connect stations on False Creek, Granville Island, Stamp's Landing, and the Hornby Street Dock.

If you want to take a cab, it is best to call one of the main companies such as Black Top or Yellow Cab, as hailing a taxi in the streets is rarely successful. However, Vancouver is a great city for cyclists, with plenty of bike paths, including the 10-km (6-mile) road around Stanley Park. There is a park-and-ride service for bikes here, similar to the one elsewhere for cars.

Fares are the same for bus, SkyTrain, and SeaBus in the Vancouver area, but the price varies according to time of day and the distance you travel. Adult fares are cheaper after 6:30pm, and all day Saturday, Sunday, and holidays. There are three zones in the city, and the price of the fare depends on how many zones you cross. The off-peak adult fare in zone one is Can $2.75. For Can $9.75 a Compass Day Pass provides unlimited use on all buses, SkyTrain and Seabus. You can purchase one online, by phone, or at Compass vending machines throughout the city. Children under 5 ride free, and those between the ages of 5 and 13 pay less (as do students with a valid GoCard); seniors over 65 also get concessions. A transfer ticket is free and lasts for 90 minutes of travel.

SkyTrain traveling over the city bridge in Vancouver on a summer evening

The scenic approach to Château Frontenac in Quebec City is best appreciated on foot

Ottawa

Fortunately for visitors, many of the capital city's major tourist attractions are within walking distance of Parliament Hill. Ottawa's sidewalks are both wide and clean, and you can do most of your sightseeing on foot, using public transportation to cover the longer distances. The region of Ottawa-Carlton operates **OC Transpo**, a 130-route bus network. OC Transpo uses a smart card system, called Presto. Passengers top up their card with credit, and then touch their card to the readers upon boarding a bus or O-train. When boarding a connecting bus, tapping the card to the reader will not charge the card again. Fares using Presto are Can $2.80 on regular routes and Can $3.80 on express routes. In contrast, standard cash fares are Can $3.45 and Can $4.90. All routes meet downtown at the Rideau Centre, and the stops are color-coded according to the route.

If you are using a car, there are several reasonably priced municipal parking lots – look for a green "P" sign. Taxis can be booked by phone or hailed at stands outside major hotels. Bicycles are a good way to explore a city that has some 150 km (93 miles) of scenic paths. The Rideau Canal, which crosses the city from north to south, is bordered by delightful walking and bike paths.

Calgary

Calgary transit operates buses and a light-rail transit system known as the C-Train. For a flat fare of Can $3.25 you can transfer to either using the same ticket, although day passes for around Can $10 are good value for visitors hoping to see several sights in one day. The C-Train travels north to the University and airport, and south along Macleod Trail. It is free in the downtown section between 10th Street and City Hall (buses are not). Maps are available from the **Calgary Transit** offices, where you can also buy tickets. C-Train tickets can be bought from machines located on the rail platforms.

If you wish to travel mostly within the city center, walking and public transportation are

Logo for the C-Train
in Calgary

your best options. However, the city's blocks are long, (Calgary spans a large urban area) and any trip to the outskirts and beyond requires a car. There are several rental companies, including all the major outlets. Weekend car-rental rates are cheaper than weekday car rental. Cabs are expensive here and cannot be hailed on the street, but they can be picked up at hotels or ordered by telephone.

Winnipeg

Many of Winnipeg's attractions are within a 20-minute walk of one another in the downtown area, centered on the crossroads of Portage and Main streets. **Winnipeg Transit** operates an efficient bus system, which is also ideal for reaching farther-placed sights. There is a flat fare of Can $2.70, or you can purchase a weekday pass for Can $23.50 from convenience and drug stores as well as the Transit Service Centre based in the underground concourse at Portage and Main. The center is open weekdays between 8:15 am and 4:45 pm, and offers detailed information and a free route map of the city. There are also several pleasant bicycle paths that run through the city as well as to outlying districts.

Quebec City

The charming narrow streets of the old town are best seen on foot, especially since most of the historic sights are located within a small area of the walled city. If you need to travel farther to see one of the more distant sights such as the Musée du Québec, the bus system is frequent and reliable. Fares are cheaper if you buy a ticket before boarding and are on sale at several outlets in grocery stores, costing Can $2.95 per person. There are also one-day passes for Can $8.25. The bus station is in the Lower Town on Blvd. Charest E. Most of the main routes stop centrally on the Place d'Youville in the Old Town.

Taxi stands are located in front of the major hotels or outside city hall. Horse-drawn carriages or *calèches* may be hired for a gentle trot around the Old Town, but expect to pay Can $60 for 40 minutes.

Halifax

The compact city of Halifax is best explored on foot or bicycle, which can be hired for a half or full day. Driving around is difficult: parking is hard to come by. To reach outlying districts, there is the **Halifax Metro Transit** bus and ferry system. The ferry route between downtown Halifax and Dartmouth is a wonderful and inexpensive way to enjoy the harbor. Fares are cheap, with a flat fare of Can $2.50 charged downtown. It is also possible to purchase budget books of 10 tickets for Can $20.

Charlottetown

Prince Edward Island is linked to the mainland by bridge and ferry. Crossing by bridge to the island is free, while a fare of Can $45.50 per vehicle is collected when leaving.

The ferry service runs from Pictou, Nova Scotia between May and November. There is a shuttle bus service from Halifax that travels to the island by ferry. The island's public transportation system is limited to a bus service in Charlottetown run by **Charlottetown Trius Transit** (the fare is Can $2.25 per sector). However, touring by car is most popular, and it is a good idea to reserve a car during the busiest months of July and August. Several companies offer organized bus, walking, and cycling tours.

Confederation Bridge to Prince Edward Island

St. John's, Newfoundland

In comparison to most of Canada's cities, parking is easy in St. John's. It is possible to buy a parking permit from one of many well-placed machines. They take quarters (25 cents) or dollar coins. All major car-rental companies have vehicles at both the airport and downtown locations.

The local bus service is run by Metrobus, and tickets cost Can $2.50 every trip. If you are planning on spending some time here it is worth investing

in a 10-ride card for Can $22.50. By riding on two routes, such as one downtown and one on a suburban bus, you get a bargain tour of the city.

Bus traveling over Harbour Bridge in Saint John, New Brunswick

Train Travel in Canada

The Canadian rail network is run by the government-owned VIA Rail Canada. The service has been significantly reduced since the late 1980s, when many cross-country services, along with other lines, were cut. VIA Rail still provides a service on the famed 1950s *Canadian*, a beautifully restored train that travels across the country between Toronto and Vancouver, passing through stunning Rockies' scenery between Jasper and Kamloops.

Increasingly, Canadians fly long distances or use their cars to cover most of the shorter hauls. For visitors, traveling by train remains a wonderful way to see large parts of Canada (especially in those trains that have glass-domed observation cars). Smaller commuter networks around the major cities are also useful for visitors who wish to explore an area in detail.

Specialty trips on the *Rocky Mountaineer* travel through the Rockies

The Canadian Rail Network

Via Rail Canada Inc. operates Canada's national passenger rail service. Despite the closing of several lines, there are still 400 trains every week, which cover some 13,000 km (8,000 miles) on major routes between Vancouver and Toronto, traveling on to Montreal, Quebec City, and Halifax. It is possible to cross the country by train – a trip that takes five days – by connecting up with these lines. The longest continuous route remains the Vancouver–Toronto trip on board the stylish and luxurious 1950s *Canadian*, with its observation and dining cars. Places with no road link, such as the town of Churchill in northern Manitoba, rely on the railroad. Trains from Winnipeg to Churchill run on Sundays and Tuesdays and take 48 hours.

VIA Rail operates both long-haul trains in eastern and western Canada, as well as inter-city trains in the populous Ontario Corridor, from Quebec City to Windsor, passing through Kingston, Montreal, Niagara Falls, Ottawa, and Toronto. This is a fast service that offers snacks and drinks on board most trains.

It is easy to travel onward to the United States, as VIA connects with the American rail network, Amtrak, at both Montreal and Vancouver. For tickets from Montreal to Albany or New York, and tickets from Vancouver to Seattle, Eugene, or Los Angeles, you'll need to book with Amtrak. VIA Rail and Amtrak jointly run the Toronto–New York line through Niagara Falls, which takes over 12 hours including a two-hour stop at the border. You can get to Chicago from Toronto via

Buffalo. The VIA station in Windsor is only a few kilometers from the Amtrak station in Detroit.

Smaller Networks

Visitors should also be aware that VIA is not the only passenger rail service in Canada. The larger cities all have useful local commuter lines. Vancouver has the West Coast Express, while Toronto's Go Transit covers the numerous towns in the commuter belt as far as Kitchener, Barrie, Hamilton, and Oshawa, and Montreal also has a metro system (*see p410*).

Specialty Trips

There are several lines that offer visitors the chance to enjoy Canada's best scenery in comfortable, often luxurious, trains. Among the best trips is the **Algoma Central Railway** in Ontario, which runs through northern Ontario's spectacular scenery. The day-trip tour runs through the stunning Agawa Canyon from Sault Ste. Marie daily from late June to mid-October. The route is particularly popular in late September and early October, when the blazing fall colors are at their most intense. On Saturdays in February and early March the Snow Train makes the trip to Agawa Canyon through mammoth snow drifts and ice-covered forests.

The **Polar Bear Express** starts in Cochrane in northern Ontario and heads another 300 km (186 miles) north through boreal forest to isolated Moosonee, from where visitors can take a motorized canoe to Moose Factory. An overnight stay is recommended.

The most spectacular train ride in Canada is probably in British Columbia, where, from mid-May until early October, the *Rocky Mountaineer* runs excursions to and through the Rockies. These trips operate entirely in daylight with nights spent in hotels rather than sleeping on the train. Most routes run from Vancouver. You can continue all the way to Halifax by taking the *Rocky Mountaineer* to Jasper and then switching to the VIA's *Canadian*.

From June to September, the charming little **Train de Charlevoix** threads its way along the Saint Lawrence River from Quebec City to La Malbaie. At times the track hugs the shoreline between water and cliffs in otherwise inaccessible territory, but it also passes through some lovely coastal villages in a region known for its artisan food. The scenic 125-km (78-mile) journey can be taken as an overnight round trip or broken up with stays and activities along the way, with accommodation ranging from hotels to tents.

Travel Classes

On long-distance VIA rail routes there are two main classes of travel available, Economy and Business, and a variety of Sleeper classes. Economy and Business offer comfortable, reclining seats in cars with wide aisles and large windows, as well as blankets and pillows for overnight trips. Passengers in Economy and Business classes also generally have access to

Maple leaf on VIARail logo

one of the onboard snack bars or restaurants. Sleeper classes offer a range of options from double- and single-berth bunks to double bedrooms, which convert to luxurious sitting rooms. VIA services in Western Canada, such as the *Canadian*, include meals.

Tickets and Bookings

Reservations for rail travel can be made direct through VIA Rail or other train operators' websites. There are a variety of discounts available, if you book in advance. There are two main VIA travel passes available. The Canrailpass System covers the entire country from coast to coast and as far north as Hudson Bay. The System pass is valid for seven one-way trips over a 21-day period. Canrailpass Corridor covers the busy area from Quebec City to Windsor (at the border with Detroit), giving access to Montreal, Toronto, and Ottawa and all the stops between. The Corridor pass allows for seven

one-way trips within a ten-day period. Both passes are available as either Supersaver, which is cheaper but has fewer seats allotted, and Discounted, which allows for more flexibility, as more seats are available. It is a good idea to reserve seats in advance in the summer, as there are a limited number for pass holders. Children travel for half price, there are special youth rates for those between 12 and 25, and those over 60 receive a discount too.

DIRECTORY

Algoma Central Railway
Tel 1 800 242 9287.

Amtrak
Tel 1 800 872 7245. W amtrak.com

Polar Bear Express
Tel 1 800 265 2356.
W ontarionorthland.ca

Rocky Mountaineer
Tel (604) 606 7245.
W rockymountaineer.com

Train de Charlevoix
Tel (418) 240 4124.
W traindecharlevoix.com

VIA Rail
Tel 1 888 842 7245. W viarail.ca

Principal Rail Routes

VIA Rail is the main provider of passenger rail services throughout Canada. It is possible to reach all the major centers of the country, and regional operators link up with most town's outlying districts.

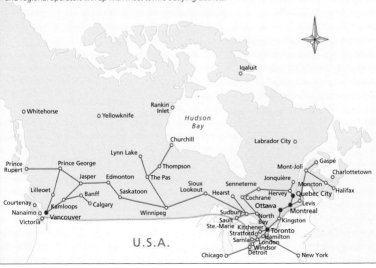

Traveling by Bus

Buses are the least expensive way to get around Canada using public transportation. Most bus routes west of Toronto are run by Greyhound Canada, including the epic trip along the Trans-Canada Highway (Hwy 1) between Toronto and Vancouver. East of Toronto, there are several smaller companies that cover most areas. Although a long bus trip can mean one or more nights spent sitting upright, the buses are generally clean and comfortable, and offer plenty of rest stops. The network is also reliable and efficient, with buses usually arriving on time. In more remote regions, check timetables in advance, as there may be no service or only one bus a week.

Long-Distance Buses

Buses covering long distances provide a cheaper and often faster option than the railroad. The main operator, Greyhound Canada, carries more than two million passengers each year to most of the towns and cities across the country. Although Greyhound lines operate in the west and center of the country, many routes are linked to bus lines in the east, and in the United States. Through trips using Greyhound tickets from Vancouver onto Vancouver Island are possible with BC Ferries Connector and Tofino Bus Lines; Pacific Coast Lines and Sunshine Coast Connector also run services westwards from Vancouver. East of Ottawa, Greyhound links with Orleans Express and Maritime Bus. DRL runs buses in Labrador and on the Newfoundland mainland,

and communities in northern Ontario have been serviced by Ontario Northland buses since the trains stopped running in 2012. Greyhound's Express service offers a faster, highway-based service on buses that have more leg room, movies, music, and snacks.

Greyhound bus logo

Although smoking is prohibited, most long-haul buses stop every three to four hours, so that travelers can leave the bus for a break. Rest breaks or driver changes take place at both bus and service stations, where you will find a variety of facilities ranging from restaurants and cafés to snack vending machines. All the buses are air-conditioned and have washrooms. Buses also offer passengers the advantage of picking up and arriving in convenient downtown areas.

Discounts and Passes

Greyhound tickets are cheaper when booked online over two weeks in advance. Children under 12 are charged 75 percent of the full fare, and toddlers under two travel free. Seniors over 65 receive a 10 percent discount. However, the deals are better when traveling as a group or family. One person pays the

full walk-up fare, and up to three people can join them at 50 percent off. High-season black-out periods may apply.

Bus Stations and Reservations

Buses from different carriers all operate from the same stations, making it easy to connect with other bus lines and municipal transit services. Reservations are not usually needed, since buses are filled on a first-come, first-served basis. Passengers are advised to be there at least an hour ahead of departure time, leaving plenty of time to buy tickets and check their luggage. Do not panic if the bus fills up; it will generally be replaced with another one right away. Buying tickets in advance does not guarantee you a seat, and you will still have to line up to board the bus. Priority boarding is available at some bus stations for an extra Can $5. Go to the ticket desk no more than 45 minutes and no less then 20 minutes before your bus is scheduled to leave.

Most bus stations have a small restaurant or café, where reasonably priced snacks and meals can be purchased. On long-distance journeys it is a good idea to take some food with you, otherwise you will have to rely on the sometimes over-priced, unappealing food available in service stations. At the larger stations it is possible to rent luggage lockers, leaving you free to explore unencumbered by suitcases. In the major cities such as Toronto, you have the choice of boarding in the suburbs or in the city center. Choose the city center, if you can, since the bus may be full by the time it reaches outlying districts. Always ask if there is an express or direct service to your destination, as some trips involve countless stops en route and can seem very

Buses waiting on Ottawa's Parliament Hill

Tourists on a bus trip to the Athabasca Glacier, near Jasper

long. A small pillow or traveling cushion, a fleece or sweater (to counter the sometimes-fierce air-conditioning), and a good book or magazine can often help to make a long trip more comfortable.

Bus Tours

There are several tour companies that offer package deals on a variety of trips. An extensive range of tours is available, from city sightseeing and day trips to particular attractions, to expensive, luxury, multi-day tours including guides, meals, and accommodations. There are specialized tours that focus on such activities as glacier hikes, whitewater rafting, and horseback riding. A typical ten-day tour of western Canada may take in everything from a cruise to Victoria, a hike in Banff, and a picnic beside Lake Louise, to a trip to the Columbia Icefield, or a look at the history of gold-rush country in the Cariboo region. Most companies will send you detailed itineraries in advance, and it is a good idea to make sure that there are no hidden extras such as tips, sales taxes, and entry fees – these are often included in the price of the package. Some of the most beautiful scenery can also be seen on regular Greyhound routes, such as those in the Rockies.

DIRECTORY

BC Ferries Connector
Tel 1 888 788 8840.
W bcfconnector.com

DRL (Newfoundland)
Tel 1 888 263 1854. W drl-lr.com

Greyhound Canada
Tel 1 800 661 8747.
W greyhound.ca

Sunshine Coast Connector
Tel 1 844 613 8222.
W sunshinecoastconnector.ca

Maritime Bus
Tel 1 800 575 1807.
W maritimebus.com

Orleans Express (Quebec)
Tel 1 888 999 3977.
W orleansexpress.com

Pacific Coach Lines (BC)
Tel (604) 662 7575, 1 800 661 1725. W pacificcoach.com

Tofino Bus Lines
Tel 1 866 986 3466.
W tofinobus.com

Bus-Tour Companies

Brewster Travel Canada
W brewster.ca

Great Canadian Holidays
W greatcanadianholidays.com

Bus Routes

This map shows the main bus routes across Canada. It is possible to travel right across the country along the Trans-Canada Highway using Greyhound Canada and the bus companies that operate east of Toronto.

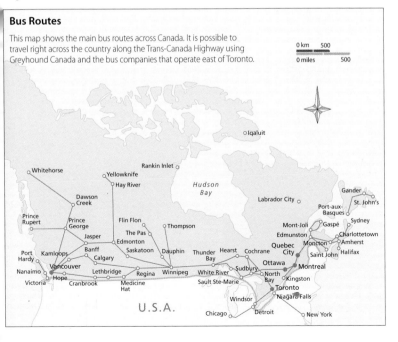

Driving in Canada

It is a good idea to rent a car when visiting Canada. Other modes of transportation will get you around the cities and from one rural town to another, but once you arrive in a remote country area, a car is the best way of exploring. Tours of regions such as Quebec's wild Gaspé Peninsula *(see pp148–9)*, or British Columbia's Okanagan Valley *(see p321)* are best made by car. Several aspects of Canadian life reflect the fact that this is a driver's country: there is an excellent, well-maintained highway network, and many places have huge out-of-town malls. However, city-center traffic congestion means that visitors to the major cities of Toronto, Vancouver, Montreal, and Ottawa may find that public transportation is quicker and cheaper than driving.

Arriving by Car

Many people drive to Canada from the US. The border here is the longest in the world. There are 13 major crossing points, the two busiest being from Detroit to Windsor and at Niagara Falls. Most of the highways entering Canada connect to the Trans-Canada Highway, which is the longest highway through the country, running for some 7,821 km (4,860 miles) from Victoria, BC, to St. John's in Newfoundland. Customs control ask that visitors declare their citizenship, their place of residence, and proposed length of stay. You will be asked to show your passport and visa *(see pp398–9)*. It is a good idea to fill up with less expensive fuel on the US side. It is also possible to enter the country from the Alaska side by the famed Alaska Highway *(see pp266–7)*, which crosses the Yukon and ends in British Columbia at Dawson Creek.

Driver's Licenses

An up-to-date driver's license from your own country usually entitles you to drive in Canada for up to three months. There are some provincial variations: in British Columbia, New Brunswick, and Quebec your license will be valid for up to six months, in Prince Edward Island for four months, and in the Yukon for only one month. It is advisable to carry an International Driving Permit (IDP) with your license, in case of problems with traffic officials or the police.

Insurance

Whether driving a rental or your own car you will need proof of insurance coverage, which is compulsory in Canada. If you are using your own car, it is advisable to check whether your insurance is valid in Canada, as this may save money. The minimum liability cover is Can $200,000, except in Quebec, where it starts at Can $50,000. Most rental companies offer collision damage waiver and personal accident insurance for an additional charge; it is a good idea to have both. If you are driving a private car that is not registered in your own name, you will need to carry the liability insurance card or "pink slip" for that particular car. For a rental vehicle you must carry the company's official documentation for the same reason. Arranging summer rentals and insurance in advance is recommended.

An RV passes mountains and forests on a trip through Banff National Park, Alberta

Car Rental

Rental cars are available just about everywhere in Canada. Most major agents such as Avis, Hertz, and National, have offices at airports and in towns and cities across the country. Among the less expensive options are booking a fly-drive package from home, or there may be discounts if you rent your car in advance. The cost varies greatly, depending on the season, type of vehicle, and length of rental. Ask about hidden costs such as drop-off charges, and taxes, depending on which province you are in. When picking up your car you may be asked to show your passport and return airline ticket. The minimum age for renting a car is usually 21, but often under-25s are not permitted to rent certain luxury cars or SUVs. You will need a credit card for the deposit; it is all but impossible to rent a car in Canada without one. Children under 18 kg (40 lb) require a child seat fixed in place with a seat belt. Most companies will arrange for one, given notice. The biggest rental firms offer a wide choice of vehicles, from two-door economy cars to four-door luxury models. Bear in mind that nearly all rental cars in Canada have automatic transmission. Manual models are unusual, although cars with specially adapted hand controls for disabled drivers are available from some of the larger companies. RVs (Recreational Vehicles) or camper vans can also be rented, but they are more expensive. They should be booked well in advance if you intend to travel in summer.

Fuel and Service Stations

Fuel prices are about 25 percent higher than in the US (but still half those in the UK), especially in cities and large towns, although rural areas often charge more. Unleaded gas and diesel only are available in Canada. Rental companies generally provide a full tank on departure, and give you the choice of paying for the fuel in advance or on return. Gas stations are often self-service, which can be a problem, if you need a mechanic. In major cities and along the Trans-Canada Highway, some stations are open for 24 hours, but in rural areas they often close at 6pm and are few and far between, especially in northerly regions. It is a good idea to fill up before setting off. Credit and debit cards are widely accepted.

Rules of the Road

Canada's highway system is well maintained and has mostly two-lane all-weather roads. They are clearly numbered and signed. Most highway signs are in English, and some bilingual, except for those in Quebec, where they are only in French. A good road map is essential and can be obtained from any auto club such as the **Canadian Automobile Association (CAA)**, which is affiliated with other similar clubs in the world. It is worth checking the rules of the road with them, as there are numerous small provincial variations. In Canada you drive on the right. You can turn right on a red light everywhere, except in Quebec or where indicated otherwise (such as for cycle lanes.) The speed limits are posted in kilometers-per-hour (km/h) and range from 30–40 km/h (19–25 mph) in urban areas to 80–120 km/h (50–75 mph) on highways. On multi-lane highways you pass on the left for safety. Some provinces require cars to keep their headlights on for extended periods after dawn and before sunset, for safety reasons. Seat belts are compulsory for both drivers and passengers.

Winter driving in the north involves special procedures because the roads are

Moose warning sign on a highway

extremely hazardous due to ice, and some are passable only during the summer months.

Winter Driving

Canadian winters are harsh, and you should always check road conditions and weather forecasts before setting out on trips. Drifting snow and black ice are frequent hazards in winter or in northern regions. When driving in remote areas, make sure you have a full gas tank, and carry blankets, some sand, a shovel, and emergency food, such as chocolate bars, in case you get stuck. Jumper cables (jump leads) are also useful, because extreme cold can drain a car battery quickly. Snow tires are recommended in freezing conditions and required by Quebec law in the winter months. Studded tires are also useful and are permitted in most provinces. Check with local tourist offices.

Large animals such as bears and moose can be a hazard for drivers, especially in parts of British Columbia. Take extra care when you see deer or moose road signs, as these indicate an area where animals are most likely to appear suddenly.

General Index

Page numbers in **bold** refer to main entries.

108 Mile Ranch, hotels 358

A

Abbaye Cistercienne (Oka) 154
Abbaye Notre-Dame du Lac (Oka) 154
Abbaye Saint-Benoît-du-Lac 152
Aboriginal people *see* Native Canadians
Above Lake Superior (Harris) 168
Acadia University 91
Acadian Peninsula **85**
Acadians 64, **68–9**
 Acadian Wax Museum (Caraquet) 85
 Annapolis Valley 91
 Carleton-sur-Mer 148
 Chéticamp 99
 expulsion of 68, 91
 Festival Acadien de Caraquet 45
 flag 35
 history 52, 53
 Village Historique Acadien **84**
Adams, Bryan 27, 41
Admission prices 399
Advocate Harbour, restaurants 365
Aga Khan Museum (Toronto) **192**
Agawa Canyon Tour Train 229
Ainslee, Lake 96
Air travel **406–9**
 domestic flights **408–9**
Aircraft
 Canada Aviation and Space Museum (Ottawa) **201**
 Canadian Warplane Heritage Museum (Hamilton) 212
Airports 406–7
Ajawaan Lake 255
Alaska Highway 59, **266–7**, 340
Alberni Inlet 291
Alberta
 history 55
 see also Central Canada; Rocky Mountains
Alberta Badlands 252
Alcan Highway 336
Alcohol 360–61, 400, 402
Alexander Graham Bell Museum (Baddeck) 97
Alexander Graham Bell National Historic Site 98
Alexandra Bridge (Gatineau) **158**
Algoma Central Railway 414, 415
Algonquin Art Centre (Algonquin Provincial Park) 15, **208**
Algonquin Logging Museum (Algonquin Provincial Park) 15, **208**
Algonquin Provincial Park 10, 15, **208–9**
 hotels 354
Algonquin tribe 49, 51
Allen Sapp Gallery (The Battlefords) 256
Allison, Susan 40
Ambleside 283
Ambulances 403
American Falls 216
American Revolution 52
Amherst **90**
Amish 33, 222, **223**
Ammanites 223
Amtrak **415**

Amusement parks
 Centreville (Toronto) 192
 La Ronde (Montreal) 130
 West Edmonton Mall 254
Anabaptists 280
Anahareo 254
Anderson, Patrick 41
André, Brother 127
Angel Glacier 14, 294, 312, 315
Anglo-French hostilities **52–3**
Anishinabe people 247
Annapolis Royal 17, **91**
 restaurants 365
Annapolis Valley 68, 91
Anne, Saint 142
Anne of Green Gables 17, 40, 86, 88, 89
Antigonish
 hotels 350
 restaurants 365
Antigonish Highland Games 45
Antiques shops 386, 387
Appalachian Mountains 29, 149
Aqghadluk 39
Aquariums
 Marine Centre and Aquarium (Shippagan) 85
 Ripley's Aquarium of Canada (Toronto) 174, **177**
 Vancouver Aquarium 279
Archaeological sites
 Colony of Avalon 74
 L'Anse-aux-Meadows National Historic Site 77
 Petroglyphs Provincial Park 206
 Wanuskewin Heritage Park (Saskatoon) 250
The Arches (Northern Peninsula tour) 77
Arctic wildlife 31
Armstrong, Jeanette 41
Arseneault, Angèle 34
Art 27, **38–9**
 Group of Seven **168–9**
 Inuit Art and Culture **330–31**
 shopping 387
Art Gallery of Greater Victoria **287**
Art Gallery of Ontario (Toronto) 12, 27, **182–3**
 street-by-street map 180
Art Gallery of Windsor 214
The arts 26–7
Arts Commons (Calgary) **297**
Ashevak, Tommy 39
Ashoona, Qaqaq 39
Aspy River Valley 98
Assemblée Nationale (Quebec City) **136**
Assembly of First Nations (AFN) 26, 37
Assiniboine Park (Winnipeg) **242**
Assiniboine tribe 251
Athabasca Falls 313, **314**
Athabasca Glacier 306, 314
Athabasca Valley 315
Athapaskan people 49
Atlantic Canada **62–101**
 The Acadians 68–9
 map 64–5
 New Brunswick, Nova Scotia, and Prince Edward Island 81–101
 Newfoundland and Labrador 70–79
 travel 65
 wildlife 66–7

Atlin Lake 325
Atlin Provincial Park 325
ATMs 404
Atwood, Margaret 27, 41
Audy, Lake 248
Aulavik National Park 343
Aurora Borealis 328, 332, **341**
Austin, James 186
Auto clubs 419
Automatists 39
Autumn 46–7
Autumn, Algoma (MacDonald) 168–9
Autumnfest Outdoor Festival 46
Auyittuq National Park **344**, 392
Available Light Film Festival (Yukon) 47
Avalon Peninsula **74**

B

Baddeck 17, **98**
 restaurants 365
Badlands 252
Baffin Island **344–5**
 map 344–5
Baie-Comeau **146**
 restaurants 369
Baie-Saint-Paul 16, **143**
 hotels 352
 restaurants 369
Baker Lake **343**
Balfour Report 59
Ballet 389, 390–91
Baltimore, Lord 74
Bamfield 292
Banff 14, **307**
 festivals 44, 47
 hotels 358
 restaurants 380
Banff National Park 11, 14, 237, 303, **304–7**
Banff Park Museum (Banff) 307
Banff Summer Arts Festival 44
Bank notes 404
Bankhead 305, 306
Banking 404
Banks Island **343**
Banting, Dr Frederick 58
Barachois Falls 76
Barker, Billy 324
Barkerville Historic Town 324
 hotels 358
Barkley Sound, hotels 357
Barry's Bay **207**
Bars 391
Bas St. Laurent, restaurants 369
Baseball **42**, 43
Basilique-Cathédrale Notre-Dame-de-Québec **138**
 street-by-street map 134
Basilique Notre-Dame-de-Montréal 12, 110, **116–17**
 street-by-street map 114
Basketball **43**
Bastion Square (Victoria) **285**
Bata, Sonja 186
Bata Shoe Museum (Toronto) 12, **186–7**
Bathurst Inlet 25
Batoche National Historic Site **256**
The Battery (St. John's NF) **72**
Battle of Crysler's Farm Memorial 204
Battle Harbour **78**
Battleford 33, **256**
The Bay Centre (Vancouver) **286**

Mennonites **223**
  Mennonite Heritage Village
    (Steinbach) 244–5, **246**
  St. Jacobs 222
Merritt, David 82
Métis 25, 32, **55**, 243
  rebellions 54–5, 256, 257
Michal and Renata Hornstein
  Pavilion (Musée des Beaux-Arts,
  Montreal) **122**
Michelangelo, *Pietà* 143
Midland, hotels 355
"Midnight sun" 328
Mies van der Rohe, Ludwig 178, 180
Miette Hot Springs 14, 313, **315**
Miette Valley 315
Mile End (Montreal) 119
Miles Canyon 57
Military Museums (Calgary) **299**
Mills, Richard, *Sans titre* 120
Milne, A.A. 242
Milne, David 38
Minas Basin 90, 91
Mingan Archipelago National Park
  146–7
Minnewanka, Lake 305, 306
Mint
  Royal Canadian Mint (Ottawa) 197,
    200
  Royal Canadian Mint (Winnipeg)
    242
Miquelon *see* Saint-Pierre and
  Miquelon Islands
Mirabel Airport (Montreal) 406–7
Mirimachi, restaurants 366
Mirvish, Ed 178–9
Miscou Island 85
Miscou Lighthouse 85
Mistaya Canyon 306
Mitchell, Joni 27, 41, 187
Mobile phones 405
Mohawk people 32, 36
Mol, Leo 242
Molson Amphitheatre (Toronto) 175
Monastère des Ursulines (Quebec
  City) **139**
Monastère des Ursulines (Trois-
  Rivières) 153
Moncton
  festivals 45
  hotels 351
  restaurants 366
Money 404
Monroe, Marilyn 187
Mont Saint-Pierre, Gaspé Peninsula
  tour 149
Mont Tremblant 155
Mont-Royal (Montreal) 111
Montagnais First Nation 145
Montague, restaurants 366
Montcalm, Louis Joseph de 52, 53
Monteregie, restaurants 371
Montgomery, Lucy Maud 40, **89**
  Cavendish Home 11, 17, **88**
Montmagny 147
Montmorency Falls 10, 16, **143**, 155
Montreal 104, **110–31**
  2 days in Montreal **12–13**
  airports 406–7
  climate 46
  entertainment 390–91
  festivals 44, 45, 47
  history 50, 51
  hotels 351–2
  maps 21, 112–13
  restaurants 367–9
  St. Lawrence Seaway 109
  shopping 386–7

Montreal (cont.)
  travel 113, 410
  Vieux-Montréal: street-by-Street
    map 114–15
Montréal Orchestre Symphonique
  41
Montreal Tower (Montreal) 129
Moodie, Susanna 40
Moore, Henry 182
  Draped Reclining Figure 182
Moose Jaw **249**
  hotels 356
Moraine Lake 304, **307**
Morisseau, Norval 39
Morissette, Alanis 27, 41, 389
Moriyama, Raymond 186–7
Morrice, James Wilson 38, 122
Morris, Edmund 38
Morris, William 121
Morton, Desmond 49
Mosaic – Festival of Cultures
  (Regina) 44
Mosquitoes 403
Motherwell, William R. 248
Motherwell Homestead National
  Historic Site 248
Motor racing, Grand Prix du Canada
  (Montreal) 44
Motorhomes 349
Mount Edziza Provincial Park 325
Mount Fernie Provincial Park 301
Mount Revelstoke National Park 303
Mountains *see* by name
Mounties *see* Royal Canadian
  Mounted Police
Mourning Dove 41
Mud Creek Trail (Prince Albert
  National Park) 255
Muddock, J.E.P. 257
Mulroney, Brian 61
Multicultural Canada **32–3**
Muncho Lake Provincial Park 262,
  317
Munro, Alice 27, 41
Murray, Robert 39
  Sculpture 39
Murray Premises (St. John's NF) **72**
Musée Heritage – Saint Pierre et
  Miquelon 74–5
Musée McCord (Montreal) **121**
Museum of Contemporary Art 193
Museums and galleries
  admission prices 399
  opening hours 399
  Acadian Wax Museum (Caraquet)
    85
  Aga Khan Museum (Toronto) **192**
  Alexander Graham Bell Museum
    (Baddeck) 96
  Alexander Graham Bell National
    Historic Site (Baddeck) 98
  Algonquin Art Centre (Algonquin
    Provincial Park) 15, **208**
  Algonquin Logging Museum
    (Algonquin Provincial Park) 15,
    208
  Allen Sapp Gallery (The
    Battlefords) 256
  Art Gallery of Greater Victoria
    (Victoria) **287**
  Art Gallery of Ontario (Toronto) 12,
    27, 180, **182–3**
  Art Gallery of Windsor 214
  Banff Park Museum (Banff) 307
  Bata Shoe Museum (Toronto) 12,
    186–7
  BC Sports Hall of Fame and
    Museum (Vancouver) 275

Museums and galleries (cont.)
  Beaverbrook Art Gallery
    (Fredericton) 17, **83**
  Bell Homestead National Historic
    Site (Brantford) 222
  Bethune Memorial House **223**
  Bytown Museum (Ottawa) **198–9**
  Campbell House Museum
    (Toronto) 180
  Canada Agriculture and Food
    Museum (Ottawa) **200**
  Canada Aviation and Space
    Museum (Ottawa) **201**
  Canada Science and Technology
    Museum (Ottawa) **201**
  Canadian Museum of History
    (Gatineau) **159**
  Canadian Museum of Human
    Rights (Winnipeg) **242**
  Canadian Museum of Nature
    (Ottawa) **201**
  Canadian War Museum (Ottawa)
    15, **199**
  Canadian Warplane Heritage
    Museum (Hamilton) 212
  Casa Loma (Toronto) 12, **190–91**
  Cave and Basin National Historic
    Site (Banff) 14, 307
  Centre Canadien d'Architecture
    (Montreal) **126**
  Centre d'histoire de Montréal
    (Montreal) 12, **118**
  Centre des sciences de Montréal
    (Montreal) 12, **118**
  Château Ramezay (Montreal)
    12–13, 115, **116–17**
  Confederation Centre of the Arts
    (Charlottetown) 89
  Cranbrook History Centre 302
  Craigdarroch Castle (Victoria) **287**
  Cumberland County Museum
    (Amherst) 90
  Dawson City Museum (Dawson
    City) 340
  deGarthe Gallery (Peggy's Cove) 93
  Dionne Quints Museum (North
    Bay) 207
  Dory Shop Museum (Shelburne)
    92
  Doukhobor Discovery Centre
    (Castlegar) 322
  Dr. Elizabeth LeFort Museum
    (Chéticamp) 99
  Dundurn Castle (Hamilton) 212
  Eagle Aerie Gallery (Tofino) 292
  Emily Carr House (Victoria) **286**
  The Exploration Place Museum
    and Science Centre (Prince
    George) 316
  Fisheries Museum of the Atlantic
    (Lunenburg) 81, 92
  Fisherman's Life Museum
    (Jeddore) 93
  Fort Dauphin Museum (Dauphin)
    248
  Fort La Reine Museum and
    Pioneer Village (Portage la Prairie)
    247
  Fort Qu'Appelle Museum 248
  Fort Wellington National Historic
    Site (Prescott) 204
  Fraser-Fort George Regional
    Museum 14
  Fundy Geological Museum
    (Parrsboro) 90
  Gardiner Museum (Toronto) 12, **186**
  Gateway Labrador Visitor Centre
    (Labrador City) 79

Acknowledgments

Dorling Kindersley would like to thank the following people, whose contributions and assistance have made the book possible:

Main Contributors
Paul Franklin is a writer and photographer for both Canadian and world travel guides, he lives in Nova Scotia.
Sam Ion and **Cam Norton** live and work in Burlington, Ontario. A successful travel-writing team, they contribute to newspapers, magazines, and brochures.
Philip Lee has worked as a travel writer for over a decade, and is the author of numerous articles and travel books about countries throughout the world. He has lived and traveled extensively through the US and Canada and is now based in Nottingham, England.
Lorry Patton lives and works in British Columbia, having been travel editor of *BC Woman* magazine. She currently runs an online travel magazine, which includes BC, and lives on the Gulf Islands just outside of Vancouver.
Geoffrey Roy is an award-winning freelance travel writer and photographer, based in Surrey, England. He has published numerous articles on Northern Canada.
Donald Telfer is a Saskatchewan-based travel writer with over 20 years' writing experience of Central Canada. He contributes regularly to a variety of Canadian and international newspapers and magazines.
Paul Waters was a Montreal-based journalist, who wrote extensively on Quebec and was travel editor for *The Gazette*.

Additional Contributors
Bruce Bishop, Alan Chan, Katharine and Eric Fletcher, Helena Katz, Ffion Llwyd-Jones, Sandra Phinney, Michael Snook.

Additional Photography
Tim Draper, Bert Hoferichter, James Jackson, Alan Keohane, Gunter Marx, Ian O'Leary, Cylla Von Tiedman, Enrique Uranga, Matthew Ward, Peter Wilson.

Additional Illustrations
Stephen Conlin, Eugene Fleury, Steve Gyapay, Chris Orr, Mel Pickering, Peter Ross.

Cartography
ERA-Maptec Ltd, Dublin, Ireland.

Proof Reader
Sam Merrell.

Revisions Team
Louise Abbott, Gillian Allan, Emily Anderson, Claire Baranowski, Sonal Bhatt, Hilary Bird, Ilona Biro, Louise Bolton, Julie Bond, Lola Brown, Barbara L. Campbell, Divya Chowfin, Vivien Crump, Flannery Dean, Hannah Dolan, Gadi Farfour, Emer FitzGerald, Joy Fitzsimmons, Camilla Gersh, Emily Green, Mohammad Hassan, Andrew Hempstead, Dr. Stephen Henderson, Jessica Hughes, Marie Ingledew, Shobhna Iyer, Zafar ul Islam Khan, Steve Knowlden, Kathryn Lane, Jude Ledger, Patrick Lejtenyi, Hayley Maher, Bhavika Mathur, Shubhi Mittal, Casper Morris, Mary Ormandy, Clare Peel, Helen Peters, Marianne Petrou, Adrian Potts, Rada Radojicic, Mani Ramaswamy, Lee Redmond, Lucy Richards, Toby Saltzman, Sands Publishing Solutions, Azeem Siddiqui, Rituraj Singh, Susana Smith, Jaynan Spengler, Mark Stevens, Anna Streiffert, Rebecca Taylor, Geordie Telfer, Priyanka Thakur, Rachel Thompson Stuti Tiwari, Helen Townsend, Vinita Venugopal, Nikhil Verma, Lisa Voormeij, Candice Walsh.

Additional Picture Research
Rachel Barber, Marta Bescos, Ellen Root

Special Assistance
Canada Map Office, Ontario; Canadian Tourism Office, London, UK; Claude Guerin and Danielle Legentil, Musée d'art contemporain de Montréal; Jim Kemshead, Tourism Yukon; Wendy Kraushaar, RCMP Museum, Regina, Saskatchewan; 'Ksan Historical Indian Village & Museum, Hazleton, BC; Leila Jamieson, Art Gallery of Ontario, Toronto; Antonio Landry, Village Historique Acadien, New Brunswick; Marty Hickie, Royal Tyrrell Museum, Drumheller, Alberta; Mary Mandley, Information Office, Sainte-Marie among the Hurons; National Air Photo Library, Ottawa, Ontario; Liette Roberts, Manitoba Museum of Man and Nature, Winnipeg; Mark Sayers; Ernest D. Scullion, Aeriel Photography Services, Scarborough, Ontario; Visit Canada, London, UK; Jennifer Webb, UBC Museum of Anthropology, Vancouver, BC.

Photography Permissions
Dorling Kindersley would like to thank everyone for their assistance and kind permission to photograph at their establishments.

Picture Credits
a = above; b = below/bottom; c = center; f = far; l = left; r = right; t = top.

Works of art have been produced with the permission of the following copyright holders: © Bill Vazan *Shibagua Shard*, 1989 sandblasted sheild granite 189c.

The publishers would like to thank the following individuals, companies, and picture libraries for their kind permission to reproduce their photographs:

123RF.com: citylights 416bl; **Air Canada**: 406cla; **AKG, London**: 57bc; **Alamy Images**: Rubens Abboud 296tr; Philip Bird 1c; Bill Brooks 363tl; Scott Dimond 294; Ron Erwin 343tl; Jeff Greenberg 385t; Marshall Ikonography 90–1; Gunter Marx 362cla; Mediacolor's 386cla; Megapress 386tl; Don Johnston 162-3; Pictures Colour Library 13bl, 386br; Robert Harding Picture Library Ltd/Roy Rainford 8cla; Rolf Hicker Photography 226tr, 240tr, 321cla; Andrew Rubtsov 193tl; Stephen Saks Photography 363c; Steve Shuey 332; John Sylvester 96c; Travel Pictures 118tl; David Trevor 192tl; David Wei: 384cr; Darwin Wiggett 80, 338–9; **Alamy Stock Photo**: All Canada Photos 340tl, CharlineXia Ontario Canada Collection 44clb, Terrance Klassen 65cr, Ton Koene 330-331c, North Wind Picture Archives 52tr, Sorin Papuc 67ca; **Aux Anciens Canadiens**: 370br; **Avalon**: Andrea and Antonella Ferrari 161t. **Bearfoot Bistro**: 383tr; **Bell Homestead**: 222tl; **The Bison Restaurant & Terrace**: 380bl; **Bistro Le Coq**: 361tl; **Anchorage Museum of History and Art**, Anchorage, Alaska: B74.1.25 56tr; Courtesy of **The Anne of Green Gables Museum**, Silver Bush, Park Corner, Prince Edward Island: 89br; **Art Gallery of Ontario**: 182tr; Edgar Degas *Grande Arabesque*, bronze 180bl; Paul Gauguin French 1848–1903; Lawren H. Harris Canadian 1885–1970 *Above Lake Superior* c.1922 oil on canvas 121.9 x 152.4 cm Gift from Ruben and Kate Leonard Canadian Fund 1929 © Mrs. James H Knox 168br; Paul Kane *Scene in the Northwest* (1845–46) The Thomson Collection 183br; J.E.H. MacDonald Canadian (1873–1932) *Falls, Montreal River* 1920 oil on canvas 121.9 x 153cm Purchase 1933 Acc no 2109 Photo Larry Ostrom 169tr; Henry Moore British (1898–1986) *Draped Reclining Figure* 1952–53 original plaster 100.4 x 160.4x

68.6 cm Gift of Henry Moore, 1974. The work illustrated on page 182cla is reproduced by permission of the Henry Moore Foundation; Robert Gray Murray (b1936) To 1963 painted aluminium, 2 units, tubular column H271.1cm planar column 275.0cm Gift from the Junior Women's Committee Fund 1966 65/60.1–2 39cb; Photographic Resources 38br; Peter Paul Rubens *Massacre of the Innocents* (1609-11) The Thomson Collection 182clb; Tom Thomson Canadian 1887–1917 *The West Wind* 1917 oil on canvas 120.7 x 137.2 cm Gift of the Canadian Club of Toronto, 1926 183crb; **Axiom**: Chris Coe 28cl, 37tc, 92cr, 209br, 241tl/cra, 243ca/bc, 251tr, 281t, 314tr, 336cr/bl, 361br. **Bard on the Beach Shakespeare Festival**: David Blue 390br; **Bata Shoe Museum**, Toronto: 187bl; **Brasseurs de Temps**: 370tr; **Bridgeman Art Library**: Emily Carr (1871–1945) *Skidagate, Graham Island, British Columbia* 1928 (oil on canvas) Gift of the J. S. Mclean Collection by Canada Packers Inc. 1990 39tl, Maurice Galbraith Cullen (1866–1934) *On the Saint Lawrence* 1897 (oil on canvas) Gift of the Reuben and Kate Leonard Canadian Fund, 1926 38cl; British Library portolan by Pierre Descaliers Canada: *from the voyage of Jacques Cartier* (1491–1557) *and his followers c.1534–41* 50cla, *Jacques Cartier* (1491–1557) *French navigator and discoverer of Canadian River St. Lawrence* (steel engraving after a portrait in St. Malo) 50b; Hudson Bay Company Lieutenant Smyth (19th Century) *Incidents on Trading Journey: HMS Terror Making Fast to an Iceberg in Hudson's Strait*, August 18th, 1836 167tl; medal commemorating the British capture of Quebec, 1759 (bronze) 53bl; engraving by Jean Antoine Theodore Gudin (1802–80) *Jacques Cartier* (1491–1557) on the St. Lawrence River, 1535 7; litho by Howard Pyle (1853–1911) *The Capitualtion of Louisbourg, illustration from 'Colonies and Nation'* by Woodrow Wilson, pub. in Harper's Magazine, 1901 53tl, Benjamin West (1738–1820) *Willaim Penn's Treaty with the Indians in November 1683* (oil on canvas) 36tr; Stapleton Collection engraved by Carl Vogel (1816–51) *Indian Hunting the Bison, plate 31 from volume 2 "Travels in the Interior of North America"*, 1844 (aquatint) by Karl Bodmer (1809–93) (after) 36crb, engraved by Charles Geoffroy (1832–82) *Assiniboin Indians, plate 32 from volume 2 of "Travels in the interior of North America 1832–34"*, 1844 (acquatint) by Karl Bodmer (1809–93) (after) 251bc; **British Columbia Archives**: Province of B.C. Photo 53crb. Courtesy of **Calgary Transit**: 412clb; **Cephas**: Fred R. Palmer 106tr; Pascal Quittemelle 106bl; TOP/Hervé Amiard 34bc; **Le Chien Noir Bistro**: 375br; **CinCin Restaurant & Bar**: 360cl; 378tr **Clayoquot Wilderness Resort**: 349t; **Chives Canadian Bistro**: 366bc; **Colorific!**: Randa Bishop 403br; Terence LeGoubin 229tc; Black Star/ Richard Olsenius 78br; Michael Saunders 107bl; Geray Sweeney 29b; Focus/Eric Spiegelhalter 325tr; **Corbis**: 35tl, 39bc, 54cl, 56cl, 69br, 213t, 215tr, 236bl, 254bl; Craig Aurness 236–237; David Bartruff 331b; Bettman 55bl, 57cr, 58br; Bettman/UPI 207b; Alan Copson 110, 124–5; Peter Harholdt 330bl; Hulton Deutsch collection 6–7, 60fcr/bc/br; Wolfang Kaehler 330cl; Lake County Museum 237crb; Library of Congress 51tr/cb; William Manning 132; Alan Marsh 150; Masterfile/Frank Krahmer 206br/Jeremy Woodhouse 201t/ Michael Mahovlich 374tc; Wally McNamee 129cra; New York Public Library Picture Collection 50ca; PEMCO-Webster & Stevens Collection Museum of History and Industry, Seattle 57t; UPI 41cla; **Delta Montreal**: 352tc; **Depositphotos Inc**: frizio 61bc, pictureguy 266bl; **Discovery Harbour**: 223b; Courtesy of **destinationlabrador.com**: 79crb; **Adrian Dorst**: 260cl, 292cra, 293cb; **Dreamstime.com**: Ahkenahmed 67tr; Michel Bussieres 175cra; Ckchiu 389t; Jerry Coli 42cl; Jiong Dai 402bl; Debsta75 249c; Songquan Deng 5cr, 220–1; Dennizn 111b; Tom Eagan 77cr; Eddygaleotti 262br; Elena Elisseeva

223cla; Rusty Elliott 67cla; Fallsview 396-7; Chris Hill 210; Ivansabo 265bc; Ritu Jethani 143tr; Wangkun Jia 15t, 22, 26tl; Josefhanus 328bl; Brian Lasenby 263cla; Pierre Leclerc 263tl; Chu-wen Lin 10cl; William Manning 268; Martinmark 47bl; Maudem 147cl; Paul McKinnon 42br, 97br; Meunierd 127br, 136cla; Mirceax 128tr; Mkoudis 17bl; Nelugo 309–10; Jaroslav Noska 27tr; Pdrocha 45cb Philippehalle 16t; Photawa 398b; Norman Pogson 11bc; Porbital 31cr; Quoc Anh Lai 305tc; Yelena Rodriguez 47tr; Jason P Ross 14cr; Howard Sandler 30tr, 201br; Brandon Smith 238; Paulo Tardao 208cl; Thevirex 190tr; Vdvtut 5cla, 175bl; Valentino Visentini 175tl; Simone Winkler 156–7; Sara Winter 4crb; Wwphoto 242tr; **Robert Estall Photo Library**: 83br, 106–7, 108c, 160br; **Mary Evans Picture Library**: 53cr, 57tr, 166tr; **Fairmont Château Laurier**: 199tr; **Fairmont Hotels and Resorts, Canada**: 348t, 349b, 354b, 357tl, 359tr, 381tl; **Les Fougères**: 371tc; **Four Seasons Centre for the Performing Arts**: Sam Javanrouh 178tl; **P. M. Franklin**: 29tr, 31ca, 66ca, 69tr/cr, 99t; **Winston Fraser Photos**: 74br, 106cl, 107crb, 109tr, 233br, 254tl, 340br, 405clb, 407cl; Black Star 161c; Canada In Stock 223tr; Ivy Images/Don Mills 46cr, 66br, 68tr, 69tl, 78crb, 79tl, 155cr; Ivy Images/Don Mills/© Gilles Daigle 84t,/© Sylvain Grandadam 395tl, /© Tony Mihok 44br/© Dan Roitner 87br; T.Klassen Photography 242c, 246tl, 257tc; **Fundy Restaurant**: 365br. **Genoa Bay Cafe**: 377tr; **Getty Images**: Barrett & MacKay 70, 244–5; Wayne R Bilenduke 37crb; De Agostini Picture Library 51c; Grant Dixon 345tl; Keith Douglas 324tr; Krzysztof Dydynski 171b; Werner Forman 331cra; Tom Hanson 26cb; Henry@scenicfoto.com 2-3; Pierre Longnus 317t; Yves Marcoux 102–3; mbbirdy 170; Dennis McColeman 198cl; George Pimentel 27bl; Boris Spremo 37bl; Lisa Stokes 346–7; Stringer / Nick Didlick 61cr; Superstock 276–7; Taxi/Walter Bibikow 12tr; Michael Wheatley 258–9; **Goderich**: 226bl; **Gotham Steak House & Cocktail Bar**: 379tr; **The Great George Hotel**: 350bl; Courtesy of **Greyhound Canada**: 416ca; **Lyn Hancock**: 342cla, 344b, 345br, 392bl; Jeff Greenberg 266cb; Norma Joseph Frgs 237br; Maurice Joseph Frgs, Arps 417tl; Alan Marsh 382b; R. McLeod 325b; Roy Rainford 184tl; Walter Rawlings 309cr; Geoff Renner 235tl; Ian Tomlinson 45t, 298bl; Dr A.C. Waltham 334b; Explorer 160tl/Patrick Lorne 148bl; Publiphoto Diffusion 30cl/ Paul G. Adam 144t/Yves Marcoux 147t; **Hilton Hotels and Resorts**: 351tl; **Hornblower Niagara Cruises**: 217bl; **Hotel le Saint-James**: 352br; **David Houser**: 78tl, 79cl, 147br, 149bl; **Hudson Bay Company Archives**, Toronto: 166bl; Provincial Archives of Manitoba 166b, 167cra; **Hulton Getty Collection**: 60tl, 99cb, 108clb. **Inuit Art Foundation**, Ontario: Sarah Joe Qinuajua, Puvirnituq *A Polar Bear Meets A Woman* QC1985 Black Stone Cut 330tr; **iStockphoto.com**: RyersonClark 32cl. **Jasper Tourism and Commerce**: 312tr; Hugh Levy 313ca. **Wolfgang Kaehler**: 148tr, 149br; **Robin Karpan**: 25tc, 232tr, 235cr/br, 236tr, 240bl, 242bl, 247br, 248l/bc, 249b, 250tl/c/b, 253t/b, 254cra, 255cla/cr/b, 335tl, 343br; **Joseph King**: 271br, 279t, 324bl; **Kobal Collection**: *Rose Marie*, MGM 237tr; *Anne of Green Gables*, RKO 40cl. **Frank Lane Picture Agency**: Dembinsky 30crb; Michael Gore 67crb; John Hawkins 67br; David Hosking 234clb, 264tr, 301br; Maslowski 30br; C. Mullen 147c; Mark Newman 31crb, 264cb; C.Rhodes 31bc; M.Rhode 82c; Leonard Lee Rue 31clb, 160c, 317cr; Sunset/Brake 82tl, 344cl;/T.Leeson 264bl; John Watkins 66cb; David Whittaker 264ca: Terry Whittaker 30clb; **Hotel le Priori**: 348cr; **Leisurail/ VIA Rail Canada**: 415ca; **Lil' Baci Restaurant**: 372br; . Courtesy of the **Manitoba Museum of Man and Nature**: 243clb; **Arnold Matchtinger**: 190bl; **McCord Museum of Canadian History**, Montreal: Notman Photographic Archives 59tc;

McMichael Canadian Art Collection: Photo Arthur Goss/Arts & Letters Club 169br; A.V Jackson (1882–1974) *The Red Maple*, 1914 oil on panel, 21.6 x 26.9cm Gift of Mr. S. Walter Stewart 1968.8.18 168tr; 193br; **Musee d'art contemporain de Montréal:** Natalie Roy *Les Dentelles de Montmirail*, 1995 (detail) Soutiens-gorge et jupon sous acrylique et bois 32 x 300 x 35cm Denis Farley et Natalie Roy Du Compagnonnage du 2 juin au septembre 1999 ©SODART/DACS, 2011 120tr; Richard Long *Niagra Sandstone Circle*, 1981 32 pierres de gres © Richard Long 120cl; **Musée des Beaux-Arts de Montréal:** 122tr; Laurent Arriot *Teapot* Photo Christine Guest 1952 DS 41 122bl; El Greco *Portrait of a young Man* 1945.885 123c; Harmensz van Rijn Rembrandt *Portrait of a Young Lady* 1949-1006 122cla; courtesy of the **Museum of Anthropology**, Univeristy of British Columbia, Vancouver, Canada: photo: Bill McLennan 280clb, 280b, Red Cedar Totem Poles in Great Hall, Haida and Tsimshian (Canada) 280tr; Wooden Frontlet Bella Bella, (Canada) H.R. MacMillan Purchase 281crb. **National Archives of Canada:** C-011371 55tc, C25739 267cra; **National Gallery of Canada**, Ottawa: 202cla, Davidialuk Alasua Amittu (1910–76) *The Aurora Borealis Decapitating a Young Man* c.1965 purchased 1992 © La Fédération des Cooperatives du Nouveau-Québec 202; Louise Bourgeois *Maman* 1999 © Louise Bourgeois *Trust* 199tl; Jackson Pollock (1912–56) *No. 29* c.1950 purchased 1968 © ARS, NY and DACS, London 2011 203tc; Francesco Salviati *Virgin and Child with an Angel* c.1535–1539 203crb; Tom Thomson (1877–1917) *The Jack Pine* c.1916–1917 purchased 1918 203ca; **Natural History Photographic Agency:** Brian and Cherry Alexander 67clb; Dan Griggs 29cr, 167bc; Stephen Krasemann 30bl, 66tr, 265br, 336tl, 337t, David E. Myers 24br; T.Kitchen and V.Hirst 31tr/bl, 66crb, 265ca/tr/cb, 266cla; Jean-Louis Le Moigne 265bl; Dr. Eckart Pott 264bc; Kevin Schafer 66bl, 335c; John Shaw 67bl, 264br, 304bl, 324cla; NorbertWu 293cl; **Naturpress:** Roberto Olivas 341tl; **NBA Photo:** 43ca; **New Brunswick Tourism:** 84br; **North 44°:** 373tc; **Northern British Columbia Tourism Association:** 316br; **Num-ti-jah Lodge:** 381br. **Olive et Gourmando:** 369bl; **Opéra de Montréal:** Yves Renaud 391tl. **Parks Canada:** Claudette Bue 222cr; Claude Picard *Acadians working the fields* commissioned by Canadian Heritage 68–69; **PA Photos:** AP/Aaron Harris 390cla; **The Pearl Eatery:** 367tr; **Peter Newark's American Pictures:** 48, 52–53, 52cl/bc, 53tr, 54tr, 55br, 56bl, 58t/cl, 59clb/bl, 68cl/bl; **Photo Library:** Robert Harding Travel/Alison Wright 345cr; **Pictures Colour Library:** 408cl, 411b; **The Pointe Restaurant:** 378br; **Provincial Archives of Manitoba:** neg no. CT16 55crb; **Prince of Wales Hotel:** 358bc; **Publiphoto:** 61tl; Y. Beaulieu 35c; J. P. Danvoye 145br, 149tl; Claude A. Girouard 145bl, 146bc; Jean Lauzon 60crb, 148cla; D.Oullette 146tl; M. E. F. /Boulion 145cra; S. Clement 34cr; G. Zimbal 35br. **Raymonds Restaurant:** 364bc; **Regié des installations Olympique:** 129tl; **Retna Pictures:** Steve Granitz 389bc; Phil Loftus 41b; Micheal Putland 40br;

Rex Features: 41tr; **Ripley's Aquarium of Canada:** 174cla; **Robert Harding Picture Library:** 31cl, 37tl, 109cr, 262clb; Image courtesy of the **Royal British Columbia Museum:** 288cla/cl, 289t/cra/crb; © Peter and Mabel Fox 288crb; Courtesy of the **Royal Canadian Mounted Police Museum**, Regina: 236cl/br; © **Royal Ontario Museum:** 188cla, *Man's painted caribou-skin coat*, Innu, Quebec-Labradorc. 1805 188clb; David McKay 188c; **Royal Tyrell Museum**, Drumheller: Alberta Tourism Parks,Recreation and Culture 234cla/br, 234–5, 234tr, 235cra; 252ca/clb/br.; Courtesy of the **Sainte-Anne-du-Beaupré Museum:** 143bl/tl; Courtesy of **Scotiabank:** 404clb; **Sheraton on the Falls:** 356br; **Spectrum Colour Library:** 337br, 340c; **Spectrum Stock:** Ottomar Bierwagen 46tl; Ron Erwin 228tr/b; Henry Kalan 228c; Norman Piluke Photography 229br; **STA Travel Group:** 400crb; **Tony Stone Images:** Wayne R Bilenduke 329br, 341crb; Cosmos Condina 23b, 304br; Richard Elliot 267bl; John Edwards 177b; Suzanne and Nick Geary 418br; Sylvian Grandadam 109tl; David Hiser 257br, 331tl; Paul Souders 267tl; Jess Stock 43br. **Superstock:** age fotostock / Guillem López 27c; agf photo 331tr; Barrett & MacKay All Canada Photos 365tl; Russ Heinl 194; Rolf Hicker 318, 326-7; Dave Reede 230-1; **Swiss Hotel, Ottawa:** 355tl **Donald I. Telfer:** 30cr, 246br, 247tl/cr, 248tr, 249t, 256t/b; **Travel Alberta:** 305cr, 316tl. **University of Toronto:** J.B Tyrrell Papers, Thomas Fisher Rare Book Library MS Collection 26 234bl. **Tourism Winnipeg:** 240bl; **Tuck Shop Bistro:** 369; Two Guys and a Pizza Place: 376br. **Vancouver Public Library, Special Collections:** 13220 56–7; **Victoria University** in the University of Toronto, Canada: Lawren S. Harris *Autumn Algoma*, 1920 © Mrs. James H. Knox 168–9; **Village Historique Acadien:** 85tl/tr/bl. Courtesy of **Western Union Money Transfer:** 404cr; **Westjet:** 409c; **Willensky's Light Lunch:** 368tl; Collection of the **Winnipeg Art Gallery**, Canada: Frank H. Johnston *Edge of Forest*, 1919 watercolour, tempera on hardboard 52.2 x 62.8cm L26 Ernest Mayer 168cl; **World Pictures:** 1c. **Yukon Government Communities:** 334cra.

Front endpaper: **Alamy Images:** Scott Dimond Lcl; Steve Shuey Ltc; Darwin Wiggett Rcra; **Corbis:** Alan Copson Rtr; William Manning Rtc; Alan Marsh Rtl; **Dreamstime.com:** Chris Hill Lbr; William Manning Lbl; Brandon Smith Lbc; **Getty Images:** Barrett & MacKay Rca; mbbirdy Rcrb; **Superstock:** Russ Heinl Rbr; Rolf Hicker Lcla.

Jacket
Cover images: Front and spine – **Getty Images:** All Canada Photos. Back – **Dreamstime.com:** Chu-wen Lin.

All other images © Dorling Kindersley.
For more information see: **www.DKimages.com**

Special Editions of DK Travel Guides

DK Travel Guides can be purchased in bulk quantities at discounted prices for use in promotions or as premiums. We are also able to offer special editions and personalized jackets, corporate imprints, and excerpts from all of our books, tailored specifically to meet your own needs.

To find out more, please contact:
in the United States at: **specialsales@dk.com**
in the UK at: **travelguides@uk.dk.com**
in Canada at: **specialmarkets@dk.com**
in Australia at: **penguincorporatesales@penguinrandomhouse.com.au**

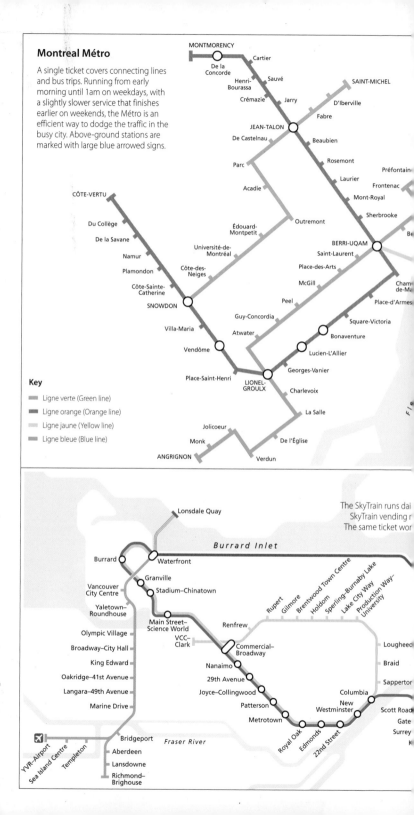

Montreal Métro

A single ticket covers connecting lines and bus trips. Running from early morning until 1am on weekdays, with a slightly slower service that finishes earlier on weekends, the Métro is an efficient way to dodge the traffic in the busy city. Above-ground stations are marked with large blue arrowed signs.

MONTMORENCY
De la Concorde
Cartier
Henri-Bourassa
Sauvé
Crémazie
Jarry
JEAN-TALON
De Castelnau
Parc
Acadie
Édouard-Montpetit
Outremont
SAINT-MICHEL
D'Iberville
Fabre
Beaubien
Rosemont
Laurier
Frontenac
Préfontaine
Mont-Royal
Sherbrooke

CÔTE-VERTU
Du Collège
De la Savane
Namur
Plamondon
Côte-Sainte-Catherine
SNOWDON
Côte-des-Neiges
Université-de-Montréal
Villa-Maria
Vendôme
Place-Saint-Henri
LIONEL-GROULX
BERRI-UQAM
Saint-Laurent
Place-des-Arts
McGill
Peel
Guy-Concordia
Atwater
Square-Victoria
Bonaventure
Lucien-L'Allier
Georges-Vanier
Charlevoix
La Salle
Place-d'Armes
Champ-de-Mars

Jolicoeur
Monk
ANGRIGNON
De l'Église
Verdun

Key

- ▬ Ligne verte (Green line)
- ▬ Ligne orange (Orange line)
- ▬ Ligne jaune (Yellow line)
- ▬ Ligne bleue (Blue line)

The SkyTrain runs dai
SkyTrain vending r
The same ticket wor

Lonsdale Quay

Burrard Inlet

Burrard
Waterfront
Granville
Vancouver City Centre
Stadium–Chinatown
Yaletown–Roundhouse
Main Street–Science World
Olympic Village
Broadway–City Hall
VCC–Clark
Renfrew
Rupert
Gilmore
Brentwood Town Centre
Holdom
Sperling–Burnaby Lake
Lake City Way
Production Way–University
King Edward
Oakridge–41st Avenue
Langara–49th Avenue
Marine Drive
Commercial–Broadway
Nanaimo
29th Avenue
Joyce–Collingwood
Patterson
Metrotown
Royal Oak
Edmonds
22nd Street
New Westminster
Columbia
Lougheed
Braid
Sapperton
Scott Road
Gate
Surrey

YVR–Airport
Sea Island Centre
Templeton
Bridgeport
Aberdeen
Lansdowne
Richmond–Brighouse
Fraser River